To the memory of Isabel Alexander

CULTURE AND PEDAGOGY

*INTERNATIONAL COMPARISONS
IN PRIMARY EDUCATION*

ROBIN ALEXANDER

Blackwell
Publishing

350 Main Street, Malden, MA 02148-5020, USA
108 Cowley Road, Oxford OX4 1JF, UK
550 Swanston Street, Carlton, Victoria 3053, Australia

First published 2000 by Blackwell Publishing Ltd
First published in the United States of America 2001
Reprinted 2002, 2003

Library of Congress Cataloging-in-Publication Data

Alexander, Robin J.
  Culture and pedagogy : international comparisons in primary education / Robin Alexander.
      p.   cm.
  Includes bibliographical references (p.) and index.
  ISBN 0-631-22050-X (hb : alk. paper) — ISBN 0-631-22051-8 (pb. : alk. paper)
  1. Comparative education. 2. Education, Elementary — Cross-cultural studies. I. Title.
LB43.A44   2001
372—dc21   00-057908

A catalogue record for this title is available from the British Library.

Set in 10 on 12.5 pt Sabon
by Graphicraft Ltd, Hong Kong
Printed and bound in the United Kingdom
by Athenaeum Press Ltd, Gateshead, Tyne & Wear

For further information on
Blackwell Publishing, visit our website:
http://www.blackwellpublishing.com

Contents

List of Plates   vii

List of Figures   ix

List of Tables   xi

Acknowledgements   xiii

Note   xvi

Introduction   1

Part I   **Settings**   7

    1   The Comparative Context   9

Part II   **Systems, Policies and Histories**   47

    2   Primary Education in France   49

    3   Primary Education in Russia   64

    4   Primary Education in India   82

    5   Primary Education in the United States of America   101

    6   Primary Education in England   120

    7   Primary Education and the State   154

Part III **Schools**   173

    8   Buildings and People   175

    9   The Idea of a School   195

    10   Beyond the Gates   227

Part IV   **Classrooms**   263

    11   Comparing Teaching   265

    12   Lesson Structure and Form   297

    13   Organization, Task and Activity   320

Contents

14	Judgement, Routine, Rule and Ritual	356
15	Interaction, Time and Pace	391
16	Learning Discourse	427

Part V   Reflections   529

17	Culture and Pedagogy	531

Notes	571
Bibliography	604
Index	626

Plates

The plates appear between p. 528 and p. 529.

1. School exterior (Russia), with Lenin.
2. School exterior (India), children on their way to lessons.
3. Playground (England).
4. Playground (India).
5. Playground (France).
6. Internal play area (Russia).
7. Family Center playground (Michigan).
8. Child's view (Russia).
9. Child's view (France).
10. Child's view (India).
11. Child's view (Michigan).
12. Whole class teaching: music (England).
13. Groups in a whole class setting: art (France).
14. Whole class teaching: mathematics (India).
15. Grouping for mathematics (England): one group works with the teacher, the others work independently with textbooks and apparatus.
16. Teacher's view (Russia): orthodox desk layout, posture, hand-raising (left) and answering (right).
17. Teacher's view (India).
18. Teacher's view (France).
19. Growing apart? Different tasks, different outcomes (England).
20. Staying together? Same task, different outcomes (India).
21. Listening (Michigan).
22. Working in groups: classroom Reading Center (Michigan).
23. Working as a class: one child reads aloud while the others follow the text (Russia).

24. Working as a class: mental arithmetic with *l'ardoise* (France).
25. Working in pairs: worksheet mathematics with clipboard (England).
26. Sharing ideas: this is the correct way to solve the problem (Russia).
27. Sharing ideas: this is how we thought about the problem (Michigan).
28. Sharing ideas: book reviews (England). Roald Dahl waits his turn.
29. Queueing for marks and *bons points* (France).
30. 'How do you spell . . . ?' (England).
31. Monitoring (England).
32. Staying alert: mid-lesson exercise with variations (Michigan).
33. Staying alert: mid-lesson exercise without variations (Russia).
34. Visual values: the Co-operation Quilt (Michigan).
35. Visual values: the skill of painting (Russia).
36. Physical/moral values: courage and co-operation on the climbing wall (France).
37. Physical/moral values: competitive team games – kickball, or baseball with feet (Michigan).
38. Physical/moral values: fitness and posture (Russia).
39. Whole school assembly (England): 'Imagine what it is like to be blind'.
40. Whole school assembly (India): deep breathing.

Figures

1.1	Goals for the millennium	25
2.1	The education system in France	50
3.1	The education system in Russia	65
4.1	The education system in India	84
5.1	The education system in the United States of America	102
6.1	The education system in England	121
13.1	An action-based framework for the analysis of teaching	325
13.2	Classroom plans	326–32

Plan 1   Hamilton Primary School, England (lesson 11.13, discourse sequence 16.11)

Plan 2   St Teresa's School, England (lesson 11.16, discourse sequence 16.13)

Plan 3   Cheetham School, England

Plan 4   St Etienne Elementary School, France

Plan 5   Coulanges Elementary School, France (lesson 11.3, discourse sequence 16.9)

Plan 6   Montagne village school, France: 5 and 6 year olds (combined école maternelle and cours préparatoire)

Plan 7   Chanderi Primary School, India (lesson 11.4, discourse sequence 16.2)

Plan 8   Ferozabad School, India: morning and afternoon sessions

Plan 9   Kursk School A, Russia (lesson 11.7, discourse sequence 16.4)

Plan 10   Moscow School B, Russia: room re-arranged for art lesson

Plan 11   Thoreau School, Michigan (lesson 11.2, discourse sequence 16.16)

Plan 12   Emerson Elementary School, Michigan (lesson 11.10, discourse sequence 16.15)

Plan 13   Thoreau Elementary School, Michigan: multi-age class of
          45 children (grades 2, 3 and 4) with four adults
Plan 14   Hawthorne Elementary School, Michigan: three layouts,
          including that for lesson 11.11, discourse sequence 16.17
          (middle plan)
13.3   Cross-cultural continua: functions of wall-mounted teaching
          materials   333
13.4   A preliminary framework for classifying learning tasks   347
14.1   Cross-cultural continua: forms of classroom assessment   373
14.2   Cross-cultural continua: agents of classroom assessment   374
14.3   Cross-cultural continua: criterial emphasis of classroom assessment
          (other than formal tests) – the balance of cognitive, affective, social
          and behavioural considerations   377
14.4   Cross-cultural continua: criterial emphasis of classroom assessment
          (other than formal tests) – the balance of convergence/precision
          and divergence/creativity in pupils' expected responses   377
14.5   Mapping classroom routines, rules and rituals   384
15.1   The relationship between organization and interaction   407
15.2   Monitoring: an analytical framework based on the *Five Cultures*
          data   410
16.1   Transcription conventions used in sequences 16.1–16.7   440
16.2   Classroom discourse: organization, function and form   517
16.3   Pedagogic control in *Five Cultures*   522
17.1   Curriculum metamorphosis   552

Tables

1.1   Education and human development: five nations and the rest of the world (1997)   45

13.1   Task profiles of primary school lessons in five countries, based on an analysis of all lessons observed   348

13.2   Task demand in 40 primary school lessons from five countries, based on an analysis of eight language and mathematics lessons from each country   349

13.3   Percentage of time spent by primary pupils on ten generic learning activities in ten English primary classrooms   352

13.4   Pupils' learning activities in 40 lessons in five countries, based on an analysis of eight language and mathematics lessons from each country   354

14.1   Criteria for differentiating pupils within primary classrooms   362

14.2   Pupil differentiation in primary schools, based on observation and interviews in the *Five Cultures* classrooms   363

15.1   Type and frequency of teacher–pupil interaction, based on systematic observation of the lessons of ten English primary teachers over two weeks   395

15.2   Rate of each type of teacher–pupil interaction in ten classes, based on systematic observation of ten English primary teachers over two weeks   395

15.3   Balance of interactions in primary school lessons in five countries   398

15.4   Teacher and pupil utterance length in 25 lessons from five countries   399

15.5   Balance of teachers' different interaction purposes in primary classrooms in five countries, expressed as proportions of all those interactions observed in each country which involved the teacher   400

15.6   The changing pattern of interaction during a lesson – France (Coulanges: lesson 11.3, French)   402

15.7 The changing pattern of interaction during a lesson – Russia
(Kursk A: lesson 11.7, Russian)   403

15.8 The changing pattern of interaction during a lesson – Michigan
(Thoreau: lesson 11.12, mathematics)   403

15.9 The changing pattern of interaction during a lesson – England
(Ogden: multiple focus lesson: language, maths, art)   404

15.10 The changing pattern of interaction during a lesson – England
(Kirkbright: lesson 11.15, Literacy Hour)   404

15.11 The changing pattern of interaction during a lesson – England
(St Teresa's: lesson 11.16, Numeracy Hour)   405

Acknowledgements

This book has been a long time in the making and owes much to many. Several organizations gave financial or institutional support to the research project whose data provide much of the book's raw material. The Leverhulme Trust funded the larger part of the fieldwork in France, India, Russia and the United States. The British Council's Delhi and Paris offices awarded me travel grants; they and the Moscow office also gave me considerable help in setting up my programmes of interviews and school visits. The University of Leeds sanctioned my leave of absence to undertake the non-UK fieldwork, and the University of Warwick released me for two terms to make a start on writing the book. Warwick too, through its Research and Teaching Development Fund, supported the translation and transcription of the videotapes and audiotapes.

The Ministry of Education for the Russian Federation (now the Ministry of General and Professional Education) invited us to Russia, facilitated our contacts with institutions in Kursk and Moscow and provided invaluable information; Yuri Albetkov (International Section), Margarita Nikolaevna Kostikova (Teacher Training Department) and Irina Anatoloyevna Petrova (Primary Education Department) were especially generous with their time and wisdom. Also in Moscow we received unstinting help from Alec Bessey at the British Council and important insights from Nikolai Dimitrivich Nikandrov, Natalia Feodorovna Vinogradova, Alexei Alexeivich Leontev and Merem Biboletova, all of the Russian Academy of Education. In Kursk the Rector and staff of Kursk Pedagogical University arranged matters comprehensively for us, covering everything from accommodation to visits and meetings and warm hospitality. Particular thanks are due to Alexander Nikolaevich Huden and his fellow members of the Faculty of Pedagogy and Primary Education at the university: they worked out the details of our programme, organized transport, accompanied us to schools, and were always on hand to answer questions. I learned much from them. Above all, I am grateful to our guides, interpreters and good friends Natasha Achkasova, Anna Ivanova and Sergei Pupenko.

The Government of India's Ministry of Human Resource Development (MHRD) invited us to Delhi and at MHRD I am especially grateful to Mr H. C. Bajeva and

Dr R. V. Vaidyanatha Ayyar. Our base in India was the National Council of Educational Research and Training (NCERT) in Delhi. I thank NCERT's Director (Professor A. K. Sharma) and the many staff who helped and advised us there. However, at NCERT I am most indebted to Daljit Gupta, Manju Jain, K. C. Nautiyal and Kamlesh Rai for arranging and accompanying us on our visits to schools, for interpreting and for answering our many questions. As always, the British Council gave sterling support and I thank especially Tony Davison and Kanta Vadehra; also our three drivers, Mohammed Husein, Hazari Lal and Seurish Massey. I am also grateful to the UK Government's Overseas Development Administration and Department for International Development and to the European Commission for enabling me to maintain contact with India since our initial fieldwork through the assignments I have undertaken in Delhi and Maharashtra in connection with the Government of India's District Primary Education Programme. Barbara Payne of DfID and Mervi Karikorpi of ECEPO, both in Delhi, have been especially helpful in this regard.

In France the British Council was once again in the vanguard. This time it is Sharon Memis and Claire Dellière whom I must thank, particularly for their handling of the Paris leg of our fieldwork and for arranging interviews at the Ministry of National Education and other sites. At the Ministry I gained much from Gérard Bonnet, Yves Guérin and Maurice Dubrulle; at the Paris Institut Universitaire de Formation des Maîtres (IUFM) from Ginette Jollivet. In Nice we were given generous hospitality by the Nice IUFM for the duration of our fieldwork and for this I thank the director and staff, but especially Joseph Giordani, the IUFM's Directeur Adjoint. He, Jacques Moulary and M Jourdanet arranged our school visits and other interviews and meetings. My special debt of gratitude in France, however, is to Chantal and Michel Lemosse, who looked after us and advised us before, during and after our visit.

In the United States we were based at Michigan State University in East Lansing. I am considerably indebted to Michael Sedlak for organizing our accommodation there and for overseeing all the arrangements for our meetings with MSU faculty, our visits to schools and our interviews with staff at Michigan State Department of Education and in the school districts of Lansing, Holt and Flint. At MSU we also had valuable support and guidance from Robert Floden, Fran Barger, Sonya Gunnings-Moton, Doug Campbell, James Spillane, Anne Soderman and Julie Ashi. Michael Sedlak laid on a couple of seminars at which I benefited from exchanges with a larger number of MSU faculty. At state and district levels Ann Hansen, Nancy Mincemoyer, Maxine Hankins Cain, Samuel Lopresto, Nathel Burtley and Linda Borgsdorf provided us with essential professional and administrative perspectives.

Once I started writing the book I gained much from the comments of colleagues who read drafts of the chapters dealing with the five systems of primary education, their histories and cultural contexts: Alan Blyth, Anne Corbett, Jean Drèze, Neal Finkelstein, Robert Floden, Leonid Illushin, Chantal Lemosse, Michel Lemosse, James Muckle, Denzil Saldanha, John Shotton, Brian Simon and Joan Simon. Needless to say, any errors or eccentricities of fact or judgement in those chapters are mine and mine alone. Also during the course of writing I have benefited from dialogue with a far larger number of people than I can possibly list, though I would single out Johanna Crighton, Julian Elliott, Julia Evans, Kathy Fiddes, Maurice Galton, Jonathan Hodge, Neil Hufton, Leonid Illushin, Malcolm Lister, Alison Sealey and Michele Schweisfurth (who also helped with some of the preliminary data analysis) and Joseph Tobin. In England Alison Moore of Leeds University assisted the organization of the first phase of the fieldwork; Paul Blewitt, Archivist to the Moravian Church, responded to my queries about Comenius; and at Blackwell, Sarah Bird, Martin Davies, Ally Dunnett and Lisa Eaton sustained their faith in this project throughout.

In the matter of providing intellectual sustenance, however, I must acknowledge a particular debt to Alan Blyth, Joan Simon and Brian Simon in England, Michel Lemosse in France and Denzil Saldanha in India. Sadly, Alan died shortly before this book went to press: more than anyone he deserves credit for establishing primary education, against the grain of academic snobbery, as a field of serious scholarly endeavour in the UK, and throughout the 1980s and the 1990s he was an astute and constructive commentator on my own work. Coming from France's leading expert on British education Michel's comparative perspective was invaluable, and indeed his knowledge of the intricacies and oddities of the English system was humbling. With Denzil in Delhi, Mumbai and Warwick, I had many illuminating exchanges about Indian and English education and culture. And in long conversations at their house Joan and Brian were never less than thoroughly stimulating on English and Russian education, on Russian psychology, on the history of pedagogy, on UK government policy, and on much else besides.

It is always frustrating that the ethics of research prevent one from thanking in person those who have been most closely involved in it. In this case I refer to the many dozens of teachers and close on two thousand children in the five countries whom we observed, interviewed, recorded and videotaped. They accepted our scrutiny and questioning without complaint and the warmth of the welcome that many of the schools gave to us compounds our indebtedness.

Karen Lennox accompanied me on all the fieldwork visits, made the video recordings, took the photographs of which a small sample appears in this book, helped with the transcription and analysis, and – having shared my experience of visiting all the schools – provided a constant sounding board for my treatment of what we found there. To her, finally, this book owes a greater debt than I can possibly express.

Note

To protect their identity, the names of schools have been changed and in the discourse extracts in Chapter 16 pupils have been given letters rather than names.

To frustrate attempts to identify participants from the illustrations I have used a mixture of photographs taken as part of the project but in lessons other than those principally featured and photographs taken in schools which were not involved in the project at all.

Introduction

The discipline of comparative education has existed in recognizable form since the early nineteenth century, though in Britain it remained relatively marginal to the work of university departments of education. By the late 1980s, however, academic comparativists were feeling the pressure from those with a more urgent interest in how British education compared with that of other countries. During the 1980s and the 1990s Her Majesty's Inspectorate (HMI) made a series of brief forays into the education systems of countries such as France, Germany, Japan, Italy and the United States, from each of which came lessons for education in Britain.[1] These excursions were nothing new. In 1859 Matthew Arnold, poet, guardian of high culture and inspector of schools, was asked by the Royal Commissioners 'to inquire into the state of popular education in England' and to do so by reporting on the systems of France, Holland and the French cantons of Switzerland.

In words which have a prophetic resonance for the kinds of sweeping comparison which were being made during the 1990s, Arnold found that in French primary schools 'the walls are barer than with us . . . The reading and arithmetic are better than ours, the arithmetic in particular being in general much more intelligently taught . . . and much more intelligently apprehended . . . The information about geography and history is decidedly inferior.[2] And in making his case for a proper national system of basic education in England he pronounced that 'by its form and by its contents, by its letter and by its spirit, by its treatment of reason and by its treatment of prejudice, in what it respects and what it does not respect, the school legislation of modern France fosters, encourages and educates the popular intelligence and the popular enquiry'.[3]

By the end of the following century, alongside the overseas excursions of Arnold's successors in the inspectorate and the more cautious judgements of academics, international comparison had acquired a harder edge. The Organization for Economic Co-operation and Development (OECD) had devised educational 'indicators' to facilitate comparison of the performance of its member countries.[4] The World Bank was using comparative data to judge the cost-effectiveness of different kinds of funded intervention in development education and to separate 'promising avenues' from 'blind alleys'.[5] The United Nations had nominated education as one of the three principal components of its Human Development Index to show the extent of the gulf among the world's nations in respect of basic human needs and rights.[6] And testing agencies had devised instruments to enable governments to compare the academic performance of pupils of given ages and in given subjects across a large number of countries.[7] On the basis of the latter evidence the performance of English pupils and schools was judged to be inadequate, especially in those very 'basics' of reading and number which had dominated teachers' and pupils' time and attention at the primary stage for the past century.

But the chief spur to the growth of the industry of international comparison was globalization. The imperatives of the global economy forced governments to confront hard questions about the relationship between a country's showing in the league tables of educational and economic performance. It was then a short step – in some countries made shorter by the political urge for scapegoats and a quick fix – from judging that economic and educational performance had declined to presuming the existence of a clear-cut causal link between these two trends, and thence to arguing that the way to make good national economic deficiencies was to borrow the educational policies of a country's more successful economic competitors. Thus by the mid 1990s the British government had espoused the simple nostrum that the key to enhanced standards and economic competitiveness was an unrelenting concentration on basic skills in literacy and numeracy, to be taught mainly through that 'interactive whole-class teaching' which was used in schools in Germany, Switzerland, Hungary, Taiwan and Japan.[8]

I shall examine the merits of these arguments later. Here I prefigure just four elements of a critique of this kind of thinking: the cause–effect relationship between teaching strategies, educational league tables and national economic performance is far from proven; yet the need for informed international educational comparison is now inescapable; pedagogy could well be one of the keys, though not the only one; and there is far more to pedagogy, and to the effectiveness of pedagogy, than making a simple choice between whole class teaching, group work and individual attention.

The empirical core of this book is a comparative study of primary education in England, France, India, Russia and the United States, using data gathered in those countries during 1994–8. It took place in the political context outlined above, though it was first conceived in 1992, well before the moral panic about league tables and teaching methods that was exploited by both major political parties in the run-up to the 1997 general election. Unlike those research projects that capitalized on these fears it was not primarily concerned to deliver 'best buy' formulae for school and classroom effectiveness. Rather, it set out to extend into the international arena lines of enquiry which had preoccupied me in the context of close study of primary education in England over many years and which required a much broader canvas: the structure and purposes of primary education; the nature of primary teaching and the thinking of primary teachers; the classroom experiences encountered by primary pupils; the language of the classroom; the relationship between the world of the classroom and the world of educational and social policy;

the impact on these of culture and history.[9] Though pedagogy was to be the core of the study, and though I hoped to identify the pedagogic lessons of these kinds of comparison, the purpose was to be interpretative rather than normative or prescriptive.

Nobody embarking on a study of education in countries and cultures other than their own does so (or at least nobody ought to do so) without being acutely aware of how little, despite their best endeavours, they end up knowing. Academics in cognate fields such as anthropology, history or politics tend to be specialists in just one country, and the knowledge they profess is part of a cumulative tradition built up by others as well as themselves within the boundaries of a well-established discipline. Though a few comparative studies have ranged convincingly over several countries, studies such as those of King (seven countries),[10] Archer (four)[11] or Green (four)[12] concentrate their attention on the macro or national level and say little or nothing about the day-to-day workings of schools, still less hazard analysis of pedagogy. Indeed it is perhaps a weakness of comparative education as a discipline (and of the three cited, only King would call himself a comparativist) that so many of its proponents have neglected what is arguably the most important part of the educational terrain, the practice of teaching and learning, and what is possibly the most elusive theme of all, how such practice relates to the context of culture, structure and policy in which it is embedded.

There are other understandable reasons for this neglect. Comparative study of the work of schools, teachers and children presents problems of access, cost, language, methodology and indeed physical stamina in comparison with which a programme of policy analysis based on documentation is relatively plain sailing.

Naturally, there are exceptions to the tendency to focus on policy rather than practice, including several that I shall refer to in this book. Comparativists such as Tobin (Japan, China and the United States),[13] Broadfoot (France and England)[14] and Muckle (the Soviet Union and Russia)[15] do bite the methodological bullet and progress beyond structure and policy to the classroom. Their studies illuminate their national contexts all the more effectively for documenting the grassroots human detail.

I have no illusions about the intellectual risks of going where relatively few have ventured: five countries rather than one or two, the classroom as well as the system, practice as well as policy. To do this kind of work makes heavy demands on an individual's capacity to garner, understand and synthesize material from very diverse sources, disciplines and of course cultures. And there is the constant spectre of seeming naive, presumptuous or simply too tidy in the face of what even insiders find baffling or contrary. As one of the characters in Susan Richards' illuminating account of life for ordinary Russians after the collapse of the Soviet Union remarks, in some exasperation: 'Understand! . . . You are speaking like a Westerner. Logic-ally. But life here is not logical'.[16] Or, as a teacher no less pithily observed while I was collecting data for the five cultures project in the southern Russian city of Kursk: 'You will understand nothing about Russia until you have tried to live for a year on a Russian salary'.[17] What then did – could – this project attempt? Its stated objectives were to:

- undertake a comparative analysis of primary education in five countries – England, France, India, Russia and the United States – which exhibit marked contrasts in respect of their geographic, demographic, economic and cultural characteristics, while sharing a formal constitutional commitment to democratic values
- focus such study on educational policies and structures on the one hand and school and classroom practices on the other
- locate the analysis of practice within two pupil age-groups, six to seven and nine to ten year olds, so as to examine issues of comparability and gain a purchase on progression in teaching and learning through the primary phase as a whole
- examine the scope of intended and actual learning at the primary stage in each country but concentrate in particular on language and the teaching of literacy.

The broader goals which it was hoped these objectives would address were to:

- unravel further the complex interplay of policies, structures, culture, values and pedagogy
- develop a theory and account of pedagogy which might have general application
- make a distinctive contribution to the discipline of comparative education
- differentiate what is universal in pedagogy from what is country specific or culture bound, and thus more clearly define the possibilities and limitations of international comparisons in education and of what one country can learn, borrow or adapt from another
- provide information and provoke insights which would be of value to policymakers, researchers, practitioners and others committed to the universalization and improvement of primary education.

Data were collected at three levels, the system, the school and the classroom, using a mixture of interviews, semi-systematic observation and – for later translation, transcription and analysis – videotape and audiotape. These data were supplemented by school and country documentation, photographs and daily journal entries. The core of the material consisted of 37 'level 1' interviews together with material from 30 schools: 61 interviews, fieldnotes from 106 lesson/session observations, 130 hours of videotape. The English data were more extensive than those from the other four countries because they included both material collected in 1995–8 specifically for the project and the revisiting of field notes, videotapes, audiotapes and lesson transcripts from three earlier projects: a 1985–7 study of the thinking and dilemmas of experienced primary teachers, the 1986–91 study of policy and practice in primary education in Leeds, England's third largest city, and the 1990–92 CICADA study of change and continuity in pedagogy and pupil-teacher discourse following the 1988 Education Reform Act.[18] In addition to the core project material therefore, we had available for analysis or re-analysis tapes of a further 60 lessons in 30 schools and a wider penumbra of data from another 40 schools. The contexts for the fieldwork were:

- England: three northern local education authorities
- France: the *régions académiques* of Nice and Paris
- India: Delhi and the states of Haryana and Uttar Pradesh
- Russia: Moscow and the *oblast* of Kursk
- United States: three school districts in the state of Michigan.

The United States has a highly decentralized education system and although I do refer to federal policy it therefore made sense to concentrate our attention at state and district levels.

More precise details of the *Five Cultures* methodology appear in the chapters where data are presented and discussed. I also discuss there some of the more intractable problems of this kind of study: the 'typicality' of data which emphasize depth of focus rather than breadth; working through interpreters (as we did in India and Russia); recording, translating and transcribing classroom talk; and undertaking comparative discourse analysis using translated material.

Throughout the study the notion of *culture* is paramount. If making sense (rather than, say, transplanting policies) is one's principal goal in a study of this kind then culture and history have to be the basic frames within which one's attempts to understand and explain are set. Though there are undoubted cross-cultural continuities and indeed universals in educational thinking and practice, no decision or action which one observes in a particular classroom, and no educational policy, can be properly understood except by reference to the web of inherited ideas and values, habits and customs, institutions and world views which make one country, or one region, or one group, distinct from another.

The same can be said of *language*. The power of language in shaping what is distinctive about teaching and learning in a particular country is readily evident. When to this proposition one adds two others – that the first stage of compulsory schooling is a particularly potent arena for cultural transmission and socialization, and that 'it is in the discourse between teacher and pupils that education is done, or fails to be done'[19] – it will be clear why in a comparative study of educational processes neither culture nor language can be given the status of mere 'factors' but must be handled as central and pervasive.[20] It is no accident that the chapter on the classroom discourse of teachers and pupils is by far the longest in the book. It marks the study's culmination, the point where the relationship between culture and pedagogy is most effectively demonstrated, by teachers and children if not by me.

So a project of this kind is fraught with risks of one kind or another, and it is important to stress its exploratory nature. However, exploration and speculation are by no means poor relations to the confident marshalling of facts, figures, causes and effects. I am as concerned here to build theory as to make claims about practice, and indeed see the tasks as interdependent. The book's instrumental goal is to enhance our understanding of primary education and to provide insights which will enable those concerned with it, whether policy-makers, administrators or practitioners, to improve the quality of young children's learning and its relevance to the uncertain world they face. The allied theoretical goal is to develop a coherent account of pedagogy that embraces the art, science or craft of teaching, the values and ideas by which teaching is informed, and its contexts of culture and history. To do this requires that I keep the discussion constantly on the move between micro and macro, school and state, classroom and culture.

The book is divided into three main parts, representing the three levels – system, school and classroom (Parts II, III and IV) at which data were gathered. These are sandwiched between chapters which place the study in its international and comparative context (Chapter 1) and review and reflect on the ground covered (Chapter 17). The fieldwork data start to dominate the analysis only when we move to the school level in Part III. Thereafter, as we progress from school to classroom and from lesson structure to teaching act and teacher–pupil discourse, the book is increasingly data driven.

Readers will soon perceive that there could be two books here, one about primary education and the other dealing with pedagogy, conceived broadly and without any necessary reference to the education of pre-adolescent children. It is also evident that the book falls naturally into two halves and could therefore appear as two volumes. One volume (Parts II and III) would deal with school and state; the other (Parts IV and V) with teaching and learning. Keeping these themes together may make for a weighty publication, but this is what I prefer, for the theory of pedagogy towards which I work depends on an understanding of how nation, school and classroom are intertwined. An account of primary education that neglects this relationship does not take us very far.

The photographs are an important part of the book – my only regret is that there are so few of them – for they may convey what words cannot. At one stage I half toyed with the idea of presenting the discourse extracts in Chapter 16 with minimal commentary, so as to allow this most important part of my data to speak for itself. That was not really feasible – after all, having decided to select these particular extracts from a much larger body of transcribed material I was under an obligation to say why. And the commentary does not prevent readers from making their own sense of the extracts, particularly as I have provided abundant contextual information to help them to do so. I would encourage this, for although I have chosen to interpret the classroom discourse in a particular way, I have no monopoly in this enterprise.

The photographs allow reader engagement in this less fettered way. Again they have been selected from a much larger number, and again there is a purpose behind the way they have been presented. One, since this is a comparative study, is to point up similarities and differences, and this is why the photographs appear in groups rather than singly. The rest is up to the reader. Like the discourse extracts, they repay study in their own right, quite apart from what I say about them.

Part I
Settings

1

The Comparative Context

Prelude

It is 8.15 on a Monday morning. Nearly three hundred children aged 6–11 are converging on an elementary school in the affluent residential quarter of a coastal city in southern France. They are well dressed – fashionably and expensively so in many cases – well nourished and loquacious. Parents accompany many of them. At 8.28 their teachers come out of the modern two-storey building. The pupils line up in the covered part of the playground where the school is raised on pillars to provide shelter in poor weather. They follow their teachers into the classrooms, and another day starts. First is registration, then French or mathematics, today as on Fridays preceded by civic education. The pace is brisk, the teacher's manner business-like. At 11.30 most of the teachers and children go home for a protracted lunch break, returning for a second three-hour stint – science, perhaps, or history, geography, art, music or physical education – at 1.30.

The same routine, give or take minor variations, is repeated in a considerably less pristine new town some ten miles away, with a mixture of low-rise housing and low-cost tower blocks and a high level of parental unemployment, especially among the many families of North African origin. It is repeated, more or less, in the one-teacher *classe unique* school in a mountain village some thirty miles distant, whose 22 pupils, 24 hours earlier, joined their fellows from the next village in a day's skiing. This school shares a building with the *Mairie*, and its lessons are interrupted from time to time by errant phone messages for the mayor. The other has a brand-new building with hexagonal classrooms and a state-of-the-art climbing wall.

The classroom settings in which the various groups of children work are some-what more variable than the routines which structure and punctuate the day. They are all spacious, light and well equipped, but in some the desks are arranged in rows facing the blackboard, in some the children work at tables in groups of four or six facing each other, and in others the tables are set, boardroom-style, in a hollow square. In one room the walls are covered by children's paintings, wordlists, work in progress and notices; in another the blank spaces are punctuated only by the odd poster advertising one of last year's exhibitions or concerts. These physical arrangements reflect a similar diversity in the modes of instruction adopted by the teachers. Some lessons deviate not at inch from the formal didactic structure of *la leçon*. In others there is structural fluidity and collaboration between pupils. In some classrooms, strict social distance is maintained between teacher and taught, while in a few the younger pupils address their teachers by their first name. In every room, however, the blackboard provides the focus and constant point of reference, and it is actively used (rather than merely viewed) by the pupils as well as their teachers.

Crossing several national boundaries and time zones we find a recognizable variant on this routine taking place in a large town in southern Russia (in Britain it would be designated a city but in Russia only Moscow and St Petersburg merit this accolade) close to the Ukrainian border. Here, some fifteen hundred pupils aged 7–17 circumnavigate the street's potholes, puddles and battered lorries, make their way into the school compound past the white-painted statue of Lenin – seated for once, and with his arm round a small boy, rather than standing with coat flapping, beard jutting and arm outstretched to the revolutionary horizon, as in the town's main square – and up the steps of the large three-storey building. The corridor to the school's primary section is lined with photos of prize-winning pupils and former directors, slogans about the motherland and world peace, and – in unselfconscious juxtaposition with Lenin – 'Through our sufferings we have achieved that New Thought which is necessary if we are to bridge the gulf between political practice and the moral and ethical standards which are common to all mankind: M. S. Gorbachev'. This sentiment has survived Gorbachev's vilification, just as Lenin's statue has survived the collapse of the Soviet Union.

The children play – even more boisterously than their French peers – in one of the large spaces outside each group of classrooms which serves as an indoor playground during the long winter, but their manner changes the instant they are summoned into the classroom for the first of their 40-minute lessons. Warm coats are removed, and the crisp, clean and relatively formal attire is in marked contrast to the jeans, trainers and designer clothing we have seen in France. The children stand by their desks, sit only when instructed by their teacher to do so, quickly and efficiently arrange books, book rests and pens in a preordained pattern, and silently await their instructions. Their day, like that of the French children, starts with the native language and mathematics. Their classroom is tall, with large, curtained windows down one side, on the ledges of which are houseplants with trailing foliage. The desks are arranged in rows, facing the large blackboard with its triptych of carefully prepared panels and, to one side, the teacher's desk. Above and around the board are lists of letters and numbers, together with a picture of a child seated at its desk with ramrod-straight back, which the children emulate without prompt by the teacher. Its superfluous caption reads 'Sit leaning slightly forward. Do not touch the desk with your chest. Put your elbows on the desk. Place your feet on the floor. Lean on the lower, strengthened edge of the chair back'. The wall at the back of the room, which the teacher can see but the children cannot, is filled with an atmospheric picture of birch trees in autumn.

In similar buildings and classrooms in other parts of the town, in the three-class village primary school with just 60 pupils which – unusually – occupies its own building, in the brand new school on a collective farm surrounded by the vast emptiness of the steppe, and in the Moscow gymnasium specializing in modern languages, the ambience and routines are pretty well identical.

Much further east and south, in the Indian state of Haryana, children and teachers are picking their way from one rickety stepping stone to the next along a narrow and muddy footpath wedged between two buildings. Alongside their path runs an open sewer. At one end of the ginnel is a snarling, hooting maelstrom of traffic – buses, lorries, cars, auto-rickshaws, scooters, bicycles, carts drawn by oxen, and pedestrians and cows. At the other is a square of one-storey buildings grouped round a pump from which women and children are collecting water in jerrycans and used Bisleri bottles. Beyond is the school: a small, dusty courtyard with the school building – two classrooms and a veranda – on one side and a lean-to with three bays on the other. Over four hundred children share this space, divided into morning and afternoon shifts. There is a class in each of the two rooms and in each of the lean-to bays; there are two more on the veranda and in the courtyard. The chanted responses of one class merge into those of the next. Most pupils here are the children of illiterate migrant workers who live in the slums and transient shanty town surrounding the school. They are seated one behind the other on worn *tat-pattis* or runners, close-packed and cross-legged, with slates resting on satchels that in turn rest on laps. The teacher stands at a portable blackboard.

Some distance north, in a suburban enclave of New Delhi, 600 children aged 6–11 have assembled in a large, shady and well-brushed courtyard. Each is immaculately dressed in the school's uniform of red and blue. The school's female head teacher, who uses a public address system, leads the assembly, which combines patriotism and culture in equal measure. Around the courtyard are the classrooms: small, bare, whitewashed, devoid of furniture except a blackboard, a cupboard and the runners on which the children will sit cross-legged. Each room accommodates anything from 30 to 50 pupils. Running the length of each block is a veranda on whose walls are lists of 'humble requests' to parents about school uniform and homework, attendance and absence figures for every class, recorded daily, and assorted maxims: 'Great ideals create a great mind' . . . 'The way that an insects eats away at clothes is the same way that jealousy destroys a human being' . . . 'You will reap what you sow. You cannot expect flowers to grow where you have sown seeds of thorns' . . . 'At the time of judgement a human being should remain impartial.'

The assembly ends with a display of dancing and singing by a group of girls. The music and choreography are traditional, taught by a teacher whose parents, grandparents and great-grandparents were musicians. The theme, however, is modern: through words and movement the assembled children are reminded of the importance of personal hygiene and a healthy diet.

In the neighbouring state of Uttar Pradesh, we are in a village school with mixed age (or 'multi-grade') classes. Here, too, the day has started with assembly, and here too, the classrooms are – by Western standards – small, crowded and sparsely equipped. In each, the teacher will shortly embark on an unvarying routine of rote learning and drill. She points in turn to each letter or number on a chart or the blackboard (for here, too, the daily priorities are literacy and numeracy), asks what it represents, how it sounds or what it adds up to, and receives back the chanted unison response, usually repeating this antiphony five or six times before she moves from one written symbol to the next.

In a township on the edge of the capital of one of the Midwestern states of the USA, the school's 340 children arrive on foot, by bicycle or in a succession of yellow buses. Today they are returning after an enforced day's leave caused by a blizzard. The school is single storeyed and built round a central courtyard. The large field in which it is set is surrounded by low-density houses and the occasional shopping mall, along streets laid out on the grid pattern into which most of the state was divided when it was first settled in the 1830s, although this settlement is a much more recent overspill from the state capital a short distance away by car. The building contains not only classrooms but also two gymnasia, specialist rooms for science, music, art, and speech therapy, a newly furbished media centre housing a library, study carrels and a computer laboratory with fifteen workstations. It also has a suite of offices for clerical staff and the school's principal together with consulting rooms for the ancillary team of nurse, psychologist, social worker and counsellor.

The school's entrance foyer is liberally adorned with messages: '101 ways to praise a child' . . . '101 ways to love a child' . . . 'x was a good listener during conflict negotiation meetings' . . . 'Making reading together a family tradition' . . . 'Peace is nurturing' . . . and, a triple juxtaposition which is surely without ironic intent but is the more striking for that: 'Popcorn 50c' . . . 'No guns in our schools – Crime Stoppers of mid-Michigan will pay up to $500 reward for information leading to arrest' . . . 'The new 3Rs: we are Respectful, Responsible and Ready to learn'.

The classrooms are large and every wall is covered with teaching material, notices or children's work. The furniture consists of a mixture of informally disposed tables at which the children work in groups, specialist areas for art and language, an information technology area with five computers, and a carpeted corner with easy chairs and sofas in which the class assembles for stories and other collective activities. The children enter in twos and threes, greet the teacher and each other with equal informality, exchange news, take off coats, hats and boots, fetch the journals in which they will write their latest news, settle themselves randomly on the chairs – not for these children the upright posture of their Russian peers – and begin, intermittently, to write. While they are doing this, the teacher checks the register. This done, the children stand and, hands on heart, face the national flag for the Pledge: the one unvarying ritual of this and every day.

The ritual is repeated across the state in a much larger elementary school of over 700 pupils, located in an industrial city whose main employer – the automobile industry – has fallen on hard times. Many of the parents are on the minimum wage of $4.50–$5.50 an hour and over half the pupils qualify for free school lunches. All the school's pupils, the principal and about half of the teaching staff, are black. The principal himself is ubiquitous, energetic and dominant. Here, too, the entrance area and corridors have their messages, but now their burden is attending and achieving rather than caring and sharing: 'Spiderman says good attendance is important'; lists of pupils in each class grouped under the headings of 'Perfect attendance', 'Good conduct' and 'A and B grades'; information about after-school activities; photographs of pupils over the futures to which they aspire: 'Erica – teacher', 'Jonathan – attorney', 'Courtney – doctor', 'Tehquin – jazz musician', 'Sophia – ballerina', and (seated in front of the US flag) 'Lauren – president'.

To England, now, and a school in what was until 20 years ago a village but is now a sprawling dormitory of near-identical detached houses from which many parents drive into the neighbouring city each day to work. The modern, single-storey school building stands in extensive grounds, part of which has been landscaped by the parent-teacher association as a wildlife conservation area, complete with pond. The school's entrance area is welcoming and attractive, but the building's main focal point is the large hall at the centre of the complex, in which the school's 300 pupils and 11 teachers meet daily for assembly and which also doubles as a gymnasium and refectory. Around it are the classrooms, the staff room and separate offices for the head, deputy head and school secretary. A second focal point is provided by an internal courtyard which has been laid out by the pupils as a Japanese garden and in which some of the older pupils prefer to sit and converse during the morning, lunchtime and afternoon breaks rather than submit to the supervised anarchy of the playground. Every wall of every classroom is covered with carefully labelled and mounted examples of children's work – writing, art, science investigations, activities arising from a recent school trip. The storage units below this 'display' (for that is what this use of wall space is invariably called by English primary teachers) are topped with its three-dimensional items. In addition every class has a library, a bulging storeroom and at least one computer. The children come into the classroom at any time from 8.50, chat with the teacher and each other and collect a reading book from their personalized tray in one of the storage units. Ten minutes later, the teacher checks their names in the register, deals with various items of housekeeping, then summons the children's attention to explain their tasks for the first hour or so. Once this is done, the children work in their groups from cards, worksheets or textbooks, and the teacher moves from one group to the next, quickly during the first few minutes to establish that the tasks are fully understood, then spending longer with each group and with individual children in the group as the lesson proceeds, not standing over the children but crouching down or pulling up a chair so that her head is close to theirs. Her manner is quiet and conversational; the children's, mostly, likewise.

A few miles away, in an older two-storey block on a bleak 1960s housing estate, the visitor negotiates the locked door and security intercom to find beyond the less pristine exterior a similar internal ambience to that of the first school, although here it belies a daunting catalogue of social and behavioural problems which the head links to the area's low per-capita income, high unemployment and high crime rate. The other contrast is spiritual: everywhere are the images and words which remind one that this, a Roman Catholic school, is shaped by church as well as state, by religious imperatives as well as those of the National Curriculum, annual tests and Office for Standards in Education (OFSTED) inspections. The classrooms reveal the

familiar ecology of displays and groups, but in one, once the children have settled
and the register has been taken, the teacher commands their attention with the still
novel greeting 'Welcome to the Literacy Hour!'. She then embarks on her version of
the formula which the government has recently prescribed for every primary child,
teacher and classroom in the country – 15 minutes of whole class 'shared text
work', 15 minutes of whole class 'focused word work', 20 minutes of individual
work during which the teacher concentrates on just two of the class's six groups,
and a final ten-minute plenary to review what has been accomplished.

Finally, to a terraced street of back-to-back red brick houses in one of the country's largest cities, once part of the industrial hub of empire, now striving to recreate
itself as a centre for the service and retail sectors, education, culture and even
tourism. The street – and the many others arranged in a dense grid across this part
of the city – is Victorian, but the school is modern. It is a complicated, low-ceilinged,
single-storey affair of 'home bases' and 'practical areas'. Children spill over from
one into the other, and – since each practical area is shared by two classes – from
one class into the next, and no one space seems quite large enough for its purpose.
Here, too, the Literacy Hour now rules, together with its companion the Numeracy
Hour – or, more correctly, a sliding scale from 45 minutes for the youngest pupils
and an hour for the oldest – with a similar structure of timed lesson stages and
whole class teaching and a strong emphasis on mental arithmetic. These novelties
apart, the school's most striking feature is its inhabitants, for nearly half of the
children are from Muslim families whose roots encompass villages in Pakistan as
well as these red-brick urban streets, and the colour and formality of their traditional
dress contrast with the jeans, sweatshirts and trainers worn by the white children.
Here, then, the implementation of the government's Literacy Hour is complicated, for
the children as well as the teachers, by the context of bilingualism, and the school's
corporate values must accommodate to the imperatives of a multi-ethnic and multi-
faith community.

Brave New Millennium

Shortly before the end of the second millennium the UK government launched its
blueprint for the beginning of the third. Dismissing both 'naive reliance on markets'
and 'old-fashioned state intervention' – the doctrines of its Conservative and Labour
predecessors – New Labour announced the discovery of a 'third way'[1] and nailed its
colours to the mast of the 'knowledge-driven economy'. In the global economy, the
government asserted:

> Capital is mobile, technology spreads quickly and goods can be made in low cost
> countries and shipped to developed markets . . . British business therefore has to compete
> by exploiting capabilities which competitors find hard to imitate. The UK's distinctive
> capabilities are not raw materials, land or cheap labour. They must be our knowledge,
> skills and creativity.[2]

Specifically, the four capabilities most urgently required were enterprise and entre-preneurship, the exploitation of science and technology, key and managerial skills, and information and communications technology.

The 1998 Competitiveness White Paper, in which this case was presented, was an initiative of the government's Department of Trade and Industry (DTI), although the requirements it placed on the education service were clear enough. In parallel, the Department for Education and Employment (DfEE) launched its own vision, that of a 'learning age . . . of information and global competition' requiring 'ingenuity, enterprise, design and marketing skills' and exploiting the UK's leadership in information and communications technology (ICT) and biotechnology.[3] A National Skills Task Force (New Labour's pervasive use of the language of the military campaign merits a study in its own right) was recruited to draw up a National Skills Agenda. Its aim was

> The establishment of a national culture of high skills and an education and training system able to deliver appropriately and at the right time. We live in an age of global competition and constant change. We must seek to achieve a high skill, high value added economy as the recipe for national competitiveness. For a truly dynamic economy, we must keep the skills of our people 'ahead of the curve'.[4]

The skills in question were set out under three headings: *generic skills* which are transferable across occupational groups and which include the 'key skills' of communication, application of number, problem-solving, team-working, ICT and the capacity to improve one's performance; the more specific *vocational skills* needed to work within a particular occupation or group of occupations; and *job-specific skills* for distinctive positions within an occupation. Formal education would concentrate on the first two categories.

Dovetailed with this were the government's requirements for basic education, spearheaded by their drive to raise standards in literacy and numeracy in the primary years. Literacy and numeracy would then form the base of a skills pyramid whose superstructure would comprise what the Qualifications and Curriculum Authority (QCA) called – in an effort to give coherence to the deluge of 'skills' recipes pouring out of think tanks and governmental departments – *basic skills* (literacy and numeracy with oracy), *key skills* (communication, application of number and ICT), *wider key skills* (working with others, problem-solving and improving one's performance), and *adult life and generic skills* (other skills required in the world of work).[5]

This response to the challenges of change begs a number of questions. How far is the received analysis of the global imperative valid and just? Are the skills which have been identified the skills which are actually needed? Is the new skills vocabulary sustainable, or is it indefensibly reductionist? (Interestingly, the UK Confederation of British Industry [CBI], which one might have expected to endorse the government line, took a more traditional, less skills-oriented approach, arguing the need for curriculum balance and a strong emphasis on personal development[6]). And is the endorsement of the old 'basics' of literacy and numeracy as the bedrock of the 'new' primary education appropriate?

This chapter considers particularly the first question, embedding it in a wider consideration of how the current English system of primary education relates to its national and international context. This will take us to the matter of how this system compares with those of other countries, to the problems and possibilities of making such comparisons, and thence to the five countries which provide the lens for this book's analysis of primary education at the levels of policy and practice.

The Ages of Primary Education

Eric Hobsbawm sees the period 1870–1914 as 'in most European countries, the age of the primary school' – an age of nation-building in which primary or elementary education became universal and compulsory, and states exploited its power to 'teach all children how to become good subjects and citizens'.[7] For Britain, the imperatives of social cohesion were balanced with those of economic prosperity. National identity in part grew, and of course still grows, out of international comparison and economic competition. Economic warfare reinforced identities which, in Linda Colley's analysis, had been forged by the long succession of military wars during 1689–1715 and cemented by Protestantism: the enemy was both without and within.[8] During the first 'age of the primary school' it was the industrial and economic might of Germany, and especially Prussia, which Britain most feared, although Britain was at least a world power and there was always an empire to fall back on. During the third age of the primary school – for so the period from the mid 1980s seems to be shaping up, after a second age which established primary education as a distinct phase – the picture is a good deal more complex and fragile.

Yet on balance one of the defining characteristics of English primary education as it developed during the twentieth century was not its national, still less its international consciousness, but its insularity and parochialism. Elsewhere, Hobsbawm portrays the twentieth century as 'An age of unparalleled and marvellous progress scientifically and technologically' and 'Without doubt the most murderous century of which we have record, both by the scale, frequency and length of the warfare which filled it . . . but also by the unparalleled scale of the human catastrophes it produced, from the greatest famines in history to systematic genocide'.[9]

How a state system for educating young children might have responded to these enormities is unclear. That it could have responded more adequately to the march of science and technology is beyond dispute. Yet for much of its history, indeed until the last decade of the twentieth century, neither featured in more than a small minority of English primary schools.

If the period 1870–1914 was the (first) age of the primary school, it was also the age of a minimalist conception of what primary schooling should attempt to achieve: 'The duty of a state in public education is . . . to obtain the greatest possible quantity of reading, writing and arithmetic for the greatest number'.[10]

This view, from the 1861 Newcastle Commission Report on elementary education, dominated the discourse of English primary education not just for the remainder of the nineteenth century but also, arguably, into the twenty-first. The only real alternative was that offered by the progressive movement and endorsed by the Hadow and Plowden reports of 1931 and 1967, respectively.[11] But this alternative looked not outward to society, still less to the world beyond Dover. Its values were bounded by a preoccupation with the child, the family and the community. The Plowden Report, which brought into the mainstream of primary education ideas about children's development and needs which had hitherto informed only the minority progressive counter-culture, found that it could say nothing about society other than to be vaguely 'hopeful and fearful' about its future and commend that schools respond by promoting 'flexibility' and 'adaptability'.[12] But these, as I noted in 1984, are at best extremely difficult objectives to achieve in any operable sense and, at worst (since the words are frequently invoked but rarely explicated), are a device for dodging serious social analysis.[13]

Plowden, therefore, effectively washed its hands of the vital question of the relationship between education and society. Others at this time – only a few others, it has to be said – voiced similar reservations to mine. White, for example, noted that the English primary teacher 'of all members of the teaching profession, has traditionally been the least aware. Her typical milieu has been the world of art and crafts, of movement and drama, of learning to read and count. It has typically been a cosy, inward-looking world, quite cut off from the complexities of politics'.[14]

This is not the place to rehearse the reasons for this professional introversion. They had to do partly with the character of primary schools as institutions, partly with the now long-defunct system of teacher training which isolated future primary teachers from the mainstream of higher education in training colleges whose ethos, in Taylor's often-quoted words, was one of 'social and literary romanticism . . . suspicion of the intellect and the intellectual; a lack of interest in political and structural change; a stress upon the intuitive and the intangible, upon spontaneity and creativity . . . a hunger for the satisfactions of interpersonal life within the community and the small group, and a flight from rationality.'[15]

The isolation and inwardness, then, were as much ideological as situational. In fact, for much of the postwar period English primary education kept in uneasy equilibrium a dual legacy – of nineteenth-century elementary education and of the progressive counterculture. The one sought to produce a workforce which was functionally literate and numerate but socially conformist and politically docile, while the other celebrated individual fulfilment, although not social empowerment.

This hybrid[16] held good throughout the 1970s and into the 1980s. It remained untouched by the growing but intensely pessimistic global consciousness of a period which was dominated by the Cold War, Vietnam, the threat of nuclear catastrophe, post-colonial instability, war and famine in Africa, the growth of militant fundamentalism, and the alternative Armageddon of an imploding 'spaceship earth' overwhelmed by the multiple crisis of overpopulation, resource depletion and environmental degradation;[17] a period when Hobsbawm's 'Golden Age' of postwar growth and social reconstruction (1945–75) gave way to an era of 'decomposition, uncertainty and crisis'.[18] English primary education remained immune to all this. It also remained immune to the UK's economic crises of the mid and late 1970s which produced the inevitable backlash of blame heaped upon education in general, and on the values of progressive primary education and egalitarian comprehensive education in particular.[19] It began to emerge from its cocoon only with the dramatic change from educational *laissez-faire* to direct government control which was initiated by Margaret Thatcher's government from 1987 onwards, and accelerated by the Blair administration a decade later.

Even then, although the government's agenda for primary education was by the early 1990s unambiguously societal and economic rather than individualist, the overall scope and balance of the English primary curriculum had changed relatively little. The old 'basics' of reading, writing and number were consolidated, and the arts and humanities, although increasingly squeezed by the new arrivals of science, IT, design and technology, retained a place which – local pockets of purist progressivism apart – had in truth never been much more than marginal.

It was the encroachment of the particular kind of international consciousness denoted by the word 'globalization' which looked most likely to produce radical change to a model of primary education which had displayed remarkable continuity in its fundamentals for over a century. One symptom was the growing obsession with – and panic over – international league tables of educational attainment. Another was the insistence that nothing, and certainly not anything as *passé* and elitist as the notion of a rounded education, should get in the way of literacy and numeracy. A third was the language of targets and standards. Yet another was the reduction of all school learning to batteries of workplace-oriented 'skills' – as pointed up at the beginning of this chapter. It is time to look in more detail at the phenomenon that fuelled the new educational instrumentalism.

Globalization

Giddens rehearses the arguments in favour of the proposition that globalization marks a quantum leap in the world's economic and social relations, especially where the developed Western and Pacific Rim economies are concerned. He sees it as a combination of processes: the expanded role of world financial markets, turning over more than 'a trillion dollars a day . . . in currency exchange transactions . . . the communications revolution and the spread of information technology . . . the transformation of time and space in our lives' in which 'distant events, whether economic or not, affect us more directly and immediately than ever before . . . [and] decisions we take as individuals are often global in their implications.' It is also a process which subjects nations and states to acute dilemmas of identity and which threatens to undercut social solidarity and replace it by 'institutionalized individualism'.[20]

Giddens' account, however, is relatively cautious, and balances prediction with social concern in equal measure. Far more gung-ho and morally agnostic is the 1998 report from the Royal Society of Arts (RSA). In this, according to my sampled word count, the most frequent adjective is 'new', the most frequent verb is 'will' (rather than the more prudent 'may' or 'might') and the most pervasive phrase is 'in the new world'. No distinction is drawn between the trends that are desirable and those that are undesirable: all are simply bracketed together as inevitable.

Globalization is an unstoppable juggernaut. With a gleam in its corporate eye the RSA report welcomes

> A world where there are few fixed boundaries between public, private and voluntary; we will no longer make assumptions about what belongs to a sector or a place. Most people will be working, but fewer will have jobs; the days of the 'job-shaped' job and the job-based career are numbered . . . Technology will make the skilled globally mobile. More and more organisations . . . will be virtual organisations . . . Much of this change has begun. It will not stop . . . Managing uncertainty will be the name of the game . . . Information and communications technology will transform the face of education . . . Flexible working will breed a new kind of employee . . . The new skills will be in managing the virtual workforce.

And, of particular note in the context of this book:

> In the new world, the education system will be built around information and communications technology . . . will use a new, IT-based pedagogy . . . developed by education specialists, psychologists and technologists as well as business . . . will [have] a competence-based curriculum.

Unfortunately, having said all this, the report pulls the rug out from under its (virtual) feet with:

> In the new world of our vision, the only thing anyone can be certain about is the constancy of change.[21]

Reduced to their essentials, the common elements in this and similar analyses are two: global economic interdependence and competitiveness; and the limitless potential of information and communications technology. The common omission is any acknowledgement of the human and social downside of these developments, especially for those – individuals, groups, nations, states, continents even – who will be neither beneficiaries nor participants, including (in Nelson Mandela's telling estimate) the two-thirds of the world's population who have never used a telephone, let alone e-mail or the Internet. (The extent to which Internet use in 1998 was dominated by the mere 19 per cent of the world's population who live in OECD countries, especially the United States, is shown in the United Nations' *Human Development Report* 1999.[22])

This apart for the present, there are two kinds of critique or counter-prediction to the above with which, in an educational context, we need to engage (the third is to dismiss globalization as a chimera, or at best a continuation of a process which started a century ago, but that is probably not an option). One critique accepts the broad definition of globalization as 'the interconnectedness of capital, production, ideas and cultures at an increasing pace'[23] but sees it as, in its own terms, fraught with danger and risk as well as opportunity. The other views a definition of globalization that focuses only on its economic and informational aspects as seriously deficient and in need of extension.

Thus, Kennedy warns of the danger of globalization running out of control, disadvantaging those unable to compete and leading to nationalism and protectionism. He points to the massive and growing income disparity between workers in the United States and Europe and those in the successful Pacific Rim economies. He sees a potential Third World workforce of about 1.2 billion people poised to enter global production and labour markets, most earning less than US$3 per day (as compared with the *per diem* average of $85 for workers in the United States and Europe). As a consequence of these trends he predicts wholesale industrial transfer from West to East, a 'colossal depressive force' on wages in the richer countries, heightened competition spilling over into trade conflict, political instability, public discontent, and the rise of nationalism and fundamentalism in those countries unable to compete. And he – like others – asks whether Marx was not, after all, right.[24]

By and large, and as one would expect, historians seem more alive to the social risks of globalization than do economists. Thus, noting that while historians tend to be 'agnostics about the future, hence virtual pessimists, economists and business people tend to be optimists,' Landes debunks the assumptions that 'the world will continue to get richer . . . the poor will catch up with the rich . . . islands of growth will become continents . . . knowledge will solve problems and overcome material and social difficulties along the way' – arguing instead that global industrial diffusion will lead to a 'levelling down of wages, increased inequality of incomes and/or high levels of (transitional?) unemployment'.[25]

And, reminding us that 'other things being equal, it is the rich who poison the earth' he revisits the ecological doom scenarios of the 1970s. Giddens, too, couples ecology with globalization in his list of dilemmas confronting the 'new' social democratic politics of Blair and his counterparts in Germany and France, rehearsing the now familiar scenarios of global warming, resource depletion and food degradation.[26] (In the latter case he cites BSE: since Giddens' book appeared public anxiety in the UK has switched to the genetic modification of food, and since the food market is one increasingly international market among many, biotechnology can be added to the list of the mixed blessings of globalization.) The point is made more forcibly by Landes, who credits the Green Revolution of the 1960s–90s with seeing off – for the time being at least – Malthus's (and Ehrlich's) more pessimistic predictions of global famine but asks whether biotechnology can continue to deliver on the promises of its advocates without destroying the environment.[27]

However, aside from its caution in the face of unguarded economic optimism, the historical perspective on globalization has one crucial advantage over the economic one: it concerns itself first and last with human agency and human consequences. On this basis, as Landes notes, 'if we can learn anything from the history of economic development, it is that culture makes all the difference', and this provides the clue to how the new economic order is, and will be, differently handled in different countries and regions. He contrasts East Asian entrepreneurship with, in post-Soviet Russia, '75 years of anti-market, anti-profit schooling and insider privilege [which] have planted and frozen anti-entrepreneurial attitudes. Even after the regime has fallen people fear the uncertainties of the market place and yearn for the safe tedium of state employment.'[28]

However, not all the economists are as optimistic as Landes claims. I have referred to Kennedy above. Hutton argues that a global financial market without global financial regulation will spiral out of control, and in turn he cites the testimony of arch speculator George Soros to the US House of Representatives in 1998 that 'financial markets are inherently unstable' and 'the belief that financial markets, left to their own devices, tend towards equilibrium . . . is false'.[29] By 1999, there was increasing public concern about the need for financial controls, a concern which New Labour, at least at the time of writing, seemed unprepared to countenance, despite Prime Minister Blair's dismissal of 'naive reliance on markets.'

Other Worlds

Clearly, then a definition or vision of globalization as an economic-cum-informational bonanza is pretty wide of the mark. On this at least, economists and historians agree. It is therefore unfortunate, to say the least, that the more restricted and uncritical view has had such a prominent airing in educational circles.

Perhaps the most comprehensive corrective to naive futurology is provided by Manuel Castells in his formidable trilogy *The Information Age: Economy, Society and Culture*.[30] In setting the scene for a searching analysis of the condition of the world at the turn of the millennium Castells presents economic globalization and the IT revolution as two events among many – albeit powerful and pervasive ones – which are transforming our lives and consciousness. His full list includes:

- the technological revolution centred on IT
- economic globalization and interdependence, and the resulting reworking of the relationship between economy, state and society
- the collapse of Soviet statism, the demise of communism, the consequent loss of the historical opposition to capitalism and the transformation of global geopolitics
- the restructuring of capitalism, with increased flexibility, networking and decentralization
- the decline of the power of organized labour relative to that of capital
- increased individualization and diversification of working relationships
- increased participation of women in the workforce, although often under discriminatory conditions
- state intervention to deregulate markets and dismantle the welfare state
- increased global economic competition
- the reshaping of the world's economic blocks with the rise of the Asian Pacific, the consolidation of the European Union, and the decline of the Third World and the former communist bloc
- uneven development not just between the world's north and south but everywhere
- the globalization of organized crime
- the use of the new technology to enable individuals to satisfy hitherto unachievable needs and desires, including those which were formerly illicit or taboo

- the decline of patriarchy, the emergence of gender as a contested domain, and the redefinition of relationships between women, men and children
- the spreading through societies of environmental consciousness, and its consequent hijacking for political advantage
- a crisis of legitimacy for political systems and for politicians vis-à-vis electorates
- the crisis of individual and collective identity resulting from all these changes, especially social, cultural, religious and ethnic identity, the search for new identities through emphemeral social groups and the resurgence of the older identities of religious fundamentalism
- the rise of nationalism, racism and xenophobia
- social fragmentation, social exclusion, the breakdown of communication, the alienation of groups and individuals, all as a consequence of the crisis of identity
- the emergence of millenarism in a variety of guises and through a variety of gurus: technology new age prophets, postmodernists, political and religious extremists.[31]

Much of this Castells summarizes as 'a bipolar opposition between the Net and the Self', or between the 'abstract, universal instrumentalism' of global economic and information networks on the one hand, and those individual and collective identities which are deeply rooted in culture and history.

It is a daunting scenario, and one which engenders precisely the feeling of helplessness in the reader which Castells charts more generally in society, particularly Western post-industrial society. Yet he argues as strenuously against the nihilism and extreme individualism of the postmodernist analysis as he does against the naive technological determinism of the kind I illustrated earlier. Nothing, in his view, is inevitable; humans can and must take control.

From the standpoint of basic education it is clear that to view the challenge of the information age as merely one of making tomorrow's citizens computer literate falls pitifully short of what is needed. Although IT literacy is a necessary tool for survival in the new global/informational economy, and the UK government was right to initiate high-profile developments in this regard,[32] the equally pressing and much more taxing problem for education is how to respond to the human and social dimensions of the conditions which Castells and others investigate, especially the crisis of meaning and identity, the growth of individualism, and the loss of social consciousness and cohesion. If today's children and tomorrow's adults cannot relate meaningfully to each other and have no real sense of who they are, where they belong, where they come from or where they are going; if they find their world fragmented, hostile and alienating; if individual and collective morality are meaningless concepts; if they find that their only way of coping is to escape into the virtual reality of the web, downloading more and more information but knowing less and less; then basic education will have failed, and dismally.

Castells' analysis, then, is daunting but not apocalyptic. The warnings he sounds are a proper and inevitable consequence of acknowledging the multi-dimensionality of the economic and information revolutions, and of placing them in some kind of historical and cultural context. And his analysis is shared by others. So, for example, historians David Landes and Eric Hobsbawm, both referred to above, arrive at a similar prospect by a different route;[33] as does sociologist Krishan Kumar;[34] and the briefer account of the dilemmas of modern society and polity provided by sociologist and New Labour guru Anthony Giddens devotes a substantial part of his case for the 'third way' to addressing issues such as individual and collective identity, individualism, social solidarity and social inclusion/exclusion. His prospectus combines a reinvigorated and active civil society, a renewal of democracy and a strengthening of family and community, among other ingredients.[35]

Rather more pessimistic is journalist Melanie Phillips, who focuses on some of the intellectual and social symptoms of the current crisis (for that is how she sees it) – the twin scourges of cultural relativism and postmodernism, the decline of individual and collective morality, the breakdown of the family, the threat to liberal democracy.[36] Her explanatory canvas, however, is unacceptably narrow. Despite the fact that what she charts can be treated as part of the wider condition of Western post-industrial society and has international as well as national roots, she deals exclusively with Britain and indeed lays much of the blame at the door of UK state education, its apologists and its 'establishment'. In this sense, although her analysis is useful in its account of some of the conditions which must give educationists cause for concern, it is seriously deficient in its analysis of cause, effect and solution. And although she – like HMCI Woodhead – cites Matthew Arnold in support of the cultural imperative in education ('the best that has been thought and said in the world'[37]) the real genealogy for her polemic is the political scapegoating of the 1960s–70s Black Papers.[38] Arnold, of course, although he had a European rather than a merely British consciousness and indeed knew several European education systems at first hand, was addressing not the circumstances of global interconnectedness which we perforce must consider in the 2000s, but those of industrial and bourgeois Britain in the 1860s.

These examples are given to buttress my argument that if we are to rethink basic education for the global era we shall need a perspective on the world which is rather more generous in its apprehension of time, space, social structure, human relations and the connections between them than UK governments in recent years have been prepared to allow. Moreover, although I referred earlier to that majority of the world's population which is disenfranchized by poverty, it has to be said that any account which confines itself to globalization – which is after all essentially a Western invention – runs the risk of ethnocentrism on a grand scale. By way of a very different starting point, therefore, we should inject into the discussion some rather different realities.

So, as an indication of how unlevel is the playing field of the global economy, we might note that the per capita GDP in 1999 ranged from US\$29,010 in the United States to \$410 in Sierra Leone, with the average of \$992 for the least-developed countries against the industrialized country average of \$23,741.[39]

This is stark enough. However, in its synoptic *The Progress of Nations*, the United Nations Children's Fund (UNICEF) ranks countries not by their position in the economic league table but by the condition of the children. This yields a set of statistics with massive and telling disparities. For example, accurate national population figures are essential to the planning of social and educational provision, yet while in Europe an average of 98.8 per cent of births are registered, in southern and eastern Asia only 76.5 per cent are. In the USA 89 per cent of children are immunized against measles; the figure for Niger is 21 per cent. The under-five mortality rate varies internationally from 4 to 320 per 1,000 live births and the maternal death rate from 0 to 1,800 deaths per 100,000 live births. As one indicator of the conditions and rights of adolescent girls and women, while in France the number of births for every 1,000 teenage girls is 8, in India it is 109 and in Guinea 229.[40] And if we take adult literacy as the yardstick for educational progress we can note that although from 1960 to 1990 the number of literate people in the world doubled, this achievement was neutralized by population growth, leaving a staggering figure of 800 million illiterates.[41] Indeed, by other calculations, one-sixth of humanity, and one in four adults in the developing world is illiterate, and the numbers are growing.[42]

More specifically, we find that primary school enrolment maps closely with GDP, giving an average of 91 per cent enrolment for high income countries (with most Western countries actually at or near 100 per cent), and a 54 per cent average for low income countries. Broken down, this figure yields individual country enrolments as low as 10 per cent for girls and 20 per cent for boys in some of the poorest countries. Worldwide in 1999, 125 million children – equal to the total school-age child population of North America and Europe – never attend school; another 150 million children start primary school but drop out before they can read and write.[43] And those children who do enrol, and who stay (low enrolment is often followed by high dropout) are taught in classes averaging 40:1 in low-income countries and 20:1 in high-income countries, although the range is of course much greater, with low-income country averages of 50:1 or 60:1, and individual class ratios in some of these countries frequently over 100:1. In contrast, we find average pupil–teacher ratios of between 12:1 and 25:1 in the richest countries.[44]

These differences are combined within the Human Development Index (HDI) developed from a much larger array of statistical indicators to provide 'a measure of the same level of vulgarity as GNP . . . but a measure that is not as blind to social aspects of human lives as GNP is'.[45] The HDI 'reflects achievements in the most basic human capabilities – leading a long life, being knowledgeable and enjoying a decent standard of living'. It uses just three variables: life expectancy, education and income. On this basis, Canada heads the list with an HDI value of 0.932 as compared with Sierra Leone's of 0.254 (1997 figures).[46]

From tip-the-iceberg figures such as these it is clear that our interdependent world is also a polarized world. It is polarized in terms of income, life expectancy, health, welfare, gender, class, caste, access to schooling, educational attainment, adult literacy, employment, access to democratic processes, freedom from violence, human rights, and countless other indicators of the real and fundamental inequalities between the world's gainers and losers which make the word 'globalization' so profoundly misleading; especially as, historically, gainers and losers are inextricably linked by the ties of colonialism, exploitation, hegemony and dependency, and both gain and loss are self-reinforcing spirals which are reversed only with difficulty.

What helps to drive home the implications of all this for education is to juxtapose two visions for our millennial year 2000 (Figure 1.1). The first contains the six National Education Goals announced by the Bush administration in 1991 (later extended and enshrined in the United States Educate America Act of 1994 which we discuss on pages 104–5).[47] The second comprises the goals adopted by the 1990 UNICEF-sponsored World Summit for Children.[48]

Goals 2000

- By the year 2000, all children in America will start school ready to learn.
- By the year 2000, the high school graduation rate will increase to at least 90 per cent.
- By the year 2000, all students will leave grades 4, 8 and 12 having demonstrated competency over challenging subject matter including English, mathematics, science, foreign languages, civics and government, economics, arts, history and geography, and every school in America will ensure that all students use their minds well, so that they may be prepared for responsible citizenship, further learning, and productive employment.
- By the year 2000, United States students will be first in the world in mathematics and science achievement.
- By the year 2000, every adult American will be literate and will possess the knowledge and skills necessary to compete in a global economy and exercise the rights and responsibilities of citizenship.
- By the year 2000, every school in the United States will be free of drugs, violence, and the unauthorized presence of firearms and alcohol and will offer a disciplined environment conducive to learning.

Target 2000

- Reduction of infant and under-five child mortality rates by one-third of the 1990 levels, or to 50 and 70 per 1,000 live births respectively, whichever is less.
- Reduction of 1990 maternal mortality rates by half.
- Reduction of severe and moderate malnutrition among under-five children by half of the 1990 levels.
- Universal access to safe drinking water and to sanitary means of excreta disposal.
- Universal access to basic education and completion of primary education by at least 80 per cent of primary-school-age children.
- Reduction of the adult illiteracy rate to no more than half its 1990 level, with emphasis on female literacy.
- Improved protection of children in especially difficult circumstances.

Figure 1.1   Goals for the millennium

Alternatively, we might take the resounding declaration of the 1990 Jomtien World Conference on *Education for All* that basic education should be universalized by 2000 – a declaration that by 1996 was so far from fulfilment that OECD shifted the date to 2015, and even that looked optimistic.[49] The World Education Forum, meeting in April 2000, stuck to a target date of 2015 for universalizing primary education and added 2005 for achieving equal access for boys and girls.

In sum, although for a country such as the UK globalization demands a rethinking of the educational as well as the economic agenda, that agenda cannot be confined to increasing national economic competitiveness and maximizing informational capacity and skills, necessary although these manifestly are (and I understand fully the reasoning that without these other aspirations may become a luxury). Globalization has human, social and environmental as well as economic and informational consequences – indeed the economic consequences are human, social and environmental or they are nothing – and it is by its nature a force for destabilization which challenges or undermines established identities at every level from individual to collective and national.

Moreover, globalization, even if it is more comprehensively defined, is at best a partial picture of those global realities which demand attention in an interconnected future. On present estimates, the majority of the world's population will be affected by globalization to some degree but will not benefit from it, and indeed many will be positively disadvantaged by it. For every winner in the new global race there could be many more losers, just as there were in the old. These questions, too, demand attention if basic education is to fulfil the promise of universalization. Its agenda is moral as well as pragmatic. A country needs to be civilized as well as solvent.

International Comparisons in Education, Old and New

Placing education in the context of the disparities in human development between the world's richest and poorest nations allows one kind of educational comparison. The 'international horse race'[50] provoked by the league tables of national test scores in reading, number and science permits another. International comparison between educational systems more generally has a long history, although it is only recently that it has been motivated by concern for others rather than national self-interest. Comparing, of course, is one of the most basic of conscious human activities: we necessarily and constantly compare in order to make choices and to judge where we stand in relation to others and to our own past. In the more specific context of education it is important to distinguish the comparing, importing and exporting of ideas, which is an activity intrinsic to educational development, from the task of attempting to devise rules and procedures for doing so in a systematic way. In the former context we would place the influence of Greece and Rome on medieval monastic learning and later, rediscovered, on classical humanist education from the Renaissance onwards. We would also locate here the pan-European development of scientific and vernacular education following the Reformation, especially the influence of Bacon, Descartes, Locke and Comenius; here, too, Rousseau, Pestalozzi, Herbart, Froebel and, more recently, Montessori, Dewey and the peculiarly Anglo-Saxon variants of progressivism which emerged in Britain and the United States; or the influence of the American common high school on the development of secondary education in Europe. Likewise – as saw briefly in the Introduction – Matthew Arnold's attempt to broaden the debate about popular education in England with his reports on education in France, Switzerland and Holland. The examples are numerous, for educational ideas have always had strong international currency, and this shows itself at both ends of the macro–micro continuum, in the striking similarities in the education systems of countries that are otherwise very different,[51] and in the fine detail of classroom practice.

There is also a more Olympian justification. By 'making the strange familiar' we 'make the familiar strange' and thus increase our understanding of our own society, culture and ways of educating. At the same time, it must be noted that educational comparison is not merely incidental, a by-product of idle human curiosity as it were. For those who have responsibility for the education of others, be they policy-makers, administrators, researchers or teachers, comparison is actually essential to educational progress. Whether we are talking of whole education systems or of the day-to-day encounters of teachers and pupils, education by its nature requires hard choices of both a technical and a moral kind. To make such choices requires an awareness of options and alternatives, together with the capacity to judge what is most fitting in a given set of circumstances. The vocabulary of possibilities is vastly increased and enriched if we extend it beyond the boundaries of one school to others, one region to others, one culture to others and one country to others. Education positively requires, and positively benefits from, a comparative imagination and comparative understanding.

Despite this, comparative education as a more or less systematic intellectual discipline is usually traced back no further than 1817, to Marc-Antoine Jullien's *Sketch and Preparatory Survey of a Work on Comparative Education*, which set down a procedure for assembling and disseminating comparable information on different education systems.[52] Michael Sadler's work can be placed in this more recent tradition in as far as it entailed comparisons that were consciously disciplined. His accounts at the end of the nineteenth century produced insights and principles which comparativists still quote a century later – and with good reason:

> In studying foreign systems of education we should not forget that the things outside the schools matter even more than the things inside the schools, and govern and interpret the things inside . . . The practical value of studying in a right spirit and with scholarly accuracy the working of foreign systems of education is that it will result in our being better fitted to study and understand our own . . . No other nation, by imitating a little bit of German organisation, can thus hope to achieve a true reproduction of the spirit of German institutions. The fabric of an organisation practically forms one whole. That is its merits, and its danger. It must either be taken in all, or left unimitated . . . All good and true education is an expression of national life and character.[53]

King sees the development of comparative education over the past 200 years as having four phases: to inform the development of particular institutions (universities, schools and so on); to guide the process of universalizing whole sectors such as elementary education; to place the evaluation of national systems in an international context; and to guide national educational policy. This expanding role, then, has been increasingly directed at policy and the solution of policy problems.[54] In this, comparative analysis can serve a corrective or supportive function in the policy process, providing, in Phillips' words 'authoritative objective data which can be used to put the less objective data of others (politicians and administrators, principally) . . . to the test'.[55]

However, although King is right to point up the instrumentalism which has motivated much educational comparison, he somewhat blurs the distinction I have made, and which I consider it essential to make, between those comparisons which are opportunistic and methodologically unselfconscious and those which, while not necessarily any less instrumental, are framed – as were Sadler's – by a strong sense of the exercise's risks and limitations and its consequent methodological imperatives. Moreover, it certainly cannot be assumed, as Phillips implies, that professional comparativists are by virtue of their job more objective than politicians or administrators. For a start, the latter frequently have access to information to which academics can gain access only with difficulty, if at all; and the comparativist's claims to 'authoritative' objectivity – whatever that is – must be tested no less searchingly than those of politicians and administrators.

In any event, the constituencies are not nearly as clear cut as Phillips suggests. National politicians in the UK – that is to say, Members of Parliament – are, by and large, well-educated and intelligent people; many have good academic backgrounds and some indeed are former academics. There is also a certain amount of interchange between academic and administrative roles, particularly, as it happens, in the international field (the UK Department for International Development and the British Council provide many examples). Not a few academics – this author included – find themselves serving as national policy advisers. And there are both academically inclined politicians and politically motivated academics. The divide, then, is one of outlook, approach and allegiance rather than occupational group.

We now have a context in which the activity of international educational comparison, as it stands at the turn of the millennium, can be situated. The discipline of comparative education continues to develop, and indeed after several decades of relative marginality within the field of educational studies it is experiencing a dramatic revival.[56] The reasons for this have little to do with the discipline as such, and everything to do with that internationalization of educational discourse that is part and parcel of globalization. Yet there is still a clear fault-line between the 'old' and 'new' comparative education. The former – although it honours the likes of Arnold, Darlington and Sadler who were inspectors and administrators – is first and foremost an academic pursuit which aims to expand the sum of our knowledge and understanding of the educational endeavour and whose policy applications are subsidiary to this aim. The new comparativism is policy-oriented from the outset and sees little virtue in undertaking comparative research unless it addresses directly the agendas of those whom 1990s researchspeak calls 'users' (policy-makers and practitioners) and comes up with solutions to the problems which these constituencies identify. Thus it is probably more helpful to make our distinction not in terms of 'old' and 'new', for academic comparative education has in many respect reconstructed itself to take account of new social science paradigms and methodologies, while – as noted above – there is nothing particularly novel about internationally informed policy, but by differentiating *comparative education* (the discipline) and *policy-directed international educational comparison* (the activity, pursued by whatever means are thought appropriate). Crossley simplifies this to a distinction between 'comparative' and 'international' research.[57] My caveat would be that some of the latter is too overtly politicized to justify the label 'research'.

This distinction enables us to locate the impatience – and ignorance – of David Reynolds, who during the 1990s became one of New Labour's most influential educational advisers. He writes despairingly of

> The frankly inept contribution which the comparative education discipline has made over time . . . the presence of a large body of theories, without any apparent empirical backing . . . a large range of descriptive case studies of individual schools which it is impossible to synchronize together because there are no common measures of outcomes or processes utilized . . . descriptions of the range of educational, political, economic and cultural phenomena within different countries, with no attempt ever made to assess the contribution of the educational system as against that of other factors.[58]

Quite apart from the cavalier inaccuracy of most of these claims, especially the one about evidence, this stance is problematic in other respects, for Reynolds in essence contends that there is no place for speculative theory in our attempts to understand other cultures and how education is conceived and undertaken within them; that unless individual researchers in different traditions and different countries co-ordinate their activities within a common analytical framework they might as well go home; that educational phenomena can validly be compared only in terms of measurable processes and outcomes; and that political, cultural, economic and educational aspects of a society are not worth studying unless they can be factor-analysed.

In other words, Reynolds does not make a case *against* comparative education so much as one *for* his preferred mode of international educational comparison. On this basis he can safely ignore the kinds of problems that vex comparativists and to which his own study is no less immune than theirs: for example, misinterpretation or over-interpretation of results in a research field whose inherent frailties are compounded by barriers of culture and language; ethnocentrism; selective borrowing.[59]

However, from this book's standpoint the most fundamental weakness in Reynolds' approach, and in the way international educational comparison was being used more generally in the 1990s UK policy context is his – and its – handling of culture. He says (the italics are mine):

> We do not . . . know yet what is the exact contribution of the *educational* system and of the *cultural* and *social* systems to the very high levels of educational success enjoyed by other societies, although most observers would credit the system at least as much as the society.[60]

Separating the cultural, educational and social into three apparently independent and free-wheeling 'systems', which can then be translated into a collection of factors for the purposes of statistical correlation, is conceptually untenable. Life in schools and classrooms is an aspect of our wider society, not separate from it: a culture does not stop at the school gates. The character and dynamics of school life are shaped by the values that shape other aspects of our national life. The strengths of our primary schools are the strengths of our society; their weaknesses are our society's weaknesses. Or, as Boyer put it, 'A report card on public education is a report card on the nation. Schools can rise no higher than the communities that serve them'.[61] Culture, in comparative analysis and understanding, and certainly in national systems of education, is all.

The compartmentalization of culture is unsatisfactory not only in a broad conceptual sense. If the argument were only one of how the word 'culture' should be defined it would be hardly worth making, in this context anyway. More important are the educational consequences of this view. At national level it enables governments to legitimate their claim that questions of quality in education can be resolved by attacking pedagogy while ignoring structure and resources. It allows them to deny that a government's broader social and economic policies impact in any way on what teachers do, or can do, in the classroom. (Conversely, it allows teachers to excuse or underplay their own agency and to blame government policy or resourcing levels for matters over which they have more control than they may be prepared to admit.) At classroom level it encourages the view that pedagogy carries no educational messages or values of itself, but is merely a value-neutral vehicle for transmitting curricular content; and it discourages vital questions about the importance of 'fit' between pedagogy, the children being taught, and the knowledge domains from which curriculum experiences are drawn. Effective teaching arises from attention to cultural, psychological, epistemological and situational considerations, not merely organizational and technical considerations.[62]

Thus, in the context of the interest in primary education in countries that are as culturally different as the UK and Japan, treating culture as an independent variable in a statistical calculation encourages the assumption that an educational strategy can be detached from the values and conditions which give it meaning and ensure its success, transpose it to a context where these may be diametrically opposed, and yet expect it to deliver the same results.

Comparative Education and Educational Comparison

In contrast to Reynolds' waspish rejection of the entire discipline of comparative education, caveats and all, Patricia Broadfoot subdivides its activities into five categories:

(1) Studies which provide detailed empirical documentation of educational phenomena in a particular, typically national, setting.
(2) Studies which provide (1) above but which are contextualized in terms of the broader international debates, theoretical frameworks and empirical accounts of the issues.
(3) Studies which are designed as explicitly comparative, based on a coherent rationale for their selection in order to illuminate 'constants and contexts'.

(4) Studies in which the contexts being compared are themselves theorized as part of wider social science debates on, for example, the relationships of system and action, power and control, culture and the creation of meaning.

(5) Studies which use comparative research to inform theory.[63]

This contrasts with, or complements, Noah's identification of the methodological range of comparative studies as including:

> Work that is primarily descriptive . . . work that seeks to be analytic or explanatory . . . work that is limited to just one, or a very few, nations as well as . . . work that embraces a wide scope . . . work that relies on non-quantitative as well as quantitative data and methods . . . and work that proceeds with explicitly-formulated social science paradigms in mind as well as in a less formalised manner.

Noah's methodological spectrum can be systematized as a set of four dimensions which cross-cut Broadfoot's five study types (the order of the last two is reversed to achieve a more logical sequence of decisions):

(1) *Purpose*: descriptive – analytic – explanatory.
(2) *Scale*: one country – a few countries – many countries.
(3) *Paradigm*: formalized – less formalized.
(4) *Methods and data*: quantitative – qualitative – mixed.

Broadfoot's framework, useful although it is in pointing up issues of scale and purpose, does however confirm the fault-line identified above, although from the other side: for here, if comparative education informs anything beyond itself it is theory rather than policy. However, this exclusiveness, although theoretically more coherent than Reynolds', is in its own way as unsatisfactory, for it seems to discourage comparativists from making the effort to tackle real-world educational problems, or from pursuing the relationship between educational analysis and its application. Instead, comparative education remains sealed within its disciplinary confines, dangerously giving comfort to those who portray the academic study of education as a world that talks only to itself. It is a pity that it should be Broadfoot who unintentionally confirms this view, for her own comparative studies of teachers, teaching and assessment in England and France have real-world applications which are as direct as they are significant.[64]

On the other hand, the British comparative education establishment does now seem to have opened its doors to a stance which is economically and politically more engaged. Watson powerfully argues the need for reconceptualization of the entire field in the light of new global imperatives.[65] Crossley makes a case for a rapprochement between comparative and international research as differentiated above,[66] and this ought to be encouraged by the establishment of the British Association of International and Comparative Education (BAICE) in 1998 in which – crucially – academic comparativists come together with those closely involved in the politics of educational development, aid and consultancy.

My own stance – although I am conscious that after the foregoing it may sound a trifle sanctimonious – is one of triple commitment within the field of primary education: to the pursuit of understanding, the improvement of policy and the amelioration of practice. These objectives are not incompatible, and like many academics working at the interface between study pure and applied I have always found it deeply unhelpful that in British intellectual life they should be treated as though they are. The amelioration of policy and practice can motivate the work of the educational researcher, but it need not compromise it.

Broadfoot's and Noah's frameworks can be used as a cue for attempting something similar in respect of the comparative counter-culture. If there are five kinds of comparative education, there also seem to be, existing outside the comparative education discipline, five kinds of policy-directed international educational comparison, each classifiable in terms of the four methodological dimensions derived from Noah:

(1) system-level factual information and databases (descriptive/many countries/no paradigm/mixed quantitative and qualitative data)
(2) system-level indicators of input, process and output (analytic/many countries/ statistical paradigm/quantitative
(3) international league tables of educational performance (analytic/many countries/ educational measurement paradigm/quantitative)
(4) effectiveness studies (explanatory/a few countries/effectiveness paradigm/ quantitative)
(5) value-for-money studies (analytic/many countries/cost-benefit paradigm/ quantitative.

This is a hierarchy of aspiration. To understand requires that we have, at the very least, information (1). To judge how well we are doing requires us to judge outcomes in relation to input (2). Alternatively, it requires us to be able to compare our outcomes with those of other countries (3). To improve our performance entails knowing which practices are most effective (4). And to do so within budgetary constraints necessitates careful costings of those strategies deemed most effective in order that we can judge which gives best value for money (5).

We have, then, three frameworks for bringing some semblance of order to the field of international comparison in education. I started by distinguishing comparison as a basic human activity from comparison as a discipline pursued in accordance with shared assumptions, rules and procedures. I then differentiated the 'old' and the 'new' comparative education, but found this less helpful than to separate them according to the constituency within which they originated, or which they addressed, or to which they owed their principal allegiance: hence *comparative education* and *policy-directed educational comparison*. Next, I explored study categories, using Broadfoot's classification of studies undertaken within the discipline of comparative education; to this I added my own parallel classification of policy-directed studies; and Noah provided a basis for differentiating the methodological orientations of the studies in both lists.

Because Broadfoot's framework can be explicated by reference to the extensive literature of comparative education, I do not need to elaborate it here. My own classification of policy-directed studies, however, does require elaboration: partly because the domain is more recent, partly because the classification is novel, but mainly because this, for the present, is where the political power resides.

Factual information and databases

First, there is the assembling and collating of comparative factual information about different national systems. One example is the work of Eurydice, the Education Information Network of the European Union (EU). One of their publications is a helpful compendium of information and statistics relating to pre-school and primary education in the EU, and covers matters such as the ages and stages of education, the distribution of time during the school year, week and day, the aims, content and time requirements for national curricula, and contingent matters such as textbooks and teaching methods.[67] This kind of data is now available on compact disc, and through this format the range of information is, potentially and actually, vastly increased. Material from the UK's Qualifications and Curriculum Authority (QCA) and the United Nations Children's Fund (UNICEF) provide data on, respectively, 16 and 80 countries.[68]

However, what may seem to be the lowest common denominator and least contentious area of policy-oriented comparative study – collating information from official documents – is not without its problems and, surprisingly perhaps, needs to treated with the same kind of caution as more obviously questionable kinds of data. For example, the Eurydice document gives us this statement about the school curriculum in the UK:

> In England, Wales and Northern Ireland, the Secretaries of State have proposed the following criteria [for the development of the curriculum]: rather than being provided with detailed proposals, schools should be given significant opportunities to develop their educational programme according to their own schemes of work . . . a broad and flexible statutory framework . . . consideration of what has been learned about child development, good educational practice and the results of research.[69]

Bearing in mind that this statement was published in 1994, when the National Curriculum was exerting its tightest grip on schools and teachers, British readers will recognize it for the stunning travesty of the truth that it is. This is not a matter of perspective: the legal position in respect of the curriculum is crystal clear, and dramatically different from that presented above. 'Detailed proposals' are what the National Curriculum is all about; schools do not have anything approaching the degree of flexibility indicated; and educational research, other than that which toes the party line, has been all but banished. One wonders whether this version of the balance of state and school control over the curriculum was the genuine mistake of an out-of-sorts archivist or a piece of deliberate DfEE misinformation. Either way, it should give us pause for thought. If the status of the educational fact at this most basic level is shaky, how do we judge the higher-stakes empirical studies?

The difficulty for this kind of information-gathering is that it is a long way removed from verifiable practice. It is as reliable as the – usually official – providers of the information wish it to be, and both the QCA and UNICEF data reveal examples of statements purporting to represent the truth about a given system which are little more than policy-apologists' spin. This is especially the case when the data are statements of policy rather than statistics. On the other hand, both are also good examples of the strengths and limitations of a typical product of the information age. The data are interactive, and they can be corrected, updated and disseminated much more easily and rapidly than can the print equivalents; yet they require contextual knowledge to be properly understood and interpreted, and – no less important – for their veracity to be tested.

Indicators of input, process and output

Since 1987, the Organization for Economic Co-operation and Development (OECD) has been developing international educational indicators in respect of what it terms inputs, outputs, processes, and resources, the latter being both fiscal and human.[70] By 1998, this endeavour had produced the fourth edition of the compendium *Education at a Glance*, with its linked volume of statistics.[71] *Education at a Glance* conceives of education in terms of six broad considerations: the demographic, social and economic context; expenditure; student access, participation, progression and completion; the transition from school to work; the learning environment and the organization of schools; student achievement and the labour market outcomes of education. The basic structure of context, input, process and output is similar to that in earlier editions, but with the important exception of the process section each has been progressively refined.

There is no denying the value of the OECD volumes as a resource for comparative research, let alone policy. But what we can get out of such an exercise depends on what has been put into it. Thus, in the 1995 edition, the wide range of *outcomes* at the primary stage was reduced to a single indicator, reading scores at age nine (education at a glance indeed), while to these was added, in the 1998 edition, the results of the TIMSS comparative study of mathematical achievement at age 11. That, apparently, was as far as primary education went. Similarly, the real-life complexity of school and classroom *processes* is subjugated by reducing them to a collection of indicators whose rationale is either immensely subtle or non-existent: teachers' salaries, teachers' age and gender, intended teaching time, the distribution and balance of power and responsibility as between national government, regional/local government and schools; and the availability of computers in schools. *Education at a Glance* gives us a great deal of information about the financial and demographic context of schooling, and in these terms is an excellent resource but it offers precious little insight into schooling itself, let alone teaching and learning, and – a significant omission in this kind of study – only fleeting glimpses of the cause–effect relationship between the various inputs, processes and outputs, arguably the main reason for collating all this information in the first place.

In the volumes dealing in greater detail with indicators of quality for schools, teachers and learning, OECD do go beyond reading and mathematics scores and the distribution of curriculum time.[72] But because they stay firmly within the bounds of what can be quantified and then measured the focus remains skewed both in terms of what is included and how it is analysed, and this is a particularly serious problem in respect of the content, dynamics and outcomes of teaching and learning, much of which inconveniently resists such treatment. Even time on task, a 'process' indicator much favoured in school effectiveness research as both apparently objective and amenable to calculation, is much more problematic than it may seem. Supposing one can guarantee that when one observes children 'on task' they actually are (for who knows what is going on in children's heads when their eyes are apparently glued to a book?) how does one effect a calculation of the hours per year spent on task? Like this, perhaps:[73]

$$\text{TIONTA} = \left\{\frac{\text{SPERLEN}}{60} \times \text{SSCHPER} \times \text{SDAYSYR}\right\} - \left\{\frac{\text{TORDERT}}{60} \times \frac{\text{SDAYSYR}}{5}\right\} + \left\{\text{YAHWKT} \times \frac{\text{SDAYSYR}}{5}\right\}$$

Even with knowledge of what the letters in this formula signify, one has to recognize that there is a rather tautologous and self-validating character to enterprises of this kind. They usually start from indicators that have featured in earlier studies, often for no reason other than that such indicators have been shown to be technically feasible. These indicators are then built into new research designs, and thence provide the framework for further research, which in turn consolidates their position. Thus, what happens to be within the bounds of statistical computation comes to define the very nature of teaching itself, and armed with such definitions of 'quality' policy-makers, presumably, can simply touch the relevant input, process or output key and feel they have the entire system under control. Note the way, incidentally, that all the OECD indicator studies have *quality* on their covers but inside are all about *quantity*.

International league tables of educational performance

In 1995–6, OFSTED commissioned a review of internationally comparative studies of educational achievement involving England. The resulting report by Reynolds and Farrell[74] caused a considerable political and media stir: it highlighted the poor performance of England in relation to several of its economic competitors, and it postulated reasons why this should be so.

The report lists and summarizes the results of the test programmes of the International Association for the Evaluation of Educational Achievement (IEA) and the International Assessment of Educational Progress (IAEP) which started in the 1960s and whose most recent instalment at the time of writing is the Third International Mathematics and Science Study (TIMSS) of 1996–7. It concludes that these justify serious concern about the performance of English children in science and mathematics, especially the latter, and above all in arithmetic.

Alongside the devastating certainty of that judgement Reynolds and Farrell catalogue some of the technical flaws in the IEA and IAEP studies – poor sampling, missing data, excessively variable response rates, and lack of between-country comparability in test items and administration procedures – which are so serious as to make one wonder whether the test results were worth reporting at all. Surprisingly, they do not see their judgement on the state of mathematics education in England as in any way compromised by these flaws.

In advance of its publication, Keys claimed that the TIMSS study would avoid these problems,[75] and the results as published and analysed do indeed show a dramatic technical improvement. They also dictate a more careful reading than their public reception allowed, for England was close to the top of the league table in science, and while below the international mean in number was above it in geometry and in data representation, analysis and probability.

This key outcome was ignored. When the TIMSS results were published, just before the decisive and dramatic 1997 general election, good news about education was the last thing New Labour wished to hear. Their 'education, education, education' platform was firmly predicated on 18 years of unremitting Conservative failure, and as Margaret Brown noted:

> . . . the rather complex message that science scores had improved as maths scores degenerated would have prevented any simple attributions of blame. It was left to the researchers who conducted the study to point out that since the previous surveys the data showed that pupils were devoting 20 minutes per week less to mathematics and 20 minutes more to science. Thus maybe the unintended side effects of the national curriculum were the real cause of the decline.[76]

If Brown's explanation is correct, then the 1997 UK government's response may guarantee that in the 2004 league tables – to be based on the TIMSS 2003 data – there will be an equally notable difference between performance in mathematics and science at the primary stage, but it will be skewed in the opposite direction. The government's Numeracy Strategy, imposed on all primary schools in England from September 1999, will almost certainly yield improvements in basic number, the aspect of mathematics on which teachers are required to concentrate most. However, since the introduction of the Numeracy Strategy, and its companion the Literacy Hour, are at the expense of the wider curriculum, it is probable that performance in science at the primary level will be depressed from its good showing in TIMSS (whose first test programme was undertaken in 1995, six years after science was made a National Curriculum core subject and thus at the point when the cohort of pupils tested had been taught science as required by the National Curriculum ever since their arrival at school). At the time of writing, the UK government is unwilling or unable to acknowledge that its policies may carry this risk.

Effectiveness studies

From 1997, 'effectiveness' became the adjunct to New Labour's pursuit of higher educational standards. The UK government appointed a Standards Minister and a

Standards Task Force, and established within the DfEE a Standards and Effectiveness Unit. At the same time, a new branch of educational inquiry, school effectiveness research, was making large claims about its potential to deliver answers to the question of what kinds of schooling and teaching have the greatest impact on children's learning. This research would cut through the methodological qualifications and caveats that characterized previous school and classroom research and would thus appeal directly and unambiguously to policy-makers and practitioners.

Thus, by little more than a terminological sleight of hand two agendas merged: a government's proper wish to raise standards, and the legitimate ambitions of a particular group of academics. The result was a degree of intellectual hegemony which, underpinned by tight central political control, frustrated rather than enhanced the development of pedagogy as practice and field of enquiry.

The first wave of school effectiveness research was largely non-empirical. It consisted of territory demarcation and the collating of those few empirical studies that, as defined by school effectiveness researchers themselves, were deemed relevant to the endeavour.[77] Effectiveness was defined very simply, as a statistical calculation of the gain in output over input:

> We define effectiveness in two dimensions [graph shows axes of input and output] . . . The 'quality' dimension is modelled as the average score of each school on output (corrected for input) and is represented by the intercept (each school has a different intercept). The 'equity' dimension encompasses the compensatory power or selective quality of schools. Some schools can better compensate for input characteristics than others. This dimension is represented by the slopes of the within school regression of input on output.[78]

Those studies which conformed to this statistical paradigm were extensively reviewed in the publications of the school effectiveness group which established itself in the UK and then networked across several other countries. In a parallel venture, OFSTED commissioned an extrapolation of the 'key characteristics of effective schools' from school effectiveness research from a group at the University of London Institute of Education.[79] This came up with 11 factors:

(1) professional leadership (of head)
(2) shared vision and goals
(3) a learning environment
(4) concentration on teaching and learning
(5) purposeful teaching
(6) high expectations
(7) positive reinforcement
(8) monitoring progress
(9) pupil rights and responsibilities
(10) home–school partnership
(11) a learning organization.

Each of these was subdivided. Thus 'professional leadership' included 'firm and purposeful', 'a participative approach' and 'the leading professional', while 'purposeful teaching' was explicated as 'efficient organization', 'clarity of purpose', 'structured lessons' and 'adaptive practice'.

Hamilton's devastating critique of this exercise sees it as predicated on a pathological view of schools as sick institutions in need of clear policy prescriptions presented as 'magic bullets or smart missiles'; he faults the methodology of aggregating findings from studies conducted by different methods, at different times and in different countries; and rejects 'the suppositions and conclusions of such research . . . as an ethnocentric pseudo-science that serves merely to mystify anxious administrators and marginalize classroom practitioners'.[80]

In my view, the aggregation is not only indefensible (it yields, for example, a model of an all-powerful but collegial school head which, whatever its currency in the UK or USA where most of the reviewed studies were undertaken, makes no sense in those countries, like France, where school heads have more limited jurisdiction); it is also reductionist and banal. Not one of the factors listed above takes us beyond what the common sense of a layperson would have predicted.

Notwithstanding government patronage, the promise of school effectiveness research as defined by its proponents has yet to be realized. The most prominent school effectiveness group has put together an International School Effectiveness Research Project (ISERP)[81] whose statistical paradigm is compromised from the outset by sampling problems – between five and twelve schools, serendipitously identified, are deemed representative of each of the nine countries involved. On the other hand, the project has at least confirmed some of the factors in effective teaching which emerged from other classroom research, notably the importance of organizing classroom time and space as economically as possible, maximizing childrens' opportunity to learn, and generating challenging and focused pupil–teacher interaction. We shall return to these matters in our substantive discussions of pedagogy in later chapters. Meanwhile, I would add the following further reservations to Hamilton's.

First, and perhaps most important given its international and comparative claims, school effectiveness research does not deal more than cursorily with culture. I noted this in my reference to Reynolds' work earlier: Fuller and Clarke represent school effectiveness researchers as 'policy mechanics' in search of discrete, culture-free variables.[82]

Second, for inherent methodological reasons, school effectiveness research is unable to engage with the purposes, meanings and messages which elevate pedagogy from mindless technique to considered educational act. Teaching is presented as value-neutral and content-free.

Third, there is a degree of arbitrariness in the variables which the paradigm includes and excludes, as can be seen in Creemers' frequently cited model.[83] In fact, most are derived from literature searches, so the model – being merely a representation of what other have chosen to write about or investigate – is by no means as comprehensive as it appears or claims.

Fourth, there are obvious technical questions to be addressed in ISERP and related studies: sampling, the use of questionnaires rather than observation as the basis for identifying effectiveness factors, the highly mechanistic approach to such classroom observation as is undertaken.

Fifth, there is a spurious absolutism to the terminology of school effectiveness – 'success', 'failure', 'improvement', and of course 'effective' itself, which conceals the technical deficiencies of the research and implies a degree of homogeneity in schools, classrooms and lessons which cannot be sustained empirically.

Sixth, school effectiveness research is unacceptably exclusive and tacitly rejects the principle of cumulation which is vital, in any discipline, to the advancement of knowledge. Its literature makes little or no reference to the much longer and more substantial tradition of pedagogic research that has attempted to address the same question – what teaching makes the most difference – but by different means.[84]

Finally, the claim that this particular branch of educational research is a discipline in its own right is premature. It has little of the internal dialectic of conflicting theories and methodologies which give a discipline the hard edge of scepticism which is essential to its vitality, and this weakness is compounded by the field's resistance to ideas which lie beyond its tightly drawn boundaries. School effectiveness research is not a discipline but a club. Its exclusivity in the context of UK educational policy is not helpful to the cause of educational improvement.

Value for money studies

The least ambiguous application of the input–output approach to shaping policy decisions about educational practice is provided in the context of aid to developing countries. It is relevant here partly because those in donor countries such as the UK have a moral/political as well as a financial interest in knowing how 'aid' is conceived, calculated and distributed on their behalf – Keith Watson of course argues a familiar case[85] when he writes of aid as a 'two-edged sword' which assists developing countries while maintaining the gap between donor and recipient nations and benefiting the former in tied purchasing of equipment and training by as much as 70 per cent – but more particularly because the aid scenario illustrates in an extreme form some of the problems of policy-oriented comparative research which we are examining here.

In the aid literature, education inputs, processes and outcomes are reduced to their barest essentials as a basis for calculating the cost-effectiveness of particular kinds of intervention. Thus, Lockheed and Verspoor's influential World Bank study of primary education in developing countries identifies five main educational variables – curriculum, learning materials, teaching time, teaching quality and teachability – and divided aid options under these headings into 'promising avenues' for investment and 'blind alleys'.[86]

This is not as far removed from the UK situation as it might seem. Three of the 'blind alleys' identified by Lockheed and Verspoor have their counterparts in political and inspection discourse in the UK during the late 1990s: using the 1995–2000 curriculum moratorium recommended in the Dearing Report[87] to 'improve' (i.e. to entrench) the National Curriculum rather than 'adjust' or question it, dismissing class size as a factor in educational quality, and advocating initial teacher training courses that cut out all except training in the basics and whole class teaching.

However, since no aid agency can conceivably ignore the powerful impact on both education and economic productivity of the human, social and environmental factors which also define a country as 'developing', the educational modelling of donors such as the World Bank reaches much further in its lists of contextual factors than do the 'rich nation' indicators of OECD referred to earlier. We know, for example, how closely in a country such as India the maps of illiteracy, poverty and high fertility coincide, and the way that improved education correlates closely with increased per capita income, health, nutrition and fertility control.[88] Knowing this should remind us that the argument about the extent to which educational quality and learning achievement are related to non-school factors such as socio-economic status and income may have been overplayed during the 1950s and the 1960s but is certainly not dead. Rather, successive governments in the UK engineered an education 'debate' that absolved its own social and economic policies from any responsibility and directed blame for failures in the education system at teachers, schools and teacher trainers.

International Comparison and Educational Policy

I have identified two broad domains of international educational comparison. They are different in kind and purpose. The discipline of comparative education originates in academe, goes wherever its participants, individually or collectively, wish it to go, is validated by the criteria of academic research and scholarship, and while in many cases it has – and is intended to have – applications to policy and practice, this is not a necessary condition, for its principal aspiration is the accumulation and refinement of knowledge. In contrast, policy-directed international education comparison, as its label signals, originates in the policy context and/or has policy problems and their solution as its principal focus. It may look to academe for methodological validation but what matters more is the extent to which it is seen by policy-makers to engage with their agenda (and indeed to take that agenda as a 'given' rather than as problematic), and whether it meets policy-driven definitions of relevance. Its principal aspiration is the accumulation not of knowledge which stands the test of verification or falsification, but of information which others will deem useful. Academic comparative education risks abstraction and marginalization; policy-directed educational comparison risks trivialization and appropriation. The first is likely not to be taken seriously enough; the second is likely to be taken more seriously than it warrants.

To some extent, the distinction I have made runs through the entire field of educational research at a time when – in the UK at least – educational research is under attack for its supposed ideological bias and irrelevance, and government and its agencies are either (the Teacher Training Agency) seeking to determine its precise course or (OFSTED) to write it out of the script altogether. Clearly, comparativists need to examine how they stand, and how they ought to stand, in relation to policy and practice.

This takes us to the context of policy applications. In the UK during the last decade of the second millennium, international comparison offered policy-makers the tempting prospect of both plausible explanations and viable solutions. The explanations tended to be monocausal and linear, and to jump incautiously from correlation to causality. Thus, with international league tables of both economic and educational performance now conveniently available, it was assumed that a country's position on one was determined by its position on the other. On this basis, Britain's poor economic performance in relation to certain Pacific and European countries during the 1980s and the 1990s could be put down to the fact that Britain, or at any rate England, also underperformed relative to these countries in the IEA comparative test programmes. The solution was clear: adopt strategies that would raise the average test scores of British children, and Britain's economic future would be assured.

The next stage was to identify the means to raise the test scores, and here again simple correlation provided the basis for the conclusion which was reached. A country wishing to improve its test scores relative to those of its competitors could do so simply by copying the educational practices of those competitors. Since the most striking pedagogical contrast was the much heavier use of whole class teaching in the classrooms of the Pacific Rim and continental Europe, it was assumed that a shift to this method in English primary schools would make the desired difference, reverse years of national decline and simultaneously propel Britain up the league tables of educational and economic performance.

In 1996, when this line of argument became prominent in the UK – a development not unconnected with the imminence of the 1997 general election – it was adopted without reservation by the 'new' educational comparers. HMCI Woodhead insisted on prime-time television that 60 per cent whole class teaching in mathematics and 50 per cent in the rest of the curriculum would do the trick; he, the then Secretary of State Gillian Shepherd, the future Secretary of State David Blunkett and numerous journalists visited primary schools, in Barking and Dagenham, which were implementing a version of the 'interactive' whole class mathematics teaching used in some schools in Switzerland and Germany[89] and announced that they, too, had found the solution, each striving to out-do the other in their desire to appropriate the ideological territory which up to now the Right had held uncontested, and its associated pathology of progressive teaching methods, neglect of the basics, self-serving and incompetent teachers, ideologically suspect teacher training, and irrelevant research. With this degree of political consensus the outcome was inevitable: an even greater emphasis on reading, writing and number in the primary curriculum, and the imposition, through the Literacy and Numeracy Strategies, of what was termed, somewhat tautologously, 'interactive whole class teaching' (what whole class teaching is *not* interactive?).

Let us take this argument a stage at a time. Brown, Halsey *et al.* set the current debate in historical context (Halsey writes from a lifetime's experience of charting the relationship between education, the economy and society):

> The intellectual history of attempts to chart the link between education and economic productivity has been strewn with good intentions and theoretical and empirical failures . . . it is difficult, if not impossible, to demonstrate a causal relationship between education and economic productivity.[90]

Similarly, Levin and Kelly, writing of the United States – which in the educational league tables does only modestly, yet remains the world's strongest economy:

> The general notion that the competitive economic position of the United States can only be sustained if we out-compete students from other countries in scores on achievement tests is naive and hardly supported by the empirical data.[91]

More specifically in relation to the TIMSS results, Robinson demonstrates that the relationship between mathematics attainment and per capita GDP is in fact very weak, and that the generally unremarked anomaly of England's good showing in science is perhaps a more significant indicator of future prospects. In any event, he sees the faster economic growth of the Pacific Rim countries as primarily a process of catching up which is unlikely to be maintained.[92] Indeed, by 1998–9, the foundations of the Asian Tiger miracle were beginning to look decidedly shaky.

If we move to to the pedagogical strand of the argument we encounter similar difficulties. Galton, like Reynolds and Farrell, finds the IEA test programmes to be fraught with problems of consistency and reliability. If, as Keys claimed, these were eliminated in TIMSS, the earlier difficulties effectively prevented TIMSS from being more than a 1995 snapshot and thus weakened the claims of the programme as a whole to chart trends over time.[93] The potential usefulness of international league tables of educational performance, the third in my list of policy-directed comparative studies, is considerable. Its actual usefulness at this stage seems more limited.

This compromises one part of the 'new' comparers' pedagogy-performance analysis. The other is damaged by the fact, as I have argued elsewhere, that there is in truth no statistical correlation between whole class teaching and educational performance, since whole class teaching is the most universal of teaching methods in basic education, widely observable in countries at every point on the educational league table, and for that matter in poor nations as well as rich. (Indeed, if we were so minded, we could construct a case *against* whole class teaching on the grounds that it is associated with poor educational and economic performance: the case is not entirely facetious, as we shall see when we consider primary education in India.) There may well be something *within* the particular versions of whole class teaching deployed in countries such as Germany, Switzerland and Taiwan, but it is more likely to be the generic properties of this teaching mode – for example the structure of lessons and the form of pupil-teacher discourse – than the organizational formula of whole class teaching as such. In any event, single-factor analyses are as pointless in these discussions as are naive correlational claims.[94] If whole-class teaching is a pedagogical universal, or near-universal, we need to penetrate well beyond its organizational form to discover precisely how it engages children's minds and promotes, or fails to promote, their understanding.

I noted earlier that education, like other fields of human activity, has developed through the comparison, exchange and diffusion of ideas and practices, often and demonstrably across international boundaries. This is a fact of life. But if it is, wherein lies the objection to the particular spate of educational borrowing and lending which the economic circumstances of the 1980s and the 1990s provoked in several of the world's richer countries?[95]

There is indeed no objection to educational borrowing and lending as such: far from it, for without it we are the poorer, intellectually, culturally and – just possibly – economically. The objection concerns the thinking that provokes borrowing as a policy response, and the way the borrowing is done. First, as we have seen, the insistence that British primary schools should copy the educational practices of the country's more successful competitors was based on a suspect testing programme allied to naive correlation and the drawing of unsustainable conclusions about educational and economic cause and effect. The case, then, was never convincingly argued, merely asserted. Second, having been asserted, it was then translated into policy and imposed on the nation's schools as part of a complex agenda which had to do, variously, with discrediting the pre-1997 government, delivering on the 1997 government's election pledges on educational standards, destabilizing the educational establishment, and consolidating the power of the new educational elite in government and its ancillary agencies: the Department for Education and Employment, the Standards and Effectiveness Unit, the Teacher Training Agency, and the Office for Standards in Education.

Five Cultures

The episode I have described is less about educational ideas than about the nature and distribution of power, and indeed about the relationship between education and the state. This is the central theme for the next six chapters. First, however, let us recontextualize the five-nation empirical study that informs the book as a whole.

I mentioned above that the *Five Cultures* project marked the logical next stage in a programme of empirical and theoretical research which I initiated during the late 1970s. This research had a number of preoccupations which I wished to take into the international arena: the relationship between educational policy and practice; the balance of historical change and continuity in the evolution of public education; the context of professional and political power; the values, purposes and content of primary schooling; the nature of teaching and its conceptual and ethical basis; the question of what kinds of teaching are most worthwhile and what classroom practices have the greatest leverage on children's learning. However, going international both enables preoccupations such as these to move into another dimension and allows for new preoccupations to develop and be pursued. I can best make sense of these by returning to the three classification systems I presented on pages 30–1.

The *Five Cultures* research aspires to the third, fourth and fifth categories of Broadfoot's model (page 30). That is, it seeks to identify similarities and differences within and between the five countries' approaches to primary education; it addresses meta-questions such as those I have defined as 'preoccupations' and by so doing it hopes to contribute towards the development of a sustainable and useful theory. In terms of Noah's methodological categories (page 30), the research is somewhat untidy in its purposes since it describes, analyses *and* attempts to explain; its scale is self-evident – five countries; its paradigmatic basis is eclectic and therefore no doubt impure; and it employs both quantitative and qualitative methods and data. Finally, since it is not a policy-directed study it is congruent with none of the five policy-directed categories listed on page 31. Nevertheless it exploits the data that some of these categories have produced. In any case, the 'five cultures' research, and this book, do not ignore policy or policy applications. On the contrary, policy analysis is a prominent theme and by making it so I would hope that the book may be at least as helpful in the policy arena as those studies which are tied more directly to the policy agenda of this or that government or party.

Why five countries rather than the more usual one or two? There is a numerical answer. To compare two drops us into the polarizing mindset from which it is hard to escape. To compare three invites what Tobin calls the 'Goldilocks effect' (in respect of its primary education this country is good, this one is bad but this one is just right).[96] To compare five is more difficult but has the vital advantage of enabling one to present similarities and differences as continua rather than as poles. And if the five are sufficiently diverse it makes the uncovering of educational universals, which is a goal of this study, a realistic pursuit.

But why these five? England is there because the condition of primary education in England concerns me most directly. For the rest, the five countries offer similarities, contrasts and intriguing connections.

The countries are well spaced out on a number of global continua: geographical size, population, GNP/GDP and economic development; history and culture. In the educational arena there is the continuum of centralization–decentralization, along which England has moved rapidly and dramatically to the point where from being not far from the United States, the most decentralized of the five, it is now in many respects more centralized than France or post-Soviet Russia; the continuum of position on the international league tables of educational performance; and that of pedagogy, with each country having its distinct place in relation to Anglo-American and central/eastern European pedagogic traditions. In this matter the United States represents one extreme, Russia the other.

The connections are as fascinating as the similarities and differences, although more elusive. In all five countries there are the common legacies of the drive to mass education following the first Industrial Revolution. France and England, although now together in Europe, remain torn between confrontation and co-operation. The United States and India share educational legacies of British colonialism. France, the United States and Russia have ties of revolutions that although different in their form and consequences all had discernibly British connections. Historically all five countries have participated in the lively international trade in educational ideas and practices yet these have been domesticated and acculturated in very different ways.

My final justification takes us back to globalization. We have here five countries and four economic blocks confronting each other in the arena of global competition. That, as we noted, is the way some Western governments choose to represent the world and its future for the purposes of determining educational goals at the turn of the millennium. It is a simple enough view, with simple policy implications: construct a basic education which will maximize national competitive success in the 'basics', whether old (literacy and numeracy) or new (science and information

Table 1.1 Education and human development: five nations and the rest of the world (1997)

	Life expectancy at birth (years)	Adult literacy rate (%)	Primary enrolment ratio (% of age group)	Secondary enrolment ratio (% of age group)	Real GDP per capita ($)	Human development index (HDI) value
France	78.1	99.0	99.9	98.7	22,030	0.918
India	62.6	53.5	77.2	59.7	1,670	0.545
Russia	66.6	99.0	99.9	87.6	4,370	0.747
UK	77.2	99.0	99.9	91.8	20,730	0.918
USA	76.7	99.0	99.9	96.3	29,010	0.927
Developing countries	64.4	71.4	85.7	60.4	3,240	0.637
Industrialized countries	77.7	98.7	99.9	96.2	23,741	0.919
World	66.7	78.0	87.6	65.4	6,332	0.706

Source: United Nations (1999), pp. 134–7, 176–9.
The Human Development Index (HDI) combines three variables: life expectancy, educational attainment and income.

technology), and forget about wider notions of what it means to be educated or at best reduce them to token status. I have argued that if we are serious in our claims about global interdependence this view is unacceptably narrow. Arguably it also attends too exclusively, even by its own definition of what matters, to the short term. But most critically, it leaves out of the calculation of cost and benefit the ethical dimension of both international interdependence and education.

Some who have been aware of the *Five Cultures* research have said that although they understand why the United States and France should feature alongside England, they are baffled by the inclusion of India and Russia except in so far as these countries provide valuable contrasts. That is a sufficient reason, but we should also note that in the year 2000 the condition of children in India or Russia is more globally representative than that of children in England, France or the United States (see Table 1.1). Castells' study of globalization reminds us of 'the complex set of linkages between the characteristics of informational capitalism and the rise of inequality, social polarization and misery in most of the world . . . New information technologies tool the global whirlwind of accumulation of wealth and diffusion of poverty.'[97] In an interconnected world, as in an interconnected society, the comfort of some and the privation of others are also connected. We are all in this together. On the question of what binds and divides humanity Marx may or may not have been right, but Donne certainly was.

Part II
Systems, Policies and Histories

2

Primary Education in France

Introduction

The scene is now set. Basic primary education is a universal aspiration. It is profoundly important for individual liberation, economic advancement and social progress, although it is by no means a universal achievement. If we are to understand how primary education might be reshaped for a changing and interdependent world we need a perspective which is global and comparative, not merely national. Without comparison we simply refashion the world to fit our individual, collective or political interests and remain imprisoned by local or national habits that are too deeply ingrained to allow us to countenance alternatives.

The case for a deliberate and explicit comparative consciousness in education, which goes beyond the instinctive comparing which informs everyday thought and which is open to examination by others, is now generally accepted. However, the previous chapter's discussion of the 'old' and 'new' comparative education and their role in UK educational policy-formation shows that comparing and the comparative consciousness are by no means synonymous. Comparing can be as reductionist an act as not bothering to compare.

In this chapter we initiate our own exercise in educational comparison, trusting that readers will reserve judgement until the book's final pages on whether we have attained the higher ground staked out above. The entire exercise, as I indicated earlier, is a journey through five different national systems of primary education, from structure and policy at the national level to the transactions of teachers and pupils in the classroom. In this and the remaining chapters in Part II, four basic questions are considered. What is the essential character of primary education in France, Russia, India, the United States and England, when considered as national educational systems, that is to say as agglomerations of structure, policy, values and mechanisms of control? What were their origins and how did they develop? What are their main similarities and differences? How can these be explained?

The present chapter pilots a sequence which is followed for all five countries. Each starts with a factual distillation of the country's system of primary education

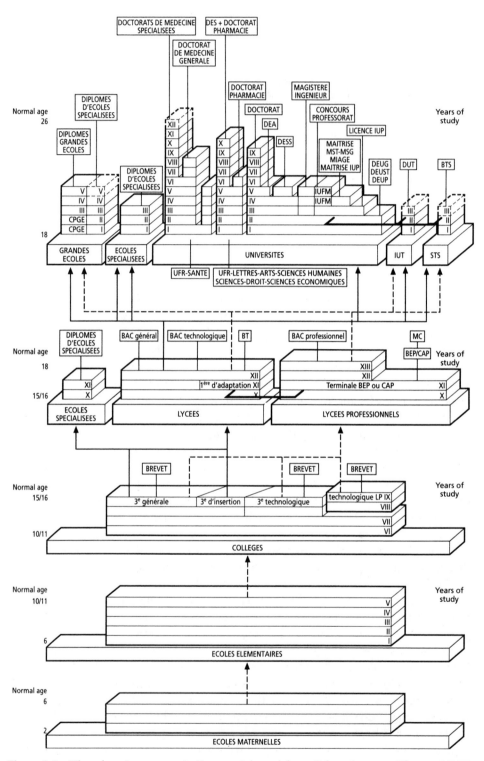

Figure 2.1   The education system in France. Adapted from *Education at a Glance: OECD Indicators 1996*. Copyright OECD, 1996.

as it stands at the turn of the millennium, concentrating on demography, structure, policy and control and drawing on data from international agencies, from national governments, and (in the case of the highly decentralized United States) from state and local administrative authorities. The second part of each chapter traces the system back to its historical roots, seeking to identify the forces that prompted or constrained its development, and the ideas by which it was influenced. The chapters close by reassessing this legacy in terms of the values which the contemporary system of primary education embodies and the problems which, as a system, it encounters.

I have decided against the usual practice of a lengthy preliminary chapter which sets out a theoretical framework. That is provided in Chapter 7, after the last of the five accounts. In fact the themes that I deem significant – notably *power*, *control*, *culture*, *values* and *identity* – will become evident enough to the reader without my announcing them. Having revealed themselves in this way, their treatment in Chapter 7, which will develop the themes and discuss the lessons we can draw from system-level comparisons between the five countries, ought to be more meaningful. Further, by coming at that point in the book Chapter 7 will provide a bridge to Parts III and IV, which concentrate on schools, classrooms, teaching and learning.

Context, Structure and Control

In 1999 France (metropolitan France together with its overseas territories) had a population of 60,082,000 and covered an area of 551,500 square kilometres. France is the second smallest of the five countries dealt with in this study, although even so it is considerably larger than England and indeed the entire United Kingdom, and has a third of England's population density. The per capita GNP in 1998, at US$22,320, was the second highest of the five countries and 5.8 per cent of this was spent on education.[1] France is divided into 22 regions, each of which contains several *départements*. Of these, metropolitan France (that is France minus its overseas territories) has 96.

The structure of the French education system is shown in Figure 2.1. Since 1967, education has been compulsory for children aged 6–16, although the system's guiding principles – that a school should be *laïque, gratuite et obligatoire* (secular, free and compulsory) – were laid down in the Ferry laws well over a century ago. Free state education for children at the equivalent of the English primary stage is provided by *l'école primaire* which children attend until 11 years old. The preceding optional nursery stage for ages 2–6 (*l'enseignement préélémentaire*) comprises a mixture of public and private nursery schools (*écoles maternelles*) and infant classes (*classes enfantines*). By 1998 the attendance rate at these among 3–6 year olds was nearly 100 per cent.

The French system, as is well known, is highly centralized, although as a result of recent legislation, notably the *loi de décentralisation des établissements publics locaux d'enseignement* (1983), the balance of responsibility has begun to be shifted downwards to the 28 regional *académies* and (in the case of primary education) to the

36,532 local *communes* which deal with schools. The national government determines national education policy. The central educational administration – the *Ministère de l'éducation nationale* – has two ministers and nine directorates and is responsible for framing the system's objectives, defining curricula, recruiting, training and managing teaching and other staff, national school inspection, assessment, quality assurance and planning. Planning is supported by extensive documentation of regional and local variations in school intake, provision and outcomes, giving particular attention to those respects in which there is deviation from the fundamental principle which centralization aims to secure: that of equal access to an education of consistent quality for all pupils 'regardless of their social, cultural or geographical background'. With this principle in view, according to one of our Ministry interviewees, the Ministry has to judge whether the differences it identifies represent 'diversity, disparity or inequality'.[2]

The ministry delegates certain aspects of school organization and administration: *lycées* (upper secondary schools) to regional *académies*, *collèges* (lower secondary schools) to *départements*, and primary schools to communes. The *commune* owns, builds, equips and repairs the primary school building and employs ancillary staff, although not teachers. The *académie*, presided over by its *recteur*, handles, in respect of primary education, teacher training (initial and in-service), the implementation of national policy, and inspection. These operations are controlled by *l'inspecteur d'académie*, and the actual inspection is undertaken by *inspecteurs de l'éducation nationale* (IEN), answerable through the *l'inspecteur d'académie* and *le recteur* to *les inspections générales* (IGEN) at the ministry in Paris.

Within each school the lines of control and accountability are different in one important respect from those in England. Each teacher is responsible not to the school head but directly to the *académie* and thence to the ministry. The head therefore has a considerably narrower range of responsibilities than his or her English counterpart and this difference has an important bearing on the character of the schools themselves.

Following endorsement of decentralization in the 1989 *loi d'orientation sur l'éducation* – commonly known, after the then minister, as the *loi Jospin* – the government promulgated *le projet d'école*.[3] The 'school project' was intended to provide a framework for school development and action planning which would reconcile national requirements with local circumstances and needs. It would also encourage schools to move towards a greater level of collegiality. In 1990 the ministry decreed that this process should be taken further: each school was required to set up a *conseil d'école* containing teacher, parent, *commune* and *académie* representatives and chaired by the school's director. The school council determines the school's timetable and internal regulations, formulates and approves the *projet d'école*, approves the uses to be made of the school premises outside school hours and reviews policy matters such as choice of textbooks and provision for children with special educational needs.[4]

Goals, Curriculum and Assessment

Primary schools normally contain five classes or (in larger schools) parallel sets of classes: *cours préparatoire* (CP), *cours élémentaire première année* (CE1), *cours élémentaire deuxième année* (CE2), *cours moyen première année* (CM1) and *cours moyen deuxième année* (CM2). In rural areas the *communes* either concentrate all pupils from a cluster of neighbouring villages in one school or share them by level among several single class (*classe unique*) schools so that the age spread in each is not too great. In 1996–7 France had over 41,412 primary schools, with an average pupil–teacher ratio of 19.5:1.[5]

The *loi Jospin* also introduced the idea of cycles to generate greater continuity, flexibility and developmental appositeness within each of the phases of compulsory education. At the pre-elementary and elementary stages there are three cycles: *le cycle des apprentissages premiers* (C1 or first learning cycle) covering most of the nursery phase; *le cycle des apprentissages fondamentaux* (C2 or basic learning cycle) covering the last year of the nursery phase, CP and CE1 (ages 5–8); and *le cycle des approfondissements* (C3 or consolidation cycle) covering CE2, CM1 and CM2 (ages 8–11). This allows different ways of grouping children into classes, for example by age (one teacher for a year group, as most commonly in England) and by cycle (one teacher for a three-year age group). By attacking the historical rigidity of age-based pupil grouping and classification it was also intended to reduce the frequency of *redoublement*, the practice of making pupils repeat a year.[6]

In the 1989 law, the goals of public education in France were defined to

- transmit knowledge and enable pupils and students to acquire appropriate work habits and study skills
- prepare individuals for a civic and working life by developing judgement, individual and collective responsibility, adaptability and creativity
- acquire a general culture although cultural, artistic and civic activities
- obtain a high level of recognized qualification.[7]

More specifically, the elementary stage is held to be chiefly concerned with: mastery of the French language, spoken and written; development of citizenship; personal autonomy, work habits, study skills and self-evaluation; and induction into the disciplines.[8]

The curriculum is centrally prescribed. Following legislation in 1975, 1989 and 1994, the subjects and *horaires* (weekly time requirements) were confirmed as follows:

Cycle 2 (ages 6–8)

- French (9 hours)
- mathematics (5 hours)
- discovering the world (science, technology, history, geography) and civic education (4 hours)

- artistic education (visual arts, music, drama, dance and *les images* – discovering, exploring and understanding visual images, including photography, cinema and television), plus physical education and sport (6 hours)
- supervised study (*études dirigées*) (2 hours).

Cycle 3 (ages 8–11)

- French (9 hours)
- mathematics (5.5 hours)
- history and geography; civic education; science and technology (4 hours)
- artistic education (visuals arts, music, drama, dance, *les images*), plus physical education and sport (5.5 hours)
- supervised study (2 hours).[9]

In the third year of Cycle 2, the nine hours for language were expected to include one hour for a foreign language, and in Cycle 3 this allocation could vary between one hour and one hour and a half. Average recreation breaks were set at fifteen minutes each half day, and the midday break, conventionally two hours, was to be determined at *académie* level.[10] The 26 hours are disposed in various ways across the six days Monday–Saturday, by agreement between the *commune* and the *inspecteur d'académie*. The commonest arrangement frees Wednesday and Saturday afternoons.

Ministry curriculum statements differentiate three kinds of competence to be achieved through elementary education: language competence, discipline-based competence, and cross-curricular competences (*compétences transversales*). The latter include *attitudes* (personality development, acquisition of autonomy, social learning, desire to know and eagerness to learn), *fundamental concepts of space and time*, and *methodological competences* (memory, work habits, and the handling of information).[11]

Assessment became an important feature of the French system during the 1990s. The national system includes mass diagnostic assessment of 8 year olds each September, that is to say just before the mid-point of the elementary stage (further national tests are taken at ages 11 and 15, when pupils begin *lycée* and *collège*); continuous teacher assessment as the basis for promotion from one class or cycle to the next, typically including weekly tests; and end-of-year sampled testing for the purposes of national monitoring or international comparison. As a result of the Jospin reforms of 1989–90, teachers are required to record pupils' progress in their cumulative individual report books (*livrets scolaires*). The *livret scolaire* is sent home regularly for parents to see and sign and provides a basis for teacher–parent discussion about pupils' progress. To encourage precise and consistent teacher assessment the Ministry publishes detailed objectives for each subject and cycle-specific handbooks containing banks of assessment items coded by subject, field and objective with guidance on marking.[12]

It will be seen that French teachers work to precise curriculum specifications, calibrated by level and year. In the past the levels were hurdles which each pupil had to surmount before being allowed to move on to the next class – the terminology of 'grades' and 'standards' in other countries (not just in England under the Revised Code) – reminds us how common this practice still is. We have noted that its concomitant, *redoublement* – making less able or successful pupils repeat a year – was discouraged by Jospin, although it still occurs, with problematic consequences for some pupils, especially in the context of social exclusion.[13] Streaming by ability, however, is banned at the primary stage, and the Ministry has set its face against the associated apparatus of published results and league tables installed in England after 1988. In France, assessment at the primary stage is diagnostic rather than summative, and it is used in order to evaluate the performance of pupils, not of teachers or schools.[14]

At the time of writing the organization and relationship of schools, the curriculum and the structure of the school day are the subject of a government-initiated review instigated by Minister of Education Claude Allègre. *La Charte pour bâtir l'école du XXIe siècle* ('Charter for building the school of the 21st century') has enunciated three broad principles to govern the evolution of primary education: continuing concentration on the 'basics' of speaking, reading, writing and arithmetic; making the structure and rhythms of schooling consistent with those of childhood, and structuring the school day so as to take account of changing social conditions and equalize children's opportunities to benefit from education; rethinking the role of the primary teacher so as to provide him/her with greater freedom of choice over pedagogical matters, and making related changes to initial and in-service teacher training.[15]

Origins and Development

History being what it is, several of the French education system's defining characteristics predate the event which is generally credited with its creation. The Revolution inherited *étatisme* – the controlling, interventionist state machine – together with clerical dominance, a hierarchical and elitist teaching profession with the *agrégation* as its sternest test and ultimate prize, a Cartesian belief in education as the training of the mind, but also Enlightenment ambitions to establish a genuinely national system of education.

During the Revolution the case for primary education – free, universal and egalitarian – was initially pressed by Enlightenment *philosophe* Condorcet. His 1792 plan for public education was to replace a church-controlled patchwork of provision with a framework which would at the same time liberate minds and produce good citizens. The plan was overtaken by events – the fall of the Legislative Assembly in 1792, the Revolution's radicalization and growing violence, and the rise of Napoleon. Napoleon's vision for education was of a piece with his vision for government: strong central control, an elaborate bureaucracy, and a concentration on those aspects and stages of education that would consolidate the fledgling state and the position of those who ran it.

The education of younger children, on this analysis, was far less of a priority than the building of systems of secondary, technical and university education which would have a direct and instrumental purchase on the needs of the state: military schools, schools of medicine, law, science, mining and engineering, *collèges*, *lycées*, and the University of France. Primary education languished until the Restoration of 1815–30, a period which was notable for two milestones in the development of French primary education, one pedagogical, the other political.

In 1815 liberals set up the *Société pour l'Instruction Elémentaire* to propagate basic instruction for the poor using the monitorial method of Joseph Lancaster, whose school in Borough Road, Southwark, had been visited by a French deputation in 1814. This challenged the two methods which were firmly in place before the Revolution: *l'enseignement simultané* (the simultaneous method) which was favoured in the larger church schools, and *l'enseignement individuel* (the individual method) which was used, perforce, by the mainly lay teachers, *les petit frères*, in the rural schools. Reboul-Scherrer suggests that whole-class teaching (for this is what the simultaneous method was) had signalled competence as well as the luxury of a school with several teachers, while the individual method was generally associated with incompetence, as the lone village teacher struggled to keep the triply disparate members of a large class (mixed age, mixed attainment and mixed motivation) occupied.[16] One of the most enthusiastic advocates of *l'enseignement mutuel* was the Duc de la Rochefoucauld, who had fled to England during the Revolution and whose translations of Lancaster's *Improvements in education as it respects the industrious classes* (1803) was widely distributed in France under the title *Amélioration dans l'éducation des classes industrielles de la société* by the *Société pour l'Instruction Elémentaire*. This society was set up in 1815 expressly to disseminate the Lancasterian method and by 1820 there were 1500 monitorial schools, mainly concentrated in the industrial cities.

Partly in response to this movement, 1816 saw the introduction of an important counter to absolute central control whose legacy persists, two centuries on. An educational *ordonnance* decreed that each *commune* should 'provide a primary education for all its inhabitants, and in the case of the poor this shall be provided free' and that committees should be set up to supervise this effort. An annual state grant of 50,000 francs was provided to support the latter objective and during the first few years the *Société pour l'instruction élémentaire* had the larger share of this.[17] By 1830 somewhere over half of France's communes had responded and the survey of primary education commissioned by Minister of Public Instruction Guizot recorded a national network of some 42,000 primary schools run by the church and, increasingly, by communes.[18] However, this system remained for the time being separate from the rest of the educational structure: primary schools were for the common people, secondary education was for the bourgeoisie, and the higher primary schools established by the *Loi Guizot* of 1833 made little impact until later in the century. The *Loi Guizot* also set out the basics of the primary curriculum – reading, writing, spelling, grammar, composition, arithmetic, weights and measures, and – as a crucial concession to the church – religious education.[19]

This, in essence, was the system which won Matthew Arnold's approval in 1859, although by then monitorial pedagogy had been largely superseded by a return to *l'enseignement simultané* or a combination – *la methode mixte* – of simultaneous teaching, more or less homogenous groups and monitorial support or supervision.[20] Interestingly, Arnold endorsed France's particular combination of central direction and local engagement, pronouncing on one that 'on certain capital points the State in France has by its legislation and administration exercised a directly educative influence upon the reason and equity of its people' while on the devolution of the control of individual primary schools to the communes he commented that 'a school system, once established in a locality, invariably renders school matters a subject of interest and occupation with the inhabitants of that locality'.[21]

In passing we might note that the early history of primary education in France provides one of those ironies with which comparative education abounds: the cause of primary education in France (as in Spain, Italy, Denmark, Sweden, the United States, Norway and several other countries) was greatly boosted by a movement which originated in England;[22] yet for many more decades England remained behind all these countries in establishing its own proper system of primary education.

There is another. It is salutatory and possibly depressing, to note that debates about the balance and relative merits of whole-class teaching, group work and individual attention, which figured prominently in English research and policy interventions during the 1980s and the 1990s, had been initiated in France almost two centuries earlier. It is also intriguing to track a characteristic Anglo-French divergence on this matter. By the late twentieth century French primary pupils were taught mainly by the whole class method (to which schools reverted after their brief flirtation with the monitorial system) but their teachers were being encouraged to use more group work; at the same time English primary teachers were being urged to shift the balance away from group and individual work towards whole class teaching. The pressure for pedagogic change is as likely to be ideological as methodological. 'Modernization' may mean abandoning the prevailing method, whatever it is, rather than addressing the question of which method or combination of methods is educationally the most sound.

Despite its advanced state of development by comparison with England, primary education in France remained the system's Cinderella for much of the nineteenth century. *Instituteurs* – primary teachers – were from the same peasant background as their pupils and found their work and indeed their lives tightly constrained by the combined forces of *maire* and *curé*,[23] especially during the period after the revolutionary year 1848.[24] French primary education had to wait until the Third Republic of 1870–1914 and, specifically, the Jules Ferry laws of 1879–86, to come of age. Yet despite their modest status, primary teachers occupied an important role as *les hussards* (hussars) *de la République* and much was expected of them.[25]

The *loi Ferry* of 1882 established the three principles on which basic education in France still rests. It became *laïque, gratuite et obligatoire* – secular, free and compulsory. For Ferry, 'the first duty of a democratic government is to exercise control over public education'.[26] Communes were required to establish (separate) schools for both boys and girls of six to twelve years of age. Religious instruction was removed from the curriculum, clerical influence was reduced, and teacher and mayor forged a powerful alliance as the front line of republican principles and virtues, helping to secure the bourgeois state against both the clerical/monarchist right and the revolutionary left.[27] Ferry was also progressive pedagogically. Prost suggests that his concern with democratization and secularism was allied to a belief in teaching methods which would 'excite and awaken the spontaneity of the child . . . instead of imprisoning him in rules already made.'[28]

This, in essence, was the system which survived three republics and France's devastation and occupation in two successive world wars. The legislated changes of the twentieth century built on the Ferry foundation that in turn consolidated the slow but steady progress achieved since the Revolution. Thus, compulsory schooling was extended first to 14 years and then, in 1967, to 16 years of age. The anomaly of separate systems which these changes exacerbated – primary, upper primary and secondary – was removed by the Haby reforms of the mid 1970s which established a single route, the *collèges uniques*, for all 11–16 year olds, although as with the establishment of comprehensive schools in England after 1965, implementation was slow, uneven and in places fiercely resisted.[29] Haby's reforms were followed by a re-assessment of the curriculum under Minister Savary and a standards drive led by his successor Jean-Pierre Chevènement, from 1984. He directed schools to concentrate more on reading, writing and arithmetic, but also restated the importance of Republican values and brought back weekly lessons in civic education.[30]

Lionel Jospin, a successor to Chevènement and later prime minister, turned his attention to the structure of the system itself. By then *étatisme* was in partial retreat: Gaston Defferre's 1982 law on decentralization had paved the way by increasing the powers of regions, departments and communes across a wide range of decisions and services, and Jospin's *loi d'orientation* of 1989 replaced monolithic central control of education by a system of national directives which would provide the framework within which schools would devise their own policies and practices. Schools were expected to prepare *projets d'école* – development plans – which attended to local circumstances and needs,[31] and the rigid matrix of subjects and school years was modified into the system of cycles described earlier.[32] France, then, challenged the principle of central control at the same time as England capitulated to it – a coincidence which has allowed the development of an illuminating series of comparative studies by Patricia Broadfoot and her colleagues at Bristol University, to which we shall refer shortly.[33]

Control, Values and Identity

In a later chapter I take issue with the method used by the OECD – a head-count of educational decisions regardless of their significance or impact – to assess the balance of educational power and control as between national government, regional or local administration and schools.[34] We know that France is widely perceived to be highly centralized in education and other matters; and that the Mitterrand government instituted a programme of devolution to regions, departments and communes. We have also established that since the early nineteenth century the communes themselves have provided an important forum for local involvement in education, and that this was greatly consolidated once the Ferry laws established the secular principle and gave primary schools agency for the transmission of Republican values. How, post-Jospin, do we assess the place of primary schools in the educational power structure of France, and where do they stand in the web of culture and values?

When I posed this question in interviews with senior Ministry of Education officials, I received somewhat conflicting answers, which itself is a useful indicator of change. One official was prepared to argue that the balance of power was now – since Defferre and Jospin – shared equally by school, *académie* and ministry, quantifying it as one-third to each. But another expressed it rather differently:

> The real power is still with the Education Ministry . . . At local level, for primary teachers, the inspectors are all-important because they assess the teacher in his or her work, and they are always there, so they know their teachers well and they know their schools. They are perhaps the most efficient link in the chain, yet they don't have the most power, for they are also loyal civil servants and they are attentive to the Ministry's wishes. They ensure that decisions adopted at national level are complied with.

A third official felt it necessary to draw a distinction in this regard between curriculum and teaching method:

> The curriculum is the same in every classroom in France, so, yes, it's highly centralized still. On the other hand, the way the curriculum is implemented in the classroom is the responsibility of the teacher, and only the teacher – it is nothing to do with the head, for example . . . and anyway the method is not important, it's the result which counts.

The latter point was underlined by a colleague:

> It is our principle to leave the teacher free to choose the methods he or she wishes to use. What we are interested in is how effective his or her work is, rather than the method . . . what we want is that the children should achieve the standards defined in the curriculum.

On the other hand:

> An inspector does not have the power to say 'Use this procedure or this method'. But an inspector can say 'Your method is not suitable for the pupils. Your pupils are not progressing. You must come to a training course'.

Thus, working from the *académies* but answerable to the Ministry the inspectors secure compliance with ministry directives on curriculum content and time allocations, while they may restrict teachers' autonomy in matters of classroom method where they feel it deviates from what is required to deliver on those directives and the associated standards, providing the ideological corrective of retraining. In fact, the role of school inspectors in France subtly and obliquely combines authority with dialectic in a way that contrasts starkly with the much more overtly authoritarian approach of OFSTED in England. A senior *inspecteur général* in Paris put the matter in almost Cartesian terms:

> The inspector first checks compliance then assesses quality. But it's not a question of whether the method is good or bad, but of whether it exists: whether a teacher who is giving an arithmetic lesson knows exactly what he intends, and why. The inspector makes a note of what the teacher does, as he goes along, and at the end of the inspection there is an interview between the inspector and the teacher, a sort of interactive examination – because it is possible that the inspector has not quite understood the teacher's intentions and method – when the inspector asks the teacher to assess himself and then questions him about why he did what he did, taking specific examples from the lesson.

Underlining the way the 'text' for this characteristically French oral examination is the lesson as given rather than a pre-existing lesson template, the same senior inspector stressed that

> There are criteria, and all inspectors have a full year's training in how to do the job and what to look for, but we don't have a check list. This would be like doing an inspection by correspondence – you turn up with a list of items and put a cross by them. We think this is dangerous and we are trying to prevent it: two or three departments have adopted the practice and we are going to ask the Minister to prohibit it.

This, then, is the paradoxical sting in the tail: the power to direct from the centre remains, even – or especially – in defence of what this inspector invoked as *la liberté*: 'one goal, many routes'.

Defining the balance of power in absolute terms, then, is difficult if not impossible. The system remains centralized, yet devolution to the regional *académies* and those local ties and alliances which are centred on the commune provide a counterbalance which is probably more solid and effective than the equivalent levels in the English administrative structure (which would range from large urban LEAs to the village parish councils which have no say whatever in educational matters). In any event, as the reference to *la liberté* revealed, the system is underpinned by broader values that have no equivalent in England, and it is to these that we turn now.

It may be pushing a bit far the sense of relative ideological coherence conveyed by the French system to see the Ferry principles of *l'école laïque, gratuite et obligatoire* as entirely of a piece with the revolutionary cry of *liberté, égalité, fraternité,* for it took nearly a century for the revolution to deliver the basic human rights enshrined in Ferry. Nevertheless, the signpost is clear enough: in France nation, citizenship and education are closely linked, and the state takes it upon itself to secure and deliver all three.

State and nation, of course, are not coterminous. We know the boundaries of the state of Great Britain and Northern Ireland but the character of the British nation is much more elusive (and, as noted earlier, much discussed and debated at the time of writing), for whereas states are physical entities, nations are 'cultural communities constituted in people's minds by the sharing of history and political projects'[35] and indeed by much else that is suggested by the notion of culture. It would be unwise to argue from the British experience of nation-state dissonance – let alone from the nightmare of post-communist Yugoslavia – that in France nation and state map onto each other with a reasonable degree of fit.

Nevertheless, *la France* does signify a combined sense of state and nation which is vastly more comprehensive and multi-layered in the ways it draws in geography, history, rural and urban landscape, ways of life, ideas, language, literature and values than anything conveyed by 'British'. In public discourse that sobriquet is more commonly redolent, at best – or worst – of post-imperial angst, the heritage industry or the jingoism of Thatcher and the tabloids.

If this is so, then certain emphases in French education make immediate sense: the commitment to *culture générale* (in the *lycées* more than at the primary stage, admittedly), the linked crusade (for example under Minister of Culture Jack Lang during the 1980s) against American cultural imperialism, and indeed the very notion of a Minister of Culture; the explicit inclusion of citizenship as a goal and civic education as the means; the absolute priority given to pupils' schooling in the French language, the bouts of concern that its 'purity' be defended, and the way that language in French basic education connotes something considerably comprehensive in its reach and vital in its everyday purpose than the officially approved English concept of literacy. (Note that 'speaking' heads the list of 'basics' in the 1998 Allègre charter for the twenty-first century: in England, oracy initiatives are no sooner devised than shelved.)[36]

General culture, citizenship and the national language are elements of a public education which one would expect to be emphasized in any context where national identity is deemed important, and indeed we shall see how they have their counterparts in post-Soviet Russia. More distinctive to France is the emphasis on discipline-based knowledge, fundamental at the secondary stage, diluted although still strong in the primary curriculum. Here the genealogy is as much Enlightenment as Revolution, and the liberating power of reason serves a multitude of purposes.

It is this strong rationalist charge borne by *les disciplines* which is most evident – and impressive – to outsiders visiting French schools or talking with French educationalists. The authority of received bodies of knowledge with their distinctive canons, laws and procedures is allied to the authority of the teachers who deliver them. They combine in that 'inspired academic pedagogy' whose role is to 'transmit knowledge and train intellects' and which so impressed Matthew Arnold ('The intelligence of the French people is well known . . . it is the source of their highest virtue'[37]) and many since. Ardagh notes that 'even poorer children, while not so often reaching the lycée, have been put through sufficiently rigorous mental hoops in their primary schools for a foreigner to be frequently impressed by the working man's articulateness and grasp of ideas'.[38] Indeed, Arnold, an early educational tourist, squared the circle of rational pedagogy and rational state:

> The text of an English Act of Parliament never carried to an uneducated English mind anything but bewilderment. I have myself heard a French peasant quote from the *Code Napoléon*; it is in everyone's hands; it is its rational form, hardly less than its rational spirit, that the Code has to thank for a popularity which makes half the nations of Europe desirous to adopt it.[39]

There is a very different way to view this tradition, however, for the paradox of this form of intellectual liberation – if this is what it achieves – is that it is non-negotiable. Knowledge is received, not negotiated or reflexive. It is also embedded in a structure that is highly selective and meritocratic. It is thus no coincidence that one of the most sustained critiques of education as cultural and social reproduction comes from France, where, for Pierre Bourdieu, 'the educational system reproduces all the more perfectly the structure of the distribution of cultural capital among the classes'.[40]

The close articulation of identity, culture and language within a centrally-determined curriculum can never sit other than uncomfortably with pluralism, and from time to time matters come spectacularly to a head. Thus, in 1989, when a school director expelled three Muslim female pupils for wearing the *chador*, his action exploded into a national crisis – *l'affaire du foulard* – which exposed sharp conflicts between the values of national identity, group difference, secularism, liberty, religious tolerance and gender equality, and required the arbitration of the *conseil d'Etat*.[41] A decade later the fault-line was the French language. In May 1999 the socialist-led coalition government signed up to a Council of Europe charter which, in line with the general European and Western trend towards inclusionist social policies, committed schools to the teaching of regional and minority languages, while maintaining the dominance of French. This provoked accusations that the government had breached the republic's constitutional commitment to culturally indivisibility and linguistic homogeneity, and stoked the ever-smouldering fires of nationalism and regionalism. At the time of writing the row continues and the affair remains unresolved: Prime Minister Jospin asked President Chirac to revise the constitution to make it compatible with the Council of Europe charter: Chirac refused.[42]

It is part of the purpose of this study to explore how far macro-level claims about the relationship between culture and pedagogy can be sustained when one examines what goes on in the classroom, and if so, by what pedagogical mechanisms the reproductive role of education is secured. For the moment, however, we are teasing out the broader ideas and values that are to be put to the test in this way, and of these, in France, education of the mind, discipline-based knowledge, general culture, citizenship and language seem to be pre-eminent. Their precise force within day-to-day primary education comes from the chemistry of pedagogical content allied to pedagogical process. Since one is centrally prescribed but the latter is not, that chemistry is likely to be an uncertain one.

Moreover, it is clear that in France, as in many other countries, the primary tradition stands somewhat apart from the educational mainstream. Napoleon's vision largely excluded it; and for much of the nineteenth and the twentieth centuries the standing and level of education of primary teachers was low, despite their distinctive place in the civic and political life of towns and villages and their role as guardians of Republican values. Only with the establishment of the IUFMs (*Instituts Universitaires de Formation des Maîtres*) in 1990–91 did primary teacher training move from the relative isolation of the *école normale* (training college) tradition into some degree of proximity with the academic mainstream, and that transition was by no means easy. The universities, by and large, resisted the IUFMs (and primary teachers) as a threat to *les disciplines* and to educational standards – in which, traditionally, disciplinary purity and rigour were deemed to be the central component – and although the old status distinction between *instituteurs* and *professeurs* was made less evident once, from 1991, primary teachers were permitted to call themselves *professeurs d'école*, primary and secondary teachers continued to inhabit what were for most purposes vastly different cultural and professional universes.

The French teaching profession remains hierarchical and deeply conscious of the nuances of status which make the *agrégation* a qualification fit not just for the best *lycée* teachers but also for presidents and prime ministers. For their part primary teachers are only just emerging from two centuries of relegation to the bottom of the professional pyramid, although a recent survey in *le Monde* suggested that for all that they are the most contented group in the teaching profession. In the year 2000, the salaries, training and qualifications of a *professeur d'école* are at last comparable to those of a *professeur de collège*. Yet the bumpy ride experienced by the IUFMs on their journey from bitterly contested idea to uneasy institutional reality revealed the strength and breadth of the political, academic and professional alliance that was determined to maintain the long-established status differentials.[43].

In contrast with the struggle over professional status, and the fierce debates, from 1968 onwards, about the hegemony of *les disciplines*,[44] problems of underachievement, the handling of poverty and cultural diversity,[45] and differentiated teaching,[46] there has at least been one zone of harmony. One of the striking features of French education, as Corbett and Moon point out, has been the degree of national consensus over the system's aims.[47]

3

Primary Education in Russia

Context, Structure and Control

Even shorn of some of the old USSR republics, Russia remains, in terms of area (17,075,400 square kilometres), by far the largest country in the world. In 1998, however, its population was a mere 146.9 million (and falling[1] giving it the lowest population density of the five countries in this study (8.6 persons per square kilometre, compared to 386 in England).[2] This population, however, is culturally and ethnically immensely diverse: that over eighty languages are spoken gives some indication of this. By 1998 per capita GNP had fallen to US$3,950, or 13.5 per cent of that of Britain and 8.3 per cent of that of the USA.[3] In the same year education spending accounted for 4.4 per cent of this, although public expenditure on education, both in real terms and as a proportion of GNP, has fallen since 1990[4] and still further since a peak of 7 per cent in the early 1970s.[5] On the other hand, it is higher than in the early 1980s.[6]

That the Russian Federation has been undergoing profound and traumatic change and transformation since the dissolution of the Soviet Union in December 1991 is self-evident. The education system has experienced both reform and the fallout of economic turbulence, although there are powerful continuities too, and what one finds on the ground is not necessarily congruent with the intentions of Moscow-based legislators, reformers and officials.

The structure of the Russian education system is shown in Figure 3.1. Unlike many other systems, it does not sharply differentiate the primary and secondary phases, but presents instead an uninterrupted core of free and compulsory general (or basic) secondary education from age seven (or, for about 20 per cent of children, age six) to age 15, which with a further two years of upper secondary education in gymnasia or two-stage secondary schools comprises the standard 7–17 'ten-year course'. Separate primary schools such as those that exist in England and in many other countries are therefore not the norm, except in isolated villages. Instead, the characteristic form of provision is a large all-age school with a primary or elementary stage or course covering the first three or four years. There is pre-school and

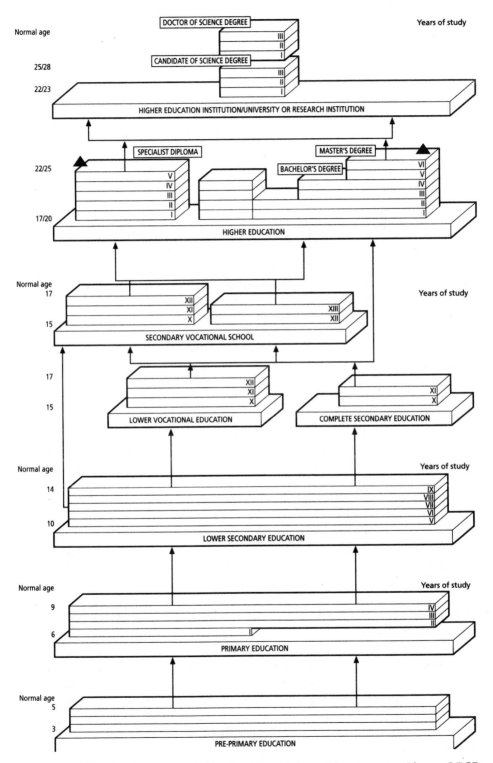

Figure 3.1 The education system in Russia. Adapted from *Education at a Glance: OECD Indicators 1996*. Copyright OECD, 1996.

kindergarten provision for children aged one to three and three to six or seven. An extended (six-year) primary course is currently (1999) under discussion. In 1996 Russia had over 70,000 schools of which about 16,000 were separate primary schools. The number of pupils in general daytime education was 21,500,000.[7]

Under the Soviet regime, kindergartens, like compulsory schooling, made an important contribution to *vospitanie*, a key element in Soviet education which combined upbringing, the education of character and the development of communist morality. Kindergarten provision remains distinctive and well supported. However, because an increasing number of kindergartens are private and a proportion of the costs of public kindergarten provision has now to be borne by parents, since the early 1990s there has been a marked decrease in enrolments.

The administration of this geographically vast system is complex, although because of its origins within a highly centralized command structure it secures remarkable consistency in provision. There are four levels: federal, regional, municipal and school. At the apex is the federal government with its legislative and executive chambers and the Ministry for General and Professional Education (MGPE), formed in 1996 from the former Ministry of Education and the State Committee for Higher Education. In 1999 the MGPE had nine deputy ministers, 21 divisions and eight independent bodies. At the intermediate level are the 89 administrative subjects including republics, *oblasti*, *krai*, autonomous *oblasti*, autonomous *okrugi*, and the cities of Moscow and St Petersburg. These administrative subjects vary in size and status: republics are headed by presidents, *oblasti* and *krai* by governors and cities by mayors. At the municipal level large urban areas have several *rayony* with separate departments of education while rural areas have one *rayon* and a simpler structure.

The federal level has direct responsibility for policy and strategic planning across the system as a whole. Its remit includes goals, curriculum, textbook requirements, standards, monitoring, quality assurance, financial planning, manpower planning, teacher training. Contingent central agencies such as the Russian Academy of Education co-ordinate research, curriculum specification and the preparation of textbooks and other teaching materials. The regional level, which has its own government, defines regional policies and programmes, manages teacher training other than that undertaken by universities, and organizes the publication of teaching materials. The 1,800 city and *rayon* governments at municipal level construct, manage and control the schools, implement federal and regional requirements, develop curricula, assess and pay teachers (or not, as the case may be) and deal with student enrolment.

The schools themselves allocate pupils to classes, choose textbooks from the approved range available, make decisions on teaching methods and assessment, hire and fire staff and determine the manner in which the required curriculum will be implemented, subject to centrally-determined specification of the number of hours to be allocated to each subject. In these matters they have a degree of budgetary discretion. Primary teaching is generalist for the core curriculum, with some specialist provision for subjects such as music, physical education and foreign language. Schools are headed by directors, with, usually, a senior teacher in charge of the primary phase.

Since the 1992 *Law on Education of the Russian Federation*, which eliminated the state monopoly of education, there has been a substantial shift towards decentralization and diversification. There is an expanding private sector, and the responsibilities now vested in regional and municipal governments, and in the schools themselves, are real and growing. Schools are now allowed to charge for certain services that they provide over and above what is required of them (teaching English at the primary stage, for example). Nevertheless, 'federal' in Russia and the United States has very different constitutional and operational force, and the transition to a more decentralized model is marked by uncertainty about the new arrangements on the one hand and the persistence of old habits and assumptions on the other.[8] It also exacerbated the 1997–9 crisis over teachers' salaries, since many *rayony*, particularly in rural areas, failed to collect taxes or pass on grants from central government, or were simply corrupt.[9]

Goals, Curriculum and Assessment

The 1992 Law on Education, amended in 1996, set out the new system's goals. *Obrazovanie* (education) was defined, as it was under the Soviet system, as including both *obuchenie* (instruction) and *vospitanie* (upbringing), although the 1992 law relegated the latter, with its inevitable overtones of Soviet indoctrination, from pre-eminent to subsidiary status.[10] The 1996 amendment adumbrates six governing principles:

(1) the humanistic character of education, the priority of universal human values, human life and health and the free development of the personality; the guiding spirit of citizenship, diligence and respect for human rights; love of family, environment and the Motherland
(2) a unified federal, cultural and educational 'space' which protects and develops ethnic and regional cultures and identities within the multinational state
(3) universal access to education, and adaptability of the system to student needs
(4) the secular character of education in state and municipal educational institutions
(5) freedom and pluralism in education
(6) democratic state control together with with institutional autonomy.[11]

Elsewhere the 1996 amendment emphasizes differentiated and individualized instruction which matches children's interests and abilities and the maximizing of pupil choice. There is considerable emphasis on the kind of citizenship education needed to build the new humanistic civic culture and reshape national identity, with a strong compensatory thrust away from corporate values towards individual self-realization.[12]

The character of primary education has been under review since the establishment of the Russian Federation in 1991. During the 1990s the Ministry espoused a shift from 'knowledge-centred' to 'learner-centred' teaching, the reality and tensions of which we shall examine in later chapters. At the same time, primary education continues to 'lay the foundation of pupils' functional literacy, equip them with basic skills and experience in communication and academic work, and introduces the basic principles of domestic and world culture'.[13]

In keeping with the move to a more decentralized structure, the 1992 law set out a three-tier curriculum with federal, regional and school components. The federal component, or 'basic curriculum', provides the common core for all schools and takes about 60 per cent of teaching time. This 'helps form the pupils' personal attributes in accordance with the general ideas of mankind and cultural traditions, and also creates unity throughout Russian education as a whole'.[14] The regional component or 'regional basic curriculum' is intended 'to meet the aims of national, regional and local social/cultural particularities and traditions'[15] in Russia's 89 administrative subjects; it can include regional or minority language and literature together with regional history, geography and arts. It is allocated about 30 per cent of the timetable. The remaining 10 per cent is at the discretion of the school and facilitates options and advanced study in particular subjects.

For the primary stage the Ministry's 1993 resolution on curriculum 'standards' (which holds at the time of writing) defines the curriculum as being structured round six aspects of 'personality culture':

(1) cognitive culture
(2) communicative culture
(3) moral culture
(4) aesthetic culture
(5) work culture
(6) physical culture.[16]

Perhaps the most critical variant in the curriculum as specified, bearing in mind Russia's linguistic diversity combined with its historic commitment to foreign language teaching, is the arrangement for language. The Ministry defines four permutations of Russian, native language and foreign language within the curriculum field 'language and literature', always securing a minimum of 50 per cent of language time for Russian as the national language.

Typical weekly time allocations for the curriculum as a whole are

Class 1 (ages 7–8)

- language and literature (8 hours)
- mathematics (5 hours)
- arts (art, music) (2 hours)
- physical education (2 hours)
- technology (2 hours)
- compulsory studies, by choice (5 hours)
- options (2 hours)

Class 3 (ages 9–10)

- language and literature (8 hours)
- mathematics (5 hours)
- art (1 hour)
- music (1 hour)
- social studies (history, social studies) (1 hour)
- science (science, physical geography) (1 hour)
- physical education (2 hours)
- technology (2 hours)
- compulsory studies, by choice (3 hours)
- options (3 hours)[17]

('Technology' here is not straightforward. It is the legacy of the gender-specific Soviet 'labour' and since the early 1990s has tended to mean what schools want it to mean.[18])

This gives a weekly total of 26 hours in grade 1 and 27 hours in grade 3 (by grade 14 the weekly total is 38 hours). Lesson time is an invariable 45 minutes.

At the time of writing there is no national system of assessment, although I have noted elsewhere that Russian schools appear to hold their own in the international league tables of pupil attainment in reading, mathematics and science. A United Nations team suggested that by the late 1990s the system was 'running on air' and that Russia's excellent results in TIMSS largely reflected the inherited achievement of the Soviet era:[19] this proposition, disturbing in its implications for the future, deserves to be tested. The Soviet system maintained quality and standards not by measuring learning *outcomes* (the preference of UK governments since 1988) but by strictly controlling the system's *inputs* – the content of the curriculum as prescribed and experienced at each grade, the timetable, textbooks, teacher training – and by establishing a culture of maximum commitment and effort among both pupils and teachers. As a result, apart from certification at points of student transfer or graduation there is no inherited tradition of standardized testing. Instead, assessment is very much a school-level issue and since, unlike France, it is not at this level the subject of central government requirements, we shall need to postpone further discussion of assessment until we consider the *Five Cultures* school and classroom data. During the post-Soviet period of transition both the World Bank and OECD in their reviews of Russian education urged the federal government to develop standardized assessment as a basis for monitoring and quality assurance and to shift from a notion of educational 'standards' specified as content to be covered and numbers of hours to be taught (as above) to one which defines outcomes, minimum levels of learning or benchmarks.[20] This may well be sensible – and the development work is now well under way – but it is also a fairly typical example of the kind of Western cultural colonialism to which international agencies feel they are entitled by virtue of holding the trump card of credits and grants. By the late 1990s, Russians were voicing growing resistance to this hegemonic pressure and were showing a desire to reassert the values of Russian culture and education.[21]

Origins and Development

Russia presents a much more extreme case than France of the thesis that social transformations, however radical, manage to ensure continuity as well as change. However, in Russia's case the scale and trauma of those transformations make it hard to assess the balance of change and continuity, and may lead to what look like contradictory judgements. Thus Lloyd argues against an overemphasis on continuity –

> Continuity is ... precisely what Russia has lacked, and cannot have. Its history has been one of shocking discontinuities. The Soviet experience was the greatest breach with a country's past traditions and culture the world has seen.[22]

– while at the same time he stresses the tsarist genealogy of those conditions and structures which seem quintessentially Soviet:

> Soviet rule was itself the inheritor of tsarist, absolutist traditions which the early Bolsheviks believed could be wholly transcended and which ... Stalin selectively renewed and strengthened ... Nikolai Berdyavev ... said of the 1917 revolution that the past was repeating itself, only behind masks.[23]

He is probably right on both counts: the contradiction is not of argument but of Russia's history. In fact, the tsarist legacy was a closely meshed triumvirate of political autocracy, nationalism and religious orthodoxy, and parallels between the tsarist and Soviet regimes go deeper than mere analogy. The Russian Orthodox Church was, unlike Protestantism and Catholicism, a national rather than a world religion, Slavophile and anti-Western,[24] the bulwark of 'Holy Russia', responsible until Peter the Great for transforming the country into 'one vast monastery, under the rule of the tsar-archimandrite'.[25] In this respect, as Hobsbawm notes:

> In turning himself into something like a secular Tsar, defender of the secular Orthodox faith, the body of whose founder, transformed into a secular saint, awaited the pilgrims outside the Kremlin, Stalin showed a sound sense of public relations.[26]

This is not far from the judgement voiced more earthily by Russians themselves, for example to Colin Thubron – 'Of course Communism's a religion. It's never existed as anything else. It has its own dogma, its own prophets, and even its own embalmed saint'.[27]

In the more particular context of education, the tsarist–Soviet continuities included strong central control in the context of Archer's 'inpenetrable polity'[28] and forms of education which revealed what several have called the 'schizophrenia' of the tsarist era – the juxtaposition of anti-Western, Slavic culture and values with conscious Europeanization as represented most tangibly in the ventures of Peter I, Catherine II, and indeed the architecture of St Petersburg,[29] and as embodied in the Russian and Soviet *gymnasium* and in forms of pedagogy, which like the gymnasium itself, were imported from Germany.[30] Catherine herself was German and there are documented contacts with Enlightenment France (including Voltaire and Diderot) and with England, and indeed a history of importing foreign teachers that goes back at least to the sixteenth century and Boris Godunov. At the elementary stage, the English monitorial system, one of the most successful educational exports of all time, became fashionable in the first quarter of the nineteenth century and even found its way into Pushkin's *Tales of the Late Ivan Petrovich Belkin*.[31]

However, the more lasting educational connections and influences were German, especially where secondary, technical/vocational and university education, and the development of teacher training and pedagogy were concerned.[32] The latter, as we shall see when we examine the work of Russian primary teachers in detail in later chapters, was an influence of profound and lasting importance.

It is as well to emphasize the limited scale of the earlier educational ventures, however, for under the tsars most Russians outside the aristocracy and bourgeoisie were illiterate and by the end of the reign of Peter the Great, notwithstanding his reforming zeal, the country had only 110 secular elementary schools and the serfs, of course, remained uneducated.[33] And, unlike Western Christianity, which was above all a religion of the written word, Russian Orthodoxy was until relatively late – the mid-sixteenth century – run by a mainly illiterate priesthood. Given all this, the most remarkable achievement of Soviet education was its almost complete eradication of illiteracy within the space of a few decades: among males, for example, literacy levels rose from an 1897 figure variously put at 21, 28 and 40 per cent to 94 per cent in 1939.[34] Among the population as a whole the 1939 literacy level was 81 per cent.[35] Although there is disagreement over the precise literacy base on which the Soviet system built, there is no dispute about the sharp differences between groups that the global figure conceals: female literacy levels were much lower than male, rural much lower than urban.

The key events in the development of the modern system of Russian primary education can now be summarized. Until the late nineteenth century provision for public elementary education remained minimal. The brief liberal thaw of the early 1860s under Alexander II – the period of reform which Figes sees as the tsarist equivalent of Gorbachev's *perestroika*[36] – culminated in the 1864 Elementary School Code which provided for a combination of Ministry and *zemstvo* (elected local government assembly) administration, school boards and the goals of 'strengthening the religious and moral understanding of the people and of disseminating the essentials of useful knowledge'.

However, the *zemstva* were variable in both their will to reform and the resources they were prepared or able to allocate, and in any case the 1865 Secondary School Code, which introduced 'classical' and 'real' or 'pro' gymnasia (the latter directly modelled on the German *Realschule*) was given far greater attention and priority. Moreover, the reforms were limited in their reach as to both class and gender: serfs and girls (except those in the upper classes) continued to have at best limited access.

Perhaps more important than the legislative reforms during this period were the ideas with which they were associated, for they constituted an ideological seed which bore fruit after 1917. Thus, Ushinsky – 'the father of the Russian primary school'[37] – who was strongly influenced by the Western philosophical tradition, by the schools he had visited in Germany, Italy and France, and especially by Pestalozzi, anticipated key Soviet educational preoccupations such as *vospitanie* and the labour-oriented curriculum.

The 1860s reforms themselves were short lived. An unsuccessful attempt on the life of Alexander II heralded a clampdown on liberal thinking and on progressive experiments such as Tolstoy's school at Yasnaya Polyana, and after the second and successful attempt in 1881 repression returned and by a decree of 1887:

> The gymnasia and progymnasia . . . shall be freed from the attendance of the children of drivers, footmen, cooks, laundry-women, small traders and other persons similarly situated, whose children, with the exception perhaps of the exceptionally gifted ones, should not be encouraged to abandon the social environment to which they belong.[38]

The grounds for barring these groups will have resonance for those familiar with the debates about the universalization of elementary education in Victorian England (not to mention the tripartite principle of the 1944 Education Act, even down to the view of the grammar school as an escape route for clever working class children).

During the final decade before the Revolution, however, public primary education at last got going – although long after it had been established in the United States and most European countries. Nicholas II responded to pressure for reform by introducing the Universal Primary Education Law of 1908. This made education free and compulsory for boys and girls aged 8–11, a ten-year period being allowed for the completion of the reforms in acknowledgement of the fact that at that point neither the buildings nor the teachers were widely available. The government appointed a strong bureaucracy of officials and school inspectors to ensure *zemstvo* compliance and to maintain control from the centre, and by the outbreak of the First World War literacy levels were rising rapidly and there were four types of primary school: one-class lower primary schools in remote areas concentrating on the bare minimum of reading and writing; one-class schools with a four-year curriculum in reading, writing, arithmetic, history, geography, religion and science, alongside two-class schools which added a further two years and science; and four-year schools which provided the fullest range of elementary provision but which did not give automatic access to secondary education.

Thus, although some of the formal structures and attendant pedagogical ideas were in place before the 1917 Revolution, primary education was not truly universalized until then. From then on, education was given the highest priority, being expanded at all levels. Administrative power was devolved, nominally at least, to regional, provincial and local authorities, although in fact it was largely vested in the new ministry, or People's Commissariat of Enlightenment (acronymed *Narkompros*). The church was disestablished and the curriculum was secularized. The complex patchwork of four kinds of primary and two kinds of secondary school was partly rationalized into the Unified Workers' School which was divided into five divisions: lower primary, primary, upper primary, pro-gymnasium and gymnasium. Parallel secondary schools with eight-year programmes emphasizing languages or science/technology were set up. Textbooks were taken under government control, nominally to purge them of tsarist and clerical remnants.

Archer identifies three phases in the evolution of Soviet education between 1917 and the 1970s, coinciding with the rules of, respectively, Lenin, Stalin and Khrushchev.[39] In relation to the development of Russian primary education the first is of particular importance, not just because it bore most strongly and dramatically the imprint of the revolutionary regime, but also because at the primary stage the canvas was still relatively empty: it was, to all intents and purposes, the first stage in the development of Russian, as well as Soviet primary education.

This period – 1917 or so until Stalin's defeat of Trotsky in 1928 – was one of conscious and indeed (to quote visiting Fabians Beatrice and Sidney Webb) 'luxuriant' educational experiment.[40] Nadezhda Krupskaya, Lenin's wife, was a member of Narkompros and encouraged the importing of American progressive ideas, including John Dewey's project method and Helen Parkhurst's Dalton Plan. Dewey, strongly promoted by S. T. Shatsky, proved remarkably influential at the highest levels of the regime.[41] This was the era of the activity-based 'complex method', of 'pedology' – developmental psychology allied to intelligence testing – of the nurturing of political consciousness through the Little Octobrists and the Young Pioneers, and of debates about the proper balance of individualism and collectivism. It was also the era of L. S. Vygotsky, A. R. Luria and A. N. Leontiev, figures of world importance in the development of psychology and pedagogy.

With Stalin the shutters came down on both experimentation and Russia's brief flirtation with Western progressivism. Dewey's democratic humanism was outlawed, and economic ambitions shifted the emphasis from a common general education for all to a two-track system that separated future factory workers from those heading for higher education.[42] A distinctly Soviet curriculum was established by 1932, and traditional teaching methods, framed by the standard 45-minute lesson, had been reinstated. After 1934 the curriculum was made rigid and uniform, with no differentiation apart from the special provision for children talented in music, art and dance which had been inherited from the pre-revolution era. In 1936, the Communist Party Central Committee disowned the new psychology and Vygotsky's seminal study *Thought and Language*, despite its clear Marxist credentials.[43] It did not reappear until 1956, 22 years after his death.[44]

Over the next two decades the textbook pattern of Soviet education was firmly established. The debate about the balance of individual and collective goals and interests within the Soviet curriculum was resolved by asserting the primacy of the collective. Largely through the agency of Anton Makarenko, *obrazovanie* (education) was subsumed within *vospitanie* (upbringing) and the moral/social goals presaged in the previous century by Ushinsky were given the harder edge of strict training in communist morality. Individual differences and genetic endowment were to be transcended by the more powerful shaping forces of education. For the pupil, what counted was effort rather than innate ability. There was to be no streaming or setting. Makarenko's emphasis on the collective ethos of school and classroom was extremely influential. It was grounded in experience (rather than mere ideology) and the account of his school gave his work credibility beyond the Party apparatus.

During this period, too, the modern schooling structure and curriculum were consolidated. By 1930, universal compulsory primary education was required throughout the Soviet Union; by 1939 seven-year schooling was available to most children and ten-year schooling was the goal in towns and cities: by the 1950s, when a group of English HMIs toured selected schools in Moscow, Leningrad and Baku, the curriculum and textbooks were centrally prescribed, and education, although formally a matter for each republic, was effectively shaped in Moscow.[45] Primary education was preceded by a distinctive pattern of kindergarten and, for some, pre-school. Strong ideological commitment to the comprehensive principle meant that most children attended the common school and that children of all abilities encountered the same 'general education' curriculum. Alongside this, however, the new science of 'defectology' sustained institutionally separate special education for those with particular physical and learning difficulties, while special-profile schools (common schools with enhanced curricula in subjects such as languages, science or music) catered for specific talent. Muckle quotes official insistence (in 1988) that these did not contravene the common-school principle. However, the issue was contentious and special-profile schools were fiercely attacked in the Soviet press on just these grounds.[46]

The system was consolidated further – and to a degree gradually liberalized – during the 1960s, the 1970s and the 1980s. The common school was reinstated under Khrushchev, and the system of special schools for talented children was extended to include physics, mathematics and modern foreign languages. Shortly before the collapse of the Soviet Union, Muckle found the ten-year school firmly established throughout the USSR except (as in 1999) in some rural areas. The curriculum for the primary years (ages 6/7–10) had been revised in 1984 and comprised first language, mathematics, the world around us (family, school and community), nature study, art, music, physical culture and labour and vocational training, and the Ministry spelled out time and content requirements for each in detail and backed these with approved textbooks. *Vospitanie* pervaded all aspects and was reinforced through the parallel activities of the Octobrists (ages 7–9), Pioneers (ages 9–14) and the communist youth organization Komsomol.[47]

During the 1980s, too, serious root-and-branch reform was mooted. The 1984 *Guidelines for Soviet School Reform* proposed lowering the school starting age to six, broadening the concept of general education to include both polytechnical education and a stronger emphasis on cultural and aesthetic development, raising teachers' salaries and investing in buildings and infrastructure. There were growing calls for a more humane and creative 'pedagogy of co-operation'. These reforms had limited impact and were in any case overtaken by the wider *perestroika* movement.[48]

The New Russia: Control, Values and Identity

With the demise of the Soviet Union in 1991, we enter the most recent stage in the development of basic education in Russia. The legacy was an effective system of compulsory, free and secular schooling, controlled by the state and enshrining a distinctive mix of instruction and moral training underpinned by a strong collective ethic. In assessing the positive gains of Soviet education as a whole (from a Western perspective), the OECD team which reviewed Russian education in 1997 cited effective kindergartens, high levels of literacy, scientific, mathematical and artistic achievement, and extensive extra-curricular and supplementary education. They noted – as in the previous chapter we noted – the conscious shift to a more individualistic and humanistic regime in the Federation's 1992 and 1996 education laws, and the way each formally adopted goal – individualization, differentiation, democratization, human rights – represents almost the antithesis of what went before.[49]

Like the World Bank, OECD strongly commended the efforts at decentralization we noted earlier, although the Bank proposed a different way of sharing the curriculum cake between federal, regional and local authorities. Moreover, the Bank – as, given its dominance by free-market ideology one would expect it to – found the curriculum inappropriate to the needs of the market economy. Literacy, numeracy and science, they asserted, were not enough, and the emphasis on fact-acquisition needed to be replaced by problem solving.[50] In similar vein, both OECD and the Bank argued that quality control mechanisms should shift their focus from the Soviet preoccupation with regulated and standardized inputs to greater emphasis on the monitoring of processes and outcomes.[51]

In these and other respects, Western agencies display an incomplete understanding of the Soviet educational legacy, which they may well presume to be ineluctably communist in its values and consequences for as long as it retains features of Soviet pedagogy, and indeed of the older Russian and European traditions with which Soviet educational ideology and practice were combined. The difference in how 'standards' are defined is not simply a matter of efficiency. To seek to guarantee absolute consistency of input is itself consistent with the goal of securing success for all and with collectivist values and the emphasis upon effort rather than ability. To argue that the only 'correct' way to define standards is in terms of measured outcomes is to assume the primacy of Western concepts of individualism and individual ability, neither of which, as we shall see, is anything less than problematic in the context of primary classes of twenty to thirty children. The superficiality of the OECD's and the World Bank's engagement with school and classroom processes is further confirmed by their accounts and critiques of Russian pedagogy, which OECD simply dismisses out of hand as 'old fashioned'.[52] We and they need to be reminded that Russian notions of standards, and Russian pedagogy, have proved themselves capable of matching many Western countries on measures which those countries themselves, rather than Russia, have defined.[53] Russian pedagogy, in particular, is the product of traditions which go back not just to Soviet reformers such as Makarenko, but also to Ushinsky and a broader European tradition which is humanistic and democratic in its core values and can be traced back to Pestalozzi and Comenius. It merits the careful and sympathetic study that this book will try to provide.

The ethnocentric or ideological interventions of international agencies dramatically highlight the problem of values and identity in Russia during the period of transition. If, as is commonly suggested, autocracy, nationalism and orthodoxy speak to something deep in the Russian psyche, so that throne, fatherland and altar find both communist as well as tsarist manifestations, where in post-Soviet Russia are these to be found? In the revival of the Russian Orthodox Church? In the commonly voiced hankering for strong leadership? (Several of those I interviewed openly regretted the passing of Stalin but thought in all seriousness that Margaret Thatcher would make a more than passable substitute.) In the recovery of the Communist Party under Gennady Zyuganov or the rise of right-wing nationalists such as Vladimir Zhirinovsky? Or, conceivably in Vladimir Putin, who won his 'strong man' election credentials through his prosecution of the Chechnya war and the annihilation of its capital Grozny?

Or maybe we should look to those invocations of birch forest, autumn sunshine and companionship – whether conjured up in song, or glimpsed through the alcoholic haze of those endless and increasingly maudlin toasts which came to form an inevitable adjunct to the gathering of the *Five Cultures* Russian data? (We might note in passing that most Russian folksongs are in minor keys and when harmonized the parts have a way of converging on a plangent unison rather than a contented triad. However, an ethnomusicologist would no doubt point out that since this is a common feature of all such music, regardless of mood, any melancholy is in the ear of the hearer.)

Part of the answer is only too evident on the streets and in the appalling demography of downward-spiralling life expectancy, poverty, vagrancy, crime, violence, declining diet and health, and rising divorce rates.[54] It is there, too, in the lives of children. By the late 1980s, and even more seriously during the 1990s, child mortality rose, children's health deteriorated, especially once they reached school age, childhood diseases more characteristic of wartime reappeared, and homelessness reached epidemic proportions. By 1992 there were an estimated 10,000–20,000 homeless children in St Petersburg alone, and neither orphanages nor the many temporary shelters could cope, there and elsewhere.[55] (This figure, however, is strongly disputed by our contacts in St Petersburg.)

Yet somehow, despite this, and despite deteriorating school buildings, lack of textbooks and other materials, and the sufferings endured by teachers themselves, we shall see how schools managed to maintain a remarkable illusion of civic normality during the 1990s, more so at the primary stage than secondary, admittedly. But at this level, given schools' traditionally powerful moral agency and the disappearance of the Octobrists, the Pioneers and Komsomol, the questions are well put by Anthony Jones:

> What should replace the old, politically-based system of morality? What are to be the new sources of moral upbringing, the new values which will provide a guide to appropriate behaviour? . . . How are educators who themselves do not know what freedom is going to educate free people?[56]

Let us consider some of the elements in the 'old' morality. Framing and sustaining the work of schools were family and community. Bronfenbrenner's classic comparative study of child rearing in the Soviet Union and the United States stresses the seamlessness of family, community and *vospitanie*. Families were close, physically warm and protective, and socialized children into obedience and self-discipline.[57] By then – 1960–61 – the efforts of the family were once again in harmony with those of the collective after the excesses of the Stalinist era for ever emblematized by the figure of Pavlik (Pavel) Morozov, the boy who in 1931 denounced his father, chairman of the village Soviet, for accepting bribes in return for counting rich peasants as poor ones. Pavlik was murdered by his brother and grandfather and became the consummate Soviet saint and classroom icon who put party and fatherland before family. The story may be apocryphal: after *glasnost* Russian researchers began to query the evidence.[58]

Pre-school and kindergarten education emphasized collective living and playing and, as their necessary adjunct, the development of self-reliance. Once the child entered the primary school *vospitanie* began in earnest as a programme of training in personal and social morality in the contexts of school, home and community. Bronfenbrenner quotes the official manual on *Vospitanie* produced by the Soviet Academy of Pedagogical Sciences (now the Russian Academy of Education) which sets down detailed objectives for different age-ranges under five general traits: communist morality, responsible attitude towards learning, cultured conduct, aesthetic culture, and physical culture and sport.

Although, as we saw in the previous chapter, the 1990s government of the Russian Federation demoted *vospitanie* from an overarching educational goal to a subsidiary one, the 1960s programme quoted by Bronfenbrenner remains highly relevant to our analysis. First, if just one of the 20 goals listed for 7–11 year olds (atheism) is removed, the remainder stand as a statement of the attributes of the socially responsible, autonomous and balanced individual which would undoubtedly find favour in many non-communist cultural and political contexts. (The list for the 16–18 age group, however, is a different matter, being far more overtly Communist.[59]) Second, explicit party ideology excepted, the list overlaps the 1993 post-Soviet resolution on curriculum 'standards' I cited in Chapter 2, not least by defining the entire school curriculum in terms of the development of 'personality culture'.[60] Third, and most important, if *vospitanie* is a suspect concept in the Ministry of Education, we shall see that in schools and primary classrooms it is not.

For despite Jones' sense of a moral vacuum, and all those Western media images of civil dislocation and dissolution (which nearly always come from the streets of Moscow and St Petersburg, rarely from other towns in Russia, and never from schools and homes) the continuities are pervasive and powerful. The political overtones of *vospitanie* notwithstanding, it was frequently invoked by teachers, and in interview the Director of Primary Education at the Ministry of Education identified 'the development of the personality' as the central goal of this stage of education, interestingly arguing that Soviet pedagogy, by concentrating on basic skills, had neglected personality development. In this, which seems paradoxical in the light of how Soviet education made much of personality development, she appeared to be tacitly distinguishing between moulding the personality to the requirements of the collective and allowing it to develop autonomously. She may have intended the more individualistic connotation, but our teachers, by and large, did not.

Nikolai Nikandrov, Vice-President of the Russian Academy of Education – in both his writing and in interview with us – argued that the collapse of communism and the privations of the 1990s had generated a crisis of values: there had been a move away from communal values towards individualism and materialism, goals perceived as essentially Western and underscored by the Americanization of media, shops and entertainment. Yet despite this, and the undoubted stresses to which marriages and families were now subject, the family remained the anchor, cited as the most important value by 90 per cent of respondents to a *Moscow News* poll in 1993.[61]

Within the schools, too, although Ministry rhetoric is strong on 'humanization' and the need to shift from what Nikandrov calls the 'pedagogy of command' to the 'pedagogy of co-operation',[62] we shall see how the traditional relationship between teacher and pupil remained relatively secure, notwithstanding teachers' own espousal of the new democratic rhetoric.

This brings us to the vital question of control, and back to Archer's preoccupation with change in centralized and decentralized systems. Clearly, Soviet education was an archetype of cultural, social and political reproduction, and it sought to achieve this by exerting a strong measure of control from the centre, backed by a variety of mechanisms to secure and check compliance at each level of the system down to the classroom. On the face of it this should have ensured that what was delivered at the periphery was exactly what was mandated at the centre.

The true picture, is – and remains – somewhat more complex, and four countervailing or at any rate moderating forces emerged from the *Five Cultures* 'level 1' interviews. First, although Stalin's accession ended the 1920s decade of 'luxuriant experiment', even during the period of his repressive rule the system could be mildly subverted, and sometimes in surprising places. Thus, one of our respondents recorded that:

> It was a period of strict conformity to *vospitanie* and *obrazovanie* as defined by the Party: no experimentation, no innovation. Only the talented and the courageous experimented. But in one school I knew well during the 1940s an exceptional teacher introduced new ideas and methods. I must tell you that the school was attended by the sons of both Khrushchev and Mikoyan.[63]

Second, and more generally, the problem with macro-analysis of educational systems and educational change is that by ignoring the school and classroom levels of educational action they tend to imply that policy and practice are synonymous and indeed that policy as stated is somehow more 'real' than what people do with it. Although Stalinist surveillance will have kept most teachers firmly in line during the 1930s and the 1940s, the gap may have widened during the Khrushchev thaw and Brezhnev's final years, in classroom culture and the messages of the hidden curriculum, if not in curriculum content. The same respondent identified a growing divergence between rhetoric and reality during the latter stages of the Soviet regime and suggested that in respect of the 'humanizing' pedagogical reforms introduced by the Yeltsin government in the 1990s this had become a yawning gulf. The problem, in his view, was partly the time-lapse inherent in all centre–periphery reform movements, partly the countervailing power of long-established habits and routines, but partly also intellectual and conceptual.

Developing this last point, he suggested that during the Soviet period some, at least, of those in high places understood this:

> X went to the Minister and asked for the ideas of Y to be introduced to schools. The Minister said 'All right, but after one year you will need to cancel the programme'. 'Why?' 'Because I know our teachers and you don't: they aren't up to it'.

This resonates strongly with the findings of British and American research. In England, for example, Plowdenite progressivism in its pure form was implemented to a fairly limited extent. Bowdlerized, it reached somewhat further, but more widespread still was the phenomenon of progressive rhetoric sustaining practice which was less 'traditional' or 'progressive' than merely mediocre or muddled. The potential or actual gulf between teachers' 'espoused theory' and 'theory-in-use' is a constant and well-established phenomenon.[64]

Fourth, to construct the scenario in terms of a centre–grass-roots relationship is seriously to underestimate the influence of those at intermediate levels. Our Russian interviews revealed two significant brakes on government reform intentions. The first was and is close – very close – to the Ministry. One respondent suggested that in Russia the government could not but depend very heavily on experts:

> In Russia, politicians can't influence school practice as much as people think because the country is very big and politicians change jobs so quickly. The first thing they do when they come to the Ministry is make themselves familiar with the research. They rarely have their own view; they take their ideas from leading researchers and school directors, and they form their image of the system from these. And they don't really intrude into our research and training work.

Further, the very device which is so often cited as evidence of the iron hand of government controlling teachers' actions – centrally produced textbooks – is open to some degree of professional manipulation by an alliance of textbook writers and teachers:

> The Academy of Pedagogical Sciences – now the Russian Academy of Education – worked out the national curriculum and prepared the textbooks. But as a researcher developing textbooks I had no right to present them for publication unless I could demonstrate that I had worked with teachers in preparing them, tried them out over several years, and made modifications to ensure that they could be used effectively. The government has a view of the curriculum but that is as far as it goes.

Of course, in this account, which was a little suggestive of the civil service view of ministerial understanding expressed in the British television comedy series *Yes, Minister* (in which the minister is a puppet manipulated by officials), we must allow for the possibility that the Academy's view of its influence may have been inflated. Equally, the account may attribute to the Academy a greater reforming zeal than it actually displayed. Others suggest that during the Soviet era, and right through until its change of title and management in 1992, the Academy, along with the ministry, was a decidedly conservative force. During the crucial period of educational debate about the new 'pedagogy of co-operation' in the late 1980s, the Academy was strongly criticized for obstructing reform.[65]

However, there are other levels at which government intentions can be frustrated. Teachers are trained, they are answerable to the local authorities that employ them, and they receive in-service training. In the city and *oblast* where we gathered much of our local and school-level data, we became aware that outside Moscow and St Petersburg this cycle of career and professional development is very much a closed circuit. Most of the teachers we interviewed and observed had attended school in the same town as their parents, and were trained to teach at the town's pedagogical institute by lecturers with a similarly local pedigree. Having been trained there, they returned to the schools as teachers, and at regular periods undertook in-service training where their lecturers were those from whom they had received their pre-service training, who had attended and taught at their schools. All this time, for in Russia student and teacher mobility is very limited, they were living at home with their parents. In these processes, we were given to understand, party membership and patronage used to play a large part and, residually, still did.

When we interviewed the Federation's Director of Teacher Training, she confirmed this analysis and, moreover indicated what we were not in a position to test, namely that it was and is replicated in most towns and districts in Russia. For a reformist Ministry, breaking through the dense local carapace of self-reinforcing values and practices sustained by professional, family and – until recently – party networks, was seen as a major challenge.

We might also suggest that this reality calls into question the new culture of decentralization, as endorsed by both the Ministry and those international agencies which hold the purse-strings of aid. Decentralization in theory empowers grassroots initiative and creativity. Yet our findings suggest, first, that these local professional hierarchies could be extraordinarily powerful and resistant to any challenge to their position within the local and regional professional and political structure; second, given this, that power may be devolved to local level but may well penetrate no further.

This would tend to confirm the view of one of our Moscow interviewees that the main influences – and constraints – on teachers' practice were textbooks, teacher training, in-service training and research as mediated through these. In contrast to their immediacy, national policy remained vague and partly understood. We can confirm, then, the critical importance of centralization–decentralization as a key to understanding state education systems, but in addition to the problems raised by my earlier comment on the OECD analysis we can add another. To list the powers formally wielded or the decisions taken formally at each level of the system is insufficient: we must understand also the dynamics of their relationship and the subtle transformations of policies and ideas which those dynamics permit. In Russia's case we found the local level to be critical, for it combines professional and pedagogical hegemony with administrative and financial control.

Postscript: the National Doctrine of Education, 2000

In Russia, educational practice may not change very quickly but policies certainly do. Shortly after this book went to press the Ministry of General and Professional Education published the draft of a new *National Doctrine of Education in the Russian Federation*.[66] This followed more than two years of political argument about the proper direction of education reform, a period which was also punctuated by ministerial resignations and dismissals.

The draft *National Doctrine* was a statement of aspiration. It dealt in principles rather than practice, and certainly provided nothing new on matters as detailed as curriculum and time allocations. It retained the general thrust of the 1996 amendment to the 1992 Law on Education – human values, Russian culture, Russian language, secularism, pluralism, individualism, universal access, patriotism, environmentalism, democratic principles and democratic control – while purportedly addressing some of the problems and failures of the 1990s, not least in the fraught sphere of educational finance. Thus it envisaged protected salaries, salary increases and pensions for teachers and other education workers together with the stabilization of institutional finances. It also ambitiously prescribed free provision at every level of education from pre-school to vocational, higher and post-graduate and reiterated earlier commitments to the 12-year course. All this was to be paid for by a three-stage increase in educational spending, starting with a target of 6 per cent of GDP by 2003 and rising to 10 per cent of GDP by 2025.

The draft *National Doctrine* emphasized science and the new technologies, especially IT, more strongly than did earlier statements. It also displayed a greater consciousness of the global market place and Russia's need to reinstate itself 'as a major power in the field of education, culture, science, high technologies and economics'. To support these goals provision would diversify, teaching would be individualized and post-secondary education would become more competitive.

Yet the draft *National Doctrine* attempted to address social as well as economic and infrastructural problems and to this end it maintained the traditional Russian emphasis upon civic responsibility, morality, the partnership of family and school, and the linking of education and upbringing. *Vospitanie* – and no doubt much more besides – lived to fight another day.

4

Primary Education in India

Context, Structure and Control

With one billion inhabitants in 2000, India has the largest population of the five countries in this study and, after China, is the second most populous country in the world.[1] It is also large geographically: at 3,287,590 square kilometres, it is 24 times the size of England, although it is considerably smaller than either Russia or the United States. Among the five countries its population density is second only to that of England.[2] Despite this, and despite the scale of densely populated conurbations such as Bombay, Calcutta and Delhi, it is as well to remember that the reality of life for the majority of the population (73 per cent in 1997) remains rural.[3] In 1998 per capita GNP was US$1,700, or just 5.8 per cent of that of the USA, and of this 3.3 per cent went to education.[4] Despite its low ranking in these particular economic league tables, India's many disparities include massive differences between rich and poor, exacerbated by geography, class and caste; between world-beating hi-tech cities such as Bangalore and Hyderabad[5] and low-tech subsistence farming; between world-class universities and training institutes, and rural primary schools, some of which exist in name only, having neither buildings nor teachers.

Like Russia, India is a country of immense cultural, ethnic, religious and linguistic diversity. The usual figure of over a hundred languages is probably an underestimate, since many are minority tribal languages spoken, but not written, in the remoter parts of the six 'tribal states' (Octavio Paz rates the 1927 British linguistic survey, which yielded no fewer than 179 languages and 544 dialects, more reliable than surveys undertaken since Independence,[6] while the Government of India gives a figure of 1,000 languages and dialects[7]). Hindi and English are the two 'official languages' but the 1947 Constitution lists 14 'principal languages', of which Hindi has by far the largest number of speakers (about 39 per cent of the population), with Bengali, Gujarati, Marathi, Tamil, Telegu and Urdu coming closest, but a long way behind, being spoken by between 5 and 8 per cent, and the frequency list tails off from Kannada, Malayalam, Oriya and Punjabi to Assamese, Kashmiri and Sindhi (0.2 per cent).[8] Each has major concentrations in particular states and territories, and even Hindi, which to an outsider might look relatively universal, is in fact the majority language of the north only, that is, of India above a line drawn roughly from southern Gujarat to northern Orissa.

Caste, religion and tribe further differentiate and divide. Although caste is a Hindu institution, Hindus comprise some 85 per cent of the population and the hegemony of caste extends much further than this, across religious groups as distinct as Muslims, Sikhs, Jains, Buddhists, Jews and Christians. The scale of social exclusion represented by the caste system needs underlining in the context of the Indian government's aim of universalizing basic education: *dalits* or Untouchables number 150 million, 15 per cent of the country's population, and by the late twentieth century they were becoming increasingly militant.[9]

Politically, India is a union of 25 states and seven union territories within a federal parliamentary democracy. Within each state there is generally a four-tier administrative structure – region, district, block and village – and since 1992 many states have introduced a measure of local self-government in rural areas in the form of the *Panchayati Raj*, or village council. The Constitution deals with the balance of power between national and state government through its three lists: the Union and State Lists cover those areas on which, respectively, national government and state governments legislate exclusively; the Concurrent List includes those areas – education being one of them – where power is shared. There is substantial devolution of powers and resources from federal to state level, and for this and historical and cultural reasons the quality of educational provision, and the outcomes of this provision in terms of measures such as adult literacy, are as varied as every other aspect of the country. The education budget is largely the responsibility of the individual state governments, with the result that there is considerable statewise variation in expenditure on education, including elementary education. Credits and grants from international agencies, notably the World Bank, the European Commission, UNICEF, the UK government's Department for International Development and. the Netherlands government, have supported the Government of India's drive to universalize elementary education.

Recent initiatives, especially the Government of India's District Primary Education Programme (DPEP), as its name implies, have encouraged this process of devolution, making districts, block and village clusters the focus for development efforts and encouraging local ownership through village education committees (VECs). DPEP is a significant intervention and the extent of support it receives from the international agencies and national governments referred to above make it, at the time of writing, the world's largest initiative in basic education. But the DPEP experience also points up the tension between two commitments: to devolution on the one hand, and to the universalization of primary education, the reduction of inequalities of gender, caste and tribe, and the eradication of illiteracy on the other – a commitment which can be fulfilled only if action at district and village level is combined with unambiguous policy, clear leadership and substantial resource investment from GOI and the state government.

In a country where statistical differences rarely raise technical problems of significance because the raw numbers are so large, the scale of India's basic education

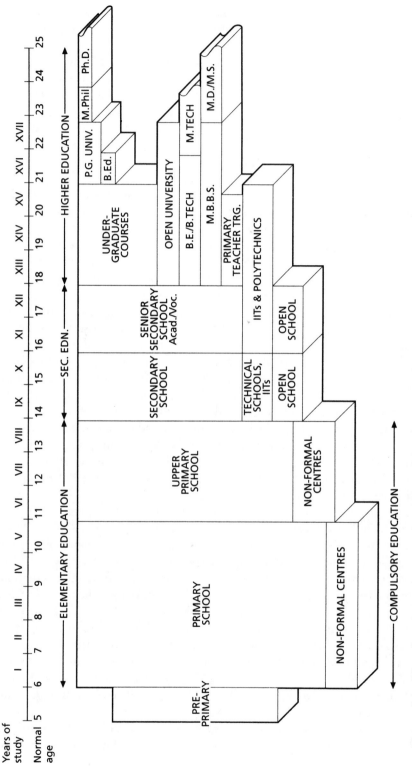

Figure 4.1 The education system in India. Adapted from *Education for All: The Indian Scene*. Copyright Ministry of Human Resource Development, Government of India, 1993.

problem is incontrovertible: in 1993 India had the world's largest number of out-of-school children (22 per cent of the global total) and about one third of the world's adult illiterates. Alarmingly, 36 per cent of men, but 61 per cent of women, were unable to read or write; less than 30 per cent of adults had completed eight years of schooling; one-third of all children aged 6–14 years were out of school; only 72 per cent of schools had *pucca* buildings; enrolment and dropout of girls and members of scheduled castes and tribes was running much higher than the overall figures; and, crucially, there was a high coincidence across the central and northern 'Hindi belt' states of the key educational and social indicators: low school enrolment and low pupil retention, high illiteracy, high gender disparity and – the factor which consistently reduces numerical gains to proportional stasis – high fertility.[10]

As one critical example of the geographical variation, female literacy in 1991 was 8 per cent in parts of Rajasthan and 94 per cent in the Kottayam district of Kerala; and to drive home the gains of female literacy across the board we can note that in India a mother's primary education correlates with markedly decreased infant mortality and smaller family size.[11]

At the same time, the improvements in respect of all these measures, and the achievements of both central government and individual states, have been substantial: non-participation in elementary education, for example, has been reduced to its 1993 figure of 22 per cent from 50 per cent at independence. Universalization of elementary education, however, remains in 2000 some way from achievement.

This is the background against which the structure, administration and content of primary education in India can now be summarized.

The structure of the education system in India is set out in Figure 4.1. Notwithstanding the diversity of context and unevenness of provision referred to above, the structure of public education in India is broadly the same across the entire country. Free and compulsory elementary education for children aged 6–14 is divided into primary (usually classes 1 to 5, or ages 6–10+) and upper primary or middle stages (usually classes 6 to 8 or ages 10+ to 13+). The precise division varies slightly between states. The upper primary stage can be free standing or combined institutionally with either primary or secondary. In many rural areas, however, upper primary provision may be available but children's use of it may be frustrated by distance, and this is a major contributory factor in the high pupil dropout after class 5.[12] A limited range of pre-school and nursery provision is available, mainly in the cities, and alongside public schooling there is a significant tradition of non-formal education in rural areas and private schools, again in the cities.

In urban areas, primary schools may be large, with one or more classes for each age group, but in rural areas the norm is a one-teacher, or at most a two-teacher school. In 1986, 60 per cent of India's primary schools had no more than two teachers and only 15 per cent had five or more.[13] More recent figures show considerable improvement, however, although multi-grade pupil grouping and teaching remains the norm in such circumstances.[14] In every case generalist class teaching, as in England, is standard practice, although in some well-staffed schools there may be specialist support for subjects such as music. Classes are large: one recent survey calculated an average (assuming full enrolment) of 68:1, with a range of between 9:1 and 168:1.[15] Another gave the slightly more optimistic figure of 52.4:1.[16]

Goals, Curriculum and Assessment

The 1950 Constitution aimed for free, compulsory and secular education for all children up to the age of 14, and safeguarded the religion, language and educational choice of minorities. The 1986 National Policy on Education restated these commitments and set out the broad goals of public education; to:

- promote all-round development, material and spiritual
- refine sensitivities and perceptions that contribute to national cohesion, a scientific temper and independence of mind and spirit, thus furthering the goals of socialism, secularism and democracy enshrined in the Constitution
- develop manpower for different levels of the economy.[17]

The 1986 Policy was also egalitarian and inclusionist. It sought to:

- remove disparities and equalize educational opportunity
- use education as an agent of basic change in the status of women
- equalize the educational development of scheduled castes, scheduled tribes and other minorities
- integrate the physically and mentally handicapped with the general community as equal partners.[18]

The same Policy announced a 'new thrust' for elementary education:

- universal access and enrolment
- universal retention of children up to 14 years of age
- a substantial improvement in the quality of learning.[19]

This 'substantial improvement' was glossed as improved buildings and equipment, increased staffing, and

> ... a warm, welcoming and encouraging approach in which all concerned share a solicitude for the needs of the child ... a child-centred and activity-based process of learning ... children should be allowed to set their own pace ... a policy of non-detention ... corporal punishment will be firmly excluded ... and school timings as well as vacations adjusted to the convenience of children.[20]

A series of five-year plans has sought to reduce the gap between aspiration and reality, most recently by launching a series of initiatives targeted at those states and districts where provision, enrolment and retention are poorest, where inequalities are most marked, and where literacy levels are lowest. In this, although the policy is national its implementation is intended to be local, and the Panchayati Raj Act of 1992 committed states to decentralized planning and fully representative government at district level and below.

In parallel with the bid for universalization through decentralization, the federal government during the latter decades of the twentieth century aimed to produce a system which in terms of entitlement and content was national and which would promote a strong sense of national cohesion and identity. Core components were identified which would underpin all provision, regardless of location and circumstance:

(1) the history of India's freedom movement
(2) the constitutional obligations
(3) other content essential to nurture national identity
(4) India's common cultural heritage
(5) egalitarianism, democracy and secularism
(6) equality of the sexes
(7) protection of the environment
(8) removal of social barriers
(9) observance of the small family norm
(10) inculcation of the scientific temper.[21]

These ten 'common core components' were intended to inform the subjects in the required curriculum rather in the manner of the 'cross-curricular themes, skills and dimensions' in the 1998 version of England's national curriculum, although their actual character was very different. The primary curriculum itself was defined in 1991 as including six subjects with weekly time allocations as follows:

(1) language: Hindi or regional language (30 per cent or 7.2 hours)
(2) mathematics (15 per cent or 3.6 hours)
(3) environmental studies (science and social studies) (15 per cent or 3.6 hours)
(4) work experience (a combination of technology, craft and positive work attitudes (20 per cent or 4.8 hours)
(5) arts (art, craft, music, drama, dance and rhythm) (10 per cent or 2.4 hours)
(6) physical and health education (10 per cent or 2.4 hours).

The National Council for Educational Research and Training (NCERT), the lead national body for educational research, testing, in-service training and the production of curriculum specifications and materials, elaborated each subject as a comprehensive and detailed set of Minimum Levels of Learning (MLLs) for the end of the primary stage and Minimum Learning Outcomes (MLOs) and content for each year, set out in teaching units. These are therefore intended to provide at the same time syllabuses for teaching, targets for end-of-year attainment, and criteria for assessment.[22] The model has been heavily criticized in some quarters as being daunting, unrealistic and inoperable,[23] although that is not our concern here.

There is no national system of assessment, although there is a substantial pro-gramme of national monitoring and the impact of the District Primary Education Programme is being judged in part through a programme of testing in language and mathematics. Some states have examinations after classes 5, 7 or 8 and most do so not later than class 8. Otherwise, assessment is a school-level issue. At the same time, a vast array of social and educational data is gathered by the federal and state governments, and by agencies such as the National Council of Educational Re-search and Training and the National Institute of Educational Planning and Admin-istration (NIEPA) for the purposes of monitoring and planning. Much of it this information is provided by teachers, who double in rural areas as census agents. Because schools and districts gain financially from favourable enrolment and at-tendance figures, the reliability of school-level information is regarded as suspect.

Origins and Development

To understand the Indian system of primary education we need to superimpose on the cultural diversities, social divides and economic inequalities a historical timeframe which has at least three distinct stages.

Conventionally, since India's British colonial past remains such an obvious residual influence on its contemporary educational patterns and practices, accounts of these tend to confine themselves to the impact of colonization and independence, imply-ing in effect that there was no popular education in India until Macaulay's Minute of 1835. To do this, however is to underplay both geography and history. British hegemony before Independence, and Hindu nationalism after it, varied considerably in their impact from one region to another, the British were not the only colonizers, and above all India had, and has, highly significant and deeply-rooted indigenous patterns and traditions of education.

To split Indian educational history so conveniently, too, is to compound British and European hegemony in more subtle ways, and to risk accusations of what Edward Said calls 'orientalism' – writing about Asia from the standpoint of Western culture, values and politico-economic interests.[24] In a book which deploys hegemony as an interpretative device, and which will be generally critical of the cultural colonialist tendencies being displayed by international (that is to say, Western) aid agencies in India (and indeed Russia) even as I write, it would be unwise not to be acutely sensitive to this risk.

Unfortunately, this is easier said than done, for, as Landes points out, 'Some of the most important work on Indian history has been done by Indian scholars, yet these, ironically, have had to rely almost exclusively on European records and accounts. Almost no documentation comes down to us from the Indian side.'[25] In seeking to explain why this should be so he notes that while pre-colonial India was far from illiterate and thus had records, it was a *hieratically* rather than a *generally* literate society and therefore generated documentation which centred on the imperative of religious continuity and conformity rather than secular change and enquiry.[26]

But then perhaps this is perhaps the key to understanding not just the difficulties of Indian educational history but also important aspects of the character of Indian education itself. Thus Kumar's scholarly polemic on the intertwining of colonialist and nationalist ideas in Indian education makes it clear that one reason why the *pre-colonial* educational legacy must not be left off the balance sheet is its dominance by priestly concepts of teaching, learning and knowledge whose legacy is still evident.

The pre-colonial era, then, is the first of the evolutionary stages identified above. Although there is evidence that literacy and literacy instruction have been present in India for over four thousand years (Goody suggests since about 2200 BC[27]) – to the extent that collapsing such an immense span of time into a single stage seems decidedly presumptuous – the paucity of primary sources other than the religious texts themselves, means that for 'pre-colonial' it is sensible to read 'the period before the arrival of the English in the late sixteenth century'. On the basis of nineteenth-century accounts by C. E. Trevelyan (brother-in-law of Macaulay and great-uncle of historian G. M. Trevelyan), James Mill (father of John Stuart Mill) and William Arnold (Matthew's brother) – the familial networking of the English establishment is nicely illustrated here – Kumar characterizes the indigenous system as village based and village controlled, with instruction relatively individualized within groups of up to about thirty pupils of different ages, often using the monitorial method, thus freeing the teacher to work with individuals and small groups.

Teachers had a fair measure of autonomy as to the selection of texts and the pacing of pedagogy in respect of individual needs and progress.[28] In accordance with the Brahmanical tradition, the teacher commanded respect both as an adult and as source of knowledge. Equally important for our understanding of later developments, the book and the text – secular as well as, self-evidently, religious – were sacrosanct. They were to be savoured and illuminated rather than interrogated.[29]

The central role of the religious text, and of the models of teaching and knowledge which it provided, may be important to our understanding of later developments for two further reasons. First, the mode of transmission was oral – through constant recitation and repetition, backwards and forwards from teacher to pupils, texts were committed to memory. Second, a pedagogically powerful feature of the sacred texts of the dominant religion, Hinduism, was their use of doctrinal formulae (*sutras* or threads) and lists, a habit for which Paz finds ready evidence in contemporary Indian life: 'Essential, too, is an affinity for nomenclatures, numbers, categories, and lists, whether of shapes, tastes or sensations, philosophical ideas or grammatical figures. Logic, grammar, aesthetics and erotics are alike in this predilection for catalogues and classifications'.[30]

We shall discover the resilience and pervasiveness of these various aspects of the pre-colonial educational traditions when we examine in later chapters the contemporary language and ritual of Indian primary classrooms. That their influence was pedagogical rather than structural or systemic is not really surprising, given the sub-continent's dispersed and variegated political structure before the colonial period, and the way the colonizers combined administrative integration with divide-and-rule policy. However, there may well be a more general systemic legacy that penetrates the administrative *process* if not its structure. Thus, it has been suggested that the bureaucratic elaboration which characterizes Indian government and many Indian institutions owes at least as much to Hinduism as to the British civil service mindset, and indeed it was something the British were able to exploit.[31] In any event, apart from possible parallels between Vedic texts and official documents and procedures (of which one should probably be careful not to make too much), the more obvious legacies are those of caste and gender, to which few organizations – and certainly few public organizations such as schools and education authorities – are immune.[32]

It is therefore also important to stress that such liberation as indigenous education offered was countered by restricted access. Nayar cites sources suggesting that during the second millennium BC the Aryans provided eight years of education for both boys and girls, to take place mainly within the family.[33] Stein confirms this, noting that in the pre-Vedic period women had higher status than at any time subsequently, daughters as well as sons were educated and women had more equality in day-to-day affairs, and greater rights in marriage and inheritance.[34] However, during the Brahmanical period (from about 1500 BC) the caste system and the Brahmanic codes combined to deny education both to lower castes and to girls, and that the period from 500 AD to 1800 was one of progressive deterioration in the status of women in particular, as the Brahmanic social order came to define the social structure not just of Hindus but also of other religious groups, Buddhists, Muslims and Christians included.[35]

Turning to the second stage, then, let us consider the fate of the indigenous education system at the hands of the British.

It is one of this book's several pieces of international symmetry that at exactly the time when one of Thomas Arnold's sons was evaluating popular education in France, another was doing the same in India. Both complained of the absence of that indispensable tool of empire, geography (the British understood the importance of maps and overland communications at least as well as the Romans, in whose language and literature members of the colonial service were steeped); and both had much to say about the moral purposes of literacy. Kumar notes that William Arnold complained that children in Punjab learned to read for memorization and repetition rather than understanding and intellectual transformation,[36] which in the light of the preceding paragraphs is interesting because in Punjab the dominant religion was Islam rather than Hinduism, the language was Persian rather than Sanskrit and the texts in question were those of classical Persian lyric poets such as Sa'di and Hafiz. The cultural contrast between Sufi mysticism and Hindu concretism could hardly be greater.

By then, however, (1859) Macaulay had already decided that the British investment in Indian popular education would have to be a limited one. Made president of the Commission of Public Instruction in 1834, his Minute on Education famously announced a year later that

> It is impossible for us, with our limited means, to attempt to educate the body of the people. We must at present do our best to form a class who may be interpreters

between us and the millions we govern; a class of persons, Indian in blood and colour, but English in tastes, opinions, morals and intellect.[37]

Nor was this by any means the first British intervention in popular education in India. We have noted that the monitorial system, or *l'enseignement mutuel*, spread from England to France and other European countries during the period 1815 to 1830 or so. In fact, some would argue that it originated in India when army chaplain Andrew Bell, who during the 1790s was Superintendent of Egmore Vale Military Academy in Madras, had children learn their letters by tracing them in sand trays under the supervision of older or more able pupils. Bell's *Experiment in Education*, published in 1796, was explicitly acknowledged by Joseph Lancaster (who opened the Borough Road school two years later) in his 1802 *Improvements in Education*.

Mutual instruction is not incompatible with the authority ascribed then or now to Indian teachers, and in a primary school in Uttar Pradesh I myself observed children tracing numbers in the sand of their outdoor classroom, instructed by their teacher and helped by their fellows – a 1990s variant on a 1790s experiment. Whether or not this originated with Bell or predated him is unclear, although the bitter dispute of the early nineteenth century back in England, over whether Bell or Lancaster was the true originator of the monitorial method, seems to have ignored the probability that Bell had witnessed something of the kind in Madras and had merely modified it. Indeed an Indian account of rural education during the mid-nineteenth century portrays mutual instruction taking place some years after the Madras system although Kumar suggests that this, in essence, was how village schools in India had operated for generations.[38] In the face of the various claims and counter-claims over ownership of mutual instruction, it seems reasonable to suggest that it is an obvious enough pedagogical formula and could well have been used in many emerging education systems without the monitorial imprint.

To return to Macaulay. The standard, benignly utilitarian view – that Macaulay was chiefly interested in training the growing army of Indian clerks and administrators[39] – is contested by those who see his decision as reflecting the wider and more ruthless motives of empire. For a start, he presumed the inherent superiority of the English language over Sanskrit as the medium of instruction and of European culture and civilization over those of Hinduism and Islam, and cited the 'Westernizing efforts' of Peter the Great in Russia:

Within the last hundred and twenty years, a nation, which has previously been in a state as barbarous as that in which our ancestors were before the Crusades, has gradually emerged from the ignorance in which it was sunk, and has taken its place among civilized communities . . . The languages of western Europe civilised Russia. I cannot doubt that they will do for the Hindoo what they have done for the Tartar.[40]

and

I have never found one [orientalist] . . . who would deny that a single shelf of a good European library was worth the whole native literature of India and Arabia. The intrinsic superiority of the Western literature is, indeed, fully admitted by those . . . who support the Oriental plan of education.[41]

This, after all, was the same Macaulay who produced *Lays of Ancient Rome*, one of the most rousingly popular volumes of narrative poetry of its time. Nurturing Anglophilia, and especially the virtues of a classical education – rather than merely teaching the English language – was the natural project for someone with his essentially public school worldview, and no doubt generations of Indian children chanted 'Lars Porsena of Clusium/By the Nine Gods he swore' with the same mixed sense of bafflement and pleasure as their British contemporaries (for *Horatius* was, if nothing else, at least eminently chantable).

Scrase goes further: the task for the colonial rulers, he argues, was to use education to consolidate power, and an important element in their strategy was to domesticate indigenous cultural elites such as, in Bengal and particularly Calcutta, the *bhadralok* ('higher people'), exploiting their caste-based interest in learning and their aversion to manual labour. Thus, the new education was suffused by *bhadralok* as well as British values, and it both manifested and strengthened the culture of the Anglophile Indian bourgeoisie, and especially the Anglo-Indians, on which British power depended.[42] The same pattern was repeated in the other towns – Madras and Bombay – in which the British were most securely established. After 1858, the Indian English-educated middle classes could enter the Indian Civil Service (ICS).

This imperialist patronage, however, had mixed outcomes: it secured the empire and buttressed India's burgeoning bureaucracy; but it also provided the seedbed for the development of the nationalist movement, the Congress Party, the drive to Independence, and the still-continuing 'bourgeois revolution' which Stern, following Barrington Moore, sees as the dominant pattern of change in Indian society.[43]

Kumar is particularly scathing about the view – 'theoretical feeble and historically untenable' he deems it – that producing clerks was the chief purpose of colonial education, still less its main outcome. He points not only to the way education served the colonial imperatives of subjugation and stability but also to its diverse and contradictory consequences: socialization into colonial values on the one hand, socialization into rejection of those values on the other. Shotton is no less critical of the received wisdom, and notes that 'education in India under British rule produced dissenters and ranters, great political thinkers and writers, highly successful businessmen and intellectual giants, not only office lackeys'.[44]

Of course, we are talking here of forms of education available to an already privileged minority, forms which had their purest expression in private schools and universities expressly modelled on their English counterparts. *Primary* education in India, as in Britain, had a much less exalted pedigree. Kumar sees the two forms as different sides of the same coin. Both were rooted in a concept of order in which the counterpart of dominance was acquiescent subordination, or that very English condition of 'knowing one's station'. The good life enjoyed by the minority was preserved by forms of education for the majority and which secured obedience, conformity and respect for property. The main function of literacy was – in this restricted but very British sense of the word – moral.[45]

The problem, however, was – as Macaulay had noted – that resources for mass education would not stretch beyond the immediate needs of the colonial state apparatus. For much of the colonial period, then, primary education was thin and patchy, and such government provision as was available was supplemented – and often qualitatively outpaced – by indigenous schooling and by the efforts of the Christian missionaries, especially in the south.

The missionary schools were particularly significant for girls, since although the British might deplore the social and religious equilibrium they were reluctant to disturb it. Their attempt to suppress *sati* in 1828 was an extreme case, met stiff opposition, and was only partly successful (even today cases are reported in Indian newspapers). Where the education of girls was concerned, such efforts as were made could gain little headway against 'social impediments such as purdah, child marriage, parental indifference to daughter's education, distrust of the Western system and fear of conversion'.[46] From the 1850s onwards a sequence of commissions, policies and resolutions – the Hunter Commission of 1882, the Government of India Education Resolutions of 1904 and 1919, and the Hartog Committee of 1929 – deplored the male–female disparity in school enrolment and provision, although Usha Nayar suggests that the issue only really took hold once women became involved in the Independence movement and once that movement itself annexed the education of girls as a campaign issue.[47]

Alongside these three versions of basic education – indigenous, colonialist and missionary – the teaching of arts such as music and dance maintained its distinctive continuity. Today, set against mainstream government school teaching, it provides the most dramatic pedagogical contrast imaginable, and as clear an illustration as one can hope to find of my general thesis that national systems of education, however radical the efforts of reformers, display not just a mixture of change and continuity, but also considerable longevity at their deeper levels of values. Traditional teaching of music and dance uses a very different pedagogical model – apprenticeship, imitation and disciplined practice – from the dominant school models of rote and recitation.

A system of education is only as effective as its teachers; a colonial system of education maintains the trajectory of the colonizers only if its teachers themselves are tightly controlled. Whereas the indigenous systems accorded teachers both status and autonomy, the colonial (and post-colonial) systems gave them neither. Primary teachers were badly paid. The pay differential underscored the extreme inequality of the power relationship: after the Indian Education Service was established in 1896, a primary inspector might earn one hundred times as much as a primary teacher. Equally important, the right of the former to tyrannize the latter was unquestioned.

In an attempt to raise the standing and quality of primary teaching, if not its financial rewards, the British exported to India both the pupil–teacher system and normal schools. Kay-Shuttleworth, the originator of both schemes, had opened Battersea Training College on the model of the French *école normale* and German *Normalschule* in 1840, and in 1846 introduced the pupil–teacher system to provide the normal colleges with a ready flow of suitably qualified trainees, and to hasten the phasing out of the monitorial system.[48] In India, implementation was slow: by 1870, only 4,346 students were enrolled, most of them male. The training was, and remained for over a century, very basic. Entry qualifications were low, the training instrumental and mechanical in the extreme. Its core was a Herbartian model of 'the lesson' that was applied strictly to the planning and delivery of all aspects of the prescribed syllabus. Herbart's influence on primary school pedagogy, in other countries as well as India, is considered in a later chapter.

With Independence, from 1947, came the third stage in the development of India's system of primary education. The colonial system was relatively small, and varied in quality and reach from one region to another. The number of indigenous schools had declined in proportion to the expansion of Department and Grant-in-Aid schools.[49] Overall, 'only 14 per cent of the population was literate and only one child out of three had been enrolled in primary school. The low levels of enrolment and literacy were compounded by acute regional and gender disparities'.[50] The system, such as it was, was bureaucratized and hierarchical. Teachers compensated for their lowly status and restricted professionality by asserting the Brahmanical residues of absolute authority and unquestioned textbook knowledge. In other respects – large classes instead of small, prescribed rather than autonomous pedagogy, a curriculum detached from rather than grounded in children's everyday realities – the model was that not of rural India but of urban, industrial Victorian England.

The independence movement was strongly committed to the universalization of basic education.[51] Within the movement, however, there were differing views over what 'basic' should encompass. Tagore wished to counter the exclusiveness and inequity of colonial education with a model that achieved universality through intellectual autonomy and that pursuit of truth for truth's sake that he admired in the Enlightenment and Western science. This was to be allied to a version of child-centredness which owed much to those same individuals who shaped the English progressive vision – Rousseau, Pestalozzi, Froebel, Dewey, Montessori and, more specifically in relation to the *ashram* which he established, the Elmhirsts of Dartington. The core values were childhood autonomy and community.

In contrast, Gandhi rejected Western education in even its more benign forms as the engine in the machine which had made India what under the British it had become: exploited, violent, impoverished, and above all divided by wealth, class and caste. He espoused a vision which centred on community and a craft knowledge which dignified the manual and creative skills of lower castes and thereby gave them a better chance to succeed against the odds set by a system which historically favoured upper-caste values, knowledge and occupations. His inspirations outside India were Ruskin and Tolstoy (after whom he had named one of his South African communities and with whose school at Yasnaya Polyana he was familiar). Gandhi also wanted to liberate teachers and pupils from the tyranny – as he saw it – of the textbook and return to a more autonomous, oral, *guru* ideal of teaching.

Countering both these versions of an alternative to colonial style public education was the more pragmatic line taken by Nehru. Western-educated, like so many in the independence movement, he espoused a modernizing programme which enabled

India to engage on equal terms with the West rather than turn its back on it, and which recognized that industrialization was unstoppable.

All these currents – indigenous, colonial, anti-colonial, idealistic, pragmatic – helped shape the post-1947 system as it was described in Chapter 3. Article 45 of the Constitution committed the state (that is, the Government of India, the state governments and the regional and local administrative authorities acting together) 'to provide, within a period of ten years . . . for free and compulsory education for all children until they complete the age of fourteen years'. Article 29(1) protected minority languages, Articles 29(2) and 30(1) protected individuals from discrimination on the grounds of religion, race, caste and language; Article 46 obliged providers to devote special attention to the needs and rights of Scheduled Castes and Scheduled Tribes. Other articles framed those dealing with education with more general commitments in respect of equality of opportunity, gender discrimination and child labour. The Constitution's 42nd Amendment (1976) invoked the principle of 'concurrency', or legislative and administrative partnership in respect of education between the national and state governments, and this was glossed in the 1986 National Policy on Education so as to specify more clearly the role of the Union (national) government in shaping the 'national' character of education, defining national manpower needs, and securing through monitoring and policy initiatives such consistency in provision as these were deemed to require.[52]

Since 1947, a sequence of five-year plans has re-stated the commitment to universal elementary education (UEE), defined most recently as 'access to elementary education for all children up to 14 years of age; universal participation till they complete the elementary stage through formal or non-formal education programmes; universal achievement at least of minimum levels of learning'.[53] However, by 1999, notwithstanding the massive advance from the baseline left by the British, universalization remained a long way off and the statistics on enrolment, retention and literacy showed the extent of the ground still to be covered, especially in rural areas, in the urban slums, for girls, and among children from scheduled castes and tribes.[54]

Control, Reform and Universal Elementary Education

Before considering some of the reform efforts in greater detail, let us return to the question of the balance of power and control in national education systems, for it bears particularly on a system, such as that in India, which is both vast and confronted by a daunting reform agenda.

We saw how 'concurrency' is manifested in a division of labour between the Ministry for Human Resource Development in Delhi and the 25 State Government Education Departments, together with the seven centrally administered union territories. Central government determines policy and also supports specific initiatives, state governments bear most of the expenditure, and the system's day-to-day administration is in the hands of the district education offices. The 1986 National Policy on Education aimed to refocus the work of the Central Advisory Board on Education (which predated independence), to give greater impetus to the training of planners and administrators, and to enhancing the roles of school heads, and to encourage community involvement. In the case of primary schools, the government's advocacy of decentralization consolidated district-level powers in respect of pre-service and in-service teacher training as well as school staffing and provision. Decentralization generally – not just in education – was given a firm nudge by the 1992 Panchayati Raj Act, which gave significant powers to the *panchayat* or village council, and required states to constitute these in such a way so as to counter the tradition of excluding women, lower castes and minorities. Panchayats have to set up village education committees (VECs) to oversee the work of the primary school and, through micro-level planning and house-to-house surveys do their utmost to increase pupil enrolment and retention and parental participation. The implementation of the decentralization policy, however, and the effectiveness of local participation, is – to say the least – extremely uneven.

Where, then, does power really lie? The OECD decision-matrix analysis is unambiguous: in 1998, decisions on 'organization of instruction', 'personnel management', 'planning and structures' and 'resources' were overwhelmingly concentrated at 'provincial/regional' (i.e. district) level. Schools had relatively little say even in the 'organization of instruction', the one area most commonly devolved to that level in other countries.[55] This analysis is consistent with one undertaken some twenty years previously, for UNESCO.[56]

On the other hand, the OECD analysis seriously understates the very real influence of the national government and its agencies, especially on the curriculum and textbooks. These are effectively controlled by a pyramid of institutions with a research, training and advisory brief, headed by the National Council of Educational Research and Training in Delhi, which works closely with the Ministry on the one hand and with the various State Councils of Educational Research and Training (SCERTs) on the other hand. At the base of the pyramid are the District Institutes of Education and Training (DIETs) which were established under the 1986 National Policy on Education and which took over the mantle of the old normal colleges. In 1988, NCERT produced a National Curricular Framework, then revised all subject syllabuses and textbooks, and by 1990 had published a detailed set of 'Minimum Levels of Learning' – in effect terminal objectives – for each subject at the primary stage.[57] These activities are supported by extensive in-service programmes at both state and national levels in which NCERT's influence is often very strong.

Although this scenario manifests something of a centre–periphery tension (not forgetting that there are state 'centres' as well as a national one) what is not in doubt is the sense that primary school teachers – and especially, in comparison with many other countries, primary school heads – lack autonomy in all but the most basic matters. This was confirmed in the *Five Cultures* project interviews. One senior Ministry official talked frankly about the way the general shift to decentralization had further empowered districts and was strengthening community involvement but had left heads and teachers as underpowered as ever. Another senior national interviewee saw heads as 'weak and uninfluential' and provided a scenario – essentially a rural composite – of teachers subject to considerable local pressure and interference and the tyranny of wayward and doctrinaire district inspectors, some of whom were not averse to bribery. In this context, he argued, teachers do not necessarily welcome the decentralization that elsewhere is heralded as a panacea, because it increases rather than diminishes the extent to which they are vulnerable to such pressures. Indeed, PROBE reports that teachers have actively lobbied for greater central intervention to reduce their vulnerabilty and guarantee a greater degree of consistency.[58]

Other interviewees spoke of an acute problem of teacher motivation linked to exceptionally low status and the way they were viewed as little more than low-grade technicians. With poor motivation came poor performance, unreliable attendance and a host of other manifestations of a low level of professionalism that caused opinion to diverge on whether teachers in the Indian primary system were the problem or the symptom. For his part, Kumar is in little doubt: teacher autonomy and status, high before colonization, were drastically weakened by the British through a combination of centralization, bureaucratization, low pay, rudimentary training and the tyranny of textbooks. Under colonial rule, primary teachers became 'meek dictators', preserving their traditional classroom authority but in respect of a vastly reduced remit. This state of affairs remained largely untouched by Independence, by the policy of universalizing elementary education, and by 1990s measures to secure decentralization.[59]

The 1999 PROBE report on basic education in India, based on a detailed study undertaken in 1996 in the five states that contain between them 40 per cent of India's population (Bihar, Himachal Pradesh, Madhya Pradesh, Rajasthan and Uttar Pradesh), confirms and fills out this picture. The report catalogues problems which frustrate the working of concurrency: inadequate resources; overstretched administration; mechanisms for teacher appointment and transfer which are riddled by incompetence, patronage and corruption; infrequent, unfocused inspection in which teachers get little feedback and the inspector's task is restricted to checking compliance against a tick-list. Particularly serious for educational planning, staffing and resourcing is the fact – recorded by PROBE but also confirmed in the *Five Cultures* interviews – that in many schools not subject to external or peer checks (small rural schools, typically) teachers may inflate enrolment and attendance figures.[60]

The PROBE report is generally rather critical of disparities between the Government of India's optimistic presentation of its major reform and intervention initiatives such as Operation Blackboard – which was launched in 1986 and aimed to provide a minimum level of accommodation, staffing and equipment for every primary school – and the situation on the ground. However, Indian material on educational reform seems relatively free from the grosser layers of spin and doublethink which became the hallmark of the British government as part of the 1980s and the 1990s centralization drive. In India, the problem is less one of mendacious government rhetoric than of the way the system's vast scale, combined with the sheer remoteness of many schools, and managerial deficiencies at the operational levels of district and below, present immense challenges to the process of policy implementation and, incidentally, also make it hard to judge the reliability of those statistics on which the targeting and efficacy of policy interventions depend.

It is in this light that we should mention the Government of India's District Primary Education Programme (DPEP), launched in 1994 with support from the World Bank, the European Community, UNICEF, and the UK and Netherlands governments, and at the time of writing the world's largest education project. DPEP aimed to universalize access, increase enrolment, maintain attendance and raise achievement in primary education; to give particular attention to equalizing opportunity and provision for historically disadvantaged groups – girls, the disabled, and children from scheduled castes and scheduled tribes; to maximize community involvement in primary education, especially at village level; to provide and upgrade school buildings; to raise levels of school resourcing and equipment; to support teachers and schools with training, networking and resource centres; to strengthen and build capacity for planning, management and evaluation at every level; and to improve the quality of teaching itself.[61]

The models of pedagogy and pedagogical renewal enshrined in DPEP are not without their problems. However, there is little doubt that DPEP is having a considerable and often dramatic impact in those states, districts, blocks and villages where it is working well (the intensity and frequency of the monitoring undertaken by both the Government of India and the multilateral and bilateral agencies means that in this instance exaggeration can fairly readily be exposed[62]). At the time of writing, however, DPEP is confined to a minority of India's districts, and it is finite. Long-term sustainability of progress achieved within DPEP states and districts once the programme is finished, and DPEP's capacity to influence thinking and practice in non-DPEP states and districts, will be its sternest tests.

The basis for reform initiatives such as DPEP is not unchallenged. The PROBE study argues that access, provision, enrolment and retention are massively uneven between states and districts (in fact this is clearly understood by the government and guides the targeting of DPEP resources); that there is a widespread problem of state inertia and official apathy which consistently frustrates national policies and initiatives; and that overall progress towards universalization is unacceptably slow, and certainly by comparison with a country such as China, whose problems of poverty and illiteracy were in the 1940s similar to India's but which is now not far off 100 per cent literacy in the younger age groups.[63]

This is uncomfortable enough. However, the PROBE study goes further and exposes what it regards as the more persistent 'myths' of Indian elementary education: that parents are not interested in securing a good education for their children (some, say PROBE, are not, but most are); that non-attendance is caused by child labour (child labour is indeed a blight, argue PROBE, but it provides only a partial explanation for the high levels of non-attendance);[64] that elementary education is free (legally it is, admit PROBE, but the added costs of books, slates and so on can be a major burden for poor families with several children); and that schools are available and the problem is enrolment (PROBE insists that lack of even basic provision in many areas remains a serious problem). To counter these 'myths', PROBE provides an analysis which suggests that schooling, rather than parenting, is the crux of the matter (this recalls a comparable shift in consciousness in the United States and the UK during the 1960s and the 1970s), and that for many parents and children the combination of expense, large classes, unmotivated and absent teachers, an overburdened and meaningless curriculum and an oppressive pedagogy are deeply alienating and account for many of the difficulties of enrolment and retention.[65]

Interestingly, in our interviews, members of the education service itself at district and school levels were more ready to blame parents than were senior national officials and researchers. One district director of education made much of family breakdown, another of alcoholism (a condition mentioned by several teacher interviewees), and none commented on the part the school itself might play, except in respect of resource levels, and they were someone else's responsibility. It could be argued that district officials and teachers knew the situation on the ground rather better than those in air-conditioned offices in Delhi, or that each party was simply succumbing to that most basic instinct – to deflect blame from self to others.

Clearly, the scenario is hugely complex, for every pathology of Indian primary education can be countered by another, and the danger of correctives is that they can understate other problems. Thus, Nayar and her colleagues in the Department of Women's Studies at NCERT have documented in detail since the department's inception in 1979 the historic and persistent disadvantaging of the girl child in India, at home, in the community, in education, in the arena of legal and civil rights, and in employment. The scale and severity of the problem is undeniable; its longevity – the 3,500 years from the later Vedic period onwards – is daunting. On the other hand, they reckoned the 1980s to be the turning point in the fight against discrimination, the period when bland egalitarian rhetoric gave way to policies of positive and precisely targeted intervention.[66]

Nautiyal disputes the claim that the crisis of primary education in India is essentially a rural one, and has revealed the massive scale of the problems of enrolment, retention, literacy and provision in the urban slums of Delhi and other major cities, showing that in the slums, as in many rural areas, the problem is the school as much as the home.[67] For him, this section of the population, unlike those that now feature in policies and intervention strategies, remains largely ignored.

Ambasht tellingly extended for us the vocabulary of pupil recruitment and retention, arguing that the phrase 'drop-out' tacitly attributes blame for non-attendance to the child, whereas in fact children may be withdrawn by parents to work or look after siblings ('pull out'), alienated by their experience of schooling ('push out'), or prevented from attending by, for example, parental membership of a migratory labour force, as in the construction industry ('stay out'). Like the PROBE team he wished to shift the emphasis from a parental deficit model to one which attends to the quality of schooling. He identified six factors which between them persuade many families, especially in remote areas, that primary schooling is not for them, or make it difficult for many children to succeed at school: timing (the school year is not in harmony with the seasonal work cycle); location (too many schools are further than the required 1.5 kilometres, and even those that are close may be sited in – for lower caste children – socially hostile zones; teachers (barriers of education, caste and geography); language (disparity between the home language and the regional standard language); curriculum (perceived as irrelevant and culturally biased); textbooks (likewise). To these, another NCERT interviewee added factors specific to teachers: low status, poor motivation, low commitment, widespread absenteeism (which in a one-teacher rural school means no school), inadequate grasp of the content to be taught, lack of professional induction, lack of opportunities for in-service development and training, and large classes.

Clearly, for all that the established patterns of gender, caste and class militate against the values of universal and egalitarian basic education, there is a growing consensus that as currently constituted the provision of such education simply fails to speak to the condition of a substantial proportion of India's population. The language of textbooks, and the realities they purvey, are one symptom; the priorities and messages of the curriculum are another; the legacies of pre-colonial village teaching, the colonialist import of minimalist elementary schooling, and the enfranchising idealism of Independence, each of which we explored above, provide superimposed and conflicting frames of reference for these and other problems. Thus the divergence of values is in its way as pressing a matter as the quality of provision. Although improving provision is immensely costly, it is at least theoretically amenable to a resource-led solution – buildings, equipment, training, teaching materials – and to related infrastructural improvements in planning, administration and evaluation. However, the values question – in any country, but above all in a country with India's history, India's diversity, and India's depth of historical divisions of region, race, religion, caste and gender – is much more intractable. The case of India reinforces this book's central argument that the interaction of culture and pedagogy is not just critical to an understanding of public education, but is also one of the keys to its success.

By way of oblique commentary on this catalogue of alternative diagnoses and solutions we might note the judgement of M. C. Chagla, one of the country's most respected post-Independence education ministers:

> We know the problems; we know the answers, or at any rate most of them. In many cases we also know how to implement. What is lacking is the moral courage to start implementation.[68]

That seems a harsh judgement, and one which the architects of the 1990s reform initiatives, especially the District Primary Education Programme, would surely contest. Implementation has started: the problem, increasingly, is the *sustainability* of reform and its ability to reach to the furthest corners of this immense and complex country. As if to counter any suggestion that it lacks the will, the Government of India is about to launch a no less ambitious initiative to build on DPEP through *Sarva Shiksa Abhiyan* and achieve at last the promised universalization of elementary education.

5

Primary Education in the United States of America

Context, Structure and Control

The United States covers 9,363,520 square kilometres and has 280 million inhabitants, giving it a low population density relative to all the other countries in our study except Russia. Like Russia and India, but for different reasons, its population is immensely diverse. Relatively few are descended from the native inhabitants who preceded settlement from Europe and the enforced immigration from Africa from the sixteenth century onwards. By 2000, the citizens of the United States came from a greater diversity of races and nationalities than most other countries, yielding a broad ethnic breakdown of 83.4 per cent white, 12.4 per cent black, 3.3 per cent Asian and Pacific and 0.8 per cent native American. The school population in 1994 was 64.5 per cent white non-Hispanic, 13.86 per cent Hispanic, 16.32 per cent black, 3.64 per cent Asian/Pacific and 1.05 per cent native American/Alaskan.[1] The national figure conceals wide variation in regional distribution. Thus, by way of example, in California 50 per cent of school students are of Hispanic background.

The United States is the world's consistently strongest economy and the richest of the five countries considered in this study, in 1998 generating US$29,340 per capita GNP,[2] of which 5.5 per cent went to education, although it spent less per capita on primary education than, for example, Switzerland, Denmark, Canada and Austria.[3] However, in educational spending as in other matters there is also considerable variation across the 50 states, for this is a highly decentralized country and under Amendment 10 of the United States Constitution 'the powers not delegated to the United States by the Constitution, nor prohibited by it to the States, are reserved to the States . . .' Education is among the powers so reserved. As a result, we find – for example – that in 1998 the state of Utah spent US$3,632 per elementary/secondary pupil while New Jersey spent US$10,140, nearly three times as much.[4] The federal government does devise national education policies and does invest in education, and both policy and resourcing impact on the individual states. Yet state laws and district decisions have a far greater impact on the day-to-day work of schools than pronouncements from Washington and for this reason most of this book's

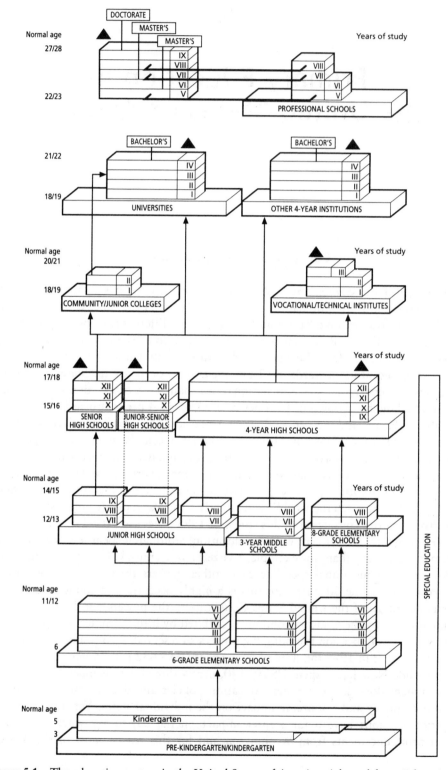

Figure 5.1   The education system in the United States of America. Adapted from *Education at a Glance: OECD Indicators 1996.* Copyright OECD, 1996.

discussion of the day-to-day detail of primary education in the United States will concentrate on just one state – the 'Wolverine' or 'Great Lake' state of Michigan, which has a population of 9,817,242 and at 147,136 square kilometres is slightly larger than England.

Despite decentralization and the consequent diversity of values, resourcing and provision, there is a fair measure of overall consistency in the education system's structure, which is set out in Figure 5.1. Education is organized on three levels: elementary (including pre-school and primary), secondary and post-secondary. It is free and compulsory from elementary to the end of secondary, although the period of compulsory attendance varies between 9 and 13 years (in Michigan it is from age 6 to age 16). The terms 'elementary' and 'primary' can signal different age ranges as one moves from one school district to another. Nationally, elementary generally includes kindergarten, primary and lower secondary – ages 5–13, or kindergarten to grade 8 (K-8) – with primary schools typically including the age range 5/6–11, or grades K-6. In the three Michigan school districts featured in this study the primary stage was K-5 in two and K-6 in the third.

Decentralization, as we have noted, is the striking feature of the American education system. This is the nation of over 83,000 governments: one federal, 50 state, 83,000 local, including some 15,000 school districts to co-ordinate the work of 110,000 schools, of which about 60,000 are elementary.[5] Despite growing levels of federal investment and increased state intervention, and larger claims that federalism is dying or is being replaced by shared sovereignty,[6] the school districts, and the schools themselves, remain powerful brokers of the character and quality of public schooling.[7] This power is fiscal as well as constitutional. The principal funding source for most schools is state and local taxes, and in our three school districts federal funding counted for under 1 per cent of school district income.[8] In school districts in receipt of special support, for example where there is a large proportion of children on Title 1 programmes aimed at breaking the link between family poverty and low school achievement, the federal share may be rather larger. Nationally, the federal share in 1993–4 was 7 per cent. However, although Title 1 is the largest source of federal support it remains a small proportion of the whole by comparison with more centralized systems.

When one combines the funding balance with the relatively small size of many individual school districts and the fact that many key positions in the education service are filled by public election rather than behind-the-scenes appointment, it is clear why local accountability is such a prominent feature – and such a powerful lever – in the US school system.

The federal government does frame laws which bite at local level, notably in recent years on issues such as special education (Federal Law 94–142), but generally its legislative programme in education enables and empowers rather than requires, and it has to achieve its goals by persuasion and lobbying rather than by coercion, by funding special programmes which states can buy into (thereby accepting certain conditions). State departments of education are usually headed by a chief state school officer who distributes the state funds which account for about 50 per cent of school funding and interprets and implements the wide range of state laws and requirements on matters such as attendance, certification, transportation, curriculum and assessment. District school boards and district superintendents of schools prepare schooling budgets, determine curriculum within state guidelines, hire teachers and other personnel, provide and maintain buildings, and purchase school equipment and supplies. Two of the school districts dealt with here, one of which was the second largest in Michigan, had 33 elementary schools, while the third had just six. These figures contrast with the 200–400 primary schools in a typical local education authority (LEA), the UK equivalent to the US school district. Only the largest city school districts in the United States have such large numbers of schools.

The elementary schools themselves vary in size from large urban to small rural, with the national average in 1994–5 at 471 pupils. In the same year the average pupil–teacher ratio was 19:1 (20:1 in Michigan). Schools are generously staffed by international standards, with a variety of subject specialists, nurses, librarians, psychologists, social workers and counsellors working alongside the teachers. Yet, as always, there is considerable national variation and levels of staffing and resourcing in many urban schools are much lower. The teaching mode at the elementary stage, as in our other four countries, is generalist, and pupils are grouped sometimes by year group and sometimes on a multi-age basis, although nearly always the classes are mixed ability.

Goals, Curriculum and Assessment

It follows from all this that educational goals promulgated at federal level have limited force or at least that the route from national goal to classroom action is even more complex and uncertain than in centralized systems. However, goals at this level do exist, most notably as the six National Education Goals for the year 2000 set out by the Bush administration following the 1983 report *A Nation at Risk* that called for reform in order to raise educational standards.[9] The six 1991 goals (or, more properly, targets) were subsequently extended by the Clinton administration and passed into law as the 1994 Educate America Act:

- By the year 2000, all children in America will start school ready to learn.
- By the year 2000, the high school graduation rate will increase to at least 90 per cent.
- By the year 2000, all students will leave grades 4, 8 and 12 having demonstrated competency over challenging subject matter including English, mathematics, science, foreign languages, civics and government, economics, arts, history and geography, and every school in America will ensure that all students use their minds well, so that they may be prepared for responsible citizenship, further learning, and productive employment in our Nation's modern economy.
- By the year 2000, the Nation's teaching force will have access to programs for the continued improvement of their professional skills and the opportunity to acquire the knowledge and skills needed to instruct and prepare all American students for the next century.

- By the year 2000, United States students will be first in the world in mathematics and science achievement.
- By the year 2000, every adult American will be literate and will possess the knowledge and skills necessary to compete in a global economy and exercise the rights and responsibilities of citizenship.
- By the year 2000, every school in the United States will be free of drugs, violence, and the unauthorized presence of firearms and alcohol and will offer a disciplined environment conducive to learning.
- By the year 2000, every school will promote partnerships that will increase parental involvement and participation in promoting the social, emotional and academic growth of children.[10]

These goals, the other four laws in the Clinton education package, the associated initiatives on national educational standards, including benchmarking, and the increased level of federal funding for earmarked initiatives, represented America's most comprehensive attempt at systemic educational reform to that date. States were invited to sign up to the reforms, and most did. Federal funding was made available to support state initiatives and in years 2–5 of the programme most of this was passed to individual districts and schools. In Michigan a major programme of curriculum reform, specifying 'core curriculum content standards' for all subjects, culminated in a restatement of the National Education Goals[11] and the state monitored progress towards their achievement.[12] Other states took similar decisions.[13] However, alongside these were broader statements that tended to emphasize self-fulfilment and citizenship as much as academic achievement. Thus, Michigan's *Vision Statement for K-12 education* committed the state system to producing

- literate individuals
- healthy and fit people
- responsible family members
- productive workers
- involved citizens
- self-directed lifelong learners.[14]

At district level the message was similarly varied. One of our three districts committed itself to the education of individuals who

- are competent communicators, skilful problem solvers, and critical thinkers
- are civic-minded and prepared to make ethical decisions
- have a career motivation, a knowledge of our global and technological society, an appreciation for the arts and humanities, and a desire for lifelong learning

while individual schools added a further, and not necessarily identical or even compatible, value-orientation.

As with goals, so with the curriculum: there is no national curriculum and the operative legislative level is the state. However, reviews show that across the United

States, as across England before the introduction of the 1988 national curriculum there is a reasonable consistency in the range of subjects covered and the amount of time allocated.[15] Thus in July 1995 the Michigan State Board of Education adopted 'model content standards for curriculum' and related benchmarks, but stressed that these 'are not a state curriculum, but are specifically designed to be used by local districts as they develop their curricula'. They comprised:

- language arts: reading, writing, speaking, listening, viewing
- mathematics
- science
- social studies: history, geography, civics, economics, inquiry, public discourse and decision making, citizenship
- arts education: dance, music, theatre, visual arts
- technology
- career and employability skills.[16]

Although in Michigan it was left to individual districts and schools to maintain curriculum breadth, other states actually required this. By and large state core curricula introduced during the 1990s rarely contained less than language, mathematics, science and social studies (the latter always strongly civic in its goals and content) and by and large it was the arts which tended to be most vulnerable.[17]

The allocation of time across the curriculum is left to districts and schools, although states set minimum numbers of school days to be eligible for full state funding. The school year generally runs from September to June, with holidays at Christmas, Easter and in July–August. Schools usually open from Monday to Friday for a teaching day running from 8.30 to 3.30 with breaks for recess and lunch. Elementary school lessons vary considerably in length.[18]

Most states combined their introduction of core curriculum requirements with the specification of standards to be achieved by given transition or exit points. Thus, the Michigan content standards and benchmarks translate these into expected learning outcomes for early elementary, later elementary, middle and high (roughly equivalent to the ends of the four Key Stages in England). Nationally, standardized testing – for many decades a substantial industry in the United States – expanded dramatically from the 1960s and was endorsed as a critical element in the achievement of *Goals 2000*. However, apart from programmes such as the National Assessment of Educational Progress (NAEP), which has sample tested 9, 13 and 17 year olds since the 1960s for the purposes of national monitoring and international comparison (and in which state participation was voluntary), most formal assessment to date has been administered at state and district levels. By the late 1990s national assessments were being strengthened, with particular attention being given to reading and writing.

At the same time, states were developing tests to measure progress towards the state-level common standards in the core subjects, in accordance with *Goals 2000*. In Michigan, the Michigan Education Assessment Programme (MEAP) tests children at Grade 4 in reading and mathematics and Grade 5 in science. Results are published for districts and schools, and these are set alongside the results of other test programmes that districts opt into. In our three districts these included the Iowa Test of Basic Skills (for early grades), the Stanford Achievement Test in language and mathematics, and the Scholastic Aptitude Test (the latter two, confusingly, both acronymed SAT and causing added problems for English readers familiar with a rather different version of SAT).[19]

The two levers in the drive to raise standards, then, are the specification of content and standards, and testing to establish whether those standards have been achieved. In the United States, the means by which schools strive, with varying degrees of success, to achieve the standards – that is to say, school and classroom processes – may also be subject to scrutiny, but rarely if ever of a kind which is as comprehensive, public or punitive as that administered in England by OFSTED. There is much emphasis on peer accountability, and the UK government's arbitrary denial of 'right of reply' to OFSTED inspectors' judgements would not, I imagine, go down well in the United States.

Origins and Development

Until very recently the US and English education systems tended to be bracketed together as paradigms of educational decentralization, relative mavericks on a world stage where the norm for state educational systems was and is state control. Indeed, notwithstanding the great power clawback initiated by Margaret Thatcher in 1987–8, that is how OECD was still managing to present the English system in 1998.[20] Decentralization, it was generally believed, was what Anglo-Saxon polity was all about.

We shall see that in the United States the last two decades of the twentieth century marked increased levels of state and federal intervention in educational matters. Nevertheless, the American system remained firmly rooted in the local community while in England the national government seized control, tightened it, and tightened it still further. How could local decision-making and a high degree of professional autonomy survive in one country while in the other they crumbled almost overnight?

Margaret Archer argues that in decentralized systems

> . . . the profession rapidly becomes an active participant in the formation of education policy . . . the process of professionalization occurs early . . . independence enables the profession to make substantial internal innovations on the basis of its own experience, the teaching experience it faces, and the collective goals it faces.[21]

If indeed the process operates in this way, then professionalization should provide an effective counter to centralizing tendencies, but in England that did not happen either. What we need perhaps to do, therefore, is make less of the similarities and more of the differences, and of these the starkest and most dramatic is that America had a revolution that yielded a written constitution while England did not.

In one country, therefore, local control and a high degree of political accountability are inalienable; in the other they may be offered or denied on the whim of the government of the day. For the crux of the matter is that the two versions of democracy (about which we hear a great deal of self-satisfied rhetoric on both sides of the Atlantic) are very different. In the United States, democracy claims to be – and perhaps sometimes is – about the daily exercise of bottom-up power; in England it is about what happens on the one day every five years when the electorate is given its brief say in the matter of who should wield absolute power on its behalf for the next five years, and even then a first-past-the-post voting system effectively ensures that British governments gain their parliamentary majorities from a minority of the popular vote. For admittedly partisan commentators such as Jonathan Freedland, the American Revolution and constitution are where the real and perhaps unbridgeable differences between the two countries start, although – the cruellest irony for English democrats – the American democratic ideal grew from the English tradition of radical dissent.[22]

Appropriately and necessarily, therefore, we start our brief survey of the development of primary education in the United States with the colonial period. The original 13 colonies were closely tied to the English crown and had limited powers of self-government. On the other hand, and of considerable importance for the later development of public education, they were predominantly Protestant, and nonconformist at that. Although the Church of England was prominent in Virginia and the Carolinas, the colonies' religious complexion was fundamentally Puritan, with an increasingly varied admixture of Quakers, Presbyterians, Catholics and – with the arrival of settlers from continental Europe – Lutherans, Calvinists, Mennonites, Moravians and other sects. Most shared a belief that children should be taught reading and religion.

The forms that such schooling took varied according to the traditions of the church in question. Most were one-room establishments teaching the four Rs. Some were fee-paying; others were maintained by church or community. Most deployed a rudimentary pedagogy; some however, especially in Pennsylvania and Massachusetts, were influenced by the work of Francke and Comenius. Although institutionalized schooling was generally restricted to colonists' sons, the Moravians pioneered the education of girls, and Robert Young documents in some detail a correspondence on the education of Indians according to Comenian principles at Harvard (established in 1636) which involved the Governors of Massachusetts and Connecticut and Comenius himself.[23] Indeed, Comenius' *Orbis Pictus* provided the model for American elementary school primers well into the nineteenth century.[24]

The first legislation for elementary education was the Massachusetts Act of 1647 which required all settlements in that state with more than 50 families to establish an elementary school to keep the devil at bay: 'It is one chief project of the old deluder, Satan, to keep men from a knowledge of the Scriptures, as in former times by keeping them in an unknown tongue, so in these later times by persuading them from the use of tongues'. Not surprisingly, the teacher's main task was reading and writing.[25] However, under this and similar acts attendance was not compulsory, and provision was generally restricted to boys.

Good identifies three patterns of colonial school administration, reflecting the different forms of settlement. Something approaching a system of public schooling along recognizable lines and subject to legislation developed first in New England where settlements were compact, governance was well advanced, and the occupational structure demanded it. The Middle Colonies, with their mixed populations and faiths, developed church and parochial schools; and in the south, whose scattered populations were less favourable to the development of local schools, and where the divisions of class and race cut deepest, private education (and thus education only for the privileged minority) was the norm.[26]

It was this variety of form and function which provoked attention during the revolutionary period and the early decades after independence, although it has to be said that if there was a priority it was not elementary education but the desire to reverse the migration of young men to European (and especially British) universities where they might acquire 'a partiality for aristocracy or monarchy'[27] and a distaste for the as yet fragile values of republicanism. Education, then, had a direct role to play in the consolidation of the new United States, and, as Green comprehensively shows, state formation was the imperative, above all others, which extended and shaped the provision of public schooling during the post-revolutionary period.[28] The argument for this – rather than education for its own sake – as the principal motivation would tend to be supported by evidence that the colonies, especially New England, already had exceptionally high levels of literacy before the end of the eighteenth century.[29]

Thus Thomas Jefferson: 'Enlighten the people generally and tyranny and oppression of body and mind will vanish like evil spirits at the dawn of day'. Thus, too, Noah Webster: 'You have an empire to raise and support by your exertions and a national character to establish and extend by your wisdom and virtues. To effect these great objects it is necessary to frame a liberal plan of policy and build upon it a broad system of education'. And more directly and pithily, Benjamin Rush, for whom the task of education was to 'convert men into republican machines'.[30] The two strands are equally significant: the Enlightenment belief in the relation between freedom of mind and freedom of action, and the more focused concern that new political forms required political education, and that without instruction 'in the principles of liberty and government' the revolution would falter.

Of the various republican founding fathers, Webster is particularly interesting to us for his grasp of the importance of language in fostering national identity, although the sheer rhetorical power of the Declaration of Independence – 'We hold these truths to be self-evident: that all men are created equal; that they are endowed by their Creator with certain unalienable rights, that among these are life, liberty and the pursuit of happiness' – will have escaped none of them. Jefferson had encouraged 'judicious neology'; Benjamin Franklin proposed a *Scheme for a New Alphabet and a Reformed Mode of Spelling*; but Webster went further: 'Our honour requires us to have a system of our own, in language as well as government . . . a language of North America, as different from the future language of England, as the modern Dutch, Danish and Swedish are from the German, or one from another'. His *American Speller*, which introduced many of the rationalizations with which we are familiar today (theater, center, color, wagon, defense, etc.) sold over 80 million copies during his lifetime, and his *American Dictionary of the English Language* aimed to eradicate many of the eccentricities of English pronunciation, 'giving every letter in a syllable its due proportion of sound . . . and . . . making such a distinction, between syllables, of which words are composed, that the ear shall without difficulty acknowledge their number'.[31]

The parodox of the preoccupation with nation-building was the persistent fact of decentralization – an inevitable consequence of colonization, and an essential adjunct of the further settlement of the Midwest and West. Education was nationally important, but there was to be no national system of education, for, under the Constitution's Tenth Amendment 'The powers not delegated to the United States by the Constitution, nor prohibited by it to the States, are reserved to the States respectively, or to the people'. By 1791 only eight of the 14 states had written education into their state constitutions. Most required a school or schools to be established out of public funds in every county, with low fees and sometimes provision for poorer children to be taught free.

Moreover, as has frequently been pointed out, 'all men' in the Declaration of Independence meant some men but not others, and certainly no women, African Americans or Native Americans, and public education was no less discriminatory (Benjamin Rush argued, in vain, that women should be given equal access to education). The pattern for elementary education during the early republican period then, despite the fine words, was essentially an extension of colonial provision: community-centred in rural areas, organized by churches and charities in towns and cities. In the rural areas the district system – initially a one-teacher school controlled by a local board – was also the pattern most suited to the constant outward movement of frontiers and people; in the towns and cities charity schools provided the basis for the development of public schooling, as charities expanded their provision, opened schools to the poor, sought and gained public funding, and eventually became in effect the public system of basic education. The ubiquitous monitorial system, or rather the Lancasterian version of it, spread rapidly through the urban public schools from the early 1800s, and especially during 1818–38, when Lancaster himself lived in the United States.

As always, however, the South was different. Class and racial divisions kept schooling highly stratified and frustrated the development of public schooling on anything like the scale of the north-eastern states.

By the 1830s, the system, or more correctly, systems of American elementary education entered an era of expansion and reform. Pressure increased, especially in the north-east, for its extension to the working classes, and during the 1830s large numbers of schools were set up, often on the monitorial principle. The fact that they were mostly fee-paying generated further pressure for forms of basic education which were not only available but also free, and the debate centred on the principle of the common school as the most appropriate expression – and one of the surest guarantees – of the American democratic principle.

Under the Constitution the point of leverage for the extension of public education was the individual state. Massachusetts was the first to establish a state board of education, in 1837, and others followed, although many of them with some reluctance: the District of Columbia and Vermont in the 1860s, 14 states in the 1870s, ten in the 1880s, but many Southern states did not enact elementary school legislation until early in the twentieth century. Moreover, as noted earlier, most public provision excluded girls, Blacks and Native Americans. Nevertheless, the United States was decades ahead of England in establishing and implementing the principle of free and compulsory education. Like France, but unlike England, that education was also secular.

The common elementary schools then provided the foundation for common high schools, that distinctively American institution which reputedly influenced the pattern of secondary schooling in many other countries, including the Soviet Union. At the same time teacher training was established and extended along European *Normalschule/Ecole normale* lines, and through such institutions the ideas of Pestalozzi, Froebel, and especially Herbart, achieved considerable currency.

So far, in as far as this kind of retrospective tidying-up is admissible, we have identified three phases in the development of American primary education: colonial, early republican, and the period of expansion and consolidation. Together, allowing for the considerable time lag between the reforming zeal of the east and northeast and the conservatism and resistance of the South, these take us to the end of the nineteenth century. As the campaigns for public education intensified, so opinion divided more sharply between those who sought equality of access and provision through uniformity and therefore centralization, and those who resisted this as 'Prussianization' and a threat to local and religious distinctiveness.[32]

With a national system more or less established, the arguments increasingly turned from provision and control to goals and content. The next discernible phase was the first and more significant of two waves of progressivist reform which swept American schools during the twentieth century. It centred on the ideas of John Dewey – cuttingly described by Simone de Beauvoir as 'the only philosopher recognized in America', and criticized by her for preferring the narrowly practical to the speculative and metaphysical.[33]

Unlike English progressivism, which was mainly preoccupied with the individual, the American progressive movement of the late nineteenth and early twentieth century was concerned with social reconstruction. In this it was of a piece with, rather than (as in England) detached from wider debates about the good society. The pedigree – *pace* de Beauvoir – included, as well as Dewey, the emerging discipline of psychology as pioneered by William James, and the philosophical pragmatism of C. S. Pierce. In the context of the growth of a would-be science of teaching centred on Herbartianism (that is, a somewhat bowdlerized version of Herbart's ideas), James argued – against both the scientific claim and the historical legacy of rote learning – that the teacher's role should be a creative and intuitive one. This line was continued by Dewey who in *The School and Society* claimed that 'the ordinary schoolroom, with its rows of ugly desks placed in geometrical order . . . is all made "for listening"; it marks the dependency of one mind upon another'.[34] His alternative, 'democratic pedagogy', made knowledge relative, the child an active agent in his or her learning, and the school a workshop or laboratory. Antithesizing the strict stages of the Herbartian lesson plan, which systematized teachers' instruction, he focused instead on children's thinking as a process of problem solving. In *Democracy and Education*, Dewey pressed further his objection to the prevailing pedagogy of fact-cramming, and argued for a version which, in fostering reflection and scientific enquiry, was congruent with the way a democracy, too, should develop.

Dewey's opponents advanced objections which had, and have, considerable reson-ance in England: his views on teaching were labelled 'soft pedagogy'; his epistem-ological relativism was attacked as anti-standards and anti-teacher; his supposed rejection of moral absolutes was in 1929 savaged by the Pope, no less. However, the real problem – again as with progressive education in England – was not so much the founding ideas as what the teachers and others did with them. They were taken up in a big way in teachers' colleges, especially (through W. H. Kilpatrick) at Teachers' College, Columbia, and provided a new rationale for teacher training. They were celebrated in the work of the newly established Progressive Education Association (PEA). And, progressively (*sic*) adapted, debased, corrupted and bowd-lerized, they were used to justify a wide range of practices that bore little or no relation to Dewey's original pedagogic ideas. In any event, the movement was much wider than Dewey, encompassing also the curriculum reformism of Franklin Bobbitt and the child-centredness of Harold Rugg.

As in England, ideas that purported to liberate increasingly enslaved. They lost their intellectual clout yet were nevertheless enforced as professional orthodoxy through the mechanisms of teacher appointment and promotion. Dewey himself warned that 'an educational idea which professes to be based on the idea of free-dom may become as dogmatic as ever was the traditional education which was reacted against'[35] while his widow noted that Dewey's followers, in the end, 'could not see their idol for the incense they sent up'.[36]

The movement, however, penetrated deep into the system. Ravitch argues that 'by the 1940s, the ideals and tenets of progressive education had become the dominant American pedagogy . . . teachers in training learned of the epochal struggle between the old-fashioned, subject-centred, rigid, authoritarian, traditional school and the modern, child-centred, flexible, democratic, progressive school . . . progressivism had deteriorated into a cult whose principles were taught as dogma and whose critics were treated as dangerous heretics'; although she, too, identifies a gap between progressive rhetoric and classroom practice.[37]

The postwar decline of progressivism was rapid and politicized. In 1938, the Committee on Un-American Activities was set up to investigate subversion from both right and left. After the war it was hijacked by the McCarthy anti-communist witch-hunt. Progressive educationists were lumped together with liberals, pacifists, socialists and of course Communists as subversives.[38] The *coup de grâce*, however, was the launch of the Russian Sputnik in 1957, which most commentators agree dealt a devastating blow to America's first-nation complacency.

However, the issue was not simply science, mathematics and educational com-petitiveness. It is true that these sparked off a major curriculum reform movement in which subjects re-asserted themselves and curriculum planning was heavily sys-tematized along the lines presaged by Ralph Tyler, and taken to its logical extremes by Benjamin Bloom and his colleagues in the behavioural objectives movement.[39]

But US progressivism had outstayed its welcome for other reasons. If its wellspring was social reconstruction, its societal vision seems to have been far too unfocused and unspecific for postwar America, and especially for the growing crises of race, poverty and the city.[40] For 1957, it will be recalled, was also the year of the Little Rock confrontation over the admission of black students to high school, one of many such tests of the Supreme Court's 1954 'Brown decision' which found racial segregation of public schools unconstitutional.

The educational agenda, then, became a civil rights one, and the failure of white political leaders to support the civil rights cause led to growing polarization, militancy and violence.[41] At the same time, the rights spectrum widened to take in poverty and disadvantage more generally, and the 1960s – the decade of Kennedy and of Johnson's 'Great Society' – also became the decade of theories of compensatory education, massive federal and state intervention programmes and heated academic debates about cultural 'deprivation', 'disadvantage' and 'difference'.

But the later 1960s were the era of Johnson's greatest disaster abroad – Vietnam – as well as his greatest achievements at home. The war dramatically raised the political temperature, the US Civil Rights Act was passed in 1964, and the civil rights and anti-war movements converged on the fateful year 1968, when Martin Luther King and Robert Kennedy were assassinated and middle America roused itself and elected Richard Nixon as President.

This was the turbulent backdrop to the emergence of progressivism in another guise, and one which bore much more exclusively on elementary schools than had its Deweyistic predecessor. This time the model was imported rather than home grown. The 'open education' movement was based on a highly romanticized view of the English form of progressivism endorsed by the Plowden Report of 1967 and practised in a minority of primary (ages 5–11) and indeed mainly infant (ages 5–7) schools in England's most comfortable rural and suburban heartlands. Nothing further removed from the urban crisis of the United States could be imagined, but then that was precisely the point: by a breathtaking and implausible leap of logic it could be argued that open education English-style – integrated day, topics, groups, individualization, teacher as facilitator, discovery learning, creativity, display and so on – was why when Birmingham, Alabama was rioting Birmingham, England was not.

In the early 1980s (for although Ravitch suggests that official endorsement began to wane in the mid 1970s, the newly converted were not prepared to give up that easily[42]) I rather unkindly – but I hope not xenophobically – wrote of

> . . . planeloads of professors and teachers, the latter in pursuit – in between the Tower of London and Anne Hathaway's cottage – of easy credits for master's degrees and doctorates, descending on primary schools in Oxfordshire, Leicestershire and the West Riding of Yorkshire. One Oxfordshire primary head finally called a halt when he arrived at his school one morning to find a coachload of US teachers waiting, direct from Heathrow and uninvited.[43]

For to an English reader or observer the enthusiasm of Featherstone, Silberman, and Rathbone, and those teacher educators who acted as couriers for the visiting teachers, was naive and overblown – and for reasons which they themselves, given their experience of the earlier versions of progressivism, should have understood.[44] On the other hand, it is as well not to overestimate the reach of the open education movement. Many schools were barely touched by it, if at all.

The final stage in this fourth of my educational Cook's Tours takes us to 2000. By 1980, the sense of what was problematic in the system increasingly centred on the issue of standards. The 1983 report *A Nation at Risk* warned of 'a rising tide of mediocrity that threatens our very future as a nation and as a people'.[45] In 1988 President Bush met state governors to agree *Goals 2000*, one of which was to place America 'first in the world in mathematics and science achievement'. The accumulation of international test data, much of it through organizations such as the International Association for the Evaluation of Educational Achievement (IEA), the International Assessment of Educational Progress (IAEP) and Educational Testing Services (ETS), placed United States students below many of its economic competitors in the key areas of reading, mathematics and science. And as in England, experts in international comparison were on hand with ready explanations, pronouncing American culture as defective as American pedagogy.[46]

Control, Values and Identity

So now, at the turn of the millennium, where in this country of 83,000 governments[47] does educational power lie, and by what values is it driven? The formal position is as set out earlier: the United States looks to be the archetype of decentralization. However, Kirst identifies two periods when local control has been compromised by the pressure of national interests. During the first two decades of the twentieth century, the sheer scale of immigration from Europe led to a concerted drive to imbue the new Americans with old American (that is to say, WASP) ideals;[48] then, from the mid 1960s onwards, the parallel agendas of civil rights, standards and international league tables once again demanded a more than local response. The result was a marked increase in state-level intervention. Thus, for instance, from 1966 to 1976, 35 states passed accountability legislation, and the 1965 Elementary and Secondary Education Act gave states a veto over district applications for federal support. At the same time, although its financial contribution remained small in comparison with that of the states, the federal government itself was able to exert leverage through earmarked funding and by working for consensus on matters such as national goals.[49] *Goals 2000* is a good example of the latter process at work.

But local control has had to respond to other pressures. The second half of the twentieth century saw teacher unions asserting increasing influence at every level down to the individual school, to the extent that Kirst concludes that by the 1990s the autonomy of school districts and the historical muscle of superintendents were squeezed from below as well as from above – that is, by local collective bargaining contracts as well as state legislation and reform initiatives.[50] To an outsider, the uniquely American concept of 'systemic reform', an adjunct to the 1990s educational standards drive, exactly captures the situation's essence. In England or France, educators and policy-makers talk of 'reform' only, for its reach across the entire system is taken for granted. In the United States, the idea of 'systemic reform' speaks to a condition of fragmentation and policy frustration to which the only response is a drive for greater homogeneity.[51]

The *Five Cultures* state- and district-level evidence from Michigan supports but also extends this analysis. There, districts and schools were caught between not just state and teacher unions, but a variety of interests and pressure groups, the most heavyweight or volatile of which were actively courted by state politicians. At the time when we collected Michigan school-level data, the state's Republican governor was ideologically committed to consumerism and marketization in education and at the same time was particularly sensitive to the demands of the religious right, a considerable force in Michigan.

The acute tensions of a society which is both pluralist and decentralized – for decentralization will tend to force value plurality out into the open while in a centralized system value differences may remain concealed or suppressed – were exemplified in the debate about the raising of educational standards in Michigan. The pursuit of standards demanded clearly specified learning outcomes and the setting of curriculum targets. The phrase 'outcomes-based education' (which was merely an updating of those 'terminal' behavioural objectives inspired by the Bloom taxonomy to which I referred earlier) was the sensible shorthand. However, to the religious right 'outcomes-based education' was anathema because, in their view, it handed values teaching over to the schools.

In several interviews, confessing myself to be baffled by this anxiety, I sought but failed to receive a convincing explanation. The religious right, like the political right in England and the United States, was convinced that phonics teaching would raise reading standards. But to talk of its consequences in terms of 'outcomes' was to risk tangling with a contrary agenda, and we were told that educators found they could get by instead by speaking of 'performance', 'results', 'standards' or – in the case of curriculum specification – 'indicators of learning': any word or phrase, in fact, as long as it was not 'outcomes'. Somehow, outcomes-based learning had become equated with the inculcation of secular/humanist values and the spectre of the school undermining the influence of family and church. American public schooling is explicitly secular, but 'secular' in this context has negative rather than positive connotations. It does not indicate a positive course of action: only territory to be avoided.

The state's response to the extreme electoral sensitivity of this matter was to keep values of all kind at arms-length and if necessary to legislate against them, and if the word 'outcomes' had to be used then legislators and administrators covered their backs by stipulating exactly what it should mean. Thus the State of Michigan Enrolled House Bill 5121 determined that 'The state board [of education] and the board of each school district shall ensure that the Michigan Educational Assessment Program (MEAP) tests are not used to measure pupils' values or attitudes'.[52] Elsewhere, the same bill asserts that ' "Outcomes" means measurable pupil *academic skills and knowledge*'[53] (my italics: we all know that academic skills and knowledge are never value-free, and that subjects such as language arts and history are value-saturated, but this formula apparently did the trick). For those at the cutting edge the matter was more problematic (the interviewee was a senior officer in Michigan's State Department of Education):

> Well, in some legislation it's been said that you will not teach values other than those essential in our society, so some teachers said 'OK, we are not going to teach any values at all' and we all said 'You can't do that – school is about values. Are you not going to correct the kid that writes on the wall? I mean that's values, that's property rights. Are you not going to teach things such as honesty, respect for each other, you know a whole lot of things that are not impinging on home values but ought to be the values of the people?' So a lot of communities are coming together and saying 'All right, what are the values that we want our kids to have when they leave, and what are the ones we are going to let alone?' In the State Department we can talk about democratic values, but we have to stay out of the controversial areas.

In the end, however, it is the temperature of a particular community which will determine how such matters are resolved. Another state-level interviewee:

> We have laws against teaching religion in our schools, but in one school this guy used to have pictures of Jesus in the classroom and he would do prayers and stuff but no one in that community ever complained. But I had to investigate one case where this far right religious group said that schools were teaching witchcraft because they celebrated Hallowe'en[54] and they allowed books in the library about witches and goblins and ghosts and wizards. And now there is a group that wants to teach creationism as science – science, not social studies.

In Michigan – and no doubt in other states – the documented shift towards increased state and federal intervention in education is complicated by the contrary impulse of the political right. Thus on the one hand Michigan had introduced a state-wide testing programme (MEAP) in the early 1970s, and by the 1990s was implementing quality assurance mechanisms, benchmarking, state standards and the state core curriculum to which we referred earlier, all of which spelled inexorable centralization. On the other hand:

> We have got a Republican governor and this republican agenda saying 'Get rid of the State Department of Education, get rid of national standards, we think people ought to control schools locally and government should get out of people's hair'. Our governor is interested in choice, and charter schools, and vouchers, and giving private dollars to fund non-public schools, and just when we were starting to get more state guidance and regulation and a new kind of thinking about quality, we have 'Get rid of all that and let people do what they want to do locally.'

The Michigan interviews convey a sense of the transience, unpredictability and lack of continuity in educational policy; of how hard many decisions have to be fought, and of the way that the fight engages the community, not merely professional politicians. Business mobilizes, teachers unionize, religious groups and parents lobby, and politicians both court and tread a tightrope between them all. In other words, the Freedland claim of an active democracy operating right down to community level is not as romantic as it may seem.[55]

However, the outcomes may be rather different from the gradualist, incremental pattern of educational change that Archer sees as the concomitant of decentralization.[56] Admittedly, her models of decentralization were not the United States, but Denmark and pre-1988 England. Decentralized England was very different from the decentralized United States in that it was characterized by limited political literacy and limited activism at community level. Power was indeed devolved from central to local government, but it almost always stopped there, and the discontinuities of the electoral cycle were more than compensated for by the considerable power wielded by unelected permanent officials. In the American version of decentralization, the political power exercised at grass-roots level can make the process of educational reform much more tortuous and inconclusive than any British politician would be prepared to tolerate.

All this suggests that in the context of American public education 'the values question' is anything but academic. We start with the inherent volatility of the cultural melting pot; add the tensions between traditional WASP hegemony and the countercultures and contrary identities of race, ethnicity, gender, religion, region and locality; season with the considerable disparities of wealth and educational provision; then ensure that political decentralization and grass-roots activism keep the whole pot on the boil. Small wonder – as we shall see in the *Five Cultures* classrooms in later chapters – that the playing-out of values and value-tensions was a much more overt element in the pedagogy of the American classrooms than of those in the other four countries.

For the differences are substantial. In 1994 the gap between the richest and poorest 20 per cent of the population was wider than in any other industrialized country (only Britain came close).[57] Of the population of the United States, 12.8 per cent (32 million), could be officially classified as poor, and poverty was not random but went with geography: south/north; rural and inner city/suburban. One third of the population was other than white non-Hispanic. Nearly 60 per cent claimed to be religious (the comparable figures for France and the UK were 22 and 23 per cent).[58] Cutting across these differences are the dominant values of freedom, individualism, self-help and anti-statism that demarcate the United States so sharply from the social democracies of Europe. A 1991 survey found that 72 per cent of Americans valued freedom above equality and only 20 per cent valued equality above freedom. In Italy and Germany the figures were evenly matched; only Britain came close to the American insistence on the primacy of individual freedom.

Afterword: Whatever Happened to *Goals 2000*?

Goals 2000 was an ambitious statement, as perhaps national educational goals should be. Like New Labour's numeracy and literacy targets for 2002, *Goals 2000* came with a deadline. Thereafter, the policies followed the diverging trajectories of decentralized and centralized systems. The numeracy and literacy targets belonged not to England, and certainly not to teachers, but to New Labour. If they were achieved by 2002, New Labour would take full credit; if they were not, Secretary of State Blunkett would resign (or so he said in 1997). In contrast, *Goals 2000* were not so closely identified with the fortunes of a particular administration, for they started with the Republicans, were taken over by the Democrats, and were then passed to state governments of different political hues to work on as they wished. In turn, state education departments passed the initiative (and the funding) down to districts and schools.

This process should have produced a sense of collective ownership. If it did, then the lessons for centralizing governments such as Britain's are very clear. However, goals without strategy do not progress very far, and strategy in this case was beyond the federal government's constitutional remit. All it could do was lobby, persuade and allocate funds. Meanwhile, because the UK literacy and numeracy targets were an electoral pledge, New Labour did what it thought necessary to ensure that teachers would deliver the outcome which would help them stay in power, including cutting back the rest of the curriculum and imposing teaching methods and lesson frameworks.

In the year 2000 it seemed pertinent to check on the progress of *Goals 2000*. The Michigan State Department of Education (MDE) website indicated that 'the US is far from where it should be if we expect to achieve the . . . goals by the end of the decade' (this surely could have been predicted when the initiative was first launched) but then listed a number of partial successes and a much larger number of 'exciting programs and projects'. But on the goals themselves it sounded less convinced. On Goal 7 ('Safe, disciplined and drug-free schools'), for example, the MDE report could say only that 'Michigan data indicate that students are safer in school than outside of school'.[59] One would hope so.

Meanwhile, at federal level the publicity seemed more nervous. One document from the United States Department of Education itemized a large number of 'promising practices' which had been undertaken with federal support in states, districts and schools.[60] These display the variety one would expect in a country as diverse as the United States, but they also confirm the paradox of national targets in a decentralized system. Some of the goals had been achieved, in some schools, some districts and some states. But these were national goals, so although national success depends on local effort, local success, unless it is replicated nation-wide, is not a national achievement. But another document from the federal Department of Education showed the other face of decentralization: the values and fears of sectional interests and above all the bogey of statism. Even our old Michigan chimera, Outcomes-Based Education, is there.

Misconceptions about Goals 2000:

- *Goals 2000* will lead to a federal government takeover of local education.
- Our schools will henceforth be pushed toward a philosophy known as Outcome-Based Education (OBE).
- *Goals 2000* creates the National Education Standards and Improvement Council (NESIC), which will act as a 'national school board' and control what is taught in the classroom.

- *Goals 2000* will require the use of National Standards.
- *Goals 2000* will encourage the proliferation of school-based health clinics, and move schools away from the fundamental duty of education and into the provision of reproductive services.
- *Goals 2000* is another burdensome federal program with a multitude of rules and regulations.
- *Goals 2000* promotes opportunity-to-learn standards that focus on inputs rather than on standards for student achievement.
- The *Goals 2000* Act is the result of the liberal establishment's wish list.[61]

Perhaps in 2002 we should return to both *Goals 2000* and the UK literacy and numeracy strategies in order to compare the balance of benefits and costs in these very different approaches to educational reform.

6

Primary Education in England

Context, Structure and Control

The United Kingdom, of which England is a part, covers a mere 244,755 square kilometres, or just 1.4 per cent of the area of Russia, yet in that space are concentrated 59,009,000 inhabitants, giving it a population density well in excess of India's. However, about 50 million of these live in England, and the majority in London and the conurbations of the Midlands and the North, with the result that that the population density of Scotland and Wales is considerably lower than that of many other European countries, and even large tracts of England remain sparsely populated. In 1998, the UK's per capita GNP was US$20,640 – lower than France or the United States but much closer to those two countries than to Russia or India, and the proportion of this spent on education was 5.4 per cent.[1]

The United Kingdom of Great Britain and Northern Ireland is a recent and not wholly happy invention and its full name hints at the latter. Wales was joined to England *de facto* in 1301 and *de jure* by Act of Union in 1536. Scotland and England shared monarchs from 1603 and a century later, in 1707, a second Act of Union proclaimed 'one united kingdom by the name of Great Britain'. This became the 'United Kingdom of Great Britain and Ireland' in 1801, but acquired its present name after the establishment of the Irish Free State (subsequently Eire or the Republic of Ireland) in 1921. Among the many consequences of this history of first forcible and then legislated annexation by England is the UK's disunited system of education. This book concentrates on England rather than the UK because in educational matters England remains legally and administratively separate from Scotland and Northern Ireland, and semi-detached from Wales. Moves towards a far greater devolution of powers from the UK government in London to the Scottish parliament in Edinburgh and the Welsh assembly in Cardiff could make existing differences of approach even more marked during the first decades of the twenty-first century.[2]

The structure of the education system in the United Kingdom is set out in Figure 6.1. Free and compulsory education in England is provided for pupils aged 5–16, though an increasing proportion choose to stay on until age 18 and then to

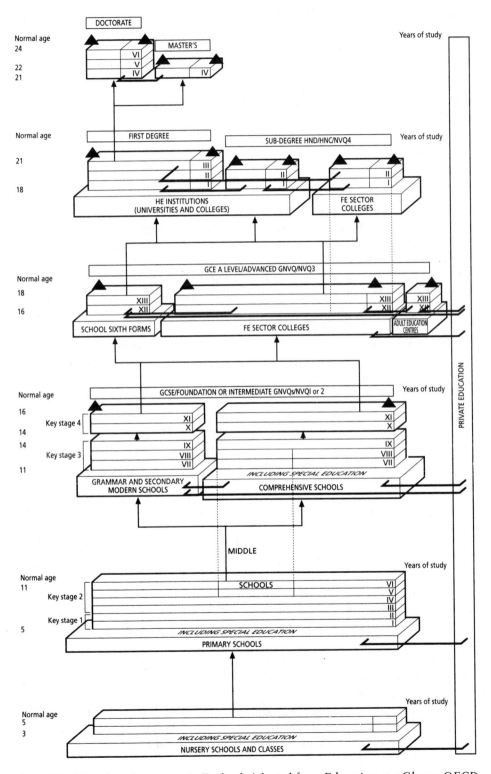

Figure 6.1 The education system in England. Adapted from *Education at a Glance: OECD Indicators 1996.* Copyright OECD, 1996.

enter higher education. Children must start primary education no later than the term following their fifth birthday, though in practice an increasing number of primary schools take children into their 'reception' classes at age four. 'Primary education' in England designates the stage from ages 5 to 11, which for the purposes of statutory curriculum and assessment is divided into Key Stage 1 (ages 5–7) and Key Stage 2 (ages 7–11). A combination of public and private pre-school and nursery education is available for children aged 3–5. Though by the mid 1990s over 80 per cent of 3 and 4 year olds were receiving some form of pre-compulsory education,[3] take-up of *public* provision varied from 25 per cent to 90 per cent, depending on the policy of the local education authority (LEA).[4]

One international database claims that 'education in England is characterized by its decentralized nature'.[5] This was certainly the case until 1988, and for decades England's was among the most decentralized systems in the world. This is not only no longer true, but it can also be argued with some justification that during 1988–98 England acquired one of the most tightly controlled and regulated state education systems in Europe.

In fact, the situation in 2000 demonstrates the difficulty of treating the notion of 'decentralization' as monolithic, for England has a split system, each part pulling in different directions. Administrative and financial responsibilities continue to be shared between central government, the 151 local education authorities (LEAs) and the schools, as under the 1944 Education Act, with LEAs providing schools and ancillary services from funds allocated by the national government. Indeed, since the 1988 Education Reform Act and related subsequent legislation a large and increasing share of LEA funding has been delegated to the governing bodies of individual schools, and the power of LEAs has been substantially weakened. Alongside this very real administrative and financial decentralization the same Act hastened direct government control of the education process itself, and this control has been progressively tightened since then by strengthening the powers of the Secretary of State for Education and Employment, and by establishing a further tier, between LEAs and national government, of government-controlled agencies. These are responsible for school inspection and quality assurance (Office for Standards in Education – OFSTED), curriculum, assessment and qualifications (the Qualifications and Curriculum Authority – QCA) and teacher training (the Teacher Training Agency – TTA). The 1997 Blair government added a Standards and Effectiveness Unit (SEU) as a non-accountable agency located inside the Department for Education and Employment (DfEE, the education ministry), and which has to some extent undercut the work of the publicly accountable QCA by taking direct control of what the government sees as its most important task at the primary stage, the teaching of literacy and numeracy.

This, then is the reality of control: decentralized administration and finance, centralized curriculum, assessment and teacher training, the latter areas aggressively policed on behalf of the government by OFSTED.

The administration of the system is complicated by, from September 1999, the co-existence of four categories of school with varying balances of funding and administrative control as between LEAs, governing bodies and charitable foundations (usually religious): 'community' schools (those owned by and funded and administered through LEAs, which are the majority); 'voluntary controlled' schools (established and owned by the churches but funded via the LEAs); 'voluntary aided' schools (church owned and established with costs shared between the governing body and the LEA),[6] and 'foundation' schools which are owned and controlled by the governing body or a charitable foundation and are funded via LEAs.[7] The difference between foundation and voluntary aided schools is essentially one of control, with the foundation having a majority on the governing body of aided schools and non-foundation members (notably parents) having the majority in foundation schools. A fully independent sector of private schools exists alongside the state system. Confusingly, private secondary schools are called 'public schools'. Their primary equivalent is designated 'preparatory'.

In 1998, England's 4 million primary age children were attending 18,230 primary schools. These ranged in size from one-class rural schools with under 20 pupils to urban schools with over 800. They included infant (pupil ages 4/5–7), first (4/5–8/9), junior (7–11), middle (8/9–12/13), combined (4/5–12/13) and, the largest category – 65 per cent of schools – infant with junior (4/5–11). The average school size was 225, and if there is a typical primary school in terms of size and organization it is the 4/5–11 primary school with one mixed-ability class for each year group, 200 or so pupils and seven or eight full-time teachers (one of whom is the head teacher).[8] In addition the school will have clerical support and perhaps part-time or occasional specialist support for certain pupils whose special educational needs (SEN) are severe enough to justify individual attention but not so severe as to require, under a system which since 1978 has sought to integrate SEN pupils, attendance at a separate special school.[9] In those parts of the conurbations with a high proportion of pupils from ethnic minorities for whom English is their second language, there may be language support staff as well.[10]

The national average pupil–teacher ratio for primary schools in 1997 was 23.4, but 32 per cent of pupils were taught in classes of over 30 and a small number (200 pupils) were still in classes of over 40.[11] The incoming 1997 Labour government pledged to reduce class sizes for 5–7 year olds to no more than 30. By 2000, teachers were claiming this was achieved simply by moving the 'bulge' into upper primary.

English primary teachers, like those in many other countries, including the other four in this study, are generalists who teach the full range of subjects, though some also have responsibility for co-ordinating their school policy and provision in their specialist subject. Since 1978 these 'curriculum co-ordinators' or 'subject leaders' have become a standard, though problematic, element in primary staffing, usually covering language, mathematics and science, though not all of the remaining subjects.[12]

Primary teaching in England – unlike, say, Denmark or Canada – is an overwhelmingly female profession.[13] In 1998, 84 per cent of England's 181,394 full-time equivalent primary teachers were women, and the proportion has grown significantly, and continues to grow, over the postwar decades (in 1981, for example, the proportion of women teachers was 77 per cent; in 1962 it was 75.4 per cent[14]). Men, however, were for a long time disproportionately represented in senior teaching posts, though the balance is now shifting: in 1981 55 per cent of primary heads were men and 50 per cent of all male teachers (compared with a mere 16 per cent of women teachers) were either heads or deputy heads; by 1994 the proportion of male primary heads was 49 per cent, by 1998 it had reduced further to 43 per cent,[15] and by 1999, in a dramatic further shift, the National Association of Head Teachers reported that nearly 75 per cent of new primary head teachers were women. However, while this breached the link between male gender and power in the profession, it also accentuated the overall gender imbalance in primary teaching as a whole.

Goals, Curriculum and Assessment

In 1997 the incoming Labour government set out its aims for the education service as targets to be achieved by 2002:

- to make education central to government policy and national life ('education, education and education')
- education to benefit the many, not just the few
- to focus on standards, not structures
- intervention in inverse proportion to success
- zero tolerance of under-performance
- partnership between government and those committed to raising standards.[16]

This of course is a statement of political rather than educational ends (and the debt to United States presidential rhetoric will be evident to American readers), but it indicates the way that raising standards, especially in relation to England's international competitors, was to shape and drive the more genuinely educational goals. These were expressed briefly but in somewhat convoluted and inelegant form in the 1988 Education Act and were restated in the 1996 Education Act:

- to promote the spiritual, moral, cultural, mental and physical development of students at the school and of society
- to prepare students for the opportunities, responsibilities and experiences of adult life.[17]

In 1997 the outgoing Conservative government initiated a review of the national curriculum. This was continued under the 1997 administration and by 1999 the Qualifications and Curriculum Authority had added four main purposes of the national curriculum:

(1) *Entitlement:* to secure for all pupils, irrespective of culture, social background or gender, an entitlement to a number of areas of learning and to develop skills, knowledge and understanding necessary for their self-fulfilment and development as active and responsible citizens.
(2) *Standards:* to establish standards for pupil performance in all subjects.

(3) *Continuity and coherence:* to promote continuity and progression in pupils' learning and facilitate the transition of pupils between schools and phases of education and provide a foundation for lifelong learning.

(4) *Public understanding:* to increase public understanding of, and confidence in, the work of schools and in the learning and achievements resulting from compulsory education.[18]

Even this was some way from a set of *educational* aims. However, the same document went on to propose two, or rather a much larger number reduced to two clusters:

(1) *To provide opportunities for all pupils to learn and to achieve* – develop pupils' enjoyment of, and commitment to, learning and achieving . . . build on pupils' strengths, capacities and interests . . . equip pupils with the essential skills of literacy, numeracy, and information technology . . . promote an enquiring mind . . . develop a sense of identity through knowledge and understanding of their spiritual, moral, social and cultural heritages and of the local, European, Commonwealth and global dimensions . . . encourage pupils to appreciate human aspirations and achievements in aesthetic, scientific, technological and social fields . . . enable pupils to think creatively and critically, to solve problems and to make a difference for the better . . . to become creative, innovative and enterprising, capable of leadership to equip them for their future lives as workers and citizens . . . develop physical skills and encourage pupils to recognize the importance of a healthy lifestyle;

(2) *To promote pupils' spiritual, moral, social and cultural development and prepare all pupils for the opportunities, responsibilities and experiences of life* – promote pupils' spiritual, moral, social and cultural development and develop their understanding of right and wrong . . . develop knowledge, understanding and appreciation of their own and different beliefs and cultures . . . pass on enduring values, develop integrity and autonomy, and help pupils to become responsible and caring citizens capable of contributing to the development of a just society . . . promote equal opportunities and enable pupils to challenge discrimination and stereotyping . . . develop understanding and respect for the environment and secure their commitment to sustainable development at a personal, local, national and global level . . . equip pupils as consumers to make informed judgements and understand their responsibilities and rights . . . promote self-esteem and emotional well-being and help pupils to form and maintain worthwhile and satisfying relationships based on respect for themselves and others . . . develop pupils' ability to relate to others and work for the common good . . . enable pupils to respond to opportunities, challenges and responsibilities, to manage risk and cope with change and adversity . . . prepare pupils for the next steps in their education, training and employment.[19]

In rather different vein, reverting to political priorities and election pledges, the government announced a series of targets for student performance and qualifications by the ages of 19 and 21, and pledged itself at the primary stage to raise standards in literacy so that by 2002 80 per cent of 11 year olds would achieve the age norms for literacy and 75 per cent the age norms for numeracy.[20] Commissioned literacy and numeracy strategies, at the core of which was a single pedagogical prescription for every primary classroom in the form of literacy and numeracy 'hours', were introduced from 1998.[21]

As for the curriculum itself, the 1988 Education Reform Act, which introduced the national curriculum, specified nine subjects for the primary stage plus religious education, a reflection of still unresolved battles over the relationship of church and state in a country with an established church of which the monarch is the titular head, and perhaps the most striking anomaly in an international context where whatever the religious character of a country its schooling and curricula tend to be secular. The 1997–9 National Curriculum review maintained the 1988 specification with slight modifications:[22]

Core subjects

- English
- mathematics
- science

Non-core foundation subjects

- design and technology
- information and communication technology
- history
- geography
- modern foreign languages
- art and design
- music
- physical Education
- citizenship

Also required

- religious education
- sex education

Citizenship was probably the most radical change. However, neither citizenship nor the teaching of a foreign language was obligatory at the primary stage. For pupils aged 5–11 the former was wrapped up within a non-statutory framework for 'personal, social and health education and citizenship',[23] most of which was to be achieved by permeating other subjects, rather in the manner of France's *compétences transversales* or the cumbersomely named but optional 'cross curricular themes, skills and dimensions' of England's first national curriculum. These were for the most part quietly overlooked in the 1993 Dearing review and received no mention in the revised version of the curriculum implemented in 1995.[24] Ironically, in a country which has no citizens, only loyal (and disloyal) subjects of the monarch, the one 'cross-curricular theme' now officially reinstated in the 2000 version of the national curriculum is citizenship, familiar under that or similar designation in many other (republican) countries.

Apart from literacy and numeracy, it is for schools to decide how much time to devote to the other subjects, how to divide the week up into lessons and how long each lesson should be. The school year consists of 190 days, divided into three terms, with breaks at Christmas, Easter and in August, together with shorter breaks in the mid-point of each term. Primary pupils attend school from Monday to Friday, generally between the hours of 0900 and 1530, and the recommended weekly minimum teaching time is 21 hours for pupils aged 5–7 and 23.5 hours for 7–11 year-olds.[25]

England has had, since 1988, a national system of assessment at the primary stage. All pupils are tested at the end of Key Stages 1 and 2 (that is, at the ages of 7 and 11) in the core subjects of English, mathematics and science. The tests are calibrated against levels of achievement for specified 'attainment targets' in each of these subjects on an eight-point scale, with levels 2 and 4 representing the expected (average) levels for, respectively, 7- and 11-year-old pupils. The government publishes the test results for each school, showing the proportion of pupils achieving level 4 or above at age 11, in the form of league tables.

Alongside the statutory Key Stages 1 and 2 tests in English, mathematics and science, schools are expected to undertake regular teacher assessments in all subjects and to incorporate these in pupil records and reports to parents. From 1998, all primary schools were required to undertake baseline assessment of children starting school, using schemes accredited by the QCA.

Statutory national inspection, as I have noted, is a further part of the UK government's drive to raise standards. In 1992 an Office for Standards in Education (OFSTED) replaced the 150-year-old system of occasional inspections by HMI (Her/His Majesty's Inspectorate) with a fuller and much more public arrangement whereby schools are assessed at least every four years and the results are quantified and published. The inspections are comprehensive, ranging from school management to teaching quality, and each year the chief inspector publishes further lists of weak, outstanding and improving schools.[26] The publication of test and inspection results within a framework and ethic dubbed 'naming and shaming' has proved highly controversial.

Origins and Development

Late start

Public primary education in England at the turn of the millennium bears the scars of many battles, some of them far from resolved. The entrenched interests of church and class repeatedly blocked, frustrated or compromised efforts to extend basic education to the children of ordinary working people. While France, America, Germany, Holland, Sweden and many other countries forged ahead during the early and mid nineteenth century in universalizing basic education, England remained without a national system almost until that century's end.

Elementary schooling, once conceded, for long remained minimal, philosophically no less than materially. Where other countries celebrated forms of primary schooling which were compulsory, free and secular, England allowed itself – and still allows itself – only the first two. Even in the late twentieth century opinion remained sharply and bitterly divided over whether primary schools should confine themselves to the inherited diet of 'the basics' (reading, writing and arithmetic), or embrace a more generous concept of what is fundamental to early learning. The political culture within which modern English primary schooling is set remains in some respects as it was a century ago – deeply paternalist, utilitarian and suspicious of change generated from within. When they are confronted with questions about the purposes which primary education should serve, how it should be organized and how resourced, many still reach unthinkingly for the Victorian doctrine of minimalism.

The question of why England, for all its economic success and relative political stability during the eighteenth and the nineteenth centuries, should have been be so slow to universalize basic education, has exercised many. The power of the established church was one barrier; class-based resistance another. But it can also be argued that because England industrialized first, and without either mass education or significant state intervention, a vital pressure to change was removed, one to which all its competitors were subject: to acquire as rapidly as possible the technology and skills needed to catch up. It was individual entrepreneurship and inventiveness that put Britain ahead of the game in the first Industrial Revolution. It was through state action – including the fostering of elementary, scientific, technological and vocational forms of public education – that countries such as Germany and the United States were able first to recover the ground lost and then rapidly to pull ahead. Britain, meanwhile, lived on borrowed time and the spoils of empire, ignoring evidence of its industrial and economic decline.[27]

Roots

Despite its relatively recent arrival, primary education in England has a considerable genealogy, though most of it has been at the margins of educational development. The dominance of the church was established early, through monasteries and schools attached to cathedrals and collegiate churches. In the ninth century King Alfred sought to arrest the decline in learning by commanding the translation into English of important texts and by urging the use of the vernacular, rather than Latin, to spread literacy. If his campaign did not amount to anything approaching popular education, it undoubtedly contributed to the evolution of the English language.[28] The Norman Conquest set back these incipient reforms substantially, not least by what can be described – with the dismal hindsight of the twentieth century – as a campaign of ethnic cleansing. However, during the twelfth and the thirteenth centuries clerics lost their monopoly of literacy, which diffused down through the lay classes as far as artisans, though rarely beyond, and seldom outside the major centres of population. (Latin) grammar schools were supplemented by parish schools, song schools and a variety of informal arrangements, with seven as the preferred starting age, though from such opportunities girls, as well as the peasantry, were largely excluded.[29]

Lawson and Silver rate the establishment of Winchester College in 1382 a landmark, for it included places for *pauperes et indigentes*, as, 60 years later, did Eton.[30] However, the number of poor and needy who benefited from endowed places there, in parish schools, chantries and elsewhere, was undoubtedly small in relation to the total population. At the same time, education was reaching further down the social scale, and during the fifteenth century the urban merchant classes and their guilds increasingly sponsored apprenticeship with reading and writing, and during this period the imperatives of commerce ensured that literacy penetrated furthest among merchants, craftsmen and artisans.[31] Graff cautions about the lack of firm figures, but estimates that by 1500 urban male literacy in England stood at about 25 per cent, national male literacy at 6–12 per cent, and female literacy significantly lower. On the other hand, within particular groups such as merchants, the figure for males could well have been as high as 40 per cent.[32] Literacy was no longer the monopoly of the church, and Caxton's introduction of the printing press in 1476, following its invention by Gutenberg in Germany, 30 years earlier, rapidly ensured that church control of the texts on which the development of literacy depended, too, was broken.

Graff also warns against overstating the impact of printing as the single development demarcating ancient from modern, or mediaeval from renaissance. Printing alone cannot account for the social, political and economic changes of this period, and must be seen, alongside the growth of literacy, as part cause, part symptom and part consequence of these changes.[33] Nevertheless, it greatly facilitated the spread of the ideas by which events critical to the onward march of education – notably the Reformation – were informed and manifested. Printing was a vital ingredient in the growth and dissemination of religious and intellectual countercultures. More specifically, it speeded access to the vernacular versions of the Bible and prayer books that were to serve as foundation texts – indeed the very rationale – of popular schooling.

The first serious push for education at state level in England came with the conjunction of the Reformation, the printed word and Tudor state-building. Joan Simon shows how with the Reformation control of church education passed to the crown, while at the same time the state intervened to reorganize local schools and to enforce the secular as well as ecclesiastical rule of a church of which the monarch was now the head.[34] By royal injunctions of 1559 schoolmasters had to subscribe to the royal supremacy, the Thirty-Nine Articles and the Book of Common Prayer, as from 1616, did graduands from Cambridge and Oxford. Education, then became a means of consolidating both church and state.[35]

No less significant during the Tudor period and subsequently was the considerable expansion of educational opportunity through endowments and charities. The beneficiaries, through the many grammar schools founded during this period, were the sons of the better-off, but poorer children (girls as well as boys, though not the poorest) also benefited from the petty schools (*petites écoles* in France) which, as their alternative name of ABC schools indicates, concentrated on basic reading. The dominant method for teaching reading, from the sixteenth century until well into the nineteenth, was described in 1588 by William Kempe as '*Prosodia*, in pronouncing of letters, syllables and words with the mouth, and *Orthographia*, in writing of them with the hand'. Children learned to read first, orally and catechistically, then to write.[36]

Blyth suggests that this period was also important for its incipient demarcation of primary education's distinctive 'elementary' and 'preparatory' traditions. He cites Richard Mulcaster's early use of 'elementary' (in *The First Part of the Elementarie*, 1582) to denote schooling which was finite, while the petty schools frequently had a dual purpose of providing a complete elementary education and preparing pupils for entry to grammar schools.[37] This distinction is of fundamental importance, as we shall see shortly; later elementary education retained these two forms until well into the twentieth century and in rural areas especially the all-age elementary school was for many children the only educational provision available. (Several of the older inhabitants of my own village experienced this form of schooling).

If printing was one watershed between ancient and modern in education and the Reformation the second, the scientific revolution of the early seventeenth century was undoubtedly the other. In *The Advancement of Learning* (1605) and *Novum Organum* (1620) – both brought together in *De Augmentis Scientiarum* (1623) – Francis Bacon redrew the map of knowledge and immeasurably advanced the cause of inductive scientific enquiry. In *New Atlantis* (1627), published a year after his death, he set out his case for state support for scientific research and for the establishment of Solomon's House, an institution dedicated not, in the mediaeval tradition, to the preservation and transmission of knowledge but to its enlargement through observation and experimentation. These ideas had a profound influence on Comenius, whose interests within education included not only pedagogy narrowly defined but also ways – through encyclopaedias and scientific societies – of containing, organizing and disseminating human knowledge. At the behest of merchant-turned-philanthropist and intellectual entrepreneur Samuel Hartlib, Comenius was persuaded to visit England in 1641–2 in connection with his scheme for the establishment of a college for scientific research on Baconian lines. This institution was to be the centrepiece of a general reform of education in both England and New England.

Comenius' visit was curtailed by the growing crisis between Parliament and King, a crisis which led to the Civil War of 1642–5, the execution of King Charles I in 1649 and England's brief flirtation with a kind of republicanism under Oliver Cromwell. However, the baton was picked up by Hartlib, G. W. Leibniz, Robert Boyle, and John Milton, whose support in the cause of educational reform Hartlib had enlisted. Milton's *Tractate on Education* (1644) was short, and literary rather than scientific in its educational orientation, but his support for the cause of educational reform – as Cromwell's secretary – was useful and in 1648 Parliament actually debated a scheme for a national system of education.[38]

The eventual outcome was the founding of the Royal Society in 1662, after the Restoration. A national system of education had to wait a good deal longer. As for the impact of these ideas and events on the development of *primary* education, it was at best oblique, for it is fair to say that debates about education, in England as in other countries, have until relatively recently concerned themselves more with what follows the primary stage, tacitly reinforcing the view that primary is about reading and writing and the real education comes later. Nevertheless, I record this episode because it embodied a critical combination of ideas which continued to eat away at established interests and mindsets and gradually to filter down into thinking about popular basic education: scientific enquiry, teaching as a principled activity, the challenging of clerical hegemony and the traditional curriculum, the humanizing of school discipline, and even – through the pamphlets of Hartlib, Winstanley, Dury, Dell, Petty and of course Milton – the establishment of universal, free and compulsory education. If the Restoration of 1660 prevented such ideas from being realized as policy, the fire of dissent and reform had at least been lit, the Puritans had seized the initiative, and the idea of popular education had become a practical possibility. And if England was unable to benefit for another two centuries, at least America could.

Green argues that the Restoration marked the point at which educational development in England and the rest of Europe began to diverge. From that point on, other countries made steady progress while England stagnated.[39] It is true that the 1662 Act of Uniformity – which required clergy, dons and teachers to declare their allegiance to the established church and state and to teach only with a bishop's license – reinstated the church as the arbiter of educational development, drove dissent and experiment largely underground, and of course put paid to further talk of a national system of education. On the other hand it also gave nonconformity the impetus to flourish with greater vigour and tenacity, and nonconforming schools and academies began to spring up all over the country, in defiance of the law and often at considerable risk. The pressures on them were eased somewhat by the Toleration Act of 1689, which gave nonconformists freedom of worship in recognition of their part in the revolution of 1688. Meanwhile, the educational thinking liberated by the Renaissance and the Reformation continued, and though Locke's *Some Thoughts Concerning Education* (1693) contemplated only the education of the sons of gentlemen, and was thus firmly within the bounds of acceptable reformist talk, it was an important early example of genuinely child-centred analysis, arguing that education required an understanding of children's characteristics and needs, that it should attend to what is most useful for them to learn, and that it should replace rote by activity.

The real educational recession set in towards the end of the century and lasted until 1780 or so. The universities and grammar schools declined, popular education was viewed with deepening suspicion on the grounds that it made the people dissatisfied with their lot, fuelled dissent, and invited disturbance to the established social order. In this, church and gentry forged a powerful and inpregnable alliance.

Yet, despite this, charity schooling for the poor spread significantly, and though – as in the case of the Society for Promoting Christian Knowledge (SPCK) – the motivation was to tighten church hegemony and social control by making the poor god-fearing, this could not be achieved without also making them – after a fashion – literate.

The figures for literacy during the eighteenth century reflect a complex picture. Overall, literacy increased, but there was considerable regional variation, and female literacy remained lower than male. In some areas literacy actually declined while in others it increased, and overall literacy rates mapped closely on to social status and occupation. But while labourers and servants remained mostly illiterate, artisan literacy increased rapidly. Everywhere, print and access to print was a major factor. Books, newspapers, tracts, pamphlets, chapbooks, ballads and handbills multiplied, and in multiplying they spread down and across the social structure.[40]

The struggle for mass elementary education

With the final decades of the eighteenth century came the start of the upheavals that would eventually yield a public education system in England. The Enlightenment encompassed human perfectibility, the power of ideas, social justice – and education. The 1790s pamphlet war of Tom Paine, Edmund Burke, William Godwin, Mary Wollstonecraft, William Wordsworth and others centred on revolution – 'Bliss was it in that dawn to be alive / But to be young was very heaven' – but also on education[41]. Paine costed in detail a six-year system of education for the poor – 'A nation under a well instructed government should permit none to remain uninstructed. It is monarchical and aristocratical government alone that requires ignorance for its support'.[42] Joseph Priestley was a key figure in the dissenting academy movement and in the Lunar Society of Birmingham. William Godwin was the product of one such academy. Mary Wollstonecraft took issue with Rousseau over women's education, attacking what we would now call the sexism of his differentiation of the education of Sophie and Emile: 'Strengthen the female mind by enlarging it, and there will be an end to blind obedience; but, as blind obedience is ever sought for by power, tyrants and sensualists are in the right when they endeavour to keep women in the dark, because the former only want slaves, and the latter a play-thing'.[43] And, in his sensational 1808 Royal Institution lecture, Coleridge set out a radical prospectus for a state-funded national system of education extending beyond basic literacy to 'form the habits' of the whole person and provide the essential foundation for a liberal society.[44] Others did not agree: Godwin and Priestley, for instance, opposed state education on the grounds that governments would use it to advance their own interests rather than those of the people, and this suspicion of state educational hegemony was a persistent and powerful strand in the thinking of other groups too.

The case of Joseph Priestley is particularly important in our context, for it takes the education debate physically out of the metropolis and into the rapidly growing towns and cities of the industrial revolution. The Birmingham Lunar Society, the Literary and Philosophical Societies in Manchester, Newcastle, Lichfield, Derby, and several other towns, organized meetings and lectures, developed considerable libraries and provided a vital context for the discussion of ideas and social and economic reform. The first volume of Brian Simon's monumental history of English education charts the emergence and influence of such groups in considerable detail.[45] They laid the foundation for that civic involvement in self-improvement that was later to become a significant part of Victorian urban life.

From the 1780s, educational provision for the poor was extended beyond the charity schools by the burgeoning Sunday school movement. The objective was 'habits of industry and piety' and for these reading, but generally not writing, was required – for while reading aided instruction writing, like speaking, invited autonomous reflection. One of the leading figures in the evangelical Sunday school movement, Hannah More, was criticized for teaching the masses to read, but tracts such as her *Village Politics* illustrate her conviction that the existing social order was just and education should seek to uphold it.[46]

The Sunday schools in turn paved the way for one of the most influential educational developments of the first half of the nineteenth century, the monitorial schools. We have already noted the controversy over whether Lancaster or Bell invented the monitorial system, and whether Bell's Madras experiment – which actually preceded Lancaster's by a couple of years – was based on earlier indigenous arrangements in India. The argument is less important in itself than for the rivalry between Anglicanism and nonconformity that it signals in the growing battle for children's minds and souls. Lancaster was a Quaker, Bell a Church of England clergyman. The methods of the latter were adopted by the National Society for Promoting the Education of the Poor in the Principles of the Established Church (established in 1811 – the title needs no further elucidation) in direct response to the early successes of the Royal Lancasterian Society, founded in 1808 and renamed the British and Foreign Schools Society in 1814.

Monitorial schools under the aegis of one or other of these societies rapidly spread across the country. Their rivalry helped in the rapid expansion of popular education, though it also frustrated the establishment of proper public provision. James Bonwick gives a lively first-hand account of his experiences as a pupil at Lancaster's Borough Road school, starting with 'the very primitive Oriental style of sand marking' – tracing letters in the sand tray – and working his way up through the school's eight classes until he himself became a monitor. The routines were elaborate and highly regimented. Over all the children hung the portrait of George III, 'The Patron of Education and Friend of the Poor' with his no less gracious endorsement of Lancaster's methods: 'It is my wish that every poor child in my dominions be taught to read the holy scriptures'. Reading, then, was a means to a particular end, and the Bible provided the point of reference across the entire curriculum: 'Our only reading was . . . selections from the Bible . . . [In geography] the Scripture Maps received prominent regard' . . . In Science . . . our reading was absolutely confined to Bible extracts'.[47]

These methods provoked adverse reactions, too. In 1808, Coleridge stunned the audience at one of his Royal Institution lectures with his attack on Lancaster's system of penalties and punishments, hurling Lancaster's book on the floor 'and exclaiming "No boy who has been subject to punishments like these will stand in fear of Newgate, or feel any horror at the thought of the slave ship" '. Lancaster threatened to sue, the Royal Institution passed a motion of censure, and the Church of England was no doubt delighted.[48]

More measured were the reservations of mill owner, philanthropist and proto-socialist Robert Owen, whose legendary schools at New Lanark offered a broader curriculum, a more humane regime and – most importantly – an image of an infant stage of education separate from mainstream elementary education and conducted on very different lines. Inspired by the New Lanark model, an Infant School Society was founded in 1824, and the schools established under its banner espoused continental rather than English models, especially the ideas of Pestalozzi. Blyth suggests that Owen 'can claim to be the real founder of developmental primary education in England'.[49]

Thompson judges, however, that Owen was paternalist rather than radical, and records Hazlitt's warning that the highly placed patronage he enjoyed was conditional upon his ideas and practices being confined to New Lanark and in no way threatening to disturb the status quo. In his judgement, Owen's socialism simply failed to engage with the realities of power, class and capital.[50]

But the ultimately more significant comment on the extreme limitations of early nineteenth century basic schooling, including the monitorial schools, was the development of working-class collective consciousness and the autodidact culture. Increasing numbers attended parish, Sunday, National and British schools; but for many of them this was not enough: 100,000 copies of Cobbett's *Grammar of the English Language* were sold in the first few years following its publication; to each copy sold many are likely to have had access.[51] Thompson estimates that 'something like two out of every three working men were able to read after some fashion in the early part of the century, although rather fewer could write', and charts in detail the growth and influence during the first half of the nineteenth century of the alternative education provided by pamphlets, the theatre, reading groups, mutual improvement societies, mechanics institutes, and the Methodist and Evangelical movements. However, he rates the religious influence motivational rather than intellectual.[52] Simon, too, shows how the conventional 'top-down' history of the development of public education in the nineteenth century seriously underestimates the extent and influence of both the workers' movements and the many organized contexts for self-improvement, the dissemination of knowledge and the forging of consciousness.[53]

Meanwhile, Hazlitt was being vindicated. In 1807 Samuel Whitbread tried, but failed, to gain Parliamentary support for a bill to link factory and educational reform. In 1816 Lord Brougham, working with the British and Foreign Schools Society, succeeded in persuading Parliament to set up a select committee 'to enquire into the Education of the Lower Orders in the Metropolis'. This exposed the weaknesses of the endowment and charity systems and the lack of educational provision generally, led to the appointment of the Charity Commissioners and thence to England's first public education bill – the 1820 Bill 'for the better education of the Poor in England and Wales'. Brougham's bill, too, failed, scuppered by the combined forces of the Church of England, the non-conformists and the gentry, each of whom saw state provision as a threat to their own ascendancy. The best that could be mustered was Commons approval in 1833 for a grant of £20,000 to support voluntary agencies in their task of building 'School Houses for the Education of the Children of the Poorer Classes in Great Britain', the money being distributed through the British and National societies.[54]

On the other hand, this was a foot in the door of state provision, for it was the first time public money had been voted for education, and from then on the annual grants provided a modest supplement to voluntary effort. In 1839 a Committee of the Privy Council on Education was set up with Dr Kay (later Sir James Kay-Shuttleworth) as its secretary; it was charged with overseeing the use of the annual grant, and this oversight was exercized on the basis of information provided by inspectors. Thus, slowly and piecemeal were two elements of the modern system introduced: national funding and national inspection. Neither, however, was allowed to disturb church control.

However, in small but significant ways the new committee added to the patchwork of provision. Grants were available first for school buildings, then (from 1843) for furniture and equipment, then (from 1846) to replace the monitorial system by pupil teachers who could compete for Queen's scholarships to training colleges. By the 1850s, the stage was set for the last act in the convoluted drama of English public primary education.

In 1858, a commission was set up under the chairmanship of Lord Newcastle to 'enquire into the present State of Popular Education in England, and to consider and report what Measures, if any, are required for the Extension of sound and cheap elementary instruction to all classes of the People'. The Newcastle Commission reported in 1861. It rejected compulsory education, opposed any interference with the church-dominated voluntary sector, but proposed that the arrangements for paying the grants to schools should be modified to include a substantial element of what came to be called 'payment by results' – payment made conditional on children's performance in tests conducted by the inspectors. Children under six were subsequently exempted, thus preserving by a whisker the distinctive character of infant education as it had developed since the 1820s. Robert Lowe's justification of the Code – 'if it is not cheap, it shall be efficient; if it is not efficient, it shall be cheap' – entered the English educational consciousness and was still being evoked to damn government policy on primary education at the end of the twentieth century.[55]

Opposition to this formula (it can hardly be called a principle) was eloquent and well placed. Kay-Shuttleworth (now retired) and Matthew Arnold were two of the most prominent critics. Arnold – at some risk to his position of HMI (no OFSTED inspector in 2000 would dare to step out of line as Arnold did) – inveighed not only against the formula, but also what he saw as the entirely specious reasoning behind it. In words that were to resonate strongly with the arguments about primary school standards in the 1990s, he argued that the elementary schools were being expected to 'cram into the space of two or three years the instruction which ought to occupy five or six'[56] and contested the claim that standards of literacy would rise if teacher concentrated on the 3Rs alone. His sentiments initially seem patrician and paternalist, but this is the author of *Culture and Anarchy*, so there is a sting in the tail:

What renders impossible the attainment by so many of a power so considerable – a power which is a real lasting acquirement for the whole life – is the utter want of care for books and knowledge in the homes from which the majority of them come forth . . . in a word, the general want of civilization in themselves and in those among whom they pass their lives . . . It is the advance of them and their class in civilization which will bring them nearer to this power, not the confining of them to reading lessons, not the striking out of lessons in geography or history from the course of our elementary schools. Intelligent reading . . . is not very common even among the children of the rich and educated class. When children in this class possess it, they owe it not to the assiduity with which they have been taught reading and nothing but reading, but partly to natural aptitude, far more to the civilizing and refining influences, the current of older and educated people's ideas and knowledge, in the midst of which they have been brought up.[57]

Arnold went on to demonstrate – quoting the Commission's report – that 'the Revised Code . . . will not do what it proposes to do . . . and even if it were to do what it proposes, the means by which it proposes to do this would still be objectionable'.[58]

I have quoted Arnold at length, not to imply that he alone was instrumental in ensuring the Code's subsequent demise but because the form of his opposition to the Code captures certain continuities in English primary schooling which outlasted both the Code and elementary education: minimalism *versus* breadth; class-based assumptions and expectations about what children from particular backgrounds can or cannot do; even the argument, which I myself had to press to the House of Commons Education Select Committee in 1999, against the minimalist prescriptions of one of Arnold's more notorious successors, that 'the way to raise standards in literacy and numeracy is to raise the standards of *teaching* in literacy and numeracy, while embedding those subjects in a broad curriculum which will provide the necessary context for the application and consolidation of the skills in question'.[59]

The Elementary Education Act of 1870 introduced by W. E. Forster (Arnold's brother-in-law) is often presumed to have established, at long last, a proper system of public elementary education (in 1970 many primary school pupils were actually required to celebrate the Forster Act's centenary on these grounds, rather as at other times they are expected dutifully and subserviently to celebrate royal weddings). It did not: it was a compromise which provided neither free nor compulsory schooling; nor did it challenge the hegemony of the Church of England, but merely plugged the gaps in the voluntary system with public elementary schools provided and supervised by school boards.

On the other hand, the Forster Act started the ball rolling. By the end of the century nearly 2,500 school boards had been set up, education had been made compulsory to age 10 in 1876, 11 in 1893 and 12 in 1899, illiteracy had substantially diminished, and payment by results had finally disappeared, to be replaced in 1900 by a single block grant. The quality of provision was variable: the prevailing image of the board schools remains cheerless and punitive – something later progressives were keen to exploit ('rigid timetables, clanging bells, silent cloakrooms, cramping desks and absurd rules . . .').[60] However, some of the autobiographies collected by John Burnett record as by no means isolated exceptions those schools where individual teachers strove to provide those 'civilizing and refining influences' all but outlawed by the Revised Code – a wide range of literature, science, French and music – suggesting that for some children at least 'the later elementary school was often a livelier, more original and imaginative institution than has sometimes been supposed and that not a few children emerged from it with a genuine love of learning and a considerable ability to write'.[61] The fact that teachers of this calibre and vision existed is testament to the power and pervasive-ness of alternative patterns of working-class education as well as to formal provi-sion and training. Moreover, under many school boards extra classes and higher grade schools extended the educational opportunities available for working-class children, providing for many a vital stepping stone to grammar schools and/or skilled occupations, and in this and other ways boards were able to use their local-ized control to exercise a certain amount of discretion in how they interpreted the requirements laid upon them.

The Balfour Act of 1902 replaced the 2,500 school boards by 318 local education authorities – a change that was fiercely contested by many of the boards. Even more strongly contested – by non-conformists – was the protection given to the voluntary (church) schools by making local education authorities responsible for maintaining them and paying their teachers, out of taxes paid, in part at least, by the non-conformists themselves.[62]

Elementary to primary

With elementary education established, the focus shifted to what followed – or for many children did not – and elementary education stagnated. After the 1902 Act pupils' opportunities for transition from elementary to secondary schooling de-pended on the availability of free places and scholarships, a situation that was incompatible with demand, let alone social justice. The move for 'secondary educa-tion for all' (the title of R. H. Tawney's 1922 policy document for the Labour Party) aimed to create 'a system of universal secondary education extending from the age of eleven to that of sixteen . . . Nothing less . . . will satisfy the demands of the workers of this country, nothing less is urged by the most eminent educationists; nothing less will enable the community to make the best use of its human re-sources'.[63] The Hadow Report of 1926 accepted the 'end-on' principle, proposing that compulsory education is divided into primary and secondary stages, with trans-fer at age eleven.[64] However, the system remained selective: 'modern schools' were to operate in parallel with the grammar schools, and the Board of Education, in accepting Hadow, also made it clear that it viewed the modern schools as element-ary in all but name.[65] 'The hereditary curse of English education' Tawney had complained, 'is its organization along lines of social class'. It was to be another generation before something along the lines of the American or continental com-mon secondary school became established in England.

The Board of Education Consultative Committee under Hadow then turned its attention to primary education. Its 1931 report was Janus-faced. Promisingly for the belated development of primary education as a distinct phase of education, it featured and endorsed some of the new educational thinking of the previous two decades, drawing on both the emerging disciplines of developmental psychology and Freudian psychoanalyis and a strand of progressivism which owed something to Dewey and his colleagues in the United States ('The curriculum is to be thought of in terms of activity and experience rather than knowledge to be acquired and facts to be stored')[66] as well as to European luminaries such as Rousseau, Pestalozzi, Herbart and Montessori. The New Education Fellowship was founded in 1920 to celebrate and give practical meaning to their ideas, and the 1920s and 1930s witnessed some radical educational experiments, not least in the independent sector, with the founding of schools such as Summerhill (1921), Dartington (1925), Frensham Heights (1925), Bryanston (1928), and Millfield (1935). Indeed, the climate of opinion was sufficiently sympathetic to 'the new education' for the Froebel Society to insist that Hadow's famous 'activity and experience' statement, which by the 1960s and the 1970s had become a progressive shibboleth, be presented in a subtly but significantly more extreme form than originally drafted: in the draft the formula was inclusive – 'activity and experience *and* knowledge to be acquired and facts to be stored'. In the final version the one excluded the other.[67]

Polarities of this kind, many of them unhelpful if not downright untenable conceptually, subsequently became embodied in what I have called 'primaryspeak' – the public language of progressive primary education during the 1960s, the 1970s and the 1980s: knowledge (as we have seen) versus experience, child centred versus subject-centred, formal versus informal, didactic versus exploratory, whole class teaching versus individualization, teaching (bizarrely) versus learning, and of course the ultimate standard around which the opposing troops were to rally, traditional versus progressive.[68]

To return to Hadow: the Froebelians' victory was illusory, for Hadow was also much influenced by committee member and notable psychologist Cyril Burt, who believed that the normal or bell curve defined exactly the distribution of human intelligence and advocated streaming from the ages of eight or nine to enable primary schools to provide the required foundation for selection for separate kinds of secondary schooling at eleven. Not coincidentally, for Tawney's 'hereditary curse' usually manifested itself, conveniently, in tripartite form to reflect the stratification of English society (middle/upper working/lower working perhaps, rather than upper/middle/lower), Hadow accepted Burt's argument that where school size allowed there should be three streams, A, B and C.[69]

The sense that new ways of thinking about primary education would be tolerated only if they left untouched the more fundamental elements of the old order recalled New Lanark. It also anticipated research findings of the 1970s, the 1980s and the 1990s that otherwise 'progressive' primary teachers who were wedded to a doctrine of individualization and the maximization of every child's potential held low expectations of the educational potential of inner-city children which were grounded in deeply ingrained and unexamined assumptions about social class.[70] Between Hadow and the late 1960s, when streaming began to be phased out in primary schools with the introduction of non-selective secondary education, the Burt view prevailed: intelligence was measurable and fixed, and school organization was expected to reflect this belief.

The Education Act 1944 finally buried elementary education (in name at least), required all local education authorities to provide secondary education, presaged the prolongation of compulsory schooling to fifteen and then sixteen, required private schools to be registered and inspected but otherwise left them untouched, and modified the arrangements for supporting voluntary schools. The curriculum was divided into 'religious' and 'secular' components: religious education and a daily act of (Christian) worship were made compulsory; the rest was for local education authorities to determine. The Act's requirement that secondary schooling should be provided according to pupils' 'ages, abilities and aptitudes' left open the question of how it should be organized. Although there were isolated early experiments in 'multilateral' or common secondary school organization in Anglesey (1953) and London (1954), governments of both major political parties, and local education authorities in the 1940s and the 1950s, broadly accepted that three kinds of ability/aptitude required three kinds of school – grammar, modern and technical, as foreshadowed in the 1943 White Paper – and that children should be selected for them on the basis of tests at the age of 11.

Primary education after 1944: the battle for hearts and minds

The development of English primary education after the Second World War had three clear phases. In the first, from 1945 to the late 1960s, what was in European terms a remarkable degree of curriculum freedom (compulsory religious education apart) was heavily constrained by two forces: history and the backwash of selection at eleven. Both ensured the dominance of the 3Rs, and a century of deeply ingrained elementary minimalism ensured that what was offered alongside literacy and numeracy sometimes amounted to not very much. Nevertheless, this was also a period of quickening curricular and pedagogical experimentation, fostered largely through a growing network of inspectors, LEA chief education officers and advisers, and college of education lecturers. As a result, innovation was concentrated in specific areas – the West Riding of Yorkshire (Alec Clegg and Arthur Stone), Oxfordshire (Robin Tanner and Edith Moorhouse), Leicestershire (Stewart Mason), Bristol (Marianne Parry), and London (Christian Schiller, John Blackie, Marion Richardson, Mollie Brearley) – rather than evenly spread.[71]

The Plowden Report of 1967[72] marked the culmination of the first phase of postwar development and the opening of the second. Though more conservative on curriculum matters than is often claimed, Plowden nevertheless endorsed and legitimated the progressive tide in which such figures played a prominent part. Its opening – 'At the heart of the educational process lies the child' – challenged the elementary legacy and heralded a shift in perspective which the report sustained throughout its detailed discussion of children's development, their home circumstances, their vulnerability to disadvantage and deprivation, and the culture and organization of schools and classrooms. No less important, the report received strong representations on the damaging consequences of streaming for children and their educational prospects,[73] and as a result reversed the recommendation of Hadow. Plowden's tone is immensely confident, and understandably so, for support for its

version of primary education extended across the educational and political spectrum
(the enquiry was commissioned by a Conservative minister, chaired by a Conservative
local councillor, and reported to a Labour minister):

> A school is not merely a teaching shop, it must transmit values and attitudes. It is a
> community in which children learn to live first and foremost as children and not as
> future adults . . . The school sets out . . . to devise the right environment for children,
> to allow them to be themselves and to develop in the way and at the pace appropriate
> to them. It tries to equalize opportunities and compensate for handicaps. It lays special
> stress on individual discovery, on first-hand experience and on opportunities for cre-
> ative work. It insists that knowledge does not fall into neatly separate compartments
> and that work and play are not opposite but complementary.[74]

Most of the elements in 'Plowdenism' are captured in this extract: child-centredness,
school as a micro-community, individualization, learning by discovery and experience, the preference for a seamless, integrated curriculum over traditional subjects,
creativity, the learning potential of play; but also the dogmatic tone – 'this is how
things are and how they should be' which delighted many at the time but also
opened the doors to the same hardening of ideas into orthodoxy which we noted
earlier in relation to the American progressive movement of the first half of the
twentieth century.

The pedigree of the progressivism of mid twentieth century English primary schools
was highly eclectic. We can readily trace a continental European line from Rousseau,
Pestalozzi and Froebel to Montessori. In curriculum matters we find Dewey. Piaget
is adduced to legitimate the strong emphasis on the ages and stages of children's
development. But there are also four uniquely English components. First, the separ-
atism of the infant school tradition running from Owen and Wilderspin to Susan
Isaacs and Dorothy Gardner. Second, the romantics' rejection of the Enlightenment
elevation of reason above feeling. Third, the arts and crafts movement, especially
and appropriately as reflected in the rural Oxfordshire variant of progressive
primary education for which Robin Tanner provided both inspiration and focus.
Finally – and most important of all in relation to how progressivism came to be
construed politically from the 1970s onwards – the English tradition of radical dissent going back through Fabianism and Morris to Blake and the non-conformists,
an intellectual line which stood in opposition to the establishment might of church,
class, wealth, power and patronage.[75]

The backlash was not long in coming. The economic confidence of the 1960s
gave way to the recessions of the 1970s. The Right sought a scapegoat, and found
it in their persistent caricature of anarchic primary schools neglecting to teach
the basics of literacy, numeracy, conformity and deference. Displaying their own
numeracy problems they even managed to blame the 'permissiveness' surrounding
the 1967 Plowden Report for the 1968 student disturbances which affected English
as well as French and American universities.[76] Researchers began to unpick both the
philosophical shakiness of progressive thinking and the operational problems of
progressive practice. Researchers and inspectors also discovered that claims, or fears,
of a Plowden takeover were wide of the mark.

Meanwhile, the political right and its press were more than happy to present single cases such as the 1975 William Tyndale affair[77] as symptomatic of a disease infecting the entire system. When in the Leeds study, undertaken a decade later, we reported in detail on the classroom practice of a sub-sample of teachers in ten out of England's 20,000 primary schools, one national newspaper generalized wildly to claim that 'The education of millions of primary school children has been blighted in the name of an anarchic ideology'.[78] Plowden itself had found barely 10 per cent of schools which conformed to its vision, and studies a decade later found that while the language of primary education may have changed out of all recognition, the practice had changed rather less. As the 1992 'three wise men' report summarized matters:

> The commonly held belief that primary schools, after 1967, were swept by a tide of progressivism is untrue. HMI in 1978, for example, reported that only 5 per cent of classrooms exhibited wholeheartedly 'exploratory' characteristics and that didactic teaching was still practised in three-quarters of them. The reality, then, was more complex. The ideas and practices connoted by words such as 'progressive' and 'informal' had a profound impact in certain schools and LEAs. Elsewhere they were either ignored or . . . adopted as so much rhetoric to sustain practice which in visual terms might look attractive but which lacked any serious educational rationale. Here they lost their early intellectual excitement and became little more than a passport to professional approval and advancement. The real problem was not so much radical transformation as mediocrity.[79]

The link between rhetoric and professional patronage came through strongly in the 1986–91 study of primary education in Leeds, England's third largest city. It was uniquely a primary (rather than secondary) problem: the 1944 Act had passed the power to determine the 'secular' curriculum to LEAs; the progressive movement operated as a network of gurus who inspired unquestioning discipleship, and would-be gurus who insisted on it. Primary teachers, as an historically underpowered and dependent profession, were vulnerable to pressure from all of them.[80]

Government control regained

As in the immediate postwar period, English primary education during the final decades of the twentieth century was framed by legislation. The Labour government of the mid 1970s initiated the process of centralization, the Conservative governments of 1979–97 established its legislative framework, and their New Labour successors plugged most of the remaining loopholes of school and teacher autonomy. A long succession of government discussion papers and consultation documents, occasionally leavened by a more considered offering from the national inspectorate, paved the way for the introduction of the national curriculum. The 1988 Education Reform Act laid down requirements for curriculum and assessment at ages 7, 11, 14 and 16, and, in parallel, for arrangements for governance and finance which greatly reduced the power of local education authorities. Control of curriculum passed to agencies directly accountable to, and appointed by, central government: first, in tandem, the National Curriculum Council and School Examinations and Assessment

Council, then the combined School Curriculum and Assessment Authority, and finally, in 1997, the Qualifications and Curriculum Authority (QCA).

With curriculum under firm control, the government strengthened its leverage first through teacher training, then through inspection. From 1984 the government required all pre-service programmes of teacher training to be accredited by a newly established Council for the Accreditation of Teacher Education (CATE) in accordance with statutory criteria. CATE was also an advisory body, and when it began to offer advice the government did not wish to hear it was replaced in 1994 by the Teacher Training Agency (TTA), which was both more powerful than CATE and more directly under ministerial control. The broad accreditation criteria progressively refined from 1984 to 1993 were now translated into a full-fledged national curriculum for teacher training, and absolute compliance with this was enforced by giving TTA control of the allocation of funds and trainee places, and subsequently funding for in-service training as well.

The education system had been subject to inspection since 1839 by Her/His Majesty's Inspectorate (HMI). During the 1970s and the 1980s, HMI had increasingly supplemented its individual school and teacher training inspections with national surveys and monitoring and annual reports on the state of the education system as a whole. Though it operated in standard civil service style and tacitly endorsed the policies of the government of the day, HMI would from time to time deliver explicit or coded messages that were more critical, especially on resource issues. In 1992, as part of the centralizing drift allied to the rhetoric of marketization, and possibly because HMI were not as malleable as government wished, they were summarily abolished and replaced by an Office for Standards in Education (OFSTED) which began work in 1993. A rump of HMI were retained for survey work and the head of OFSTED was given the title of Her Majesty's Chief Inspector of Schools (HMCI), which erroneously implied continuity of ethics and procedure from the HMI system. OFSTED was established as a non-ministerial government department whose remit was tied closely to the implementation and validation of government policy. England thus lost its independent inspectorate. The powers of OFSTED were considerably greater than those of HMI and under its second HMCI it wielded these with increasing ruthlessness, taking full advantage of open reporting and prime ministerial patronage to name those institutions, and indeed those individuals, of whom it – or rather HMCI personally – approved or disapproved. Growing disquiet about the actions of OFSTED and the pronouncements of its head prompted the House of Commons Education and Employment Committee to launch an enquiry into OFSTED in 1998. This reported in 1999, and its carefully modulated language does not disguise the committee's concern about the direction taken by the new inspectorate. In particular, the report proposed reining in the chief inspector, requiring him/her to speak from evidence rather than opinion or prejudice, and arguing for more genuine parliamentary accountability in respect of the appointment of the chief inspector and OFSTED generally.[81]

Pedagogy was the ultimate prize for any government wishing to secure a level of control of the educational process as close to absolute as – given the stubbornness of the human spirit and the wayward chemistry of classrooms – is feasible. In 1991, exploiting the furore surrounding the Leeds report, the Conservative government commissioned the so-called 'three wise men' report on teaching at the upper end of the primary phase.[82] For all its strictures on poorly conceived and ill-executed practice, the report came down firmly on the side of professional judgement where pedagogical decisions are concerned, reminding teachers – and the government – of Secretary of State Kenneth Clarke's assurance that 'questions about how to teach are not for Government to determine', and arguing a research-based case for 'fitness for purpose' as the principle which should guide teachers' application of general pedagogical principles to the solution of specific classroom challenges.

The Conservatives honoured Clarke's assurance. New Labour did not feel obliged to do so. Its 1997 election platform included the pledge to raise the tested performance of 11 year olds in literacy and numeracy to specific levels by 2002. To ensure delivery on this pledge and to avoid the electoral consequences of failing to meet the literacy and numeracy targets, New Labour was willing to risk relying neither on the last remaining vestiges of teacher autonomy nor on 'fitness for purpose'. A single national lesson formula – the 'literacy hour' – was prescribed for all literacy teaching for 5–11 year olds from September 1998, and a similar 'numeracy hour' was introduced in September 1999.[83] At the same time, the government reduced the requirements of the primary national curriculum in all subjects except English and mathematics in the belief that this would make delivery on the 1997 pledge as near certain as was possible.

At the end of the century, then, English primary education was firmly established as a distinct educational phase whose potential impact on Britain's educational and economic performance – not to mention the fortunes of the majority political party – demanded the closest possible control by government and surveillance by its agencies. It was not so much the *standing* of primary education that had improved as its perceived strategic significance. Had it been otherwise, the debate about 'standards' would have focused on the quality of primary education overall, rather than – as actually happened – merely on pupils' test performance in literacy and numeracy. And had it been otherwise, government would have been less ready to ride roughshod over professional opinion.

What, then, was the outcome of a transfer of educational control which was more rapid and decisive than in any other of our five countries, or indeed than in many other countries worldwide? And how could it have happened?

The second question is easier to answer than the first. The English social infrastructure has little constitutional protection – it is protected by law, but laws change – and Britain's first-past-the-post voting system rarely produces a situation in which coalitions are needed to achieve a viable government or in which daily deals and compromises are thereafter necessary to keep it in office. That combination makes possible radical overnight changes in policy, regardless of popular or parliamentary feeling, as Margaret Thatcher most convincingly demonstrated in her successful campaigns to privatize the energy, telecommunications and transport industries, to part-privatize health and 'marketize' education. In the latter case, the 1987 consultation exercise on the proposed introduction of a national curriculum, local school financial management, higher education, education in London and related matters, all of them of considerable and far-reaching significance, yielded over 20,000 written responses, many of them unequivocally hostile. The government took little note of these, nor of the 16,500 hostile responses to the consultation on the subsequent Education Reform Bill,[84] nor of the massive campaign in which minority opposition parties, teachers, parents, churches and local education authorities united in solid opposition to a number of the bill's most important measures. Thatcher's impregnable majority ensured that the Act passed into law with relatively little difficulty.

Naturally, Labour's education spokesman Jack Straw (later the New Labour Home Secretary) also inveighed against the bill: 'Under the disguise of fine phrases like "parental choice" and "decentralization" the Bill will deny choice and instead centralize power and control over schools, colleges and universities in the hands of the secretary of state in a manner without parallel in the western world'. However, his party was quick to learn the lessons of this episode, and once in power took the process of centralization far further than the Conservatives had ever contemplated.[85]

Thus, when we consider Margaret Archer's 1979 use of England as an archetype of educational decentralization,[86] not only does it read somewhat curiously in the light of what followed, but we must wonder whether the balance of power before the 1988 legislation was as clear as it seemed.

Where primary education is concerned, for instance, Archer's theory that decentralization generates professional engagement is true to only a limited extent. For one thing, it ignores what Thatcher's government clearly recognized (and resented), the considerable power wielded by local education authorities. In the United States, such local power is a constitutionally embedded – and indeed constitutionally celebrated – check on the powers of state and federal government; in England it was merely an obstacle to be removed. Moreover, the same historical processes which placed a reluctant England last in the queue to universalize basic education also produced a primary teaching force whose education, training, social class background and gender combined to create a professional culture of subservience and dependence.

The Leeds study clearly showed the first of these conditions – LEA power – interacting with the residue of the second – teacher dependence – in a way which counteracts the Archer thesis that change in decentralized systems is in the nature of things incremental. In fact, at the level of educational *practice*, the history of change in English primary education has been closer to the stop–go scenario that is the characteristic of centralized systems. On the other hand, at the level of *policy*, comparison of, say, curriculum change before and after 1988 vindicates the Archer thesis, for up to 1988 change was indeed gradual – indeed painfully slow – while after the 1988 Act the school curriculum, especially at the primary stage where there was little of the countervailing influence of professional subject interest groups, became a wildly swinging pendulum. The swings reflected not just shifts in policy from one administration to the next, but also mid-administration trimming as ill thought-through policies constructed with an eye to securing electoral advantage revealed their weakness in operation and were hastily modified, re-packaged or even abandoned, leaving teachers and others to pick up the pieces. Each stage in the halting and increasingly violent progress of the educational stop–go cycle was heralded as a 'tough new initiative designed to raise standards'.

This suggests that we need to look at the pathology of educational control at two levels – policy and practice – and where change in the latter is concerned come to a clearer understanding of local forces for change and stasis and of the way the professional culture of teachers acts on both. Where the primary teaching force is concerned political power has always been a major determinant of professional thought and action, and whether it emanated from local or national sources was less important than the fact that it existed and had to be responded to.

Perhaps the critical difference, then, has been one of outcome. In a regime of LEA patronage and preferment, such as conditioned many teachers' responses to the progressive 'revolution' of the 1960s, the 1970s and the early 1980s, the impact of external power was on the individual: a teacher conformed, succeeded and got on, or he/she did not, but others in the same school might respond differently and thereby have totally different career paths. Where control moves up from local to national level, it is the career of the school (and even the LEA) rather than the individual teacher which is at stake: if the pupils of teacher X underperform in the Key Stage 2 tests, or if two of a school's eight teachers underperform in front of the OFSTED inspectors, it is the school which drops down the league table and is pilloried in the local press. The ideology of individualism that was central to 1960s–70s primary progressivism was nicely mirrored by an emphasis on individual professional accountability. By 2000, there was a similar correspondence between the ideology of whole class teaching and unitary national models of curriculum and pedagogy and the emphasis on corporate accountability.

'Corporate accountability' is a much-sanitized version of the reality of public exposure which centralization generated. It is no coincidence that the central post-war myth of English primary education – that it was subverted by extreme forms of progressivism allied to left-wing ideology, both of them the outcome of an 'educational establishment' conspiracy of academics and LEA advisers – followed a similar trajectory from the mid 1970s onwards to that of the process of increasing government control. Political objectives and news values coincided. Government interest prompted media coverage; media coverage prompted government interest. Policy changes are best justified in terms of a deficit pathology; a deficit pathology was what the press were happy to provide; and so on.

The tale of press and government collusion in the fostering and maintenance of this myth, in the defaming of leading educationists, and in the sustained discrediting of primary teachers, teacher trainers, academics and LEA officers, is instructive but hardly edifying. We are too close to events to tell it here.[87] The closest equivalent from another culture would be the anti-communist witch-hunts of 1940s and 1950s America; by the 1990s England even acquired, in the form of the chief inspector of schools, its own Joseph McCarthy.

Elementary and Primary: Conflicting Legacies, Confused Identities

So much for the control of England's system of primary education: what, at the turn of the millennium, of its character?

History invariably leaves its mark. Combining hubris and ignorance in equal measure the educational modernizers of the 1960s, the 1980s and the 1990s presumed that their reforms would eradicate all traces of what had preceded them. But three things are abundantly clear: in English primary education as currently constituted each of the different stages of its development remains clearly discernible; this process of historical hybridization has created significant and remarkably persistent tensions and anomalies; and the first step to achieving genuinely radical reform is to recognize this.

Alan Blyth, as we noted earlier, identifies three formative traditions in English primary education: *elementary, preparatory* and *developmental*. 'Elementary' is all about minimalism: a limited education, at modest expense, for those who can afford nothing else. 'Preparatory' reorients this as a first stage of two or more, and offers the prospect of a ladder of expanding opportunity. 'Developmental' connotes a philosophical alternative to elementary, centred on assumptions about children as children, their nature and their needs.

To these three I have added *progressive, behavioural/mechanistic, classical humanist,* and two variants of the twentieth-century concern that primary education should address societal needs and circumstances: *adaptive/utilitarian* and *reformist/ egalitarian*.[88] I separated 'progressive' from 'developmental' to distinguish the philosophical and psychological strands in the rather loose array of ideas we conventionally and rather too conveniently throw together as 'progressive': the ideas of, say, Dewey and Piaget are very different, and need to be respected and studied as such. 'Behavioural/mechanistic' marked a recurrent strand in official attempts to call teachers and schools more closely to account which first emerged in its most primitive form as 'payment by results' in the 1860s; then returned, refined by psychometry, as the behavioural objectives and testing movements imported from post-Sputnik America during the 1960s; it was kitted out afresh in the 1980s and the 1990s as the amalgam of national curriculum assessment and OFSTED inspection, both of which leaned heavily on quantitative accounting paradigms. 'Classical/humanist' is the Arnoldian strand, which reminds us to temper a narrowly drawn view of 'the basics' with a more generous concept of liberal education, though by the 1980s some saw it as class-bound, nostalgic and unresponsive to cultural pluralism. My two variants of societal imperatives are also recurrent. They represent the perennial conflict between those who believe that education should prepare children to take their place in a society whose social and economic order is fixed and preordained, and those who see this order as open to challenge, not least through education; between those who define society by its economic needs alone, and those who place the economy in a wider frame of culture and values which also demand analysis and an educational response.

The point I wish to make is that 'elementary' stands apart from all the others. We have seen how progressive thinking comes and goes and how at different times education shifts from an adaptive/utilitarian to an egalitarian emphasis, then back again. We have witnessed the different manifestations of the mechanistic outlook. We have heard the debates about high culture, mass culture and cultural relativism. In the light of these we might even wish to suggest that at the time of writing the values informing official prescriptions for primary education are utilitarian, mechanistic, populist and philistine. And we can anticipate, or hope, that at some future date different values will prevail. But what makes the elementary strand different from all these, and therefore more permanent and pervasive, is that it has *structural* as well as ethical and procedural reality. English primary education in 2000 is nineteenth-century elementary education modified – much modified, admittedly – rather than transformed. Elementary education is its centre of gravity. Elementary education provides its central point of reference. Elementary education is the form to which it most readily tends to regress.

The structural continuities from elementary education are six: funding, ages and stages, teaching roles, the curriculum as a whole, the prevailing concept of curricular 'basics', and the religious component. I comment briefly on each of these in turn.

First, primary schools may be much more generously funded than were their elementary forbears, but they remain funded at substantially lower levels than secondary, thus making it virtually impossible to entertain alternative modes of teaching to the class teacher system operating on the basis of 100 per cent contact time. Although New Labour began substantially to erode the related primary–secondary differentials of larger class sizes and more limited pay prospects, it left the balance of funding between the two sectors to LEAs, despite the recommendations of Hadow in 1931, Plowden in 1967, Commons Select Committee reports in 1986 and 1994 and the 1992 'three wise men' report.[89]

Second, Hadow's 'break at age eleven' tidied up the earlier arrangements. The post-1988 'key stages' (ages 5–7 and 7–11) rationalized the old infant/junior division that in turn stemmed from that between infant and elementary. Overarching both is an assumption that primary education is a distinct and coherent phase, requiring the same educational strategies regardless of whether the child is four or 11 years old. The blanket application of the literacy and numeracy hours in 1998 and 1999 showed the persistence of this monolithic thinking.

Third, the dominant teaching role in primary schools, as in elementary, remains that of the class teacher – one person teaching the whole curriculum to a large class for a full year and sometimes more. Although the limitations of the class teacher system in respect of a modern curriculum have been under discussion since the Plowden report, funding arrangements prevent the introduction of alternatives and, no less significantly, the system inspires deep loyalty regardless of its limitations because out of it grows the essence of the distinctive professional identity of primary teachers. For that reason as much as because of the funding restrictions, the options of specialist and semi-specialist teaching are rarely entertained, and the compromise of specialist curriculum co-ordinators or subject leaders has limited impact.[90]

Fourth, the primary curriculum, like the elementary curriculum, remains sharply divided into two components: the 'basics' and the rest, or what in 1984 I called 'Curriculum I' and 'Curriculum II'. The division is fundamental: it is one of time allocations, priority, seriousness of purpose and quality. Curriculum I is safeguarded, Curriculum II is vulnerable. Even the progressives' celebration of creativity and the humanities in the 1960s and 1970s did little to disturb this. In 1988 Curriculum I was augmented by science, but the notion of 'core' and 'non-core' subjects in the national curriculum is merely an updating of elementary Curriculum I/II thinking, and by 1997 there were signs that science – arguably a crucial component of a modern basic curriculum – was once more vulnerable as New Labour's literacy and numeracy strategies reverted to the old divide and gave its policy the creakingly unoriginal spin of 'back to basics'.[91]

Fifth, and relatedly, the notion of 'basics' as reading, writing and arithmetic remains unchanged. The primacy of literacy is self-evident, but it is significant that the position of spoken language within a concept of language basics remains far from secure. (The French national curriculum places 'speaking' at the very top of its list, and we shall see in later chapters just how important for children's learning this emphasis is.) And, as I noted earlier, the elementary school assumption that literacy and numeracy are equally important and should have equal weight and equal teaching time remains impervious to argument to the contrary.

Finally, there is the moral core of elementary education. Christian religious education – if not, any longer, instruction – remains predominant, notwithstanding the countervailing circumstances of secularism, humanism and cultural and religious pluralism.

Each of these reinforces the others. The funding arrangements make alternatives to the class teacher system impossible to implement, even when teachers wish to introduce such alternatives. This system, by taxing teachers' subject expertise and planning ingenuity to the utmost, creates problems of curriculum manageability. The problem of curriculum manageability is resolved by reducing the curriculum rather than tackling the staffing and funding issues that cause it. As I noted in respect of the government's January 1998 decision to cut back the primary curriculum to enable teachers to deliver on its election pledges in respect of literacy and numeracy:

> There are two ways to read (this) decision. One, upbeat and optimistic, is to see the new 'flexibility', and the strong hints of a slimmer curriculum to be introduced from 2000, as a sensible and realistic response to the situation which schools face. By this analysis we have at last a government which listens to what teachers say. The alternative reading, however, is that the curriculum has been used as the safety-valve, as a way of side-stepping once again the historical problems of primary school funding and staffing and of defusing the professional anxiety and resentment which this legacy has created. On this basis, children have been denied their right to the kind of education which ought to be the hallmark of a civilized society, and educational entitlement has been sacrificed on the altar of political expediency. The doctrine of 'cheap but efficient', one century on, has resolved the growing mismatch between educational task and professional resources by trimming the education rather than increasing the resources.[92]

Thus, the contemporary structure of primary education reflects the dominant values of the system's formative phase, over a century ago; and both contemporary structure and inherited values condition and constrain contemporary educational discourse. It is in this sense that I would argue that the elementary legacy reaches far deeper than those of progressivism, classical humanism and so on; that it is the fixed point around which other values revolve, and – to consolidate the metaphor – the source of the gravitational pull to which all such values in the end remain subject.

This cannot be the entire story, for had there been a fundamental value-shift outside the education system, the inherited nexus of structure and values would surely have weakened to the point where they became vulnerable to seismic movement. We need to consider the extent to which elementary school structures and assumptions remained the core of English primary education because they spoke to more pervasive social values.

Here we confront the possibility of a paradox: deeply rooted values in a country which in other respects shows every sign of being in a value-vacuum. There are those who claim that the problem for England is that by the 1980s it had all but lost those collective values which made for social cohesion in earlier decades and centuries. Melanie Phillips is one such who argues that common morality and shared identity have been routed by individualism and moral relativism.[93] Linda Colley shows how British (as opposed to English) identity is a relatively recent invention, forged from war and religion during 1707–1837. She suggests that the late twentieth-century crisis of national identity (in which, as Castells shows, Britain is far from unique[94]) has occurred because

> ...the factors that provided for the forging of the British nation in the past have largely ceased to operate ... Protestantism, that once vital cement, has now a limited influence on British culture, as indeed does Christianity itself. Recurrent wars with the states of Continental Europe have in all likelihood come to an end ... And, crucially, both commercial supremacy and imperial hegemony have gone.[95]

In this chapter we have seen the impact of Protestantism on the development of public education, both as a protracted conflict between established church and the nonconformists, and in the consolidation of Anglican hegemony in elementary and primary education through to the legislation of 1944, 1988, 1996 and no doubt beyond. It is also clear that governments have little stomach for tackling this anomaly for as long as church and state remain constitutionally intertwined. Yet – and this is a matter of history rather than belief – the religious requirement in the curriculum of state schools, or at least the particular form that it takes, *is* an anomaly in the kind of society which England has become, and it nicely exemplifies Ringen's assertion that 'Britain is a thoroughly modern society with thoroughly archaic institutions'.[96]

We also saw how, compared with three of our other four countries, including those – Russia and India – which have experienced cultural upheavals far more traumatic than anything experienced by Britain, the values purportedly under-pinning state education in England are confused, contradictory or at best anodyne; that is, if we go by legal and official statements (we shall test later the extent to which such confusion and contradiction penetrate down to the levels of the school and classroom). Muddled values, presumably, portend uncertain identity.

Primordial Values

To return to the paradox, if it can be shown that England at the turn of the millennium faces a crisis of collective values and national identity (which, put that way sounds uncomfortably glib, anyway), how *does* one make sense of the largely unquestioned persistence of the elementary school core of primary education? To answer that, we must avoid being seduced by postmodernist visions of universal flux and consider what else in the social fabric of England has *not* changed.

Smelser suggests that this is precisely the point: the British condition was a combination of change and paralysis, alternately nudged forward and held back by the 'special pattern of primordialism in British society'. Its three fundamental dimensions were social class, religion and region.[97] This chapter's account has highlighted the first two of these. The third has been less obvious here, but can readily be pointed up: the industrial revolution, the growth of anti-Anglican dissent and the rise of the working-class movement were all located away from the nation's capital, in the Midlands and North. Antagonism between London and the rest of the country has always been strong, and this remains the case, though the boundaries of metropolitan wealth and power now need to be drawn more widely to include the whole of south-east England. It is a mark of the persistence of this aspect of Smelser's 'special pattern of primordialism' that in the year 2000 Prime Minister Blair felt the need to leave his London fastness and announce that the North–South divide no longer existed. His claim was treated with derision by all but his most loyal supporters.

Our account of the role of the Church of England in all this seems to sustain another part of Smelser's thesis. English and continental European Protestantism have had a very different impact on education. In Central Europe, Scandinavia and the Low Countries the Protestant churches often headed the drive for literacy and educational reform. But in Britain, the Anglican Church was also the political establishment. It exchanged the Pope in Rome for the monarch in London. It stood 'midway between the authoritarianism of Catholicism and the anti-authoritarianism of radical Protestantism'.[98] It thereby opened the door to further anti-authoritarian dissent, to schism and to a situation in which

> ... the development of British primary education was shaped, and probably inhibited, because religion and the state had not extricated themselves from each other structurally, and were in conflict over this matter throughout the [nineteenth] century.[99]

However, as its congregations dwindled, so the Church of England struggled with its own problems of identity. By the 1980s it was less a pillar than an irritant to the political establishment. Archbishops and bishops openly criticized Thatcher's Falklands War triumphalism and the damage caused to Britain's social fabric by her policies. They upbraided both main political parties for their disdain for the problems of the poor, the old, the unemployed and the homeless. They attacked government for failing to take radical steps to combat environmental degradation and global warming. They urged New Labour to write off third world debt. They pursued an independent line on a wide range of policies ranging from transport to health – and education. And they refused to join the lemming-like rush to portray the communications revolution as an unmitigated good.

Of the three of Smelser's dimensions which in 2000 continue to bear on public education that leaves class. The claims of Prime Ministers Thatcher, Major and Blair

– and for that matter Prince Edward (his very existence proves him wrong) – that millennial Britain is classless can be dismissed as political ploys, alongside their calculated appeals to 'middle England' and 'the people'. Study and everyday experience both suggest otherwise. The analysis of Adonis and Pollard is particularly pertinent in our context because it traces the link between class and education, showing the still striking correspondence between the hierarchies of education, occupation, wealth and power, especially in politics, the law, the military and the civil service. Adonis and Pollard also show how the divide between state and private schools was at the turn of the millennium stronger than at any time since 1945, and how this included the primary phase as well as the more familiar contrast of comprehensive and public schools.

Cannadine, too, tracks the linked hierarchies of education and nation, and strikingly (if rather speculatively) points up the pervasiveness of a triadic vision of society – upper, middle and lower class, Arnold's 'barbarians', 'philistines' and 'populace', the 1944 Butler Act's tripartite secondary system of grammar, technical and modern – and the way each maps on to the other. (I noted earlier, however, that this does not work quite as well as it should, since the upper classes sent their offspring to private rather than state schools). Earlier in this chapter we noted how the primary school streaming system of the 1940s and 1950s prepared the ground for secondary school tripartism, and can now remind ourselves of the way during the postwar decades the coincidence of class, perceived ability and educational destination became a recurrent theme in social research.[100] However, Cannadine's argument is more subtle than this: he traces not one but three fundamental ways in which British society has divided itself and has been seen by its members to be divided:

> The first was hierarchical, which described society individualistically as an interlinked, finely layered and elaborately graded procession; the second was triadic, which divided it into three collective constituencies, usually upper, middle and lower; and the third was the dichotomous, which saw society as polarized between the two extremes of 'patricians and plebs' or 'them and us'. Across the centuries, these three models have been astonishly resonant and appealing, not only at a popular level, but also among intellectuals and commentators.[101]

He follows the rise and fall of each version of social stratification and shows how they continue to suffuse contemporary institutions, consciousness and social relations to a powerful degree.

Primary education – and this is the nub of my explanation for the persistence of the elementary ethic – emerges from the bottom level of all three versions of class. The fight for public education in the nineteenth century was a fight for – and against – the education and enfranchisement of working people. The parish and elementary schools were on the lowest rung of an educational hierarchy which was headed by the universities of Oxford and Cambridge, and even educational reformers such as Kay-Shuttleworth were in no doubt about the clientele of the forms of schooling for which they campaigned: 'For each class of society there is an appropriate education' he said, and elementary schools were definitely for 'the people' rather than 'the upper classes' or 'the middle classes'.[102] The education that mattered, for the people that mattered, took place elsewhere.

Primary teachers were trained, when eventually proper training became widespread, in institutions (normal colleges, training colleges and finally colleges of education) which were well outside the university sector and from which the universities kept their distance, none more so, again, than Oxford and Cambridge. Primary teaching until the 1960s was almost exclusively a non-graduate profession. It was also – and remains – a predominantly female profession. The feminization of primary teaching has undoubtedly contributed to its historically low status, but in the larger matter of the place of primary education in the educational hierarchy it probably cannot be regarded as more than a contributory factor.

In the schools themselves, though primary education eventually became much more socially representative, and many parents in the second half of the twentieth century were happy for their children to attend primary schools before transferring them to private secondary education, stratification revealed itself in ways which were less obvious but no less powerful in their impact. Sharpe and Green showed how teachers' judgements on the needs and abilities of children in inner city primary schools were conditioned by their assumptions about social class, and they simply expected less of working class than middle class children.[103] King demonstrated the process by which infant teachers built up 'typifications' of their pupils in which class was a key factor in defining children's ability and behaviour, and everyday discourse was shot through with unexamined assumptions about 'nice' children from 'good' homes.[104] These tendencies emerged, too, from the Leeds study where teachers held lower expectations of 'disadvantaged' inner city children than of others, yet also tended to avoid discussion of high ability on the grounds that somehow it was socially elitist.[105] More generally, a 'cultural deficit' view of certain social groups is a pervasive theme in postwar educational research. By the 1990s it had surfaced as a political issue, rather than one confined to academic journals, and the chief inspector of schools had alerted the government to the seriousness of the problem of underperformance among white working class boys.[106]

To return to the question of why English primary education's core of elementary structures and values remains as resistant to change as it does, I am suggesting that there are many factors at work. Social structure shapes educational structure. Structures shape consciousness, and consciousness does not care to be unsettled. Societal and educational values are not independent but exist on a continuum. Assumptions about *what* primary education is for shade into assumptions about *who* it is for. All such assumptions are conditioned by individual and collective experience, and schooling is one experience we all share so the past continues to assert its hold. Professional identities must be defended and thus are to a degree inherently anachronistic. Change costs money and is therefore resisted on pragmatic grounds. Above all, in certain fundamentals English society has changed rather less in the past century than people believe, assert or admit.

The obvious objection to this line of reasoning is that, whatever its origins, primary education by the late twentieth century had become thoroughly colonized by the aspiring middle classes of suburbia and the commuter villages, and the established middle classes of the fashionable metropolitan enclaves. Outside the minorities of inherited status and acquired or inherited wealth, primary schools had become broadly representative in their pupil intake of the population as a whole.

This is true. But the geography of middle-class colonization is *not* representative. Primary schools are neighbourhood schools, and neighbourhoods segregate along the boundaries of class. For the middle class that matters, what goes on in primary schools in inner cities and overspill council estates is neither here nor there, for these are working-class schools, and those with money to do so buy themselves into very different communities. In an affluent middle-class neighbourhood the school can become, *de facto*, a preparatory school, and its values and aspirations can match its clientele. But in those areas which being mixed are demographically closer to the national picture, matters may be more problematic: crucially so when an affluent and vocal middle-class enclave abuts a working-class ghetto, as in many parts of London where those who are, or wish to be, close to the centres of national power and influence tend to settle.

It is here that the tensions between pauper educational structure and middle-class values and requirements, or between elementary and primary, are most evident, and it is here that the most strident complaints about 'standards' are heard. Speaking directly to the anxieties and prejudices of parents in this group (which includes many of their own number) press and politicians will happily blame the professionals – teachers, teacher trainers, LEAs – for the schools' perceived inadequacies and for problems of standards, carefully massaging that tired old myth of a 'progressive takeover'. For their part the teaching unions accuse the government of not resourcing the schools and of not paying teachers at the levels needed, or of requiring them to teach an unmanageable curriculum.

Each group correctly perceives that the quality of teaching is a vital factor in the quality of learning and that resources may, positively or adversely, affect both. Some will also understand that the resources of teacher time and expertise are no less significant than salary levels. Neither government nor teachers go further and consider the extent to which the inherited structure makes primary schools *inherently* vulnerable to the damaging consequences of insufficient time and inadequate expertise. Government cannot because to modernize the structure would be inordinately expensive;[107] teachers will not because the structure is what gives them their identity.[108] It is much easier for government, its agencies and apologists to conjure up a progressive conspiracy and for teachers to indict an overloaded curriculum. And the government that accepts both explanations, as New Labour did in 1997–8 (when it allowed its chief schools inspector to peddle anti-progressive mischief while blaming its Conservative predecessors for the curriculum) appeases both middle England and the teaching profession. At some point, however, middle-class opinion may become dissatisfied with this level of political opportunism and start probing deeper. It may also become less than happy that the price their children pay for reasonable though not exceptional standards in literacy and numeracy is an impoverished and unbalanced curriculum. That will be the point at which government might with profit address the growing misalignment of structure and task in primary education, if not the doggedly persisting chasm between elementary and primary.

7

Primary Education and the State

Primary Education as a Formal System

I opened Chapter 2 by posing four basic questions. What is the essential character of our five national systems of primary education? What were their origins and how did they develop? What are their main similarities and differences? How can these be explained? From the first two questions we spun each chapter's two main threads: contemporary and historical. The other questions frame what follows.

Let us consider first our five patterns of primary education as *formal systems*, that is to say as structures which governments devise (or more commonly inherit and modify) for planning and delivering education to young children, that are administratively mediated and policy referenced, and which derive their legitimacy from being sanctioned by legislation and paid for from public funds. Despite the national differences in geography, population, economy, culture and language there are commonalities as well as contrasts, some of them of a kind to merely to be noted, others worth registering as significant.

In all five countries basic education is free and compulsory, although in one, India, the shortfall in pupil enrolment and retention remains a severe challenge, especially in rural areas, in urban slums and among girls and members of scheduled castes and tribes. The span of compulsory education in the five countries varies, starting at ages 5, 6 or 7 and ending at ages 14, 15 or 16. Non-statutory pre-school provision is available in all five countries: very uneven in India, comprehensive in France, Russia and the United States. England's belated attempt to universalize at least the opportunity for pre-school education is perhaps offset by the fact that here the starting age for compulsory schooling is one or even two years earlier than in many other countries. Primary education takes place in designated primary schools in four of the countries, but in Russia (its more remote rural areas apart) 'primary' denotes a phase rather than an institution, and one which is shorter than elsewhere.

Infrastructure is a useful comparative indicator of investment. At one extreme is the United States, at the other India, with Russia confronting growing infrastructural problems as a consequence of the 1990s economic collapse. However, in the United

States decentralization and a high level of dependence on the vagaries of state and local taxation make for considerable inequalities in provision at this level. In contrast, perhaps the most consistent system in respect of infrastructure is France, not just because of its high level of educational expenditure relative to GDP, but because in France consistency of provision is the explicit concomitant of that *égalité* which is the bedrock principle of the entire system, and which is secured and maintained by central control.

Goals, Curriculum and Assessment

Making due allowance for the merely rhetorical function of stated educational goals, we find nevertheless some striking differences in the educational missions that these five states set for themselves. France balances citizenship, knowledge, general culture and work-related qualifications. Russia exorcises the memory of not one but two absolutist regimes and stresses human values, human rights, humanistic education, freedom, pluralism and democracy; but it also taps the deeper and more permanent Slavic appeal of family, soil and motherland. India asserts, alongside personal development and fulfilment, the national imperatives of secularism, democracy, equality and social cohesion for which its constitution firmly stands. The United States, which by virtue of a rather different constitution is denied a national educational system, has used that constitution instead to shape not the content of education but its conduct and organization at community level; on to this it has latterly grafted a set of goals which respond to the perceived crises of national anomie and international competition. Finally, in the matter of formulating educational goals at least, England has twice taken the wooden spoon: first, when in the 1988 and 1996 Education Acts it propounded a meagre brace of goals which were even more meaningless as touchstones for practice than they read; then, in 1999, when in the context of national curriculum review it over-compensated and threw down a statement so comprehensive – a veritable rag-bag of values – as to have not even a rhetorical purpose.

Their rhetoric apart, one notable difference among the five sets of goals is how they each relate to national consciousness and identity. The French, Russian and Indian statements are consonant, albeit in different ways, with national identities forged in revolution and enshrined and safeguarded in constitution. They are pretty well what one would expect. In contrast, the American and British cases manifest two very different kinds of constitutional vacuum, of commission and of omission. In the United States the constitution proscribes federal intervention in education, so that educational goals become the business of state, community and school rather than national government – at least, that is, until they are overriden by what the federal government claims to be the national interest. Even then, the federal government is anxious to ward off any suggestion of statism. But in Britain the vacuum is one of omission. There is no constitution, no clear sense of national identity or purpose, merely a blank sheet on which civil servants can inscribe whatever versions of the nation's educational goals suit, for the moment, the temper or the electoral calculations of their political masters and mistresses: goals which are abbreviated to the point of redundancy in 1988 under a prime minister who decrees that 'there's no such thing as society; there are only individual men and women, and there are families';[1] and are then expanded to the point of inoperability in 1999 under a successor with a grandiose post-imperial mission to build a new Britain, seemingly severed from its historical and cultural roots.

National education goals, as we shall see when we move into the schools and classrooms, relate to local educational practice obliquely and sometimes surprisingly; beyond that they serve as a cultural and political weather-vane, sometimes revealing much more than their bland language suggests, or indeed than their authors intend.

Turning to the primary curriculum, which is perhaps a truer measure of national intentions and priorities than the goals themselves, we find first some well-documented similarities, especially the prominence consistently given to literacy and numeracy. Even here, however, there are two differences to be noted: between those countries – France, Russia, India – which although rating numeracy important give absolute priority to literacy, and the one – England – which treats literacy and numeracy as equivalent; and between those (including England) which define literacy mainly in terms of reading and writing and others (notably France and Russia) which give no less prominence to the spoken word. I have already noted how heavily the unexamined habits of history weigh on innocent educational phrases such as 'the basics', so that in England, 140 years on from the Newcastle Commission and the Revised Code, few people yet question, or dare to question, the continuing hegemony of its view that 'the duty of a State in public education is to obtain the greatest possible quantity of reading, writing and arithmetic for the greatest number'.[2] However, for the time being we must regard as open the question of whether giving numeracy parity with literacy is truly justified by the national and international circumstances of the twenty-first century. Certainly this view is not shared by many of Britain's economic competitors, including several who – despite this, and with delicate irony – manage to outperform Britain in the mathematics league tables.

The combination of similarity and difference extends to the curriculum as a whole. The basic primary curriculum mix is literacy, numeracy, science, humanities, arts, physical education. Yet at this level too there are three important differences.

First, central specifications allow schools different degrees of latitude in how requirements should be interpreted and implemented. France and Russia reserve time for options, England does not: there the curriculum is what is specified, no more, no less.

Second, subjects are grouped in different ways and allocated different amounts of time. Thus, considering that 'no period in history has been more penetrated by and dependent on the natural sciences than the twentieth century'[3] the variation in attention given to science may seem surprising. It is relatively strongest in the English national curriculum (as the 1995 TIMSS results confimed[4]), but is accorded only parity with the humanities and social studies in France and Russia. But to be surprised is to neglect the cultural contexts in which curricula arise and to presume that the surface transnational similarities at the level of subject labels noted by Benavot and others[5] betoken global consensus at the level of curriculum substance. They do not, and England and France represent contrasting paradigms in this regard. In England the curriculum core includes English, mathematics and science; in France the equivalent 'première groupe de disciplines' at the primary stage comprises French, history, geography and civic education.[6] On the one hand we have the imperatives of economy and employment; on the other those of civil society and citizenship. At the level of comparative curriculum listings the nuances may be delicate and within a given week the difference in time allocation may be modest, but over the entire span of compulsory education their cumulative impact on each pupil's consciousness, as well as on his or her understanding, will be considerable.

The reference to perceived societal imperatives takes us to the third major difference in the specifications. There is a further group of three subjects whose place is rather less certain and predictable. Thus, civic or citizenship education was until 1999 much more explicitly signalled in France, Russia, India and the United States than in England. Here it was rarely mentioned, still less made a curriculum requirement, until it was belatedly added to England's national curriculum in 1999. That this occurred was largely a result of the insistence of one man, Bernard Crick – political scientist, biographer of George Orwell, and, as it happened, friend and former teacher of the then Secretary of State for Education, David Blunkett.[7] Arguably, without Crick's personal intervention England would have remained internationally atypical in this regard. Even then, although citizenship became compulsory for secondary schools, it remained optional for primary.[8]

Thus, too, modern foreign languages: here again England's position is anomalous – less obviously so among our five countries (there is no serious tradition of foreign language teaching at the primary stage in India and the United States, either) than in comparison with international provision more generally. Certainly, among members of the European Union, England is nearly unique in failing to include a foreign language in basic education until the secondary stage.[9] But the most singular curriculum anomaly is religious education, which in many countries – including four of our five – is not so much not included as explicitly excluded on the grounds that where the state protects freedom of religion, belief and values, public education must be secular.

As with the stated educational aims, I do not want to invest these national curriculum lists with more significance than they can bear. In any case, the curriculum beyond the labels and inside the classrooms is far more important, and this is the reality to which we shall attend in this book's later chapters. Yet it seems not unreasonable at this point to identify this particular curriculum cluster – citizenship, foreign languages, religious education – as another cultural indicator or weather vane, alongside the national educational goals which governments espouse and those parts of the curriculum which they designate as the core. For citizenship and religious education both signal particular although contrasting values in respect of how the individual stands in relation to society, while the presence and extent of foreign language teaching conveys an equally important message about how one society stands in relation to others.

If we turn now from curriculum to assessment, we find considerable variation across the five countries in respect of how far assessment is treated as a state concern rather than, or as well as, a professional one. As is to be expected, national assessment is a significant part of the centralized French system, as indeed it has been since 1988 in England. Yet if we wish to deduce that national assessment is inevitable in centralized systems – an essential cog in the machine of government control, perhaps – we shall have to explain the anomaly of Russia, which was until the early 1990s the archetype of centralization and yet had – and has – no proper system of national assessment; and indeed the further anomaly of the United States, with its fiercely guarded tradition of local control running alongside a highly-developed assessment culture.

In England, the motivation to shift from *laissez-faire* to national assessment at the primary stage after 1988 reflected both the urge for greater political control and nervousness about the international league tables. Yet to understand why governments' desire to secure accountability takes such different forms we need to consider, as part of the accountability package alongside assessment, inspection. France has both national assessment and inspection, although in the latter it now maintains a much lighter touch and a more open stance than England. Russia at the time of writing has neither, India has rudimentary national assessment coupled with a highly uneven pattern, across all its states and districts, of local inspection. On the other hand, it has a well-developed tradition of educational data-gathering which is all the more remarkable when one remembers India's size and population and the geographical and linguistic barriers to nationwide communication. The United States has a long tradition of standardized assessment, mostly applied at state, district and school levels, latterly extended into the national arena. England has a very long (160 years) tradition of central inspection, which from 1992–3 was revamped as something altogether more aggressive and comprehensive. But national assessment of pupil performance – at the primary stage, anyway – was only added in 1988.

In France, the imperatives of equality and consistency required the state to give equal attention to monitoring inputs, inspecting processes and assessing outcomes. In England, since 1988, the same imperatives have been partly subverted by government paranoia about a supposedly hostile 'educational establishment', with the result that by 1999 the policing of school and classroom processes by OFSTED had escalated almost out of control and provoked a parliamentary enquiry.[10] In the United States, local community accountability between school board, school and parents dictated the use at that level, but only at that level, of standardized assessment, while national anxiety about international competitiveness extended assessment to state and even national levels, although on a voluntary basis. At the same time, process inspection was at best rudimentary, perhaps because when accountability is highly localized informal and grapevine knowledge make it redundant, and in any case the relative intimacy of the educational culture encourages *moral* and *professional* rather than exclusively *contractual* accountability.[11] In Russia, the most interesting case of the five on this matter because it was until the early late 1980s both the most centralized and the least assessed and inspected, state control focused almost exclusively on inputs. By prescribing and controlling curricula, timetables and textbooks on the one hand, and the training, appointment and promotion of teachers on the other, the state ensured both consistency of provision and a way of policing that provision which was highly effective because it was internal to the school and permanent rather than – as is the case with inspection – external and occasional.

Centralization and Decentralization

This brings us to the final point of comparison that is allowed by the first part of this account of each of the five systems of primary education: control. The World Bank sees decentralization as a growing international trend: 'The emergence of modern economies, the rise of an urban, literate middle class, and the decline of both external and domestic military threats have created nearly insurmountable pressures for a broader distribution of political power'.[12] Here, a discriminating vocabulary is necessary. It is neither valid nor helpful to assert vaguely that England and France are 'centralized', the United States is 'decentralized' and India and Russia lie somewhere in between. As we have seen by comparing budgetary and curriculum control in England, the locus of control can vary from one aspect of education to another. Thus, Dale differentiates the activities of *funding, regulation* and *delivery* in state education, and although he warns that as categories they are relatively coarse, they do at least provide a credible basis for mapping the more specific decisions and acts which are undertaken at each level of an education system.[13]

The World Bank uses two broad sets of measures, *fiscal* and *electoral* decentralization. On this basis, if we take the sub-national share of public expenditure for each country, we find the following percentages: India 51.1, USA 46.4, Russia 37.6, UK 27.0, France 18.6.[14] Electoral decentralization is shown as a gross number of local jurisdictions. This, unfortunately is not helpful, since it indicates merely that in large countries there are many such jurisdictions and in small countries rather fewer. We can try setting these against population figures to create a crude index of local jurisdictions per person, and on that basis England in 1997 had far fewer per person than any other of the five countries, the United States and India show up as highly decentralized, but France destroys the measure by appearing to be more decentralized still. It depends, then, on what one means by a 'local jurisdiction'.

For its 1998 set of international education indicators the OECD developed a framework for determining the level at which each of some 38 educational decisions are taken in 33 countries. The levels were defined as *central* (national government), *intermediate* (state, provincial/regional, and sub-regional), *local* and *school*. The decisions were grouped in four domains: *organization of instruction, personnel management, planning and structures* and *resources*. Internationally, this analysis showed that while schools tend to take most of the decisions about the organization of instruction, decisions within each of the other domains are spread across much less evenly across the other levels, although the trend to decentralization is in general a growing one.[15]

On this basis, OECD defines the balance of centralization–decentralization as dramatically different in those four of our five countries which it features. In France, interestingly in terms of its usual image, the OECD analysis portrays a genuine balance between national government, *académie* and school; in the United States the overwhelming majority of decisions appear to be taken at local level; in England, the majority is represented as being taken by the school, although a significant proportion is attributed to central government and the LEA; and in India the schools seem to have very little power when compared with most of the other countries surveyed, and most decisions are apparently taken at state level.

There are four difficulties with this kind of analysis. First, for the purpose of defining whether a country is more or less centralized OECD treats decisions that are vastly different in terms of their scale and significance as equivalent. To say that in France, numerically, the decisions are split more or less evenly between central government, *académie* and school is to imply an equal distribution of power that is almost certainly misleading. Second – and I fear that this is now becoming something of a refrain – close examination of the OECD's matrix shows that some decisions are allocated to the wrong levels. Thus, for England, OECD claims that *all* (100 per cent of) decisions about the organization of instruction (teaching time, textbooks, pupil grouping, support for pupils with learning difficulties, teaching methods and assessment) and all decisions about personnel management (hiring and dismissal of staff, staff duties and conditions of service, fixing of staff salary scales, influence over staff careers) are taken at school level. This is so seriously incorrect – consider assessment, conditions of service, salary scales, the temporal and pedagogical requirements of the government's literacy and numeracy strategies, which account for 40–50 per cent of instructional time in the primary school – as to call into question the validity of the entire exercise.

The third problem is that although the OECD framework qualifies its placing of school-level decisions by differentiating those made 'within a framework set by a higher authority', those made 'after consultation with other bodies' and those made 'in full autonomy' this reflects only the statutory position and takes no account of the way that power, influence, pressure and patronage suffuse all education systems, even those which are most fully devolved. The cheerful designation of 'in full autonomy' to most of the instructional decisions in English primary schools simply ignores the power-coercive climate of state education in England during the 1980s and the 1990s, and the pressure towards pedagogical conformity which LEAs were able to apply during the four preceding decades.

Finally, the fact that the information on which the OECD analysis is based was presumably supplied by government agencies probably explains both its inaccuracy and – in the case of England – the apparent eagerness to claim a far greater extent of professional and school autonomy than actually exists, for OECD countries are generally keen to display their democratic credentials.

Despite all this, the balance of central, regional, local and school control remains an important dimension of national systems of primary education; but it needs cultural and historical perspectives to enable us to move beyond surface comparisons of the five systems to a deeper understanding.

Beyond Systems: the Struggle for Control

No discussion of the emergence of state education systems can ignore Margaret Archer's searching account of the origin of public education systems in Denmark, England, France, and Russia.[16] Her study is framed by a sociological preoccupation with the relationship between macro-level structure and micro-level interaction, and with the defining processes of power and control; it traces each system back to its roots in conflict among interest groups in the eighteenth and the nineteenth centuries; and by comparing the four histories it builds and sustains a general theory of the evolution of state education which is both explanatory and predictive.

The crux of her analysis is this same distinction between centralized and decentralized systems, viewed now historically and politically rather than administratively. Both kinds of system arise out of the 'interaction of dominant and assertive groups' which constitute 'the "guidance mechanism" responsible for repatterning the relationship between education and society and transforming the internal structure of education itself'.[17] The groups include ruling elites, churches, government bureaucracies, dissenters, entrepreneurs and professionals. Centralized systems emerge when the dominant groups, by a process of 'restriction', destroy earlier monopolies through legal constraints and then state power. Decentralized systems reflect the alternative strategy of 'substitution' in which monopolies are outflanked by the creation of rival institutions and subsystems.

Hence the establishment of a unitary system in France eventually underpinned by the principle of laïcité (secularism), but the emergence in England of parallel Anglican, nonconformist and secular subsystems (what Archer calls a 'multiply-integrated' system) and the survival in that country, right into the twenty-first century, of the protected status of religious instruction in the school curriculum.

Once the system is established, the different groups involved – governing elites, professional interest groups and external interest groups – interact in different ways and with inevitably different outcomes. In centralized systems educational change is achieved mainly by political manipulation; in decentralized systems, it is achieved by a combination of political manipulation, 'external transactions' and 'internal initiation'. However, the process of change is frustrated, mediated or accelerated in either context according to the degree to which the state framework is 'impenetrable', 'semi-permeable' or 'accessible'. In an impenetrable polity only favoured sections of the political elite can negotiate for change; where polity is semi-permeable government supporters have access; where it is accessible, political opponents also have a voice.[18]

Archer's analysis not only helps us to understand the sharply contrasting cases of, for example, decentralized America or centralized France or Russia, as these systems have emerged to date; it also sheds predictive light on the continuing processes of change and reform. For a state's political complexion changes (Archer portrays France's Second Empire as impenetrable, the Third and Fourth Republics as accessible, and the Fifth as semi-permeable), and with it the pace and extent of change which is possible. However, her general thesis is that when these fluctuations are ironed out the patterns of educational change in centralized and decentralized systems are markedly different: decentralized systems achieve, out of the interaction of state, community and school, change which is progressive, sustained and incremental; centralized systems operate on a stop-go pattern in which long periods of stability or stagnation are punctuated by sudden shifts.[19]

Finally, Archer postulates a growing trend of convergence between the two types of system, with centralized systems reducing standardization and encouraging diversity and decentralized systems restricting diversity and seeking tighter co-ordination.[20]

Applied to the current condition of the five countries in this study, Archer's theory is persuasive, especially as one of the countries (England) has experienced not so much convergence as revolution. Its case in 2000 is very different from that portrayed by Archer in 1979 and to compare the processes of change and reform in English primary education during the 1970s with those of the 1990s is highly instructive in this regard. However, like all theories worthy of attention, Archer's has provoked criticism,[21] and one line of commentary is especially germane to this book's concerns.

Like Margaret Archer, Andy Green is exercised by the puzzle of the differential development of state education systems. He tests and rejects cause-effect explanations revolving round industrialization, bureaucratization, the rise of Protestantism, the Enlightenment, and the growth of democracy, finding too many anomalies and too many problems of faulty chronology to sustain any of them on their own, although the influence of all of them is conceded. What in Green's opinion each of these – and Archer's explanation – lacks is a coherent view of the character of the states within which the various systems developed.[22]

For Green, in fact, it is to the state itself, rather than to this or that national movement or trend, that we should look to understand how and why state education systems develop, for 'it is in the specific national forms of *state formation*, of which educational development is a part, that the key to the uneven and distinctive development of education systems lies'[23] (my italics).

The nineteenth century, then – the century of mass public education – was the watershed between a highly differentiated, voluntaristic pattern of education in each of Green's case countries (England, France and the United States) and forms of public education which were constructed in part to generate and consolidate national consciousness:

> The nineteenth century education system came to assume a primary responsibility for the moral, cultural and political development of the nation. It became the secular church . . . It formed the responsible citizen, the diligent worker, the willing taxpayer, the reliable juror, the conscientious parent, the dutiful wife, the patriotic soldier, the dependable or deferential voter.[24]

The critical mechanism for Green is Gramsci's application of Marxist theory to modern society, born particularly of his experience of communism and fascism in Italy. Gramsci's central illuminating device is *hegemony*, which applies not only to political predominance between states – the example of the former Soviet Union's influence in Eastern Europe used to be the one most frequently cited in the West, while this was countered by reference to the dealings of the United States with Western Europe and Latin America – but also to social relations within them. And it is the way that Gramscian hegemony moves beyond a simple polarity of domination and subordination into a combination of force *and* consent that, for Green, makes it particularly potent as a means of understanding the role of public education in the emerging or changing nations of the nineteenth century.

Thus, emerging public education provided a means for social control, and it developed first and fastest in those countries where national cohesion and manpower requirements were most urgent: those which confronted external threats or were undergoing internal destabilization and transformation. Prussia used it to promote first militaristic state-building and then economic transformation, while France used it to consolidate the new social order initiated by its revolution of 1789–91.[25]

The cases of America and England look to be more difficult to explain in terms of Green's thesis, but Gramscian hegemony allows its application in less centralized and authoritarian contexts too. In the United States, as we have seen, the constitution's Tenth Amendment required educational decentralization. But while in the United States public education was less directed towards the production of state functionaries than in was in either Prussia or France, it nevertheless faithfully reproduced and spread republican and capitalist values during the periods after independence from Britain in 1776 and the Civil War of 1861–65, especially – as a time-bomb which exploded only in the second half of the twentieth century – the values of the white, Anglo-Saxon, Protestant bourgeois ascendancy.[26] In Britain the case was different again. The country entered the nineteenth century with no obvious spurs to the development of public education: the state was firmly established by the early years of the eighteenth century and Britain had been first to industrialize. Britain's early start in state formation and industrialization thus prolonged and made increasingly redundant and counterproductive (in state terms) its pre-industrial patterns of education.[27]

Culture, Power and Social Control

We carry forward from these abbreviated summaries of two key works some important concepts to help us understand the development of the five national systems of primary education and the resulting contemporary relationship in each country between primary schooling and the state: *centralization/decentralization*; *interest groups*; *impenetrable/semi-permeable* and *accessible polity*; *incremental* and *stop-go* patterns of change; *state formation*; *hegemony*. Let us turn now to a second cluster, whose centrepiece is *culture*.

'Culture' itself was for Raymond Williams 'one of the two of three most complicated words in the English language'.[28] Generally we start unpicking its complexity by distinguishing two major usages of 'culture': the first of them anthropologically comprehensive – culture as values, beliefs, ideas, institutions, networks of relationships, patterns of behaviour, and artefacts; the other more restricted and artistic-cum-literary – the art, music, literature, the humanities – but with powerful Arnoldian connotations of relative worth shading into assumptions about class and status. We then find that we are left with a residual baggage that stubbornly refuses to be tidied into one or other of these definitions. One clue to the difficulty is the frequency with which the word carries appendages of one kind or another: adjectives which demarcate, claim, reject, compare and in any event tacitly evaluate kinds of culture – 'high', 'popular', 'mass', 'majority', 'minority', 'youth', 'ethnic', 'gender'; nouns which indicate what people and groups do with culture and what culture does to people – cultural 'capital', 'reproduction', 'transmission', 'oppression', 'politics', 'relativism'; prefixes which place culture temporally, spatially or taxonomically – 'postmodernist culture', 'subculture', 'micro-culture'. More recently, the word has acquired such pervasive usage that it can be appended to virtually any sphere of activity to signal its distinctiveness and otherness – 'business culture', 'institutional culture', 'professional culture', 'research culture'.

For the purposes of examining the place and functioning of education, we need to deploy both extended and more restricted senses of the word 'culture'. That is to say, schooling and curricula select from a society's spectrum of values and ideas and this selection informs and pervades curriculum, teaching and assessment. At the same time those in receipt of this selection are themselves already located somewhere in relation to it (inside or outside) as members of one or another cultural group or segment, defined perhaps by gender, class, race or ethnicity. And the encounter takes place in an institutional setting – a school – which, as a micro-culture both conveys its own messages and filters and perhaps subtly modifies those coming in from outside. Thus schools and classrooms are both cultural channels or cultural interfaces and microcultures in their own right.

To understand precisely what an education system, its constituent organizations (governments, administrative authorities and schools) and its participants (policy-makers, officials, teachers and pupils) *do* with culture requires us to address the relationship of social structure and power. The sharpest demarcations of the state–school relationship emphasize the school's role as a direct instrument of state control. For Althusser the school is no less than an *ideological state apparatus* (ISA) which serves to reproduce the power and ideology of the state and socializes children into the prevailing mores and economic structure.[29] For Bowles and Gintis, schooling in capitalist countries (with the United States as their archetype) reproduces through the educational process, especially through the hidden curriculum, the psychology and social relations of production, setting up the relationship of subordination and domination, and socializing both conformist, deferential and rule-following future workers and autonomous, rule-making future managers and decision-makers.[30]

For Bourdieu and Passeron, schools and teachers are agents of *cultural reproduction*, transmitting and thus reinforcing as *cultural capital* the dominant (middle-class) culture, as reflected in both the hierarchy of subjects and curriculum content and the messages of classroom relations.[31] In this, the language of 'pedagogic authority' or 'magisterial discourse' has a critical role in maintaining a teacher–pupil relationship of dominance – subordination/dependence, legitimating as *linguistic capital* Latinate linguistic structures and 'bourgeois parlance' and devaluing 'common parlance' or pupil vernaculars and thus perpetrating *symbolic violence* against working-class pupils.[32] Bourdieu and Passeron developed their ideas by reference to schooling in France, where the concern with linguistic forms which drives their theory of pedagogic communication may seem more convincing – as we shall see when we look closely at the language of the classroom – than in England or the United States where teachers tend to elide formal and vernacular language. However,

Bernstein's work, grounded in a theory of the relationship between language, pedagogy and class, provides an Anglo-Saxon variant of the Bourdieu and Passeron thesis. Bernstein's later work moves from a traditional account of social stratification to one which identifies the different 'disseminators of social control' in the new middle class – 'regulators', 'repairers', 'diffusers', 'shapers', and 'executors' – and unravels the agency of 'pedagogic discourse (using both 'discourse' and 'pedagogy' in their broadest senses).[33]

Giroux summarizes 'the practice of ordering, licensing and regulating that structures public schooling' in terms of four trends:

(i)   An epistemic arrogance and faith in certainty sanctions pedagogical practices and public spheres in which cultural differences are viewed as threatening.
(ii) Knowledge becomes positioned in the curricula as an object of mastery and control.
(iii) The individual student is privileged as a unique source of agency irrespective of iniquitous relations of power.
(iv) The technology and culture of the book is treated as the embodiment of modernist high learning and the only legitimate object of pedagogy.[34]

Macedo takes a sharper view still of the 'culture of the book', using Hirsch's *Dictionary of Cultural History: what every American needs to know* to expose the 'poisonous pedagogy' of approved curricula which in his (Macedo's) view peddle lies and deny students access to alternative versions of their history and culture. He exemplifies this process by contrasting approved and alternative versions of American democracy, the treatment of Native Americans, Hiroshima and Nagasaki, and American involvement in the Vietnam War.[35]

Somewhat at variance with this strict transmission/reproduction view of schooling, with its classical Marxist genealogy and its assumption of working class and pupil passivity or collusion, are theorists such as Apple and Giroux, who provide the corrective of *resistance* to account for the contested and oppositional character of much school and classroom life. Grand theories of cultural reproduction take little or no account of the dynamics and tensions of pedagogical relationships, or of the strongly negotiative character of many curriculum transactions, or of the way that classroom power is not invariably one way. Giroux argues that the Bowles and Gintis view of cultural reproduction is over-determined: 'Not only does their argument point to a spurious "constant fit" between schools and the workplace, it does so by ignoring important issues regarding the role of consciousness, ideology and resistance in the schooling process.'[36]

From this more open reading of the society–school relationship Apple argues that 'the key struggle is against the use of education to dominate and subordinate' through the 'commodification of culture'.[37] To contest and counter this tendency Apple and Giroux propose developing and enlisting a *critical pedagogy* which 'links teaching and learning to forms of self- and social empowerment that argue for forms of community life that extend the principles of liberty, equality, justice and freedom to the widest possible set of institutional and lived relations.'[38]

However, pervading much of this kind of analysis is the Gramscian idea of *hegemony*, in which the ideas and the values of the dominant class or group in society come to predominate not just through overt mechanisms of political and social control but also by suffusing general consciousness and becoming accepted as right and inevitable. Despite the potential of critical pedagogy, the idea I shall particularly want to test is the application of hegemony to the practice of education as most clearly expressed by Giroux:

> Pedagogy is . . . a technology of power, language and practice that produces or legitimates forms of moral and political regulation, that construct and offer human beings particular views of themselves and the world . . . Pedagogy is about the intellectual, emotional and ethical investments we make as part of our attempt to negotiate, accommodate and transform the world in which we find ourselves.

Although this posits a process of cultural shaping, it remains open as to its precise force, avoiding the poles of pedagogy as ideological state apparatus and – at the other extreme – of pedagogy as successful resistance. As we look more closely at each system of primary education and at the patterns of schooling and pedagogy they contain and allow, we may be able to place what we find along this notional continuum. In doing this, we shall find not only variation between countries but also – of critical but relatively neglected importance in this kind of analysis, which tends to confine itself to macro-level theory – variation between one classroom and another, one teacher and another. It is in the micro-level analysis that we shall begin to discover the true potential of pedagogy to change rather than merely reproduce.

In all this, however, we need to heed Margaret Archer's warning that 'we must not fall into the trap of certain sociologists of education and assume that because reproduction is attempted then its success is a foregone conclusion.'[39] What schooling and pedagogy seek to achieve and what they actually achieve do not necessarily coincide. We have only to look at the stubborn persistence of independent thinking in totalitarian regimes to recognize this. Once we enter the classroom we shall need to place alongside grand theories of resistance, or for that matter notions of the indomitability of the human spirit, explanations which are altogether more prosaic. Teaching, for instance, is often a far from efficient process.

Identity

The final concept I want to inject into the analytical frame at this stage is *identity*. As I write this, in the United Kingdom, elections have taken place for the new Scottish Parliament and Welsh Assembly against a backdrop of Welsh and Scottish nationalism on the one hand and English nervousness and collective self-doubt on the other.[40] In Germany, by way of contrast, the opening of the rebuilt Berlin Reichstag marks the final symbolic act in the reunification of that country's East and West. Meanwhile, confidence in the European project, in as far as this is accurately reflected in national voting patterns in the 1999 European parliamentary elections, varies from one member state to another, although in Britain it is impossible to tell whether the exceptionally low poll in 1999 signals contentment, indifference or disenchantment. In the Balkans, the Serbian Milosevic regime has brutally and systematically pursued its policy of 'ethnic cleansing' against the Kosovan Albanians, murdering civilians, torching villages, and depriving survivors of their identity not only by forcibly ejecting them from their communities but by separating them from those collective 'apparatuses' – churches, political parties, trades union, civic groups of one kind or another – which place them within civil society.

In Europe at the turn of the millennium, then, national identities are increasingly fluid and contested. But for Hobsbawm, identity is called into question not just as a consequence of particular events such as development of the European Union or the collapse of the USSR and the realignment of its former satellite states, but also by more generalized changes – globalization, the decline of collective consciousness, the rampant growth of individualism, and our loss of historical memory:

> The destruction of the past, or rather of the social mechanisms that link one's contemporary experience to that of earlier generations, is one of the most characteristic and eerie phenomena of the late twentieth century. Most young men and women at the century's end grow up in a sort of permanent present lacking any organic relation to the public past of the times they live in.[41]

To Castells, whose analysis is contemporary rather than historical yet overlaps Hobsbawm's in this matter, economic and informational globalization restructures our consciousness 'around the Net and the Self':

> Global networks of instrumental exchanges selectively switch on and off individuals, groups, regions and even countries, according to their relevance in fulfilling the goals processed in the network, in a relentless flow of strategic decisions . . . it follows a fundamental split between abstract, universal instrumentalism and historically rooted, particularistic identities.[42]

Into the vacuum step the 'prophets of technology', the postmodernists and other millenarists whose 'implicit assumption is the acceptance of full individualization of behaviour, and of society's powerlessness over its destiny.'[43]

We saw something of this in the triumphalist determinism of the ICT-centred 'new education' at the start of this book's first chapter. But we have seen too the counterculture: the reassertion and reforging of collective identities in the face of change, instability and the shifts in power which provoke and accompany them: the rise of nationalism, territorialism and religious fundamentalism; the growth of environmentalism and other grass-roots political movements; the repositioning of collectivities based on race, ethnicity and gender; the emergence of the cultural politics of difference.[44]

Identity is a vital part of any consideration of state education. Historically, states have used their controlling stake in mass education to consolidate national identity on the one hand and to differentiate subnational identities on the other. At school level the hegemonic process suffuses curriculum and pedagogy, perhaps in the way suggested by Giroux above, perhaps by some other means: in any event curriculum and pedagogy convey messages to children about what knowledge, what ways of thinking, talking and acting, and – through assessment – what achievements and what people are of greater and lesser worth.

So, in France, what it is to be French is, and has long remained, an explicit focus for national educational goals and curricula (citizenship, general culture, the disciplined mind) and for structure (consistency and equality of provision at every level from primary school to university, and a competitive and meritocratic ethos from secondary level onwards). Yet from time to time intimations of a less consensual reality come to the surface: for example, the collision between secularism and religious freedom, and between national identity and individual rights, as manifested in *l'affaire du foulard* in 1989 (the controversy over whether Muslim girls should be allowed to wear their headscarves, as ordained by their religion, in secular state schools), or the 1999 dispute over the teaching of regional and minority languages in schools (we touched on both matters in Chapter 2). To portray France as the archetype of cultural reproduction is to over-simplify, yet as the most consistently centralized education system of the five, and the one with the most durable view of its purposes, the conditions for this line of analysis seem to be right.

In post-Soviet Russia the situation is both more fluid and less easy to interpret. The country's educational policies read as a conscious inversion of those of the preceding era (humanism, pluralism, individualism, decentralization); yet the prescribed curriculum also retains that era's collectivist and normative preoccupation with social and moral development, motherland and citizenship. Decentralization, meanwhile, represents a paradox: it powerfully signals the new order, and responds to Russia's immense ethnic and linguistic diversity; yet in so doing it makes it possible, at the level of the republic, *oblast*, *krai* and *okrug*, for the old order to continue virtually unimpeded within the closed political and administrative system that each such unit can so easily become. The possibility that Archer's 'semi-permeable' if not 'impenetrable' polities will persist at this level is strengthened by the Russian population's relatively low level of geographical mobility.

There are similar tensions in India, although for very different reasons. Here we have a large country whose vast population divides along lines of race, language, religion, caste, gender and wealth; which is culturally ancient yet – in its present form – constitutionally young; which decentralizes education to state and district levels yet whose provision is ostensibly underpinned by very explicit appeals to all-Indian history, culture and unifying political ideals of independence; whose primary schools manifest an uneasy combination of absolute Brahmanical authority, relative teacher powerlessness, indigenous values and imposed colonial structures. The stated goals for primary education seek to balance national values and local cultural and linguistic differences. Government policies – especially those of interventions such as DPEP – strive for a similar balance: to respect cultural difference while overcoming the divisions and inequalities that are its concomitant. Yet, from the 1999 PROBE research emerges a sense that the well-known problems of recruitment and retention within the groups targeted in such policies – girls, scheduled castes and tribes, the rural poor – require explanations which address much more even-handedly the gulf of culture, meaning and identity between family and school.[45]

In the United States what it means to be American (and by extension 'un-American') is a pervasive element in both political and popular rhetoric. The appeal to patriotism is insistent and relentless. Yet offsetting a genuinely national identity are the claims of race, gender and religion (a potent element in American life) and the cultural roots of the many nationalities from which America's mainly immigrant 'melting-pot' society has descended. In such a context of pluralism it is inevitable that the version of Americanism on offer will speak more sympathetically to some groups than to others, and that some will feel excluded or belittled by it. Moreover, part of the essence of American identity is a highly decentralized polity and a fierce combination of individualism and anti-statism. All this makes for a heady and possibly contradictory mix. The result, as I have already noted in respect of policy debates in Michigan and as will become more apparent when we examine life in elementary school classrooms in that state, is that values, the core of identity, are very much out in the open. It is hard to imagine a term such as 'poisonous pedagogy' arising in England.

England, in its own terms and in the light of the foregoing, is a strange case. If a well-developed sense of national identity is to be desired, England would seem to have the advantages of historical longevity, political stability and geographical intimacy. Yet in no country of the five does analysis of the educational system and its historical development convey a stronger sense of confusion about the kind of person the state, through its schools, seeks to produce. The manifest goals and values of the English education system are anodyne or contradictory, and public expressions of Englishness range along a continuum of mindlessness from jingoistic flag-waving to the replacing of historical consciousness by a prepackaged 'heritage'. Meanwhile national values are invented and discarded at the drop of a political hat by the likes of Margaret Thatcher, John Major and Tony Blair. The devolution of powers to Scotland, Wales and Northern Ireland highlights what those countries have by way of identity but England does not. Cultural and ethnic minorities develop their community networks while others bemoan the loss of community more generally. Some speak of Englishness as something that is intrinsically understated and therefore not easy to explicate for educational purposes. But if this is so, English culture and identity are as acutely vulnerable to – for example – the American cultural colonialism encouraged for economic reasons by successive governments as the fragile English countryside is vulnerable to imported agri-business farming practices. Yet cutting across all this is the defining English fact of class, which both divides and binds. At the turn of the century the vacuum or conundrum of identity in England is an open door to political appropriation; the more so as in England education is now more tightly controlled by central government than in any other of our five countries.

Temporal and Spatial Continuities

In all five countries we found significant historical continuities yielding a many-layered present. Often such continuities survived political earthquakes. Thus, in

France, statism outlasted one revolution and in Soviet Russia autocracy another. In the United States, meanwhile, decentralization was itself a conscious act of revolution. We also saw how as voluntarism gave way to state control governments were forced to deal with the expectation of the voluntary providers – usually the churches – that they would have a continued role. In France the battle for secular education was not won until 1882; in England the matter – it is no longer a battle, although perhaps it ought to be – has still not been resolved. In Russia, India and the United States the springboards for the establishment of the secular principle were revolution and independence.

As to the substantive details of primary schooling, both curriculum and pedagogy have long roots. Literacy has always been the core of the primary curriculum, although the rationale for making children literate has at different times responded to imperatives ranging from the exclusively religious (keeping the devil at bay by enabling children to read the scriptures) to the economic. The transition from voluntarism to public education made the primary curriculum a potential instrument of state policy. In France, Russia, India and the United States the forging of a new national identity was an overt objective, and in this the curriculum tools included language teaching, civic education and moral development. Here cultural reproduction first required cultural transformation or at least adjustment. In England, in contrast, the curriculum of public primary education for much of its history looked back rather than forwards – to preserving the hegemonies of religion and hierarchy, and to buttressing the inequalities of class. Only towards the end of the twentieth century did British governments begin to understand and exploit the power of the curriculum as an instrument of cultural transformation. The transformation they sought, however, rested on an impoverished and restricted view of culture.

The history of primary education in these countries is alternately about minimalism and entitlement. Where public provision arises in the context of pre-existing private schooling, it tends, to begin with anyway, to be minimalist; for it is targeted at those without wealth or influence. Hence the recurring pattern in primary education systems of large classes, generalist rather than specialist teaching, and a restricted curriculum. Once public primary provision becomes mainstream provision, once it offers an automatic ladder to secondary and higher education and is therefore used by a wider social spectrum, minimalism begins to give way to a broader curriculum and to arguments about children's entitlement to a rounded education provided by properly trained professionals. It is instructive to track how far each system has progressed along this route. In all five countries it is possible to discern the pauper legacy, even if only faintly now, but in England and India it is more pronounced than elsewhere, and in India our respondents insisted that given choice and income parents almost invariably bought out of government and into private schooling, seeing government primary schools as second rate and second class. There are residual problems of status for primary teachers in France – its long history of educational entitlement notwithstanding – and in Russia, India and England. This residue seems least evident in the United States, where although elementary schools have retained the class teacher system it is not uncommon to find class teachers almost outnumbered by specialist and support staff.

However, although India is the most extreme case of the five in as far as low resourcing levels have kept buildings, staffing, equipment, training and teaching at a relatively basic level, the persistence of earlier structures and assumptions cannot be explained by reference to resource levels alone. In India, we found clear echoes of both pre-colonial and colonial versions of pedagogy, and the example of England, which I examined in some detail, is probably not unique. Here we saw how the crucial first period of public primary education left its mark not just on structures but also on ideas and attitudes. That these should prove more durable than those associated with any of the subsequent waves of reform, I suggested, can be explained by reference to the persistence of those deeper structures in the wider society – notably class – from which the distinctiveness of English primary education derived.

Comparative studies of educational systems and practices by definition compare and contrast. They deal in similarities, differences, and commonalities, and they explore ways of explaining these by reference to both context and theory.[46] Less commonly, comparative studies uncover and trace *connections* between those systems and contexts that have been selected for comparison. There are no doubt those who find a lateral venture of this kind unsatisfactory, for it muddies the water of comparison by implying that systems are not sealed or free-standing but actually influence each other.

As I have worked through the system-level accounts of primary education in the five countries, I have pointed up instances when education in one country was clearly influenced by what was going on in one or more of the others. Thus, for example, the monitorial system may well have originated in India, was developed in England, and was exported to Russia, France and the United States (and Sweden, Denmark, Switzerland, Italy, Spain, Canada and Australia). For a while it was the pedagogical bedrock of basic education in a large number of countries. The development of secondary education in Russia was influenced before the 1917 revolution by the German *Gymnasium* and after it by the American common high school. The latter also provided a model for common or comprehensive secondary education in other countries, including England. Teacher training in all five countries owes something to the French *école normale* and the German *Normalschule*, not merely by the informal transmission of ideas but by direct importation of models (for example, to England and India by way of Kay Shuttleworth).

Progressivism proves to have been a genuinely international commodity. Rousseau's *Emile* was widely read. Pestalozzi's school at Yverdon was much visited and imitated. Tagore's ashram ideal in India was much influenced by the Elmhirsts' Dartington in England. Dewey's ideas were highly favoured during the 1920s period of 'luxuriant experimentation' in the Soviet Union. They also fed English progressivism during the same period, gaining legitimation through the Hadow and Plowden reports in 1931 and 1967. The second wave of English progressivism – the 'Plowdenism' of the 1960s and the 1970s – was exported to the United States as it stood, unmodified.

And so we might go on (and back) almost indefinitely. I make these connections – and once we investigate classroom pedagogy there will be many more – for three reasons. First, I wish to counter the postmodernist belief that the globalization of ideas is a recent and necessarily electronic phenomenon. Second, I feel it important to offer a cautionary and revisionist perspective on the phenomenon of 'cultural borrowing', which comparativists since Sadler have universally condemned as unacceptable. Cultural borrowing happens, it has always happened. Few countries, if any, have remained hermetically sealed in the development of their systems of basic education, and the remarkable similarities which exist in respect of – for example – the primary curriculum are no coincidence. This is not to say that one should be sanguine when a government minister or adviser proposes transplanting a particular educational policy or practice as it stands from, say, Taiwan or Germany to London; rather that one's response should be tempered by historical and cultural awareness. On this basis one will know which sorts of educational ideas travel and implant themselves more and less successfully, and one will understand why this should be so.

Finally, I want to give advance notice of a later preoccupation, the idea that there are clearly discernible supranational versions of pedagogy which owe their character to the traffic of people and ideas, and to highly formative individual encounters, at certain critical periods in educational history. In this matter the history of educational thought is no different from the history of thought more generally. Nor is there any reason why it should be, although it is both intriguing and depressing to note that while the finest minds engaged themselves in the long struggle for universal basic education, once provision as such was universalized many of them lost interest in what was provided.

Part III
Schools

8

Buildings and People

During the 1990s schools in England were seldom allowed to be just schools. Each must face the world wearing its obligatory judgemental tag – 'outstanding', 'effective', 'improving', 'failing', 'weak' or the ominous 'requiring special measures' – as if to suggest that schools would do a good job only if they lived in constant fear of being named, praised or shamed.[1] For its part, the UK government took to spinning even its most benign policies as 'tough' – as if to signal that schools would regress to a natural state of fecklessness or incompetence unless they were whipped into line. English primary schools in the 1990s were regarded rather as English elementary school pupils were regarded in the 1870s – as irredeemably tainted by original sin.

In this and the following chapters, however, we shall suspend such judgements – on schools and on policy towards schools – until we have reached a clearer understanding of what primary schools actually are and how they operate. We shall concern ourselves as much with the *idea* of a primary school as with its objective, bricks-and-mortar reality. This idea, or ideal, varies not just from one country, or indeed one school, to another, but also over time.

The 1967 Plowden Report's much-quoted 'A school is not merely a teaching shop; it must transmit attitudes and values'[2] was, up to a point, correct. Schools do of necessity transmit attitudes and values, but not – as Plowden believed – because they have a moral obligation to do so over and above an ostensibly separate activity called 'teaching', but because teaching is itself about the transmission of values. Some of those values are predicated on notions of what it is to be educated; some concern the idea of a school itself.

So while in the England of 1967 Plowden went on to stipulate the values and attitudes which the primary schools of that and the following decade ought in its view to transmit ('a community in which children learn to live first and foremost as children and not as future adults . . . to be themselves and to develop in the way and at the pace appropriate to them . . .' and so on), by the 1990s these values had given way to the nostrums of school effectiveness. Schools were no longer communities whose members were bound together by social and affective as well as educational ties, but quasi-commercial organizations characterized by 'firm and purposeful leadership', 'a strong commitment to academic goals', close control of their members' use of time, high expectations, and 'a consistent focus on teaching, learning and achievement'.[3] Just two years later New Labour was beginning to distance itself from even this uncompromising model, declaring impatiently that 'We know what it takes to create a good school' and 'Standards matter more than structures . . . The preoccupation with school structure has absorbed a great deal of energy to little effect. [We should now] create a climate in which schools are constantly challenged to compare themselves with other schools and adopt proven ways of raising their performance'.[4] By the turn of the millennium, the UK policy line had shifted from a concern with the kinds of places that schools were or ought to be to what they achieved and where those achievements stood on local and national league tables of relative success and failure.

Schools exist to promote learning. That being so, the standards they realize in this regard (leaving aside for a moment how such standards are defined and judged) are self-evidently much more important than structures as such. That is to say – and this in common-sense vein is presumably what the UK government's message-mongers were getting at in 1997 – what a child learns at school matters much more than how that school is organized. As purveyor of the most influential images of UK primary education for the 1960s, the 1970s and the early 1980s, Plowden did indeed expound at length and in detail on school climate and classroom process while it said curiously little about outcomes. In this respect it created an unfortunate legacy. In my own research in one English city and its primary schools during the late 1980s and the early 1990s, I found an institutionalized obsession with the 'learning environment' which appeared to pay more attention to school decor, classroom organization and display than to learning, and indeed tended to judge the latter against aesthetic rather than educational criteria.[5] The shift from what was celebrated there as 'the quality learning environment' to a greater concern with 'standards' was no doubt proper and overdue.

However, structures, no less than school effectiveness 'factors', are not merely institutional means to educational ends: they also speak for themselves. Ideally, school structure and environment make manifest educational goals, and both goals and context then speak with one voice, reinforcing each other. Schools perform the task of educating, but they are also, as institutions, educative, and in this sense Plowden and its heirs were right to argue the benefits of attention to the context of learning and the relationships upon which learning depends. Not uncommonly, however, school structures are at variance with educational goals, frustrating or even contradicting them, and sowing in the minds of their pupils anything from mild confusion to rampant alienation.

To dichotomize 'standards' and 'structures' may serve a convenient political purpose, but it is in fact no more helpful to our understanding of what kinds of institutions primary schools are or ought to be than was Plowden's dichotomizing of 'teaching' and 'values', or indeed that report's tacit caricature of teaching as mere fact transmission. In pursuit of both kinds of understanding we probably need to choose different starting points.

In this book's analysis, as has already been indicated, the idea of culture is central, and central to culture is the relationship between structures, ideas, values and action. In educational policy, structure is subsidiary to standards; but in seeking to understand the distinctive institution we call a school, both structure and definitions of standards are subsidiary to culture. In the three chapters which comprise this section of the book, I shall use the *Five Cultures* school-level data to examine in turn five linked aspects or dimensions of primary school culture: *space, time, people, ideas and values*, and *external relationships*. The last aspect, which we shall consider in Chapter 10, reminds us of another of the book's preoccupations: the relationship between the worlds inside and outside the school, between educational practice, local circumstance and national policy, between micro and macro. Chapter 10 therefore views the school–state relationship opened up in earlier chapters through the other end of the investigative telescope.

Organizing Space

The *Five Cultures* data include material from fieldwork in thirty school buildings in five countries and from an additional sixty or so English schools. Of these, most were free-standing primary or elementary schools, although in Russia all but the smallest village schools were all-age establishments in which the space for primary education consisted of a suite of classrooms, usually on an upper floor.

The size of school buildings usually relates to the numbers of pupils they accommodate, and there is a consequent tendency for urban schools to be larger, often considerably larger, than rural. Usually, but not always: in India building size and pupil numbers did not necessarily coincide, and the instances we encountered of schools operating on a shift system were, we were given to understand, not untypical. In one, 425 pupils were divided between morning and afternoon shifts, giving expected session enrolments of 245 (five classes) and 180 (four classes) to be accommodated in two permanent classrooms, a lean-to building, a veranda and a playground. The Russian schools, being all-age, were largest, while in France and England we visited typical examples of the many one- and two-classroom schools that cater for rural children. In India, one- and two-room schools are the largest single category, although a significant (but fast declining) proportion of schools have either *kachha* (makeshift) buildings or no buildings at all.[6] There, as noted in Chapter 5, initiatives such as Operation Blackboard and the District Primary Education Programme have made the move to *pucca* buildings with at least two classrooms a national priority.

Building design varied considerably. The closest we came to uniformity was in Russia and India. In Russia, the typical school was a two- or three-storey block with a central entrance door and foyer, long corridors widening at intervals into substantial play areas for pupils' use during the long, dark and inhospitable winters. Opening on to the corridors were the classrooms, high, rectangular, and brightly lit from one side by tall windows. In India, the smaller schools were flat-roofed blocks with two or three adjacent rooms opening onto a veranda and a patch of open ground; the larger schools had two, three or four wings around a central courtyard, each wing consisting of veranda and several classrooms, and one also containing an office for the head teacher.

In France, Michigan and England, in contrast, building design was less predictable. In Michigan, all the elementary schools we visited or noted *en route* were dispersed, single-storey affairs with low-pitched roofs. In France, as in England, the older buildings tended to be tall and barrack-like. In England many nineteenth-century elementary school buildings are still in use as primary schools. They are characteristically red brick without, glazed tile within – the materials proving equally impervious to weather and to children – and many still have their original entrance porches segregating 'boys', 'girls' and 'infants'. The newer buildings reflect changes in post-war educational and architectural fashion: prefabricated boxes with conventional classrooms from the 1950s and the 1960s, open-plan or part open-plan structures from the 1970s and the 1980s, with small 'home bays' for each class and shared 'activity areas'. In France, the newest building we visited was a complex structure on two levels over the familiar covered play area, whose network of interlocking hexagonal classrooms was guaranteed to confound the cartographically challenged.

All the schools had outdoor spaces. In France and Russia, these were usually asphalt playgrounds. In France the building sometimes projected over part of the playground to provide protection in poor weather without the need to bring the pupils indoors, or for teachers to have the additional burden of those 'wet playtimes' which are a routine imposition on their English colleagues. The usually unpaved open spaces of Indian primary schools ranged from the large random *maidan* to immaculately tended courtyards with mature trees and plants in earthenware pots. In England, the urban primary schools in high-density neighbourhoods had, as a minimum, a playground. Suburban and rural schools usually had playing fields as well, as did their American counterparts, often with climbing equipment.

What is it about a school building that signals 'school'? In England and Michigan the educational architecture of all periods was quite distinctive; but in Russia a school could equally have been an office block – only the label over the main entrance and the piece of Soviet-era statuary at the gate gave it away. (Although even the labels managed to make Russian schools sound like factories – 'School 1275', 'Gymnasium 46'.) In India a multi-purpose vernacular architecture combined with the way schools often turned inwards to courtyards rather than outwards to the street made them indistinguishable at that vantage point from other buildings; while in France schools – apart from the more adventurous modern buildings – tended to be curiously anonymous structures, fronting directly onto the street and conveying the business-like message that here was just another building for people to work in, no more and no less special than its neighbours. Indeed, we found ourselves using the phrase 'business-like' to describe much more of French primary education than buildings alone.

Thus far we have attended to the total structure. Structure begins to reveal intention and function once one steps inside. Here, country-specific generalization is in order, regardless of the different character of the school buildings themselves. Entering a French primary school provides a relatively low-key experience: there may be welcoming signs but equally there may not be. A notice will direct you to the office of the *directeur* or *directrice* but that, apart from the odd concert or exhibition poster, may be as far as it goes. In England, in contrast, the entrance area traditionally signals what a school thinks it stands for. It conveys explicit messages which you must read and interpret before you engage with the people who work there. Once you gain access (during the 1990s, and especially after the massacre of 16 primary school children and their teacher at Dunblane in 1996, many schools tightened their security and installed entry phones) you are confronted by notices extending a welcome either cautious ('all visitors must report to the office') or unqualified ('welcome to our school'). These lead to elaborately mounted displays of children's work, some of it three-dimensional and suspended from the ceiling, together with, if the school is competitively-inclined, which many profess not to be, trophies won at inter-school sporting events. Also prominent will be lists of expectations, and sometimes rules and sanctions.

> *Our expectations.* Always treat other people in the same manner you would like them to treat you. Always polite. P & Q [peace and quiet]. Do as you as asked. Listen when teacher is talking. Line up beautifully. Sit sensibly and still. Always own up and tell the truth. Work hard. Be organized.

> If we see a bully we stick up for our friends. We tell a grown-up in private. Rubbers are banned except for art work – we use brackets when we make a mistake. At Cheetham we try to be patient, polite and kind. Good manners are very important to us. We do not like rough games in our playground. Any fighting is sorted out by Ms T. We leave our toys at home, but we do bring books and extra work to show our teacher.

> *School rules.* Move quietly and sensibly around school and be ready to settle to work quickly. Do as you are asked the first time. Listen silently when someone is speaking to you. When you are working only the people in your group should be able to hear you. Keep your hands, feet and all other objects to yourself. Take care of all property and the whole-school environment.

> *School sanctions.* Class-based sanctions. Quiet room. Sent to the head teacher. A letter will be sent home. Parents will be called in.

This value placed on visual impact was even more marked in the Michigan schools, where the entrance and circulation areas were often covered with material, but the tone was significantly different from the equivalent spaces in English primary schools. In Michigan the emphasis was moral rather than aesthetic, and three messages predominated: caring, sharing, and celebrating success:

> With the right amount of love, support and encouragement from you our students will achieve their dream.

> *Peace is nurturing* – making peace is the everyday struggle to be kind, just and responsible . . . first in ourselves, then in our homes, then in our world.

> *Wonderful ways to love a child* – Give your presence. Laugh, dance and sing together. Allow them to love themselves. Listen from a heart space. Create a circle of quiet. Giggle. Don't hide your tears.

> *101 Ways to praise a child* – Wow. Way to go. Super. You're special. Outstanding. Excellent. Great. Neat. A+ job. You're a treasure. You're sensational. A big hug . . .

Heather was a good listener during conflict negotiation meetings. Tyler – good listening skills . . .

Perfect attendance – Michael, Kimberley, Brandon, Omar, Cinnamon, Shamika (most improved).

Good conduct – James, Robert, Sheree, Anthony, Giovanni, Tiffany.

In Russia, the tone of such material was again moral, but in a different way. There were pictures of star former pupils – and often of former teachers, signalling that in this country teachers, too, are important – together with assorted slogans and extracts ranging from the overtly political to the broadly nationalistic.

On relating to parents: contact is the key! The older I become, the more dear my parents become. If your relationship is moving towards failure, you yourself must find the key to making contact. Parents have their ideas on what constitutes good and evil, and children theirs.

How to fight stress. The main thing is not to bottle up turbulent emotions. Do not allow stress to prevent you from fulfilling your tasks. Anticipate stress and fight it!

Has Earth anything more fair to offer than a kind deed illuminated by the lofty light of disinterestedness? Is there any feat greater than offering self-sacrificing service without demanding or needing reward?

Our country has succeeded in bringing about political reforms. The main one is to form a state that functions in accordance with constitutional law, and to provide a leadership which fulfils that law . . .

The new political thought requires – Preservation of human civilization in the face of the threat of nuclear annihilation. Practical conclusions from an acknowledgement of the world's diversity and interdependence. The strict respect of the right of people to a a free choice about their destiny. The understanding that it is possible to resolve quarrels between states without military means, and that it is important to balance different interests.

In India, in contrast again, there was little visual material. This is partly because of the absence of indoor circulation space – the climate allows the courtyard to serve this purpose, and the veranda roof, where it exists, provides protection against sun and monsoon rain – and partly because relatively little visual material is used in Indian primary schools more generally (there was very little on the interior walls, either). What we saw tended to combine random improving quotations from, for example, Gandhi and Tagore with the occasional notice of a more directly instrumental kind, such as a daily attendance chart.

Great ideals create a great mind.

The way an insect eats away at clothes is the same way that jealousy destroys a human being.

You will reap what you sow. You cannot expect flowers to grow where you have sown seeds of thorns.

Requests to parents / guardians. Special attention should be given to children's personal hygiene – a clean mind is developed in a clean body. A proper school uniform should be worn – uniform is the symbol of unity. A habit of sending children to school on time should be encouraged. Children should be encouraged to follow the school rules. A hearty thank you for your suggestions and co-operation.

Invaluable quotations. The wise learn from others' misfortunes, while fools learn from their own (Gandhiji). Laziness and progress are always in conflict (Nehruji). Obedience is the way to progress (Lal Bahadur Shastri).

All the schools had classrooms. Here is where children and teachers spend most of their time. We can and will infer a certain amount from how classrooms are arranged, but before that we should note the striking differences in the internal spaces which schools possessed, apart from their classrooms. The Indian formula was the simplest: classrooms, veranda and courtyard. Then came France: playground, classroom, circulation space, cloakrooms, staff room and perhaps director's office. The Michigan buildings were the most complex and variegated: classrooms and cloakrooms, one or even two gymnasia, library, offices for principal, secretary and others, specialist rooms for subjects such as music, art and science, and for support activities such as speech therapy, special needs and counselling and so on. In Russia, the accommodation was somewhat simpler: classrooms, offices, gymnasium, hall with stage, perhaps doubling for dining, and specialist rooms which were used more by the schools' secondary than their primary pupils. In England the accommodation centred on multi-purpose classrooms, occasionally supplemented by libraries and specialist teaching rooms, administrative offices, and a hall combining the functions of gymnasium, dining room and – most important – venue for the bringing together of all the school's pupils and teachers.

There are two critical differences within all this variation. First, is the degree to which classrooms as the core teaching spaces are supplemented by specialist accommodation – which possibly reveals as much about available resourcing levels as about educational philosophy. Second, and indisputably a matter of educational philosophy, there is the existence of a central space upon which all of a school's members converge for events which signal that a school is indeed 'more than a teaching shop' or a collection of classes. In this matter, the French schools were at one pole, those in England at the other. In France the business of schooling has traditionally started and finished with what goes on in classrooms (although things are changing in this regard, as we shall see). In England, schools have always attached considerable significance to the collective life and collective acts of the school as a whole, above all to the daily 'assembly'. The Indian primary schools shared and no doubt inherited this trait, although there the arena for daily assembly is the courtyard rather than a covered hall. In Russia and Michigan there were occasional, but much less frequent whole school events, although the spaces for them existed. In Russia the bringing together of all the school's pupils and teachers marked a special occasion; in England it was a daily commonplace.

Now to the classrooms. Self-evidently, resourcing is a major factor. The Indian classrooms were small and minimally furnished: whitewashed down to pupils' shoulder height and black below, they contained at most a blackboard, a teacher's desk, *tat pattis* or runners on the floor upon which the children sat cross-legged and worked (but rarely desks), and a cupboard. Much of what was available was dilapidated. The Michigan classrooms were the most lavishly furnished and equipped, with tables and chairs for pupils, sofas and easy chairs, teacher's desk, television, video, computers (we counted seven in one classroom, and this in a school with a separate IT laboratory with a further 25 computer work-stations), overhead projectors, screen, maps and a sink, together with abundant supplies of books, equipment, consumables and other materials, all of them stored in dedicated and labelled units allowing security, visibility or access, depending on the nature of the materials and the purposes they served.

However, while the quantity and quality of classroom furniture and equipment tells one story, its *disposition* tells another. Resourcing levels, as betokened by school buildings and equipment, signal economic factors and political priorities over which teachers have little influence and no control. The decision on how building and equipment are to be arranged and used is an educational one.

Most of the classrooms were variants on two basic kinds of layout: rows and groups. UK research reminds us not to jump to over-hasty conclusions about the pedagogical significance of either of these arrangements – children may be seated in groups but work individually, and they may be seated in rows but work co-operatively.[7] This is what Galton describes as the difference between *base* (where children sit) and *team* (how and with whom they work):[8] it is essential to study teaching in action rather than draw inferences from classroom geography alone. Nevertheless, we have here a first-order indicator of classrooms' pedagogical centre of gravity. At one end of the continuum were the Indian classrooms, where children sat one behind the other on the *tat patti* (not even in pairs as in Russia), interacting with the teacher or the blackboard but rarely with each other. Here, teacher dominance was accentuated by the fact that he/she alone had a desk, and stood while they sat on the floor, producing a height differential of some three feet and ensuring that children invariably looked up to speak to the teacher while the teacher looked down to address the children. At the other extreme were the Michigan classrooms. Here the teacher's desk was frequently pushed to one side, the blackboard might be in another part of the room, and the teacher, by moving about, sitting with groups and speaking to the class from wherever he or she happened to be, reinforced the implied shift from didactic to collaborative pedagogy. In these classrooms there was no obvious focal point for pupils' attention.

The Russian classrooms represented the fusion of geography and pedagogy in its purest form. In none of the 16 Russian classrooms in which we undertook fieldwork was there the slightest deviation from the formula which is confirmed in other contemporary studies or those from the Soviet era.[9] Here pairs of desks were aligned in rows facing what was clearly the focal point of the classroom: the teacher's desk to one side, notices to the other, the blackboard in the centre. The latter was often a complex triptych of hinged outer leaves, sliding centre sections and a mixture of white and chalkboard surfaces, sometimes with curtains so that the boards' front as well as back surfaces could be prepared in advance and concealed until they were needed. The unambiguous focus of these classrooms was underscored, as we shall see later, by the conduct of the lessons.

That leaves England and France. In both countries there was more variation in classroom layout than we witnessed in the other three (although we were given to understand that in the United States more widely, in indeed in some other school districts within our chosen state of Michigan, rows rather than groups were readily evident as the layout norm). In France, although the blackboard had the same kind of prominence as in Russia (and was used in similar ways), we also found class-rooms more variously disposed than this would suggest. Desk groups were in fact more common than rows, but we also recorded horseshoe plans and mixtures of the three. England appears to be once more in transition in this regard: in the early 1980s, in London, Mortimore and his colleagues recorded a mixture of rows and groups. In the late 1980s, in Leeds, I found nothing but groups. In the mid 1990s, Galton found mainly groups, but with a small number of horseshoe plans. In the *Five Cultures* English classrooms we found the same apparent shift, and a greater tendency than in the 1980s for teachers to rearrange furniture to meet different purposes. In this matter, the government's literacy and numeracy strategies were beginning to exert some influence.

The horseshoe arrangement, in which children face both each other and the teacher, is thought to be more flexible than either rows and groups in allowing individual work, collaborative activity and whole class teaching without the need to move furniture. It was commended by the UK government's Numeracy Task Force on the basis of a project in the London Borough of Barking and Dagenham that in turn sought to emulate mathematics teaching in Switzerland and Germany.[10] However, McNamara identified it as a useful option some years earlier than this.[11]

From where children sit in relation to each other and to the teacher we can gather – subject to the caveat expressed earlier – something of the dominant forms of pedagogic interaction. But in two of the countries seating might also relate to cur-riculum content. In the English and American classrooms space was frequently subdivided to meet specialist requirements. Most had carpeted meeting areas where the whole class would sit on the floor to receive instructions, engage in discussion or listen to a story. Some had bays, areas or simply tables for art, science, computing, technology or other activities which have specialized material requirements – the primary equivalent of the subject rooms in secondary schools. Most had a reading or library corner. Closer examination showed, as it did in the Leeds and ORACLE follow-up studies, that in some classrooms the idea of curriculum-specific space was taken further than others: in one classroom there might be a carpeted area and a reading corner; in another these together with zones for most other subjects.[12] In some of the Michigan classrooms, where this practice was taken to its furthest extremes, the zones were labelled in a way which suggested that a classroom was almost a school in itself: 'reading center' (with books displayed and shelved, and easy chairs), 'writing center' (with paper, card and writing implements), 'listening center' (with tapes, tape recorders and headsets), 'computer center' (banks of between three and seven monitors and keyboards), 'math center', 'science center', 'art center', 'office center'. Other Michigan teachers with more conventional classroom layouts said that they intended to move to a 'center-based approach' in the not-too-distant future.

The existence of specialist curriculum zones or centres within a classroom in which, by virtue of the class-teacher system, all or most subjects are taught, has an important consequence for pupil location. Children no longer have set places, but become peripatetic, changing position according to the task in hand. In turn, this means that their belongings must be stored separately, rather than in 'their' desks, and indeed the concomitant of grouping in this context is that tables replace desks and units containing ranks of individually assigned trays replaces desk storage space. In consequence, and having critical implications for classroom management and the use of time, these kinds of classroom are characterized by a high degree of both teacher and pupil mobility. This in turn takes time from the teaching day and requires the development of appropriate routines. In Russia, however, pupils sat in the same place for every lesson, and movement was confined to standing up to answer questions and coming to the front to work at the blackboard. In France, which in this matter, as in a number of others, finds itself somewhere towards the mid-point of the two continua of classroom geography – rows/groups and curriculum-specific zoning – there was little or no zoning, but some changes to seating according to teaching circumstance.

Looking up to the classroom walls from where pupils sit, move about or work, we find large and potentially usable spaces between windows, doors, blackboards and furniture. In England, what is placed in these spaces is called 'display'. The word carries a peculiarly English charge – and an appropriate one in many classrooms – suggestive of ostentation, window dressing or peacockery, so to apply it across cultures would be quite wrong, and we shall have to be content with the neutral but more cumbersome 'wall-mounted materials'.

In the Russian classrooms enlarged photographs of landscapes provided a backdrop and served the same decorative function as the ubiquitous pot plants. Above or beside the blackboard would be numbers, the Cyrillic alphabet and a reminder of the importance of sitting up straight. For the main part, the wall material consisted of rules and reminders. In India, as I noted above, the walls were mostly unadorned; the exception was the occasional moral, rather than procedural, injunction. In most of the English classrooms the walls were used very much as a showcase for children's (and teachers') finished work, and in this matter the word 'display' exactly fits the function since high priority was attached to the quality of presentation, and work was rarely attached to the walls without first being mounted not just once but sometimes twice or thrice – a degree of material extravagance which would be neither conceivable nor possible in India or Russia. In France, however, we found a wider range: from rules and reminders to the more transitory collections of 'work-in-progress' where words, problems, information, drawings and so on were pinned up, referred to over the next day or so, added to and then taken down and replaced by others. These might be punctuated, somewhat inconsequentially in terms of the basic curriculum, but of wider significance in terms of *la culture générale*, by posters for concerts, festivals and local exhibitions of art or archaeology. In Michigan we tended to find an eclectic, and frequently exotic, mix: no surface left uncovered by children's finished work, work in progress, number lines, alphabets, exhortations and pocket homilies, usually relating to attitudes and relationships, and, in every classroom, the Stars and Stripes and the Pledge, focus for an unvarying daily ritual.

With these different spatial and mural geographies in mind we can begin to invoke some of the differences in classroom ecology. They will become clearer still when we have explored the interactions that they frame. We can sum up the main differences, to this point anyway, in terms of two dimensions: *focus* and *ambience*.

In India, Russia and to a lesser extent France, the focus was *unitary*: one class rather than several groups or many individuals, a relationship between that class and the teacher, and one activity pursued at any one time. In England, Michigan and to a lesser extent France again, the focus was *multiple*: several sub-groups rather than simply one class unit, different kinds of relationships, both within groups and between groups, between individuals and the teacher, and several activities pursued at any one time.

Judging ambience is a subjective matter, but in this section of the chapter I have started with the physical properties of schools and classrooms and am trying to infer no more from these than what they most obviously and perhaps intentionally convey to an observer.

The ambience conveyed by the physical disposition of the Indian classrooms is neutral: but for the blackboard, *tat pattis* and store cupboard the space between their four bare walls might be used for anything. They are a setting only, and have no individual stamp. One classroom is much like another, and a classroom in India is much like any other public space in which ordinary people are required to congregate for some purpose or another, be it receiving an education or buying a railway ticket.

One Russian classroom is much like another, too, but here the distinct educational purposes are manifest and unambiguous. These are places in which to work, to work hard, and to work together. Of this the formal layout, the convergence of all sightlines on the blackboard, and the messages on the walls all provide an unwavering reminder. Yet as places to work they are not the least bit cheerless. There are pictures, plants, curtains and above all a great deal of light, for the windows in every Russian classroom that we visited filled one whole wall of the four, from desk height to ceiling. In contrast, some of the large, low-ceilinged modern classrooms in England and Michigan were so inadequately fenestrated that they required artificial light throughout the day.

Once we reach the United States, too, the ambiguities start to creep in. The multiple focus conveys multiple realities. Look one way and you see a computer laboratory; look the other and you see the cosy domesticity of a sitting room, complete with rugs, sofas, easy chairs, television and table lamps; at the margins the apparatus of the storeroom, the shelves and bookcases needed to classify and contain the vast armoury of equipment; in one corner, apparently, a shrine to patriotism; in between an apparently random collection of chairs and tables. Is this a place for work, for play, for worship, or for rest and relaxation? Perhaps it is all of these at once, and perhaps we shall find that the role of the teachers who work here is similarly unconfined. Moreover, and in strong contrast to India and Russia, each

Michigan classroom bore its teacher's personal aesthetic stamp. Teaching space, like the teaching itself, was individualized.

In between these extremes are France and England. The English classrooms read like a pale imitation of the Michigan ones (the actual direction of influence is the other way round, since the high-visual-premium, multiple-focus elementary school classroom is in fact an import from 1960s England) but with a narrower spectrum of options, and the English primary teacher's obsession with labelling ensures that every space and every object ('our reading corner' . . . 'Sandra's drawer' . . . 'Mark's coat' . . . 'Red Group' . . . 'large paint brushes' . . . 'round-ended scissors' . . . 'plain paper') tells you its function unasked. Nevertheless, there is frequently an unre-solved competition over function: is a classroom a workplace or a gallery? The tension stems from the fact that in England, as in Michigan, teachers personalized 'their' classrooms and expected to be judged on how the classroom looked as well as how they taught. In England I came across an LEA officer who judged the suitability of a school head to be short-listed for an advisory post on the strength of the quality of the 'display' in the school's entrance hall. This, I think, would be inconceivable in France, India or Russia.

The French classrooms are clearly classrooms rather than lounges, art galleries or ticket halls: the only question is what kind of classroom. A few that we visited expressed the cheerless and regimented minimalism which was commonplace in French elementary schools until quite recently ('cheerless', though, is arguably an ethnocentric judgement and there is plenty of scope for good cheer in a barracks); most conveyed a sense of both instrumentalism and collegiality; a few at the other end of the spectrum had, by virtue of shifting furniture layouts and the transitory and unpolished character of what went up on walls and as quickly down again, more of the feel of a workshop or studio.

Organizing Time

The child's experience of schooling is bounded by time as well as space. Primary schooling is but a fleeting fragment of a lifetime, but to a child it is an eternity. 'The magnitude of 7000 hours spread over six or seven years of a child's life is difficult to comprehend', said Philip Jackson in his 1968 classic *Life in Classrooms*:

> Aside from sleeping, and perhaps playing, there is no other activity that occupies as much of the child's time as that involved in attending school. Apart from the bedroom (where he has his eyes closed most of the time) there is no single enclosure in which he spends a longer time than he does in the classroom.[13]

Jackson said much more than this, and his book is a closely observed, timeless and engaging account of the complexities of classroom life and the way it utterly enfolds and subjugates those who live it. Jackson' thesis turns on

> . . . the three facts of life with which even the youngest student must learn to deal . . . the *crowds, praise* and *power* . . . that . . . collectively form a hidden curriculum which each

student (and each teacher) must master if he is to make his way satisfactorily through the school.[14]

Actually, Jackson also devotes considerable attention to the rule of the clock and could reasonably have made *time* a fourth 'fact' of school life and a fourth component of the hidden curriculum.

Most of the child's time in school is spent in the classroom, and it is therefore in the context of our discussion of pedagogy (which starts in Chapter 11) that we shall examine most closely the use of time in primary education. All five countries have officially declared norms for the total time a child at a given stage of education must spend in school (these are given, country by country, in Chapters 2–6), but other events than lessons may punctuate the day, and some of these may consume amounts of time that are by no means insignificant: play, break or recess; lunch; whole school activities such as assembly. The assembly, as we show below, is a peculiarly British phenomenon. It was also exported to India, and in both countries it is one of the day's pivotal points. It has no equivalent in France.

Beyond the identification of the basic categories of primary school time – lessons, whole-school events, break/recess, and lunch – we can define the comparative use of time by reference to four dimensions:

(1)   time concentrated – dispersed
(2)   time elastic – rigid
(3)   lesson length regular – irregular
(4)   lessons short – long.

The dimension *concentrated/dispersed* is best illustrated by comparing the English and American schools with those in Russia. In the English and American schools, children, especially older children, spent long periods in the classroom at a stretch, and there might be just three breaks from study during the day: for morning play/recess, for lunch, and for afternoon play/recess. Indeed, in both countries it was not uncommon for pupils to work right through the afternoon session, say, from 1.20 to 3.10, or from 1.15 to 3.30, without a break. In contrast, in the Russian schools there was a brief break between every lesson and a longer break for lunch. There were also occasional short breaks for exercise and/or relaxation during lessons, especially for the younger children. These were intended to keep them at a peak of concentration.

Elastic time/rigid time. In Russia and India, and to a lesser extent in the French schools, the divisions of time were precise and predictable. Indians themselves talk jestingly or resignedly about the infinite elasticity of 'Indian time', usually in the context of delays experienced or anticipated at the hands of officials, or, self-deprecatingly, to explain a missed deadline. In the schools, however, Indian time was as rigid as Russian time. In the American and English classrooms, in contrast, lessons had a habit of extending beyond their expected limits, usually so that a line of enquiry could be pursued further or a piece of work could be finished. By the late 1990s this had become far less common in English primary classrooms than it was in the 1960s and the 1970s, when temporal flexibility had been counted a professional virtue, and the folklore still made frequent reference to the bad old days of rigid timetables and clanging bells. The national curriculum and public accountability brought back timetables, and bells too, sometimes.

Lessons were *regular* or *irregular* in length. Again there was an East–West divide. All the lessons we observed in India were the same length, as they were in Russia, within a margin of five minutes either way. This is not to say that all subjects were allocated the same time within a day. If schools wished to spend more time on mathematics, Russian or Hindi, they might include two such lessons in the day, either consecutive (the double lesson) or separated by others. In the other three countries the variation in lesson length could be considerable.

Finally, absolute lesson length – allowing, that is to say, for 'elastic' time – varied considerably. We observed some lessons of under 30 minutes in all the countries except Russia and India, for in those two countries the standard lesson length was 45 minutes and 30 minutes respectively. On the other hand it was never longer than this, while in the other three countries lessons could be considerably longer. In Michigan and England we observed several sessions which lasted for up to 90 minutes, as we did, though less frequently, in France. Although for want of a better term I have called this dimension *short–long*, no judgement is implied about whether the lengths of lessons were appropriate. To Russian teachers a 45-minute lesson is neither short nor long: it is exactly the right length for what it has to contain and accomplish. But it is shorter, sometimes considerably shorter, than some lessons observed elsewhere.

Underlying these differences were equally contrasting beliefs and assumptions about both learning and the curriculum which we shall explore more fully later: the presumed limits to children's span of concentration and the proper way to optimize it; the timetable as a standard framework which a school constructs for all its teachers, as opposed to something teachers construct for themselves and their unique circumstances; knowledge as received and bounded on the one hand, reflexive and organic on the other; teaching as predictable, and learning as open ended.

Organizing People

It is time to place on our educational stage its main actors. They fall into two groups – children and adults; and three role sets – pupils, teachers and ancillary staff. The middle role set subdivides into teacher and head teacher, director or principal. (Hereafter, except when discussing a particular country, we shall use the generic term *head* for the office which is called *director* in France and Russia, *principal* in the United States, *head master* or *head mistress* in India and *head teacher* in England.)

It used to be the case in England that the boundaries between and within these groups were closed and impermeable. Taylor's study of primary teachers in the early 1970s identified two 'zones of influence', those of the head (the school as a whole) and the class teacher (the classroom).[15] By the mid 1980s the introduction of curriculum co-ordinators and whole-school planning had begun to erode the boundaries of both zones: class teachers worked with heads on whole-school matters, and in turn worked with each other in the classroom. However, the Leeds research, which charted *inter alia* deliberate attempts to break down these boundaries,[16] revealed them to be more resistant to change than other commentators had claimed,[17] and the long and as yet unresolved debate about subject leaders has confirmed the more cautious reading.[18]

Before we attempt such judgements on a comparative basis, however, we need some facts and figures. To illustrate the range we take one or two schools in each country, providing contrasts where appropriate. All schools have been given pseudonyms. The Russian schools have letters rather than numbers to convey something of their titular anonymity without causing confusion over whether, for example Kursk's School 42 is School 23 redesignated or the real School 42.

Coulanges School in Nice has 275 pupils aged 6–11. They are organized into eleven age-based classes: two parallel classes for each year but three for the youngest group (age 6–7) reflecting the beginning of a local population boom which will now work its way up through the school. There are 15 adults, including a teacher for each class, a *directrice*, a teacher who works with small groups of children with special educational needs, a secretary and a caretaker. Montagne school in the Alpes-Maritimes has just 22 children aged 5 and 6 (it combines the last stage of *l'école maternelle* with *cours préparatoire* (CP), which is the first stage of *l'école élémentaire*). They are taught by one full-time teacher and an assistant. The children work sometimes together and sometimes in year groups in adjacent rooms, with the teacher moving between the groups and deploying the assistant as necessary. They come from two neighbouring villages whose communes have taken the decision, in conjunction with the *académie*, to treat the two schools as in effect a single split-site campus, with 5–6 year-olds on one site and 7–11 year-olds in the other, rather than have two self-contained establishments each catering for the full 6–11 age range, or closing one school and concentrating all the pupils from both villages in the other. The school occupies the ground floor of the *mairie* and lessons are occasionally interrupted by errant official phone calls.

Kursk School B has 1,554 pupils aged 7–17 shared among 60 classes. The staff numbers 90 and includes the director, 4 deputy directors, the head of the primary section, specialist teachers, generalist primary teachers, psychologists, 'defectologists' who work with children with special educational needs, technicians, secretaries and others. The primary classes (termed 'grades') are age based. Obolensky School is almost that relatively rare establishment, a free-standing primary school: it is in fact the primary department of the secondary school which stands close by, but it has its own head, 3 classes containing 66 children aged 6–9, and 3 other teachers.

Purana Primary School in New Delhi has 620 pupils aged 5–11. There are 17 classes and 17 teachers, together with a headmistress, 5 nursery staff, and 6 ancillary staff including watchman and sweepers. Its pupil–teacher ratio, at 36.5:1, is good by Indian standards, so it is probably useful to contrast it with Ferozabad Primary, in the state of Haryana, which has 425 pupils, 9 classes and 9 teachers including the head, and a pupil–teacher ratio of 47:1. The school also has a sweeper (part time). Further out into the state there are village schools with a nominal roll of 70 and one teacher.

Thoreau Elementary School in a suburb of Lansing, the state capital of Michigan, has 320 pupils aged 4–12. There are 12 'multi-age' classes, two for kindergarten (ages 4–6), and between two and three each for grades 1–5. The ages overlap – 5/6/7 at Grade 1, 6/7/8 at Grade 2, and so on. Counting the number of staff is something of a challenge, even – he admits it – to the school's principal: there is the principal, a teacher for each class, 7 'co-teachers' (teaching assistants), 3 special needs teachers, a secretary, and several part-time professional staff: teachers for music and physical education, reading consultant, speech therapist, librarian, nurse, counsellor, psychologist and social worker. There are also 'noon supervisors' who police the school and playground during the midday break, canteen staff, crossing guards and two custodians (one for days, the other for nights). In and out of the school on a more or less constant basis are students and faculty from a neighbouring university, and the school is designated a Professional Development School along the lines of the recommendations of the Holmes Group.[19]

Hamilton Primary School on the edge of a cathedral city in the north of England has 312 pupils aged 4–11. They are in 10 classes, most of which are age based, although two have a mixture of 5 and 6 year olds. It has a head teacher, 10 class teachers, a secretary, 2.5 non-teaching assistants, a part-time special needs support teacher, 6 canteen staff, a caretaker and a 'lollipop lady' (the familiar title has a decidedly undignified ring after 'crossing guard' although the friendly image is deemed important. The title derives from the lollipop-shaped stop-go sign with which road crossing patrols in England control the traffic). Cheetham Primary School, in a different city which was formerly one of Britain's great industrial centres, has 210 pupils age 5–11 divided between 7 age-based classes and a 26-place nursery. It has a head teacher, 9 full-time teachers, 3 full-time nursery assistants, 5 special needs assistants, 3 bilingual staff giving support to children for whom English is the second language, a caretaker and of course the lollipop lady. The range of support staff, and although smaller than Hamilton it has more adults, reflects its circumstances: this is an inner city school and 40 per cent of its pupils are from Muslim Asian families originating in Pakistan. It qualifies for additional support and some of this (the 'Section 11' complement of bilingual staff) is provided for outside the school's budget. Finally, Tilty Church of England Primary School: a village school with 38 children, 2 classes (ages 5–7 and 7–11), 2.5 teachers (2 full time and 1 half time), together with part-time secretarial support.

This basic comparison yields some equally basic, although significant, variables. The schools studied ranged in their pupil population from 19 to nearly two thousand. The Russian schools were the largest, but they incorporated both the primary and secondary stage. The largest of the *Five Cultures* primary schools was the 705-pupil Hawthorne Elementary in Michigan. The age range varies in accordance with the national arrangements outlined in earlier chapters, although there is a certain amount of flexibility at the bottom end: in Russia, children started at the age of 7 in our urban schools and 6 in the rural school; the kindergarten, nursery or *école maternelle* was sometimes physically separate from the primary school, and sometimes incorporated into both buildings and school structure and staffing.

As we noted in the Leeds research, judging pupil–teacher ratios is more complex than it may seem. Dividing the number of pupils in a school by the number of classes yields the average class size. Beyond this basic operational statistic there are the ratios of teachers to children and adults to children (for it is clear that not all members of a school's staff are teachers, and some are in the shadow zone between teaching and non-teaching staff). Class sizes were significantly smaller in our rural schools, except in India, where they were much larger. India also had the widest class size fluctuations – between 36 and 70. Those for Russia, France and Michigan were, at 22–26, fairly comparable; the classes in our English schools were somewhat larger – thirty or so.

However, class size cannot be taken in isolation from other staffing provision. If one detaches from a school's staffing complement those adults other than the head and class teachers, one arrives at what might be termed a 'support index'. This was lowest in India and highest by far in Michigan, with Russia and England following and the French schools trailing slightly. On the other hand, although the support index in our French schools was lower than in England or Russia, most of the French classes we observed had 20–22 pupils and none had more than 24, significantly fewer than the observed English average. The differences reflect budgetary circumstances as well as educational priorities, for support staff are often cheaper than teaching staff. The French approach was to concentrate the budget on schools' central teaching function: teachers, books and equipment. In all but the largest French schools heads, too, had a class. In England, as the 1999 OFSTED survey points out, the number and proportion of support staff rose markedly during 1994–8, and by the latter year there were 40 per cent more nursery assistants, support staff for children with special needs and from ethnic minorities, not to mention administrative and clerical staff.[20] But most strikingly, in our Michigan schools support staff invariably outnumbered the class teachers, and the ratio of pupils to those adults undertaking a teaching or teaching support role (that is, excluding custodians, canteen staff and so on) could be as low as 9:1. This, together with the fact that these schools were also the most generously equipped, illustrates the extent of the gap between the resourcing levels of the Michigan schools and those in the other four countries, although this is modest in comparison with the resource chasm between Michigan, England, Russia and France on the one hand, and India on the other.

We noted variations in pupil groupings. In these five countries, single-year age-grouping was the commonest basis for determining membership of a class, although the village schools in France, England and India – in common with small schools worldwide – were forced to adopt a multi-age/multi-grade strategy, and in England and Michigan multi-age grouping was sometimes adopted from choice. Thus in one of our three Michigan school districts multi-age grouping had been adopted as district policy for all 5–8 year olds (K-3, or Kindergarten to Grade 3), and was strongly defended in a school district publication as being a cardinal principle of 'developmentally appropriate education'.[21]

The policy is interesting because its justification to parents conflates age and grade:

> Previously your children attended schools that used a graded system (1st, 2nd, 3rd grade etc.). This system had been in existence since 1848. It was implemented during the Industrial Revolution . . . Children were placed in grades based on their birthrates and chronological age . . . Each year students entered school 'differently-ready' . . . [Yet] they were all expected to be 'made the same' at the end of 180 days . . . In the multiage system grade levels are eliminated . . . the classroom lessons and activities are prepared to meet the needs of individual students, rather than in the graded system in which students had to change to fit into an existing curriculum . . . Multiage classrooms are good for students because they are 'child centered'.[22]

'Grade' here is the equivalent – structurally, historically and ideologically – of the 'standards' into which English elementary schools were divided under the 1862 Revised Code. Grades and standards were, and in many countries remain, hurdles which have to be cleared before a child is permitted to move on to the next grade (hence 'making the grade', and the French practice of *redoublement*). But of course – as is now the case in England – pupils' transition from one age-related class to the next is not necessarily tied to their performance in age-related tests. In England, pupils *move up* a grade (i.e. from one class to the next) regardless of whether they have *made* the grade (i.e. achieved the expected standard).

The Flint multi-age policy, with its claim to child-centredness, is one manifestation of the reasoning which supported 'vertical grouping' in English primary classrooms in the period between the 1960s and the 1990s (some schools still use it out of choice rather than necessity); the endorsement of *les cycles à l'école primaire* by France's Ministry of Education is another. In France, elementary education is now officially divided into two cycles (see p. 53) and schools can choose how these should relate to pupil organization and the distribution of teachers' responsibilities. Classes may be age-based, but with a different teacher each year, in which case teachers of classes within a cycle are expected to work closely together (in the same way that English primary schools now often have teams for Key Stage 1 and Key Stage 2); alternatively, the teacher may stay with the same class from the start to finish of a cycle; children may be grouped by cycle rather than age, with one teacher for each year; or these strategies may be mixed so as to allow differential grouping for certain subjects and children.[23] In Russia, by way of comparison, we were told it was common for teachers to see the same class through the first three years of the primary stage.

Other pupil grouping variants include streaming and setting. There was little evidence of streaming in any of the schools we visited, although in England streaming was the norm at the upper end of primary schools until the late 1960s. The surprising exception was Russia, where we encountered on the one hand fierce opposition to the principle of streaming under any circumstances and on the other schools which formed classes by dividing each age cohort into an upper and a lower stream in each school year (pupil differentiation emerged as a problematic area in Russia, as we shall see). There were, however, several examples of setting by ability for certain subjects, especially mathematics and literacy, and the UK government has given this practice strong support by presenting the extension of setting as a specific political target to be achieved by 2002:

> By 2002 ... we will have ... schools setting pupils according to ability and further development of innovative approaches to pupil grouping.[24]

The other 'innovative approaches' commended in this document include 'target-grouping' (changing groups in line with their differential progress towards weekly targets), and the 'fast-tracking' of able pupils towards qualifications ahead of their age cohort.[25]

On the basis of this evidence, then, the grouping of pupils for teaching purposes, and the way such grouping relates to pupils' perceived development and ability, looks set to be one of the fault-lines revealed by our international comparison.

The organization of teaching staff may be another. In the early 1980s I showed how the typical English primary school had a simple and relatively flat management structure consisting essentially of just two levels, the head and the class teachers.[26] By the 1990s, I was able to present a more complex picture. The classic two-tier, two 'zones of influence' structure, which from the Leeds evidence I termed *type 1*, had given way in many schools to variants on both two and three-tier models. This was the result of the growing specialization of curriculum-related management roles in English primary schools after the 1978 HMI Primary Survey,[27] the general shift to more participatory approaches to whole school decision-making, and pressure towards delegation created by the exponential increase in the demands placed on schools by central government after the 1988 Education Reform Act. Deputy heads' roles, ill-defined until the 1980s, were filled out to provide the beginnings of a counterpoint to the head–class teacher axis (*type 2*); schools began to set up senior management teams (*type 3*) larger schools established quasi-departments based on school years, national curriculum key stages or school subjects (*type 4*) departmentalization produced an explicit level of management between senior and junior (*type 5*); and, as the most developed form, schools moved from a management *hierarchy* to a management *matrix* whose two main axes were the curriculum and pupil age-grouping (*type 6*).[28] In this, although the class teacher system continued to predominate, their management structures had come to resemble those of many secondary schools.

The *Five Cultures* data from English schools confirms the trend towards either more complex hierarchies or a matrix approach to management. The other four countries provide useful contrasts. In all our schools, as we have noted, the core school roles were, as in England, those of the head and the generalist class teacher. The degree of subject specialization entertained or provided was more variable. This was partly a function of school size and staffing levels, for historically the class teacher system exists – as noted in Chapter 6 – for economic rather than educational reasons, and it will persist for as long as resourcing levels do not permit an alternative. This was clearly the case in India, although we worked in one school where a specialist taught music. But where resourcing *did* permit different configurations, as in the American and Russian schools (the latter had plenty of subject specialists on site by virtue of encompassing the full school age range) generalist teaching roles might also be a matter of choice. In France (as in England) our teachers stoutly defended the generalist teaching role on educational grounds: actually, given the high level of boundary-maintenance among teaching staff, they could hardly do otherwise. In Michigan, as in England, specialist teachers were used for a minority of subjects, usually music and physical education. In Russia, where primary education was based within predominantly specialized teaching communities, the primary teachers each had 'their' class, and taught those classes Russian, mathematics and one or two other subjects. However, they might hand their pupils over to specialist teachers not just for music and physical education, but also for history, geography and art.

Moroever, because the Russian all-age schools were usually considerably larger than the separate primary schools in the other countries, they inevitably had more developed forms of senior management. Typically, below the director and working with him/her as a senior management team were four or five deputy directors with responsibilities for areas such as primary education, secondary education, extra-curricular activity, research, science, technology – and, most distinctively, for *vospitanie*, or moral upbringing, that critical legacy from the communist era. Moscow may have demoted *vospitanie*, but schools had not.

To summarize, then: primary schools in four of our five countries operated on the basis of the familiar counterpoint of head and generalist class teachers. In the French and Indian schools that counterpoint was of a piece with the classic two-tier, two 'zones of influence' model of English primary schools before the 1980s, except that neither Indian nor French primary heads wielded the same amount of power as their English counterparts. In Michigan the high resourcing levels produced in effect two parallel and numerically comparable professional groups, class teachers and support staff. The class-teaching role nevertheless remained dominant and this, combined with the extent of the head's authority, placed the management structure and culture of the Michigan schools not far from those of the English schools.

In these matters Russia stood somewhat apart. There we found a greater tendency to subject specialization, although still within the generalist norm, but because the schools were larger and catered for both primary and secondary pupils, the management context was very different. School directors were inevitably more remote, the senior management tier was weightier, and senior management roles were themselves highly specialized.

9

The Idea of a School

We have noted that the fabric of a school, the way it is equipped and physically organized, and the kind of material with which its walls are adorned, all convey messages of relevance to our quest to uncover and explain cross-cultural differences and commonalities in primary education. The balance and organization of a school's teachers, pupils and support staff takes us further. The way pupils are grouped, where this reflects conscious principle rather than a pragmatic response to pupil numbers or resource limitations, reveals assumptions about how children develop and learn, how they should relate to each other and what counts as educational progress. The timetable for the day, week or year signals the school's educational priorities, but also tells us something about how knowledge and learning are conceived. Through the interviews with heads and class teachers, supplemented by meetings with parents, we were able to go beyond such partly inferential judgements and uncover important variations in respect of the *idea* of a primary school, in the key values which shape the relationships between its members, in the way being a head, a teacher or a pupil are defined, and in the educational goals which teachers claim to pursue.

I say 'claim' not to imply that statements of goals provided by teachers and schools are to be distrusted as so much rhetoric but because we now know something of the complexity of the relationship between what Argyris and Schön many years ago called teachers' 'espoused theory' (the ideas to which they give allegiance and which they communicate to others) and their 'theory-in-use' (the ideas which, in the privacy of their classrooms, actually inform their actions).[1]

In a study undertaken with a group of experienced English primary teachers during 1986–7, we used lesson videotapes and the technique of progressively focused interviews to examine the thinking beyond the espoused theory. At that time we found the public language of primary teaching still dominated by the 1960s–70s slogans and shibboleths of post-Plowden child-centredness, many of them sharply adversarial or dichotomous – 'children not subjects', 'learning not teaching', 'the child's view of the world, not the teacher's', 'flexibility', 'spontaneity', 'discovery', 'integration', 'individualization' 'groupwork', and so on. Each had their function:

slogans generated and reinforced professional solidarity, shibboleths secured, or sought to secure, professional approval and career advancement in the context of hierarchy and patronage.[2]

One of the more intriguing aspects of the recurrent fuss about 'traditional' and 'progressive' teaching in England is the way it takes this public professional language at face value and presumes that it has a precise and isomorphic relationship to what teachers and children actually do in classrooms. It is easy to be critical of 'primaryspeak' – as I myself have been[3] – but it is also essential to understand it for what it is, a form of language which has public rather than private purposes and which may say little more about the day-to-day business of teaching than the Hippocratic Oath says about the day-to-day conduct of medical practice. On the other hand, in a context of educational debate which, in England since the 1970s at any rate, has become increasingly polarized and politicized, primaryspeak provides a convenient aunt sally for the contrary slogans of 'back to basics', 'zero tolerance of failure', 'standards not structures' (an oppositional counterpoint to 'children not subjects'), 'intervention in inverse proportion to success', as well as a suitably flabby punchbag for the combative absolutism of 'targets', 'standards' and 'effectiveness'.

In the 1986–7 study we found the teachers operating in an intellectual and practical context sharply at variance with the easy certainties of primaryspeak. The teachers revealed an acute sense of the competing imperatives of teaching: of the daily struggle to reconcile differing expectations about what they should do and how they should act – from government, inspectors, parents, peers, pupils and self; of the way that experience and a growing sense of the complexity of human development and learning widened rather diminished the gap between what they sought to achieve and what, despite being armed with both experience and skill, they were able to deliver. The private professional language of these teachers gave voice to both uncomplicated values and complicated realities. Teaching, even at its most ostensibly formulaic, was about identifying and resolving dilemmas.[4] In subsequent research, undertaken in 1988 and 1991, we confirmed the centrality of dilemmas and dilemma-consciousness in primary teachers' thinking and uncensored discourse, but found that the particulars changed in response to the changing educational climate beyond the school walls.[5]

It is possible that this reflected a uniquely English state of affairs. In planning the *Five Cultures* interviews, however, I presumed that it might not, and that while I should not expect to encounter the same dilemmas or indeed the same extent of dilemma-consciousness among primary teachers in the other countries, I should almost certainly need to anticipate the possibility of their existence and of the use of public forms of professional discourse to disguise or suppress them.

We can note at this point that the teachers we interviewed in Russia and India more commonly deployed a public, formulaic language to describe and explain their ideas and practices than did the teachers in France, the United States and England, and that in Russia and India the gap between expressed claim and observed reality tended to be more marked than elsewhere. The reasons are likely to be methodological as well as cultural, for in those two countries interviews were conducted through an interpreter while in the other three they were not. Apart from transforming the interview dynamic and making it difficult to establish the kind of easy rapport which is necessary before interviewees will speak freely about what they feel as well as what they do, about what they really believe as well as what they are expected to believe, the context of simultaneous translation tends to exert a constant pressure towards formality of utterance, on both sides. Certainly, we came away from several of the Russian interviews, in particular, with a frustrating sense that we had penetrated no further than the espoused theory. The dynamics of interviews apart, this is not really surprising when one considers the relative novelty for the Russian teachers of uncensored and unguarded conversation with strangers.

Combining interviews with observation and the collection of documentary and pictorial evidence gave us a basis for triangulating what teachers said with what they did, and with what others said and did. Nevertheless, if interviewing has certain inherent limitations, as it does, then these are inevitably compounded when the interview is conducted through an intermediary. This certainly does not invalidate data gained in this way, but it does require us to be cautious in its use.

How, then, did our teachers understand the idea of a primary school? Their responses formed a commentary on the theme of *community*, or rather on Tönnies' distinction between *Gemeinschaft* (a social group united by a sense of common ties, common purposes, common values and interdependence) and *Gesellschaft* (an association of individuals whose members have a practical relationship but in which there is no superordinate sense of community and community values to bind them together).[6]

France

In this matter, the French schools were clearly at one end of the continuum. In its classic form a French primary school is an organizational device for delivering the curriculum required by the Ministry. Its pupils are divided into a given number of classes, each of which is directed by a teacher. Beyond that, the school's identity is not a strong one. What prevents the extension of identity into the realms of community which was such a prominent element in the accounts we had from Michigan, England and Russia, is a combination of central direction, externalized teacher accountability, and a relatively underpowered concept of school headship.

Let me develop these claims. One of the French heads put it succinctly:

> The curriculum is the same in every classroom in France. On the other hand, the way the curriculum is implemented in the classroom is the teacher's responsibility, and only the teacher's responsibility. Provided you comply with the curriculum you can organize things as you want in the classroom.

So here are two components: central directives on curriculum, and a high degree of teacher autonomy on method (an analysis confirmed in the comparative studies of French and English primary education by Broadfoot and her colleagues[7]). That autonomy is not absolute, but, crucially, the teacher's line of accountability runs not within the school to the head, but directly out of the classroom to the inspector-ate, bypassing the head. As another teacher argued:

> How we teach is up to us, and our superior – that is, the inspector. The head of the school has only an administrative role. The head can't dictate, but the inspector can.

Even the matter of who teaches which class, which in the other countries was determined by the head, reflects the autonomy principle, although only up to a point:

> I choose to teach this age-range, each year. The established teachers have a choice, but the new ones don't.

– a fact confirmed in another school:

> Everyone chooses the class they want but when you're new you have to take what's left over. This class wasn't my choice. I'm better teaching older children.

This individualistic, externally referenced notion of teaching is not an organiza-tional aberration: it is of a piece with the principles of equality and consistency in educational provision which affects all provision from primary school to university and goes back via the Ferry laws to Napoleon:

> ...a school can be called a school in the sense that if everyone works the way they want to work, everyone must achieve the same result. So it is a national school, be-cause the curriculum is the same everywhere, and when children leave their local schools they must have the same skills. So, it is a school. If you go to this school, or if you go to a school in Lille, the children may *do* different things but when they leave the school they have *learned* the same things. There are different ways of reaching the same goal and each of us is free to choose the way. But it's the same school, because everyone has the same knowledge.

This head's argument, then, allows us to suggest that while in England 'school' signifies both the building and the activities which take place within it, *l'école* in France is somewhat more disembodied, an intellectual as much as a physical reality, closer perhaps to the use of 'school' to denote a collection of academics in an English university (school of law, school of engineering, and so on, as an alternative to 'department'). *Gesellschaft*, then, gets closer to the nature of the professional relationship in French primary schools, but not to this head's intimation that while in a physical sense France has over 41,000 elementary school buildings, there is only one French elementary school. Constitutionally, France is indivisible (hence, as noted earlier, the French education system has a problem in coping with the politics of difference, whether in religion or language). So too, unless this teacher was seeking to subvert her interview by indulging in metaphysics, is the idea of *l'école*.

We might note here the parallel with French universities, descendants of the single Imperial University and the University of France, both abolished long ago but

– as Judge notes – leaving individual universities with a much more limited identity than their English counterparts.[8] The post-1968 reforms gave universities greater autonomy, but John Ardagh finds French individualism and resistance to institutions as such a powerful antidote to the development of community values of the kind nurtured in English and American universities. 'For us' he reports a Grenoble student as telling him, 'this campus is just a place of transit for getting a degree. We have no urge to build it into some cherished Alma Mater'.[9]

The proposition is supported by the division of labour. The head of a French elementary school, one of them told us, is

> ... a link between everyone – between the *mairie* and the school, between the *académie* and the school, between the parents and the school, between teachers and other teachers, between the caretakers and the teachers, between the school dinner service and the teachers. I am a kind of pivot.

This is the expression of the French concept of school, and the concomitant idea of headship, in its purest form. In practice, the teachers are not totally autonomous. The need to staff every class, as we have seen, means that while established teachers choose their class, new teachers pick up what is left. Further, most of the French teachers talked of attempts within their schools at *harmonization* – meetings at intervals varying from fortnightly to monthly or even termly at which teachers

> ... discuss methods and attempt to harmonize them, especially teachers taking classes at the same level. For example, the teacher next to me and I try to teach the same things in more or less the same way. It is not required that we should do this, but we consider it important.

The Ministry itself, as we saw in chapter three, has attempted to move schools to a more collegial culture. Following the Jospin *loi d'orientation* of 1989, the *projet d'école* was promulgated as a framework for school development planning. In one of our schools, at Juan-le-Grand, the *projet* was taken very seriously. There the head defined an effective school as 'one which thinks and acts together', confirming our view that – in her words – 'in France it is possible for schools to be collections of closed, isolated classrooms' and objecting to the fact that it was so. Each week, for one hour, all the teachers in this school met to discuss matters of shared concern, and pedagogy was prominent among them. Sometimes they would invite a member of the inspectorate or the IUFM to talk with them. The staff had followed the *projet* guidelines and produced a plan that outlined the school's most pressing problems and set out objectives and strategies for attending to them. In the year in question, they were giving particular attention to written communication, space, time and measurement in mathematics, and to promoting dialogue with parents.

Yet despite this change, the range of collective activities and events was limited in comparison with what went on in the other four countries. A school's *conseil d'école* was a formally constituted governing body; its *conseil des maîtres* brought teachers together. Conspicuously absent were activities that brought together all a school's teachers *and* its pupils. There were of course school visits, sporting events and school exchanges, but no school assemblies or their equivalent. Each morning, noted one teacher:

> The children go straight to their classrooms. They stay in their classrooms. At lunch time most of them go home. At the end of the day they all go home.

This situation, which – as I have noted – is at the far end of the community–association continuum, means that many of the matters which concerned teachers in our other countries, especially in England and the United States, impinged little if at all on the French teachers. The French schools had a limited range of school-level policies and few whole school activities. In consequence teachers' roles were more narrowly and instrumentally defined than in other countries. School management structures were rudimentary not from inadequacy but because the framework of assumptions about what schools and teachers were and how they should act demanded nothing more elaborate than this.

One of the heads suggested that the matter went deeper than this:

> It's a matter of liberty. Freedom of expression goes very deep in the French mentality. If you tell French people to do such-and-such, they will refuse. If you tell them we have to achieve such-and-such but you can do it how you like, they will probably agree.

Whether the *projet d'école* can steer the necessary line between collective action and personal autonomy remains to be seen, especially now that the boundaries of the teaching role are being challenged by changing social circumstances. For example, most of our French teachers voiced concern about the way they were having to deal with the consequences of family breakdown, one of which was the transfer of moral agency from home to school. They were not happy about this:

> Schools are having to play a role which should not be theirs. More and more teachers are having to teach children to behave, because the family no longer plays a part. More and more we have to face problems relating to behaviour rather than education. It's a kind of abdication (*démission*) by parents. Children used to be taught rules of behaviour in the family. Now the parents are abdicating and schools are having to take over their role, even if they don't want to. In as much as a school is like a smaller version of society, if the rules aren't observed the school cannot operate. So we are obliged to teach them the rules.

However, although the sands had begun to shift, our teachers were clear that the core educational values remained, and must remain, intact. Central to these were qualities of mind:

> When they leave school they should always be searching for something – with regard to learning, with regard to life, with regard to society, with regard to the world around them.

An educated person is someone who has learned much from the stock of knowledge but has also acquired human values and has become a citizen and can think. Someone who has, as Montaigne said, *une tête bien faite et une tête bien pleine.*

The literal translation – a head well made and well filled (although this is a misquotation[10]) – does not convey completely what this school director was driving at in terms of the combination of knowledge, culture, judgement and civic responsibility which, in her view, being educated the French way ideally produced. The formula, repeated in similar terms by several other teachers in the French schools, was strikingly different to what we were offered in England. Nor, in England, would a statement of educational aims or values have sought the validation of a sixteenth-century essayist, even one admired – as Montaigne was – by Bacon, Shakespeare and Matthew Arnold. This is not to suggest ignorance of such figures among English primary teachers; it is more that in England educational values are justified by reference to future change rather than historical continuity, and to what people can do rather than what they know and how they think. In millennial England, we hear much of 'skills' and of 'information' of the pre-packaged kind that can be downloaded from the web, little of knowledge and even less of understanding.

United States

In the matters explored so far, Michigan provided as sharp a contrast with France as it is possible to imagine. For a start, our Michigan schools generated a wealth of documentation in which 'the school' as agency featured prominently. The school was corporately sentient as well as extant – it 'expected', 'believed', and 'hoped'; it had a 'mission', prominent within which was the idea of community itself, and this embraced not just teachers and pupils, but also those outside the school's walls; it reduced boundaries not just between school and the world beyond, but within the school itself:

> The mission of this school is to provide students, prospective teachers, practicing educators, families and community members with opportunities to use learned knowledge to interpret new situations, to solve problems, to think and reason. Working together as a community of learners, we will create an equitable learning environment that will promote educational growth and development as lifelong processes. To achieve these goals in meaningful ways will require creative thinking about organizational structures and professional roles. Collaborative study supports and promotes the development of deeper understanding of persisting educational problems and fosters a questioning stance. This collaborative relationship is based upon mutual respect and appreciation for the expertise of all concerned in an effort to build an exemplary educational extension network for the 21st century.

And at another school:

> At our school, all people are teachers and learners . . . Our culture encourages mutual support, professionalism and collegiality.

Here, the specific statements on each area of the curriculum actually transformed community into an epistemological mantra:

> In Math, by working and learning together . . . In Literacy, by working and learning together . . . In the Arts, by working and learning together . . .

And whereas in France *les disciplines* were an intellectual domain set apart from the children's everyday experiences, one into which they would be inducted by the teachers, in the Michigan schools, as the mission statement of one of them put it:

> . . . the curriculum consists of important ideas and skills, including students' own questions and interests.

As in Russia, schools publicized and celebrated individual achievement in documentation and in material displayed in the building, but in the Michigan schools the achievements which gained most of this particular kind of praise were those of the team player and the joiner, rather than the star individual: 'President of Junior Board of Education and Student Council' . . . 'National Honor Society' . . . 'captain of baseball and football teams' . . . 'junior Board of Education' . . . 'school choir' . . . 'cheerleading' . . . 'community volunteer' . . . 'track team' . . . 'cabinet member' . . . 'Civitan Club' and so on.

Thus the idea of community pervaded schools' espoused definitions of knowledge, pedagogy and pupil achievement. Yet this was also a culture which nurtures individualism to a high degree. The apparent collision between these two values within the schools was well understood by one of the Michigan heads, and the communal emphasis can perhaps be understood in part as a response to individualism:

> In our country we have put such an emphasis on individual rights that there has been a loss of a common standard of quality, of the shared vision of what's important. Quality suffers because we're trying to accommodate everyone's whim.

We shall see later how within the classroom the conflict between the values of individualism and community could become even more marked.

Not surprisingly, the Michigan schools had collective events to reinforce their collective values. As in England and India, the word 'assembly' was used to signal a bringing together of teachers and pupils, and in our Michigan schools assemblies enabled pupils and classes to share work, to do presentations, and to meet people from the wider community. However, these had only partial equivalence to English or indeed Indian primary school assemblies, for in the United States the religious element required in England was absent, the assembly was an occasional rather than (as in England and India) a regular occurrence, and the class itself provided an important collective forum. There, as we shall see, the language of inclusion and collaboration was prominent, and it was within the classroom that the day's most important collective ritual was celebrated:

I pledge allegiance to the flag of the United States of America, and to the Republic for which it stands. One nation under God, indivisible, with liberty and justice for all.

In the classroom, too, tannoy announcements punctuated the teaching process to provide a form of school assembly by proxy, issuing reminders, making announcements, welcoming newcomers and visitors, cheering successes, and celebrating pupils' birthdays:

> Good morning. Could I have your attention please. It's Student of the Week time. Will those students named as Student of the Week on Friday please come down to the display case in an orderly fashion . . . Here's Mr C with another announcement.

> Morning boys and girls. I hope you're off to a real good start today. We are having a different procedure in the lunch room today because we are going to start using the salad bar. I need to go over the rules for using the salad bar. The rules will be posted by the salad bar and there will be adults down there to help you too. But I just want to kind of go over the rules so it doesn't come as a real shock to you. First of all, we don't want you to pick up the food with your hands. Second . . .

> (Some minutes later) . . . So we would appreciate your co-operation in this matter. Thank you and have a great day.

Pressing the matter further, the strength of the community emphasis in the Michigan schools came from the way there were two levels, or circles of community – outer and inner, the school and the classroom. The values of inclusion and sharing were strong at whole school level, but stronger still once one entered the classroom.

Judging the character and the relative strength of the messages of classroom and school is important. In Michigan, the messages at the two levels were consistent, powerful, and mutually reinforcing: belonging, sharing, caring, and striving for the collective good were what mattered. In France, while that kind of message did not characterize the school-level culture, such as it was (and our French teachers would surely have regarded tannoy announcements like those transcribed above as a gross intrusion into the business on teaching), collective values could be heard, although in a relatively muted form, in some of the classrooms, for at that level solidarity becomes an imperative if not an aspiration, and our French teachers spoke of the need to establish social roles and behavioural norms and rules not so much because these were educationally desirable in the longer term but in order that classrooms could function here and now.

Yet the relationship of school to classroom values in the Michigan schools was not one of straightforward symbiosis. Clearly, heads expected, and were expected, to embody the superordinate values of the school and in this sense they had a distinct zone of influence. In Thoreau Elementary the principal saw himself as the only person with the 'big picture', the one who knew what everyone expected and whose job it was to reconcile all these expectations and strive to mould them into consensus policies of a kind which could be translated into viable practices. This was by no means easy: much of the time he was looking outwards to the community and responding to varied and often vocal demands coming from parents, pressure groups, the school board and local and state politicians. Within the school he was acutely conscious of the influence of the teacher unions, and of the demands of a culture in which every issue embodied a value dilemma, and perhaps the makings of a value-conflict, which needed to be resolved. And if no dilemma was immediately apparent, other teachers hinted, someone would be sure to spot one. At one point in his interview he vented his frustration at the problems this almost obligatory dissensus created for him as a manager:

> I'm going to get into trouble here . . . There is a real need to know who is in charge of our schools . . . There are too many people trying to dictate what goes on in schools, how they should be run. People are pursuing single-item agenda, not getting the whole picture of what it takes to educate a child . . . No matter what someone throws out the school board feels they need to respond to it . . . And now we're very happy to threaten each other with lawsuits and other kinds of intimidation, so it tends to prevent us from taking a firm stand on things we should be taking a firm stand on . . . People must know their roles and stick to them. So my school board is responsible to set policy and my responsibility is to carry it out. I'm happy with that, but I'm not happy when school board gets involved in details about day-to-day. People are muddled about their roles.

By way of illustration, Thoreau's principal recounted his struggle to gain approval from parents, teachers and the community for the school's 'new 3Rs' motto ('At this school we are respectful, responsible, ready to learn and safe'). It had taken him three months.

At Emerson Elementary the struggle to achieve consensus over basic school values had led to the principal being forced to take sick leave after the school staff had failed collectively to determine a viable policy on the management of pupils' anti-social behaviour. As one of the teachers reported:

> The principal is a very gentle, nurturing, kind-hearted person and that's her basis for building discipline. But this doesn't work for 100 per cent of the kids. Some of the kids need hard-line consequences after behaviour has escalated. And there's been frustration in the staff of not getting that kind of support when it escalates to the more serious levels of behaviour problems . . . The principal's not a confrontational person, but these days the principal's job is a confrontational job . . . You can confront issues without being confrontational, but you have to confront students, teachers, parents, central administration. That's why the job's there.

While one principal had skilfully negotiated the values minefield which seemed to be a central fact of Michigan elementary school collective life, and a second had failed to see the minefield for what it was and had been caught by flying values shrapnel, a third had decided that a confrontational situation called for a confrontational response. Hawthorne Elementary was a large, all-black school in a decaying General Motors town with high levels of poverty, unemployment and neighbourhood crime. Only 18 per cent of its pupils' families had both parents living together; and 40 per cent of the pupils were being raised not by single parents but by grandparents, to the extent that where other schools had a parent support group Hawthorne Elementary had a grandparent support group. In the face of all this, the principal had embarked on a moral crusade. Many of his pupils were at risk, and it was his job to save them:

> My families know that I care about the children as much as they do. When children come here it's like I adopt them for my own. I make sure they get the best. I stand up for them when they're right, I get after them when they're wrong, and I call the parents and tell them so . . . I'm a very strict disciplinarian. I won't tolerate any nonsense. I won't tolerate any talking back. I won't tolerate any disrespect to the teachers. And I won't tolerate teachers disrespecting the children. Nor will I tolerate parents disrespecting us, and we won't disrespect them. They know they're welcome here, but I won't tolerate any swearing, any cursing anybody out. You can't dress any kind of way here. You can't come half-clothed or wearing shorts or bicycle tights. I won't allow that. Our children are children, and they're not going to be grown before their time. I won't allow it.

Not for him three months of negotiation over a school slogan. Not for him a version of 'community' mildly redolent of alternative lifestyles. Community for the principal of Hawthorne Elementary was a fiefdom of reciprocal relationships governed by the strictest of rules from which no member was exempt – and it was his job to enforce them:

> I don't bend the rules for anybody. I stay straight across the board for teachers, secretaries, custodians, parents, central administration – my policy is the same.

Community also demanded practical initiatives and fundraising skills of a high order: this principal had been instrumental in setting up a cradle school, 'Smartstart' integrated health services and family clinics, professional links with the local university, and a host of other ventures. To fund these he had tapped state and federal funding and persuaded trusts to part with grants of getting on for $700,000, displaying skills of entrepreneurship which would have endeared him to the hardest-nosed of educational market-reformers. He had no choice, in his view, but to accept the challenge of what our French teachers called the abdication of parental responsibilities, but he deplored the circumstances which made this necessary:

> We feed 'em breakfast and we feed 'em lunch. I figure in the next five years we'll be feeding them supper and they'll be sleeping right in the halls because there'll be nowhere to go. The foster homes are full. There are kids that walk the street night and day right now.

These Michigan examples have enabled us to contrast further notions of both what kinds of places schools are and how far their remit stretches. Critically, it seems, although the role of the French teachers and schools remained much more confined than that of their Michigan counterparts, even they were beginning to find it difficult to maintain the traditional firmness of boundary between classroom and family, between pupils' academic progress and their social development. And although the Michigan schools embraced both from the outset, they too had to accommodate to a growing imbalance in the demands of the two worlds.

Heads, even the most charismatic and dominant heads, cannot act alone in a context where schools face these kinds of pressures and responsibilities on top of an already extensive basic educational remit. The Michigan schools, unlike those we visited in France, had well-developed management structures. Senior management teams worked with principals on core policy matters. Committees and subcommittees covered areas such as curriculum and assessment. Most class teachers had cross-school responsibilities for subjects or for school development initiatives, and at any one time the number of such initiatives could be considerable, and several required collaboration not only with teaching colleagues but also with external agencies within the district school administration and the community. For those schools established as 'professional development schools' in accordance with the Holmes Group's recommendations,[11] there was an additional layer of responsibilities and management activity involving interns and faculty from the university working together on projects ranging from pre-service teacher training to curriculum development and school improvement. In respect of day-to-day teaching, teachers worked in grade-related teams, planning for the year ahead and jointly monitoring progress.

As one would expect in this country of 83,000 governments, a great deal of school decision-making was collective, relentlessly so, and several teachers commented on the seemingly endless round of after-school meetings which the democratic imperative produced. Even the principal of Hawthorne Elementary was prepared to argue that most decisions were reached collectively, especially now that the school board had devolved a greater proportion of budgetary and executive freedom from board to school level. However, he made it clear that 'site-based decision-making' meant site-based acceptance of collective responsibility, putting the matter – to staff and to us – with characteristic bluntness:

> I told them – 'If you come here with something that I don't agree with, and everybody votes to do it and I oppose it, that's fine. But if the community gets upset, and they go to town and holler about it, and I get a bad evaluation, *you* will get a bad evaluation. So whatever I get, you get. Everybody's in this boat together.' And everybody got real quiet, but they accepted that.

England

Between these extremes we can place the schools in our other three countries. The closest to the Michigan schools in terms of the two related dimensions of 'school' we are considering in this section – its character as a collective venture and the extent of its concerns beyond the narrowly academic – were those in England. There were important differences, however.

Thus, Hamilton Primary School:

> Our central concern is the child and the basis of all our dealings with each child is that children need love, respect and care.

The aims constructed on this ethical foundation were of a piece with it. The school set out ten 'academic aims' that were generic rather than subject-related and were as strongly affective as cognitive in their orientation:

> ... to achieve the highest standards of which they are capable through hard work, commitment and discipline ... to develop their individuality and independence ... to develop lively, enquiring and creative minds, the confidence to question and the ability to discuss sensibly and take account of the views of others ... to work as a member of a group ... to consider the needs of others ... to understand the interdependence of individuals, groups and nations.

Some of the French teachers might wish to contest, probably with vigour, this definition of 'academic'. Yet in the English context there is nothing unusual about either this school's goals or the way, within the one term 'academic', that they conflate academic study as conventionally defined, children's social development, and the values of community. To study, the statement seems to say, is of necessity both to develop as a person and to engage with others. Learning is affective as well as cognitive, collective as well as individual; it engages the whole child and the whole community.

The school's rules confirm this communal thrust and validate it in a way that would not be permissible in France:

> The rules are based on the Christian ethic of 'loving thy neighbour as thyself', or 'do as you would be done by'. This model of behaviour applies to everyone in the school community ...

which, as at Hawthorne Elementary School in Michigan, but in a manner which could hardly be more different, ensures that in the matter of community and the rules which govern it, adults and children have equal obligations. Some way from Hawthorne Elementary in tone this may be, but it is much further from the sharp differentiation of teacher and pupil obligations in the French schools, and from the sense conveyed there of social development, alongside academic education, as an induction into distinctly adult ways of knowing and acting.

On the other hand, the boundaries of Hamilton Primary School's community were drawn much more tightly than in Michigan. At Emerson, Thoreau and Hawthorne the community of the school merged almost imperceptibly into the community of parents and voters that it served. For the English schools there were two communities, the one inside the school and the one outside. This being so, the heads of these schools could celebrate a communal form of solidarity, but they could also impose it, without reference to parents if they so wished. If an English primary head wanted 'We are respectful, responsible, ready to learn and safe' as guiding philosophy and motto, he or she would simply tell the parents so.

To sharpen the differences between the English and Michigan schools further still, we can note that although the Michigan teachers espoused a comprehensive gamut of aims ranging from the intellectual to the social and moral, and although they were manifestly grappling with the day-to-day implications of the latter, they did not adopt the characteristic English claim to holism. Teachers in English primary schools, certainly since the 1960s, have strongly resisted the setting of boundaries to their educational remit in respect of the children they teach. The professional language of the 1960s, the 1970s and the 1980s made constant reference to 'the whole child' and 'the whole curriculum'; and the class teacher's claim to expertise rested less on curriculum and pedagogy than on 'knowing the whole child'.

The reforms and changes of the 1980s and the 1990s, as Draconian in manner as they were in substance, might seem to have put paid to all that. Yet, as mentioned in Chapter 6, even as it was pruning the curriculum in order to secure its targets in literacy and numeracy, the UK government was still keen to be seen as endorsing a set of educational values which encompassed every objective for education that it was possible to conceive. The educational goals officially defined for English state schools were, even in 2000 and the era of targets and no-frills 'relevance', vastly more comprehensive than the equivalent statements from the other four countries (and from many countries besides these). Indeed, the more the UK government cut back the curriculum at the point of delivery, the more insistently it trumpeted the rhetoric of breadth, balance, wholeness and the rounded individual, straining credibility to breaking point as it extended and ring-fenced the demands of primary school literacy and numeracy while obliging schools to continue to teach eight other subjects, and adding to these major requirements in respect of citizenship, personal, social and health education, and an enhanced commitment to the arts.

English primary schools during the 1970s and the 1980s were happy to embrace holism as a counterblast to the narrowness and instrumentalism of England's elementary tradition. But the school day is finite and the whole is not indefinitely expandable. By the late 1990s holism as a basic educational principle was beginning to backfire.

The values of the English primary school were shaped and reinforced in two arenas, the classroom and the school. I suggested that in the French schools the school-level impact on the collective educational and institutional culture was minimal. In Michigan, the school made itself felt through high-profile headship, elaborated management, collective decision-making and a strong community ethic that embraced teachers and students alike. The English schools had all of these up to a point, but with a different balance.

The English heads were, and were expected to be, both educational leaders and school managers. The term 'head teacher' in the English primary sector is not used casually, for it signifies the principal focus of the head's leadership. 'Director', in an English primary context, would be an alien, and indeed alienating, designation. So, although increasingly tested by the pressures of budgetary delegation, external accountability and central government directives, our English primary heads, like their 1970s predecessors, expected to lead as much by pedagogical example as by managerial effectiveness. Like them, too, they expected to intervene in the classroom practice of teaching staff. However, whereas under the traditional model of primary headship this was because the head's rule on curriculum and pedagogy could be as absolute as the head wished to make it, by the 1990s this was as much for reasons of external accountability, for heads by then had explicit obligations in respect of quality assurance.

Such intervention in pedagogy would have been inconceivable in the French context for both contractual and cultural reasons; and unlikely in the American one because it runs counter to what is clearly a delicate balance of principal authority, staff democracy, collective teacher strength (through the unions), and individual teacher autonomy.

In like vein, although there were similarities between the elaborated management procedures of the Michigan and English schools, the differences were no less marked. The English teachers combined classroom and cross-school responsibilities, usually for an aspect of the curriculum, a year or key stage (pupils aged 5–7 or 7–11), or a generic field such as assessment or special educational needs. The time in undertaking these responsibilities was dominated by the whole school activities of reviewing and preparing policy statements, leading staff discussions, chairing working groups, managing resources and providing information.[12] But the range of roles, groups and ventures was notably more limited in the English schools, and meetings were less frequent.

Having said that, the English teachers complained, no less than those in Michigan, about increased role diffuseness, about the way 'external' pressures (national testing, reporting to parents, OFSTED inspections, the national curriculum, the government's literacy and numeracy strategies) had eroded and compromised their core professional task of teaching, and about their sense of running faster and faster merely to stand still.

Nor was the communal ethic so insistent in the English schools. In England, 'community' does not carry anything like the historical or political charge it bears in the United States. Community was a 1960s import into English primary schools. It was to the culture of the school what child centredness was to the culture of the classroom. Its pedigree was left-of-centre rather than mainstream, with perhaps the faintest whiff of the commune (homespun Devonian rather than revolutionary French or Russian). It spoke to a pattern of consciousness centred on the quality of human relationships – *communitas* in Raymond Williams' exegesis of the term[13] – rather than to procedures for determining goals and making decisions, and indeed it might be at variance with the latter. Hence the way the ideal of community in English primary schools asserts itself most typically through an event – the assembly – which manifests hierarchy as much as fellowship.

At the same time, and perhaps paradoxically, the English schools seemed somewhat more reserved than those in Michigan about celebrating individual achievement. The traditional English school assembly, in its public/grammar school version, was highly achievement oriented, especially where academic and sporting prowess was concerned. Star pupils were singled out, lauded and applauded. Ability was identified, sponsored and nurtured, whether on the games field or, through streaming and setting, in the classroom. English primary schools from the 1960s or so spurned all that for they believed such strategies irrevocably damaged the self-esteem of those who happened not to have what it takes to excel in sport or examinations. Effort came to matter more than attainment, taking part more than winning, succeeding as a group more than succeeding as an individual, co-operating more than competing. This contrary ideology sometimes merged none too subtly with crude environmentalist theories about the influence of family and home. If inner-city children failed to do well, it was argued, it was because they were disadvantaged; if middle-class children succeeded it was because they had 'pushy' parents. It was then but a short step to presuming that inner-city children were predestined to fail, and therefore little could be expected from them, and that middle-class children would do well anyway and so did not need motivating.

The result, we know, was underachievement all round. The counter-attack – charges of anti-elitism, diehard egalitarianism and selling inner-city children short – was initiated in the Black Papers of the 1960s and 1970s, and the charges are still routinely levelled at those who are deemed to be agents of or apologists for progressivism. As if on cue, the day on which I drafted this paragraph, 19 July 1999, Education Secretary of State David Blunkett sweepingly accused all the critics of his government's homework and literacy strategies, regardless of the arguments they presented, of being closet elitists masquerading as liberals. Generally, however, the 1990s saw the beginnings of a culture shift in these matters and Blunkett's outburst can be counted a throwback to the more polarized views of earlier decades. The Leeds report of 1991 identified low teacher expectations as a major problem in inner-city primary schools. By 2000 the raising of expectations had become a political crusade and the government had introduced strategies to back it.

However, this does not mean that schools had reverted to the competitive, individualistic ethos. Whereas we found the Michigan schools managing to square the circle of individualism and collectivism by singling out for particular mention those individuals who starred as team players, in the English schools individual success remained resolutely subordinated to the success of the group.

There was similar reticence, or fudging, over the religious element that by law was supposed to inform the school assembly. Except for the church schools, on which we comment later in this chapter, our English primary schools tended to opt either for a multi-faith assembly, which presented information about different religions or enacted ceremonies from them in order to make children aware of religious differences while not fostering their commitment to any of them; or for an unambiguously secular event at which, for example, one class, or children from different classes, 'shared' with the rest of the school work recently undertaken, and the head used the occasion to press home some of the school's core values, chief among which were the communal values of collective endeavour and respect for others.

We have used France and Michigan as templates or paradigms for two sharply differing ideas of a primary school. We placed the English schools closer to Michigan, although in key particulars distinct from them. On the other hand, while there are resemblances between the English and American schools, the distinctiveness of the French schools remains intact. Let us now locate the schools we visited in our two other countries, India and Russia.

India

Indian primary schools, as mentioned in Chapter 4, inherit ancient ideals of absolute teacher authority on which have been superimposed the values and admin- istrative structures of British colonialism and Indian nationalism. To a researcher from the UK, therefore, Indian primary schools are both strange and familiar, and the tensions in the uneasy residue of the different traditions are very evident, especially within the classroom.

At school level, again, we start with superficial familiarities: the larger schools were variants on the classic 'two zones of influence' model of the English element- ary school. There were two professional roles, headmaster/headmistress and class teacher, very little if any role specialization at the latter level (except in our largest and most affluent school, in Delhi, where there was specialist support for music and one or two other subjects, although this was clearly unusual), and a simple two-tier management structure.

Thus, in response to our questions about who controlled what, the heads of the larger schools reported, much as English heads might, that the state and district determined the curriculum but they as heads shaped the school's ethos, values and goals and allocated teachers to classes. They also dictated the daily lesson timetable. In the matter of pedagogy class teachers had some say (not that there was a great deal of variation in this regard) but heads retained the option of overriding teachers' preferences:

> The teachers make their own decisions about method, but if they want to do something different and their method is better, I will give my permission.

Moreover, they maintained a running check on classroom practice, again much as in the traditional English mould, by requiring teachers to submit their weekly lesson plans for scrutiny.

In the Delhi school, which with 620 enrolled pupils was by Indian standards exceptionally large, the head had an embryonic senior management team with which she discussed school-wide policy matters. Here, however, teachers qualified as 'senior' by virtue of the length of their teaching experience rather than their formal positions, for the formal management structure was, as we have noted, firmly two-tier.

When we moved out of Delhi into the smaller schools of Haryana and Uttar Pradesh, we noted that the head's authority waned, and in this matter these schools were a truer reflection of the broader Indian situation, bearing in mind also that over vast tracts of rural India the norm is a one- or two-teacher school. Here, heads were teaching full time, and although they undertook formal responsibilities in respect of allocating teachers to classes and dealing with parents and with block, district- and state-level officers and inspectors, their influence on the classroom practice of their colleagues was minimal.

Further, they were acutely conscious of the power of the local inspector. Reveal- ingly, a district inspector was present on the day we interviewed the head of a village school and he insisted on sitting in on the interview. Throughout the interview the head paused and looked at the inspector before answering questions on school policy as if to check that she was allowed to venture her own judgement. Sometimes he corrected her answer, while at other times he even answered the question himself before she had a chance to do so. The transcript shows the interviewer trying to regain the initiative during the later stages of the interview in a way that acknowledged the situation's dynamics, by asking the same question of first the head and then the inspector. The experience was somewhat frustrating, but on the other hand the inspector's presence and dominance, and the head's deference to his authority even on matters nominally within her remit, confirmed where the power in this and similar schools really lay.

However, although the Indian heads were underpowered in comparison with their English and American equivalents, it would be wrong to draw parallels with the situation in the French schools as we described it earlier. The authority of the French elementary school *directeur/directrice* is circumscribed by history, culture and, no less important, contract. The French heads had as much authority as their formal roles required, no more and no less. In India the situation was less straightforward. There, the heads were underpowered in relation to the job they were expected to do. They were also operating within a context of many-layered hierarchy, within which there appeared to be acute consciousness of the subtle gradations of rank and status. In crude terms, our inspector was pulling rank in front of an overseas visitor; he was also asserting the defining power of gender in Indian culture. On the other hand, the heads of two other Indian schools we visited were closer in the kind of authority they exercised over teachers and pupils alike to the traditional version of the English primary head. They were both, although in different ways, charismatic. Both were clearly dedicated to the school, and although neither talked possessively – as English heads are apt to – of 'my school' and 'my teachers', their identification with the school seemed absolute. As a result these schools had a more distinctive character and a more rounded sense of their purpose and vision. In this matter, the school's socializing and moral agency – like England but unlike France – was seen as intrinsic. It also tended to be a compensating one, based on assumptions of parental deficit. In this, illiteracy might be linked to poor attitudes and fecklessness. Thus, as expressed most uncompromisingly by one head:

> The biggest problem is illiteracy. Ninety per cent of our parents are illiterate. Illiterate parents prevent their children from going forward. Parents are apathetic. The parents sometimes discourage the children from coming to school so that they can help at home. They are also poor, but this is because they drink. Most of the parents are working on dairy farms. There is a lot of money in this area. If there is poverty, it is self-made. They are wasting their money by playing cards, and on alcohol and drugs.

This was the most extreme version. Another head spoke more sympathetically of the condition of the mainly migrant families whose children she taught:

> Most of them are labourers. Some are rickshaw drivers, some work in the construction industry. Most live in makeshift huts, a few in *pukka* buildings. They are very poor.

Most belong to scheduled castes. 95 per cent of the parents are illiterate. The children's needs are very basic. Some have no clothes to wear, no shoes. They are not clean. The teachers help by buying clothes, books and paper, and by collecting shoes. They visit the homes to check on enrolment and attendance.

The latter, in fact, was a standard part of the job of most of the class teachers we interviewed. They expected, and were expected by the local administration, to spend a significant amount of time after school and at weekends visiting homes and doing their best to increase enrolments and maintain attendance levels. In the rural areas they also served as census officers.

Not surprisingly, therefore, the moral purpose of the school was expressed with a greater immediacy than elsewhere (with the exception of Hawthorne Elementary in Michigan, where there was a similar concern to compensate for problems of home and family). I noted earlier the prevalence of notices in the schools reminding children of the importance of cleanliness and punctuality. In interview the heads emphasized as prime school goals:

Discipline, cleanliness, the ability to distinguish between good and bad.

The most important thing is discipline and punctuality. When these children leave here they should behave well. They should have a good understanding of what is sensible and what is not. They should makes good decisions about their lives and be loyal towards their country.

(*Interviewer: Do you think these things are as important as academic success?*)

They are *more* important.

The partial exception to this tendency was the school in a relatively well-off area of New Delhi. Here the head saw the parents as ambitious for themselves and their children. The school emphasized academic excellence and competition, rewarding in this way handwriting, essay, dictation, science, general knowledge and discipline. English was added to the basic curriculum to meet parental demands and counter the attraction of nearby private schools. Even here, however, the school's moral agency was central and the head defined a well-educated person as one who was well mannered, well dressed and independent.

In this school, too, the head had introduced the very British device of houses to foster corporate identity and solidarity, given a keener edge by inter-house rivalry and competition. However, this particular colonial legacy was domesticated with delicate and probably unintended irony by naming the houses to honour that scourge of colonialism, Mohandas Gandhi. So the houses were not the Indian equivalents of Churchill, Nelson, Wellington and Nightingale but Truth, Peace, Non-violence and Love.

Two other elements in schools' collective life had pre-Independence resonances. One was the use of older pupils as prefects. The other was the assembly. The schools did not have assembly halls, but then except when the monsoon rain was falling they did not need them. Each morning all the school's children and teachers gathered in front of the school (if it was a simple block) or, in the case of the larger buildings, within the central courtyard. On one such occasion, in Chanderi Primary School, the 25-minute sequence was as follows:

0850:   Children march into the courtyard, a class at a time, line up in rows and sit down cross-legged on the sand
        Prayers (led by three children)
        National anthem (led by the head)
        Story on the theme of co-operation and interdependence (recited from memory by one child and explained by a teacher)
        Cleanliness inspection (teachers and monitors chosen from the older pupils move down the rows checking hair, faces, hands and clothes)
        Announcements (head)
0915:   Children march out, a row at a time

Our field notes nominate as the values conveyed on this occasion: cohesion, mutual support, patriotism and cleanliness.

In Purana Primary School the event was considerably more elaborate and protracted, although it followed a similar pattern. The head and teachers presided from the veranda on one side of the courtyard, using a public address system. The prayers were sung, with the accompaniment provided by the school's music teacher and a group of pupils. Meanwhile, in Ferozabad Primary School the assembly had an additional function, for this was a school where pupil numbers so far outstripped the available space that there were two separate shifts, and on every available inch of floor space, indoors and out, a child was sitting. So, to avoid one class disturbing another during the lessons themselves, pupils chanted their letters and numbers during assembly, and, under the supervision of older pupils, traced them in the sand. The distance travelled since basic elementary education and the monitorial system seemed, on this occasion anyway, very short indeed.

Antiphony has a fundamental place in Indian public education not just in school assemblies but also in the classroom, as we shall see. It is a powerful and constant reminder of the sacerdotal ancestry of Indian teaching. In the classroom, the teacher initiates and the pupils respond. In assemblies, a small group of pupils might initiate and the rest of the school would respond. In the following extract there was a chorus and verses, each one repeated.

You are residing within every living creature in the form of intelligent mind and illusion.
(Chanted by a small group standing at the front; repeated by the whole school)
What kind of world have you created to test us humans? (Repeated)
You are residing within every living creature in the form of intelligent mind and illusion.
(Repeated)
We are only small children. How can we possibly know your great play? (Repeated)
You are residing within every living creature in the form of intelligent mind and illusion.
(Repeated)
My boat is old and weak, so take me to the other shore dear Lord. (Repeated)
You are residing within every living creature in the form of intelligent mind and illusion.
(Repeated)

You ate Bhildi's half-eaten cherries with love. (Repeated)
You are residing within every living creature in the form of intelligent mind and illusion.
(Repeated)
You gave Drupadi clothes when she was being stripped in front of others. (Repeated)
You are residing within every living creature in the form of intelligent mind and illusion.
(Repeated)

The one thing that nobody could satisfactorily explain to us was why there should be a religious element (a Hindu one in this case) in the assemblies of a school system constitutionally bound by the principle of secularism.

Russia

In 1988, with the Soviet system still intact, although under pressure, James Muckle described the ethos conveyed by the typical Russian school environment:

> The main entrance bears welcoming notices . . . Information boards proclaim rules for pupils, responsibilities of parents and goals for the teaching staff . . . Prominent in many schools are photographs of the *otlichniki*, the pupils who have achieved top marks in all subjects . . . Slogans, political exhortations, quotations and pious wishes appear on walls; their authors may be leading politicians, artists, writers or thinkers of any country or any period, but Lenin is the most commonly represented . . . Flags and regalia of communist youth organizations are to be seen in open spaces . . . Members of staff who have served in the armed forces are often honoured in special displays.[14]

The overtly communist and Soviet furniture had disappeared from the schools we visited during the mid 1990s (save for some well-nigh indestructible statues), but many of the messages had survived, duly modified to meet the new circumstances. Thus, in Moscow's School B we found prominently displayed a lengthy statement summarizing the school's aims and commitments, together with the students' obligations and rights:

The main areas of activity in this school are:

- formulating and satisfying educational, personal developmental and social needs
- developing the individual's capabilities, and bringing up to the highest educational standards
- producing a multilaterally developed and creative personality, and organizing the child's requirements concerning self-development
- forming an educational process with a common basis but with a varied content and methods
- creating the best possible conditions for mental, intellectual, moral, emotional and physical development of the personality.

The school is called upon to:

- satisfy the population's national and cultural requirements
- educate internationalists

- give young people a genuine position in society, prepare them for an independent life, for work and creativity, for defending the Motherland, and inculcate responsibility for the fate of the country and for mankind as a whole.

In terms of the earlier discussion about the *scope* of schools' educational aspirations, this statement – like those seen in the other Russian schools we visited – has the holistic thrust of its English counterparts. Education is much more than inculcation of specific domains of knowledge and skill; it is nothing less than the development of the person.

There are important differences, however. In English primary education 'development' is taken to refer to a natural process which takes place regardless of education, although education contributes to it. Its pathway is also unique to each child. Here, education and development are one, and development is not natural and inevitable but normative and interventive. Schools do not merely teach children: they bring them up. In England, development happens; in Russia schools, parents and the community make it happen. In one culture the verb 'develop', when used in an educational context, is intransitive; in the other – Russia – it is transitive, and its direct object is the child. 'We may have disagreements with parents about methods' said the director of another school 'but not about goals: parents and teachers want to arrive at the same goal, and that goal is development.'

Hence the significance of *vospitanie*, which translates, culturally if not etymologically, as upbringing, moral education, and the fullest possible development of the personality. In official educational statements since 1991 the Soviet overtones of *vospitanie* have caused it to be downgraded somewhat, but within the schools we visited it remained fundamental. Indeed, we noted in Chapter 3 that although from the 1920s onwards it was heavily glossed to meet the needs of the communist state, historically *vospitanie* is a Russian rather than a uniquely Soviet concept. It preceded communism and outlasted it.

Yet the Soviet emphasis on culture, nation and internationalism, for which there is no English equivalent – these things simply do not feature in the educational consciousness of most English primary schools – also survives, albeit de-Sovietized; for *vospitanie* makes little sense without it. With it survives an understanding of the kind of institution a school is. So the list from which we quoted above went on to set out students' obligations and rights, and these included among others the following.

Each student has a responsibility to:

- value highly the school's honour, and protect its interests
- be intolerant of indifference, cruelty, envy and deceit, and look after the younger students.

Every student has the right to:

- express openly their opinion concerning the quality of education
- protect his/her honour and the inviolability of his/her personality

- participate in the running of the school through the appropriate bodies
- make suggestions, comments and constructive criticism of the way the school is run
- create and join clubs, sports, study groups, workshops, and other associations.

Vospitanie, then, is both taught in the classroom through the formal curriculum and enacted by the school in its daily routines and transactions. Here, in essence, are the driving values that we found reiterated in all the Russian schools we visited: education as the development of the person and the citizen; the school as a self-governing community in which both teachers and pupils have responsibilities as well as rights; the fundamentally moral purpose of both education in the classroom and the school beyond it. The interviews with school directors and teachers filled these out, but never deviated from them.

However, their expansions frequently emphasized, alongside the social and moral goals of education, two other qualities: the importance of *kultura* and being *kulturni*, the Russian equivalent of the French schools' concern with *culture générale*; and individual empowerment through a sense of purpose and the ability to communicate and hold one's own socially:

- An educated person is above all cultured, well behaved, communicates well, is creative and has a good grasp of Russian language and literature.
- We aim to make our students well educated, cultured, well developed, with clear principles to guide their lives, and versed in literature, music and the arts.
- We want them to strive always for knowledge and culture, but also to relate well to each other. We want them to be able to converse, argue and disagree, to speak in public, to communicate.
- They must know who they are, what they want and where they are going. They should have clear principles and aims.

Naturally enough, there are certain resonances in statements of the kind we have exemplified so far with values expressed in schools in our other countries; the rounded personality (England); general culture and the ability to communicate well (France); patriotism (India and the United States); morality (India); collegiality and community (United States). But the particular combination of these and other qualities, the manner in which they are glossed, and above all the way they are united within a single, comprehensive notion of development, is distinctively Russian.[15]

Let us turn now from goals and values to dynamics. We have noted that the Russian schools, being common schools for all ages in which 'primary' simply designated what went on during the pupils' first three years, were generally much larger than the single-phase primary and elementary schools in the four other countries. Inevitably, therefore, they tended towards a more complex and specialized management structure, reaching usually to four levels: director, deputy directors, heads of subject and phase (including primary), and class teachers, both generalist and specialist.

The division of labour among these levels was clear cut. The director and deputies constituted a senior management team which sorted out timetabling and teaching responsibilities (a scheduled once-weekly management meeting was common). The curriculum, as we have noted, had federal, regional and school components, the latter theoretically leaving 10 per cent of time to the discretion of each school. In our primary classes, some of this discretion was devolved further to individual teachers. Finally, teaching method was determined by each teacher, although as in India there was relatively little deviation from a common model, and the freedom enjoyed by each teacher was in practice not the freedom to devise an entire pedagogical philosophy and procedure from scratch (which is what some of our American teachers were attempting to do, at considerable personal cost) but the right to work as creatively as skill allowed within the bounds of a predetermined form.

In the following chapters, not only is Russian pedagogy explored but also the notion of pedagogic 'form' more generally. At this point, we note merely that the clearest analogy in the matter of pedagogical freedom and constraint is artistic. The difference between routine and creative teaching in our Russian schools was the difference between what Bach and his contemporaries achieved with the fugue: alike in form, but in detail and outcome very different.

Having said that, the message from Moscow was that the new creativity towards which teachers were being nudged should allow for the introduction of totally new ideas and practices, not just the refinement of the old ones. However:

> In schools now the teachers are much more free and relaxed. They can give much more of themselves. They can choose what they put into the lesson, they can give something personal to it. The lesson and the teacher carry much more freedom of feeling. No longer do you hear 'You must do this, you must do that, you must do the other'. The quality of teaching is judged by the end result. If the result is good then one can say the same of the teacher.

Thus, professional freedom is carefully qualified. As in France but unlike England, teaching in Russian schools appears now to be judged less in terms of procedural compliance, more in terms of outcomes. However, procedural prescription may be deemed unnecessary because there is widespread procedural consensus. 'Giving much more of oneself' to a lesson, as we judged it in practice, refers less to method, more to the interpretation and presentation of content. There were innovative methodological frameworks, as we shall see, and teachers were particularly keen to legitimate their practices by reference to distinguished 'scientists' or 'methodologists' such as Davydov, Elkonin and Zankov. Yet we found it difficult to differentiate the practices conducted in the names of these three from each other or from practice not dignified in this way, and we concluded that in the matter of pedagogical innovation we were witnessing the Russian variation on a universal theme: the disparity between espoused theory and theory-in-use (see page 195).

Heads frequently spoke of teacher 'collectives', and this Soviet legacy clearly remained an important part of school decision-making. It applied particularly in the domains of goals, ethos, rules and regulations, in which teachers, and indeed parents and students, were commonly involved. The school's collective agency was emphasized in myriad ways at both the overt and subliminal level, as we have seen.

There were no daily assemblies of the routine English kind (the director of one school dismissed the idea as likely to interrupt children's work, and certainly schools' timetables appeared to have little room in them for deviation from the cycle of 45-minute lessons). Instead special days were celebrated: holidays, the end of the Russian winter, national days, and – at class level – each child's birthday. Some of our fieldwork was undertaken in September, and in several schools we found ourselves caught up in the round of parties and concerts to celebrate Teachers' Day. (Having to halt the writing of notes to make an impromptu speech to an entire school from behind a table piled high with cakes, chocolate, vodka and champagne is another of the hazards of educational fieldwork in Russia). But in general, so much of school and classroom life is structured to reflect and enact communal values that a daily event to mark these might seem superfluous. This, I think, was what the school director was driving at in her dismissive comment about assemblies. It was not so much that there was no time as that there was no point; had there been, the school would undoubtedly have made the time, for:

> A school is the children, teachers and parents. A good school is one where the relationship between children, teachers and parents is good, where there is the total absence of an attitude of indifference, and everyone pays attention to everyone else.

This strikingly phrased 'absence of an attitude of indifference' allows us to point up a key cross-cultural difference in the rules which schools devised to govern the behaviour of their pupils. In the documentation for students and parents supplied by the Michigan schools, rules concentrated on the most basic levels of behaviour: 'Keep hands, feet and objects to yourself . . . no guns or knives . . . no fighting or rough play . . . no teasing, arguing, name-calling, profanity or complaining . . .' They also combined such general injunctions with rules for particular contexts such as the lunch hall ('no shoving or changing places in line . . . children are not to throw, trade, give or sell food . . .') or the playground ('no fighting, play fighting or wrestling . . . no throwing stones, ice snow, sticks or sand . . . no tree climbing . . . no fence climbing . . . no swearing . . . no hurtful or disrespectful behaviour . . .'). The rules were accompanied by procedures to be followed in the event of incursions, with penalties from mild to severe: 'First warning . . . ten minutes of time out so that you can think of better choices for your behaviour . . . loss of recess . . . call your parents . . . send you home.'

In two respects such statements were very different from their Russian equivalents. First, for all that the Michigan lists emphasized that rules were there to enable the school to function positively as a community, they were predominantly negative or prohibitory in tone. The Russian lists, in contrast, had fewer rules of the kind which forbid particular actions, and these were in any case outnumbered by positive statements of pupils' responsibilities and rights. Second, the focus of the Michigan rules suggested an overriding preoccupation with physical and verbal violence, and indeed conveyed a sense that it was an ever-present threat. The Russian lists did not balk at addressing this problem ('Students are forbidden to use physical force, intimidation or extortion to express their attitudes . . . use obscene or indecent expressions or foul language . . .') but kept them in perspective, as one, but only one aspect of the gamut of behaviour which the school sought to encourage and develop. In this, I suggest, lies part of the difference between *vospitanie* as a comprehensive and constructive venture and the Western tendency either to try to confine the teaching of behaviour to the home (as in France) or to accommodate it reluctantly but treat it as in some way pathological (as in Michigan).[16]

A Note on Church Schools

In the matter of school values, the position of schools sponsored or funded by religious denominations is obviously of some importance. American, Indian, French and Russian state schools are secular. In England, however, secularism was resisted and, as a result, not only is religious education compulsory in state schools but 'voluntary' schools established by the churches receiving partial funding from the state. In this matter England is the anomaly among our five countries.

The other four countries do have church schools, but they are firmly within the private sector. Private Russian Orthodox church schools are enjoying a renaissance after decades of suppression. In France, however, the situation is less straightforward then its revolutionary antecedents might lead one to expect. During the middle decades of the twentieth century, under presidents de Gaulle and Giscard, private schools (mainly Roman Catholic) became increasingly dependent on state aid, but as an increasing number of parents turned to these in preference to those within the state system, so opposition grew to this apparent breach of the principle of *laïcité*. Under pressure from the left, Mitterand came to power in 1981 committed to restoring full secularism. His education minister Alain Savary attempted to push through a bill to that effect which would have retained church schools but removed state aid, thus putting them beyond the reach of most families. The bill provoked, in 1984, a massive protest demonstration in defence not so much of church schools as of freedom of choice, another key republican principle. The bill was dropped and Savary's successor, Chevènement, produced and saw through a new bill that left subsidized private schooling intact but imposed certain modest restrictions on the hiring of staff.

The legal status of church schools in England made it desirable for us to include at least one such school in the *Five Cultures* fieldwork. That school was St Teresa's, a Roman Catholic school serving a mainly working-class district of a city in the north of England. We also had the opportunity to work in St Cyril's School, which was attached to the Russian Orthodox cathedral of a town in southern Russia. St Teresa's was one of a network of Catholic schools within its diocese. St Cyril's was very much a local institution, set up by two neighbouring dioceses and a seminary with support from parents, a group of whom had banded together to construct and maintain the building.

In St Teresa's, the church affiliation was evident from the physical surroundings: a statue of the saint in the entrance hall, and a crucifix above the blackboard in every classroom. In each classroom, too, there was usually a small area, almost an altar, whose messages were overtly devotional: prayers and pictures on a pinboard, statuettes of the Virgin Mary, and in one the teacher's prominent and slightly despairing plea 'Dear God, help us to fill empty heads'. Religious education was the responsibility of the priest at the church to which the school was attached and the church was a major influence on the deliberations of the school's governing body. These matters apart, the curriculum was identical to that provided in schools fully maintained by the state. The school's religious affiliation made itself evident less through structures and procedures, or indeed through overt spirituality, than through a firm and unambiguous moral orientation to matters of everyday behaviour. This meant that it was possible for a church school not to have a particularly ecclesiastical feel, and indeed the head noted that when she took over, some four years previously, 'This didn't feel like a Catholic school: there were serious behaviour problems, and relationships among children and teachers were not at all good'. Her first and continuing task was to redefine where the school stood on the attitudes and behaviour of its pupils. As she saw it, a Catholic school was most convincingly defined and tested by the conduct and relationships of its members, both teachers and pupils, rather than by its iconography or its lessons in religious education.

The situation at St Cyril's was somewhat different. There, too, the state curriculum was taught, but religion was much more pervasive than at St Teresa's. Religious education, termed 'God's Law', and including ethics, catechism and rhetoric, was a significant addition to the curriculum. The school's stated aim was to give every child a fundamental moral education based on the tenets of Russian Orthodoxy and to make this the cornerstone of a basic education of the highest quality. Like the state schools we visited, St Cyril's strongly espoused the principle of community: 'We are', said the director, 'one big family, bound together by our faith'. However, school-level events played a much more prominent part in the implementation of this ideal than they did at the state schools we visited in Russia. Each day began with an assembly led by a priest (who in this case was also the father of one of the school's pupils) and there were further collective prayers in every classroom, at the beginning and end of every lesson, and before and after meals. The classrooms were identical to those in the public schools except for the icon placed prominently above the blackboard.

St Cyril's consciously harked back to pre-Soviet times. The Motherland featured prominently in both the curriculum and the school's collective rhetoric. Old Slavonic was taught from the second year, Latin to secondary age pupils. The director told us that the school was aiming to create standards and ethos that were recognizably 'pre-revolutionary, like your grammar schools'. The language textbooks were updated versions of those written by K. D. Ushinsky, one of the leading pre-revolution figures in the development of the Russian science of pedagogy, and author of the strongly nationalistic *Rodnoe Slovo* (The Native Word), a series of readers grounded in Russian literature.[17] Although the school was fee paying, there was an entrance exam, and of this, we were told, parents approved. Teachers, although not pupils, wore uniforms. The school, then, was making a strong bid for the high ground of moral authority, nationalism and educational standards which it, and the parents who supported it, felt had been vacated by the communists and left unfilled by the regime of Boris Yeltsin. In this, perhaps, they were exploiting what some see as the deeper psychological appeal to Russians of autocracy, nationalism and orthodoxy – whether political or religious.[18]

Something of this perception of the role of church schools developed, in much diluted form and without the nationalist overtones, in England during the final decades of the twentieth century. Not all the pupils at St Teresa's were Catholic, and for those that were not, the school attracted their parents on moral as much as educational grounds, because it had none of the perceived moral ambivalence of maintained schools. The same judgement was made by significant numbers of parents in cities with large populations of Muslims. In the absence of Muslim schools, some Muslim parents preferred to send their children to Anglican or Catholic rather than maintained schools, because, in their view, such schools made morality central rather than hedged it with relativist doubt and equivocation.

The Russian public schools would no doubt argue that the state may have relinquished the moral high ground but schools had not. Our evidence would strongly support this contention. The values of the state schools we visited were overtly nationalistic, although the appeal was to culture and the soil – Mother Russia – rather than to the trappings of state. Indeed the teachers we interviewed were reluctant to be drawn on political questions other than in the most general terms – 'previously we had to do x, now we can do y' – and appeared to be seeking to instil a kind of patriotism which would transcend politics and survive the roller-coaster of events since 1991. Privately, many felt betrayed by Gorbachev, despised Yeltsin, were alarmed by Zhirinovsky, and were deeply anxious about their country's political prospects, but if anything this made them all the more determined to maintain the moral authority of their teaching.

Moroever, the concern with standards was paramount in the Russian state schools we visited. If it was compromised, argued the teachers, this was because of an acute shortage of basic resources. This was not the English teacher's perennial complaint about pay – although since many of the Russian teachers were not being paid at all for months at a stretch, let alone too little, they certainly had cause for complaint – but an absence of material basics such as up-to-date textbooks and computer software. In one school we were shown a room with 20 non-functioning computers; in another the excellent English language teaching was compromised culturally by its reliance on audio-visual material from the 1960s featuring London buses, beefeaters, pre-decimal coinage, a sparklingly rejuvenated Queen Elizabeth II, and the clipped tones of Joyce Grenfell and Francis Matthews. As for schools' moral purposes, these remained central: softened by the new and approved humanitarianism, perhaps, but never less than clear cut in their notions of right and wrong.

Conclusion

Do the differences *within* a country's educational provision allow us to talk meaningfully of a distinctively English primary school, or a distinctively French, Indian, Russian or American one? On this matter we shall have to be cautious, for the numbers of schools sampled in each country were too small to allow us to make generalizations on the basis of the *Five Cultures* school-level data alone. However, some of the dimensions of difference – for example in relation to pupil and teacher demography, resourcing, goals, timetabling, teacher roles, school management, pupil organization and curriculum – clearly relate to national trends and policies such as those discussed in Chapters 2–6, while others in domains where schools appear to have greater autonomy confirm or develop findings from earlier research studies. These two kinds of corroboration allow us to be confident that our schools were not wildly atypical.

If we were to attempt to summarize the characteristics of a composite primary school from each country, based on the school-level data and using the organizing framework adopted for this and the preceding chapter (space, time, people and values) they might be as follows.

France

Space. Dedicated elementary school; varied building plans and structures; both external and covered play areas; little or no material displayed in the public spaces; limited specialist accommodation (classrooms, gymnasia, director's office); large classrooms, well furnished and equipped; pupils at desks or tables, sometimes in rows, sometimes in groups; blackboard as focal point; classrooms not zoned for specific activities; wall-mounted materials either minimal or transient (work in progress); classrooms have unitary focus and clear work ambience. *Time*: daily lessons, play and midday meal; time concentrated; time divisions mostly fixed, although with some flexibility (lessons 30–90 minutes). *People*. Pupils aged 6–11, director, generalist teachers, ancillary staff; mixed ability classes, age based in large schools, multi-age in small schools, 20–26 pupils; pupils may change or keep teachers from one year to the next; less successful pupils sometimes repeat a year; two-tier management, director has restricted managerial role, teachers accountable to ministry via inspector and *académie*; individual decision-making, although with harmonization on basic matters and some voluntary teacher collaboration. *Values*. School as association of teachers delivering a national standard of elementary education; teaching as individualistic; school's main, and ideally sole, function is to to teach the required curriculum as effectively as possible; clear division of labour between school and home; education as the development of mind; learning as intellectual discipline; communication, citizenship and general culture.

Russia

Space. Primary department within common secondary school (some separate primary schools in rural areas); buildings tending to a standard plan and structure; internal play areas; moral and communal tone to material displayed in the public spaces, but low visual impact; moderate range of specialist accommodation (classrooms, specialist subject rooms, gymnasia, offices); classrooms light, airy and adequately furnished and equipped, but somewhat cramped; pupils in rows at pairs of desks, each with learning materials identically placed; blackboard as focal point;

classrooms not zoned for specific activities; limited and standard wall-mounted materials, part procedural, part aesthetic; classrooms have unitary focus and clear work ambience. *Time.* Daily lessons, play and midday meal; occasional whole school events; time dispersed (short, frequent breaks); time divisions fixed and identical in length (lessons 45 minutes). *People.* Pupils aged 6–9/10 or 7–10/11, director, deputy directors, generalist and specialist teachers, psychologists, defectologists, ancillary staff; mixed ability but sometimes internally streamed classes, age based, 20–26 pupils; pupils usually keep teachers from one year to the next at the primary stage; multi-tier management, significant senior management team level; collegial decision-making, teachers accountable through director and school councils to local administration. *Values.* School as community; teaching as competitive yet collaborative; education as moral upbringing and the development of the all-round personality; individual striving for the common good; communication, citizenship, knowledge, general culture, patriotism.

India

Space. Dedicated primary school; buildings tending to a standard plan and structure; external playgrounds/courtyards; moral tone to the small amount of material displayed in the public spaces; classroooms and playground/courtyard for assembly, no specialist accommodation; classrooms very cramped and spartan, with little or no furniture or equipment; pupils seated singly in rows, usually on the floor; blackboard as focal point; classrooms not zoned for specific activities; little or no wall-mounted materials; classrooms have unitary focus and clear work ambience, although in fact only the presence of a blackboard marks them out as a classroom. *Time.* Daily lessons, assembly and play; time dispersed; time divisions fixed and identical in length (lessons 30 minutes). *People.* Large schools – pupils aged 6–11, headmaster/headmistress, generalist teachers, ancillary staff; small schools – pupils, generalist teacher (s); mixed ability classes, age based (large schools) or multi-grade (small schools), 36–70 pupils; pupils sometimes change, sometimes keep their teachers from one year to the next; less able pupils sometimes kept back a year; two-tier management, teachers accountable via head mistress/master to district office. *Values.* School as community; literacy, discipline, cleanliness, obedience, patriotism.

Michigan

Space. Dedicated elementary school; varied building plan and structure, external play areas; high visual impact; predominantly communal and moral tone to material displayed in the public spaces; extensive range of specialist accommodation (classrooms, gymnasia, staff room, offices, subject rooms, libraries, IT suites, consulting rooms); large classrooms, extensively and sometimes lavishly furnished and equipped; pupils in groups; no stable focal point; classrooms zoned for a wide range of different activities; wall-mounted materials extensive and varied in topic and purpose, abundant rather than aesthetically disposed; classrooms have multiple focus and mixed ambience – work, play, rest. *Time.* Daily lessons, recess and midday meal; occasional assemblies and whole school events; time concentrated; time highly elastic, with widely varying lesson length (30–90 minutes) except for use of gymnasia and other specialist spaces. *People.* Pupils aged 5/6–11, principal, generalist teachers (some doubling as subject leaders) and specialist teachers, teaching assistants, part-time staff, special needs, psychological and counselling staff, ancillary staff; mixed ability classes, age based or multi-age, 20–26 pupils; pupils change teachers at end of year, except in multi-age classes; three-tier and matrix management, with teachers accountable through principal to school board. *Values.* School as community; teaching as collaborative; partnership between school and home; learning as sharing, making choices, exercising responsibility, and self-actualization; individualism; the team and the collective good; patriotism; wide values spectrum, with scope for conflict and contradiction.

England

Space. Dedicated primary (4/5–11), infant (4/5–7), first (4/5–8/9) or junior (7–11) school; varied building plan and structure; external play areas, high visual impact aimed for; predominantly aesthetic and communal tone to material displayed in the public spaces; moderate range of specialist accommodation (classrooms, assembly hall/gymnasium/dining hall, staff room, offices); pupils in groups except for (after 1998) literacy and numeracy hours; no stable focal point in classrooms; some zoning of classrooms for specific activities; wall-mounted materials extensive and varied in topic and purpose, with much attention to aesthetic qualities; classrooms have multiple focus and predominately work ambience. *Time.* Daily lessons, play and midday meal; assembly daily in some schools, slightly less frequently in others; time concentrated; time elastic, with varying lesson length (30–90 minutes) except for (after 1998) literacy and numeracy hours and lessons in hall and other specialist areas. *People.* Pupils aged 4/5–11, head teacher, deputy head, generalist teachers doubling as subject leaders, special needs support staff, ancillary staff; mixed ability classes, age based or multi-age in large schools, multi-age in small, 24–34 pupils; pupils change teachers at end of year, except in multi-age classes; two-tier, three-tier and matrix (year/subject) management, with teachers accountable through head to governing body and LEA. *Values.* School as community; teaching as both individualistic and collaborative; education as the development of the whole person and the nurturing of general and transferable qualities of mind ('learning how to learn'); tolerance; respect for others; school and home in partnership; rewarding effort rather than achievement.

We turn now to how the primary schools in our five countries stand in relation to the world beyond the school gates, and especially to parents, the community and the agencies of national, regional and/or local government to which they are accountable.

10

Beyond the Gates

Governments pronounce on what schools must do to meet present and future needs, but schools, too, have perspectives on these matters. As we have seen, they operate on the basis of a framework of values, theories and assumptions which they convey through the building and the way they use it, through the way they manage time, through staff roles and pupil groupings, through daily rituals and procedures, and in pedagogy.

But although each school is unique, no school is autonomous. The way a school views and relates to its pupils' families and the communities they come from is a particularly critical part of its identity; so too is the way it handles the demands and expectations of the formally constituted bodies of the state, whether national, regional or local. These two issues, again viewed through the lens of the *Five Cultures* data, will be our concern in this the last of our three chapters on the idea of a primary school.

School and Home

The *Five Cultures* study was able to explore the home–school relationship incidentally rather than in a systematic way. We did not have the resources to look in depth at the different communities within which our schools were located or at the families from which their pupils came, although we took care to include community contrasts – rural, suburban, inner city, less affluent, more affluent – when selecting the schools. However, we did discuss with heads and teachers, within the structured interview programme, their perspectives on parents and home–school relations, and in several schools groups of parents were happy to meet us and talk with us informally.

In none of the countries, and in none of the schools, were home–school relations treated less than seriously. In the 1986–91 Leeds study we found that the dealings which schools and parents had with each other tended to crystallize into four pairs of complementary roles which we designated *consultant–client, bureaucrat–claimant, equal partners,* and *casual acquaintances*. These terms are borrowed from the realm of everyday relationships so we should not need to explain them. In Leeds, where both parties tacitly consented to operate within one or other of these role pairings, the relationship was more straightforward than when one or other of them refused to play the appropriate role. So, for instance, if a parent wanted to make a formal complaint (*bureacrat* and *claimant*) but a teacher wished to have a friendly chat (*equal partners* or *casual acquaintances*); or if the parent wanted expert advice and expected the school to solve a specific problem (*consultant* and *client*) but the teacher said 'We're all in this together: it's up to you as much as us' (*equal partners*); or if the school adopted the rhetoric of equal partnership but treated parents as subordinate; then difficulties could follow.[1]

In the present study we were able to extend this typology to a general characterization of the way schools related to parents as a group, using the terms *communication, co-operation, confrontation* and *compensation* as shorthand for dimensions of the relationship and for attitudes associated with it. Communication was intrinsic, but in some schools it was extensive, two way, and informal as well as formal, while in others it was restricted to the exchange of formal messages. In the latter case the flow of information tended to be one way: school to home rather than vice versa. Co-operation was generally claimed to be a characteristic of home–school relations, and in many cases was apparently achieved. However, sometimes the relationship descended into confrontation, or was subliminally confrontational under a veneer of co-operation. Finally, in some schools, or in relation to some children, teachers saw themselves as fulfilling a compensatory role, making good parents' inadequacies.

Generalization on these matters is difficult, because parents – it is understood that children's home circumstances vary considerably and throughout this discussion the term is used generically – are not a homogenous group, and must never be treated as though they were. The ease of home–school relations, then, depends partly on the posture taken by each party – hence the value of the Leeds finding about complementarity of role – but it also depends on the degree to which the values and aspirations of the school match those of the home, and in some circumstances, no matter how hard one or both parties work to achieve meaningful communication or even partnership, the gulf may be irreconcilable.

France

Let us develop these ideas, taking each country in turn. In France, as we noted earlier, teachers felt that parents' and teachers' roles used to be, and ought to be, distinct. The division of labour was, subliminally if not explicitly, Cartesian. Schools should deliver the curriculum; and parents should ensure that their children were ready to receive it. Schools should concentrate on the child's mind; parents on the child's social, moral and spiritual development. Both parties would respect these boundaries, and their ideal relationship would be that of consultant and client. In Coulanges school, which served an affluent district of Nice, this relationship appeared to be the one most commonly enacted. There was a certain social distance between the two groups, and a formal procedure for relaying regular reports on children's progress to parents and back again. The return of these documents with the parents' comments and signature was deemed to be as essential to the reporting process as sending them out.

Having said that, teachers commented on the growing incursion of the social and moral domain into the realm of teaching, as a result of family breakdown and what they saw as parental abdication of their responsibilities. We cited the *directrice* of Coulanges school on this matter in Chapter 9, and so do not need to labour the point here except to note that the core of the concern which she and others voiced appeared to be children's lack of respect for the unwritten rules of social intercourse grounded in acceptance of adult (and especially male) authority:

> It used to be the family's responsibility to get children to understand not only that they shouldn't steal and so on, but more basic habits of communication: that children should listen when someone else is speaking, that it is logical to wait for one person to answer before another person starts to speak. They learned this because they were not allowed to interrupt their parents, and especially they were taught to keep quiet while their father was talking . . . When I started teaching, thirty years ago, I had a class of 43 children and in that class there was one child whose parents were separated. Now we have classes of 25 children and more than half their parents are separated. Children live either with their mother or their father; they change over at weekends; mothers go out to work. The stability of the family unit has gone, and with it the rules of behaviour which the family used to provide.

She was far from alone in expressing this concern, or in explaining it in these terms. The specific point she made about talking, listening and not interrupting stemmed, I suggest, not from the kind of unfocused moral outrage – 'young people these days don't know their place' – that in England prompts people to write letters to the press signed 'Disgusted', but because an acceptance of conversational conventions is particularly important in the context of the kind of teaching that French primary schools provide. The classroom culture in France, as we shall see, is traditionally an oral one. Great store is attached not just to talk, but to *disciplined* talk: to developing children's capacities to make and listen to a case, to internalize the capacity for dialectic, to understand the fundamental symmetry of *thèse, antithèse et synthèse*. 'We cannot discipline children's minds', the French teachers were saying, 'if children are not already disciplined in their conduct'.

In Montagne village school, similar procedures to those in Coulanges operated for relaying information between home and school, but the relationship was complicated (or, depending on circumstances, facilitated) by the fact that the teacher lived in the village, knew many of the parents socially as well as professionally, and had his own children at the school. The relationship shifted constantly between consultant–client and acquaintance and for this reason, demanded skill on the part of the teacher and understanding on both sides. At Juan-le-grand school, which served an urban overspill area with relatively high unemployment and a significant minority of immigrant families from North Africa, the school found itself forced into a compensatory stance and sought to deal with this not by the having recourse to the role distance and inequality of the bureaucrat–claimant relationship but by forging the mechanisms and dynamics of partnership.

In other words, although the circumstances of these and the other French schools differed, there was a general assumption that the roles of teachers and parents should remain separate, that communication and co-operation were therefore essential, but that local circumstances might intervene and wider social trends were in any event blurring the edges and making the relationship more complex.

India

The relationship between teachers and parents in the Indian schools was mostly a very unequal one. The partial exception was Purana Primary in Delhi, which served a middle-class enclave where the school understood parents' high ambitions for their children and strove to meet them, not least because otherwise it might have lost a significant proportion of its pupils to private schools. The parents we met here took an instrumental view of the school's task: schools should above all provide children with the knowledge and qualifications to gain a job, preferably in one of the professions.

Elsewhere, the school's task was portrayed unambiguously as one of compensation for illiteracy, poverty, inequality and even fecklessness. All the teachers, following the Indian predilection for precise quantification, gave exact percentages for levels of illiteracy among the parents of the children they taught, and these were seldom below 90–95 per cent. Further, voicing a typical view, the head of Chanderi Primary said:

> In India, education is of little benefit to the community. They do not see much point, as there is no job at the end of it They feel that it is better to work at the local dairy than to have education. That is why most of them have big families, so that children can help at home.

We met a group of this school's parents. They confirmed that illiteracy was a barrier, saying that being illiterate they were in a position neither to judge how well their children were doing nor to take any part in discussion about the school's programmes. Being illiterate they felt inferior, and were made to feel so. To them, then, overcoming their own illiteracy was a vital aspect of the successful education of their children. By empowering themselves in this one vital respect they could empower their children, and indeed the school as well. Yet in their district, unlike in some other parts of the country, there were no adult illiteracy programmes, and the chances of their children breaking out of the cycle of illiteracy were thereby greatly reduced. This is the situation that has led activists such as Saldanha to argue that the illiteracy problem in India must be tackled at both child and adult levels simultaneously.[2] However, contrary to what the school claimed, they were not unambitious for their children. They wanted their sons to become qualified for work as doctors and engineers.

Which brings us again to gender. These parents, like those we met at Purana Primary, wished both their sons and their daughters to achieve a good general level of education, but gave only two reasons why this was important in the latter case:

so that their daughters could marry educated men and thus better themselves and their families, and so that if they moved away from the village at marriage they would be able to keep in touch. Only the Purana parents went slightly further. They wanted their daughters to enter one specific occupation – teaching – because unlike others it would not interfere with their roles as wives and mothers.

Both fathers and mothers came to our meetings with parents in India, but the fathers sat at the front of the room and did all the talking while the mothers sat in silence behind them. We do not know what the mothers wanted for their children, although at one school one of our interpreters cut through the polite exchange of information with her own forthright assessment:

> In this country the women are not at liberty to make any decisions whatsoever. Some are not even allowed to go out without permission, let alone to make decisions about the child's education. It is the husband who decides what the child does. Even in business class families (and some 80 per cent of the community where I live are business class) the women are suppressed and are not allowed to speak for themselves or to be independent enough to go out to work.

Nevertheless, all the schools talked of parent–teacher associations, weekly or monthly parent–teacher meetings, and their unremitting task of trying to raise the levels of enrolment and attendance by visiting children's homes at the weekends. The Indian situation, as we found it, was an extreme one: teachers and parents were not equal partners, but most parents did not have the necessary confidence or knowledge of their rights to make either a consultant–client or bureaucrat–claimant relationship work. Communication was a problem, and although through enormous efforts on both sides co-operation could be achieved, the school's view of circumstances was a predominantly compensatory one.

Russia

In no country did we have a stronger sense of parent–teacher consensus than in Russia. The formal structures for consultation were established decades ago, under the Soviet system, and the parental voice in school affairs had to be listened to. Matters in the mid 1990s, though, were far from easy. At one school, teachers spoke of moving from a situation where they knew exactly where each parent was employed to not even knowing whether they had jobs at all, and suspecting that some had none or were engaged in the black economy. Many families were facing growing financial hardship and other problems which one head said that she found so distressing that she could not bring herself to talk about. Other teachers spoke openly of disintegrating marriages, homelessness, malnutrition, alcoholism and – as in France but to a more dramatic degree – of schools having to extend their role in children's moral and social development. However, unlike in France, this was something they could take to more readily – which is not at all to say that the task was easy – because through *vospitanie* schools already adopted, and were expected to adopt, a significant role in this regard.

Throughout the interviews, the Russian teachers stressed partnership with parents. The economic and political crisis of the 1990s was also a crisis of values to which teachers, children and parents were particularly vulnerable. In these circumstances, we were told, something closer than the formalities of 'partnership' was needed:

> Our parents want their children to acquire a broad base of knowledge, to be literate, articulate, to have the power of logical and rational thought, to be creative, and overall become a fully developed personality . . .

Thus far, a familiar view of the purposes of education in Russia. But then:

> Parents very much want us, them and the children to talk together as much as possible and cultivate, and feel, a genuine sense of friendship and support. Families are now becoming very isolated, and parents often ask us to meet them, and bring them together so that children can socialize and develop friendships with each other.

This isolation was aggravated by the erosion of extra-curricular activities and the disappearance of the Octobrists, Pioneers and Komsomol, which under the Soviet system strengthened peer networks as well as pursued party objectives. *Vospitanie* was always a collective concept: bringing up the individual was about developing the all-round social personality. Losing structures and contexts for social interaction meant that the quality of upbringing as a whole was diminished.

There were three ways that schools and parents together – for that was always how it was viewed – could try, against these odds, to compensate for this deteriorating situation. One was by the school's insistence, against the contrary tides of wider social upheaval, on continuity and consistency in moral and social values. The second was by modulating the relationship between parents and teachers to achieve a bond deeper than mere partnership, as outlined by the last teacher quoted above. The third was by relying on the Russian family's traditional strength and resilience – qualities which, as Bronfenbrenner noted in his classic comparative child-rearing study, have always made families a much more potent force in children's development in Russia than in the United States.[3]

United States

I hope it is not becoming one of this book's clichés for me to suggest that in many, possibly the majority of matters we explored in this study, Russia and the United States, or at least Michigan, were a long way apart. In the matter of home–school relations we can at least start with a similarity, although that will be as far as it goes. The schools in both countries had well-developed systems for bringing teachers and parents together, and for involving parents in decisions about their children's schooling.

The extent and quality of the Michigan schools' documentation in this area was impressive. Emerson Elementary School, which we can take as typical (the other schools were similar in this regard) had both parent and student handbooks, both of which were sent to parents as a single publication. They were updated each school year. The parent handbook included, alongside basic school information, guidance on what parents should do, or the school would do, in the event of any of a list of contingencies running from illness to tornado. The student handbook concentrated on personal safety, school rules and disciplinary procedures, and the combined publication ended by reminding both parents and children of their civil rights under US Federal Law. The principal also sent out weekly parents' bulletins containing a calendar of events for the week ahead, diary dates for later in the semester, information about property lost and found, and even lunch menus. There were frequent letters to parents on specific issues, all with a slip for the parents to sign and return to confirm that they had received and read it. There was, naturally, a parent–teacher association.

Moreover, much of this kind of communication ran directly between the child's class teacher and its parents and in the matter of home–school relations the principal did not act as a gatekeeper, as so often heads (and school secretaries) do in English primary schools. Thus at the beginning of the year in the same school a teacher with whom we worked issued her own prospectus for the parents of children about to start with her as first graders. It gave the timetable, information about each subject and how it would be taught, details of classroom norms and routines, and tips on how parents might support children's learning, particularly in reading. Each Friday this teacher (and others in the school) sent home with the child a folder containing the school newsletter and work the child had completed during the previous few days. Parents were encouraged to phone or call at the school any time of the day to arrange to see her, and they were given a direct contact number for the period 3.30 p.m. to 7.00 p.m.

Parents, then, were entitled and encouraged to be as involved as it is possible to be in their children's education, to have ready access to the school and its teachers, and to comment as they wished on the workings of the school and the quality of teaching their children were experiencing.

The possible downside of this became apparent when we interviewed parents at one of the schools. Parents who wished and had time to take advantage of the open-door policy become rapidly attuned to the kinds of problems which schools in England, say, would have preferred to sort out without alerting the parents: friction among teachers, difficulties the school was having in hiring staff replacements, problems of teachers' relative competence and commitment. Since not a few parents were active in other contexts locally, and had equally clear lines of communication to the local school administration, and since the administration itself put out a great deal of comparative information on how schools were performing, there was a sense in which life in the Michigan schools seemed to be considerably more public, and more publicly discussed and contested, than in the schools we visited in the other four countries. When things are going well this is an advantage and when they are not it can be a problem.

However, the real problem in home–school relations was not unique to these elementary schools. It concerned what it is not over-dramatic to call the American crisis over basic values. We have seen how the head of Hawthorne Elementary School felt obliged to take a tough stand on the behaviour of parents as well as children.

Teachers and parents, and not merely those in the tense environment of Hawthorne Elementary, were acutely concerned about personal safety, in the home and school as well as on the street. Anti-social behaviour, and the management of anti-social behaviour, loomed large in teachers' consciousness, in staff discussions, and in formal school procedures. The principal of Thoreau told us that he could no longer assume that there was consensus among parents over the values that the school should foster, and every such value had to be made explicit and negotiated. He went on:

> Ten years ago we could have taken all this for granted. Now we cannot. There's a high student turnover. The children don't have common educational experiences and certainly not common social experiences. Our minority population has changed, so our parents would like to see more minority teachers, but we don't have any, and because of contractual issues we can't just pull teachers out and replace them by minority teachers. And it's very difficult to help parents understand our daily practice, because the kind of schooling they had is quite different from what we are doing now.

To alleviate the problem the school organized meetings and parent conferences, Thoreau's principal told us,

> Those who don't come to the meetings want us to do things differently. They want to see more of the basics being pushed . . . Now we have 'schools of choice' instead of them being restricted to certain areas that were drawn on paper by someone downtown. At least with schools of choice I can say to parents 'If you want a school that's driven by a textbook, then you don't want Thoreau'.

But the differences of opinion about behaviour, school values and curriculum at Thoreau were slight compared with the situation at Hawthorne, and the principal there, as we noted earlier, had taken the view that – in terms of our earlier discussion of elements in home–school relationships – the school had a major task of compensating for the inadequacy of many pupils' family circumstances, that communication between teachers and parents was a matter of the highest priority, but that if parental co-operation could not be secured by normal means then confrontation was the only option.

The test for Hawthorne Elementary had been establishing and enforcing norms of behaviour among the students. Ten years previously the situation had been grave:

> I didn't feel I was being an educational leader because there were so many problems. I was stopping them from breaking into cars on the parking lot. I was chasing drunks out of school, I was breaking up fights. There was always something I had to watch. I was just keeping the peace.

However, at that point he ran up against state law, which he found he could circumvent:

> In Michigan you cannot discipline children. You cannot do anything to 'em. So my discipline policy is: when you get to the point where we can't handle them any more I close the classes for four days unless mother comes to sit with them all day. If mother

comes to sit with them I keep the classes open. When she comes, she can't talk to the teacher, because the teacher is teaching. She can't help the child with his work, because that's his responsibility. Her job is the discipline, and our job is to teach, and she sits right next to the child all day. A couple of days of that and Mom makes Johnny act right – she don't want to miss her job, or whatever. I've had parents come and drop them off and say 'I've got to go work'. Well, I'll bring the child down and take him to the mother's job and drop him off. I tell her 'That's your responsibility'.

And, coming to the essence of the problem:

We don't mind teaching them, but we can't raise them too. Parents have to have some measure of responsibility for the child.

This was the problem that was beginning to impinge on the professional con-sciousness of some of our French teachers. In Russia, however, although we were told that teachers and parents were increasingly fearful of what was happening beyond the school gates, and personal safety, not an issue in Soviet days, was now a major cause for concern, we did not have this sense of a fractured society spilling its detritus into the school. On the contrary, the schools preserved a remarkable atmosphere of stability, normality, security and above all continuity. The roots of this achievement are various – a greater degree of general consensus about what schools should be doing, perhaps a higher traditional level of respect for education, the strength of the Russian family as an institution, its resilience in the face of levels of privation and suffering which most Westerners can barely imagine, and the close and sustained involvement of parents in their children's upbringing.

But a central focus for explanation, when we come to compare our American and Russian schools, must be the relationship between education and upbringing. In the Michigan schools the two were separate and teachers were fighting to keep them that way. One was the province of schools, the other of parents. When in Michigan upbringing and education converged as a consequence of that parental 'abdication' one of our French heads talked about, there was not a unification of values and effort, but a collision. In Russia, education and upbringing were already a unitary process, and for this reason, alongside the others I have suggested, the Russian schools were perhaps better able to cope with the educational fallout of families struggling to survive the trauma of a nation in transition.

England

Until the 1980s, few English primary schools had prospectuses, parents played a limited role in school governance, and although the far-from-apocryphal sign 'No parents beyond this point' had disappeared from most school gates, the extent to which parents and teachers co-operated could vary considerably from one school to another. Schools were as accountable to parents as their heads allowed them to be.

Mandatory accountability to parents began with the 1980 Education Act, which required schools' governing bodies to include parent representatives. Under the 1986 Act the proportion of such governors was increased and governing bodies took on an explicit role in relation to schools' internal management. Initially this remit covered matters such as admissions and discipline; from 1988 it was extended further to include the school's goals and curriculum, the budget, development policy, and the hiring and deployment of teachers and others staff.

At the same time, successive Conservative and Labour administrations promoted the 'marketization' of state schooling. Through open enrolment (the English equivalent of Michigan's 'schools of choice') which replaced the strict zoning policies applied by most LEAs until the 1980s, through the publication of inspection reports, test results and performance league tables, and the possibility of parents voting to take schools out of LEA control and into direct ('grant-maintained') government funding, the governments of the 1980s and the 1990s completed the cultural shift they sought. Parents were now consumers, and schools competed for their custom in the educational market place. As consumers, their rights were ostensibly protected by a 'Parents' Charter'.[4]

The paradox of all this is that the new educational market was free only up to a point. Its logical conclusion was full privatization, but these schools were, and were to remain, state schools. So parents gained the choice of which state school they would send their children to at the same time as they lost the right to choose the kind of education their children would receive. Schools competed not to meet the different parental aspirations that the new consumerism ought to have revealed, but to provide the same curriculum and, from 1998, the same teaching methods. The much-vaunted differences between schools, which were essential to a meaningful concept of freedom of choice, were therefore differences in *quality* rather than *content*. Marketization proceeded hand-in-hand with a drive for uniformity of input, process and outcome, justified by the rhetoric of standards. By 1997, when the Blair government pledged itself to raise standards in literacy and numeracy to specific levels by 2002, using methods which government rather than teachers would prescribe, it could almost be suggested that teachers had become not so much agents of the state as tools of New Labour's drive to get itself re-elected. To this drive, parents, being school governors as well as consumers, were also recruited.

The educational rhetoric of the period betrayed similar contradictions in relation to parent–teacher relations and our earlier home–school typology. The guiding principle of teacher–parent relations was, if official documentation was to be believed, one of partnership, but the educational climate of the 1990s, whipped up by the alliance of HMCI Woodhead at OFSTED and Prime Minister Blair in Downing Street, fostered consumerism in its most hostile and combative form: parent–consumer as claimant determined to sue for his or her rights, rather than client; teacher as time-serving and barely competent bureaucrat, rather than skilled and conscientious consultant. The tables had been well and truly turned: if primary schools during the 1960s, the 1970s and the 1980s could be criticized for operating on the basis of a deficit model of the home, parents at the turn of the century were being encouraged to take a deficit view of the school – guilty of the charge of incompetence until proved innocent.

But parents, families, communities and cultures remain resolutely different, and it is therefore not surprising that our English schools used whatever latitude they were able to retain to project a unique character and a unique response to local circumstances and needs.

At St Teresa's, the Catholic school featured in Chapter 9, the head expressed her task starkly as one of compensation and remediation: 'We've got a housing sink, a drugs problem, and half the criminal element of the city are on our roll'. At Kirkbright, a traditional coal-mining community was still adapting its social structure and employment patterns to the closure of its last pit. It was not yet clear what should replace established parental aspirations for their children's education, but since few of the parents had taken their own education beyond the minimum school leaving age, envisaging an alternative in which the 1997 government's ideal of lifelong learning might be fostered was far from easy. As the head of Kirkbright noted:

> The government says parents should help their children with their homework, and now with their reading and maths, but I don't think government understands at all what they are asking of parents whose own education is limited. It's going to take more than one election cycle to change the understanding of parents like ours.

Again, as at St Teresa's, the task at Cheetham dictated basic parent education before there could be any thought of genuine partnership. Nearly half the pupils at Cheetham School were from Muslim families of Pakistani origin. A significant proportion of the rest were

> . . . children who've been to four or five schools, children who've missed chunks of their curriculum, particularly science and maths . . . more and more displaced families, more and more tenants rather than owner-occupiers, coming into the areas with great social needs. There are many broken families. There's a high crime rate – we have special funding to help us work with parents to reduce crime, and we're one of only six schools in the UK to get such a grant. I've seen the decline in just six years. The expectations of these families who are constantly on the move are much lower than the more stable Asian families.

The head of St Teresa's felt that the apparatus of accountability – inspections, tests, league tables – was

> . . . a 'leafy lane' system. It favours the schools which are well-off, comfortable and look tidy; where the children speak nicely, where they're not hung up on drugs or in need of child protection . . . those schools come off better.

This perception of double disadvantage was shared by the head of Cheetham:

> We're very vulnerable here over standards and have really to be clear about our goals and our practice, because KS2 SAT results can put us in a very bad light, despite all our efforts. All that anybody wants to know is Level 4 – nobody wants to know about moving towards Level 3, about value-added.[5]

and

> We know as well as OFSTED and the government that high expectations are crucial. But we're getting fed up with being preached at about this, because we're in a no-win situation: *we* have high expectations, but many of our parents don't.

The last observation deserves comment. In the 1986–91 Leeds study we reported evidence of low expectations among some teachers of inner-city children. This was widely publicized nationally. However, we also argued:

> At the same time, some of the root causes of the problem may well be beyond the reach of individual teachers. The impact of poverty on a child's life and educational prospects is far greater than the rather clinical phrase 'social and material disadvantage' can ever convey. The teaching of reading has been in the public arena for some time now, and the brunt of the political and media attack has been borne by primary teachers and teacher trainers. While our evidence underlines the need for a considerable sharpening of the educational response, it also suggests that without a change in the political, social and economic circumstances which lead to poverty and dislocation, some teachers will continue to fight a losing battle.[6]

This is a familiar and contentious topic of post-war educational debate in both England and the United States. In the mid and late 1980s, when we interviewed the Leeds teachers, studied their school policies and observed their classroom practices, the family/home deficit view was still quite widespread within the primary teaching profession. By the mid 1990s and the late 1990s, when we interviewed our English primary teachers for the *Five Cultures* project, the climate was very different. By then, teachers were sensitive to any suggestion that they were using family circumstances and social disadvantage as an excuse for poor teaching. Research studies and inspection evidence had reported on schools that had succeeded 'against the odds'. The idea of 'value-added', resisted by the Conservative adminstrations of 1979–97, had been accepted by their Labour successors. LEAs such as Birmingham had initiated major policy drives to raise the standards of schooling and achievement in the inner city. The government was about to launch its Education Action Zones (EAZ) through which partnerships of businesses, parents, schools, LEAs and community organizations would tackle specific educational problems in deprived rural or urban areas.[7] A more balanced and realistic account of this particular nexus of problems at last seemed possible.

This was the background to the anxieties expressed by the heads of St Teresa's and Cheetham, and indeed Kirkbright (the school in the former mining community). All these heads knew perfectly well the tight-rope they walked between drawing attention to genuine and sometimes intractable social problems which militated against their best efforts and being accused of using these as an excuse for poor teaching and low test scores.

In the very different environment of Hamilton Primary, a school of the kind that the head of St Teresa's disparagingly called 'leafy lanes' – it served, that is to say, a suburban, relatively affluent neighbourhood – it was not only the teachers who registered anxiety about the pressure of the government's test programme and market-oriented policies which pitted school against school. They were less concerned about the standards which testing would reveal than about the impact of the testing process and the pressure which the associated 'naming and shaming' policy placed on teachers, for they appreciated that stressed teachers are less effective teachers. Representatives of the parents whom we interviewed said that the school's parents had come to terms with the national curriculum and testing as such, and felt confident of the way the school was handling them. Having done so, they were more preoccupied with wider aspects of the question of whether their children were getting a good deal: class sizes; mixed-age teaching (as noted earlier, changing local demography had created a bulge in pupil numbers which could only be met by mixing year groups); school finance. Under the post-1988 budgetary delegation Hamilton found itself – like other English primary schools – forced to make hard choices over the appointment of teachers: whether to recruit a young, inexperienced teacher and save money for other purposes, or to buy experience but thereby lose out in other areas of the school's work.

As in Michigan, Moscow and Kursk, there was growing anxiety among English parents about their children's safety, especially on the streets. The vast increase in motor traffic since the 1980s had been a constant anxiety. In the neighbourhoods of St Teresa's, Cheetham and Ogden there was a drugs presence. Almost everywhere, by the 1990s, there was a collective sense that young children could no longer roam freely in the way their parents and grandparents had.

If in launching and extending the marketization of state schooling during the 1980s and the 1990s the UK government thought this would make parents more aggressive in the demands they placed upon schools (bureaucrat–claimant), it may have miscalculated. We heard evidence that external pressures – a financial crisis resulting from the combination of primary school funding levels and budgetary delegation, an OFSTED inspection – could sometimes bring teachers and parents together, united in the face of a common threat or enemy.

As for the marketing process itself, the material provided by our English schools was not unlike that we saw in Michigan. Hamilton, for example, produced an attractively presented and lucidly written 'School Prospectus' containing a wealth of information from broad policies to detailed procedures, together with special booklets – 'Starting School' and 'Helping Your Child' – for parents of children entering the reception class. It disseminated other material on a regular basis. All of the schools we visited held frequent meetings with parents on a range of matters, reported on a teacher-to-family basis about the progress of each pupil, had parent–teacher associations (PTA) whose principle function was to raise funds to supplement the school budget, and encouraged parents to call or visit the school to discuss any matter which concerned them. This, by the 1990s, had become the expected and indeed required pattern of home–school relations. In some schools parents worked as unpaid volunteer assistants: this was particularly evident at Cheetham, where the presence in school of adults from the local Muslim community went some way towards redressing the cultural imbalance among the mainly white and indigenous teaching staff.

In 1999 there was a further tightening of the screws of centralization, this time in the area of home–school relations itself. The Blair government decided to make the relations between teachers quasi-contractual, although this time pushing some of the responsibility back upon parents to modify the rather one-sided bureaucrat-claimant relationship fostered by the preceding Thatcher and Major administrations. From September 1999 all schools and parents were required to enter into 'home–school agreements' setting out parental obligations in respect of matters such as the child's homework, behaviour and attendance. Parents as well as teachers expressed disquiet, for the initiative was clearly aimed at the minority of parents who fail to support the efforts of their children' schools, yet all parents were – in the words of a dissenting head – 'being tarred with the same brush'. The difficulty for the government was that it seemed genuinely to want full partnership between parents and teachers, because it understood the benefits which would follow, yet it knew that without some kind of nudge the problem of the minority would not go away. On the other hand, true partnership is entered into voluntarily, and legislating to control the home–school relationship could make it more, not less problematic.[8]

Comparisons

It seems fair to assert that, in England, the institutional relationship between home and primary school was transformed during the last two decades of the twentieth century. The initial impetus came from documents like the Plowden report that made the case for partnership on strictly educational grounds. At that time, the mid 1960s, the phrase 'public accountability' was rarely used or heard and the home–school movement was both idealistic and voluntary. Parents and teachers should collaborate rather than perpetuate the elementary school culture and confront each other through the playground railings, argued Plowden, because the child's learning would benefit, and this was manifestly in everybody's best interests. The earlier in the child's life that parents engaged in an educative relationship with their children, it was argued, and in an educative partnership with teachers, the more the school would achieve. This, allied with the universalization of nursery provision and specific programmes of compensatory intervention, would begin to reduce the gross inequalities in opportunity and achievement between children from different social backgrounds.[9]

By the end of the century, nursery and pre-school provision in England had been greatly extended, although not universalized in the way that, for decades, had been the case in France and Soviet Russia, and the compensatory movement had risen, fallen and risen again. At the same time the culture of voluntary co-operation between home and school had been eroded by the drive for formal accountability allied to the ideology of marketization and consumerism. By 2000, the relationships between parents and primary teachers were closer and more comprehensive as to their content, but also more complex and potentially fraught.

Comparisons with France, India, Russia and the United States have helped us to broaden our perspectives on these matters. The parallels between what we found in some of our English and American schools, in respect of the stance on both home–school relations and the associated procedures, are evident. They are also hardly surprising, since English approaches to early learning and urban deprivation have been strongly influenced by American thinking and practice. There has been little interest in emulating, or inclination to emulate, the practices of France or Russia. Yet they provide highly instructive alternative paradigms. The holistic and inclusive ideology of post-1960s English primary education contrasts with the careful delineation of the respective roles and functions of teachers and parents which we found, albeit now under some pressure, in France. At a time when the teaching role in English and American primary schools appears to be spiralling out of control, the French model is well worth investigating. English educational holism also bears comparison with the rather different kind of holism implied by *vospitanie* in Russia. In England, primary education is conceived as education, not upbringing; yet it includes objectives in the domain of personal and social development which overlap considerably the tasks of parents. However, it is not – or not yet – *vospitanie*, for its goal remains the development of the 'person' (whatever that means) rather than the citizen.

Everywhere we found questions being raised about parental roles and responsibilities *vis-à-vis* those of the school. Indian teachers outside the middle class urban enclaves saw their role as essentially that of compensating for parental deficit, cultural as well as educational – that is to say, in respect of matters such as gender equalization as well as the eradication of illiteracy. French teachers were concerned that parents were abdicating their authority in the domain of basic socialization and the inculcation of self-discipline, and that this was putting at risk the traditional French concept of education as the development of qualities of mind. The American teachers were worried about the breakdown of family life, the additional burden it placed on them as teachers, and growing threats to the physical safety and moral well-being of their pupils. Russian teachers, notwithstanding *vospitanie* and a high degree of consensus among parents and teachers over basic educational values, priorities and procedures, feared not so much voluntary parental abdication as that parenting was becoming a forced casualty of the 1990s trauma of social and economic transition. English and American teachers made much of partnership but were also aware that in the context of heightened accountability (and, in the United States, litigiousness) the relationship could all too easily deteriorate into confrontation. Although we saw plenty of evidence of warm and constructive relationships between home and school, the potential for tension in the relationship was seldom far away.

School and State: the Schools' View

In Chapters 2–6 we outlined each country's national system of primary education before examining its origins and development and assessing its current condition. In Chapter 7 we opened up some theoretical perspectives on the relationship between education and the state in order to place the five countries' unique systems and circumstances within a common framework of interpretation and explanation.

Our analysis pivoted on the issues of *control, culture* and *identity.* Once tested against our country-specific data, the ostensibly clear distinction between centralized and decentralized systems proved to be open to question. Educational decision-making is never monolithic and even in the contexts of relative centralization (such as France or Russia), extreme centralization (such as England), relative decentralization (India) or extreme decentralization (the United States) power is differentially distributed in respect of different kinds of decisions – goals, policy, resources, curriculum, assessment, quality assurance and so on – across the various levels from national government to school. This did not invalidate centralization/decentralization as a key variable, but it did make it more complex to handle. Similarly, the harder-edged claims that schools are passive agents of cultural and economic reproduction had to accommodate the more reflexive notions of hegemony and resistance as we balanced state control with local power and influence and suggested that, in pluralist societies such as these five, schools are not merely cultural channels or amplifiers but also cultural interfaces where competing values meet and are resolved – or not, as the case may be. They are also microcultures in their own right.

The issue of identity proved no less problematic. Public schooling clearly plays its part, sometimes a vital part, in the development and sustaining of national identity, but none of our countries, not even France with its insistence on indivisibility, is homogeneous. To varying degrees and in different ways, the national educational project in each country was compromised by division or plurality: of religion, caste and tribe; of ethnicity, class and gender; of geography. Central control of state education may conceal or suppress such divisions but it does not eliminate them. When there is a conjunction of plurality and decentralization, as in the United States, then values are very much out in the open, everywhere and every day, within the education system as a whole and within each school and classroom.

How, then, do these matters look from the schools themselves? We explored questions of control and accountability in interviews conducted at national (or, in the case of the USA, state), local, school and classroom level, that is to say with national/state level officials, inspectors and teacher trainers, heads and class teachers. To each we asked questions about where and how decisions were taken on a wide range of matters from policy, goals and resourcing to curriculum, teaching and assessment. We heard from some of the national level respondents in earlier chapters. Here we are interested in how things look to heads and class teachers.

The most striking finding was not so much what this group said in response to such questions as how they said it, and indeed what they did not say. In schools in three of the countries, despite our prompting, control and the balance of power as between the different levels from national to school and classroom scarcely rated as an issue. In the other two the balance of control and power was not only a matter of considerable concern; it also tended to prompt an almost unstoppable flow of views whose tone was anxious and occasionally vehement, but never neutral. In centralized England, and decentralized America – for these were the two countries in question – it mattered a great deal to teachers who controlled primary education, what they did with the power they wielded, and with what consequences.

It is tempting to reach for centralization/decentralization as the reason for this striking anomaly, for England and the United States are at the extremes of this particular continuum and it might be assumed that in these contexts the location and use of power would be bound to matter most to those at the cutting edge of the system, which teachers undoubtedly are. This is surely part of the answer, but only part. Before reaching a judgement on this, let us consider briefly the three countries where teachers were less exercised by these matters.

France

In France, as we have reported, teachers registered their understanding of their situation: one system of education, one set of goals, one curriculum, one school even (see p. 198), a clear command structure, but at school level the inexorable tide of centralization was subtly and significantly modified. First there was the commune, allowing a high degree of local engagement in each elementary school. Second, since the 1980s the shackles of central control had been progressively loosened, and this process was continuing and indeed in 2000 looks likely to be taken further. Third, class teachers were accountable not to the school *directeur/directrice* but to the Ministry via the inspectorate and the *académie*. Fourth, while the curriculum was prescribed, method was not. 'One goal, but many routes' was how one of our teachers put it.

So what looked like – and is frequently described as – an international archetype of educational centralization actually left teachers with a genuine sense of professional autonomy over the things which to them mattered most: not the curriculum, about which they seemed reasonably content, but its interpretation within the classroom and its translation into learning structures and encounters. There each teacher was firmly in control and not even the school's *directeur/directrice* could intervene; even inspectors, unless something was seriously amiss, acted on a teacher's pedagogy only obliquely.

But from an English or American standpoint one might reasonably ask why the content of the curriculum, over which teachers had little control, was relatively uncontentious. After all, there are important questions of value at stake, and there is no reason to suppose that the French would be any less interested in these than their colleagues elsewhere. I say 'relatively' because we did interview teachers who felt that the curriculum was in danger of becoming overloaded. A typical response on this issue was:

> The syllabi are too crowded – not so much in the lower classes as for the older children. Next year I will have to add English or German, but we haven't been told where we find the time, for we shall still have 26 hours each week. A few years ago, they added civic education because they said there were social problems. The children were behaving badly, so they said 'Now, one hour a week of civic education'. So we should have moved from 26 to 27 hours but we didn't, even although they added an hour. And in CM1 and CM2 they added two hours of information technology, which makes 28 hours, but still within 26. And that's where we don't agree, because they say to us when we complain 'We don't want to know that: you sort it out. You're the teachers, you're the ones with the training. You know best'.

This teacher also felt that his profession was partly to blame for growing logistical problems (he refers below to the difficulty of *redoublement* in the context of the post-Jospin *cycles à l'école primaire*):[10]

> Next year I will have to do a CP [*cours préparatoire* or the first year of primary school) for those who have come with me and who can't manage to do CE1, as well as CE1 itself [*course élémentaire, première année*, the second year of primary school]. You see? That makes double lessons for us. It makes life complicated. But it's our fault. The teachers asked for cycles. They demonstrated, went on strike and everything.

No doubt such unease is replicated in schools in other parts of France. Yet note that the issue is not the content or balance of the curriculum, but its manageability. Provided that the teachers felt they were in control in the classroom, they had all the autonomy they needed: curriculum overload and *redoublement* in the new context of cycles rather than years were threats to that sense of control. Note too that this teacher was quite happy for his profession to shoulder some of the blame for the logistical difficulties he and others were facing. Such a response would be relatively unusual among English teachers.

In answer to my question about the relative uncontentiousness of the substance and direction of the French state curriculum, as an embodiment of what it means to be educated, there are two possible answers: either that a centralized curriculum is the only kind of curriculum that French teachers have ever known, so questioning it may seem inconceivable; or that they had reflected on it and found it appropriate and just. While it is undoubtedly true that what you do not know you do not miss, it is also the case that our French teachers identified strongly with the curriculum as prescribed, and especially with the central part played in it by the French language. In the interviews linked with the lesson observations they argued their lesson rationales from the inside, displaying an easy mastery of subject structure. The curriculum was the Ministry's, but it was also theirs.

Keith Sharpe offers the intriguing argument that French teachers' acquiescence in educational policy, and their identification with the system rather than an individual school, are a secular variant on Roman Catholicism. The state education system may be secular, he suggests, but its culture and authority structure are quintessentially Catholic, right down to the parallel roles of *recteur d'académie* (archbishop), *inspecteur d'académie* (bishop), *inspecteur d'éducation nationale* (auxiliary bishop) and *instituteur/institutrice/professeur* (priest).[11] We have already noted the brahmanical genealogy of Indian teaching. Given our discussion in earlier chapters about the part played by organized religion in the formation of public education systems, the possibility that the culture and organization of modern secular systems of education has cultural and organizational roots which are as likely to be religious as secular seems wholly plausible.

India

India might seem to be a rather different case, for some of the evidence reviewed earlier, and some of the comments we heard in our interviews, were highly critical of educational policy, and indeed, on grounds of relevance, scope and balance, of the curriculum and the Minimum Levels of Learning.[12] But such reservations were expressed by academics and indeed officials, rather than by teachers. The only adverse comments on curriculum that we heard from teachers were, again, about overload. One teacher of six year olds said:

> There is just not enough time to cover everything we are expected to teach. I have even had to bring some children to my home and give them extra teaching there.

But then, curriculum overload was officially acknowledged to be a problem, and had been addressed as such by a government advisory committee.[13] This teacher was drawing attention to a widely acknowledged difficulty rather than going out on a dissenting limb.

This is not to say that the Indian teachers were sanguine over the balance of educational power and their place in relation to it. But compared with England and Michigan, the mutterings and rumblings we heard were slight. Thus, my exchange with another teacher on the same problem of curriculum overload:

> My most difficult task is the lack of time to cover the curriculum. There is too much to do, and it's inflexible.
> (*Do other teachers share your view?*)
> Yes, all teachers believe that this is a problem.
> (*What do they do about it?*)
> We discuss it with the district officers and with Madam [the headmistress] and we are given some flexibility, but only if there is a genuine reason, and then we have to be inspected to make sure.

This last comment brings us close to the nub. Our French teachers were civil servants, accountable to the Ministry. The residual status differential between them and their colleagues in secondary and higher education had been disguised, if not removed, now that they could call themselves *professeurs d'école*. They fulfilled centrally determined requirements in some aspects of their work but were autonomous in others. The Indian primary teachers were chronically under-powered, had limited status, and lacked autonomy in all but the most rudimentary of matters. Unlike their French counterparts they were accountable to and through the school head, which reduced their autonomy further, yet heads themselves also had limited power and limited room for manoeuvre. Above both were the local inspectors, and above them a long hierarchy stretching up through their district to the state officials and state government and eventually to the national government in Delhi.

'Delhi is a long way off' Indians are reputedly fond of saying, and indeed for most of them it is, for to the primary school teachers what matters is not Delhi, or even the state government, but district officials and inspectors. Inspectors were present during several of our visits to schools. They were entitled to call, unannounced, whenever they liked, and indeed we were given a copy of the *Proforma for Surprise Visit of Primary Schools* used in one district. It was a checklist to enable the inspector to record pupil enrolment and attendance; the numbers of SC/ST (scheduled caste and scheduled tribe) pupils; the state of the building, its facilities and equipment, including the availability of teaching aids, textbooks, *tat-pattis*, drinking water and toilets; and the head's and teacher's fulfilment of their basic obligations in respect of maintaining supervisory diaries (head), daily lesson diaries (class teachers), and tests.

A document such as this, and the unrestricted right of access and intervention with which it is associated, confirm the extreme status differentials within the Indian system. Teachers taught the prescribed curriculum, could adopt a different teaching method only with the head's permission, and the head himself or herself was likely to be closely and sometimes arbitrarily monitored. It is a hard system to kick against.

But the other key to our understanding of Indian teachers' relative silence on the prevailing balance of power and decision-making was the sheer weight of the day-to-day problems with which they had to cope. They might quibble about curriculum overload, or – as most did – complain about the lack of resources, but these matters faded into relative insignificance when compared with the adverse impact on their work of what most took to be the most intractable problems: poverty, illiteracy, imputed and/or actual parental attitudes, under-enrolment, non-attendance, the inequalities of gender and caste.

We might add – and it is inference only, although it fits with the wider evidence – that however forthcoming they were prepared to be on other issues, and they were, teachers may have been reluctant to do more than hint at matters of status and power because they had so little of either.

It did not help that they were likely to find themselves isolated. The rural teachers in one- and two-teacher schools were an extreme (and extremely common) case, and their isolation is something the Government of India's District Primary Education Programme is attempting to address through cluster and block resource centres (CRCs and BRCs) and enhanced in-service provision. But this was also a problem in the larger schools in more populated areas. There we interviewed teachers who acknowledged the availability of in-service courses but:

> We could do with a lot more mutual participation at these seminars. Besides the set lectures we need to discuss our individual problems, but there are 35 to 40 of us in a class, and if we express our discontent we rarely get any solutions. It seems a useless exercise to voice our opinions when we know they will not be considered.

So, for reasons of resourcing or culture, these teachers were kept firmly in their place even in the context of opportunities for professional development, and although not physically isolated, they had few opportunities to engage with those around them about the dilemmas of teaching.

India, then, is like France in that teachers said little about their place in the power structure of primary education, but there the resemblance stops. The Indian teachers were tackling challenges unimaginable to their French (and English and American) colleagues, yet for this they were chronically under-resourced and underpowered. They got on with the job; and given the opportunity they hinted at their dissatisfaction rather than voiced it directly. As for the government's decentralizing initiatives,

it was possible that these might prove double edged, as one of our Ministry interviewees suggested (pp. 96–7). The 1992 Panchayati Raj Act, and reform programmes
such as DPEP, have undoubtedly strengthened the lower levels of the system, from
district offices down to village education committees, but in doing so they may well
have left heads and teachers as underpowered as ever.

Russia

In Russia, we again encountered apparent acquiescence towards the prevailing balance
of control, combined with occasional and sometimes oblique references to systemic
problems. The reticence this time was the more surprising given that the entire
system was undergoing a process of reform, much of generated from Moscow.

But again, the realities were complex, and pressure from Moscow was countered
by contrary pressures at lower levels. In any event, we noted in Chapter 3 that in
Russia (as in France and indeed in India), part of the reform package was an explicit
transfer of power to regional and local level. Instead of being monolithic and centrally determined, the school curriculum would have a balance of federal, regional
and school components.

The latter two levels were significant. We found, and noted earlier, that considerable actual power was wielded by regional and local administrations, but whereas
before the collapse of the Soviet Union they were an arm of Moscow, now they
could as readily assert their distinctiveness. We were told that in the Kursk *oblast*
the communist party remained strong, and there were hints that it had retained its
influence within the formal administrative structures for education. This was the
town of Brezhnev and Rutskoy (our first visit was only a year after Yeltsin's violent
assault on the Rutskoy faction in the Moscow White House and to many in Kursk
Rutskoy was a hero and Yeltsin a figure of contempt). It was also the site of the
biggest tank battle of what Russians call the Great Patriotic War (the Second World
War), in which catastrophic damage had been inflicted on life and property in and
around Kursk. However, the German defeat had been one of the war's decisive
moments and Kursk had gained a permanent place in Russian and world history.
Teachers and administrators operated within a local culture that was proud and
independent.

Moreover, because teachers had limited geographical mobility, their professional
world was confined and self-contained. Most Kursk teachers followed the same
route from school to Kursk Pedagogical College or Kursk Pedagogical University,
back to school as a teacher, back to in-service courses at the Kursk Institute of
Qualified Teachers which were staffed by the same lecturers from the pedagogical
college or university – and all within the one town. One or two teachers we interviewed came from Orel or even Tula, further north along the railway line to Moscow,
or from Kharkov, just over the nearby Ukrainian border, but most were Kursk born,
bred and trained. There could be, and was, a distinctly Kursk line on educational
philosophy and practice in which Kursk as a tight-knit professional community, rather
than Kursk's teachers as individuals, took full advantage of its statutory regional
and school-level discretion. It was also clear that in such a context networking and

patronage played a significant part in teacher appointment and advancement, as they had in Soviet days. More than one teacher said to us 'Getting on is all about contacts and connections'.

This was Kursk. To a degree metropolitan Moscow (where we also undertook fieldwork) was different. Certainly it was more open. But Russia has only two cities of this scale and character whereas in terms of professional and administrative culture, as senior officials at the Ministry in Moscow confirmed in interview, there are many Kursks. In any event, Moscow and St Petersburg had their equivalent centres of professional hegemony.

At the same time, the school itself was also a significant player. Local inspectors, as in India, were a force to be reckoned with, but schools were large, school directors and senior staff provided strong management, and – as mentioned in Chapter 9 – schools valued and carefully nurtured their collective institutional consciousness, their corporate pride and their sense of identity.

Thus what we found in Russia was a centralized system now in the process of sharing power and devolving decisions to regional and local levels, but in any event strongly counterbalanced by local administrations and local professional cultures which exercised a hegemonic hold over schools and teachers which was stronger than Moscow's. To an English observer, the situation was not unlike that of local education authorities in their 1950s–80s heyday, especially those with ring-fenced recruitment policies, charismatic or autocratic chief education officers, and advisers peddling educational orthodoxies to which teachers were expected to conform if they wished to gain promotion.

In this context, our Russian teachers tended to pronounce themselves happy with the curriculum, confident in their pedagogy, but concerned about generic problems such as resources and overload:

> At the moment the timetable is very demanding. We have six lessons in the morning with only short breaks between them, and the children become very tired . . .

> I would like to see fewer pupils to each class. Also we need better textbooks and more money to obtain equipment.

Another mitigating factor in the balance of power was the considerable influence of researchers and textbook writers, and indeed the professional community generally. We noted in Chapter 3 that in sharp contrast to the stance taken by the Department for Education and Employment in London, the Ministry in Moscow listens to researchers and is prepared to defer to their judgement. An extract from my exchange with the Federation's Director of Primary Education:

> (*How long should the primary stage be?*)

> I wouldn't put the question to me. Ask the academics who are working on it.

This was not a throwaway line: the balance of influence, and the division of labour, were clearly understood on both sides. Textbooks were a critical component of pedagogy, and (building on Soviet experience) the Ministry understood that one of the quickest ways to effect movement towards the more 'humanized' model of education was to disseminate new textbooks to the regions. But, in Moscow we were told that the turnover of senior Ministry officials was so rapid that they had no alternative but to lean heavily on academics at establishments such as the Russian Academy of Education to fill out the policies and translate them into teaching strategies and materials underpinned by appropriate theories. Local administrative and professional communities would then select the package they preferred. On this basis, respondents at both levels, national and local, confirmed that the key influences on teachers' practice were not policies as such, so much as policies as mediated through textbooks, combined with initial and in-service teacher training which provided a legitimating theoretical and methodological framework. Usually this was personalized – 'the theory of Academician Davidov', 'Zankov's method', Elkonin's method'.

United States

Four significant levels of control and accountability – federal, state, district and school – bore down upon the teachers in our Michigan schools, and other powerful voices, most notably those of parents and the teachers' unions, made themselves heard and had to be heeded. There was no guarantee that any two of these would be in agreement with each other, or indeed with the teachers themselves.

While the *overt* plurality of values and demands to which our Michigan teachers were subject was one striking dimension of comparative difference, another was their immediacy. The federal and state governments might seem remote from the action, as one would expect in a decentralized system. Not so the school board, the district officials and – as mentioned earlier in this chapter – the pupils' parents. Even the largest of the three school districts in which we worked was small in comparison with its equivalent administrative level in England, the local education authority. The smallest, with only six K-5 elementary schools, would not have been thought viable as an administrative unit in England. Teachers knew the superintendent of schools, the director or assistant superintendent in charge of elementary education, and other officials whose responsibilities overlapped theirs, not as mere names on documents but as people with whom they engaged directly, regularly and personally. The school board was drawn from the local community, and its members included parents of children in local schools. In turn, the board's publications ensured that parents and the community had evidence – of a kind – on which to base relative judgements of each school's progress and performance.

Our Michigan teachers displayed the usual scepticism about the contributions of the federal and state governments. The principal of Thoreau:

> The federal and state governments don't understand the needs of communities and schools. The language they use is too generalized to be useful to us – they say there's a problem with science in our schools, but we need to know exactly what problem and precisely what we need to do about it.

However, they recognized the value of federal and state funding to support special initiatives. The principal of Hawthorne worked hard to ensure that his school did not miss out in this regard, especially as some years previously it had failed to benefit financially from the district's use of federal funds to support racial desegregation in a programme which had lasted into the mid 1990s. Unlike those states and districts which had enforced cross-town bussing, often in the teeth of local opposition, his school district had created a voluntary desegregation programme centred on 18 'magnet schools', each of which offered well-resourced specialist programmes in a field such as reading instruction, mathematics, science, creative arts or foreign languages. However:

> Hawthorne Elementary was not a Magnet School . . . I was disappointed, because the Magnet Schools were hi-tech but the other schools did not have the best of everything. The board couldn't afford computers for us, and our best kids were pulled out to go to the Magnet schools.

Since then, he had fought hard and successfully to get his school on to some of the funded programmes, finding the political context distasteful but working it to his school's advantage as far as he was able:

> In this state Republicans are for the rich, Democrats for the poor. Republicans here are cutting funds for the poor. They want to bring in this voucher system to use public money to fund private schools. I don't like politics, but you have to use politics to run a school.

Special programmes apart, federal policies most commonly commanded the attention of teachers via the state and district. Michigan's curriculum policy, for instance, signed up the state to the federal government's *Goals 2000*, and the message was passed on down to the schools by way of district-level policy statements and directives.[14] The board, then, was the level of the system that was most visible to classroom teachers and seemed to have the greatest day-to-day impact on their work. Whereas schools might complain about state policies, the interface between their work and that of the school district was the one with the biggest conflict potential.

The degree of control school boards chose to exercise could vary. One principal compared the present and previous regimes in his district:

> The Board was handing down the curriculum, they were deciding the textbooks, we were using exactly what the system told us to use, and nothing else. But now with site-based management we're able to pick the textbooks we want and have multi-grade and early childhood, and discuss teaching styles, co-operative learning, professional development . . .

A teacher in another school district deplored the pedagogic consequences of this previous kind of curriculum control:

Until recently I'd always taught reading from basal books. That's when the school district selects one commercial curriculum and buys it for everybody, and every child in every classroom is reading the same book, and you bring groups of children back and they read out of the same book at the same time, from the same page. There was a lot of coercion. And the rest of the kids had to sit at their chairs and do seatwork, copy things off the board, basically do busy work so that you can focus on a small group of kids who have been labelled as 'low', 'middle' and 'high' and they all know it . . .

But now:

Each year we get core curriculum objectives for each subject from the school district. We take the objectives and make our own thematic units in reading, writing, music, etc.

The same process of devolution from district to school was charted by other interviewees. However, both teachers and officials at school board and state levels also reported contrary trends, especially in the areas of curriculum and assessment, as states responded to federal and public anxiety about 'standards' and the international league tables by enacting legislation and transmitting directives of a more directly controlling kind, and simultaneously tried their hand at systemic reform. In any event, teachers we interviewed who had worked in other parts of the United States were clear that the situation could be very different elsewhere. They spoke of districts that did not merely issue curriculum guidelines but promulgated detailed directives on both content and method. Further:

This district has a strong reputation on relationships. Administration and teachers do get along, do communicate. I mean, in some other districts it's like war. Teachers and administration forget the issues and it becomes very personal. In some districts administrators come in and say 'I want desks to be in rows'. It doesn't happen so often now, but I know some districts where it does, and 20 years ago district prescription and principal policing was the norm.

The same teacher explained this attitude:

This is less educational philosophy than a power struggle between administrators and teachers. There's an attitude in some school districts that teachers don't know best and that administrators and school boards need to make the decisions and tell teachers what to do.

Oiling the wheels, or perhaps stoking the fires, were the teacher unions, which during the 1980s and the 1990s became increasingly prominent in collective bargaining at the local level.[15] One of our teachers at Emerson Elementary was the school's representative for the National Education Association (NEA), the larger of the USA's two teaching unions. The NEA has a devolved structure to maximize impact and its members' engagement, with equivalent associations (and acronyms) at state, district and school building levels.

Within a culture which by and large eschews the deference and formality in workplace relations which are still common in England, this arrangement could make the position of a school's union representative, where problems arose, both sensitive and difficult. One such storm had been brewing over the months preceding our Michigan fieldwork and it broke shortly before we arrived. The crisis turned on disagreements about how best to handle disruptive conduct among pupils (a theme from the *Five Cultures* teacher interviews which was far more prominent in the data from the United States than from any of the other countries).

Emerson's union representative was also a close personal friend of the school's principal. The principal favoured an open, democratic, negotiative relationship among staff and between staff and pupils. However:

> I personally appreciate that. I operate better in an open system such as that. But in the case of creating a calm, pleasant environment for the children it hasn't worked. Did you go to the lunch room? I am very proud for visitors to go to our science room or our computer labs, our library or our classrooms, but I am not proud to have them walk through the much room . . . It is totally out of control. There are children running, screaming, body slamming, throwing food, leaving the lunch room without permission. That to me is unacceptable.

> (*Is the lunch room supervised? Is this the problem?*)

> No, no, because in other schools it works. I think the problem is again that the principal's style is to tell the lunch supervisors 'Don't be harsh, be nice, be nurturing, be kind . . .' There are no clear expectations and no clear consequences. If you body slam somebody in line you should have to leave the line, wait until the line is gone and eat your lunch after everybody else. But there is none of that, there are just constant reminders, 'Please talk quietly'. But nothing happens, so they don't.

As union representative for a group of teachers who were becoming increasingly concerned about the absence of a behaviour policy which would actually control behaviour, our teacher met the principal and the district's assistant superintendent to discuss alternatives. The price she paid for undertaking this duty was that other teachers immediately accused her of complaining about the principal to the administration and even, when the principal subsequently took sick leave on grounds of stress, of being in part responsible for her condition.

Decentralization does not merely give schools opportunities. It can also impose a burden. The federal government sets broad educational goals. State governments define policies and call their districts and schools to account through performance standards and testing programmes. School districts fill out the detail and deliver curriculum requirements to schools in a form that can range from the permissive to the highly prescriptive. But in this matter of children's personal and moral development, and their personal safety, which to the teachers we interviewed were problems no less immediate and intractable than standards in mathematics and science, schools were pretty well on their own, for this is the domain of values and the state of Michigan, as we saw in Chapter 5, was fearful of incurring charges from any of the state's numerous value constituencies that it was being in any respect morally partisan.

Emerson's principal chose one route, which was perhaps more consistent with the spirit of democracy and decentralization than the confrontational approach taken by the principal of Hawthorne (pp. 205 and 234). But it did not work, and the school bore the consequences. So, in more personal terms, did the principal and the NEA representative.

Yet, as the teachers we interviewed understood very well, body slamming among eight year olds in school lunch queues is the tip of an iceberg of social morality in which violence of all kinds, virtual and actual, is endemic. A 1988 study found that children witnessed an average of 18,000 violent deaths on US television (not all of them simulated) before graduating from high school.[16] In 1990 there were over 19,000 murders in the United States, and Michigan's own city of Detroit had a homicide rate higher than that of many entire European countries.[17] While I was writing this book the grim annual tally was inflated by two mass killings of innocent people, one in Atlanta and the other in Columbine High School, Colorado. Just before the book went to press a six-year-old child took a handgun to Buell Elementary School (north of Flint, Michigan, not far from one of the *Five Cultures* fieldwork schools) and killed a classmate. The same constitution which devolves responsibility for education to 50 states and 15,000 school districts, and allows families and administrators to push a further burden of responsibility for children's social, moral and behavioural development on to the schools, also permits the National Rifle Association and its Congressional supporters to block gun control even in the face of tragedies such as those which occurred at Columbine, Atlanta and Buell, thus making it harder than ever for schools convincingly to square the circle of liberty and responsibility.

From the point of view of the teachers then, decentralization did not necessarily mean liberation. In a decentralized education system the controls and constraints to which schools and teachers are subject may no less unyielding than in a centralized system. Such highly localized accountability, given the relative intimacy of the community setting, may be as difficult to handle in the context of professional freedom as in the context of prescription and constraint.

England

If the powerlessness of Congress and a possibly excessive burden of responsibility placed on teachers are two of the more questionable concomitants of the American version of democracy, then England might appear to have the answer. For by 2000 what was once devolved had been reclaimed, and the hand of firm government remained poised above the heads of all in the state education service, armed if not with a 'tough new' policy for every occasion then a heroic or withering soundbite, and ready to strike at a moment's notice in the name of educational standards.

We interviewed the English teachers in 1995, 1997 and 1998. The addition of the two later rounds was itself a symptom of the condition on which several of the teachers commented: the speed and incoherence of the policy shifts from one year, and one administration, to the next. For example:

Every time we've done the SATs something has changed. Each year you think, 'I'll concentrate on that next year' but then you get to the SATs and discover that the evidence you've collected isn't wanted, so you can never get into proper routines.

The five-year moratorium on curriculum change recommended in the Dearing report of 1993 and agreed by the Conservative government of John Major[18] was supposed to start in 1996. The 1997 Labour government of Tony Blair refused to be bound by Dearing (although it claimed the opposite) and introduced major initiatives in primary literacy and numeracy which represented reforms of the English and mathematics curriculum more radical than anything undertaken since the National Curriculum was introduced in 1988. These had considerable repercussions both for the rest of the primary curriculum as taught and the post-Dearing review that QCA undertook on the government's behalf in 1997–9.

Moreover, whereas the tidal wave of centralization since 1988 (comparison with other countries suggests that the metaphor is not over-dramatic) had always stopped short of pedagogy, now this too, as part of the literacy/numeracy package, was to be brought under government control. To complete our picture of English primary education at the turn of the millennium it was therefore essential that we both interviewed teachers about these particular reforms and observed them in action in the classroom.

In the context of two key post-1997 government initiatives bearing directly on all English primary schools – the literacy and numeracy strategies, and the related decision to make room for them by suspending schools' legal obligation to teach the previously mandatory programmes of study for history, geography, design techno-logy, art, music and physical education – the interviews yielded a continuum of response from qualified acceptance to outright opposition, complicated by reflec-tions on the part played by those at other levels of the system: unions, LEAs and teachers themselves.

At one end was the head of Ogden Primary. Conscious of the Labour Party's traditional support for local councils and local education authorities – the Con-servatives' assault on local councils during the 1980s was principally an attempt to reduce Labour power, especially in the mostly Labour-controlled cities – and their pre-election rhetoric about reinvigorating local democracy, he had anticipated a partial readjustment of the balance in favour of LEAs and schools with Labour's election in 1997. In the event, his expectations had been dashed and a felt 'a strong sense of betrayal'. For him, New Labour had picked up the baton of centralization in a manner which he was convinced would deprofessionalize and deskill:

There has been indecent haste . . . no serious work has been put into discussion. It has been decided that this is the way to do it, and this is the way it will be done. We are now delivering the curriculum, not teaching it . . . There is no consideration of the different ways that children learn, of alternative methods, of finding the right approach for each set of circumstances. This is the antithesis of 'fitness for purpose'. I agree with the government that we need more consistency in literacy teaching, but not this uni-formity. The literacy and numeracy strategies have merit as frameworks for content, but I am a teacher and I cannot teach to someone else's script.

The literacy and numeracy strategies squeezed the rest of the curriculum. The government's response, in January 1998, was to offer teachers 'flexibility' to pay less attention to the other subjects than was statutorily required. In this, the Ogden head deplored what he saw as the new culture of professional compliance:

> The NUT [National Union of Teachers, England's largest teaching union] are only concerned with making things easier for teachers, not with the quality of education experienced by children, so they go along with what the government wants regardless of whether it is right educationally . . . I talk to other heads and what worries me is the silence, the compliance of colleagues who used to talk, protest, get angry . . . Perhaps younger teachers are right and the way to cope is to be pragmatic, to care less, to treat teaching not as a profession but as a job.

The head of St Teresa's was no less scornful about the unions, this time the NAHT (National Association of Headteachers, the union of which most primary heads and deputy heads were members):

> I made it clear that I was not prepared to abandon the curriculum and most of the teachers here supported me, but the union people said that we should adopt a minimalist line . . . There should have been a more thinking response. Their's was a pragmatic response. I was very upset to receive one letter from the NAHT which simply *assumed* that everybody would be reducing the curriculum to the bare minimum. Many other heads round here were unhappy with the union line. The unions have little interest in children's learning.

In any case, she derided the government's claim of 'flexibility' as a sham:

> How much flexibility is there, anyway? It's farcical to reduce it to one side of A4 and pretend that it's other than a broad statement about a very detailed specification. It still has to be translated into learning experiences giving progression in children's understanding . . . Even if QCA don't provide the detail, we still have to, so we'll be going back to the orders which have been suspended.

The concern about the pace and incoherence of government-led educational change and the apparent lack of co-ordination between government agencies was shared by the head of Kirkbright:

> When the government came in 1997 Estelle Morris [a minister in the Department for Education and Employment] said there would be no change for change's sake, and that they would put the 'fun' back into teaching, but the pace of change has prevented that. And there's no coherence at all: you're working on a QCA document and David Blunkett [Secretary of State for Education and Employment from 1997] makes an announcement and you're back to the drawing board. DfEE, OFSTED, QCA, SEU – there's no overall timetable, they're all apparently competing with each other.

However, on specific initiatives such as the literacy strategy she was prepared both to assert her independence and exploit the leverage which such initiatives gave her:

Everyone's complaining about 15/15/20/10 [the prescribed breakdown of time in the literacy hour] but there *is* flexibility. Everything depends on how LEAs and heads handle it. I see the strategy as helpful. The file is a very useful resource for us.

The Kirkbright head took a similarly robust line on curriculum manageability, the issue on which teachers' unions had campaigned during the early 1990s and which had led to the Dearing enquiry and the new Labour government's eagerness to offer teachers 'flexibility' over the non-core subjects in return for compliance with its literacy and numeracy strategies:

There never was the problem of an overcrowded curriculum that everybody claimed. All you had to do was keep a tight focus and retain the essence of each subject. Do that year on year. It's an approach to planning I've always used. I ask teachers: 'Have you got the essence of each subject and have you taught its core skills? If not, why spend all that time on it?'

The head of Cheetham also argued that policy was there to be interpreted and adapted rather than implemented as it stood, contrasting her school's response with that of another nearby:

We defend our right to implement the literacy strategy in our own way, but one of our neighbouring schools is taking it literally. The head has even given all the teachers egg timers so that they stick to 15/15/20/10. But teachers are finding it impossible to keep on top of the planning for that and five different groups. We never merely implement. So, for example, when we are given flexibility to reduce the non-core subjects we look at the proposal, discuss it as a staff, see whether it conflicts with our aims and priorities for the school, and then make our decision.

However, reserving that freedom carries risks:

It's tricky, because we must not be seen to be rejecting advice or ignoring policy. But it's essential to get back some of the decision-making that we've lost.

The Cheetham head's sense that her school was vulnerable if it did not toe the line stemmed from its particular circumstances as an inner-city school with a significant proportion of pupils for whom English was not their first language:

It's a very difficult situation for schools that haven't had good SAT [national tests for 7 and 11 year olds] results, because the pressure on them to conform is greater, and if their results don't improve it will be argued that this is because they haven't implemented the strategy.

Or as a teacher at St Teresa's expressed the dilemma:

Schools are in a bind now that the government has combined targets and strategies. If they don't reach the targets OFSTED will say it's because they're not following the strategies, so even if you have a good reason for adapting or modifying them, it's a risk to do so: you're setting yourself up.

But government, the unions and teachers were not the only players in the struggle for control. Until the late 1980s the local tier of governance, in the form of LEAs, constituted an influence on the thinking and practice of English primary schools far greater than that of central government. LEAs controlled the purse strings, set the educational agenda, defined good practice and, in many cases, used their stake in teacher appointment and promotion, particularly at the levels of head and deputy head, to ensure compliance. The Leeds research documented these processes at work just before the legislative programme of the Thatcher and Major governments decisively swung the balance of power away from the LEAs. It is important to record this, lest it be presumed that the centralization of English public education produced a shift from professional autonomy to subordination. Decentralization in England prior to 1988 meant, for many teachers and schools, especially in the primary sector, LEA hegemony.

The LEAs which maintained the *Five Cultures* primary schools represented contrasting responses to this transfer of power from town and county halls to London. In one, which had been notable until the early 1990s for its interventionist policies allied to an effective network of inspection, advice and support, teachers complained of a lack of both support and leadership as the LEA floundered with greatly reduced resources and a debilitated management structure, having lost an empire but failed to find a role.[19] Teachers were forced to look elsewhere – to unions, universities and each other – for the guidance they so badly needed during a period of continuing change.

The other LEA was very different. Newly established as part of the 1990s rationalization of local government boundaries, it had a reputation to establish. It provided schools such as Hamilton and St Teresa's with clear guidance on the handling of successive national initiatives, including statutory and non-statutory assessment and the literacy and numeracy strategies. For St Teresa's, a Roman Catholic school that had been allowed to drift by both the church and the previous LEA, this was invaluable.

For all that, the LEA, like the schools themselves, was wary of asserting more than a limited degree of independence, for:

> They want to be a flagship authority so there's a lot of support. But there's also a lot of pressure, because, like us, the LEA has OFSTED to worry about and are thinking ahead to their own inspection. They are in a cleft stick over the curriculum. One camp wants to preserve breadth, balance and flexibility, all the qualities which the government's literacy strategy is threatening. But the other, headed by the literacy co-ordinator, is simply pushing for strict compliance with the strategy.

Undoubtedly, then, what made the English version of centralization so potent a device for imposing the government's will on the public education service was the way it was policed. By 1998, OFSTED's remit included schools, LEAs and teacher training. To these, in 1999, it added the regulation of child-care provision, hitherto administered by local councils not through their education departments but through social services. The model of inspection adopted for England, in contrast to that used in other parts of the United Kingdom and in many other countries, required strict compliance with predetermined criteria or 'standards' of effective practice, no more and no less. Inspection evidence was not open to scrutiny, let alone challenge; inspectors' judgements, many of them highly subjective, were final; the price paid for failure ranged from media exposure to institutional closure; and during the mid and late 1990s the service was run by a chief inspector whose provocative public pronouncements on the state of public education were widely acknowledged to slide seamlessly and tendentiously between verifiable evidence, unsupported claim and personal prejudice.[20] Hence this typical expression of helplessness, voiced by one of our teachers, referring to the impact on public perceptions of the then chief inspector:

> We just can't win. The Woodhead attitude has now been picked up by the parents. Children go home and complain, and the parents take the child's word against the teacher's because Woodhead has said that teachers are failing their children.

In 1998–9, the House of Commons Education and Employment Committee undertook an all-party enquiry into the work of OFSTED. The weight of its evidence and recommendations favoured modification and moderation of the OFSTED model in order to introduce sensible checks and balances without diminishing its effectiveness, and in order to reinstate a more reasoned and honest climate of educational debate.[21] Most of this the Blair government summarily rejected in its formal response to the committee's report.[22] It needed OFSTED and its chief inspector to guarantee its policies, increasingly so as these policies engaged in ever greater detail with educational practice. In a democracy, New Labour calculated, centralized policy without central control is electorally risky, and election pledges that trust to professional goodwill and competence alone are downright suicidal. Set against New Labour's paramount ambition of being re-elected in 2002, the fact that central control without accountability is undemocratic was of little consequence.

In our consideration of how teachers in each of the five countries placed themselves and their schools in the respective national structures of educational decision-making, control and influence, the English case is an extreme one. England's transition from a decentralized to a centralized education system was effected at immense speed. It was sweeping in its range, covering governance, finance, curriculum, assessment, pedagogy, teacher training, local administration and much else besides. It was ruthlessly enforced and policed. And, most questionably perhaps, it used spin, half-truth and myth as conscious instruments of policy.

Conclusion: School and State Revisited

Archer's thesis that centralized and decentralized education systems develop in fundamentally different ways, and with very different consequences for the processes of change and reform, is supported by comparative evidence from the two levels we have investigated so far, the system and the school. However, the same evidence supports the reservations we expressed in Chapter 7: educational decision-making is neither unitary nor monolithic, and even in centralized systems regional and local power can significantly moderate or even counteract central direction and control.

Our school-level interviews also raise questions about the theories of the school's agency in the processes of cultural transmission and reproduction that we considered in Chapter 7. In particular, they suggest that we need a more qualified account of the interplay of top-down *transmission* and bottom-up *resistance*[23] and that the tacitly homogeneous notion of national identity has somehow to accommodate to pluralism.

The forces of complication, moderation and modification are both structural and cultural. In terms of structure, the level or levels *between* national or state government and the schools can play a decisive part. In France the *académie* maintains rather than breaks the link between teachers and ministry. In England, the influence of the once-powerful local education authorities has been drastically curtailed and they are kept in their place by being subject to the same regime of policing and sanctions as are the schools themselves. But in India, Russia and the United States the local tier, albeit in different ways, is highly significant, and not simply because decentralization is in these three countries a matter of policy. In India, geography and low teacher status combine to give district officials and inspectors considerable power. In Russia, we found not so much a local *level* of control as an almost closed local *system* encompassing administration, schools and teacher training, both pre-service and in-service. It was a classic example of hegemony in the sense that it combined control and consent, and was reinforced by limited professional mobility, a strong local culture, and the residual habits and networks of the Soviet regime.

The latter characteristic apart, there were resonances in the Russian local administrations of the old city LEAs in England which existed during the period from 1944–88. It was the capacity of these LEAs to interpose themselves between national policy and local action which so incensed Margaret Thatcher and provoked her vengeful use of legislation to reduce their powers, most notoriously in the case of the Inner London Education Authority (ILEA). ILEA's impressive headquarters faced the Palace of Westminster across the River Thames and by continuing to do so seemed to taunt as well as challenge Thatcher's iron rule. So in 1990 she abolished it.

In Michigan, as across the whole of decentralized America, it was clear that although school boards and district officials could operate in different ways, and some chose to be much more prescriptive and controlling than others, the relationship between a school and the officials and board members of the school district was never less than critical to the school's fortunes.

But other structurally embedded elements could also intervene. In France, the United States and England, teacher unions were influential. In England there were suggestions that unions were doing deals with government which put teachers' working conditions before their professional responsibilities and allowed government to reduce the child's curriculum virtually unchallenged by the teaching profession, some at least of whom saw themselves as the guardians of that curriculum. Government was only too happy to exploit this unabashed self-interest. In Michigan, unionization reached into every school and therefore introduced the potential for conflicts of interest of a direct and personal kind.

Then there was the school itself. The collective leverage the school was able to exert within the overall framework of control varied considerably, both within and between the five countries, and in this matter the position taken by the head could be critically important. In France, the influence of the school as school was limited, for collective consciousness was low and heads' power was restricted. In India, the systemic problems of low professional status and motivation could be offset, up to a point, by strong leadership and the head's efforts to establish a collegial or corporate culture. In Russia, the size of schools and the fact that their work encompassed the higher status, higher-stakes secondary teaching as well as primary, made them forces to be reckoned with in any context. In England and the United States the traditional emphasis given to schools' corporate identity and to leadership by the head allowed schools to develop along highly individual lines, a long way removed from the French notion that while there are many primary school buildings there is only one primary school.

However remote a national, state or even local government, its reach could be greatly strengthened if it had an effective system for enforcing and policing its policies. In this matter the most overtly power-coercive inspection system of all was England's OFSTED.

The interactions of national government and its agencies, regional/local administration, teacher unions, schools, and mechanisms for policy enforcement are sufficiently different in each country to make it difficult if not impossible to formulate general predictions about the implications of centralization/decentralization for teacher autonomy and educational change. Thus I said that in France the line between teachers and ministry is relatively direct. Yet the French teachers clearly felt more autonomous and more in control of their professional destinies than did their English colleagues, who – notwithstanding the greater collective strength and identity of the English school and the by no means insignificant residual powers of the LEA – felt themselves to be directly and closely circumscribed by national government.

To understand this apparent anomaly we have to remember that the scope of educational policy is now much greater in England than in France, and that, crucially, it includes pedagogy as well as curriculum content. Pedagogy is what brings a paper curriculum to life, so it is also what gives teaching its individual stamp. It is possible to teach a prescribed curriculum in one's own way; it is rather more difficult to personalize a prescribed teaching method.

The other key difference between the situation of the French and the English teachers bearing on the matter of autonomy was the type of inspection to which each was subject. In the French model the teacher is required to *justify* his or her practices – 'One goal, many routes' – while in the England of OFSTED the teacher has to *comply* with practices prescribed by others despite the much greater diffuseness of the system's espoused values ('many goals, one route', as it were). Moreover, in France, as in Russia and the United States, there is a greater preparedness to presume that if the required outcomes are achieved the methods used to achieve them must be effective. In England, centralization has given notions of 'effective teaching' a life of their own: unless a teacher uses methods officially defined as effective, goes the official line, the outcomes will not be achieved.

Research findings on the impact of centralization on teacher consciousness in England are consistent. The manner in which the reforms were forced through, and the aspects of education on which they concentrated, increased teachers' frustration, their sense of powerlessness and – most damagingly for the pupils in their charge – their tendency to operate more on the basis of what Doyle and Ponder call the 'practicality ethic' than on principle.[24]

Russia allows further commentary on this important area of autonomy and ownership. Since teachers in the Russian schools worked to a pedagogical formula in which there was only limited variation across all the classrooms observed, it might be suggested that their situation was in this respect comparable to that of their English colleagues. It was not: in Russia, the formula had not been arbitrarily and recently imposed from the centre but had evolved over many decades, and in that process of evolution ministries, including Soviet ministries, had heeded professional and academic advice. Thus, teachers identified totally with the received view of effective teaching, for it was their method, not the Ministry's.

If professional identity is one complicating factor in the transmission of ideas, values and versions of knowledge down through an educational system, cultural plurality is another. The reproductive function of the French state education system, as posited by Bourdieu and Passeron, is effective in so far as there is a sufficient degree of consensus among the various constituencies – principally government, teachers, pupils and parents – about the validity of what is being transmitted. Whatever the claims, from the 1960s onwards, about the repressive character of secondary and higher education in France,[25] the system of primary education appears to be accorded this necessary degree of cultural legitimacy. The same might be said, within their sub-national local systems of primary education, about Russia.

England and the United States, however, would appear to be very different cases. In England, the National Curriculum remained no less contentious when it was being reviewed in 1999 than when it was being devised in 1987–8; but then in 1987–8 it had been imposed in the teeth of substantial cross-party and cross-constituency opposition. Behind the objections to the *manner* of its introduction were real and significant disputes about its driving values that in turn spoke to a condition of considerable uncertainty and disagreement about national identity and the relationship of the individual to society. But whereas the British government sought, through the National Curriculum, to impose its own essentially political answers to these questions, in the United States pluralism was not only a fact of life in the cultural melting-pot but also a condition which, in the national education system, was both celebrated and fuelled by decentralization. In England, governments may use their unparalleled powers over state education to suppress value pluralism or sweep it under the carpet; in the United States, it seems safe to predict, pluralism, and endless debates about educational values, will never be other than one of the system's most ubiquitous features.

The final comment to make at this stage is about change and reform. England's change from a decentralized to a centralized system allows us to test Archer's thesis about incremental and stop-go change. There is little doubt that the centralization of educational decision-making in England during the 1980s and the 1990s yielded a pattern of change which was characterized by wild lurches both forwards and backwards, as a succession of education ministers on the one hand sought to demonstrate their radical machismo with 'tough new' policies but on the other found that in so doing they had created problems which needed rapidly to be undone and, ideally, explained away. The reform of teacher education is a good example: each successive 'reform' from 1984 to 1999 was introduced before its predecessor had been fully implemented, let alone evaluated.[26] The speed of each change, and the lack of reference to what had preceded it, had little to do with reform, everything to do with the ambition of a succession of ministers each to make his or her mark. The year-on-year changes to national assessment, referred to and deplored by our teachers, provided another example. Then there was the fiasco of the 1998–9 National Curriculum review, when government imposed literacy and numeracy strategies and citizenship on schools without regard for their logistical consequences, then had to rationalize its way out by putting at risk the 'breadth and balance' to which it had also committed itself, at the same time trying to preserve credibility by deploying the mendacious rhetoric of 'flexibility'.

But, in contrast to this sorry tale, can we assert as a sustainable generalization that educational change in decentralized Michigan is steady and incremental, or that in centralized France it is not? On the contrary, our evidence shows that while local control may yield a more powerful sense of local ownership and therefore enable policies to embed themselves at the deeper levels of professional thinking and practice, American school boards – like pre 1988 LEAs in England – can be as autocratic and prescriptive as governments if they so choose, and if they do not so choose then the democratic process may run into the morass of competing interests and irreconcilable values. Conversely, over the decade 1989–99 the educational policy process in centralized France and centralized England ran along lines, and yielded outcomes, which could hardly have been more different.

This is why we need to take into account, when assessing the capacity of a national educational system to respond to a changing world, matters such as those raised here: the character and potential of institutions and procedures at school and local as well as national level; the professional culture of those – especially the teachers – at the system's cutting edge; issues of hegemony, autonomy and ownership; and the context of values within which this apparatus is located. Finally, we must always keep well to the fore an awareness of each system's history (see Chapters 2–6), for it is here that that we will probably find the most reliable clues to its future.

Part IV

Classrooms

11

Comparing Teaching

Typical or Authentic? Statistical and Cultural Sampling

We have now reached the classroom, the base of the pyramid of public primary education. And a broad base it is too: England in the year 2000 has one government education department, 151 local education authorities and 18,230 primary schools, but its four million or so pupils spend the larger part of their waking lives in over 150,000 classes. Across the country as a whole a typical primary school day witnesses some 700,000 lessons – or 3.5 million in a week and over 13 million in a school year – and the annual tally of lessons planned by each primary teacher and encountered by each primary pupil is over 850.[1]

If we make similar calculations for the other four countries we will find, although on a much larger scale in three of them, the same sudden spread in the pyramid's conformation as we move from the levels of educational policy and administration to the levels of school and classroom action.

In this chapter consideration is given to some of the problems which attend the exercise of making cross-cultural comparisons once we move to the classroom level. The most obvious of these is typicality: with so many thousands, or millions, of versions of teaching on offer, which of them can be said to be representative of national classroom practice? Can any of them? And does it matter?

If we treat the question as a purely statistical one, the chances of coming up with an answer which satisfies accepted sampling criteria are pretty slender, and there is little doubt that typicality in this sense would be the hurdle at which most comparative studies of schools and classrooms would fall, including several which have put their faith in a quantitative research paradigm and have taken the matter of sampling very seriously. Indeed, once we begin to take stock of the potential list of school and classroom variables, and add to these a tolerably searching catalogue of the within-country differences which frame them and bear directly or indirectly on classroom life – differences in culture, demography, geography, policy and administration, for example – we would probably be inclined to admit that as a numerical construct 'typical' English, French, Indian, Russian or American primary teaching may well be empirically unattainable.

Qualitative researchers side-step this problem by claiming authenticity rather than typicality for the individual case or cases portrayed in depth, perhaps advocating 'thick description' and the alternative certainties of ethnography.[2] Unfortunately, the education research literature is littered with small-scale studies which cite the virtues of ethnography or case study in order to dignify work which is small-scale out of necessity rather than choice, without attending to the considerable alternative discipline which ethnography ought to entail in its quest to explicate and unravel what an experience or event means to those who experience it.

If we hang onto *insight*, which is surely the most important outcome of properly conducted educational research, of whatever methodological persuasion, is there a sense in which the single educational case or the small collection of cases – where 'case' means a school, a classroom and its pupils and teacher, or even a lesson – can be both insightful *and* typify more than itself or themselves? I would suggest that two conditions, if satisfied, place this goal within our grasp.

First, we must accept the proposition that the culture in which the schools in a country or state are located, and which its teachers and pupils share, is as powerful a determinant of the character of school and classroom life as are the unique institutional dynamics, local circumstances and interpersonal chemistries which make one school or classroom different from another. For culture is not extraneous to the school, nor is it merely one of a battery of variables that can be tidily stacked to await correlational analysis. Culture both drives and is everywhere manifested in what goes on in classrooms, from what you see on the walls to what you cannot see going on inside children's heads.

Thus, any one classroom can tell us a great deal about the education system and indeed the country of which it is a part, but only if – and here I come to my second condition – the research methods used are sufficiently searching to probe beyond the observable moves and counter-moves of pedagogy to the values and meanings which these embody. Reducing teaching to decontextualized measurable behaviours may yield helpful indicators of between-country difference, but once behaviour and culture have become so decisively separated such indicators may have limited explanatory power.

This was the problem which the influential 1996 OFSTED study *Worlds Apart?* failed to resolve. Having identified between-country differences in test performance in mathematics and science, the authors embarked on what they initially admitted were hypotheses to explain Britain's poor showing in the mathematics tests relative to certain countries in continental Europe and East Asia. This was a legitimate and helpful procedure until the authors formalized their hypotheses as a multi-level analytical framework comprising 'cultural', 'systemic', 'school' and 'classroom' *factors*.[3] Because the comparative analysis of test scores had been up to that point statistical, readers were led to assume that the word 'factor' was being used in its statistical sense and that for each of the many factors listed there was available for scrutiny a demonstrated correlation with pupil achievement. In fact, the OFSTED team cited only eight published sources for their speculations.[4] Although there was much in these which was suggestive and illuminating, some were impressionistic, several predated the most relevant international test data, and few of those remaining could claim to engage in a statistically respectable fashion with the factors which the OFSTED team so confidently listed. Despite these weaknesses, *Worlds Apart?* became a significant point of reference for the 1997 government's policies on primary school pedagogy, and was thereby deemed to validate the prevailing view in policy circles of 'best practice' as value-free technique.[5]

So on the one hand we have culture as pseudo-factor. On the other hand – and a useful contrast with the Stevenson and Stigler study cited in the OFSTED report – we have the close-grained ethnographic study of a mere three schools in Japan, China and the United States (one in each country) by Tobin, Wu and Davidson, which followed an intensive programme of observation, videotape, interview and discussion. This fares rather better in the generalizability stakes than some of the studies cited by OFSTED, not because it is a statistical analysis but because it is not. The practices this particular research team witnessed and reported in Kyoto were certainly not identical to those in a nursery school down the road, let alone two hundred miles away, but their authenticity as distinctively and indeed typically Japanese pre-school practice stemmed from the extent to which any surface differences were outweighed by deeper and more abiding similarities which had their roots in the ideas, values and experiences which teachers, parents and children at the schools had *in common* – ideas, values and experiences which the researchers' painstaking close-up methodology enabled them to explicate and examine in the round.

In any case this research team were alive to the problem. They showed their videotapes to parents and teachers in other towns and cities in each country, asking them in what way the one school was typical or untypical of national practice. This procedure generated lively debate and, inevitably, each school was found to be typical in some respects and untypical in others. Interestingly, however, audiences often seemed unable to separate the objective question of typicality from that of whether they approved of what they were seeing and hearing. However, the Tobin experience confirms rather than undermines my argument about surface and deeper-layered typicality, for notwithstanding the between-school differences which his videotape audiences identified (or perhaps because of them) Tobin and his colleagues were still able to write with conviction and authority about a wide range of quintessentially Japanese, Chinese and American ideas on childhood, parenting and education, all grounded in data from one school in each country.[6]

In contrast, a national or international study which, like that of Tobin and his colleagues, seeks to engage in something more useful than merely demographic comparison, but at the same time, unlike theirs, pins its claim to authenticity on its sampling procedure alone, is likely – unless it really *is* backed by a level of resources normally confined to the development of weapons of mass destruction – neither to be representative in its own terms nor to offer much by way of insight. To generalize is not only to derive a universal statement or proposition from a particular one, but also to construct a *principle* or *theory* that has general application. Classroom research findings which are generalizable in the statistical sense are of little value unless they lead to the formulation of general principles and theories which take our understanding, and our practice, forward.

In fact, schools and classrooms are culture bound in the organizational and procedural domains no less than in respect of their values and ideas. To polarize particularity and generalizability or typicality, as tends to happen in the context of debates about the claims of quantitative and qualitative educational research, is to ignore the considerable amount which all the schools and classrooms within a given state system of education necessarily and inevitably have in common. We can start – as in this book we started – with history, policy, legislation, governance, control, curriculum, assessment and inspection (all of which exert a powerful pressure towards similarity if not uniformity), move on to school buildings, staffing and resourcing (which deviate only up to a point from national norms and set additional constraints on professional choice), touch on teachers' personal education and professional training (which follow predictable, standard and these days increasingly standardized paths) and take in their professional culture (which is likely to be normative and consensual as well as, in a strict sense, shared). By the time we reach the classroom we have a chemistry in which the common and predictable mingle with, qualify and constrain the unique, and set readily observable limits on pedagogical variability, even granted the self-evident fact that each teacher, each child, and each class of teacher and children in combination is different. We can agree with Peter Woods that every teaching situation and encounter is unique.[7] That much is self-evident. But teaching, like learning, also follows patterns; French, Russian or English teaching follows patterns that are distinctively French, Russian or English.

This, then, is the basis for our claim that the *Five Cultures* school and classroom material speaks about the national as well as the local. However, to gain some purchase on local variation we selected, or asked our contacts in each country to select, a range of schools which included both small and large, and rural, urban/ suburban and inner city. Further, to reduce the risk of an unacceptable degree of randomness in the teaching observed, we restricted our observation sessions to just two age-groups – six to seven and nine to ten – in each school and for every class observed we asked that at least one lesson should be in the area of language and literacy. The age-groups were chosen as being in the mid-points of what in England are the two main curriculum and assessment cycles at the primary stage, Key Stages 1 and 2, and were thereby intended to allow us both to contrast within a given school and country the education of younger and older primary children and to examine issues of development and progression.

If the patterns in teaching are there, and are culturally shaped, how should they be exposed and interpreted? This is not the place for a discursive treatment of the many dilemmas of classroom research, but those which pressed particularly on the present study need to be identified. The fact that not all of them were satisfactorily resolved should be admitted at the outset: 'The path to increasing certainty' said Gage in 1978, 'is not the single excellent study which is nonetheless weak in one or more respects, but the convergence of findings from many sources, which are also weak but in different ways. The dissimilar or non-replicated weaknesses leave the replicated finding more secure'.[8]

Action and Meaning

If we accept that culture is central to a comparative understanding of classroom practice then we must also acknowledge that the understanding generated by a research paradigm which relies on observation alone, or on outsider perspectives alone, may do justice neither to the teaching nor to the culture in which it is embedded. Observation is an essential tool of classroom research, but if teaching is about the exchange of ideas and meanings then we can discover only some of these by observing. To maximize our prospects of gaining access to these ideas and meanings we must listen as well as look. Communication, both non-verbal and verbal, must be studied, and the language of classroom transaction must be attended to in some detail; but, especially, we must talk with those whom we watch.

This does not mean that we should take insider perspectives on observed practice as representing some kind of objective reality, nor that the outsider viewpoint is of itself invalid. Teaching, as we have noted, follows patterns, and an outsider observing a large number of classrooms in different schools and countries is almost certainly in a better position to perceive these patterns than is the teacher or child who is located in just one school. But in interpreting the patterns we need the help of those – teachers and children – who have created the constellation of actions on which we choose to superimpose our patterns. The enterprise, then, is one of both external detachment and intersubjectivity.

In the *Five Cultures* study of schools and classrooms we focused on both action and meaning through observation and interview, and by using video and lesson transcripts were able to study the processes of communication through which meaning is conveyed. The observations covered whole school events such as assemblies, children at play and teaching. The observation of teaching was the most sustained and detailed part of the study and is described below. Each lesson observation session was followed by an interview with the teacher concerned. These interviews sought to tease out teachers' intentions for, and accounts of, the lessons in question, as well as to probe wider aspects of their thinking. The interviews with school heads, directors and principals, and with parents, on which we drew in previous chapters, addressed school aims, organization, policy and problems, and provided a grass-roots counterbalance to the official accounts of where schools stood in the hierarchy of national, state and local policy, decision-making and control.

In the context of our concern with insider meanings the most obvious omission in this programme was interviews with pupils. The case for including pupils' accounts of their education is incontrovertible. It is also the most difficult to tackle in a research context, especially where younger children are concerned, but also for logistical reasons. These problems are massively compounded in an international study. In the UK, Pollard and, more recently, Ruddock, are particularly convinced and convincing advocates of the importance of exposing the pupil perspective.[9] The 1999 Ruddock studies yield important data about how children most successfully learn which deserve serious attention in a theory of pedagogy.

We took every opportunity to speak informally with pupils, but were prevented by the extreme constraint of time to which we were subjected from formalizing these conversations as a structured sequence of interviews. Such a sequence would have raised, in Russia and India (where we interviewed through interpreters) even more serious issues of interpreter 'contamination' than we have noted in respect of the teacher interviews. Regrettably, the resources available for this research were far too small to allow us either to interview on the scale required or to build in the kinds of safeguards to the integrity of pupils' voices that are essential in the context of interpretation and translation. In a study which claims to be as concerned with meaning as well as action we must acknowledge that the relatively muted level of the pupil's voice prevents us from gaining as rounded a picture as we would have liked.

Intention, Process and Outcome

Where does teaching start and stop? We have noted national differences in the focus of school inspections. Some are preoccupied with teachers' intentions and pupils' learning, some with what pupils and teachers actually *do* in classrooms. Researchers have similar options. There is a logical or temporal progression that runs from *presage* or *intention* to *context, process* and *outcome* or *product*.[10] In his test of the scientific claims of educational research Gage points out that this progression yields six sets of variables whose relationship is theoretically amenable to scientific analysis: context–process, context–product, presage–process, presage–product, context–presage and process–product. Further, Gage notes that policy-makers are chiefly interested in only one of these relationships, that between the variables of process and product.[11] That was in 1970s America: the reach of public accountability there is now rather longer – it certainly is in England – although it is still probably fair to suggest that for most people education still means what teachers and pupils do in classrooms and what pupils learn, rather than what teachers intend and where it all takes place. Moreover, the relationship is generally presumed to be an uncomplicated and linear one: pupils learn *x* because teachers teach in manner *y*.

For systematic studies of teaching the presage–context–process–product continuum remains the conceptual frame within which choices of method and focus are made, and in Britain most such studies, including those in the more recent school effectiveness paradigm, concentrate on process and product, to a lesser extent on context, and treat presage as relatively incidental.

In contrast, qualitative classroom research places process, presage and context centre stage (although it does not use this terminology) and tends not to bother overmuch with outcomes, at least not those of the (testable) kind in which systematic studies and policy-makers are most interested. For behind the difference in focus and method lies a difference in purpose: understanding teaching as a phenomenon on the one hand, assessing the relative effectiveness or efficiency of different teachers and teaching methods on the other. Both purposes are entirely proper. It is, however, a pity that they represent opposing camps rather than partners in a discussion, for it is surely as frustrating to identify an effective teaching method without understanding how its effects are achieved as it is tantalizing to understand the dynamics of classroom action without investigating the kinds of learning to which they lead.

Five Cultures was not a school effectiveness study. It sought to describe, illuminate and explain primary education in five countries in terms of ideas about culture and power, schools, curriculum and pedagogy. It aimed to uncover relationships within education systems between the state and the educational practice conducted in its name, and to contribute to our understanding of the nature of teaching and learning. In doing so it inevitably ventured judgements about the relative effectiveness of this or that classroom practice, and although such judgements will be as unequivocal as comparative study of pedagogy permits, they will need to be carefully qualified. However, although judging the precise relationship between observed teaching and measured pupil learning outcomes was not one of the project's aims, the study nevertheless engaged with presage, context and outcomes as well as process. We recorded and collected examples of pupils' work, and in conjunction with the pupils' teachers we ventured assessments of where, in terms of their learning, the observed lessons led.

The Whole and the Parts

Researchers have become adept at dissecting teaching but poor at reconstructing it. They are now able to isolate certain process factors which correlate with tested learning gains – 'orderly atmosphere', 'opportunity to learn', 'maximization of learning time', 'clarity of purpose', 'high expectations' and so on.[12] They are rather less successful in demonstrating how these and other elements are reconstituted by teachers and children as coherent and successful learning encounters with a beginning, a middle and an end. Moreover the factorization of pedagogy has proved a boon to policy-makers and quangos caught up in the rhetoric of 'standards', for such research provides ready legitimation both for shopping lists of teacher training competencies or school inspection criteria and for disembodied nostrums like 'interactive whole class teaching'.[13] The concern here, then, is to find a way of complementing the increasing *atomization* of teaching with a convincing kind of *holism*.

Ethnography, of course, offers holistic narratives, but these are of little interest to policy-makers because they are deemed to have failed the essential policy criterion of generalizability. Ethnographers in any case tend to be not that interested in the policy applications of their work, and usually steer clear (or at least claim to steer clear) of those unambiguous judgements of quality, success and failure which policy-makers need, heading off in the opposite direction towards supposedly non-judgemental narrative and interpretation. Actually, the educational literature has more than its fair share of tacitly ethnocentric and judgemental, if not outright colonialist, ethnography.

The UK government's 1997–8 literacy and numeracy strategies, about which I have expressed certain reservations, is a significant exception to the trend towards atomization – although by accident rather than design – for at the core of each strategy is a lesson which indeed has a beginning, a middle and an end. I believe that the strategies support my claim that there may be three reasons why transatlantic classroom research (and for these purposes we probably also need to include, without intending any offence, Australia and New Zealand as well as Britain and the United States) concentrates on variables, factors and elements to the detriment of whole teaching events as these are framed and defined by teachers themselves. First, the scientific enterprise, as applied to the study of teaching, is by definition one of analysis rather than synthesis. Second, it merges with a parallel tradition of defining the skill of teaching in terms of its constituent 'competencies' which, having been identified, can then be severally taught, checked, assessed and measured. Third – and this less familiar point is allowed by a comparative perspective – the notion of the 'lesson', as something bounded, constrained by both time and formal structure and transferable from one teaching context to another, was one of the more prominent casualties of the various waves of progressivism experienced by public schooling, including public primary schooling, in both Britain and the United States during the first seventy years or so of the twentieth century.[14] Time and structure were seen as forms of pedagogical tyranny, as incompatible with the very different rhythms of developing childhood as they were with the flexibility and creativity which were the hallmark of the teacher who was able to respond to them.[15] Boundaries of all kinds, but especially temporal and epistemological boundaries, were anathema.

We shall shortly encounter the legacy of this kind of reasoning in some of the *Five Cultures* classrooms, but in the immediate context of our concern to reinstate holistic analysis of teaching, my point in registering the relevance here of the UK government's 1997–8 literacy and numeracy strategies is that they constituted a deliberate act of cultural transplantation, for the stated pedigree of the literacy and numeracy 'hours' was central European and (to a lesser degree) east Asian. So in Germany, Switzerland and Hungary, the countries cited in the rationale for the numeracy strategy, the 'lesson' has wholly positive connotations, as it does in France, Russia and India. Indeed, in these countries it would seem utterly eccentric to debate teaching, let alone effective teaching, without frequent reference to the way, within specified constraints of time and subject matter, it is structured.

It will be understood, then, that the balance and relationship of the whole and the parts in teaching were a significant preoccupations in the *Five Cultures* research. We took as the unit of observation and analysis the lesson or teaching session. In France, India and Russia, the boundaries of 'the lesson' were clear and unambiguous. In England and Michigan they were less so, and one session had a habit of shading into another, sometimes even continuing after break, recess or lunch. Where this happened we determined session boundaries by erring on the side of caution and keeping the camera and field notes running, checking with the teacher if in doubt.

Teaching as Craft, Art or Science?

During the 1990s UK education ministers and their advisers appealed increasingly to that supposed British virtue, common sense, dismissed theories of teaching, banished educational ideology and advanced 'what works' as the touchstone for classroom decisions. But this appeal to pragmatism was not what it seemed, for from 1997 it became clear that government rather than teachers would define 'what works' regardless of whether, in each of those 18,230 primary schools, 150,000 classes and 750,000 daily lessons it really *did* work. Educational ideology, then, went out by the front door and in by the back.

The attempts to soften or legitimate the government's pedagogical diktats were no more convincing than the redefining of New Labour ideology as common sense. Reynolds, for example, insisted that in both its informing principles and its day-to-day action teaching is nothing less than a science. However, the 'body of science' to which he appealed included only that pedagogical research which conformed to the rules of what he called the 'discipline of school effectiveness'.[16] And while Reynolds acknowledged that supposedly democratic governments ought not to be quite so eager as that of Prime Minister Blair to claim that when it comes to teaching the common sense of ministers is superior to that of teachers, he seemed to buttress the government's claim by suggesting that in England there is a knowledge vacuum which only government advisers can fill.[17]

I register the question of the *nature* of teaching here because it relates to the question of how classroom life is most appropriately researched. It will be immediately clear that this creates a chicken-and-egg problem. To investigate a phenomenon scientifically, ethnographically, historically or mathematically (say), one must be sure that it is of its nature amenable to scientific, ethnographic, historical or mathematical analysis, and this may to some extent foreclose some of the questions which one wishes to keep open. The purist positions on the art/craft/science question are clear. Reynolds and his colleagues see teaching as a science and are therefore at least consistent in proposing a scientific paradigm to investigate it. The UK government espouses 'what works' and is therefore also consistent, if nothing else, in its rejection of all pedagogical research, other than that which sustains this view, as a waste of time.

In the other corner are those who have been inspired by Elliot Eisner, the distinguished American educationist who in the 1960s and the 1970s developed the claims of teaching to be more akin to an art than a science, guided by 'expressive' rather than instructional objectives, and pursued this reasoning into modes of pedagogical research and evaluation which applied techniques of artistic connoisseurship and literacy criticism.[18] Teaching, Eisner argued, is an art 'in at least four senses':

> It is an art in the sense that teaching can be performed with such skill and grace that for the student as well as for the teacher, the experience can suitably be characterized as aesthetic . . . Teaching is an art in the sense that teachers, like painters, composers, actresses and dancers, make judgements based largely on qualities that unfold during the course of action . . . Teaching is an art in the sense that the teacher's activity is not dominated by prescriptions or routines but is influenced by qualities and contingencies that are unpredicted . . . Teaching is an art in the sense that the ends it achieves are often created in process.[19]

He adds that 'because teaching can be engaged in as an art is not to suggest that all teaching can be characterized as such'.[20] This is an important and necessary proviso not just in relation to such teaching as Eisner characterizes as 'wooden, mechanical, mindless and unimaginative' – that is to say, bad teaching – but because even good teaching may not satisfy all four of the conditions above. As we shall see, a great deal of teaching is governed by prescriptions and routines, or is directed towards predictable and indeed planned ends. It would be foolish to suggest that this weakens its claims to be either effective or artistic.

However, at this stage possibly the safest position to adopt, pending the explorations of the next few chapters (although it would be disingenuous to claim that I have reached this point without forming a view on the matter), is something along the lines of Gage's idea that teaching is an art with a scientific basis. It is, he argues (as do Simon and Galton), a science not so much in its actual conduct as in the principles upon which it draws.[21] These principles derive from propositions about children's development and learning and the relationship between different teaching variables within the spectrum of presage–context–process–product that is considered above. The propositions have been tested in accordance with the procedures and controls of scientific observation and, sometimes, experimentation. But once one attempts to apply such principles within the classroom, matters are rather different, for the classroom is not a laboratory, variables cannot be controlled – always assuming that one has identified all those variables which matter – and the teacher therefore needs to exercise the judgements of the artist, applying the principles flexibly and with due regard to context.

The theory has a number of loose ends to which we must return, but it is worth asking immediately why the acts of sizing up a teaching situation and making decisions by drawing on shared professional understandings and scientifically derived principles define teaching as an *art* rather than, say, a craft. Indeed when in the 1992 UK government report on primary teaching Jim Rose and I argued the importance of 'fitness for purpose' as the basis for classroom decision-making, the phrase was a conscious echo of William Morris and the craft principle of the seamlessness of the ethical, the aesthetic and the practical.[22] This, incidentally, is not at all the same as the dispiritingly – and disparagingly – reductionist 'what works' criterion advocated by later UK governments, for 'fitness for purpose' hands the decision on what works to teachers rather than reserves it for government, but also acknowledges the uniqueness of circumstance and by emphasizing purpose reminds us that the teacher must engage in educational values as well as pedagogical techniques.

Teaching-as-art also rather fixates on *process* and tends to ignore the purposes which the act of teaching serves. Teaching is conducted in pursuit of learning, and learning is a necessary condition of education. But being educated encompasses far more than having been successfully taught propositions *a*, *b* and *c*. Being educated entails coming to terms with unpredictability, speculation, paradox, ambiguity and the willing suspension of disbelief, as well as with certainty – indeed, with the naggingly uncertain core of all certainty, and the unknowability of all knowledge; and with the divergence, plurality, disagreement, dissensus and conflict which are the stuff of values. If teaching is an art, its claim to be so resides as much in its capacity to handle in a coherent and meaningful way these aspects of knowing and understanding as decisions about the balance of group work and whole class teaching. But the latter, it might be suggested, are surely more in the domain of craft, as we suggested in the 1992 report.

There is a further problem. If teaching is a science, it makes sense to research it scientifically. If it is an art, it makes sense to apply, as did Eisner, the procedures and criteria of artistic appraisal. However, whereas in respect of *definition* teaching as science is generally opposed to teaching as art, in respect of its *empirical investigation* the opposing investigative paradigms most commonly cited are the scientific and the 'qualitative', which usually means ethnography, anthropology, or something vaguely at the 'soft' end of the social sciences. This is not to suggest that art and artistic activity may not be subjected to ethnographic analysis – it can be and respectably is – so much as that although the teaching-as-art claim is often made, it is less frequently pursued through to its implications for the analysis of teaching. The work of Peter Woods is an exception in that he reconciles his claims that teaching is an art and that it is most appropriately investigated through ethnography, by asserting the shared truth claims of ethnography and art, notably authenticity.[23] But art and ethnography are manifestly not the same and there are unresolved confusions in respect of both qualitative definitions and qualitative analysis of teaching.

Clearly, this is a matter on which judgement will be deferred until our analysis of the pedagogic data is complete. But with the chicken-and-egg problem in mind it is only to fair to admit at this stage that the position from which I approached this project was that *in transaction* the act of teaching has elements of both art and craft, but not of laboratory or experimental science; but that in *conception and planning* teaching draws on general principles and laws, some of which have been validated by disciplined scientific enquiry (the art or craft of the science). However it also draws on the cumulative and collective craft knowledge of teachers in general (the art or craft of the craft); and on the personal experience, theories and beliefs of the individual teacher.

Moreover, whatever the expected knowledge base of teaching in general, when it comes to individual cases such shared or individual theories may evaporate or be compromised by the force of circumstances, or by the conflicting claims of other pressures and expectations (the 'competing imperatives' idea referred to elsewhere), some of them 'in the situation' and others emanating from outside it.[24]

This, then, is a long way from purist insistence that in this matter we have to take an epistemological loyalty test and sign up to teaching as art *or* science *or* craft. It is, however, grounded in analysis of teaching as it happens rather than as idealists believe it should happen. Too often, in posing the apparently blunt question 'What is teaching?' we do not ask that question at all, but the higher-minded 'In an ideal world what kind of an activity *ought* teaching to be?' We may be prescribing, in fact, rather than describing. We need to make a clearer distinction between defining 'the science (or art, or craft) *of* teaching' (the cumulative knowledge basis about teaching and learning in general on which, sometimes and somehow, teachers draw) and uncovering empirically 'the science (or art, or craft) *in* teaching' (the way individual teachers in classrooms, under the pressure of events, act and take decisions). We should use our prepositions more discriminatingly, as do the French.

As to the need for congruence between a theory of teaching and the methods used for researching it, the *Five Cultures* methodology was similarly eclectic (or, some might suggest, similarly inclined to hedge its bets). Lessons were observed using an observation schedule which allowed for sequential and open-ended field notes but also constrained these within columns headed 'time', 'duration' (calculated after the lesson), 'teacher activity' and 'pupil activity'. After each lesson summaries were prepared under headings specified in advance. Most of the analysis, however, was deliberately *post hoc*. The goal was to capture different versions of teaching and retain them in as full and rich a form as possible so that they could be subjected to considered analysis away from the action, bearing in mind that in an international study the action can be many thousands of miles from the place where it is analysed. Hence the conjunction of on-the-spot non-participant observation, fieldnotes, videotape, lesson transcripts, photographs, and documentation such as teachers' lesson plans and examples of pupils' written work.

The Lessons Observed, and a Different Problem of Typicality

The number of sessions which were observed, annotated and recorded was: France 20, India 19, Russia 33, United States 19, England 75 (60 from preceding projects together with 15 *Five Cultures* updates). This gave a total dataset of 166 lessons. Of these, 36 (six to nine from each country) were selected for transcription and close scrutiny (transcripts of the 60 earlier lessons from England were already available), although any logistical generalizations below are based on the full range from each country.

The Russian anomaly arose because we came away from our first and intended only round of observation in Russia suspecting that some of what we had seen were exhibition lessons planned and presented with our visits in mind. This suspicion was prompted partly by their smooth format and immaculate timing and by the impeccable conduct of the pupils, and partly by the presence in these lessons, alongside our own trio of observer, interpreter and videoperson/photographer, of between one and seven additional observers, including school directors, local administrative officials and inspectors, and faculty from the pedagogical university. Ranged down the side of the classroom they looked like managers and coaches at a football match, and some indeed were not averse to issuing touchline advice. It would be hard for any teacher, in any country, to find this prospect less than daunting or to be willing to teach other than his or her safest and most meticulously prepared lesson. We therefore returned to Russia the following year, this time as tourists rather than as guests of the government, stayed with friends in Moscow and approached schools directly and informally about the possibility of observing, videotaping and interviewing. To this they readily agreed.

Such is the historical consistency of Russian teaching that although these teachers may have agreed to receive us only a few hours before we arrived, the formal characteristics of their teaching, as we examine them below, were pretty well identical to what we had witnessed a year previously, 350 miles away and under the scrutiny of between one and seven extra pairs of eyes. Comparing notes with a colleague working a couple of years later in Perm (which is a long way from either Kursk or Moscow), we found not only a common lesson format but even the same piece of music ('Autumn', from Tchaikowsky's Opus 31 *Seasons*) being used in conjunction with seasonally inspired literature and language lessons.

The Russian case raises a rather different version of the question of typicality. Our concern earlier in this chapter was with how far a small number of schools, teachers and lessons might be typical of, and generalizable to, wider practice within each of the countries in question. We felt obliged to test this empirically in Russia, but did not do so in the other countries. However, it is also necessary to ask to what extent a lesson which is observed and videotaped is likely to yield data which is typical of that teacher and his or her pupils.

To those who have not used videotape in classrooms this sometimes seems like an insurmountable problem. In fact, teachers and children acclimatize remarkably quickly to observers and cameras, especially if the camera remains on its tripod rather than roams the room on someone's shoulder. A high tripod position and judicious use of zoom and wide-angle are more effective, and much less obtrusive, than a cameraperson stumbling between tightly packed desks or a lens looming between child and book. On previous projects we had built in acclimatization time (observation without camera followed by observation with camera whose data did not 'count', and then the real thing), but as we had found its efficacy to be negligible and time pressed, we did not do this in the *Five Cultures* classrooms. On the other hand, each class was observed and videotaped on at least two separate occasions and if we had felt, by comparing the sessions, that there was an obvious observer effect, we would have discounted the lesson in question.

Examples of Lessons

We initiate the comparative analysis of teaching in the *Five Cultures* schools by summarizing 16 of the lessons observed there. The number chosen is the minimum needed to hint at (although not to encompass in full) the pedagogical and temporal range recorded in each country. The English examples include two lessons taught in accordance with the UK government's 1998–9 requirements for literacy and numeracy.

Analytically and judgementally the summaries are as neutral as this kind of abbreviated narrative allows – which is to say that there is inevitable narrator bias but efforts have been made to keep it to a minimum, or at least to bias all the summaries in the same way. Each lesson is recounted chronologically from start to finish, and in terms of the main actions of its teacher and, collectively but not individually, its pupils.

The sequences are timed and numbered to facilitate easy reference in the comparative analysis that starts in Chapter 12.

Lesson 11.1. France: Juan-le-Grand Elementary School,
16 children aged 6–7, French (29 minutes)

The children are seated in pairs, in three long rows facing the board.

1025   Teacher brings pupils in from playground, tells pupils to read page 39 in the language textbook. They do so, silently.

1027   Teacher writes on the whiteboard a brief description of one activity from the previous lesson (voting on the names of the class's two terrapins, Caroline and Cécile). A chart from this lesson is already pinned to the board. Pupils continue to read silently.

1030   At the teacher's request, eight pupils in turn read aloud from the prepared page in the textbook. Teacher stands in front of the board, listens and comments.

1034   Teacher asks pupils to read aloud from another chart pinned to the board. This features, and exemplifies in 14 words, the sound 's' as represented by the letters 'S', 'SS', 'C' before an 'E' or an 'I', and the letter Ç before an 'A', 'O' or 'U'. One of the words listed, to connect to the previous lesson, is Cécile. Pupils read the letters and words in unison, as the teacher points to each with his ruler. They then volunteer the rules that govern the pronunciation and spellings in question.

1040   Teacher asks pupils to contribute new words containing the 's' sound. Pupils raise hands and/or call out. Most are selected to supply words.

1042   Teacher cautions three pupils for inattention, then asks pupils to identify, by listening carefully, the position (beginning, middle, end) of the sound 's' in ten words given in succession. Pupils raise hands, teacher selects.

1045   Teacher asks pupils to find words containing the sound 's' in the material pinned to the classroom walls. This material has been generated in the course of recent lessons. Pupils call out and raise hands, teacher selects. Seventeen words are correctly identified. One pupil is verbally disciplined twice, another is singled out for praise.

1051   Teacher ends the lesson and instructs the pupils to move to the library corner for singing. Pupils put their textbooks away and move.

1054   End of lesson.

Lesson 11.2. France: St Etienne Elementary School, 20 children aged 9–10, French comprehension (73 minutes)

Some pupils are sitting on their own, some in pairs, and some as groups of three or four.

0840   Pupils enter classroom, sit down and take books and pens from their bags, which they then hang on the backs of their chairs. Teacher takes register and asks about the health of absent pupils.

0843   Teacher tells class to take out reading books and to read the passage from Daudet's *Tartarin de Tarascon* on page 148. Pupils read silently.

0853   Teacher asks general questions about the author and the book, and provides further background information about both.

0855   Teacher reads the passage aloud, walking round the classroom as he reads. Pupils follow the passage in their own copies.

0858   Teacher asks questions about the structure of the passage's introduction to the main character, the description of his home and the kind of personality this description suggests. Pupils raise hands or call out; individuals are invited to answer. The school secretary comes in with query about numbers for lunch.

0909   Teacher asks a pupil to read aloud the paragraph about Tartarin's garden. He then questions the class about the way the text reveals Tartarin's character, distinguishing between explicit description of the protagonist and clues provided in the account of his surroundings. A substantial proportion of the class provides individual answers during this stage of the lesson.

0927   The passage is read aloud again, this time by a succession of pupils selected by the teacher. Teacher intervenes to correct pronunciation and comment on the fluency and expressiveness with which the pupils read. He checks their understanding of several words.

0934   Teacher gives instructions for written work. Pupils take out exercise books to write answers to two questions about the Tartarin passage. They work in silence. Some pupils go to the basin for a drink of water. The teacher circulates and monitors individual pupils as they work, asking and answering questions, making corrections, and occasionally commenting on posture. Pupils remain at their tables and raise their hands if they need help.

0946   Teacher asks pupils to stop writing and asks a succession of pupils to volunteer their answers to the two questions, which they do, several calling our eagerly in the hope of being chosen.

0952   Teacher signals end of lesson. Pupils put the books back in their bags.

0953   End of lesson.

Lesson 11.3. France: Coulanges Elementary School, 26 children aged 9–10, French composition (79 minutes)

The children are seated at paired desks pushed together to accommodate groups of four to six.

1341   Pupils enter classroom and settle at their desks.

1343   Teacher, standing at the front of the room, asks questions about the nature and structure of narrative, using a schema from Larivaille which charts its course from 'initial state' through 'interruption', 'change', 'reaction, 'equilibrium' to 'final state'. Pupils raise hands, teacher selects pupils to answer, and writes the stages on the blackboard. Teacher then asks, and receives answers to, questions about the nature of dialogue and monologue.

1348   Teacher distributes to pairs of pupils photocopies of a picture showing two men in suits seated in an aeroplane. Asks questions about the content of the picture. Pupils raise hands, teacher selects, pupils volunteer speculations on the picture's circumstances and possible subsequent storylines.

1352   Teacher distributes to each pair of pupils copies of the full Larivaille schema that he earlier summarized on the blackboard. Asks eight pupils to read the schema aloud, a section each. Other pupils respond to questions that aim to establish their understanding of the schema.

1356   Teacher instructs pupils to write stories based on the picture and which incorporate the various narrative stages together with lively dialogue. He checks that they understand the task by asking and answering further questions. He instructs the pupils to work in pairs.

1359   Pupils begin working in pairs, discussing possible scenarios. Teacher monitors the whole class from a fixed position.

1402   Teacher sits on a table at the front of the classroom and reminds pupils to tell a story rather than describe a picture. The pupils resume their discussions and some start writing. Teacher moves round the room, monitoring, talking with individuals and pairs, reading and commenting on their ideas.

1409   Teacher asks class to listen to two pupils reading the opening lines of their stories. The remainder listen; then at the teacher's invitation some comment on what they have heard.

1412   Teacher circulates to monitor pairs, interrupting to talk to class about the spelling of common words and expressions which he then writes on the blackboard. Resumes interaction with pairs, concentrating on the logical progression of their stories, encouraging the inclusion of essential facts about the characters, and correcting spelling, punctuation and grammar.

1422   Teacher stops class to encourage pupils to move onto the next stage of their stories. He then resumes monitoring and the pupils continue discussing and writing. Several ask the teacher questions, mainly about word usage and spellings. Teacher publicly praises the story of one pair and uses this to encourage the others.

1430   Teacher stops class to involve them in answering a question from an individual pupil about the correct term for a ship leaving harbour. Writes the term (*appareiller*) on blackboard and extends the question to the departure of trains, aircraft, cars and coaches. One pair's story prompts him to involve the class in speculation about incidents that could happen in an aircraft. Pupils suggest a door or luggage hold opening, coffee being spilled, an engine catching fire, turbulence, illness, leaking fuel.

1434   Teacher resumes monitoring, reading through stories, asking questions, making suggestions. Pupils continue discussion and – now – writing. After a few minutes teacher announces that pupils have ten more minutes before they will read their stories aloud to the class.

1442 Teacher stops class to question pupils on the development of a story following a dramatic incident suggested by one pair.

1445 Teacher calls pupils' attention and asks six pupils in turn to read their stories. Makes critical comments, gives limited praise, corrects words, pronunciation and grammar, accepts comments from pupils. Pupils read aloud, listen, ask and answer questions as directed. Teacher now sums up with comments about the originality of the stories produced, the need to follow the plan, to avoid repetition, make corrections and create suspense and excitement. He then sends pupils out to play.

1500 Pupils leave classroom.

Lesson 11.4. India: Chanderi Primary School, 55 children aged 5–6, Hindi (29 minutes)

The children are seated close together, one behind the other, on seven *tat pattis* running from front to back of the classroom. They face the blackboard and their satchels are beside them.

0945 Teacher brings the class to attention by telling them to clap their hands. Asks questions about meals and favourite fruits. Pupils call out answers to the teacher's questions.

0947 Teacher asks four pupils to come to the board and draw an *aam* (mango). They do so, and the others watch. Teacher asks pupil named Aarti to stand up. She asks class about the initial sound 'aa' in *Aarti* and *aam*. Tells class to look at a card she holds up which has *aam* written on it.

0950 Teacher asks three different pupils to come to the blackboard to write *aam*. They do so, and are applauded by the rest of the class.

0951 Teacher asks questions to introduce the word *aadat* (habit). Each question, here and elsewhere, is asked several times. For their part, pupils chant the answers to the teacher's questions, over and over again. Pupils now chant 'aam, Aarti, aadat, aam, Aarti, aadat . . .'.

0953 To introduce *aankh* (eyes) teacher asks what we see with. Asks questions about eyes (their number and use) before returning to the list so far. Pupils chant 'aam, Aarti, aadat, aankh, aam with an *aa*, Aarti with an *aa*' etc. Teacher then writes these words on the blackboard. Four pupils, at teacher's request, now come to the board to circle the *aa* in each word. The rest of the class applaud, then resume chanting 'aam with an *aa*'. Teacher asks class to say what they have learned so far. Pupils, individually and collectively chant 'Aam with an *aa*' etc.

0957 Teacher introduces *anar* (pomegranate). Four pupils in turn come to the blackboard to draw *anar*. Class applauds. Teacher asks questions to recapitulate on words encountered so far. Pupils chant in response. Teacher introduces *Anamika* (a female pupil's name) and *aachi* (good), establishing that both begin with an 'A'. Pupils trace the letter 'A' in the air.

1000   Four pupils come to blackboard, at teacher's invitation, to write 'A'. Teacher then writes 'A' herself and asks class to recite the sound, over and over again. Teacher writes *anar, Anamika, aachi* on the board. Three pupils come forward to circle the 'A' in these words. Class applauds.

1004   Teacher asks questions to recapitulate, and children chant in response. Teacher deals with a pupil who is upset that she has not been chosen to write or draw on the board. Wipes blackboard clean. Pupils chatter.

1007   Teacher re-establishes order by getting the pupils to clap rhythmically. Tests their knowledge of *imli* (tamarind tree). Several pupils come to the board, at teacher's request, to draw *imli*. Next, teacher introduces *ither* (here) *itni* (this many) and *itna* (this much) by referring to the pictures on the board, and establishes through questions and chanted response that all begin with 'a small I' which she then shows on a flashcard. She writes *imli, itna, ither* on board. Three pupils come to board to circle 'I'.

1011   Teacher asks questions about what has been learned. Pupils chant 'a', 'aa', 'i' and the words in which these sounds have appeared. Teacher writes the three letters on the board.

1014   End of lesson. Teacher cleans the board.

Lesson 11.5. India: Purana Primary School, 44 children aged 9–10, science (34 minutes)

The children are seated at pairs of desks, facing the blackboard.

0955   Teacher announces the topic – 'substances and their properties' and writes this on the blackboard. Teacher questions pupils about 'the three main types of substance', solid, liquid and gas.

1002   Teacher asks for examples of solids and liquids. Pupils volunteer examples. Teacher then shows pupils two glasses, one of water and the other of milk. She holds up and/or names various other objects for pupils to classify. Pupils chant 'solid', 'liquid', 'gas' as appropriate.

1005   Teacher questions pupils about the properties of gas, and hands out balloons. Pupils inflate and deflate the balloons to demonstrate presence or absence of gas. Teacher asks questions about oxygen. Pupils chant answers.

1008   Teacher produces more objects – stick, stone, milk, sugar, water – for pupils to identify as solid or liquid. Pupils do so, in unison. Teacher then demonstrates soluble solid (sugar) and insoluble solid (sand). Asks questions to establish that pupils know that some solids change. Asks for examples of soluble and non-soluble substances. Writes names of five substances on board and tells pupils to classify them by writing them in appropriate columns. Pupils do so, but several mix up the columns.

1014   Teacher tells a pupil to draw five solids on the board. While he does so, the rest of the class draws them in their exercise books. Teacher monitors and corrects.

1021 Teacher writes homework instructions on board – classifying substances, finding examples of liquids and gases, drawing shapes of solids, repeating the experiment about soluble and non-soluble substances. Pupils write down these instructions. Teacher monitors, marking earlier work.

1029 End of lesson.

Lesson 11.6. India: Sankasya Primary School, 49 children aged 9–10, Hindi (63 minutes, double lesson)

0951 Teacher introduces theme, 'good friendship'. She calls a girl to the front to read part of a story of Krishna and Sudama. The other pupils follow in their own copies of the text.

0954 Teacher writes on the blackboard several words from the extract. Pupils repeat these words in unison. Teacher summarizes moral message of the passage.

0955 A second girl is asked to continue reading from the story. Teacher writes two more words on the board, which pupils repeat in unison. Teacher identifies second message (the importance of cleanliness).

0957 A boy is asked to continue the reading aloud. He does so slowly, one word at a time, which is repeated by the rest of the class. Teacher stops him and asks him to read in sentences. Further question and answer on the extract's meaning.

1000 A third girl reads aloud. Teacher summarizes and interprets.

1003 A second boy reads aloud.

1004 Teacher questions class about the story so far. Pupils volunteer answers and one girl is called to the front to answer. Two other pupils are asked to repeat her answer to the class.

1005 Further questions are answered individually or by the class in unison. Most questions and answers are repeated, some several times.

1008 Teacher summarizes the story's message about friendship and instructs the pupils to write about their own friendships.

1009 Pupils begin writing, some on slates and the others in exercise books. Teacher walks between the rows, checking and occasionally commenting or prompting.

1019 Pupils start to bring work to the teacher at the front of the class for her to mark. The compositions are typically in the form of short sentences, numbered and one to a line: '1. The name of my friend is . . . 2. She's studying in the same class as me. 3. She is the monitor. 4. Her mother and father are doctors' . . . etc.

1022 Teacher draws the class's attention to a word which several pupils have spelled incorrectly, writing it on the board. Pupils queue, teacher continues to mark.

1037 Teacher identifies and writes on the board two further words which several pupils have spelt incorrectly.

1039   Marking continues. Those pupils not queueing are writing or chatting quietly.

1042   Teacher gives instructions for homework. Pupils copy words from the board which may be used in their homework.

1055   End of lesson.

Lesson 11.7. Russia: Kursk School A, 24 children aged 6–7, Russian (39 minutes)

The children are seated at desks in pairs, facing the board (a hinged combination of black, white and magnet boards). On the latter are placed, randomly, some (but not all) of the letters from the Russian alphabet.

0918   Pupils stand by their desks in silence, facing the teacher who is in front of the board. Teacher instructs them to be seated. They sit with straight backs, fold their arms, and wait. Teacher asks opening questions about the uses of letters. Pupils reply, now and always, by raising the forearm only, opening the hand and extending the fingers, but keeping the elbow cupped in the other hand. Two pupils are invited to answer. They do so standing at the side of their desks, speaking loudly, clearly, usually in correctly constructed sentences, and sometimes at length. They wait to be told to sit down again.

0921   Teacher points to the letters on the board and asks how they should be rearranged. Pupils answer individually.

0923   Teacher selects two pupils to rearrange the letters on the board. She questions them about the categories they are using. Two pupils sort the letters into two groups, vowels and consonants. The other pupils watch and listen in silence.

0926   Teacher asks pupils whether they agree with the classification. Some pupils signal their agreement by raising clasped hands. One pupil who disagrees is invited to the board to make the change he proposes. Teacher questions class about this change, eliciting a further distinction between hard and soft sounds. Teacher writes on board the symbols for hard and soft.

0930   Teacher questions pupils on precise pronunciation of vowels and the similarities and differences between them. Individual pupils volunteer sometimes lengthy accounts in response. Sustained question and answer move the analysis on to the rules governing combinations of hard and soft vowels and consonants in Russian.

0937   Teacher tells class that they are now going to concentrate on two new letters, '3' and 'C'. She describes them with her arm. Pupils, in unison, identify them (name and sound). Teacher then writes the capital and lower-case versions of the two letters. She questions class about the correct use of capital letters. Pupils respond individually, referring to the naming of towns, states, rivers and people, and the beginnings of sentences.

0939   Teacher asks a pupil to come to the board and categorize the two new letters phonetically (hard/soft). Other pupils manually signal their judgement that the answer is correct.

0941 Teacher tells pupils to take out exercise books. She introduces the word *rozy* (roses). She asks for a volunteer. A pupil comes to the board, sounds each phoneme in *rozy* and writes above each letter the appropriate symbol for hard, soft, voiced or voiceless. Teacher questions her as she proceeds, until she finishes by adding a line to divide the syllables.

0945 Teacher changes *rozy* to *rosy* (dew) and questions pupils on the difference between '3' and 'C' (phonetically 'z' and 's'). Pupils provide examples of these phonemes within other words.

0948 Teacher asks pupils to open reading books and find further examples.

0951 Teacher announces a game of 'squelch'. Pupils make 'gates' by holding up their hands. For each word the teacher announces they must close the gate (by folding their arms) if they hear the sound 'z'. If they fail to do so she scores a goal. Teacher then asks class to rehearse the letters and sounds they have learned.

0953 Teacher turns round one of the boards to reveal four diagrams. She asks pupils what they signify. As she points to the diagrams in turn pupils chorus the different combinations of syllable and stress which they represent. With the teacher they clap the syllable/stress combination in each diagram. Teacher then asks pupils to find and read out some monosyllabic and disyllabic words in their reading books. Pupils find words, read them out individually, and for each disyllabic word the class claps to demonstrate where the stress falls.

0956 School bell rings. Teacher announces end of lesson. Pupils stand briefly by their desks before dispersing.

0957 End of lesson.

Lesson 11.8. Kursk School B, 30 children aged 9–10, Russian (42 minutes)

The children are seated at desks in pairs, facing the teacher and the board. Throughout this lesson the teacher remains standing at the front of the classroom.

0830 Teacher welcomes pupils and visitors.

0831 Teacher questions pupils on definitions of 'biography,' 'catalogue' and 'cushion', in the latter case exploring both literal and metaphorical meanings. Now and throughout the lesson the pupils raise their hands to answer the teacher's questions, and some – but not all – stand up to do so.

0834 Teacher draws attention to word combinations on the blackboard. Pupils read them silently. Teacher asks pupils to prove that in the first line 'he arrived with a fish') the words form a 'combination' (i.e. their cases agree) rather than a random 'group'.

0836 Pupils are asked to elaborate and explain the combination/group distinction. A brief class discussion follows.

0838 The teacher asks a series of questions to establish that pupils understand that the verb is 'in command' of the first sentence and that it takes the instrumental case.

0839   Teacher and pupils work through the remaining four combinations on the blackboard ('Worship the fish', 'There wasn't a fish', 'He was talking with the fish', 'He caught a fish with the net'). Pupils are asked (a) to determine whether the verb or the noun is in command and (b) to identify the cases used (respectively, dative, genitive, instrumental, accusative). During the course of this episode the teacher is challenged by one pupil who disagrees with the answer she has accepted from another pupil. The pupil is asked to explain her objection, which she does in detail. The objection is not sustained.

0841   The teacher works on the commanding function of verbs and defines a relevant construction as a 'verbal word combination'. By moving and exchanging words on the board and by questioning pupils she establishes with them that combinations cease to exist if their structure is altered.

0843   Teacher develops the verbal command/case ending connection by changing the nouns in the word combinations under discussion. This leads to a discussion of the figurative uses of one of the words ('catch').

0847   The teacher elicits, through questioning, words to describe the action of a verb in a word combination. Pupils offer 'directs', 'governs', and 'regulates', although what she seeks is 'makes demands'.

0852   The teacher pursues the defining and describing of word combinations. Two pupils offer definitions, which are refined and agreed through question and answer.

0855   Pupils are asked to write down these definitions before opening their textbooks. A girl is asked to read aloud from page 26, which contains approved definitions of the action of parts of speech in word combinations. This leads to a discussion to establish the distinction between 'word combination' and 'sentence'.

0859   Pupils are asked to read words from the list on another section of the blackboard. Through question and answer they are encouraged to make up sentences using these words and then define the cases used. The discussion centres on instrumental, prepositional and accusative cases.

0906   The process is repeated, this time focusing on dative, prepositional, nominative, accusative and instrumental.

0911   Pupils are asked to put down their pens and sit up. The teacher invites them to summarize what they have learned. Several pupils venture summaries before the preferred formulae are agreed. The teacher praises the class for the amount it has assimilated.

0912   End of lesson.

Lesson 11.9. Russia: Moscow School B, 28 pupils aged 9–10, mathematics (45 minutes)

The children are seated at desks in pairs, facing the board, a hinged triptych with six surfaces.

0930   Pupils sit with arms folded. Teacher arranges cards on her desk. Each has an addition, subtraction, multiplication or division sum on it. She copies some of these onto the board, faces the class and tells the pupils to prepare themselves for work.

0932   Teacher asks a sequence of questions about definition: 'sum', 'addition', 'product', 'multiplier', 'difference' etc. Pupils follow the familiar routine: forearms raised, stand up when invited by name to answer, step into the gangway between the desks, declaim an answer, wait for a judgement, sit down.

0933   Teacher holds up in turn ten cards, each of which shows two numbers to be multiplied. Chooses a pupil to state the product in each case. Pupils answer when nominated. This time they are not expected to volunteer.

0934   Teacher uses a pointer to indicate in turn the arithmetical problems she has written on the board. Takes pupils through each, using the terminology rehearsed earlier, and asking pupils to propose how each solution can be checked. Some pupils volunteer answers, others are nominated.

0936   Teacher asks class to recall 'rounding up' procedure for checking more complex calculations ($298 + 136$ and $600 - 198$). Pupils volunteer answers.

0938   Teacher sets a 'real-life' multi-stage arithmetical problem and asks pupils for the answer. One pupil supplies the correct answer. She is then asked to explain how she reached it. This pupil describes the first few stages of her calculation. Another is then asked to pick up the thread until all stages of the calculation have been explained. Teacher presses pupils in turn on why one course of action rather than another was taken, and how the solution can be checked.

0942   Teacher tells class to open rough exercise books and to participate in a 'control check' on the standards they have achieved in calculations undertaken previously (in their rough exercise books the pupils must show the calculation as well as the solution). She invites those who achieved a score of five (the highest) to stand up. None do. Teacher invites those who achieved a four to stand. Several do. Teacher then announces that they will check together the working out of one of these problems, step by step. Pupils respond to her questions.

0946   Teacher questions class on two further problems in their books, involving boxes, squares and chairs. Pupils volunteer and/or are asked to supply answers and explanations about how the calculations were done, might alternatively have been done, and can be checked.

0952   Teacher writes four sums on the board. Asks pupils to calculate using 're-direction' as discussed earlier in the lesson (so that, for example, $405 + 399$ becomes $405 + 400 - 1$).

0954   Teacher tells pupils to open exercise books and check previously marked work for mistakes that she has identified in a problem about time. Those who have a mistake are asked to raise their hands. One pupil so doing is asked to come to the board, write the sum in question (2 days 14 hours + 4 days 15 hours) and talk the teacher and class through the stages of calculation. Teacher questions both this pupil and others about the calculation process and outcome.

0958   The same procedure is repeated for another pupil who has admitted difficulties. He comes to the board, and through public calculation, questioning and prompting, is guided to the correct solution and the correct way of achieving and checking it.

1003   Teacher writes on board: $5409 \times 80 + 560490 \div 7 \div 3 - 84096 = \ldots$ Invites pupil to come to board to solve the first two parts. She calculates aloud, prompted by the teacher. Three more pupils, in turn, are asked to come to the board to complete the calculation.

1012   Teacher instructs pupils to pass their books to the monitors.

1015   Class stands briefly to signal the end of this lesson.

Lesson 11.10. United States of America: Emerson Elementary School, Michigan, 24 children aged 6–7, language arts (80 minutes)

The children are seated in groups of four to ten. A trainee teacher intern assists the teacher.

1100   Pupils enter the classroom singly or in small groups over a period of ten minutes. They chat with each other or with the adults, collect their journals from a table and take them to their places, or wander round the room.

1112   Teacher gently strikes a chime bar to gain pupils' attention, welcomes the pupils, reads aloud options for lunch from the board (jumbo taco and baloney sandwich), announces the 'journal' writing task and sets her timer. The task, also on the blackboard, is 'If you could meet anyone in the world, who would it be? Why?'

1115   By now pupils are: writing solo, writing collaboratively, talking with the teacher or the intern, walking round the room conversing with others, complaining about each other to the teacher, arguing about chairs. Teacher settles pupils who are still wandering.

1118   Teacher talks with individuals about their ideas for the writing task, and about attendant matters, in this case the O. J. Simpson trial, whether Simpson is guilty and what will happen to him if he is (one boy has nominated Simpson as the person he most wishes to meet). She occasionally writes comments in a notebook.

1120   Timer bell rings. Teacher announces 'closet check' and 'attendance check'. One pupil drops the jar of marbles used to reward good attendance and work. Others are asked to help pick them up. Teacher resumes conversation about O. J. Simpson, gas chambers, electric chairs and the jury system.

1124   Teacher sorts out a fight involving spitting and chair snatching, strikes chime bar to quieten class, tells six pupils to sit, and announces that snacks (fruit roll-ups) will be passed round. After competing for their preferred snack colours, pupils start eating. Many eat, talk and write at the same time.

1127 Teacher and intern move round the class talking with pupils about their stories and cautioning those who are noisy or restless.

1136 Teacher strikes chime bar to quieten class, continues to circulate, talking with pupils about their stories and how ideas have been or should be generated. In this the importance of 'peer conference' is emphasized.

1140 Teacher strikes chime bar and asks pupils to stand for the Pledge. Pupils stand, hands on hearts, face flag in corner, and repeat the Pledge in unison.

1141 Teacher divides class into two groups for 'author's chair'. She takes one, the intern the other. Pupils settle in two circles for author's chair at opposite ends of the room, some on chairs, some on the floor.

1143 In each group, pupils are asked or volunteer to read their stories aloud. Most are one-liners. The heroes are dominated by O. J. Simpson and various members of another Simpson family (the television cartoon characters). Others have chosen not to follow this 'story starter', and read rather longer accounts of what they have done recently or what they will be doing after school or at the weekend. Teacher listens, makes the other pupils listen, asks questions about both the content and writing process, and invites pupils to do likewise. She writes assessments and 'positive anecdotals' in her notebook.

1210 Teacher terminates the discussions in both groups and brings all the pupils together for a 'group meeting' on the carpet at one end of the room. She announces the date and this leads to a discussion with the pupils about St Patrick's Day, which is the day following. Discussion then turns to the weather. Pupils enter the day's weather on a chart and discuss the dangers of fog. Teacher goes over the schedule for the remainder of the day, which she has written on the board.

1220 Teacher sends pupils out, one by one, to wash for lunch.

Lesson 11.11. United States of America: Hawthorne Elementary, Michigan, 17 pupils aged 6–7, mathematics (38 minutes)

The children are in 'co-operative learning groups' of between four and eight. For this lesson the tables have been rearranged from their previous layout of rows of pairs. For the lesson that follows this, the teacher adopts a different layout again, this time a large horseshoe. A classroom assistant supports the teacher.

0947 Teacher instructs pupils to get into their 'co-operative learning groups' for mathematics. Pupils push pairs of desks together to seat groups of between four and eight. Teacher gives each group a pack of coloured shapes, called 'granny buttons', and a square of felt. She tells two boys to change places.

0948 Teacher tells pupils to tip the shapes on to the felt and check that they are lying flat. In each group, one pupil tips and the others sort. When this is done, teacher tells pupils to put their hands in their laps. They stop talking and do so.

0949 Teacher asks preliminary questions about the number of button colours and shapes the pupils can see. Pupils raise hands to answer. Teacher sets first group task: 'How can we make these buttons, in some kind of way, look the same?' She asks pupils to 'talk about it in your groups'. Teacher and assistant circulate, asking questions, prompting lines of discussion and commenting on solutions. Within the groups some sort and talk, others watch and listen.

1002 Teacher gently rings a small handbell. Pupils stop and look at her. She briefly praises what she has seen and describes several of the solutions, then reminds the class of a book about a bear named Corduroy read the previous day, holding it up for the pupils to see. She asks a series of questions about the story, leading up to the loss of Corduroy's button and to today's task, which is to find that button. Pupils raise their hands to answer questions and some call out. Teacher then tells the pupils to put the buttons back on the pieces of felt. They do so, then put their hands in their laps and wait.

1007 Teacher gives first task, presented as a clue to the attributes of Corduroy's lost button: 'Corduroy's button is not yellow'. Pupils discuss, move buttons about, then raise their hands when their group has the answer. Teacher asks one group, and checks ('Do we agree?') with the others.

1009 Teacher provides a second clue: 'Corduroy's button is not a triangle'. Pupils discuss as before. Teacher checks, and asks pupils to speculate on the basis of the possibilities eliminated so far. They suggest that the button might be big, round, blue, red, have two holes. She then repeats the process with the remaining clues: Corduroy's button . . . has four holes, has four sides, is not small, is not blue, is not green. When just one type of button is left the pupils identify it (big, red, square, with four holes). Teacher asks pupils for the generic term 'attributes', which they supply.

1020 Teacher tells pupils to check buttons and stack them 'by attribute' in the boxes. They do so, then rest their heads on their desks and wait. Classroom assistant and one pupil collect the felt squares and boxes of shapes.

1024 Teacher tells pupils to reorganize the furniture for the next lesson.

1025 End of lesson.

Lesson 11.12. United States of America: Thoreau Elementary School, Michigan, multi-age class of 18 pupils aged 9–10, mathematics (63 minutes)

The children are seated at groups of adjustable desks, singly, in pairs or in groups of between three and five. Each desk is labelled with the name of the child who uses it.

0930 Pupils come in from brief recess. Teacher is writing a math problem on the board: 'I wanted to buy 50 math journals at Office Max. The notebooks came in packages of 3. How many packages do I need to buy? Will the packages come out evenly?

0933 Teacher stands by board waiting for pupils to settle, writes pupils' names on board as they show that they are ready, moves to computer area to help pupil save his work, cautions talkers, waits.

0936 Teacher reads aloud the math problem. Instructs pupils to work alone for five minutes, after which they may consult others. They are to think always in terms of 'problem, solution, explanation'.

0937 Pupils adopt various postures as they start work: sitting, kneeling, lounging, heads on desks while writing. Teacher visits four groups in turn and talks individually to most pupils in these about their proposed solutions and explanations. She always interacts head-to-head, sitting with pupils or crouching beside them.

0952 Teacher tells class to resume their seats for some sharing of ideas so far. She calls on two pupils to demonstrate their calculation on the board. They do so, counting on in threes – 3, 6, 9, 12, etc. up to 51. Teacher asks rest of class whether they agree, disagree, wish to ask questions or have any comments. Several pupils respond by disputing or questioning either the solution or the explanation. Teacher meanwhile provides a running commentary on each child's contribution, offering frequent praise and support. She also writes observations in her notebook. She interrupts herself and the class from time to time to remind pupils to attend, listen and look.

1001 Teacher invites two pupils who have disagreed with the previous solution or explanation to come to the board and offer their alternative. Same procedure: pupils demonstrate, share, question and discuss each other's ways of tackling the given mathematical problem.

1010 Teacher invites two more pupils to the board. Same procedure.

1023 Teacher asks a fourth pair to come to the board. Same procedure.

1028 Teacher asks class to write in their math journals 'What was difficult about this or what did you learn about this problem and the different solutions?' Writes on board, by way of prompt: 'What did you learn? What was difficult?' Pupils begin writing, some conversing with each other as they do so.

1032 Teacher tells class to close their notebooks, clear their desks and put their heads down, checks two of the math problem commentaries, tells class to stop talking and waits for them to do so. She then gives them a choice of indoor or outdoor recess, asks them to 'make suggestions', hears three, and announces indoor recess.

1036 End of lesson.

Lesson 11.13. England: Hamilton Primary School, mixed-age class of 31 children aged 6–8, English – study skills and handwriting (64 minutes)

The children are seated at tables pushed together to seat groups of three to six. A non-teaching assistant (NTA) supports the teacher. For much of the lesson the teacher works intensively with one group of six pupils, while the NTA supervises the others.

1045 Teacher gives class their instructions for this lesson, and checks that NTA knows the groups with which she will be working.

1046 Teacher sits down with the study skills group. She tells them that she has earlier asked other pupils in the class to suggest questions that might be put to a knight in armour, should he come into the classroom. She has written down some of these for the group and assures them that they will be able to raise their own questions, although later rather than now. Pupils now read two of the questions on the teacher's list ('What was a tournament?' 'What happened in the joust?'). Teacher uses these as springboard to introduce the concept of 'research', and hands round a selection of reference books on knights, castles, etc.

1049 Teacher asks pupils how they use books for finding things out. Pupils volunteer 'index' and teacher tests their ability to use an index by asking them to look up 'tournament'. On the way they delightedly discover 'toilets'. They follow up the page numbers listed under 'tournament', locate the information in question and read it out. Teacher occasionally scans rest of class, here and throughout her sessions with this group.

1053 Teacher reminds pupils of the second question, about the joust. Pupils look up 'joust' in indexes, turn to the appropriate pages, hold up pictures, share information and agree definition. Teacher interacts with each child in the group.

1055 Teacher now comes to the third question ('Did castles have toilets?'). Pupils look up 'toilets' in the index. Teacher converses briefly with NTA. Same procedure.

1058 Teacher tells pupils in the group how to work independently towards presenting their findings to the rest of the class, reads through all the questions and hands a question card to each pupil. Pupils ask teacher various questions about what they are expected to do.

1104 Teacher circulates to other group in the class, confers with NTA, checks and comments on pupils' work.

1107 Teacher returns to study skills group. Pupils are now tackling the various questions on their cards. Teacher intervenes to help as necessary, concentrating particularly on one pupil who does not find the task easy. She deals with two queries from pupils in other groups.

1115 Teacher stops the group to discuss an emerging problem – the lack of information about castle baths. She then circulates to rest of class.

1119 Teacher returns to her group, helps one pupil, checks work of another, defines a word for a third, reads part of her description of a castle keep, shows pictures of mediaeval torches, reads out definition of 'solar'. She continues to give more attention to one pupil than to others. Pupils in this and other groups are continuing to work at their tasks, talking with others as they do so, although quietly.

1129 Teacher gets up to monitor the other groups.

1133 Teacher returns to study skills group, responds to queries, checks the work of pupils who have finished, praising one and telling her to add a picture.

1137   Pupils now individually volunteer their own questions for the knight, which will be passed to the next group to undertake this task. Teacher writes these down. Pupils in this group tidy up their books and papers.

1143   Teacher stops class, gives tidying up instructions, handles the continuing trickle of questions about castle sanitation, sends groups out in turn for lunch.

1149   End of lesson.

Lesson 11.14. England: Ogden Primary School, mixed-age class of 31 children aged 9–11, English (77 minutes)

The children are seated at tables pushed together to accommodate groups of four to eight.

0905   Teacher greets the class, who have just come in, the pupils having collecting reading books from their individual trays on the way to their desks. Pupils respond in unison. Teacher deals with register, lunch numbers and cycling proficiency test entries. Pupils read silently.

0910   Teacher calls three pupils in turn to her desk. She asks each questions about what they have read so far, hears them read further and checks their understanding of the content.

0917   Teacher stands, asks all members of the class to choose a sentence containing a comma. Every pupil, one group at a time, then reads a sentence aloud. After all members of one group have read their sentences the teacher asks others to comment on the clarity and expressiveness of the reading.

0936   Teacher turns from pupils' reading to their writing. She invites pupils to comment on the quality of diary writing on a recent class trip to Northumberland. These diaries are on display. Pupils offer comments, some detailed and critical. To answer they raise hands, speaking when requested to.

0944   Teacher talks about pupils' general failure in their Northumberland diaries to write in paragraphs: hence today's exercise, a three-paragraph piece on 'My bedroom'.

0946   Teacher asks questions about the nature and appropriate use of humour in writing. Sets up schema for first paragraph on the board ('1 – Describe'). Pupils volunteer descriptive words.

0948   Teacher deals with the second and third paragraphs in the same way ('2 – How your room is special to you. 3 – Other people's views of your room'). Pupils respond to questions about what they do in their bedrooms, who is allowed in, how many have televisions, videos or computers. Teacher urges pupils to give their pieces a 'good ending'.

0952   Pupils start writing. Teacher deals with individual queries, monitors some children, fetches dictionaries from cupboard and distributes them.

0958   Pupils write, teacher monitors.

1011   Teacher asks class to stop. She reads one pupil's first paragraph aloud and commends its concentrated description. Pupils listen, then continue to write.

1013   Teacher asks four pupils in turn to read their pieces to the class. She asks questions and invites comments from pupils. Several pupils comment, briefly.

1019   Teacher collects pupils' written work and gives instructions about seating arrangements for the following lesson.

1022   Pupils go to playground.

Lesson 11.15. England: Kirkbright, 28 children aged 6–7, English (55 minutes)

The children are seated as groups of four to six. The lesson is presented as a 'literacy hour' in accordance with the requirements of the UK government's 1998 literacy strategy.

1315   Pupils enter classroom and are directed to the carpeted area, where they sit close together on the floor.

1320   Teacher sits on chair in front of them, announces 'Welcome to the Literacy Hour'. Pupils respond in slow unison, 'Wel-come-Mis-sus-New-ton'. Teacher then takes the class register.

1323   Teacher goes to the board. Points to a sequence of pictures entitled 'Follow that letter' featuring a gust of wind, an airborne letter, various distraught people and a post-box. Under this one pupil has written a story. Using a hand-shaped pointer teacher leads pupils in reading this story aloud, in unison.

1326   Teacher asks pupils to compare this version with a second one which depicts the characters in the story but which has empty speech bubbles and no narrative. She invites pupils to suggest the characters' words that might go in the bubbles. Pupils make suggestions for teacher to write in the bubbles.

1327   Special needs teacher comes in to collect children for her group.

1337   Teacher asks pupils to suggest other 'helping words' they might need for this task. Pupils volunteer 'letter', 'wind', 'catch', 'help' 'post-box' 'tired', 'strong' – all of which teacher writes on board.

1339   Teacher calls for pupils' attention and chooses a pupil to hold the hand-shaped pointer while she and the pupils read aloud the dialogue in the speech bubbles.

1341   Teacher chooses another pupil to hold the pointer while pupils read aloud words in the word bank. She tells them to use their word books, 'build up the phonemes' and write carefully. Teacher and pupils re-read aloud the words on the board. Pupils return to their tables to begin writing their own versions of the story.

1343   Teacher removes the jointly written dialogue from the board and begins to monitor. She announces that she will be mainly working with just two of the groups. On the tables of each of these two groups she places a sign – 'We are working with the teacher'. Pupils begin writing.

1345   Teacher sits down with pupils in one of her target groups, asking questions, prompting, encouraging, providing spellings.

1356   Teacher adds 'blew' to the 'helping words' list. Announces 'Five minutes to go'. Resumes working with the target groups. She also deals with queries from pupils in other groups.

1402   Teacher tells pupils to stop and 'meet on the carpet for the plenary'. Pupils come to the carpet in ones and twos.

1404   One pupil, chosen by the teacher, reads his story to the class. Teacher invites other pupils' comments on handwriting and content. Three more pupils read their stories.

1409   Teacher tells girls, then boys, to put on their coats and shoes and line up at the door for play.

1410   End of lesson.

Lesson 11.16. England: St Teresa's, mixed-age class of 29 children aged 9–11, mathematics (62 minutes)

The children are at tables pushed together to seat groups of five to eight, two groups for Year 5 (9–10) and three for Year 6 (10–11). The lesson is presented as a 'numeracy hour' in accordance with the UK government's 1998 numeracy strategy.

1040   Pupils come in from playground, find seats, and obey teacher's instruction to fold their arms and look at her.

1042   Teacher introduces first mental arithmetic exercise. She gives pupils a one- or two-digit number; they have to tell her the number needed to make it up to 100. This is handled as a relay: the pupil who correctly answers her question asks the next one, and so on.

1046   Teacher presents second mental arithmetic task. Each group has digit cards. Teacher gives them a calculation, they raise the cards showing the answer. The questions become progressively more difficult, starting with '8 + 9' and ending with '$4^2 + 14 \times 3$, halve it, round to the nearest 10 and the answer is 10 per cent of this number'. Pupils put away the digit cards when this task is completed, sit up straight and wait.

1056   Teacher presents next task: 'How many ways can you make 16?' Pupils may work with partners. Pupils start discussing this problem with those next to them. Teacher collects digit cards.

1058   Teacher calls for volunteers to write their solutions on the board. Five pupils volunteer. Teacher asks pupils if they agree with each of the solutions.

1102   The class now subdivides by age group. Teacher instructs first the 9–10 (Year 5) and then the 10–11 year olds (Year 6) on their written tasks. After explaining the Year 5 pupils' worksheet (filling in 'magic squares' to make the number 15 horizontally, vertically and diagonally), she moves to the Year 6 pupils. She asks them first to see how many squares can be contained in a 2×2 grid drawn on the blackboard, then turns to their worksheets, which extend this idea.

1108 Year 6 pupils begin work, Year 5 pupils continue. Teacher monitors individual pupils in both year groups, concentrating mainly on Year 6.

1113 First Year 6 pupil comes to teacher with task completed. She checks pupil's answers, finds them correct and extends the task to even larger grids and numbers.

1120 Teacher tells Year 6 pupils to add written explanations to the worksheet solutions. Tells them they have two more minutes.

1121 Teaching resumes monitoring and attending to the increasing numbers of pupils who are coming to her with finished work, thus preventing her from monitoring those who have not finished. Most pupils are still working, but there is a noticeable increase in pupil restlessness, particularly among the Year 6 pupils.

1127 Teacher tells pupils to finish work and gives instructions for tidying up. Pupils variously collect materials, put away work, talk, continue writing.

1130 Teacher announces the start of the plenary session. Asks three Year 5 pupils to tell the class how they have tackled their task and elicits explanations as well as solutions. Three Year 6 pupils then tell the class about their task. The teacher questions the latter pupils and the rest of the class on the sequence of differences between square numbers.

1138 Teacher instructs class to tidy up.

1139 Teacher explains and starts a second arithmetical relay game. There are four teams and pupils in turn alternately add 6 and 7 to the previous pupil's total.

1142 Pupils stand by their tables. The teacher sends them out to the playground.

Using the Lesson Examples

The 16 lessons repay study in their own right, for each tells a familiar tale in a different way. As well as conveying some sense of what the lessons were like – a poor substitute, admittedly, for being there in person or viewing the videotapes – the accounts provide essential support for what follows. They reinforce the argument about the importance of holistic analysis, reminding us that if we must lift this or that aspect of teaching out of its context in order to study it, we should remember that it can only be fully understood by reference to what, on a particular occasion and in a particular place, preceded and followed it. This is why, in the chapters that deal with elements of teaching in accordance with the framework set out at the beginning of Chapter 13, I refer to these lessons wherever possible.

We cannot ground the entire analysis in these 16 lessons, however. They are only a part of the complete dataset, and we shall need both to identify trends and differences across the full range of lessons observed in each country, and to take examples from lessons other than those included here.

Chapter 12 will demonstrate these uses of the lesson narratives. The chapter draws on the full range of data while also referring frequently to the lessons exemplified; and it takes the entire lesson as the unit of analysis in order to explore notions of pedagogical structure and form.

12

Lesson Structure and Form

Timetables and Pedagogical Clocks

Lessons, whether defined as events or performances, are framed by time. The shortest of the lessons summarized in Chapter 11 lasted for 29 minutes, the longest for 80; but the range for all the lessons we observed was between 10 and 100 minutes.

In this matter the countries fall into two groups: those, India and Russia, where lessons were regular in length, and those – England, France and the United States – where lesson length was more variable. The reason for the difference is straightforward. In India and Russia this aspect of teaching was governed by school-wide timetables, and indeed by national requirements and conventions; in the other three countries lesson length was determined by the individual teacher, except when pupils used common spaces such as gymnasia or music rooms, whose use had to be timetabled.

In India the norm, and the actual average of lessons observed, was 30 minutes, with a range of 25 to 35. In India we also observed three lessons of 60 minutes which were defined as 'double', and one appears in Chapter 11 (lesson 11.6). In Russia the range was 35–45 minutes, the average was 42 and the intention was 45. The two lessons we observed which were below 40 minutes were aberrations; their start had been delayed by circumstances which were beyond the control of the teachers concerned.

In India and Russia, then, regular lesson length was perforce deeply ingrained in teachers' and pupils' psyches. There was a predictable rhythm to the day and to each lesson, especially in Russia, and such was its steadiness and invariability that although teachers occasionally looked at their watches, they appeared to have an instinctive grasp of time, organizing their material so that it filled the 45 minutes available and conveying a sense of pace without undue pressure. These teachers seemed to have developed internal 'pedagogical clocks' governing lesson periodicity almost as an extension of the way biological clocks governed their circadian rhythms.

In contrast, although they were not subject to these external requirements (or perhaps *because* they were not), teachers in England and the United States seemed both more anxious about time and less able to control it. Some lessons ran out of time; in other lessons teachers were left with empty spaces to fill with activities which were quite obviously mere 'time-fillers'. Highly variable lesson length prevented the development of teachers' or pupils' pedagogical clocks, with the result, as we shall see when we study lesson dynamics in greater detail, that time became not only elastic but also, and crucially, negotiable. Whereas in Russia the school timetable was the ultimate arbiter of lesson structure, ruling pupils and teacher alike, in France, England and the United States structure was for teachers and pupils themselves to determine. We shall see how, not infrequently, teachers' intended strategies for controlling time were subverted by the various strategies which pupils, in their turn, had devised for extending it. The stages of lessons most acutely vulnerable in this regard were those where pupils were undertaking writing tasks, individually or collaboratively.[1]

The widest temporal variation, as I have noted, was in Michigan. Apart from the one 100-minute lesson, we observed several of 65–80 minutes. Yet the range was such that the average, at 48 minutes, was lower than in England or France (58 and 51 minutes, respectively). In England the variation was less than in France: the English lessons were either short (30–35 minutes) or long (60–75 minutes), while in France there were intermediate lesson lengths of 40–45 minutes and a wider range, of 15–93 minutes.

This, as I have said, is all about the presence or absence of externally imposed timetables or lesson time requirements. When we examine how this time was filled we encounter a similar divide: the internal structure of lessons in India and Russia was by and large as regular and predictable as their length, while in the other three countries structures varied much more widely.

Sessions and Lessons

Official norms and requirements for teaching time tend to assume that *teaching sessions* and *lessons* coincide. In some instances the time taken for pupils and teacher to settle down is minimal, and in none of the French, Indian or Russian lessons exemplified above is there a delay of more than two minutes between pupils' entry to the classroom and the start of teaching. Lesson 11.7, for example, begins at 0918 with the teacher's injunction 'Sit down and look this way please' which leads without further ado into question and answer.

The same goes for most of the larger collection of observed and recorded lessons from France, India and Russia. The endings of these lessons are no less precise. In several of the English and American lessons, in contrast, the lesson proper is framed by periods during which pupils enter the room singly or in groups of two or three, talk to each other or the teacher, often about matters other than school work, and fetch or put away materials which they will need or have used.

Thus in lesson 11.10 (Emerson) the lesson starts 12 minutes into the session. At Thoreau (11.12) the session-lesson difference is six minutes, and at Kirkbright (11.15) the intended 60 minutes of the government's Literacy Hour is reduced to a session of 55 minutes within which the lesson proper takes only 46 minutes.

To determine whether this is time wasted or intended we need both to talk to the teacher and study the interaction. From both these sources it becomes clear that the 12-minute episode at the start of the Emerson lesson (11.10) was planned rather than accidental. These were young children, and the teacher saw the encouraging of open and informal interaction, especially at the beginning of the day, as an essential part of her task of socializing as well as educating. The period of six minutes spent waiting for the pupils to settle down at the start of the Thoreau session (11.12) is slightly more complex. Clearly the teacher would have preferred to make a speedy start to the lesson. She also believed that children should work because they want to work, and for this reason insisted on waiting until every child was ready, and on not pushing the issue to the point of confrontation. The Hawthorne example (11.11) will correct any impression that there is anything inevitably American about this. This teacher not only began teaching within one minute of the start of the session: she also accomplished within that time, and with the school's youngest pupils, a complete transformation of the classroom furniture layout. For good measure she did the same at the end of the lesson.

Two circumstances made the session-lesson discrepancy more likely in Michigan and England, however. First, as noted above, the teachers themselves, rather than their schools or governments, determined the structure of the school day, so teachers were in a position, if they so chose, to treat time as either elastic or rigid. Second, there was an underlying difference in values that encouraged them to opt for elasticity. In the Russian and Indian classrooms, both teachers and teaching goals were more instrumental and focused than, say at Emerson or Thoreau, where goals were diffuse and teachers pursued a social agenda which was no less important than the academic one. Central to this social agenda was the idea that ends are best achieved by discussion, negotiation and consensus rather than by one person imposing her or his will on others. Moreover, while in the Indian and Russian classrooms the nature of the teacher's authority was clear to all, and absolute, in some of the Michigan classrooms the teachers were pursuing the more demanding and equivocal line of simultaneously requiring and negotiating, of trying to achieve educational ends by both external direction and self-direction. In the French classrooms teachers had the facility of elastic time but their more instrumental values meant that it was extended in pursuit of academic rather than social goals, and their more straightforward view of their authority meant that when they did extend time they also kept it under firm control.

Beginnings, Endings and Middles

The beginnings and endings varied in both length and character. Some introductory stages are brief, even cursory – for example, lessons 11.4 (Chanderi), 11.10 (Emerson) and 11.12 (Thoreau). Others, such as Coulanges (11.3), are extended. The distinction, in fact, is less of length than of purpose. Despite their relatively lengthy *session* introductions, the openings of the *lessons* proper at Emerson and Thoreau are extremely brief: the teachers simply tell the pupils what they must do. So where the three Russian introductions (11.7–11.9) or those at Coulanges (11.3) or Ogden (11.14) are *instructional*, those at Emerson and Thoreau are *procedural*. Depending on what is to follow, instructional beginnings may include a procedural element that sets up the task of the lesson's middle stage.

The lack of instruction in a procedural introduction is usually compensated for at the lesson's development stage. At Emerson and Thoreau the teachers followed up their brief introductions by interacting with groups and individuals. In the 'multiple curriculum focus' lesson structure which was common in England during the 1970s and the 1980s but by 2000 was becoming less prevalent (although it is represented in the *Five Cultures* data), teachers delivered merely procedural introductions yet they spent considerable time doing so because each group had a different task which needed to be separately introduced ('Now Red Group: this is what I want you to do . . .'). In classes with four or five groups this round of introductions might take 15 minutes, sometimes longer. Teachers commonly undertook a second and fairly rapid circuit of the groups to check that tasks were understood before they were in a position to engage pupils in interactions of an instructional rather than a procedural kind. In general, the more complex the organization, the higher the proportion of time spent on procedural matters.[2]

The same kind of difference between the procedural and instructional marks the concluding stages of the lessons. Some – for example Juan-le-Grand (11.1) – just stop; some, such as Hamilton (11.13) end on a purely routine note to do with tidying up; but in others the final stage is clearly of critical importance to the achievement of the lesson's goals and is extended to include not just recapitulation, as in the Russian lesson at Kursk A (11.7, 0951–0956), or a recapitulatory task (putting away the buttons by attribute) as at Hawthorne (11.11, 1020), but also collective commentary on individual work, as at Coulanges (11.3, 1445), Emerson (11.10, 1143–1210), Moscow B (11.9, 0954–1012), Thoreau (11.12, 0952–1028) and Ogden (11.14, 1011–1019) and the numeracy and literacy hours at Kirkbright (11.15, 1402–1409) and St Teresa's (11.16, 1130).

However, it is the central sections of lessons where we find the greatest variation, and these also provide the key to understanding their overall structures. These sections consist of either a single task or a sequence of shorter tasks. The latter may or may not be linked. In this sense the development stages of lessons are either *unitary* or *episodic*. Thus at Coulanges (11.3, 1359–1442) the single and lengthy central task is writing a story which implements the ideas on narrative and dialogue examined during the lesson's introduction. At Emerson (11.10, 1115–1140) the central task is writing the day's journal; at Thoreau it is solving a single mathematical problem and preparing to explain how the solution was achieved (11.12, 0937–0952); at Ogden (11.14, 0952–1011) it is writing in paragraphs. All these lessons have unitary central stages.

In contrast, the lessons from Chanderi (11.4) and Sankasya (11.6) and indeed the larger proportion of Indian lessons we observed (lesson 11.5, from Purana, is an exception) consist of a sequence of brief episodes related to the lesson's main theme but each also self-contained. That is to say, while the unitary tasks at Coulanges and Ogden had to be completed for the lesson to make sense, the central section of the lesson at Chanderi could have been halted at any time, to be resumed the following day or week. To permit this, each episode incorporated its own recapitulation (11.4, 0953–1000, and 1004–1007).

The three Russian lessons – and again this was a common pattern in all the Russian lessons which we observed – were also episodic, but in a rather different way. At Kursk A, for example, there was a sequence of episodes (11.7, 0921–0951) grounded in the introduction (0918), but these pursued a wider range of objectives than at Chanderi – differentiating, classifying and representing vowels and consonants, hard and soft sounds, voiced and unvoiced consonants, syllables and stresses. Here, as in the intensive lesson from Kursk B on word combinations, case agreement and the governing function of verbs (11.8), although it would have been possible to suspend the lesson before its end without invalidating it, this would have been much more difficult than at Chanderi, because at Kursk A the episodes were *developmental* rather than merely *reiterative* or, as at Juan-le-Grand (11.1, 1030–1051), *cumulative*. In this respect the Russian lessons from Kursk A and B are comparable to the one at Hawthorne which actually takes the developmental logic even further because the sequence of classification tasks (11.11, 1007–1020) is only complete, and the lesson can only end when by a step-by-step process of elimination the pupils have discovered all the ways of sorting the counters. In a rather looser fashion, the Hamilton study skills lesson is also both episodic and developmental in that the teacher gets the pupils to use book indexes to look up a succession of words (11.13, 1049–1137), but her intention in doing so is to move the pupils from guided towards autonomous use of books as sources of information.

In the Russian lessons, the only break in the central lesson sequences – although not the three illustrated in Chapter 11 – came when the teacher halted proceedings once, sometimes twice, for exercises. The children would stand up, move into the aisles between their desks and for one minute stretch arms, twist necks, shake hands and fingers, close eyes and breathe deeply.

It is possible for an episodic central sequence to be both reiterative and developmental. At St Etienne the pupils encountered the passage from Daudet's *Tartarin de Tarascon* no fewer than four times and in four guises. They read it silently to themselves (11.2, 0843). The teacher read it aloud to them (0855). They read it aloud to each other (0909–0934). They read it silently to themselves again (at 0934, while doing the written exercise). Each reading was followed or accompanied by questions. These progressed from the passage's context and authorship (0853) to its structure and meaning (0856–0927), taking in on the way the manner in which it should be read aloud (0927). The re-reading of the passage ensured that by the time they started their written comprehension exercise (0934) the pupils were utterly familiar with it, but each questioning episode focused on a different aspect.

Just as we can discern two – or possibly three – kinds of episodic structure, so we can subdivide those lessons whose central sections are unitary. At Coulanges (11.3) and Ogden (11.14) the writing tasks are *closed* in that to be deemed complete they have to satisfy the requirements which the teacher presents at the introductory stage. At Coulanges the pupils must write a narrative which includes dialogue and proceeds from *état initial* to *état final*, as in the teacher's schema; at Ogden they must produce three complete paragraphs, each dealing with a given aspect of the chosen topic of 'My Bedroom'. At Emerson (11.10) and Thoreau (11.12) however, the tasks are *open ended*. At Emerson the teacher moves to the plenary stage of the lesson not when the children have produced a piece of writing which conforms to pre-determined criteria but when she judges it sensible to bring children together to share their ideas, the dynamics of sharing being no less important than the ideas themselves. Likewise at Thoreau, because although solving a mathematical problem might seem to be the quintessence of a closed task, the teacher, by concerning herself more with the problem-solving process than its outcome is able to move to the plenary stage at virtually any point. Indeed, the Thoreau teacher's view of the relative importance of solving the problem and explaining how to solve it is demonstrated in the time distributions: the pupils spend 15 minutes working on the problem (0937–0952) but 31 minutes discussing how they did so (0952–1023). Moreover, at no point does the teacher indicate which of the various solutions proposed by the pupils was actually correct.

In this matter, teacher intentions are of critical importance. In another context, tasks such as naming the person one would most like to meet and justifying one's choice (Emerson), or of solving a problem which entails the arithmetical calculation $50 \div 3$ (Thoreau), would be judged to be closed. Here, however, the teachers have chosen to define them as open, or rather to make the logical imperatives of each task subsidiary to other goals which, through the tasks, the teachers hope to achieve.

It is therefore not necessarily correct to define the writing and problem-solving stages of these two lessons (11.10, 1115–1140 and 11.12, 0937–0952) as their main task, since in their interviews the teachers make it clear that they are no less concerned with social processes. However, an ambiguity of purpose and structure hangs over both lessons, as we shall see when we look at the pupil–teacher discourse. Comparing these two lessons with the shorter one at Hawthorne is instructive. At Hawthorne the teacher has a mathematical objective (identifying attributes and using them as a basis for differentiation and classification) and a broader pedagogical one ('co-operative' learning). The dialogue dwells on both, but without ambiguity. In interview the teacher stresses the generic significance of co-operative learning, and in naming one of her classroom layouts for this mode (11.11, 0947) she has transmitted her belief to the pupils themselves. Yet the lesson drives crisply towards its curricular goal and there is no question, as there is at Emerson, of that goal being made subsidiary to any other. Here, co-operation is a means to an end.

It will be seen that there is a tendency for unitary central stages of lessons to centre on *seatwork* – usually reading and/or writing tasks and sometimes collaborative group work – while episodic central stages are more commonly teacher-led and *expository*. However, in many of the Russian lessons and some of those observed in France the central episodes combined both exposition and seatwork. The latter episodes were invariably brief. They consisted of either short tasks alternating with direct instruction, or a single task broken down into stages, again alternating with direct instruction.

Thus, the longest period of sustained writing leading to the production of a complete text that we observed in the 30 Russian lessons lasted for ten seconds

short of five minutes. In contrast, the longest equivalent period in the other countries was in a lesson observed at Ogden: it lasted for 50 minutes (neither of these
lessons is illustrated in Chapter 11), and in the English and American lessons seatwork
tasks that lasted for 30 minutes or more were quite common.

Although lengthy writing tasks were less common in France, it is noteworthy that
the French data did include the extremely long central sequence at Coulanges (11.3,
1359–1442). The teacher in question had been designated *maître formateur* and his
school *école d'application* (roughly the equivalent of a teacher training mentor and
a partnership school in England, or a professional development school in the United
States). He and his colleagues worked closely with the teacher training programme
at the local *institut universitaire de formation des maîtres* (IUFM) and were judged
to provide models of practice worthy of emulation by the IUFM's trainees. Yet the
continuum of teaching in the French schools also included tight episodic structures
such as the one at St Etienne (11.2).

A crude calculation of comparative outcomes – to be treated with caution – gives
some indication of the vastly different dynamics of the Russian classrooms on the
one hand, and the American and English classrooms – and, sometimes, the French
classrooms – on the other. The written task from Ogden which took 50 minutes to
complete was composition; at Kursk School B, the five-minute written task was also
composition. The children were the same age, 9–10. We have examples of both
sets of completed work: the longest produced in the Ogden English lesson was
120 words; the longest of the compositions produced in the Kursk B Russian lesson
was 75 words. At Ogden the composition was the outcome to which the entire
lesson was directed; at Kursk B it was one part of a lesson which included direct
instruction and related tasks on spelling, grammar and syntax.

I do not wish to make too much of this. To do so would be to reduce international comparison to the level indulged in by British politicians during their
frequent bouts on the 'standards' hustings during the late 1990s ('Research has
shown that Russian pupils work harder during lessons than British children of the
same age when engaged in comparable tasks. Ergo, we must copy the Russian
methods . . .'). The two lessons were different not just in their structure and dynamics
but also in their purpose. In the Ogden lesson the writing process incorporated and
was fuelled by collaborative discussion while in the Kursk B lesson it was an entirely
individual affair. Discussion expands time, while direct instruction compresses it.
No less important, collaborative writing leads to outcomes in addition to those of
the written product. Nevertheless, differences like this raise important questions
about what I have termed 'elastic' and 'rigid' time and about the pace and intensity
of learning. We shall need to look at them in greater detail.

Finally, we can classify the examples of teaching which follow the UK government's 1997–9 prescriptions for primary school numeracy and literacy. Both lessons
(11.15 and 11.16, at Kirkbright and St Teresa's) follow a formula. The Kirkbright
Literacy Hour has four stages (starting at 1323, 1337, 1343 and 1402) and the
St Teresa's Numeracy Hour has three (1042, 1102 and 1130). At Kirkbright one stage
leads to another, and the literacy lesson as a whole is developmental. The numeracy
lesson at St Teresa's is more episodic: there is no necessary connection between the

first and second stages other than that the first provides a kind of mental limbering up for the second, and the first stage itself consists of a sequence of disconnected tasks. The second stage comprises a single problem-solving task, the pupils' response to which is discussed at the lesson's final, plenary stage.

Structures Summarized

This cross-cultural excursion into lesson structure suggests a number of propositions. In listing these I draw on both the examples cited above and the other lessons observed.

- Lessons constructed within fixed timeframes (Russia, India and the numeracy and literacy hours in England) generally have a more predictable and formulaic internal structure than those where the teacher is free to determine lesson length.

- The lessons usually have three, or at the most four main stages: introduction, development (sometimes subdivided) and conclusion. The most compressed and basic structure is the two-stage lesson consisting of introduction and development, without conclusion. Some of the Indian lessons took this form, as did many of the shorter lessons in other countries.

- While the central stage is usually the longest, introductions and conclusions may vary from the extremely brief to sequences as long as, or even longer than, the central stage.

- Introductory stages are *procedural, instructional* or *procedural/instructional*. Where an introduction is merely procedural it is usually short. The exception to this latter rule (not illustrated here) is the lesson structure, common in England during the 1970s and the 1980s and represented in the *Five Cultures* data, in which there is 'multiple curriculum focus' grouping (several groups undertaking different and perhaps unconnected tasks). In this setting the time spent on introduction can be substantial because the teacher has to attend to each group in turn. Such introductions are invariably procedural rather than instructional.

- Lesson conclusions may also be *procedural, instructional* or *procedural/instructional*. An instructional conclusion may introduce new material, although more commonly it recapitulates on what has already been encountered. Again, procedural conclusions are shorter than instructional.

- The central stages of lessons consist of a single task or a sequence of several tasks. In this respect they are *unitary* or *episodic*.

- *Unitary* central stages can be *closed*, when the learning task must be completed before the lesson can move to its next or final stage; or they can be *open ended*, in which case the next stage can start whenever the teacher feels it is appropriate to do so.

- *Episodic* central stages characteristically consist of a sequence of separate tasks which are either *self-contained* or *linked*.

- Where the tasks in episodic central stages are *self-contained*, they may be either *reiterative* or *cumulative*.

- Where the tasks in episodic central stages are *linked*, they may be *cumulative* or *developmental*. In some episodic central stages the tasks may be both reiterative and developmental.

- The unitary central stages that we observed mostly involved *seatwork* – usually reading and/or writing, and – much less frequently – collaboration between pupils. The episodic central stages were largely *expository*. They were dominated by direct instruction, sometimes punctuated by short periods of reading and/or writing.

Taking all the lessons together, we can now summarize the tendencies observed in each country up to this point.

In France, timeframes were determined by teachers and the lessons were irregular in length. Some introductions were procedural only, but most were instructional. Lesson conclusions were rarely other than instructional and recapitulatory. The central sections of lessons could be unitary or episodic. When unitary they were invariably closed; when episodic they were usually developmental.

In India, timeframes were fixed, lesson lengths were regular and lesson structures were predictable. Lesson introductions and conclusions were instructional but always very brief. Central sections were usually episodic, combining direct instruction with short periods of reading and/or writing. They were strongly reiterative, and cumulative rather than developmental.

The Russian lessons also had fixed timeframes, regular lesson lengths and predictable structures. Introductions and conclusions were instructional, with little or no time spent on procedures, which had become matters of clearly understood routine. Central sections, though tending towards the episodic, were also strongly developmental. They combined direct instruction with short reading and/or writing tasks, sometimes punctuated by one-minute periods of exercise or a game.

The lengths of the Michigan lessons were determined by their teachers, so they were irregular. Introductions were procedural or instructional, as were lesson conclusions. There were some episodic central sections, in which case they were developmental, but most were unitary. Being so, they were often open ended. Lessons usually closed with a plenary session, sometimes short, sometimes substantial.

Following UK government initiatives on primary school pedagogy taken in 1997–9, the observed English lessons included both teacher-determined and externally imposed timeframes and lesson structures. The literacy and numeracy hours had instructional introductions and recapitulatory conclusions. Their central sections were unitary. However, the strict demarcation of the stages – four in the literacy hour and three in the numeracy hour – could produce a fragmented and clock-driven structure that made the central sections shorter than intended. In other lessons, teachers created their own structures and timeframes, and here there was considerable diversity.

Inheriting a structure popular in the 1970s and the 1980s, the group-based multiple curriculum focus lessons had protracted procedural introductions followed by parallel unitary central sections and, for organizational reasons, procedural rather than recapitulatory conclusions. In the other lessons observed the central sections were usually unitary rather than episodic, and frequently open ended rather than closed.

The Origins of Lesson Structure and Form

How do we explain transnational differences such as these? Before considering cultural influences we should note a more prosaic factor: the time which teachers have at their disposal.

If, as was the case in the Indian schools, teachers are obliged to teach in units of no more than 30 minutes, then there are obvious limits to the extent of exposition which is possible, and within such constraints exposition followed by a sustained unitary task and recapitulation requires considerable skill if it is to be successfully accomplished. It is much easier to adopt the episodic structure which allows the teacher to combine direct instruction and seatwork in segments which are so short that the sequence may be suspended when time runs out without damaging the lesson's integrity, provided that each episode has also included its own recapitulation.

The skill for the teacher working within this tradition is to make the episodes cumulative and developmental rather than merely reiterative: in short to ensure that learning progresses rather than stays in the same place.

The Russian lessons are half as long again as those in India, and this extra 15 minutes allows much greater flexibility. It also permits, critically, central learning tasks of a sustained and developmental kind. However, the Russian teachers whom we observed almost always adopted an episodic structure, albeit – at best – a developmental one. Since 45 minutes allow the choice of either unitary or episodic teaching, as clearly demonstrated by the several lessons of that length which we observed in France, the decision to go for an episodic structure must be deemed pedagogical, rather than one which is forced on the teacher by circumstances. In fact, as I note below, there are also cultural reasons why Indian and Russian teachers choose episodic structures, and why the Indian episodes tend to the reiterative while the Russian ones more likely to be developmental.

In marked contrast, a teacher confronted with an uninterrupted spell of 90 minutes between the time children arrive at school and the time they leave the classroom for break or recess – as could happen in England, France and the United States – can choose to define this entire period, the equivalent of three Indian or two Russian lessons, as a single lesson. Within so expansive a timeframe virtually anything is possible – several mini-lessons, a sustained period of exposition combined with a sustained piece of seatwork and a generous recapitulation, or combinations of these. Many of the teachers we observed, especially those teaching the younger age range, broke such long periods of time down into a sequence of mini-lessons. Significantly, the shortest of such lessons were almost always oral. However, other teachers, as we have seen, chose to construct an entire 75, 80, 90 or even 100-minute session round a single task.

But the constraints and opportunities of time are only part of the story. In India, reiterative episodic teaching has, as noted in Chapter 4, a long pedigree. Some Indians themselves assert that the reiterative element, and the chanting tones in which teacher and pupils endlessly exchange words, letters and numbers, has Brahmanical origins.[3] Clarke and Fuller report the consistency across many classrooms of a transmission model of teaching in which the teacher proceeds with textbook in one hand and chalk in the other, the legacy of educational minimalism under the British as well as the pre-colonial tradition.[4] Denzil Saldanha's phrase 'the rite of rote' nicely captures the pedagogical and cultural essence of this model, and indeed hints at the difference between what is indigenous and what was imposed.[5] But if Indian teachers chose consciously to break out of this tradition, most would have to overcome four major obstacles: lack of time, lack of space, lack of resources, and large classes. The 30-minute timetable barrier makes developmental teaching difficult. Small and tightly packed classrooms confine pupils to the same small patch of floor and make collaborative learning and working with apparatus impossible, and in any case the apparatus is usually unavailable. Above all, the logistical and organizational challenges of individualized learning and collaborative group work, which are acknowledged to be difficult enough in the Western context of classes of between 20 and 30, are vastly more severe when class numbers rise to between 40 and 90.

It was therefore hardly surprising that in India we encountered the most palpable and consistent gulf between teachers' espoused theory and their theory-in-use. Nearly all teachers interviewed spoke of 'activity method', 'play method', 'joyful learning', 'individual attention', 'group work' and 'teaching aids', even when they were aware that in the lessons we had just observed and videotaped pupils were passive, classes were taught as a single unit and the only teaching aid was a blackboard.

The progressive vocabulary came from policy documents, inspectors and teacher training courses. We observed courses in action in two of the district institutes of education and training (DIETs). They delivered a mixed message, to say the least. The trainee teachers we observed and talked with busied themselves making 'low-cost, no-cost teaching aids' from cheap or recycled materials. They were instructed in the importance of activity methods and group work. The form of such instruction, however, was unremittingly didactic. The student teachers sat in rows, in large classes (as if they were at one of the schools whose methods they were supposedly preparing to transform), listened, took notes, and repeated what they had been told.

There was one important exception to the dominant Indian lesson pattern as we encountered it. We observed several lessons in music and dance which although they were constrained by the 30-minute timetable norm were in every other respect utterly different from those in Hindi, mathematics and the other core curriculum subjects. They were different because they stemmed from a second indigenous tradition that was no less venerable than the Brahmanical but has been confined in school education to the arts. Its essence is apprenticeship and its chosen methods are imitation and modelling. This is transmission teaching but what is being transmitted is not recipe knowledge for recall but a combination of knowledge, skill, insight, feeling, intuition, and the capacity both to work within form and bend form to the limit. The most outstanding example was a combined music and dance lesson in the Delhi school (Purana) where girls had devised a song on the theme of health and hygiene (a required component of the curriculum) to which they also danced using combinations of steps drawn from the repertoire of classical Indian dance. The instrumental accompaniment was provided by the teacher, who, typically in this tradition, came from a long line of musicians whose skill had been handed from one generation to the next. The quality of the final performance by these ten year olds far exceeded that in the equivalent genre in English schools, and in fact in only one other country did we see anything that approached it. This was in Russia, and even there the context was a teacher training college rather than a school. In India, however, though we saw little teaching of this kind in the classroom, we observed fragments of the evidence of it in school assemblies and, more extensively, in some of the experimental establishments such as Bal Bhawan Indian Society in Delhi.

In France, although lessons were sometimes no shorter than the longest lessons observed in England or Michigan, the structure remained relatively tightly controlled. Here, teachers had inherited, but were beginning to break away from, a notion of teaching in which the formal structure of *la leçon* was central[6] and teaching was structured so as to lead towards the acquisition of knowledge and the understanding of principles. The traditional dominance of textbook and slate, which by the late 1990s was also in abeyance, tied oral enquiry to the style and conventions of textbook questions and answers.[7] The task of the elementary school teacher was to provide charismatic moral authority as much as induction into culture and knowledge.[8]

The lessons observed by Broadfoot and her Bristol colleagues in the departments of Pas-de-Calais and Bouches-du-Rhône appear to have been much more consistent structurally than those we observed at about the same time in the departments of Alpes-Maritimes and Var, which together form the *académie* of Nice. There we found teachers adopting, testing and breaking away from the traditional lesson structure which the Bristol team saw generally replicated. They record this as an eight-stage sequence comprising (1) introduction, (2) practice of principles, (3) collective correction of practice tasks, (4) writing of rules and *points de repère* (reference points, signposts or landmarks), (5) learning the lesson, (6) testing of what has been learned, (7) collective correction of work tested, and (8) recording and reporting of results.[9] The differences between the two project samples are less significant than the point that even in a context of educational and pedagogical change, such as France began to experience from the late 1980s onwards, the long-established lesson model continued to be highly influential. Structures might become more fluid, but fundamental understandings of the nature of the teacher–pupil relationship and the central elements in successful primary school teaching remained intact.

In Russia, our teachers spoke both idealistically and pragmatically about the lesson structures that they adopted. Most cited theorists or 'methodologists' such as Davidov, Elkonin and Zankov, although they seemed somewhat vague about how the work of these authorities translated into classroom practice. Our analysis of the force of the local professional culture and hierarchy (pages 247–9) led us to suspect that this was in part, possibly in large part, a strategic espousal.

Individually, however, teachers gave clues which made sharper sense in terms of what we actually observed. 'In every lesson' said the teacher of the Russian lesson with six to seven year olds at Kursk A (11.7),

> we must both consolidate previous knowledge and teach something new. It's rather like a snowball: repetition, consolidation, new knowledge, repetition, consolidation, new knowledge. But the important thing is the new knowledge. It is through this that children grow, not by staying in the same place.

To this echo of Vygotsky ('the only good teaching is that which outpaces development'[10]) this teacher and others added ingredients from an older tradition. They stressed the primacy of 'dialogue' (or direct instruction) and the need to break learning down into small, carefully graded steps. These should steer a careful course between 'outpacing development' and retaining and maximizing children's concentration:

> As children grow older we can make the tasks longer, but when they are six or seven they lose concentration very quickly. I give them new knowledge, but I also give it to them in small quantities.

She, and other Russian teachers, also used one-minute periods of physical exercise or games to allow children to relax and recoup between such periods of relatively intense concentration.

The lesson plans we collected gave the teachers' own versions of the stages in the episodic structure to which we referred earlier. A mathematics lesson for six year olds at Grigoriev village school was planned to have (and did have) eleven stages: (1) introductory words, (2) communicating the lesson's theme and aims, (3) mental exercises (nine children at the blackboard) (4) mental exercises (remainder of class, oral question and answer), (5) checking individual work so far, (6) multiplication tables, (7) problem solving at the blackboard, (8) one minute of physical exercises – stretching and deep breathing, (9) independent work from text books, (10) summing up: what have we learned in this lesson?, (11) self-assessment. The shift from what the teacher called 'limbering up' to 'new learning' came with stage (7).

Another teacher's written plan for a Russian language lesson with nine year olds at Kursk School B ('connecting verbs and nouns') showed a similar proliferation of episodes: (1) communicate lesson theme and aims, (2) individual syntactic, word formation and phonetic analysis at blackboard, (3) dialogue on verb–noun connections with class, (4) written exercise from textbook, making word combinations from the nouns given and defining the type of combination, (5) checking examples from the exercise with children at the blackboard, (6) second textbook exercise: children work in pairs, (7) check answers orally, (8) using the same text identify and classify personal pronouns, (9) one minute's physical exercise, (10) dictation on the theme of 'autumn', emphasizing word connection and agreement, (11) short individual compositions on autumn, using step-by-step word combinations, (12) some children read compositions aloud to class, (xiv) summary of lesson: what have we learned?

The 'older tradition' on which I suggested that these teachers drew was claimed by interviewees in the Ministry and the Russian Academy of Education to be traceable back to Jan Komensky or Comenius (1592–1670). The line of descent probably goes via A. H. Francke (1663–1727), who developed and disseminated Comenius's principles of universal education and graded instructional sequences and opened schools run according to these principles in Halle. These celebrated establishments laid the basis for German secondary education, including the *gymnasium* and its attendant pedagogy, a model that Russia took over. However, Comenius influenced so many later educational figures that his ideas are as likely to have travelled from seventeenth-century Moravia to twentieth-century Russia by several routes. During the 1950s, for example, he was credited in communist Eastern Europe with having been the first person to campaign for a 'unified school system from primary school up to the highest standard . . . [in which] all children are given a general education without any discrimination of sex, social origin or property'[11] – the Soviet and now Russian general secondary school of the kind in which we did our *Five Cultures* fieldwork, in fact. Comenius, then, may well have a seminal influence on the development of Russian pedagogy; but he came to serve an ideological purpose as well.

In Chapters 15 and 17 I shall argue that Comenius's ideas are indeed central to an understanding of continental European pedagogy; for the moment we can note the clear resonance in Russian classrooms of principles first enunciated in Comenius's *Didactica Magna* of 1638:

> There should be one teacher for each class . . . Time should be carefully divided, so that each day and each hour may have its appointed task . . . The same exercise should be given to the whole class . . . All subjects should be taught by the same method . . . Everything should be taught thoroughly, briefly, and pithily, that the understanding may be, as it were, unlocked with one key . . . All things that are naturally connected ought to be taught in combination . . . Every subject should be taught in definitely graded steps, that the work of one day may thus expand that of the previous day, and lead up to that of the morrow.[12]

In Michigan, one might have expected to find echoes of formalized lesson planning and presentation of another kind, derived from Pestalozzi (1746–1827) by way of Herbart (1776–1841). Pestalozzi believed strongly in the primacy of form, but in two distinct senses: first, he was a sense-empiricist in the Baconian tradition whose cardinal principle of *Anschauung* (intuitive observation or contemplation) required that children focus in the first instance on objects – 'real, movable, actual things';[13] second, like Comenius, he was concerned with form in the presentation of knowledge and the structuring of teaching. Each subject had to be broken down into its constituents that were then reorganized in a logical relationship and presented to pupils in carefully graded steps. He was – and remains – immensely influential in his native country, Switzerland, and like those of Comenius his ideas spread across

Europe, influencing reformers as diverse as Herbart and Froebel in Germany and Robert Owen and Andrew Bell in England. They also reached Russia.

Herbart took Pestolozzi's principle of *Anschauung* and made it the bedrock of his four-stage lesson plan: *clarity*, *association*, *system* and *method*, in which teaching proceeded from first-hand observation on the basis of association of ideas. This was worked up by Prussians like Ziller and Rein, who were keen to promote the new science of pedagogy, into the 'Herbartian' lesson plan. In the form in which it proved most influential in the United States in the late nineteenth century, this plan was not really Herbart's. American Herbartianism, as translated into the recitation lesson that provided the bedrock of late nineteenth-century teacher training and manuals like those of the McMurray brothers, was more mechanistic than Herbart had intended. The five stages were *preparation*, *presentation*, *association*, *generalization* and *application*. The first two stages took the pupil from previous knowledge to new; the third and fourth synthesized past and new knowledge into principles, which were then applied.[14]

Similarly, the 'object lesson' which originated with Pestalozzi and was first disseminated by Henry and Elizabeth Mayo (who visited Pestalozzi at Yverdon),[15] soon lost its element of *Anschauung* and was reduced to the mere naming of features of objects which themselves were replaced by pictures on wall charts.[16] No less influential in England, the 'object lesson' suffered the same fate there.

The reduction of Pestalozzi's and Herbart's ideas to a purely mechanical routine for delivering rote learning to passive pupils provoked the reactions from William James and John Dewey which we noted in our account of the development of American elementary education in Chapter 5. In the first wave of American progressivism the emphasis shifted from instruction to problem solving and from an autocratic teacher role to a democratic one. In the second wave it added some of the trappings of English progressive primary education, as filtered and somewhat romanticized by Featherstone and others, and combined these with elements of Piagetian developmental psychology.

This, rather than the continental European concern with lesson form, structure and sequence, was the legacy which appeared to underpin what we observed in most of the Michigan classrooms. There, too, as we noted in Chapter 10, teachers were asserting their autonomy after decades of intervention and prescription by school boards and their administrators. Most talked of having changed from 'teaching in rows' to a less formal pedagogy, and in interview they spoke about values for longer and with far greater intensity than about structure. Their pedagogy was shaped by a belief that in teaching, affectivity is central; that children 'should believe in themselves, have high self-esteem, believe that they can learn – then the rest will be easy'; that empowered teachers educate empowered children; that the teacher–student relationship should be one of mutual respect; and that

> We have to share ideas, we have to share things, we have to share space, we have to share thinking, thoughts, feelings . . . education is building relationships.

Where the Russian and French teachers spoke of 'dialogue' (meaning direct instruction through question-and-answer designed partly to check information recall but also to scaffold pupils' understanding from one stage of learning to the next) the Michigan teachers commended the more democratic and demotic 'conversation'. This distinction is of considerable significance, and we shall return to it, via the classroom discourse extracts, in Chapter 16. Both groups of teachers held that the role of talk in learning was fundamental, but the versions of talk that they espoused and fostered were poles apart.

Some of the Michigan lessons therefore trod a narrow path between openness and closure. All the teachers planned in considerable detail, often breaking a semester's work into units of a few weeks and usually working with colleagues teaching the same grades. Yet this collegially inspired predictability had also to accommodate the unexpected, and several teachers emphasized the element of improvization, of 'feeling my way' even within a predetermined lesson sequence. The tensions this provoked were similar to those we identified with English primary teachers during the mid 1980s, who sought to combine structure with openness and flexibility, and advance planning with on-the-spot creativity.[17]

So lesson planning concentrated on devising a lesson's central unitary task or tasks, assembling the resources which teacher and pupils would need and ensuring that the organizational contingencies of 'centre-based teaching' were attended to, rather than, as in Russia, determining a lesson's precise sequence of events. That sequence was more loosely shaped, and 'structure' meant not lesson steps or stages but those punctuating activities which in other contexts might seem extraneous to the task in hand, but which here, because there was no externally imposed timetable, provided the necessary boundaries. In Russia or India the boundaries were set by clock and bell, but in one such Michigan classroom:

> Everything is pretty standardized and structured. We start off the day with the lunch count, then have our journal, then go into reading. Then we have the Pledge, the weather and the calendar. Then back to our reading, then after that we have snack and recess. Then we come back for an hour of math. It's very structured.

I would not wish to give the impression of uniformity of either values or practice among the Michigan teachers. Although the dominant values among this group were those that I have summarized, the autonomy they enjoyed also encouraged variety and eclecticism. In each of the four lessons which we observed being taught by the Hawthorne Elementary School teacher whose mathematics lesson appears as example 11.11, the instructional sequence was compact and the teacher's language was succinct and deliberate rather than extended and informal. In the particular sense that she set up *dialogue* rather than *conversation*, as distinguished above, her lessons had more in common with some observed in France than with – for example – the illustrated lessons of her compatriots at Emerson (11.10) and Thoreau (11.12).

I have suggested elsewhere that every teaching strategy has three distinct yet interconnected components: *organization*, *discourse* and *values*.[18] Teachers organize space, time, pupils and materials in particular ways to achieve particular purposes; to convey and exchange the meanings in which learning deals they deploy and encourage speaking, reading and writing of different kinds and in more or less appropriate registers; and through such organization and discourse they convey values about both the formal content of a lesson and a much wider array of human concerns or conditions, including learning, knowing, achieving, failing, behaving, relating and, indeed, being. In most of the Russian lessons, the three components seemed to be held in equilibrium, all focussed on the task in hand. But in some of the Michigan lessons, organization not only seemed subsidiary to the other two (which is perhaps as it should be) but also in constant peril of being subverted by them.

Perhaps this observation is merely ethnocentric, which brings us to the question of why the English lessons were structured as they were. In the cases of the Numeracy and Literacy Hours, the answer is obvious enough: government diktat informed by an unfocused faith in the efficacy of mid-European and/or eastern Asian pedagogy and – in the case of the literacy hour – a theory of language and language teaching which includes a rather over-accentuated distinction between word, sentence and text but is otherwise somewhat elusive.[19]

For the rest, the situation is both like and unlike what we found in Michigan. I argued in Chapter 6 that the legacy and abiding influence of nineteenth century elementary education are apparent in six aspects of English primary education as it stands at the start of the twenty-first century: funding, ages and stages, the class teacher system, the curriculum as a whole, the prevailing concept of curricular 'basics', and the position of religion and religious education.

Pedagogy does not appear in this list, for it is in the area of pedagogy that English primary schools sought to make their most conscious break with their elementary forbears. As Blyth notes, when at the end of the nineteenth century Herbartianism began to provide lesson models for the training of secondary teachers, primary teacher trainers looked instead to Rousseau, Pestalozzi and Froebel.[20] Subsequently, Montessori's principles of 'scientific pedagogy' and her view of the classroom as a 'prepared learning environment' provided inspiration for the growing early years movement.[21] The ideological and methodological divergence between the two phases of compulsory schooling in England was therefore profound. Secondary teaching developed in a way that was closer to mainstream European lines, emphasizing the timetable, lesson structure, the logical imperatives of the subject taught, and the expository task of the teacher. From the 1930s onwards, and especially during the period 1965–90, English primary teaching detached itself from this tradition, emphasizing temporal and spatial fluidity, the psychological imperatives of development, the uniqueness of the individual, the child's active agency in his or her learning, the holistic nature of knowledge and the teacher's task as facilitator.

Where lesson structure was concerned the ideology created a vacuum, or rather the notion of structure in teaching itself became suspect. Just as subjects 'compartmentalized' knowledge and understanding, so lessons – emblematized for generations of primary teachers by the tyrannical bell of the old elementary school – constrained the proper freedoms of youthful learning and enquiry.

The vacuum was filled during the middle and later decades of the twentieth century by a variety of more or less homespun theories which sought to provide a basis for organizing the curriculum and the school day without contravening the essential unity of time, knowledge and children's development.[22] Timetables became minimal, teaching focused on inclusive themes rather than exclusive subjects, and in the classrooms themselves the unities expressed themselves, paradoxically, in spatial fragmentation: areas or 'bays' were dedicated to different areas of the curriculum (similar to the 'teaching centres' we found in several of the Michigan classrooms) and children moved between these either freely or regularly in accordance with the principles of the 'integrated' or 'flexible' day (the practice generically termed 'multiple curriculum focus' teaching).[23] Some of the variants were very local, and a teacher moving from one LEA to another during the 1960s, the 1970s and the 1980s needed quickly to learn whether the new LEA had views on these matters and, if so, what ways of organizing space, time and the curriculum were acceptable to those on whose approval and patronage they depended.

On to this was grafted, from 1988, a national curriculum. Haltingly at first, then more assertively, subject boundaries returned.[24] Timetabling and systematic planning became essential if schools were to achieve national curriculum attainment targets and secure good results for their pupils (and their schools) in national tests. Subject programmes of study were not readily compatible with multiple curriculum focus teaching, although teachers could sustain the practice in more restricted form by having groups simultaneously pursue different foci *within* subjects. On the other hand, a national curriculum had no obvious implications for lesson structure, and this is why, apart from the literacy and numeracy hours, most of the lessons we observed retained structural characteristics inherited or retained from the 1970s and the 1980s.

But professional consciousness *had* changed. Those English teachers we interviewed whose formative professional experiences had been acquired before 1988 admitted to becoming less idealistic and more pragmatic. In terms of the triumvirate introduced above (organization, discourse and values), values now mattered less, organization more. The extremes of decentralization and centralization were taking the American and English teachers, and the lessons they taught, in very different directions.

Lesson Structure, Form and Meaning: towards a Complementary Analysis

I took the lesson as the starting point for our comparative analysis of pedagogy not just because for teachers and children it is what most familiarly and universally frames their daily experience of schooling, but also because it tends to be neglected in classroom research. Whether we are looking to educational research in order to *understand* teaching or for guidance on how to *improve* it, merely to identify lists of factors which correlate with others – even if those others include successful learning – is a bit like tipping the 400 pieces of a jigsaw puzzle on to the table and taking away the box whose picture is the key to how the pieces should be reassembled.

I identified the balance and character of the different stages into which the exemplified lessons seem to fall and extended the analysis to include the full range of observed lessons in each country. I then showed how these structures could be

illuminated by reference to the constraints and opportunities of time and to culturally specific traditions and theories of teaching and learning.

However, I am aware that although I have used the concept of structure loosely,
to signify the relationship of the parts to the whole, this tantalizingly divorces
structure from function and meaning. This anomaly will be corrected when, in
Chapters 15 and 16, we examine the interactions and discourse through which, in
these classrooms, meanings were conveyed and exchanged. But the structures of
pedagogical language and linguistic exchange are not the same as the larger structures of the lessons within which such language arises, and it is possible to argue
that lesson structures convey their own meanings, and that some lesson structures
convey meaning, or certain kinds of meaning, more effectively than others.

There is a further problem. 'Structure' defines and describes objects which can be
viewed as finished and assembled, but although teachers and pupils experience the
complete lesson they do so only as it unfolds, moment by moment. They can never
hold it up and view it in its entirety. Only the researcher armed with a video cassette
recorder can do that, and videotapes, like transcripts and field notes, provide images
of the lesson, viewed from a particular standpoint, not the lesson itself. The nearest
the teacher comes to such a perspective is, through the lesson plan, in anticipation
of the event.

As one does, I have searched for metaphors and analogies to help me with these
problems. How do you hold a lesson up for inspection without turning it into
something else? The concept of *form* is an alternative to structure – in the sense not
of outward shape but of the principles which determine that shape.[25] Form opens
up some new possibilities: we can look for organizing principles as well as the
(mechanical) components implied by 'structure'; we can add the prefix per- and
through *performance* engage the action in teaching as well as the structure (this
is sleight of hand, since etymologically 'perform' and 'form' probably have no connection); and we can come at the debate about teaching as science/art/craft from
another angle – the science of the art rather than the art of the science. Form is in
important artistic concept. There are art forms, and there are forms within each art
form, but the art form that to me offers the greatest potential to illuminate the
structure-in-action of teaching is music, for teaching, like music, is *performance*.

That performance can be preceded by *composition* (lesson planning) and in execution is thus an *interpretation*, or it can be partly or completely *improvisatory*.[26]
Russian lessons by and large remained faithful to the *score*, and those scores/plans
were fully orchestrated, down to the length of time to be devoted to each *movement*/episode and the names of the orchestra *players*/pupils who would be called
upon by the *conductor*/teacher (who was also the *composer*) to come to the blackboard and perform a *solo*. The lessons with long unitary central episodes, especially
in England and Michigan, had plans which were sometimes suggestive or in outline
only, and teachers *extemporized* upon them as on a *figured bass*.

For the music/dance lesson at Purana school in Delhi the musical analogy is
doubly apt: the children were exploring the tension between improvisation and
form in music itself, and the teacher was doing likewise with the 30-minute lesson
form to which her teaching was confined.

The performance of teaching can be in planning *orchestrated* and in execution *conducted* – with varying degrees of competence and persuasiveness, with participants staying together or losing their way, and with consequences which may move, excite, bore or alienate. In both its planning and execution teaching is bounded and constrained, as is music, by *time*, which far from being a one-dimensional measure as implied by that familiar variable 'time on task' is in fact many-faceted.

Time in teaching comprises the overall *time intended* and *actual time spent*, both of which we considered earlier. But lessons also have their internal time: *pulse*, *tempo* or speed, and *rhythm*. In Chapter 15, comparisons of the internal time of lessons, which I have anticipated through the examples of written composition at Ogden Primary (11.14) and Kursk School B (11.8), will lead me to argue that the critical temporal variable in teaching may well be not *absolute time* (time intended and spent, or 'opportunity to learn'). This view, or fixation, leads governments to presume that the more time a subject is allocated, and the more homework children do, the more they will learn – hence the UK government's 1997 decree that unless children spend two hours a day on literacy and numeracy and a given proportion of each evening on homework, standards will surely fall and the British economy will go into terminal decline. Instead I shall want to draw attention to the *internal time* of a lesson, its *tempo* or *pace*, or its ratio of time taken to content encountered.

Allied to tempo are *dynamics*, that subtle admixture of intensity and mood which generates (or destroys) the energy and commitment which children give to the task in hand. More of these when we look at classroom interaction in Chapters 16 and 17.

Similarly, a lesson can be dominated by one or more clearly discernible *themes*, *melodic lines* or indeed *leitmotifs*. Teachers frequently talk of lesson 'themes' when they are planning, in a general rather than a musical sense, and the two are not the same. Musical themes are configurations of notes that assume particular importance in a movement or composition and may reappear at various points modified, inverted or transfigured, but always in a way that contributes to compositional unity. Some teachers, notably in Russia and India, used thematic reiteration in this way. Leimotifs, or explicit 'teaching points' have already been illustrated – the repeated 'problem, solution, explanation' in the Thoreau mathematics lesson, for example.

Themes and lines can be *harmonically* sustained or they can be woven together in a *contrapuntal* relationship; or the lesson can descend into cacophony. Again, to develop this point is to anticipate later discussion, but I have already hinted that a characteristic of some of the American lessons was the relatively large number of ideas, values, messages and activities to which the children had to attend and which the teacher as conductor had somehow to keep in equilibrium.

The whole is bounded by *form* – and in teaching, as in music, there are many forms, from the single, long, loose programmatic movement preceded by a brief task-setting introduction and followed by a short or long conclusion – such as we found in some lessons in England and Michigan – to the formal episodic structure of the classic central European lesson plan. Here we may find the *simple binary form* of the short lesson at Juan-le-Grand (11.1), or – stretching the metaphor a bit, perhaps, but not too far – something approach *ternary* or *compound binary form* in the Russian lessons. Lessons were framed by *introduction* and *recapitulation* and might be punctuated by *rondo-form* recalls of the theme or themes. Some lessons, having completed their formal treatment of the thematic material, had a *coda*. (Some even had *intervals* to allow the audience – or were they the performers? – to marshall their energies. This being a cross-cultural study, we might care to note that there was candy in the Michigan interval but physical exercise in the Russian one.)

Beyond form in this sense are the larger musical structures and genres, and we have in our data exemplifications of lessons orchestrated and conducted as *operatic* episodes (in the Russian village school) and in India lessons which ritualized their pupil–teacher interaction as *antiphony*.

If this were merely an exercise in analogy it would be interesting but little else. However, I find the perspective genuinely useful for tackling the problem of relating the parts and the whole as I have outlined it. Especially, I find that *form* in its artistic sense illuminates the relationship between the structure and organization of teaching and its meaning; that *tempo* takes us beyond the familiar process variables of 'time for learning', 'opportunity to learn' and 'pupil time on task'; while *melody*, *harmony*, *polyphony* and *counterpoint* help us to unravel the way the messages of teaching – whether explicit or implicit, congruent or incongruent, are developed and relate to each other over the course of a single lesson. For this, the musical metaphor is a useful adjunct to the more commonly evoked dramatic distinction between *text* and *subtext* (in the same way my use of musical form can usefully be set against visual-spatial principles like *proportion* and *perspective*).

Together, these concepts also help us to unpack some of the differences between the lessons observed and recorded in the five countries. Thus, there is a clear contrast in the data between on the one hand those lessons whose themes will vary from one lesson to the next but whose length, tempo and form remain predictably and reliably the same (as in Russia, India and sometimes in France), and on the other hand those lessons which pursue the more ambitious but risky strategy of multiple and even conflicting themes within a many-layered structure and a rambling timeframe, sometimes succeeding because of the skilful way they are orchestrated and conducted, sometimes losing pace, coherence and the attention of the pupils (as in England, Michigan and sometimes, again, in France).

Again, risking comparison across the five cultures, the form of the lessons we observed became more variable and unpredictable as we moved West, or – possibly – belief in the importance of form diminished as we moved further away from Central Europe. Moreover – and this is perhaps where this kind of analysis can engage usefully with school effectiveness research – the increased variability was at two distinct levels: of *organization* and of *message* and *meaning*.

Let me elaborate this notion of layered complexity. In no lesson that I have ever observed is there not a powerful sub-theme of values relating to, for example: the extent to which knowledge is open or bounded, provisional or uncontestable; how ideas should be handled; the kinds of authority the teacher and the curriculum embody; how individuals and groups should relate to each other; and what counts as success in learning. However, we found four sharp contrasts across classrooms and cultures in respect of such message systems.

First and most obviously and predictably, they differed in their substance. Knowledge, the teacher's authority and so on were viewed and presented very differently in different cultural contexts. Second, they differed in the relative emphasis given to subject matter and affective and behavioural issues. Third, they differed in the extent to which such messages were either secure, and therefore implicit, or they were less secure and therefore perforce explicit and frequently reiterated. Finally, they differed in the manner in which the messages were conveyed.

In respect of the last two, the sharpest contrasts, as in so much else, were between most of the Russian lessons and some of the Michigan ones. In the one context the substantive messages about the nature of knowledge, teaching and learning and about behavioural norms and expectations were unambiguous yet also – bar the occasional brief reminder – tacit; in the other context they were the subject of frequent reminders by the teacher and sometimes intense encounters ranging from negotiation to confrontation.

In this a reader may wish to detect a contrast between lately abandoned totalitarianism and the confusions of the world's most self-conscious democracy. However, when I add that the Michigan classrooms also exhibited the greatest organizational complexity, we can see how this kind of analysis can refresh the parts of teaching which process–product and school effectiveness research cannot reach. Here we had a combination of organizational complexity and a contrapuntal and occasionally even cacophonous message system, with classroom exchanges veering back and forth between negotiation over the learning task and negotiation over behaviour, and some marked inconsistencies between each. It was not – as usually argued – the organizational structure *per se* which led to the general lack of pace in learning and the high levels of pupil distraction that we observed in some of the Michigan lessons, but the high level of negotiation to which the teachers were committed, and the consequently problematic and confusing nature of the messages which were sometimes conveyed. The organizational complexity simply exacerbated this.

All this, however, is to anticipate the next few chapters, but I hope that by doing so I have encouraged sceptical readers willingly to suspend their disbelief for a while longer. I hope also that the analysis confirms that the whole and the parts, structure and action, form and meaning should be kept in equilibrium; and that one is not necessarily more important than another. My excursion into musical form hints at a way of analysing teaching that is complementary to those with which we are more familiar, not dismissive of them.

There is a more fundamental case for treating this line of analysis as other than peripheral. It is hardly a coincidence that Central Europe has been a centre of gravity for both musical and pedagogical form. It is not implausible to suggest that cultures which responded to the imperatives of form in realms as diverse as music, art, literature, drama, architecture, philosophy, mathematics and science, might have applied that consciousness to education, a contingent field in which many of the great figures in these fields have had a more than passing interest.

However, in a book that encompasses India and southern Russia as well as Western Europe and North America, some may view this line of speculation as dangerously ethnocentric. It is one thing to invoke the *generalities* of artistic form as a way of

he 'comprehensive model' which informs school effectiveness research, then, is
her comprehensive nor a model. It is merely a list whose purpose teeters be-
en description and prescription when it needs to provide, unambiguously, one
he other. It does not and cannot, include everything that needs to be contained
hin a meaningful account of effective education. It provides no indication of how
ooling and teaching actually work, with the result that the path from effective-
s factor to educational action remains obscure.

n fact, if we return to the American roots of this research we find that syntheses
h as those provided by Dunkin and Biddle nearly three decades ago are rather
arer on this score. They propose a model in which presage variables ('teacher
mative experiences', 'teacher training experiences', 'teacher properties') and con-
t variables ('pupil formative experiences', 'pupil properties', 'school and com-
nity contexts', 'classroom contexts') interact with classroom variables ('teacher
ssroom behaviour', 'pupil classroom behaviour', 'observable changes in pupil
aviour') to yield product variables ('immediate pupil growth', 'long-term pupil
cts'). However, they make it clear that theirs is a model for the *study* of teach-
, not a model of teaching itself.[10]

These comments were prompted by the question which this chapter's first few
agraphs begged but did not explicitly pose: what *are* the elements in teaching
ich most merit our attention in a cross-cultural study of pedagogy, and how
they best be presented within a coherent model of teaching? Process–product
earch, of which school effectiveness research is an normative offshoot, offers a
ma facie way forward in that it has a rationale for the selection which it makes
ong the many possibilities, namely that the elements chosen are those which
relate with gains in pupil learning. But as a path to a broader understanding of
character of teaching as a particular kind of human activity it takes us only so
, as do all frameworks which merely differentiate categories of variables, whether
sage, context, process or outcome, but leave unexamined the question of how
se are reconstituted as real-time teaching.

We need, then, a framework for anatomizing teaching which keeps faith with the
listic principle advanced in the previous two chapters, is appropriate to our task
comparing pedagogy across cultures, makes conceptual sense, but is also recog-
able to those who observe and experience it, wherever they may be.

n two separate classroom studies Wragg cites the model of Johnson and
ooks in which teaching (which they define here as 'classroom management') is
scribed as

. . . that organizational function that requires teachers to perform *various tasks* [eight
are specified] involving the manipulation of certain *variable elements* [six are specified]
in a variety of *settings* [six examples are given] in the furtherance of certain *values*
[again, there are six] through the resolution of a number of *tensions* [they list six
tensions within school and between school and the outside world] that differ in nature
and seriousness according to *situational factors* [six again, relating to goals, pupils and
context] in ways influenced by the school's and the teacher's *ideological stance* [three
orientations listed].[11]

illuminating the structure of lessons, but to apply the particularities of ternary,
rondo or fugal form may seem to verge on cultural imperialism. What pedagogical
parallels might we find, for instance, if we were to take the raga as our starting
point for investigating lesson structure not just in India, but in other countries too?

There are three points to make in response to this objection. First, it does not
invalidate the application of those elements such as rhythm, pace, dynamics and
so on which are universal, albeit specific to time and place in they way they are
manifested and used. Second, when we come to the specifics, there is no disputing
the fact that the central European tradition of pedagogy had a reach and influence
in Western education (including both the United States and, by way of Germany,
Russia) which was comparable to the impact of the central European classical tradition in music on the development of Western music as a whole. Third, while Western music made limited headway in India – Indian music, like Indian sculpture, is so
vibrant and massively rooted in that subcontinent's history that Western music
would have had little impact anyway – Western pedagogy was in contrast a wholly
deliberate export. In this matter the reference to cultural imperialism is apt, for in
colonial India the British used both curriculum and pedagogy as instruments of
cultural domination. In India, our attempts to understand primary school pedagogy
as a cultural artefact must continue to focus on the collision or interweaving of
indigenous, colonial and post-independence pedagogic forms, and the evidence from
the *Five Cultures* data, as from other sources, is that all three continue to be discernible in modern classroom practice.

Finally, there is a more general point to be made about the origins of educational
ideas and practices. We are familiar with the resonances and explicit connections in
European pedagogy of Bacon, Locke, Hume, Kant and Descartes. We can trace the
impact on educational thought of great intellectual movements like the Renaissance
and the Enlightenment. In English primary education we recognize the resonances
of classicism and romanticism, especially the latter, and of the perennial tension
between imposed order and 'natural' growth.[27] In the present case we can also
perceive the contrasting educational legacies of Catholicism, Protestantism, Russian
Orthodoxy, Hinduism and communism. We note also the interventions of Tolstoy,
Tagore, Gandhi, Goethe, Milton and Coleridge alongside the more familiar figures
of Comenius, Rousseau, Pestalozzi, Herbart, Froebel, Dewey, Montessori, Piaget
and Vygotsky. The world of ideas is hugely complex, but it is also seamless.

When the definitive history of educational ideas comes to be written it will have
to engage with a canvas far broader than the usual pantheon of 'great educators'
and those interminable disputes about whether education is an art or a science
which forget where the arts and the sciences have come from.[28]

13

Organization, Task and Activity

Models of Teaching

I suggested in Chapter 11 that we shall reach a fuller understanding of teaching when we tip the balance of research attention somewhat and begin to attend to the whole as well as the parts. I then nominated the lesson as perhaps the most appropriate unit for holistic analysis and in Chapter 12 I compared lesson structure and form in the five countries studied and traced the historical and cultural origins of some the differences which emerged. Finally, I ventured a paradigm shift from the social sciences to the arts in order to find an alternative vocabulary for the analysis of form in teaching and to capture the elusive essence of the lesson as planned performance framed by time.

We turn now back from the whole to the parts. If, having defined what these parts or teaching elements are we reconstruct them as measurable variables, we can examine how at any one time a limited number of them interact.[1] If one of the variables is a measure of pupil learning outcomes, a mark gained in a test perhaps, and others are distilled from what teachers and pupils do in pursuit of such outcomes, there is a plausible basis for claims about the relative effectiveness of this or that aspect of teaching.

This is the essence of that process–product pedagogical research in which the United States has been been pre-eminent and which Wragg traces back to the 1920s or even earlier.[2] (In Britain, as it happens, recent research within this paradigm has been confined mainly to the primary sector).[3] It is also the route to exercises in aggregation and synthesis along the lines of OFSTED's 'eleven factors for effective schools'[4] or the 48-factor 'comprehensive model of educational effectiveness' constructed by Creemers and his colleagues.[5]

The OFSTED list extracts from its review of mainly US and British research classroom-level factors such as 'orderly atmosphere', 'attractive working environment', 'maximization of learning time', 'academic emphasis', 'focus on achievement', 'efficient organization', 'clarity of purpose', 'structured lessons', 'adaptive practice', 'high expectations', 'intellectual challenge', 'clear and fair discipline', 'monitoring

pupil performance' and 'feedback'. Creemers provides a fuller list up[...] an attempt to create a coherent model of educational effectiveness, he [...] four 'levels' – *context*, *school*, *classroom* and *student* – and three rec[...] meative principles: 'quality', 'time' and 'opportunity'. Creemers gives [...] to his principle of quality at the classroom level, identifying 25 'quali[...] tion' factors under the headings of 'curriculum', 'grouping procedures[...] behaviour', and setting these alongside 'time for learning' and 'o[...] learn'.

Wragg cites Philip Jackson's warning that some correlational effecti[...] are 'so low in intellectual food value that it is almost embarrassing to d[...] and there are obvious dangers in aggregating the findings of rese[...] which have been conducted in different countries and school conte[...] necessarily compatible measures and yielding correlations of unsp[...] doubt varying orders of magnitude. Even the OECD, which in its pu[...] ators of educational and economic success is generally eager to quanti[...] of education it can identify, warns policy-makers against excessive a[...] effectiveness studies can be sustained in the face of this kind of crit[...] should take seriously their claim to provide a first-order list of [...] elements which most merit attention in empirical study, profession[...] strategies for school improvement.

A research-based list of this sort would include the following: h[...] content is structured and presented; how pupils are grouped and[...] which such grouping allows for co-operative learning; how effici[...] events are managed; the way time is used so as to maximize both pu[...] ity to learn and the time they spend on task; the range and clarity [...] lesson goals; the degree to which the teacher maintains a consiste[...] basic skills, cognitive learning and learning transfer; the quality of[...] tion procedures such as questioning and explaining; the timing a[...] feedback to pupils on work undertaken, and the transition from[...] feedback to the immediate rectification of pupils' mistakes and misu[...]

Many of these factors have common-sense validity. But is this t[...] I neither wish nor need to repeat the reservations which I set out [...] or my objections to exercises in process–product correlation such a[...] during the 1990s caused the UK government and OFSTED to ele[...] whole class teaching' to the status of pedagogical panacea and seek[...] every primary teacher in the land. It *is* necessary to repeat here, h[...] elements of teaching which feature in frameworks such as those[...] rather more arbitrary than they may seem. For the items in Creen[...] are an undifferentiated mixture of what he sees as desirable in t[...] process–product research has demonstrated empirically. While th[...] of them, can claim the status of factors in educational effectivenes[...] options are no more or less convincing and complete than wh[...] teaching has spawned them.[9] Moreover, the factors that *can* lay c[...] in the model on empirical rather than theoretical grounds may[...] reason other than that they are technically amenable to statistical[...]

This injects into the debate a recognition that lurking behind the itemized behavioural and organizational factors and the anodyne and apparently unproblematic 'policies', and 'rules and agreements about classroom instruction' in the school effectiveness prospectus are values and value-tensions that teaching by its nature exposes and with which teachers somehow have to deal. Yet it falls at the level of detail because for every task, element, setting, value, tension, situational factor and ideological stance which Johnson and Brooks itemize, one can nominate several others. It is thus difficult to know whether the 'elements' and 'factors' in their model are comprehensive or merely illustrative.

Keep It Simple?

Perhaps the real problem is that in striving to construct a comprehensive model of teaching we seek what is either unattainable or, if attainable, may be so convoluted as to be unusable. Some years ago the anthropologist Edmund Leach argued that the more complex the model, the less likely it is to serve a useful descriptive or explanatory function.[12] His precept was: keep it simple; and use terms, draw analogies and define structures with discrimination so as to stay as close as possible to everyday understanding and action. Leach's plea for simplicity applied to the creation of *descriptive* models. With *prescriptive* models, however – those which are intended to be translated into a course of action – he suggested that the most effective models are also likely to be the most complicated, because they have to engage in a convincing way with real-life contingencies and with what cannot be predicted as well as with what can. In the light of this we might conclude that some models of teaching may fall between two stools in that they are too complex to provide illumination, but not detailed enough to provide a guide to practical action.

For the purposes of making sense of our cross-cultural classroom data, the task is descriptive rather than prescriptive. With Leach in mind, then, let us start by reducing teaching to its barest essentials:

- Teaching, in any setting, is the act of using method x to enable pupils to learn y.

In so skeletal a form the proposition is difficult to contest, and if this is so we may extract from it two no less basic questions to steer empirical enquiry:

(1) What are pupils expected to learn?
(2) What method does the teacher use to ensure that they do so?

For all that in teacher training programmes 'method' has common currency, in the UK it is rarely explicated and therefore means in practice what individual proponents of 'method' wish it to mean. We need to unpack it a little if it is to be useful as an analytical category which is able to cross the boundaries of context and culture. A teaching method, I would suggest, combines *tasks, activities, interactions* and *judgements*. Their function can be represented by four further questions:

(3) In a given teaching session or unit what *learning tasks* do pupils encounter?
(4) What *activities* do they undertake in order to address these learning tasks?
(5) Through what *interactions* does the teacher present, organize and sustain the learning tasks and activities?
(6) By what means, and on the basis of what criteria, does the teacher reach *judgements* about the nature and level of the tasks and activities which each pupil shall undertake (*differentiation*), and the kinds of learning which pupils achieve (*assessment*)?

Task, activity, interaction and judgement are the building-blocks. However, as they stand they lack the wherewithal for coherence and meaning. To our first proposition, therefore, we must add a second, and this unpacks 'in any setting', the other question-begging phrase in our definition:

• Teaching has structure and form; it is situated in, and governed by, space, time and patterns of pupil organization; and it is undertaken for a purpose.

Structure and form in teaching are most clearly and distinctively manifested in the *lesson*. Lessons and their constituent teaching acts are framed and governed by *time*, by *space* (the way the classroom is disposed, organized and resourced) and by the chosen forms of *pupil organization* (whole class, small group or individual).

But teaching is framed conceptually and ethically, as well as temporally and spatially. A lesson is part of a larger *curriculum* that includes both established subjects and domains of understanding which are not subject specific. Curriculum embodies purposes and values, and reflects assumptions about what knowledge and understanding are of most worth to the individual and to society. That is why governments are so interested in it, and why in decentralized or recently decentralized systems curriculum is so strongly contested. This is part of the force of 'teaching . . . is undertaken for a purpose'.

The other part comprises the purposes which are injected into the teaching act by teachers and indeed pupils. In management-speak curriculum takes just one form. It is prescribed, then implemented. In the equivalent UK government-speak it is 'delivered'. The curriculum is a package, the teacher is a postman, and the classroom is the 'point of delivery'.[13] If the package looks different at the point of delivery then it is for agents of quality control to bring the teacher–postman into line. This model grossly simplifies reality, but so too does the reproduction theorist's view of teaching as simple 'transmission' of the values of the state apparatus. Neither takes sufficient account of problems of agency.[14] For our purposes I suggest that we view curriculum as undergoing a sequence of transformations as it progresses from published document to school syllabus and teacher plan, and thence to lesson, task, activity and interaction. The final and most important act of curriculum transformation takes place inside the pupil's head. This transformative process is both inevitable and necessary, for a document expresses curriculum as an abstract generality only. We return to the idea of curriculum metamorphosis in Chapter 17.

There is one more element to put in place. Teaching in classrooms is not a series of one-off encounters. Teachers spend a great deal of time with the same class, and indeed primary teachers spend a whole year and sometimes several years (in Russia many of the teachers we interviewed stayed with their classes for the entire primary stage and thus planned and taught a three-year span of their education). Together with pupils teachers create and become incorporated within a microculture. This allows teachers to make many aspects of teaching and learning habitual in order to achieve economy of effort and efficiency in the use of space, time and resources. The evolution of the classroom microculture also allows – indeed requires – them to develop procedures for regulating the complex dynamics of pupil–pupil relationships, the equivalent of law, custom, convention and public morality in civil society. Further, teachers and teaching convey messages and values which may reach well beyond those of the particular learning tasks that give a lesson its formal focus. This element we can define as *routine, rule* and *ritual*.

Frame	Form	Act
Space		Task
Pupil organization		Activity
Time	Lesson	
Curriculum		Interaction
Routine, rule and ritual		Judgement

Figure 13.1   An action-based framework for the analysis of teaching

The complete framework is shown in Figure 13.1. The elements are grouped under the headings of *frame, form* and *act*. The core acts of teaching (task, activity, interaction and judgement) are framed by classroom organization (space), pupil organization, time and curriculum and by classroom routines, rules and rituals. They are given form in the lesson or teaching session.

Building on the system-level comparisons of curriculum in Chapters 2–6, the school-level accounts of time and space in Chapter 8, and the classroom-level analysis of lesson structure and form in Chapter 12, we shall examine the framework's remaining elements in the chapters which follow. Ideally, they should discussed within a single chapter to emphasize their interdependence, or they should have a chapter each so as not to imply that the relationship between the juxtaposed elements is more significant than that between those which are separated. Logic, however, is compromised by logistics, and instead the elements are spread across five chapters. These should be read as a sequence, but not too much should be inferred from the order in which they have been placed.

Classroom Organization: Space, Resources and Grouping

In Chapter 8 we compared the spatial features of schools in the five countries, and because one can hardly discuss the geography of a school without describing its

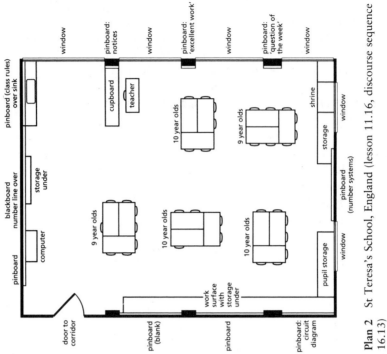

Plan 2 St Teresa's School, England (lesson 11.16, discourse sequence 16.13)

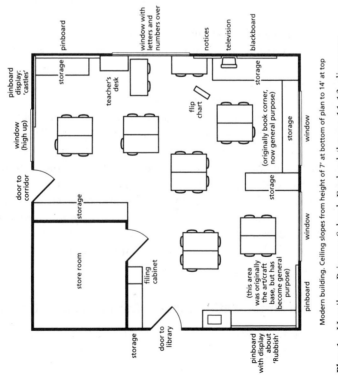

Modern building. Ceiling slopes from height of 7' at bottom of plan to 14' at top

Plan 1 Hamilton Primary School, England (lesson 11.13, discourse sequence 16.11)

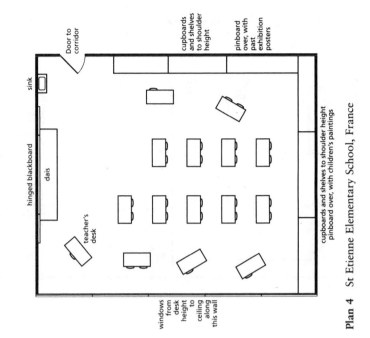

Plan 4 St Etienne Elementary School, France

windows from desk height to ceiling along this wall

teacher's desk

hinged blackboard

dais

sink

Door to corridor

cupboards and shelves to shoulder height

pinboard over, with past exhibition posters

cupboards and shelves to shoulder height
pinboard over, with children's paintings

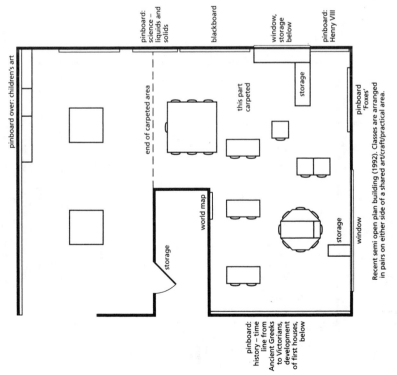

Plan 3 Cheetham School, England

pinboard over: children's art

pinboard: science – liquids and solids

blackboard

window, storage below

pinboard: Henry VIII

end of carpeted area

this part carpeted

storage

storage

world map

window

pinboard 'Foxes'

Recent semi open plan building (1992). Classes are arranged in pairs on either side of a shared art/craft/practical area.

pinboard: history – time line from Ancient Greeks to Victorians, development of first houses, below

storage

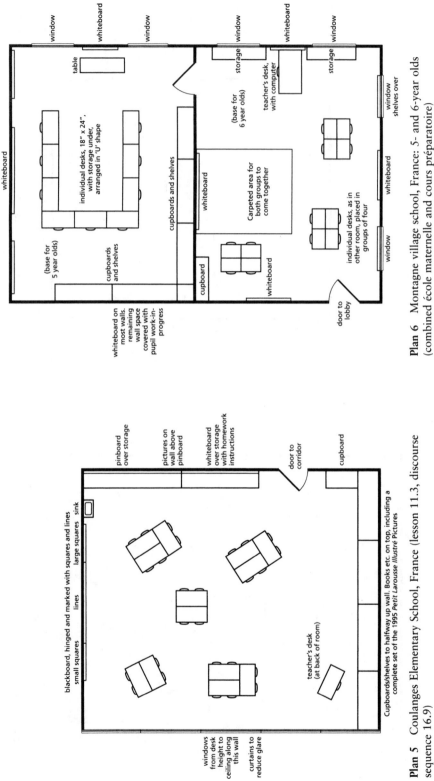

Plan 5 Coulanges Elementary School, France (lesson 11.3, discourse sequence 16.9)

Plan 6 Montagne village school, France: 5- and 6-year olds (combined école maternelle and cours préparatoire)

Plan 5 labels:

blackboard, hinged and marked with squares and lines

small squares lines large squares sink

windows from desk height to ceiling along this wall

curtains to reduce glare

teacher's desk (at back of room)

pinboard over storage

pictures on wall above pinboard

whiteboard over storage with homework instructions

door to corridor

cupboard

Cupboards/shelves to halfway up wall. Books etc. on top, including a complete set of the 1995 *Petit Larousse Illustré Pictures*

Plan 6 labels:

window whiteboard window whiteboard window

window storage teacher's desk, with computer window storage

whiteboard

table

individual desks, 18" x 24", with storage under, arranged in 'U' shape

(base for 5 year olds)

cupboards and shelves

whiteboard on most walls. remaining wall space covered with pupil work-in-progress

cupboards and shelves

cupboard

whiteboard

(base for 6 year olds)

whiteboard

Carpeted area for both groups to come together

window shelves over

whiteboard

window

individual desks, as in other room, placed in groups of four

door to lobby

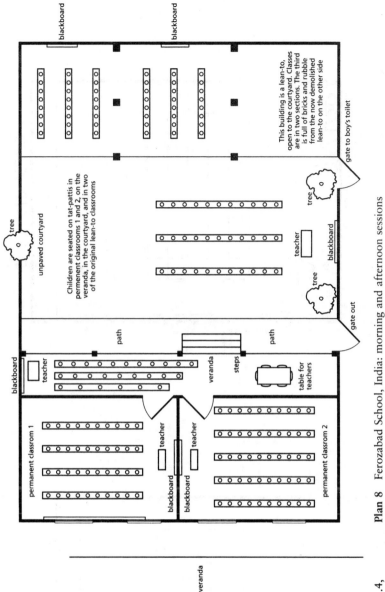

Within the plan (Plan 8):

blackboard

blackboard

This building is a lean-to, open to the courtyard. Classes are in two sections. The third is full of bricks and rubble from the now demolished lean-to on the other side

gate to boy's toilet

tree

unpaved courtyard

Children are seated on tat-pattis in permenent classrooms 1 and 2, on the veranda, in the courtyard, and in two of the original lean-to classrooms

tree

teacher

blackboard

tree

gate out

path

path

veranda

steps

blackboard

teacher

table for teachers

permanent classrom 1

teacher

teacher

permanent classrom 2

blackboard

blackboard

Plan 8 Ferozabad School, India: morning and afternoon sessions

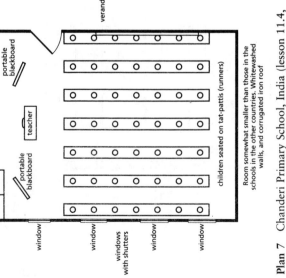

veranda

portable blackboard

blackboard

teacher

portable blackboard

cupboards charts over

children seated on tat-pattis (runners)

Room somewhat smaller than those in the schools in the other countries. Whitewashed walls, and corrugated iron roof

window

window

windows with shutters

window

window

Plan 7 Chanderi Primary School, India (lesson 11.4, discourse sequence 16.2)

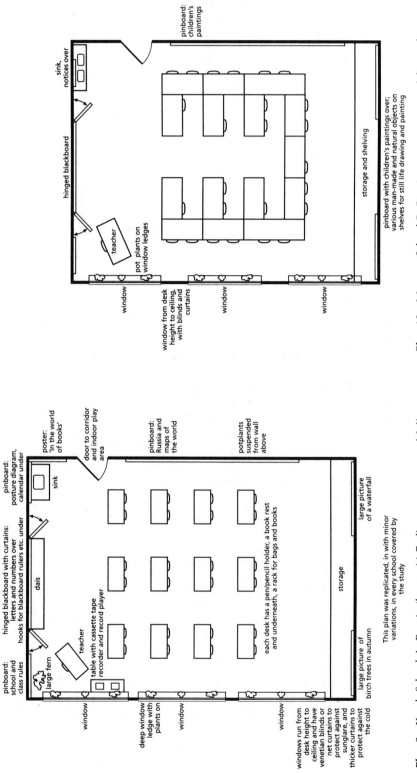

Plan 9 Kursk School A, Russia (lesson 11.7, discourse sequence 16.4)

pinboard:
school and
class rules

large fern

hinged blackboard with curtains:
letters and numbers over
hooks for blackboard rulers etc. under

dais

teacher

table with cassette tape
recorder and record player

pinboard:
posture diagram,
calendar under

sink

poster:
'in the world
of books'

door to corridor
and indoor play
area

pinboard:
Russia and
maps of
the world

potplants
suspended
from wall
above

each desk has a pen/pencil holder, a book rest
and underneath, a rack for bags and books

storage

large picture
of a waterfall

large picture
of birch trees in autumn

This plan was replicated, in with minor
variations, in every school covered by
the study

window

deep window
ledge with
plants on

window

window

windows run from
desk height to
ceiling and have
venetian blinds or
net curtains to
protect against
sunglare, and
thicker curtains to
protect against
the cold

Plan 10 Moscow School B, Russia: room re-arranged for art lesson

sink,
notices over

hinged blackboard

teacher

pot plants on
window ledges

storage and shelving

pinboard:
children's
paintings

pinboard with children's paintings over;
various man-made and natural objects on
shelves for still life drawing and painting

window

window from desk
height to ceiling,
with blinds and
curtains

window

window

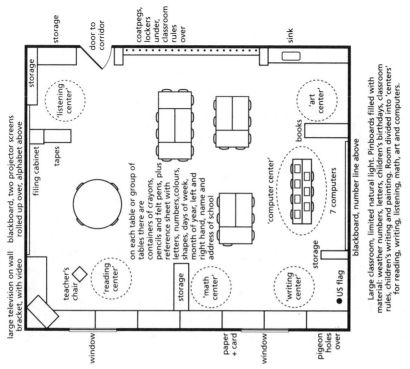

Plan 12 Emerson Elementary School, Michigan (lesson 11.10, discourse sequence 16.15)

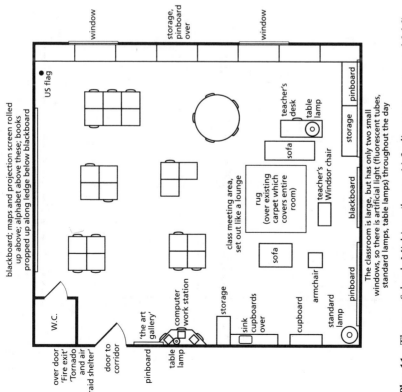

Plan 11 Thoreau School, Michigan (lesson 11.2, discourse sequence 16.16)

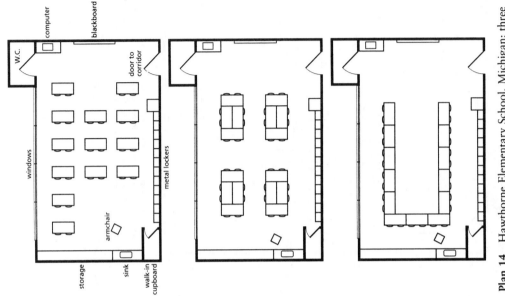

Plan 14 Hawthorne Elementary School, Michigan: three layouts, including that for lesson 11.11, discourse sequence 16.17 (middle plan)

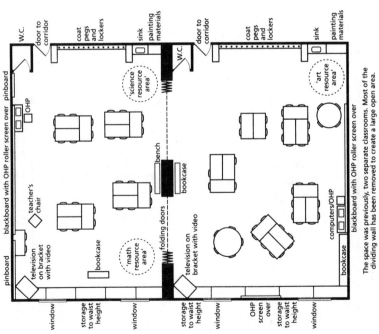

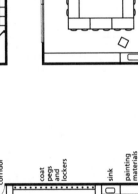

The space was previously, two separate classrooms. Most of the dividing wall has been removed to create a large open area.

Plan 13 Thoreau School Elementary, Michigan: multi-age class of 45 children (grades 2, 3 and 4) with four adults

classrooms we examined them there in some detail too. Here we are more interested in how teachers and pupils use the spaces within which they work. The discussion that follows is supported by the classroom plans in Figure 13.2.

In nearly all the classrooms the tables or desks (or in the case of India, where most classrooms had neither, the pupils) were arranged in either rows or groups. Where there were rows (Russia, India and sometimes France), these invariably faced a blackboard or whiteboard, and of course the teacher. In Chapter 8 we characterized the teaching *focus* suggested by these classroom layouts as *unitary*.

Where there were groups (England, Michigan and sometimes France) the focus was rather more ambiguous. Sometimes the collaborative seating arrangement disguised the fact that the pupils worked as a class, or as individuals within a class (rather than a group) and in such cases the focus was no less unitary than if the pupils had been seated in rows. Elsewhere, groups might be engaged in different activities ('multiple curriculum focus' teaching, as was common in England in the 1970s and the 1980s), and/or the classroom itself might be arranged so as to link particular sections of it with specific areas of the curriculum (curriculum 'bays' in England, 'teaching centres' in Michigan). In the latter cases we defined the focus as *multiple*. Generally, the French classrooms, whether their furniture was arranged in groups or rows, retained a unitary focus, while in England and Michigan we found examples of both unitary and multiple-focus classrooms.

Alongside the focus of classroom life, as this was signalled by the arrangement of furniture and the disposition of teachers and pupils, we found considerable contrast in classroom *ambience*. Wall-mounted materials ranged from sparse (India) to copious (Michigan and England) and they sought, variously, to encourage, instruct, decorate and display, generally becoming more diverse and flamboyant in style as one headed westwards from India through Russia, France and England to Michigan (Figure 13.3).

All this, together with the presence of furniture and equipment beyond the usual minimum of desks, blackboards and teaching aids, gave classrooms a pretty clear ambience even before lessons started. The classrooms in India, Russia and France were about work and work alone. Those in Michigan suggested work combined with leisure and pleasure. The English classrooms hovered somewhere between those extremes. To impute to the Michigan teachers an excessive concern for their pupils' leisure and pleasure may seem unfair: what these differences really suggest is

	Rules and reminders	Work-in-progress	Showcase
England		———————————————————————————
France	————————————————————		
India	———————		
Russia	———————————————		
USA	———————————————————————————————————————

Figure 13.3   Cross-cultural continua: functions of wall-mounted teaching materials

contrasting conceptions of what primary education – and young children's learning – are about.

Let us look at teachers' and pupils' use of space once the act of teaching introduces the dynamic of movement. Indian teaching remained at the extreme suggested by the pre-lesson layout. Pupils remained seated, one behind another, throughout most of the lessons we observed. They did so in practical lessons such as craft (designated 'work experience') as well as in the academic 'basics' of Hindi and mathematics. There was very little pupil–pupil discussion or collaboration, except when children voluntarily helped each other. A few of the lessons incorporated by design this latter-day version of the monitorial principle. The most significant breaks in the pattern occurred when children were called to the front of the classroom, singly, in pairs or as groups, to work at the blackboard or recite. Teachers, too, moved relatively little, remaining at the front of the room for most of each lesson and occasionally venturing between the rows of pupils to monitor written work.

Apart from the far higher level of resourcing, the most striking difference in the layout and use of space between the Indian and the Russian classrooms was that in the latter the pupils were placed in pairs rather than singly. It is sometimes presumed that seating children in rows dictates solitary working. In fact, several of the Russian teachers encouraged their pupils to work in pairs, and sometimes they explicitly required this, although paired activity never occupied more than a small proportion of lesson time. However, as we shall see when we look at teaching methods, the true ambience of the Russian classrooms was neither individualistic nor one-to-one collaborative, but *collective*. Pupils and teacher faced each other, maintained eye contact as far as with one adult and twenty-odd children this is possible, and such movement as occurred reinforced this ethic. Pupils stood up to answer questions, and did so not merely to the teacher but in declamatory style to the class as a whole. They came to front to explain how they had solved a problem, and did so, again, by facing the class rather than the teacher. They worked at the blackboard, and while doing this they spoke loudly and clearly so that all their peers could follow their reasoning and check it against theirs. As in India, the Russian teachers spent most of their time at the front of the room, although their monitoring of individual work was more extensive and sustained.

The only exceptions to the standard Russian layout which we observed were in lessons such as music or art. For music, pupils were more likely to be grouped in two or three semicircles, one behind the other. For art lessons, we saw the desks arranged as a horseshoe. This maintained the blackboard focus while permitting the sharing of equipment, pupil–pupil discussion and ease of teacher movement. In the one kindergarten we visited, pupils had individual tables rather than one half of a pair of desks and both teacher and pupils were much more mobile than in the primary classrooms. Stacked or folded away against the walls were beds for rest periods. Nursery and kindergarten education were not a part of this study. However, in this particular school we observed and recorded an art lesson, to which we shall return, which provided a striking pedagogical variant on the mainstream Russian model of direct instruction.

When we reach France the spatial dynamic of primary classrooms begins to become more variable and complex. We observed both rows and groups, although everywhere the focus on the blackboard and the teacher was retained. Sometimes the pupils collaborated within groups, but mostly they worked individually. In the two village schools, where there was multi-age teaching, the layouts were furthest removed from the traditional French arrangement. In Montagne, the teacher – and sometimes the pupils – moved between adjacent rooms, in one of which the tables were arranged for groups while in the other they were organized as a horseshoe to facilitate individual working, discussion and whole class teaching. The teacher also had a carpeted area where one or both age groups assembled for oral lessons and stories. In the school in the neighbouring village, which took the older children from both villages, the schoolroom was a large L-shaped open plan area in the main part of which the pupils sat in rows, while the other part was set up for group and practical work.

In the French classrooms where desks were arranged in rows, the teacher combined teaching from the front with peripatetic monitoring. Where pupils were grouped teachers spent a larger proportion of their time on the move. However, in general the French teachers were more mobile than their Indian and Russian colleagues, even when their classrooms were similarly arranged.

In the two village schools in France classroom space was used as flexibly as anywhere we visited in the five countries, including England and Michigan. Yet a mere one hour away, down from the mountains, pupils at St Etienne in Nice worked in rows, silently facing the blackboard and the teacher: 'one goal, but many routes'.

In all the Michigan classrooms the pupils were grouped, and all the classrooms had carpeted areas. There was no standard grouping arrangement, however. In one classroom there were four groups each of four pupils, and seated somewhat apart from them were three pupils whom the teacher described as having, respectively, behavioural difficulties, hearing impairment and family problems. In a second room there were six groups of between two and five pupils. In a third there were five. In a fourth, a multi-age pair of classrooms with a movable party wall, there were 45 pupils, ten groups and three teachers. In all these classrooms there was considerable mobility among both teachers and pupils – mobility, indeed, is a concomitant of multiple-focus classroom organization.

In a fifth classroom, however, the one at Hawthorne on which we commented earlier (lesson 11.11), the teacher regularly rearranged the furniture to match her pedagogy. While we observed her she paired the pupils in rows, arranged them in groups of four to six, and reorganized them as a unitary horseshoe. Alone of all the teachers we observed in those three countries in which there was significant variation in pedagogic style between and within lessons (France, England and the United States) this one Michigan teacher appeared to take the view that method and classroom layout should always align precisely with each other. If that meant moving furniture several times a day, so be it. In fact, moving furniture had become second nature to these children. It was accomplished with remarkable speed and – even more remarkable when one considers the percussive impact of metal table legs on wooden floors – almost silently.

Not for her, therefore, the situation we commonly observed in England, where pupils were everywhere seated in groups, but only occasionally collaborated, and where in the frequent context of direct instruction some pupils sat with their backs to the teacher and were able to participate only by turning their chairs or craning their necks.

In every one of the 60 classrooms observed for the pedagogy strand of the Leeds research, in 1986–91, we found children seated in groups. There were no exceptions. We also noted variations on the theme of curriculum-specific groups or bays, comparable to the Michigan 'teaching centers'. A popular arrangement involved four areas, devoted to reading, art, mathematics and language.[15] When in 1996 Galton and his colleagues followed up their 1976 ORACLE study they expected to find that the post-1988 curriculum reforms and the sustained political and media assault on progressive teaching would have impacted on classroom organization. This was not the case. As we did in both Leeds and the *Five Cultures* English classrooms, the Leicester team found that grouping was ubiquitous and curriculum-specific zoning was common. Moreover:

> What was remarkable was that, regardless of the shape, size or original purpose of the classrooms observed, the organization within them had hardly changed in twenty years. Children were still to be found 'seated in groups around flat-topped tables or desks drawn together to form working surfaces' just as they were in 1976 . . . It would appear, therefore, that two decades of classroom research, curriculum reform on an unprecedented scale, and a shift in educational thinking which has produced calls for a return to whole class teaching and more subject specialization has had almost no impact on the way in which teachers organize their pupils.[16]

Galton points out that the carpeted area might provide the setting for direct instruction. However, in the *Five Cultures* classrooms, as in those we researched in Leeds in 1986–91, the carpeted area tended to be used only in very specific circumstances, notably the start of a day or lesson (with younger pupils), and the reading of a story. Most direct instruction, especially with older pupils, took place while the pupils were formed as groups.

Galton speculates on whether this failure to modify classrooms to take account of changes in curriculum reflects conservatism or a more basic survival instinct to hang on to what one knows and can control in the face of unremitting change. Whatever the reason, it is interesting to note that in the matter of incongruence between classroom geography and method English primary teachers are not alone. The condition was common in Michigan, not uncommon in France. In India, geography and method were consistent if only because both were in part forced by the circumstances of large classes, overcrowded classrooms and minimal resources. Only in Russia did we have a sense of genuine harmony in this matter. On the other hand it was the harmony of uniformity, whereas in France, England and Michigan there was at least the possibility of harmony against the prevailing trend. In introducing flexibility into the relationship between layout and grouping, or (lesson 11.11) in getting pupils to move classroom furniture to suit the pedagogy of the moment, the teachers at Montagne, Grenade and Hawthorne Elementary were at least demonstrating that the autonomy which they and their colleagues claimed to enjoy in teaching matters was genuine. In England, most teachers chose to exercise that autonomy, or rather to forgo it, by maintaining the practices of the 1970s and the 1980s.

We have noted the considerable discrepancies in the levels of classroom resourcing in the five countries. The fact that in one Michigan classroom there were seven computers, with a further 25 in reserve in an adjacent IT laboratory, together with videos, tape recorders, and electronic calculators, while in one Indian classroom there were merely a blackboard, slates and the teacher's copy of a textbook, is as good an indicator as any of the gulf between the world's rich and poor, and of the unequal distribution of the benefits of technological globalization. The Indian teachers invariably registered their need for more resources, and when international agencies from the comfort of their thickly carpeted offices in Washington, Paris or London voice their disdain for 'chalk and talk' teaching methods in developing countries they should perhaps be more careful to discriminate between methods adopted by choice and those adopted out of necessity. From the Russian teachers, too, the most common complaint of all those voiced in interview was lack of resources, and especially the dearth of up-to-date textbooks.

Yet despite the far larger repertoire of resources available to the teachers in Michigan, England and France, we find contrasts which are useful to our understanding of cross-cultural differences in pedagogy if instead of cataloguing the full range of classroom resources we concentrate on those which might be classified as *basic* in that they sustain the teaching of most lessons. For although the Michigan teachers had at their disposal one or more blackboards and/or whiteboards, multiple sets of textbooks, flashcards, an extensive range of commercially produced charts, pictures, models and maps, overhead projectors, audio and video recorders, commercially produced mathematical and scientific equipment; and although pupils used or had access to exercise books, loose-leaf folders, worksheets, textbooks, reference books, reading books, a full range of writing and colouring equipment, arts and craft materials, computers, calculators and mathematical and scientific apparatus; the everyday technology of teaching and learning in the Michigan classrooms was much more limited than this list might suggest.

At this more basic level the most telling differences concerned the use of blackboard/whiteboard and text material. In India, the blackboard featured prominently, but it was usually small and had only one surface, so its flexibility was limited. In France and Russia (especially the latter) in contrast, there were multiple hinged or sliding blackboard and/or whiteboard surfaces, and teachers could place on these, and keep concealed until it was needed, material not just for one lesson but for several. In Russia, the teachers also exploited the metallic composition of the boards by using magnetic letters, numbers and pictures. Moreover, pupils became as skilled as teachers in the use of the board, for they were frequently summoned (or they volunteered) to come out, singly or in pairs or groups, to write, calculate and demonstrate.

The striking contrast in this matter was between France and Russia on the one hand and England and Michigan on the other. For although the classrooms we observed in the latter two countries had boards, the use teachers made of them was rudimentary, and pupils used them rarely, if ever. In some of the classrooms observed for the earlier Leeds study, teachers even covered the boards so as to render their use impossible.

Behind these differences in use, as the last example makes clear, is a difference in ideology. To English teachers during the 1970s and the 1980s, blackboards were inescapably tainted by images of elementary school didacticism. By the late 1990s, when we observed teachers implementing the UK government literacy and numeracy hours, blackboards were once more in fairly regular use. However, teachers seemed ambivalent about them, and we observed no English teachers using boards with anything approaching the skill or inventiveness of their Russian counterparts.

There was a comparable difference in the use of pupil texts. In India and Russia the standard textbook was at the heart of teaching, although in India two circum-stances militated against its widespread use. One was availability: the teachers we observed mostly taught from textbooks, and pupils were expected to have copies of some of these, but many parents either would not or could not afford to buy them. The other was growing official opposition to textbook dominance and the encyclo-paedist view of knowledge which the textbook was seen to embody. In 1993, a national advisory committee appointed by the Government of India argued for curriculum reform to go hand in hand with the abolition of the practice of 'tortur-ing young children by compelling them to carry very heavy bags of books every day to schools'.[17] Russian teachers voiced no such worries: for them the textbook remained, with the blackboard, an essential teaching tool, and at the apex of this tradition sat the textbook writers in the Russian Academy of Education. However, by the mid 1990s there were intimations of change. There had already been a massive and speedy programme of textbook de-Sovietization. On top of this the financial crisis provoked a textbook shortage, and at the same time official endorse-ment of a more 'democratic' pedagogy prompted further questions about textbook content and format, and indeed about their more general dominance.

At the furthest extreme from Russia and India in this matter was England. Because they were deemed to imply uniformity in development, learning and under-standing, and the professional ideology was at that time wedded to individualism, textbooks (like blackboards) became deeply unfashionable in English primary schools during the 1960s and the 1970s, especially once the abolition of the selective exam-ination at 11 plus eliminated overt curriculum standardization. Multiple sets of mathematical and language textbooks – graded or streamed like the 1950s–60s classes themselves – all but disappeared, and schools concentrated on building up stocks of variegated print material to serve as a 'learning resource' rather than a teaching tool. Teachers preferred, or were commanded to prefer, to recreate such material in the form of individualized worksheets and work cards, a task which for many teachers, especially trainees and those at the beginning of their careers, could consume many hours each week.

By the 1990s the tide had turned. With the introduction of a national curriculum in 1988, primary schools encountered once again standard requirements for all children, this time in the form of the programmes of study, and commercial publishers were quick to exploit the textbook potential of these, often producing them in the form of files of copyable worksheets (to retain flexibility, or the illusion of flexibility). The trend quickened with the arrival of the literacy and numeracy hours, and we observed lessons in 1998 that were almost as closely tied to textbooks as were those in Russia.

Teachers in France and the United States, meanwhile, were moving in the opposite direction. The Michigan schools informed parents of the chosen reading schemes, and enlisted their help in working through them, but several of the Michigan teachers spoke of their recent escape from the tyranny of the 'basal text' in other areas of the curriculum. At the same time, the influence of the school board and local officials in this matter remained considerable, and we had a sense that in the context of local accountability and parental and government concern about standards this was an area of tension. Daily use of a textbook guarantees only that certain areas of learning will be encountered; but from there it is a short although fallacious step to assuming that it also guarantees levels of learning outcome. In France there was similar ambivalence. All the teachers we observed used textbooks, but while some worked through them assiduously others extracted or extrapolated from more than one text to create worksheets. What we did not see in France, however, was teachers *inventing* worksheets in the manner of English primary teachers during the period from the late 1960s to the late 1980s. The French teachers were more likely to photocopy textbook pages, complete with tasks and exercises.

Clearly, the changing position of the textbook in these five countries was a manifestation of changing patterns of educational control, which is why, in this matter as in so many others, English primary schools at the turn of the millennium were treading a different path from the other four countries. However, the preceding era had left its mark on the range of print material. A high level of textbook dependence reduces the impetus (although not the need) for a school to invest in other books. In England, the legacy of the era of textbook rejection was that most primary schools built up rich and extensive libraries of reading and reference material in all subjects. By 2000 there were hints that these might be under threat: first by the return of the textbook, which required a considerable transfer of funds from library stock to secure the multiple sets which were needed, and which by their technique of summarizing or anthologizing gave schools an excuse to reduce that stock in any case; second by the web, which some argued would make print redundant. In 1998, indeed, the UK government began to make entire standard lessons available on the web, arguing that in teaching more generally, as in the matter of textbooks and worksheets, there is little point in teachers constantly reinventing the wheel.[18] Others suggested that this initiative was merely an extension of New Labour's drive to make its control of public primary schooling as absolute as possible.

Task

The question here – 'What learning tasks do pupils encounter?' – invites an exercise in classification. The lessons summarized in Chapter 11 treat aspects of language, literacy, mathematics and science. To these can be added, from the observation dataset as a whole, many more lessons in language and literacy, several more in mathematics, and a handful in each of geography, social studies, history, music, art, personal education and physical education.

Learning tasks, then, can be classified according to their *curricular content*, and this may be done at two levels, the general and the specific. That is to say, we can define, for each lesson:

- the area(s) of the curriculum to which the tasks relate, and
- the particular aspect(s) of the curriculum area(s) in question on which the teacher chooses to focus.

On this basis, we might note that the *Five Cultures* dataset includes examples in the nine curriculum areas listed above, and that, if we take the two areas of which we have most examples, the range of specific content is as follows:

- Language: reading, writing, spoken language, letters and sounds, words, sentences, grammar, constructing texts (composition), analysing texts (comprehension).
- Mathematics: counting, sorting, addition, subtraction, multiplication, division, mental operations, written calculation, fractions, problem solving.

To analyse the tasks in this way is necessary if we are to gain a purchase on how, in different cultures, the curriculum is conceived. I said that the dataset includes lessons in nine areas of the curriculum. That begs questions about curriculum labels and boundaries, about how far teachers are happy to operate within the subject terminology of the prescribed curriculum, and how far they explore relationships between subjects and indeed blur or eliminate subject boundaries altogether. A curricular analysis of learning tasks also gives purchase on the way that teachers understand a subject's internal structure and the imperatives this structure dictates for pupil learning. We find, for example, that in language tasks requiring pupils to create text (composition) or analyse it (comprehension) – some teachers pay much more attention than others to making explicit the grammatical principles on which text is constructed, and to teaching these principles systematically, perhaps even as a set of rules to be followed. Further, we find that although there was a certain amount of variation among the Michigan and English teachers in this regard, those in France and Russia were consistent in their emphasis on formal grammar, and on the idea that text is rule bound.

The example of how grammar is treated provides the pointer to a second level of analysis, which involves looking across the different subjects and aspects of subjects taught in order to discover whether the learning tasks set display *generic pedagogical* characteristics. This generic analysis might prompt us to examine

- the *number and relationship* of the learning tasks which are presented within a given lesson
- *task demand* in the sense of the *kinds of learning* which the tasks require

- *task demand* in the sense of the *kinds of knowledge and understanding* which the tasks seek to promote.

Let us now unpack and exemplify these three ways of analysing learning tasks.

Number and relationship of learning tasks within a lesson

This is our bridge from Chapter 12, for it relates learning tasks to the lessons that frame them. Looking at the central phase of lessons, that is to say at what occurs between a lesson's introduction and conclusion, we discriminated in Chapter 12 between *unitary* and *episodic* lesson structures. In unitary structures there was a single task; in episodic structures there was a sequence of tasks. Unitary tasks could be *closed,* in which case they needed to be finished before a lesson could proceed to its next stage; or they could be *open ended*, in which case the teacher would be able to halt the task whenever he or she judged this to be appropriate. Episodic tasks came, as the term implies, one after another, and they could be *self-contained* or *linked*. Where the tasks were self-contained, they could be either *reiterative* or *cumulative*. Where they were linked one to another the tasks could be *cumulative* or *developmental*.

In essence, the Russian and Indian lessons offered variants on an episodic structure, the Michigan and English lessons tended more towards unitary structures, except in the case of the UK government's literacy and numeracy hours, and the French lessons exemplified both. The episodic tasks in most of the Indian lessons were self-contained, so as to accommodate the relative brevity of the lessons, and they proceeded from one to the next on the basis of reiteration rather than development. In the Russian classrooms, in contrast, and in those French classrooms whose teachers worked within what, to them, was a more traditional lesson structure, there was a strong cumulative and developmental thrust to the way the several tasks built one upon another. By and large the Russian lessons had shorter episodes than the episodic lessons in other countries. At the furthest extreme from these variants on episodic structure were the long central sections of lessons observed in Michigan, England and occasionally in France, where teachers devised a single task. In Michigan and England unitary tasks were both open and closed; in France they were invariably closed.

Task demand: kinds of learning

To judge the nature of the demand which a task places on a pupil we ought properly to know a certain amount both about the pupil and about what has preceded the lesson being analysed. In English pedagogic research much attention has been given to how pupils respond to tasks in terms of their levels of apparent engagement or concentration, measured as time spent in relation to time available ('time on task') and their behaviour. Less attention has been devoted to examining tasks' intrinsic properties in terms of how much they ask of pupils and how what is encountered in one lesson relates to what has gone before and what the pupil already knows or can do (task demand).

The early 1980s study by the Exeter team of Bennett, Desforges, Cockburn and Wilkinson broke new ground in this regard. The team based their classification of task demand on the work of American psychologist Donald Norman, who had postulated three ways in which new learning experiences interact with what the learner already knows: *accretion*, *restructuring* and *tuning*. Accretion is the acquisition of new knowledge. Restructuring is the reorganization of existing knowledge, the adoption of new ways of looking at what has already been encountered. Tuning is the internalization, consolidation and simplification of new knowledge through familiarity and use.[19]

The learning sequence this suggests in respect of new knowledge is: accretion → restructuring → tuning. However, Norman argues that all learning necessarily includes all three processes, but at any given stage of the individual's encounter with a new idea just one of the processes will predominate. His hypothesized sequence is therefore not this simple linear one but: (i) accretion with some restructuring and little tuning → (ii) restructuring with little accretion and an increase in tuning → (iii) an intermediate period of application and problem-solving which itself generates new knowledge and thus is dominated by accretion → (iv) tuning with little or no accretion and restructuring.

Bennett and his colleagues showed how learning tasks in primary (or any) classrooms can be classified in relation to this cycle. They tied four of their task categories to stages in Norman's cycle and added a fifth. The five kinds of task were: *incremental* tasks – (i) above, mainly accretion; *restructuring* tasks – (ii) above, mainly restructuring; *enrichment* tasks – (iii) above, accretion again; *practice* tasks – (iv) above, mainly tuning; and *revision* tasks, where material is reintroduced which has not been encountered for some time, in order to minimize memory loss.[20]

The Exeter team went on to apply this model in the context of primary teachers' efforts, in the context of the then prevailing ideology of individualization, to design tasks which exactly matched each pupil's abilities and needs. They compared the demands of tasks as intended or perceived by teachers with task demands as rated by observers, and found a significant tendency for teachers to rate as incremental what were in reality practice tasks. Practice dominated the profile of tasks actually given by teachers – the issue that concerns us here. Of the 417 language and number tasks observed, 249 (60 per cent) were practice and only 104 (25 per cent) were incremental. Restructuring and enrichment accounted for just two and 24 tasks respectively (a mere 6 per cent in all), an almost unbelievably low proportion bearing in mind – if Norman is right – the part cognitive restructuring plays in moving children's understanding forward.[21]

The issue for us at this point is not the matching process as such, for we shall come to diagnosis and differentiation later, but the feasibility of a taxonomy of task demands which the notion of match invites, and the profile which results when one attempts to classify tasks as intended and as given.

The Exeter findings supported those of the earlier Teacher Education Project directed by Ted Wragg. While the Bennett team based their analysis on the full gamut of tasks, in whatever form these were presented – whether through instructions delivered orally or on the blackboard, or through worksheets or textbooks – Wragg concentrated on teachers' questions and pupils' answers, arguing that talk is the closest we can get in observational research to the protagonists' thought processes:

> Teachers talk, and that talk can be assessed for cognitive demand and for the signals it puts out to pupils about their own expected levels of thinking. Teachers ask questions, and those questions can be recorded and analysed . . . When pupils respond, or initiate, their contributions can likewise be analysed for thought-level, whether they are regurgitating facts, dealing in concepts or exploring abstract notions.[22]

Using a modified version of Benjamin Bloom's taxonomy of cognitive objectives, Wragg's team classified the task level of teacher and pupil talk among 11–12 year olds in mixed-ability secondary school classes. They found

> . . . that most task-setting provides undifferentiated work for pupils who differ widely in ability; that such task-setting contradicts the underlying philosophy of individual growth in mixed-ability classes; that few tasks make adequate cognitive demands on the able, in many cases not even on the average pupils; and that much time is spent on tasks which are simply trivial.[23]

Wragg's focus on the cognitive content of classroom talk was followed through into the Leverhulme project on primary teaching and teacher education, in which both he and Neville Bennett were involved. Together with Galton and Simon's ORACLE research, which also identified the critical importance (and relative dearth) of those kinds of classroom interaction that generate a high level of cognitive demand, it provides an analytical paradigm that we take up in our detailed account of classroom interaction in Chapter 15.[24]

Task demand: ways of knowing

Task demand as expressed by the Norman/Bennett typology differentiates the relationship between old and new knowledge, or the kinds of learning required. However, it does not differentiate knowledge itself.

The basic distinction to be drawn here is between *propositional* and *procedural* knowledge, or *knowing that* and *knowing how*. This allows one to distinguish those tasks concerned with facts and information from those designed to promote understanding. In the United States, this distinction tacitly underpinned the hierarchy of cognitive objectives produced during the 1950s by Bloom and his colleagues in an exercise whose origins and impact, and whose relationship to postwar American anxiety about declining standards, we considered in Chapter 5. The objectives hierarchy ranged up (or down) from *knowledge* (of facts, propositions, principles and so on) through *comprehension* and *application* (of knowledge and understanding to problems and situations) to *analysis, synthesis* and *evaluation*.[25] In Chapter 6 we noted the resonances of this model in UK curriculum development activity during the 1960s and the 1970s and again, more recently, in the National Curriculum;

and in India (Chapter 4) we found that the Bloom hierarchy, and the three broad families within which under the Bloom scheme the wider range of educational objectives were placed – 'cognitive, 'affective' and 'psycho-motor' – were imported to frame the government's 'Minimum Levels of Learning'.[26]

The propositional/procedural distinction allows us to add two further dimensions to the knowledge dimension of the learning task.

The first concerns the *source* of knowledge. In Chapter 8 we noted that one of the Michigan schools defined the curriculum in terms of 'important ideas and skills, including students' own questions and interests' and Chapter 11 included a lesson from Thoreau Elementary (11.12) which valued pupils' idiosyncratic routes to solving a mathematical problem above their ability to apply standard mathematical formulae, and indeed was more interested in 'process', to use another classic dichotomy, than in 'product'.

These are not isolated or eccentric examples, but stem from a shared tradition in English and American progressive educational thinking which resists the hegemony of a priori, discipline-based knowledge.[27] Thus, to use Eggleston's classification from the 1970s – when epistemological brickbats were being hurled with particular gusto over the ideological parapets of both Left and Right – knowledge can be *received*, given and non-negotiable, structured into fixed and permanent subjects and disciplines; or it can be *reflexive*, changing, negotiable and non-absolute, something created afresh by each individual's encounters with the world.[28]

This distinction bears on the question of task demand in a fundamental way, for a learning task grounded in the view that knowledge is received is by its nature likely to be much more precisely framed and tightly bounded than one stemming from the view that knowledge is reflexive. To be consistent with the latter view a task would have to be to some degree open-ended in order to respect the individual pupil's ways of knowing and understanding, and it might need to be expressed – to coin Eisner's terms – as an 'expressive objective ' or an 'encounter', rather than as a precise terminal outcome. Further, some tasks by their very nature – those designed to generate creative action or response, for example – require open-endedness in their design. This problem, indeed, was at the heart of Eisner's contribution to the 1960s–1970s debate about behavioural objectives.[29] At the turn of the millennium the stance of the UK government and its agencies – notably the Teacher Training Agency and the Standards and Effectiveness Unit – towards targets and testing requires this debate to be revisited with some urgency.

The other dimension of learning task allowed by the propositional/procedural distinction is an elaboration on the notion of procedural knowledge. Reporting on their mid 1990s follow-up to the 1970s ORACLE research on primary teaching, Maurice Galton and his colleagues shared our preoccupation with the need to find ways of categorizing the knowledge demands of learning tasks. He commended the three-level typology which Patricia Alexander synthesized from a large number of research studies and which differentiated *procedural, conceptual* and *metacognitive* knowledge.[30]

'Procedural knowledge' in this definition deviates, rather confusingly, from the standard philosophical use of the term and appears to encompass both propositional knowledge (which Patricia Alexander calls *declarative*) and procedural knowledge as more usually defined, which roughly corresponds with what she calls *conditional* knowledge. In Patricia Alexander's usage 'procedural' is a catch-all for both the acquisition of information and understanding of how such information can be used.

'Conceptual knowledge' in this typology is knowledge of ideas and of principles of definition and classification. It includes public ways of knowing such as subjects and disciplines, and subdivides into three categories to do with the communication and exchange of ideas and understanding: *discourse* knowledge (knowledge about language and its use), *syntactic* knowledge (knowledge of how to convey meaning through propositions) and *rhetorical* knowledge (understanding of register).

At the third level Patricia Alexander posits 'metacognitive knowledge' as knowledge of one's own cognitive processes, including understanding of what it is to think historically, scientifically and so on and the ability to reflect on, evaluate and regulate one's own thinking.

Knowledge of information and its uses, knowledge about ideas, knowledge about the communication and exchange of knowledge and ideas, knowledge about thinking: this typology certainly takes us further than the basic distinction between 'knowing' and 'understanding', and in fact can to some extent be mapped on to the Bloom taxonomy. Patricia Alexander's 'procedural knowledge' includes Bloom's 'knowledge, 'comprehension' and 'application'. Her 'conceptual knowledge' corresponds roughly to Bloom's 'analysis' and 'synthesis', and her 'metacognitive knowledge' to Bloom's evaluation. However, at the higher levels – for Patricia Alexander's framework, like Bloom's, is a hierarchy – she appears to go well beyond Bloom, especially in the crucial way that she defines language and metacognition as significant domains of educational knowledge.

This difference – bearing in mind that Patricia Alexander's framework is synthesized from a broad field of research and scholarship – says much about the extent to which educational pyschology has moved on from the positivism of the 1950s and the 1960s and perhaps illustrates Bruner's 'quiet revolution' which has placed the learner's acquisition and exchange of *meaning* centre stage.[31] The Bloom student was a solitary thinker operating in a cultural vacuum; the one implied in Patricia Alexander's framework is a post-Vygotskian, learning through interaction with others, beginning to understand the cultural embeddedness of ideas.

We can add one more layer. In their seminal account of the pupils' development of understanding through classroom discourse, Edwards and Mercer discuss and exemplify tasks which purport to lead towards procedural knowledge in the strict sense of 'knowing how'. In this process they examine the part played by rules and formulae, for example in mathematics or science or in language-teaching exercises in comprehension or composition.[32] This leads them to draw a distinction between *principled* and *ritual* knowledge, for the learning of rules and formulae can lead to understanding of principles and procedures and the ability to apply them critically and in novel settings, or it can lead merely to formulaic replication. 'Procedural knowledge', Edwards and Mercer argue, 'becomes "ritual" where it substitutes for understanding of underlying principles'.[33]

Now clearly one is not in a position to judge whether for the learner knowledge is principled rather than ritualized until one assesses how he or she performs the learning task and what kind of understanding he or she then displays. For it is presumably the intention of most teachers to promote genuine understanding rather than the uncomprehending application of rules or the unquestioning repetition of information. Or is it? If one takes a long view – both cross-cultural and historical – it becomes immediately evident that the promotion of ritual knowledge has always been a significant element in basic education. And in respect of our attempt to devise a framework for analysing the demands of learning tasks as presented we should note that certain tasks by their nature tend to emphasize ritual rather principled knowledge (rote learning, in other words).

However, Edwards and Mercer also point out that 'principled' and 'ritual' need not be mutually exclusive, and that there is a case and a place for the acquisition of rules and formulae on the road to principled understanding (the learning by heart of multiplication tables is one obvious example). In the same way, we might return to the earlier distinction between 'received' and 'reflexive' knowledge and suggest that these, too, are not mutually exclusive, although pedagogical extremists, whether traditional or progressive, may find it ideologically more comfortable to act as if they were. Thus in Britain at the time of writing the press is mesmerized by the antics of a group of entrepreneurs who compete for the annual Turner Prize on the basis of rejecting all received knowledge about the creative process and all preconceptions of artistic skill. However, for most of history artistic creation has been about assimilating, working within, bending and stretching received forms and conventions, and on this basis extending and moving beyond them. The same can be said of scientific creativity and indeed of knowledge generation in any domain.

It is thus probably more helpful to see 'received' and 'reflexive' as complementary ways of knowing and understanding the same thing, and in this dispensation the learner's capacity for reflexivity in respect of received knowledge squares the circle with principled knowledge. In the context of the established knowledge disciplines, therefore, the issue is not so much whether knowledge is received as what pupils are encouraged through their learning tasks to do with it, which is why the Edwards and Mercer distinction between ritualized and principled knowledge is more pertinent here. In Philip Jackson's terms, then, learning tasks can be *mimetic* or *transformative*, they can require the pupil to receive, accept and use knowledge in the form that it is presented, and only in that form, or they can encourage the pupil to translate that knowledge into something else.[34]

Let us now synthesize elements of this discussion into a framework for classifying classroom learning tasks. I propose two levels of analysis, *lesson* and *task*. At the first level we can discover a lesson's overall task profile – the number of tasks and the way they relate to each other – using the distinction between *unitary* and *multiple* tasks which I initiated and illustrated in Chapter 12. At the second level we can look at the demand placed upon pupils by each task separately, adapting the ideas of Norman, Bennett, Edwards and Mercer, Galton, Jackson and Patricia Alexander to define task demand in terms of the kind of learning a task requires and the kinds of

Lesson level: overall task profile

Unitary	closed	
	open	
Multiple	self-contained	reiterative
		cumulative
	linked	cumulative
		developmental

Task level: task demand

Kinds of learning   acquiring new knowledge
restructuring existing knowledge
applying existing knowledge
practice
revision

Ways of knowing

Received ↔ reflexive   ritualised ↔ principled   mimetic ↔ transformative

Propositional
Procedural
Conceptual
Discourse
Metacognitive

Figure 13.4   A preliminary framework for classifying learning tasks

knowledge and understanding it seeks to promote. The entire framework appears in Figure 13.4.

Lesson level: comparative task profiles

To test this way of looking at tasks I have taken first all the observed lessons from each country. The task profile of each has been analysed separately and the comparative country profiles are shown in Table 13.1. I have excluded from the analysis lesson introductions and purely administrative conclusions such as tidying up, as if these were included all the lessons could be construed as having a multiple-task profile.

I must warn immediately that scoring lessons' task profiles in this way is not an exact science, and to underline this Table 13.1 shows trends rather than observational frequencies. Yet with that caveat entered the resulting comparisons are illuminating. In the profile for the observed lessons in England we see the multiple-task structure of the literacy and numeracy hours replacing the very different multiple-task lessons of the 1970s and the 1980s. Whereas the latter might consist of several possibly unrelated tasks being undertaken *simultaneously* (by different groups), in the new literacy and numeracy lessons the whole class undertakes the same sequence of tasks consecutively. In the literacy hour the multiple tasks tend to be linked developmentally, while in the numeracy hour the first stage is self-contained.

Yet because lessons conducted in accordance with the emerging orthodoxy were a minority of those which we observed, the overall profile for England shows the other dominant 1970s–80s structure still much in evidence. In this the teacher's introduction is followed by a single, long task where pupils work at their desks and the teacher monitors groups and/or individuals in turn.

Table 13.1 Task profiles of primary school lessons in five countries, based on an analysis of all lessons observed

Tasks	England	France	India	Russia	USA
Unitary					
Closed	2	1	0	0	2
Open	2	1	0	0	2
Multiple					
Self-contained	1	1	3	1	1
Linked	1	3	2	3	1

3 = very frequently observed (over 66% of lessons); 2 = fairly frequently observed (33–66% of lessons); 1 = rarely observed (below 33% of lessons); 0 = never observed

The dominance of a unitary task profile holds for the Michigan lessons too. In contrast, in France, India and Russia the lessons were characteristically broken down into task stages. However, in respect of the form that multiple-task lessons take the differences between these three countries are greater than the similarities. In France the total number of such tasks is rather smaller than in India or Russia, but France shares with Russia a strong developmental emphasis in the way multiple tasks within a lesson are linked while in India a quick-fire succession of tasks is as likely to stand alone as to be related to each other.

Task level: task demand

To assess the cognitive demand of individual tasks we concentrated on language and mathematics lessons only, this time taking eight from each country. The judgements relate to the tasks as presented rather than to teachers' intentions. The results of the analysis are shown in Table 13.2. Again, they are presented in terms of the relative emphasis across all lessons analysed for each country rather than as tallies of the number of tasks actually observed in a given category. This is because assigning tasks to demand categories is not always easy, and while ratings of relative emphasis are reliable within the margin of error thereby introduced, a straight count of tasks in each category is not.

At first glance the differences look slight. The real gulfs between many of these classrooms will become clear only once we investigate the discourse of the teachers and pupils who work in them. Nevertheless, Table 13.2 picks up important variations. The Indian lessons were dominated by practice and revision tasks. New knowledge

Table 13.2 Task demand in 40 primary school lessons from five countries, based on an analysis of eight language and mathematics lessons from each country

Demand	England	France	India	Russia	USA
Learning					
Acquiring new knowledge	2	3	1	3	2
Restructuring existing knowledge	1	1	1	2	1
Applying existing knowledge	2	3	1	3	2
Practice	3	3	3	3	3
Revision	1	1	2	1	1
Knowledge (a)					
Propositional	2	3	3	3	2
Procedural	3	3	1	3	3
Conceptual	1	2	1	2	2
Discourse	1	2	0	3	1
Metacognitive	1	1	0	1	1
Knowledge (b)					
Ritual understanding	1	2	3	3	0
Principled understanding	2	2	1	2	2

3 = major emphasis; 2 = moderate emphasis; 1 = slight emphasis; 0 = no emphasis

was introduced a little at a time and relatively slight attention was given to restructuring and application in the context of, for example, problem solving, comprehension or imaginative writing. The Russian lessons also included many practice tasks, but alongside these the teachers insistently introduced new knowledge each lesson and equally insistently reworked and applied existing knowledge, most characteristically in the context of pupil–teacher dialogue. In the French classrooms there was a particularly heavy emphasis on application and practice. In Michigan and England, practice tasks were dominant.

Thus, everywhere primary pupils spent a great deal of time practising skills already acquired, but the critical difference came in the way this emphasis was balanced (or not) by the introduction of new knowledge and opportunities for pupils to embed such knowledge through tasks which invited application and restructuring.

As to the kinds of knowledge which the learning tasks demanded we see an immediate difference between the strong emphasis on factual, propositional knowledge (knowing that) in the Russian, Indian and French classrooms and the concern with procedural knowledge (knowing how), in the lessons observed in England and Michigan. Indeed, the content in some of the lessons in the latter two countries was extremely restricted. In the Indian classrooms, however, although most of the tasks were propositional, much less attention was given to securing understanding than in France or Russia. Moreover, at the higher levels of conceptual, discourse and metacognitive knowledge, the French and Russian lessons were notable for the level of abstraction which their teachers introduced (and which undoubtedly baffled some of their pupils) as they ventured into language about language – phonetics, grammar, syntax, principles for analysing and constructing text and so on. In this matter, the conceptual and discourse tasks which we observed in the Russian classrooms were focused mostly at word and sentence levels while in the French lessons they were equally or more concerned with text. In the English classrooms of the post-1998 literacy hour, pupils' knowledge about language was advanced at a more basic procedural or propositional level – how to use an index, knowing what a publisher does.

In all the lessons, except for some of those observed in India, teachers seemed concerned to lead their pupils to a principled understanding. In Russia and India, and to a lesser extent in France, ritual knowledge was an explicit focus of the learning tasks which teachers presented. However, whereas in Russia and France it was usually there to provide a bridge to principled understanding, in some of the Indian lessons, teachers (and no doubt pupils) remained anchored to ritual.

Activity

The distinction here between learning *task* and learning *activity*, which we applied first to the Leeds classroom data in 1986–91, is fundamental to the analysis in these chapters. It is best elucidated through examples. If we take lessons 11.9 and 11.12, we find nine-year-old children in Moscow and Michigan being given similar tasks in the context of mathematics. Both tasks required the translation of a 'real life' arithmetical problem into a numerical calculation, but the activities through which the pupils were asked to solve the problem were very different.

In Moscow School B (lesson 11.9) the pupils were expected to recognize immediately which numerical operations were called for and apply these to the problem in the context of previously learned rules and procedures. They worked alone, writing in their exercise books. Some pupils were then called upon to demonstrate their calculations to the rest of the class. The task was arithmetical problem solving, and it entailed the activities of solitary mental and written calculation first, then collective checking of solutions. There was one correct way to solve the problem, and one solution. In Thoreau (lesson 11.12), the pupils were invited to discuss possible routes to a solution with their peers and collectively to invent different ways of effecting the embedded calculation (50 ÷ 3) before 'sharing' their solutions and explanations with the rest of the class. Again the task was arithmetical problem solving, although at a more elementary level (despite the fact that the pupils were the same age as those in Moscow); this time, however, the task entailed the activities of collective discussion and hypothesizing, followed by whole-class discussion. In both activities the idea that the process might be rule bound was explicitly discouraged. The 'correct' solution to the problem was the one that worked for each pupil, subject to peer-validation in the class-level discussion.

The tasks were similar in terms of content, but different in terms of task structure (one was closed, the other open) and task demand (one was lodged firmly within the domain of received knowledge, the other was reflexive). Both involved transformative operations, but in the Russian case these were grounded in earlier mimetic tasks, while for the Michigan pupils the transformation was to be effected by their drawing as they saw fit on whatever procedural understanding they had at their disposal. The activities were also different: in the one lesson (Michigan) group discussion led to hypotheses which were then shared with the class as a whole; in the other, pupils completed individual written exercises, the answers to which, and the calculations on which they were based, were then checked at the board.

Both aspects of the learning encounter are important. The learning task is its conceptual component; the learning activity is the task's practical counterpart, or the means through which the teacher intends the child to make the required conceptual advance from what was learned previously to what must be learned now. In cross-cultural comparative analysis we are interested in both the conceptual demands which teachers place on their pupils and the activities through which these are mediated. But, arguably, some of the most illuminating kinds of comparative pedagogical analysis (within as well as between cultures) arise when we find teachers using different learning activities, and different teaching methods (for example, direct instruction, collaborative discussion) in support of similar learning tasks. In the case of Moscow School B and Thoreau Elementary, the distance between the two teachers' views of mathematical learning and understanding which each combination of task and activities revealed was considerable.

In the Leeds study, systematic observation in a sub-sample of ten classrooms over a two-week period revealed that pupils worked within a repertoire, across all subjects and tasks, of ten main activities (listed here in alphabetical order):

(1)   *collaboration* with another pupil or pupils;
(2)   *construction*, including model-making, craft, technological construction, building with preformed standardized components such as Lego;
(3)   *drawing and/or painting*;
(4)   *listening/looking*, usually at/to the teacher, but also involving other children, the television, radio, tape-recorder or class audio-visual material;
(5)   *movement* from one place to another (not simply movement of, say, the hands);
(6)   *reading*, silently or aloud;
(7)   *talking to the class*;
(8)   *talking to the teacher*;
(9)   *using task-specific apparatus*, which might range from computers and chronometers to needles and thread, but does not include such general-purpose equipment as books and paper;
(10) *writing*.[35]

Table 13.3 shows the breakdown of the activities' order of frequency, as measured by the proportion of available time spent by the observed pupils on each, over the two-week observation period.

Table 13.3 Percentage of time spent by primary pupils on
ten generic learning activities in ten English primary classrooms[36]

Activity	%
Writing	33
Apparatus	28
Reading	24
Listening/looking	20
Drawing/painting	19
Collaborating	18
Movement	14
Talking to the teacher	8
Construction	6
Talking to the class	1

These were classrooms, then, in which children spent the bulk of their time writing, reading and using apparatus, and in which they spent relatively little time in collaborative activity and structured talk. The implications of this finding for what we now know about effective learning – for which collaborative activity and structured talk are understood to be indispensable – are serious. In the Leeds study we pressed this analysis further. We first constructed a profile of each school subject to show their constituent activities and on that basis found, for example, that language teaching was dominated by reading and writing, with little attention to spoken language, and that science was the most genuinely collaborative subject. We then examined the relationship of activity to time on task, finding that some activities were much more likely than others to engage pupils' concentration.

I am not spelling out the temporal details of the Leeds analysis here because our concern at this point is with the *nature* of the learning activities undertaken in primary classrooms; pupils' and teachers' use of time is dealt with separately later. However, I trust I have given enough information here to sustain the case that a learning activity is significantly different from a learning task, and that it bears on important questions about both effective teaching and productive learning which we shall need to pursue.

The original list of activities was undoubtedly crude, for there are of course many kinds of reading, writing, listening and talking. In the Leeds research we fully understood this. The list sought to differentiate the broad range of prescribed task-related activities and their context, but not content or purposes. Remaining at this level of generality, we reapplied the analysis to the *Five Cultures* data and found that to cover the range of activities observed in the non-English countries it required considerable extension, and the direction this took is instructive in itself. For France (and, occasionally Russia) *collaboration* needed to differentiate the contexts of *groups* and *pairs*. For India we needed the additional 'talk' category of *talking as a class/ chanting* (which is clearly not the same as talking *to* the class). *Talk to teacher* in the initial classification was ambiguous, so we separated *answer questions* as a public act from *talk to teacher* on a more private one-to-one basis in the context of monitoring. *Writing* needed to discriminate *writing at desk* from children's *writing on blackboard*, which we observed frequently in France and Russia, and occasionally in India. It became necessary to separate *reading silently* from the *reading aloud* which we frequently observed in Russia and France. For Russia and – very occasionally – other countries we needed new categories of *physical exercises* and *games* (as classroom rather than playground or gymnasium activities). Also for Russia and occasionally India and the United States, we needed *peer/self-assessment* as a deliberate and explicit teaching act (naturally, as Philip Jackson reminds us,[37] pupils assess themselves and each other informally for much of the time they are in school). Although in Leeds pupils worked mostly from worksheets, to accommodate practices elsewhere we noted whether pupils were working from *worksheets*, from *textbooks* or from the *blackboard*. Finally, we needed to add, since it occurred every day if not every lesson, and invariably in the morning when pupils tended to be doing language or mathematics, the pause in the Michigan classrooms for the Pledge (defined as *national ritual*).

We might note that most of the modifications accommodated additional activities of a collective rather than an individual kind. This in itself is an important pointer to differences between England and other countries that are about to emerge.

We applied the extended framework to the same 40 language and mathematics lessons which featured in Table 13.2. Again, in Table 13.4 we indicate within broad bands how frequently the different activities were observed rather than the exact number of occasions.

We can start by picking out the anomalies, or those activities that feature prominently in one country but hardly at all elsewhere. In this category we would place the physical exercises which punctuated the Russian lessons, the ubiquitous chanting in Indian classrooms, the Pledge of Allegiance in Michigan, the bouts of public peer- and self-assessment in Russia, and, very different from all of these, the more private English practice of individual English pupils reading to their teachers *sotto voce*.

Next we can compare country profiles by focusing on the activities which we observed most or fairly frequently. Pupils in all five countries spent a great deal of time listening to the teacher and answering questions, although less so in England and Michigan than in the other three. In Michigan and to a lesser extent in France and England, but not at all in India and hardly at all in Russia, pupils worked collaboratively as groups or in pairs. Reading was a sustained act in England and France, and 'reading to teacher' apart, a largely silent one. In Russia, India and, sometimes, France, reading was more intermittent but when it occurred it was more public. In France, India and Russia, much more than in England or Michigan, pupils spoke to the class as a whole. In the latter two countries, more typically, they spoke to the teacher – and spoke conversationally rather than declaimed – while he or she moved from group to group during lessons' monitoring phases. The English, Michigan and increasingly the French pupils worked from worksheets. Those in India, France and Russia worked from the blackboard, while in Russia and France textbooks were also prominent. Finally while seatwork was a prominent activity in

Table 13.4 Pupils' learning activities in 40 lessons in five countries, based on an analysis of eight language and mathematics lessons from each country

Activity	England	France	India	Russia	USA
Answer questions	3	4	4	4	3
Assess peers/self	1	2	1	4	2
Collaborate (group)	2	1	0	0	3
Collaborate (pair)	1	1	0	1	2
Construct	1	0	0	0	1
Draw/paint	0	0	0	0	0
Games	1	1	1	3	0
Listen/look	3	4	4	4	3
Move for task purposes	1	1	1	3	1
National ritual	0	0	0	0	3
Physical exercises	0	0	0	3	1
Read silently	4	4	2	3	2
Read to class	1	3	3	3	2
Read to teacher	4	0	0	0	1
Talk as class/chanting	1	0	4	1	0
Talk to class	1	4	4	4	2
Talk to teacher	2	1	1	1	3
Task-specific apparatus	2	1	0	2	2
Work from blackboard	1	4	3	4	1
Work from textbook	1	2	1	4	1
Work from worksheet	4	3	0	0	4
Write at blackboard	1	2	2	3	1
Write at desk/seat	4	4	2	3	4

4 = very frequently observed (a prominent feature of most or all lessons); 3 = fairly frequently observed; 2 = occasionally observed; 1 = rarely observed; 0 = never observed

all five countries, in Russia and to a lesser extent in France and India, individual pupils might spend a not inconsiderable amount of time working at the blackboard.

These differences combine to confirm two points that I believe are critical to the task of locating the cultural fault-lines in our comparative analysis of pupil learning activities. First, the centre of gravity for the lessons in Russia, India and France was the class, while in England, and even more in Michigan, it was the group and the individual (although it is fair to note also that France was in transition in this respect). Second, individual pupil talk of a very public and structured kind was a much more prominent activity in Russia and France than in the other three countries. Thus, in Russia, lessons typically required pupils to look, listen, answer questions, talk to the class as a whole, read aloud, come out to the blackboard, write on it, explain what they were doing, and in relation to all these activities seatwork was just one activity among many. In England, in contrast, pupils were also required to look, listen and answer questions; but they read silently or quietly to the teacher; they talked with each other rather than to the class as a whole; they worked from group-based worksheets rather than the blackboard; if they moved around it was to fetch something they needed or to transfer from their desk or table to the carpeted area for a lesson introduction or ending rather than to expose themselves to public scrutiny or challenge.

I believe that it is the much more prominent part played by talk in the Russian classrooms – structured talk, public talk, teacher talk, pupil talk, talk deliberate rather than casual – which explains the higher incidence there, relative to the observed lessons in England, Michigan and India, of tasks which sought to advance pupils' propositional, conceptual and discourse knowledge. For knowledge at these levels can advance only a limited extent through solitary and silent written tasks, or through reading which does not lead to discussion, and it is upon talk, more than on any other of the activities that we have discussed, that pupils' conceptual and discourse understanding depends.

14

Judgement, Routine, Rule and Ritual

Judgement in Teaching: Differentiation and Assessment

There are two broad kinds of judgement that bear directly on children in schools and classrooms: *differentiation* and *assessment*. Differentiation is the process of identifying differences in children as a basis for making decisions about where, what and how they should be taught. Assessment carries on from where differentiation leaves off: it judges how and what children have learned. However, there is also a feedback loop from assessment because it also provides the evidential basis for differentiation. Very broadly, then, differentiation precedes and accompanies teaching while assessment accompanies and follows it. Together they form the continuum of educational judgement, overlapping within the teacher–pupil interactions that are the kernel of teaching.

And an explosive continuum it can be, not least in England. We saw in Chapter 6 how public education in England is rooted in historic and fundamental divisions of class, wealth, privilege and religion, divisions that in 2000 remained to a considerable degree impermeable to the political rhetoric of modernization and classlessness. The 1944 Education Act's tripartism, although ostensibly about ability and aptitude, had the effect of reinforcing these divisions. The move from selective to common secondary schooling proved a nettle which even the Labour Party, for all its egalitarian vision, grasped only with difficulty, and the renewed political conflict over grammar schools in 1999–2000 showed that in England, unlike many other countries, common secondary schooling could by no means be taken for granted.[1]

While the battles raged over the differentiating and selective functions of schooling, a parallel campaign was being fought over assessment and what assessment might or might not reveal about children's learning and the quality of teaching. The 11-plus examination was phased out during the 1960s and the 1970s, only to be replaced during the late 1980s and the 1990s by a considerably more exacting regime of tests and examinations at ages 7, 11, 14 and 16, to which were added, for good measure ('measure' being the operative word here) 'baseline' assessment at age five and the possibility of testing at ages younger even than that. Thus it was argued that through frequent testing allied to public exposure of teachers and schools standards would be raised and maintained; and thus it was that during the decade of assessment, 1990–2000, even the combined weight of tests, published results and league tables failed to mollify those who continued to insist that standards were falling. And if the test results demonstrated that standards were in fact rising, there were always those who would assert, with predictable regularity as each year's results were published, that this was because the tests themselves were becoming easier. So in 1999 the UK government felt obliged to commission an independent enquiry into the claim that

> . . . the pass mark . . . for eleven-year olds [in the 1999 National Curriculum Key Stage 2 tests] was secretly lowered to increase the percentage of pupils attaining National Curriculum Level 4, thus making it more likely that the national targets for eleven year olds would be met in 2002.[2]

Notwithstanding OFSTED's attempt to inflame the controversy and discredit the Qualifications and Curriculum Authority (the body formally responsible for the tests, and OFSTED's rival in the debate about curriculum and assessment),[3] such claims were shown to be groundless.[4] Yet government maintained the temperature on standards, lashing out at 'forces of conservatism' within the public sector, including education, and accusing teachers of harbouring low expectations of their pupils and of cloaking these and poor teaching with a 'culture of excuses which tolerates low ambition, rejects excellence and treats poverty as an excuse for failure'.[5]

By 2000, parents too were being drawn into the fray, joining teachers in complaining about the stresses caused to seven year olds by a testing system which was supposed to support their learning but which was now being used for other purposes entirely. Since the early 1990s the test results had been used to judge performance of schools as well as pupils (as in Michigan, with the publication of comparative school MEAP figures). Now, from September 2000, pupil test results were to be used to determine the pay of their teachers. The government introduced a scheme of performance-related pay incorporating 'threshold standards' whereby:

> Teachers should demonstrate that, as a result of their teaching, their pupils achieve well relative to the pupils' prior attainment. This should be shown in marks or grades in any relevant national tests or examinations, or school based assessment where national tests and examinations are not taken.[6]

So differentiation and assessment in English education are highly politicized areas of professional action, not merely complex ones. This is not to say that claims about teachers' expectations were without foundation. The HMI primary and first school surveys of 1978 and 1982 reported a pervasive combination of low expectations and undemanding teaching, especially in the 'Curriculum II' subjects.[7] Independent research, for example by King, Sharpe and Green, showed primary teachers rating individual children, and relating to them, on the basis of broad typifications of their social class background, at the heart of which was a family-home deficit theory which attributed children's relative educational success to the power of 'good' and 'poor' homes rather than to the efforts of either the children or their teachers.[8] In the Leeds study, we found that despite a programme of massive positive financial discrimination in favour of schools in the socially and materially disadvantaged neighbourhoods of that city, accompanied by serious attempts on the part of the LEA to counter the 'culture of excuses' through in-service consciousness-raising, some teachers continued to operate on the basis of unexamined assumptions about what inner-city children were or were not capable of, and there was an impermeable core to some teaching of low expectations and undemanding tasks.[9]

But at the same time, research also showed that differentiation which was structural rather than embedded in teacher consciousness could exacerbate problems of low expectations and underachievement. Indeed one of the most morally persuasive lines of attack against streaming by ability, which was common practice in English primary schools until the late 1960s, was that having labelled children 'bright', 'average' or 'slow', schools contrived to ensure that the labels stuck, sometimes for life, and few children had the confidence or self-belief to do other than acquiesce, thereby making the prophecy self-fulfilling.[10]

Elsewhere, I have offered a complementary line of analysis which suggests that problems of low expectations and underachievement at the primary stage can be traced not just to teachers' assumptions about social background, class and gender, but also to the very structure of primary teaching itself:

> There are at least two missing ingredients in conventional discussions of the relationship between teacher expectations and pupil performance: first, the curriculum experiences which the teacher provides; and second, the knowledge and skill which the teacher needs in order to do so. To this extent children's needs and teacher expertise are linked, for in the end it is the teacher, and not the child, who defines what those needs are.
>
> For as long as these ingredients are neglected we shall continue to encounter a model of children's needs couched . . . more in terms of children's problems than their latent potential. Yet as soon as we address the curricular and pedagogical issues with any seriousness we shall have to confront the question of the extent to which the class-teacher system is capable of delivering either the professional expertise or the classroom experiences which are required if the full diversity and depth of individual needs and potential in a typical class of primary children are to be identified with precision and addressed with reasonable hope of success . . . Far from vouchsafing special insights into what children are capable of, as is frequently claimed, the class-teacher system may sometimes do the exact opposite.[11]

By the 1990s the argument about the importance of teachers' curriculum knowledge was generally accepted. However, in English pre-service primary teacher training it was applied fully only in the context of the teaching of the 'core' subjects of language, mathematics and science, and there was little political stomach or professional will for addressing the implications of the argument that the class teacher system might itself be a major part of the problem.

By the late 1990s, however, international comparisons had thrown up another possible contributory factor, differentiation itself. The international review conducted for OFSTED by Reynolds and Farrell, like the three-country study of Stevenson and Stigler, suggested that the very act of celebrating each child's unique individuality, which had for long been fundamental to the philosophy of both English and American primary education, may have led to a widening of the gap in attainment between the least and most able. Among English children this was already wide by the age of seven.[12]

Indeed, we might add that the problems of low expectations, undemanding teaching and underachievement, which were consistent findings in primary school inspection and research studies during the 1970s, the 1980s and the early 1990s, may have been exacerbated by one of the procedures introduced specifically to tackle these problems. This procedure, or ideal, was what HMI called 'match',[13] and it responded to teachers' documented failures accurately to assess and meet individual differences in primary classrooms by fuelling a generation of development work aimed at creating strategies whereby 'match' could become, for each child and in each subject, as precise as possible.[14] This was the context for the 1984 Bennett study, to which I referred in our discussion of learning tasks in Chapter 13 and which revealed that even teachers nominated as 'outstanding' experienced acute difficulties in achieving reliable match of task to pupil.[15] Other studies showed that individualized teaching might give pupils individualized *tasks* but very limited and mostly low-level individualized *interaction*.[16] It was after reviewing this literature that we argued in the 1992 government discussion paper on primary teaching that

> Teachers need to reject the essentially unrealistic belief that pupils' individual differences provide the central clue as to how the simultaneous teaching of many individuals can be organized. The goals of primary education are common to all pupils. It is with this reality that planning for teaching should start.[17]

In fact, as Patricia Broadfoot shows in her detailed comparative study of assessment in French and English education, tensions between differentiation and integration are intrinsic to most systems of public education.[18] Even where (as in Russia, France and the United States) common schooling is well established, and even where (as in Russia and in many of the countries of Asia and continental Europe) teaching proceeds on the basis of what children have in common and with the intention of enabling all children to attain common standards, schools may seek both to differentiate and integrate, and to rank and select pupils for later education and employment, while playing down the differences they expose in the interests of social cohesion and political policy.

Of the several pivotal elements of teaching which I set out in Chapter 13, then, judgement in differentiating and assessing pupils is perhaps the one which is most obviously suffused with the values and value-tensions of the wider culture and society. What light did the *Five Cultures* data shed on the problem?

Differentiation

Before considering the various *forms* of differentiation, we need to be clear about their criteria. This is easier said than done, because there is a point at which formal and explicit ways of defining differences between pupils, such as age or attainment, shade off into those to which teachers may be less prepared to admit, or about which they not may be entirely conscious. Most teachers relate more readily to some children than others, identify more with their personalities and sensitivities and perhaps like them better. Not for nothing is teaching called a 'caring' profession, but caring and neutrality do not sit comfortably together. Professionalism lies in striving to care even-handedly.

Three of the criteria we observed or were told about in interview (age, ability and special needs) were more straightforward in this regard than the other two (behaviour and gender). In all five countries pupils were differentiated by *age*, except where, as in England, France, India and Michigan, there were examples of multi-age teaching. In the classes concerned, pupils might be subdivided by age *within* the class, although in all the multi-age classes we observed there were many tasks and activities for which pupils were not divided by age.

Although differences in *ability* were everywhere acknowledged, overtly differentiating pupils by ability *within* age-based classes was more common in England than in the other four countries. In England it was done through grouping, although ability groups were likely to be confined to mathematics and English. Whole class settings, as in Russia, India and some of the French classrooms, may appear to be undifferentiated, but it is perfectly possible for teachers to seat children by ability, and we encountered some evidence of this, especially in India.

On the other hand, the criterion of *special educational needs* (SEN) was more generally acknowledged and in the schools in all countries except India additional staff were available to work with children defined as having special needs. In England and Michigan, where an integrationist SEN policy was most strongly espoused, these teachers might work with their SEN charges alongside other pupils, or they might withdraw them. In France and Russia SEN children were generally withdrawn.

When we come to the criterion of *behaviour*, matters are more complex. Where children exhibit behavioural problems which are severe and recurrent, they may be defined formally as having 'behavioural difficulties' and given special attention, perhaps by specialist support teachers, often outside the classroom. This was common practice in England, France and Michigan. We observed no such children being withdrawn from the Russian or Indian classrooms, but then only very rarely indeed did we find Russian children who deviated from expected behavioural norms in the classroom setting. In contrast, in the English and American classrooms, especially the latter, divergent or anti-social behaviour, and the handling of such behaviour, were clearly perennial challenges for many teachers. Although in the context of our discussion of differentiation it might be suggested that such children differentiate themselves, it was common for teachers in England, France and Michigan physically to separate or segregate them.

The final admitted criterion for differentiation was *gender*. In some, although not all, of the Indian classrooms, as is perhaps to be expected in a country whose gender inequalities are so pronounced, girls and boys sat in separate rows. In the other countries grouping was mixed, and in England and Michigan teachers were very conscious of their formal obligation to avoid gender bias and discrimination. But this too is easier said than done. In classrooms in both countries our field notes repeatedly record boys demanding, and receiving, more attention than girls,[19] and the boys in some of the Michigan lessons were both more demanding and more aggressive in their behaviour than either boys or girls in the other four countries. But we also found teachers themselves differentiating on the basis of gender by consistently directing more questions to girls than to boys (or vice versa), or by treating one sex more indulgently or severely than the other. The most extreme case was a French classroom where a male teacher was consistently more brusque and critical in his interactions with girls than with boys. The pattern was pronounced, and it was sustained over the three lessons from that teacher which we observed.

Can gender in such circumstances be deemed a criterion for differentiation? Not in formal terms, certainly, but clearly such unacknowledged discrimination may well have a more profound and lasting impact than the overt gender differentiation of, say, separate seating.

In general, the French teachers displayed less consciousness, or self-consciousness, on gender-related issues. Whereas in English and American primary schools it has become unacceptable for male teachers to touch female pupils, this was evidently not the case in some of the French classrooms. Similarly, while English and American teachers have during the past decades become increasingly alive to the possibility and risk of the more subtle forms of gender bias in teaching, some of their French counterparts were evidently less exercised on this score. On the other hand, while 'caring' was expressed overtly in the language and behaviour of most of the English and American teachers, and their discourse was peppered with terms of affection, especially with the younger English children, the French teachers were much more brisk, business-like and on occasions severe in their interactions. Thus physical contact might accompany correction or admonition.

While the French teachers offset physical proximity by social distance, the Russian and Indian teachers maintained both social and physical distance in their relationships with all pupils.

The only other admitted criterion for differentiation which we encountered was *pupil height*. Eccentric although this may sound, it made sense in the crowded Indian classrooms in question, where the teacher placed the shortest children at the front so that they could see her and she them. The overall picture is summarized in Table 14.1.

Let us consider next the contexts within which children were differentiated and the forms such differentiation took. In their 1998 National Foundation for Educational Research (NFER) study of differentiation in primary and secondary schools, Weston *et al.* report that teachers are by no means agreed on what the word means or what in practice it might entail. While some understand differentiation, in classic 1970s terms, as being about matching task to individual child across the full spectrum

Table 14.1 Criteria for differentiating pupils within primary classrooms

Criterion	England	France	India	Russia	USA
Age, within school (year groups)	3	3	3	3	2
Age, within multi-age classes	2	2	1	N/A	1
Ability (apart from SEN)	2	1	1	1	2
Special educational needs (SEN)	3	3	1	1	3
Behaviour	2	0	0	0	2
Gender	0	1	2	1	0
Other	0	0	1	0	0

3 = frequently observed; 2 = occasionally observed; 1 = rarely observed; 0 = never observed

of ability and attainment, others confine it to specific pupils (those with special educational needs) or specific patterns of classroom organization (grouping).[20] The NFER study observed teachers at work differentiating pupils through the tasks that they set, the resources they provided, the ways in which they interacted with them and through assessment.

Differentiation in teacher–pupil interaction, as we noted in the previous section, highlights a central dilemma in English primary teaching which we exposed in the Leeds study and the project which preceded it:

> The more accessible teachers seek to make themselves to all their pupils as individuals, the less time they have for direct, sustained interaction with any of them; but the more time they give to such extended interaction with some children, the less demanding on them as teachers must be the activities which they give to the rest of the class; and the less demanding of their time and attention as teachers, the more the likelihood that the activity in question will demand little of the child.[21]

It is a dilemma to be admitted in this acute form only if one strives for individualization in teaching, so as expressed here it may be peculiar to English and American primary education. Yet in as far as all teachers, in whole class settings no less than when they work with groups and individuals, give some pupils more time and attention than others, the dilemma is intrinsic to all teaching other than one-to-one tuition.

On the basis of observation, and remaining consistent to the model of teaching which underpins this chapter's entire analysis, we identified six forms or contexts of differentiation, of which differentiation by time, attention and interaction are the most prominent. Table 14.2 presents these and their relative emphasis in the *Five Cultures* classrooms.

The first option is to differentiate pupils by *subject*. That is to say, one can separate pupils of the same age but different attainment – the most common basis for differentiation – for the entire curriculum (streaming) or for certain subjects

Table 14.2 Pupil differentiation in primary schools, based on observation and interviews in the *Five Cultures* classrooms

Differentiation	England	France	India	Russia	USA
By subject					
Some subjects (setting)	1	0	0	0	0
All subjects (streaming)	0	0	0	0	0
By task					
Different subjects and tasks	1	0	0	0	1
Same subject, different tasks	2	2	0	0	1
Supplementary tasks	2	1	0	0	2
By activity					
Same task, different activities	1	1	1	1	1
By seating or grouping	2	1	2	1	1
By teacher time and attention					
Whole class t–p interactions	2	1	1	1	2
Monitoring individuals/groups	3	2	1	2	3
By outcome					
Same task, different criteria or standards in assessment	3	2	1	1	3

3 = standard practice; 2 = frequently observed; 1 = occasionally observed; 0 = never observed

(setting). We observed no streamed classes in any of the five countries studied, and indeed most teachers were strongly opposed to the idea, especially in Russia. We observed only a limited amount of setting, usually in mathematics or language lessons, and then only in England.

Next, teachers might decide to keep pupils of all levels of attainment together for all subjects but to differentiate them by *task*. Only in some of the English and American classrooms did we find classes of pupils in which more than one subject was being taught simultaneously, and this was invariably associated with group rather than whole class teaching. It was more common to find teachers differentiating by task *within* a subject, especially in the 'basics'. Thus, a teacher of six to seven year olds at Coulanges:

There was another sheet, for those who were working more quickly. Tonight I will correct the work of those who had difficulties and provide them with another exercise tomorrow to help them. There are big differences between children in French and maths, but not so much in the other subjects. In history, geography and science, we do not expect too much of the children. We expect them to learn simple things. But in maths and French, if they get left behind, they won't be able to cope next year.

And at Chanderi:

> I give the children different tasks according to their abilities, both in the classroom and
> in their homework.

Such task-level differentiation might be combined with the provision of supplementary tasks, especially for those pupils who completed the initial tasks quickly.
Here there were considerable differences. In the Russian classrooms supplementary
tasks were not provided because the episodic structure of lessons prevented the degree
of individual divergence which made this necessary. In India, there was considerable
divergence in individual response, but supplementary tasks were usually not provided
and pupils simply waited quietly for the rest of the class to catch up (as in lesson
11.6). In France, teachers generally kept the pupils together, although the problem
of the 'early finisher' confronted those teachers who deviated from *la leçon* into the
looser unitary structure more typical of the English and American classrooms. In
these cases they usually gave the pupils in question extension tasks in the same
subject. In several of the English and American classrooms, the considerable length
of the central section of some lessons meant that some pupils finished their tasks
long before others. Considering how common this was, and how it was the direct
result of the teaching method adopted, it was perhaps striking how often the supplementary tasks provided by the teachers were clearly little more than time-fillers
(which is not to say that they were not educative) – adding a picture to a piece of
writing, fetching a reading book or, in the words of one of the teachers of lesson
11.10:

> The rule is 'Finish your own work, help a friend, and then choose something quiet
> to do'.

The next option is *differentiation by activity*. This remains a mainly theoretical
option, since if teachers differentiated at task level, they were more likely to provide
a different task, or to give the same task and allow differentiated outcomes.

Differentiation by seating or grouping, as we have seen, was a common practice
in the English classrooms (where groups might be based on ability, behaviour, or
teachers' desire to counter pupils' preference for sitting in same-sex groups), and in
India where a child's placing in the classroom might relate either to gender or
ability. Elsewhere, apart from the separation of children with special needs or behavioural difficulties to which we have alluded, the use of this form of differentiation
was marginal.

Now we come to *differentiation by time and attention*, one of the two most
prominent forms of differentiation. No teacher, anywhere, gave all their pupils
equal time and attention, in either of the two contexts within which teachers and
pupils typically interact: whole class teaching, and the monitoring of individuals
and groups. In the whole class context, several of the Russian and French teachers
came closest to an equal distribution of time across the class, directing questions at
specific pupils in turn in a manner which suggested that they aimed to engage most
if not all of them during the lesson.

Even here there were exceptions. The teacher at Coulanges, cited above, not only had additional tasks ready to support those of her children who encountered difficulties in mathematics or French and therefore looked to be in danger of lagging behind the rest of the class; she also expected to give them extra attention in the class. And by the end of the mathematics lesson in Moscow School B (example 11.9) our field note count shows that only half of the children had interacted with the teacher in the context of the lesson's direct teaching episodes, although she had interacted with many more while monitoring pupils' written tasks. On the other hand, nearly all the interactions in the former context were sustained, encompassing what by English or American standards were exceptionally long sequences of question and answer. The pupils' answers themselves were full and expository and in several cases were delivered to the class as a whole from the blackboard. Meanwhile, the remaining pupils paid close attention, and for every pupil who answered a question there were many others urgently waving their hands to signal that they too wished to do so. And in this classroom, as in others in Russia, the teacher made a point of directing questions at those pupils who had *not* raised their hands, as well as at those who had.

The message of this pattern of interaction is clear, therefore. Whether or not the Russian teachers managed to interact with every child in the context of direct instruction was perhaps not the point. More important was the fact that the teachers sought to *engage* every child, whether as a speaker or a listener. For in this context the class was working as a class rather than as 25 individuals.

This, I think, is how we square our observations that in Russian lessons teacher–pupil interaction was not evenly distributed with the firm claim made by the director of Kursk School B:

> One parent came in and complained that her child was being asked too little and that too little attention was being paid to him. She wanted the teacher to pay more attention to her child, who she thought was better developed, than to the less developed children.
>
> (*Interviewer: And you believe that all children should be given the same amount of attention?*)
>
> Of course. Although parents naturally think that their child is the most important, we don't think that this child should have more attention than anyone else.

The teacher defines as better or less 'developed' children whom English or American teachers would define as more or less 'able'. The Russian concept of development is quite distinctive, and is discussed in Chapters 3 and 9. In the same way, 'attention' in the teacher's responses above must be taken to include more than classroom interaction alone. 'Equal attention' to Russian teachers meant a common school, a common curriculum, unstreamed classes, common learning tasks, common outcomes – and, as far as is realistic – an equitable distribution of teacher time and attention while lessons are in progress. If the teacher spent more time with one child than with another in a particular lesson this was because that child deserved to achieve no less than the one who was 'better developed'. *Equalizing* rather than equal attention, perhaps.

During the relatively short periods of time when Russian pupils were engaged on solo writing tasks, their teachers monitored them. Again, the interactions were unevenly distributed, although they were also unambiguously individualized. Thus, although the pupils were not grouped or otherwise physically differentiated, one teacher told us that for the purpose of monitoring their progress and assessing outcomes in a Russian lesson she differentiated them by level and allocated her time and judged the nature of the interaction accordingly:

> First there are the children who can work independently at the task I've given them. I may not go to them at all. Next there are the children who need to be prompted from time to time, so during the lesson I'll go to them and give them a little prompt such as 'Are you sure it's a noun?' Then there's a third group. When I go to each of them I might say 'Now write everything down, then find out where the noun is, underline it and show me.' For them I must specify everything and make it concrete.

The Russian pattern can be contrasted with that observed in many of the lessons in England and Michigan, where the monitoring of individuals and groups rather than direct instruction to the class provided the principal context for interactive differentiation. Indeed, in lessons following the typical sequence of a brief whole-class administrative introduction followed by a lengthy group-based unitary central phase and a brief whole class conclusion, the monitoring phase provided the only real opportunity for teacher–pupil interaction. During this phase, typically, the dominant task-related activity – as we noted earlier in this chapter – was writing.

Three patterns of interactive differentiation emerged in the latter contexts: *planned unequal attention, planned equal attention,* and *random attention.* In the first, the teacher made a deliberate decision to attend to one or two groups only during the lesson's central phase, and the remaining pupils undertook tasks which some teachers called, out of hope rather than conviction perhaps, 'self-monitoring' (in Leeds the main characteristics of the tasks given to those children whose activities teachers chose not to monitor was they were undemanding). Alternatively, the monitoring might be undertaken by a non-teaching assistant (NTA). Thus, in the study skills lesson from Hamilton (lesson 11.13) the teacher spent most of the 64-minute lesson with just one group, engaged in both direct instruction and what I termed instructional monitoring, while the NTA supervised the remaining groups. In the Literacy Hour lesson at Kirkbright (lesson 11.15) the teacher worked with just two groups for a sustained period, as she was required to, and again in instructional mode. She signalled her intention to do so in advance by placing on the tables in question signs saying 'We are working with the teacher'.

The second variant was when the teacher sought to interact with each group, if not each individual, in turn. Of the lessons summarized in Chapter 11, the best example of this pattern was the French lesson at Coulanges (lesson 11.3). The length of the lesson (79 minutes) and of its central phase when pupils were working at their writing task in pairs (46 minutes) allowed the teacher to spend eight or nine minutes with each of the five groups, a period which made possible interactions which focused on the task rather than on procedural or routine issues, and which were sustained and searching rather than fleeting or superficial. The teacher, allowing for some random deviation to attend to individuals raising queries, made two circuits of the groups. In the first his interactions were instructional, in the second they dealt with what pupils by then had written and were more evaluative.

Note that in these two cases, as in all the lessons observed in England and Michigan and some of those observed in France, the teachers had the option of interacting with *groups* as well as with individuals and the whole class. In Russia and India, obviously, teachers interacted only with the whole class and with individuals, although their individual interactions took place both in the whole class setting and in one-to-one monitoring (see next chapter, Table 15.3).

The third pattern was random interactive differentiation. Here during the central lesson phase teachers interacted with both groups and individuals and in doing so their progress from one child or group to the next appeared to be either of a random supervisory nature or to be directed by whichever pupils sought their attention or by their behaviour required it. It is in this context that we noted the tendency, which we recorded first in the Leeds study, for those children who do not seek attention not to receive it:

> In the face of the manifest requirement that the teacher should concentrate a great deal of time and thought on certain children in their class, they have to be able to assume that the other children are able to make do with less. The most able, the oldest, the best behaved, girls – they may all, at different times, be seen as the 'undemanding ones' who can be left to their own devices, and the fact that they do just that, without drawing attention to themselves, is taken as evidence that this is both a reasonable expectation and a sensible strategy.[22]

The actual rationale may have been rather different. The Michigan teacher in example 11.10 expressed her intended strategy succinctly: 'I give them one task, then I interact with groups, responding to social and behavioural differences as much as academic'. However, if we cross-check with the categorization of the different *purposes* of interaction as these are explored in Chapter 15, we find that for this particular lesson 24 per cent were routine and 14 per cent were disciplinary (see Table 15.5). Apart from the occasional comments about procedures or noise levels which she issued to the class as a whole, nearly all of this combined 38 per cent of teacher–pupil interactions was with individuals, and in most cases the teacher was responding to something a child had said or done rather than initiating the encounter.

It is this pattern of teaching which Bennett *et al.* termed 'crisis management'.[23] His use of 'crisis' may seem unduly harsh, but the phrase at least points up the way that this kind of pedagogy – long lessons, long unitary tasks, pupils working individually but seated in groups – requires close attention to task design (so that tasks really do engage pupils for the long periods which in this kind of lesson they are expected to work at them) if the balance and content of teacher–pupil interaction is to be determined by the teacher rather than by events. In lesson example 11.10, it will be recalled, the task was to write a response to the question 'If you could meet anyone in the world, who would it be? Why?'

Thus the teacher was right when she responded 'to social and behavioural differences as much as academic' but perhaps underestimated the extent to which these, rather than academic purposes, determined much of her pattern of interactive differentiation.

The other common form of differentiation was *differentiation by outcome*. Where, as in Russia, all pupils performed the same task and the teacher intended that all should perform the task successfully, their teachers nevertheless allowed for the possibility that they might achieve different levels. In the English, French and American schools the principle of *differentiation by outcome* was acknowledged, and indeed the Western concept of the distribution of ability encourages this. However, the idea is differentially applied. The French teachers made it clear that in the teaching of French and mathematics they applied norms whereas in the supposedly less important subjects children could find their own levels. From 1998 the UK government adopted this as policy by setting level-related targets for the test performance of 11 year-olds in mathematics and English while leaving the teaching of other subjects, and children's expected levels of attainment in those subjects, to chance.

In the Indian classrooms, most teachers cited the 'one task, different outcomes' formula, but unlike France and Russia, their chances of containing the spread of attainment were limited by the combination of large classes and minimal resources. Further, teachers often used homework as a device for enabling less able pupils to catch up, but we had little evidence that this worked. Indeed, we felt that we witnessed the attainment gap widening before our eyes in those lessons where a sizeable proportion of the pupils did not understand the task, did not complete it by the end of the lesson, took it home to complete, but brought it back untouched because neither they nor their parents, who were likely to be illiterate, understood what was required or how it should be tackled. At this point the teacher moved on to the next task, the cycle was repeated, and the gap widened still further.

Assessment in the Classroom

Assessment, as noted earlier, both precedes and follows differentiation, but the two judgemental processes also overlap. Thus, in both whole class direct instruction as well as during the monitoring of groups and individuals teachers assess as well as instruct, and when they assess their judgements may feed forward as well as back. The most obvious manifestations of this latter distinction in day-to-day assessment are the grade or mark on the one hand and the oral or written comment on the other. A mark looks back and of itself provides no clues as to how the next stage of learning might build upon the one just completed. An oral or written comment is more flexible. When it is confined to the monosyllabic 'good', 'satisfactory' or 'disappointing' it conveys – save perhaps for its affective *frisson* – no more than a grade; but when it moves beyond judgement to analysis it can convey to the pupil useful information of a diagnostic or instructional kind.

Indeed, in the 1990–92 CICADA study of pupil–teacher discourse in English primary classrooms before and after the introduction of the national curriculum, we found this distinction to be pivotal to our typology of teaching. There, we distinguished between *formative* and *evaluative* feedback. Formative feedback was 'a response to a child's work or utterance containing information of a kind that furthers the child's understanding and/or satisfactory performance of the task', while evaluative feedback constituted 'praise or criticism containing no information of a kind that furthers the child's understanding and/or satisfactory performance of the task'. There was more variation between teachers in respect of formative feedback than in relation to any of the other discourse categories that featured in our analysis. Taking the 14 main discourse variables we identified two clusters, in one of which 36.3 per cent of the teachers' utterances were coded *formative feedback* while in the other cluster the figure was a mere 14.7 per cent.[24]

The second cluster corresponded more closely to those teachers in the earlier Leeds study who had revealed a pronounced tendency to be both generous and undiscriminating in their use of praise. Their feedback was evaluative rather than formative, but because – in keeping with the prevailing professional ideology of the 1970s–80s – they were anxious never to discourage pupils, they sometimes ended up devaluing the evaluation to the point where its function was merely phatic. The most frequently used epithet was 'lovely'. Clearly, after the warm glow induced by the first few of these has subsided, the child may be left none the wiser. The Michigan equivalents were 'Wow' and 'Nice job'.

Classroom assessment, then, is no mere technical device. Teachers assess by making marks on the page or by using words. Behind whatever form they use are not just objective or quasi-objective norms and standards but also assumptions about children's development, learning and motivation, and values relating to matters such as self-esteem and the relative importance of ability and effort.

The last of these, indeed, would appear to be another of our cultural fault-lines. Stevenson and Stigler contrast the Confucian belief in human perfectibility with Anglo-Saxon assumptions about fixed and innate ability. The one, they say, leads to the emphasis on effort which in their view characterizes Chinese and Japanese schooling, the other to what they claim is an endemic American educational fatalism and tolerance of low levels of effort and hard work.[25] Combine this with the belief in individualism which seems to be more prominent in England and the United States than continental Europe or Asia,[26] and with the idea that children develop in their own way and at their own speed and that learning cannot be forced, which was a central tenet of Anglo-American progressivism, and we have some radically different starting positions for the practice of classroom assessment.

In Soviet Russia, too, notions of fixed intelligence were strongly resisted. The work of Elliott *et al.* suggests a softening of this line since *perestroika* and a renewed interest in the concept of human ability, though their comparative studies also support the conclusion that English and American children may be less well motivated and more readily satisfied than their Russian peers.[27] Intriguingly, however, while our Russian teachers emphasized the importance of effort, Elliott's *student* interviewees in St Petersburg stressed ability. Comparing our data on this matter with theirs we came to the conclusion that this may have been because the importance of effort is taken so much for granted in Russian schools that students, if not their teachers, will look elsewhere to explain differences in performance.

However, other research suggests that effort and ability may have been both excessively polarized in the Stevenson and Stigler analysis and treated as semantically more stable than their cultural usage warrants. In a detailed critique of what they see as the ethnocentric use of attribution theory and theories of achievement motivation Bempechat and Drago-Severson contend that:

> Stevenson and his colleagues have pigeon-holed their findings from several Asian cultures into deductive categories which were inductively derived from American culture . . . Stevenson's work thus far has been based on the flawed assumptions that: (a) there is but one way to conceive of effort, ability and the relationship between the two; (b) across cultures, individuals share common notions of effort and ability; and (c) within cultures, there is no variation in the ways in which individuals conceive of effort and ability.[28]

We are used to debates about how 'ability' should be defined: perhaps we should treat 'effort' as a no less problematic concept. The same goes for another key term in this nexus of concepts. Muckle's study of Russian education in the last years of the Soviet regime notes what may seem a startling but, to my mind, extremely important inversion of Western views of human potential:

> Soviet teaching is intended to 'outpace' the child's development, and is supposed to be pitched at such a level that it will bring the child on from the position he has reached to that he can potentially reach, given the help of the teacher . . . It is the task of the teacher to fill this zone [Vygotsky's zone of 'next' or 'proximal' development] and that of the methodologist to help the teacher to find the right method in order to fill it. Thus the weak child has greater, not less 'potential' than the bright one, because the zone of next development is larger. An English teacher might well say that such a child 'has little potential', neatly illustrating that the meanings of that word and the Russian *potensial* are opposites rather than synonyms.[29]

Once again the message of cross-cultural analysis is that we should be extremely cautious in our handling of the vocabulary of international differences in educational performance and how these can be explained. Concepts such as 'development', 'potential', 'ability', 'effort' and 'attainment' must be regarded as no less susceptible to cultural nuance than the classroom practices with which they are associated.

With these caveats in mind we can note that the literature on French primary education would seem to place French educational values, in these matters at least, closer to those of Russia than of England and the United States. The QUEST study of Broadfoot and her colleagues found that despite some recent convergence between the values underpinning the French and English systems, English pupils are still expected to reach widely varying levels of attainment which are determined by their innate ability while French pupils are expected to strive to achieve a common level of attainment to which the only bar, children with special needs apart, is the amount of effort which they are prepared to exert.[30] The result, according to Reynolds and others, is that the spread of attainment is far wider in England than in those countries, like France, which emphasize effort in pursuit of common standards.[31]

To return to classroom assessment: emphasis on common rather than differentiated learning outcomes has an inevitable impact on assessment criteria. Comparing French and English teachers' approaches to assessing children's writing, Osborn and Planel find the French teachers expecting correctness and conformity to a predetermined plan while their English counterparts look for creativity and divergence and emphasise 'process' rather than 'product'.[32] Sharpe adds that French teachers tend to make greater use of negative language and sanctions than do English teachers, and use finite marks where English teachers make open-ended comments.[33]

The tendency to closed, norm-referenced assessment appears to be even more marked in Indian primary schools. The PROBE study notes an overwhelming emphasis on factual memorization and recall in the context of an assessment system which has the selection and 'weeding out' of all but high-flying pupils as its principal purposes, notwithstanding the egalitarian rhetoric of the national government. By the time children approach the end of their secondary schooling the pressure on those still in the system is such that the PROBE study found high levels of anxiety and depression and even cases of suicide.[34] Theirs is not a comparative study, so we do not know whether the situation is worse in India in this respect than in other countries. However, the *Five Cultures* data confirm the PROBE findings about the narrow focus of assessment at the primary stage.

Also exerting influence or leverage on how teachers assess within the classroom, then, are external requirements and procedures. We outlined these for each of the five countries in Chapters 2–6. At the time of writing France has an extensive formal assessment regime which combines start-of-year diagnostic tests, weekly tests, end-of-year monitoring and the *livret scolaire* or cumulative profile which tracks the child's school career and links with regular meetings between the child's parents and teacher. Russia specifies curriculum content and associated levels in some detail, but devolves the assessment of outcomes in respect of these to the school. A similar situation obtains in India. In the United States there is national monitoring, but the critical levels for formal assessment are the state and district, and at these levels both off-the-peg and specially commissioned testing systems are deployed in conjunction with a high level of transparency about the performance of individual schools and districts.

England combines national tests, including baseline assessment of pupils entering schooling, with published results and, until recently, performance league tables. As in the United States, aggregated pupil test performance is used as a measure of the performance of schools – and indeed countries – but in England statutory assessment is expected to bear an even wider range of purposes: reporting on the attainment of individual pupils, evaluating the effectiveness of their schools, monitoring national performance and improving teaching and learning. Clearly, the relationship between a test designed ostensibly with the first of these purposes in mind and the other three may be at best tenuous. To monitor national performance a light sample is sufficient and it is certainly not necessary to test every pupil in the land. Tests in English, mathematics and science evaluate performance in these subjects, but indicate little about the effectiveness of schools beyond this. And measuring learning provides indicators or baselines upon which amelioration or remediation strategies can be based but it does not of itself ameliorate or remedy.

Yet it is precisely this range of not entirely compatible purposes that accounts for what many of the teachers in our English primary schools called 'the burden of assessment'. It was a fourfold burden: in the weight of its demands on teachers' time; in the way it skewed the purposes and curriculum of primary schools away from breadth and balance; in the anxiety and pressure to which it subjected pupils and their parents; and in the public exposure and media pillorying to which it subjected teachers and schools as part of the 1990s political culture of 'naming and shaming' – which Labour deplored while in opposition but then pursued even more zealously than their Conservative predecessors once they gained power in 1997. The primary teachers whom we interviewed in 1986 scarcely mentioned assessment. In the CICADA interviews in 1992, and even more in the *Five Cultures* interviews of 1995–8, assessment and its use for accountability purposes were among the most prominent themes. As far as these teachers were concerned, there was too much assessment, too much was being asked of it and too much was being deduced from it.[35] Further, as we noted from the head teacher interviews (Chapter 10), schools outside the middle-class enclaves felt particularly vulnerable, because Labour's apparent acceptance of the 'value-added' principle (whereby schools are judged in terms of the progress they achieve from different starting points and in different social circumstances) had been undermined by the aggressive 'culture of excuses' rhetoric from OFSTED and Downing Street. By 1998, one of our teachers at Cheetham Primary School knew that she was breaking a New Labour taboo when she dared to say:

> The literacy hour plays down social problems and pins everything on teaching. Its message is that if you follow the model then you'll get the results, but they ignore the social side as if we're teaching in a vacuum . . . It's very hard teaching in an inner city school. It's difficult and it's draining. The problems the children bring make it a very difficult job. Yet for the government it's simply target driven. If you're not meeting your targets you're a professional failure . . . If you work in the inner city and say that the targets aren't realistic then you're accused of having low expectations.

Assessment featured in the interviews with teachers in the other four countries, but nowhere else was it viewed as so oppressive and alienating as in England. Since in several cases (notably in the Michigan schools) teachers were operating assessment regimes which demanded no less time than those in England, it is clear that the assessment 'burden' experienced by the English teachers was only partly a matter of its quantity. They found assessment burdensome because it was outside their control, because it had been imposed on them in a form and at a time that they were not in a position to question, and because – as the above quotation illustrates – it had become so comprehensively politicized.

Once we move beyond the accountability issues prompted by assessment which is externally prompted or organized (as with the Key Stage 1/2 tests in England or the MEAP tests in Michigan) classroom-based assessment raises three basic questions:

(1)   What form does the assessment take?
(2)   Who does the assessing?
(3)   What judgemental criteria are used?

Forms of assessment

It is inevitable almost to the point of being axiomatic that teachers assess pupils' learning on a day-to-day basis mostly by judging how they cope with the normal range of learning tasks rather than by giving them special tests. In France, India and Russia teachers administered brief tests, usually in aspects of language or mathematics, and often at regular intervals (weekly, for example), yet even here such tests constituted a small proportion of the total assessment effort.

This being so, one might expect the forms of assessment to reflect fairly faithfully the emphases of the *tasks* and *activities* which pupils encounter. This works more for task than activity: children are assessed on their assimilation of factual information by being asked to recall it; they are assessed on the understanding of how to tackle a mathematical problem by being asked to solve one. At the level of activity, one might expect assessment to reflect the differences of emphasis that are discussed in Chapter 13. One of the most striking of these was in the balance of oral and written activities. Certainly, where writing was the predominant activity, then it was also the predominant mode of assessment.

However, where there was more oral work, the situation was more complex, for the focus of assessment did not simply switch from writing to talk. Written work continued to provide a significant focus for assessment, but the preponderance of talk as a deliberate and intrinsic learning activity, rather than an incidental one, permitted not so much a quantitative adjustment to the ratio of written to oral assessment as a shift in the entire judgemental paradigm. When children spend most of their time on individual written tasks, assessment can be a private act that involves only the teacher and the individual child. Where talk is a central activity, assessment has the option of going public. Where the governing ideology of teaching is collective rather than individualistic, then the shift from private to public assessment is inevitable.

The broad balance of oral and written assessment is represented in Figure 14.1. In the observed lessons in England, assessment was based mainly on written work.

	Mainly oral	Mainly written
England		———————
France	—————	
India	—————	
Russia	—————	
USA		———————

Figure 14.1   Cross-cultural continua: forms of classroom assessment

In Russia, although pupils' written work was marked, the much more prominent focus and mode of assessment was oral. This emphasis extended to formal examinations for older pupils: a characteristic Russian mode is to give each candidate a set of questions to answer and allow him or her 30 minutes to prepare answers which are then given orally to examiners, who may then test them by interrogation. The teachers we observed in the other three countries combined the two forms of assessment to varying degrees although in different ways.

Agents of assessment

The paradigm shift does not stop there. If assessment is public rather than private then it allows others than the teacher to do the assessing. Teachers may continue to be the main agents of assessment, but oral pedagogy, by making the learning process visible and audible to all, turns pupils into assessors too, whether they like it or not. They listen, they look, and being human they judge.

Teachers can choose whether to exploit this opportunity. They may continue to monopolize the assessment process so that all that happens is that pupils witness the teacher passing judgement on their fellows, probably with a mixture of *Angst* and *Schadenfreude*, and develop elaborate strategies for avoiding being picked on (the hand raised eagerly but not too eagerly, the eye contact which plots a careful course between shiftiness and challenge). Or teachers may choose to translate pupils' eavesdropping into planned and invited acts of peer and self-assessment in which pupils are required to marshall their judgements around questions of evidence and criteria. By bringing these questions into the open teachers can add a vital evaluative dimension to what is being learned and at the same time greatly extend its cognitive potential. They may also deliver powerful social messages to the pupils about the importance of respecting the viewpoints of others, weighing evidence, being fair and considerate, and so on.

However, as I have noted, public assessment may be anything but democratic, and many readers will all too vividly recall teachers who use it to humiliate and tyrannize rather than to teach.

Figure 14.2 represents the continuum as we found it. In England, the teachers did most of the assessing. In Russia, while teachers were no less judgemental, they also made considerable use of self-assessment and peer-assessment, encouraging pupils

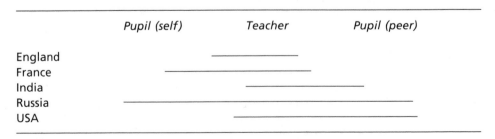

Figure 14.2   Cross-cultural continua: agents of classroom assessment

to comment on their own and each others' answers, and indeed – because pupils were often encouraged to think aloud while tackling a problem – on each others' thinking processes too. This habit started not in the primary school but, we found, at the kindergarten stage, where in one school we observed five to six year olds being asked to comment on each other's paintings. In many of the Russian primary classrooms pupils scored their own performance (on a scale of 0–5) by displaying numbers and discs, and collectively classes were invited to register their agreement or disagreement with answers and explanations. The latter device was also used in India, although there the collective applauding of answers was more ritualized than discriminating.

In the French classrooms, we saw something of the Russian tendency to peer assessment, but it was much less consistent, and we more commonly encountered situations where assessment was oral but monopolized by the teacher. In these circumstances the judgements could be uncompromising. On the other hand, there was considerable emphasis on written self-assessment, and we were shown work contracts in which pupils were required to set down targets for the week, judge how far these had been achieved and rate their progress. In Michigan, there was an emphasis on peer assessment as a continuation of the strong 'sharing' ethic that we found in most classrooms.

Such assessment, however, was sometimes fairly bland, because the prevailing ethic was also one of praise and encouragement. In Michigan, as in England, teachers praised pupils much more freely and regularly than they did in the other three countries and such praise was often without follow-up of a more informative and task-focused kind. A Russian colleague, commenting on the '100 ways to praise a child' poster which we observed more than once in Michigan (and which is apparently to be found in schools all over the United States), wryly suggested that in Russian schools the repertoire of praise contains a mere handful of words while the vocabulary of disapproval is rich and varied.

In fact, the Russian teachers were by no means reluctant to praise, but no less frequently they deployed the accepting but affectively neutral response 'Tak' (just so, correct). Russian pupils were praised if they did exceptionally well or if the teacher had reason to believe that a particular child needed strong support. Tak signalled that they had done what was required, no more and no less: that, after all was why they were in school. So cool and non-committal a judgement would have been unthinkable in the Michigan schools and unlikely in England. There, doing what was required was more likely to be greeted by hyperbole.

Criteria for assessment

Leaving aside formal tests, which everywhere tend to focus upon children's ability to deliver the single 'correct' response – a numerical calculation, a spelling, a historical date, the name of a scientific property or process – classroom assessment is notable for the wide range of criteria by which teachers judge pupils' performance and progress. And although the 'hidden curriculum' is no longer hidden (if it ever was), it continues to remind us that classroom assessments may evaluate much more than *task* performance alone. In assessing two identical pieces of work, a teacher may judge one to be better than the other because in terms of where each of the two pupils has come from it represents the greater achievement. Judgements about the learning task may be subtly qualified by judgements about the children's perceived effort and attitude, and about their relative advantage or disadvantage at the different points from which they each started. The teacher may merge within the one term 'progress' cognitive learning, behaviour, social background, and the extent to which the pupil reaches or exceeds what the teacher expected. In higher education, the pervasiveness of this tendency has resulted in many English universities requiring examiners to mark examination scripts 'blind'. In primary schools, formal tests apart, it is virtually impossible to engineer this kind of anonymity. More to the point, teachers would not want it. They expect to judge the child as much as the performance. Only then, they would say, can assessment be genuinely diagnostic.

This is one zone of potential difference among teachers and cultures in respect of the application of assessment criteria. The other is that teachers may look for different cognitive outcomes from the same task. There are several illustrations of this among the lessons exemplified in Chapter 11, perhaps the most striking of which are the lessons in mathematical problem-solving in Moscow School B and Thoreau (examples 11.9 and 11.12). The problems were similar, but while the Moscow pupils were assessed on their ability to identify the correct sequence of calculations which would lead to a problem's solution, and to apply that sequence accurately and successfully, the Thoreau pupils were expected to demonstrate inventiveness in coming up with different ways of tackling the problem.

To say that one teacher valued 'product' and the other 'process' (which is the usual way to define this difference of perspective) is to misrepresent both of them, for each teacher spent considerable time during their lessons unravelling the arithmetical processes entailed by the problems they had set. However, it does seem fair to suggest that the Michigan teacher was not acutely exercised by the matter of whether childrens' answers to the problem about the exercise books were correct, while this mattered a great deal to her opposite number in Moscow. In this sense, both were concerned with process, but while the Moscow teacher saw process as a means to end, the teacher at Emerson represented process understanding as an end in itself, and her assessment was focused accordingly. Consequently, while the Moscow teacher sought *convergence* in pupil response the Michigan teacher encouraged *divergence*.

We have identified, then, two broad value frames within which the formulation of day-to-day assessment criteria may be set. The first is about the interplay of the cognitive, affective, social and behavioural and the extent to which teachers allow their judgements in the cognitive domain to be modified by their assumptions and values in respect of the other three. The second concerns whether teachers judge pupils' work against predetermined standards and expect pupils to converge on those standards or whether they take a more relativist view and encourage divergence in pupil responses.

Figures 14.3 and 14.4 show the tendencies across the full range of lessons observed. Taking the two representations together, we find what is clearly a much more

	Strongly cognitive emphasis	Strongly affective/social emphasis
England		
France		
India		
Russia		
USA		

Figure 14.3 Cross-cultural continua: criterial emphasis of classroom assessment (other than formal tests) – the balance of cognitive, affective, social and behavioural considerations

	Convergence/precision	Divergence/creativity
England		
France		
India		
Russia		
USA		

Figure 14.4 Cross-cultural continua: criterial emphasis of classroom assessment (other than formal tests) – the balance of convergence/precision and divergence/creativity in pupils' expected responses

instrumental approach to assessment in three of the countries. In India and Russia especially, answers across a wide range of educational objectives were either right or wrong, and teachers did not hesitate to say so. In the Michigan schools, in contrast, teachers were altogether more cautious about delivering such unequivocal judgements and this showed itself in exchanges where they would receive, accept and welcome an answer but not pronounce it right, wrong, valid or invalid, for indeed nearly every answer was accorded some kind of validity.

In England, too, teachers tended to receive and to judge positively rather than negatively. In assessing written work they looked to find features on which the child could build, always seeking to keep assessment formative rather than summative, and sometimes reversing a negative judgement for fear that it might harm the child's self-esteem. 'Now what did I say about doing a graph that's all squashed up?' sternly demanded one teacher, before catching sight of the pupil's face and adding 'Well, I suppose it's all right'. In extreme cases (such as we found in the Leeds study) praise becomes a habitual or reflex response to everything a child does, in which case it ceases to serve even the purpose of motivating and encouraging the child, let alone of assessing and providing feedback on the child's progress.[36] However, when we look at the discourse we shall find that assessment becomes more subtle than this: there are ways of delivering a negative judgement while appearing to be positive, and in the English classrooms we observed, alongside undiscriminating praise, the tactic of registering disapproval or disappointment by receiving a pupil's response without comment.

In France, we encountered mixed messages. The established culture of assessment appeared to be not unlike that in the Russian schools, that is to say one that required pupils to converge upon the single correct response, solution or outcome. On occasions it could also have an edge which American or English teachers would have found acid or brutal, and we observed French teachers whose judgements of their pupils would have been deemed sexist elsewhere. At the same time, other teachers were clearly operating in accordance with the 'new' pedagogy of individualization, encouragement and creativity. Yet our sense that pedagogical values were in transition was confirmed in cases when pupils were asked to write stories in accordance with an apparently open-ended brief which were then 'corrected' not just for grammar and spelling (which in all the French classrooms were deemed important) but also for content – as if there was only one way to write the story after all.

Let us take two examples which illustrate several of these contrasting approaches to assessment. In the first, from France, we see an emphasis on cognitive outcomes, age- or stage-referenced norms, grades or marks, and a combination of teacher- and self-assessment. In the second, from Michigan, we find the emphasis shifting to affectivity and behaviour, and to individualized learning and individualized assessment criteria; we can also note the tension between professional and administrative values – those of the teacher and those of the district officials – which are identified in Chapter 10.

Accounting and self-accounting in France

Alongside baseline assessment at the start of the school year, tests twice a term and the *livret scolaire*, teachers in Coulanges regularly completed standard-format profiles on each pupil under the headings of French, mathematics, history and geography, civic education, science and technology, artistic education, physical education and sport, and cross-curricular competences. For each there was a detailed range of behaviours ('copies a text without mistake' . . . 'measures with a graduated ruler' . . . 'recognizes and respects the rights of others' . . . 'sings in tune and expressively' . . . 'works autonomously') which the teacher marked 'not yet acquired', 'acquired', or 'in the process of being acquired'. These profiles were sent home to the parents, who signed and returned them, commenting as necessary. The processes of assessing the pupils and completing the profiles was supported by a six-volume Ministry compendium *Aide à l'évaluation des élèves* which for every one of a much longer list of behaviours for each subject provided an assessment task classified by subject, level and competence and accompanied by instructions as to its administration, a commentary, and a list of typical pupil responses and how to score them.[37]

At Grenade, a village school whose teacher was influenced by Freinet's ideas about self-assessment, each pupil also had a two-weekly work contract which 'permits the child, the parents and the teacher to organize and control the work done during this period' and which had been drawn up by the teacher to include the main categories of (a) individual and (b) collective work to be encountered during the two-week period in question. The pupil noted on the contract when each piece of work had been completed. At the end of the first week the pupil was required to complete two sentences: 'I am satisfied with my progress because . . .' and 'I am not satisfied with my progress because . . .' At the end of the second week the pupil, the parents and the teacher each completed an evaluation section on the contract (*bilan de mon travail pour cette periode*) judging how much progress the pupil had made (*en progrès – stable – en baisse*).

Anecdotals in Michigan

Alongside regular student progress reports on standardized forms provided by the district administration, teachers at Emerson developed their own procedures for assessing and recording progress and for reporting to parents. As far as they were concerned, the district's forms were a chore and the in-house procedures were what they and the parents found most useful. Thus, one of the teachers at Emerson kept in her hand for much of the day a notebook in which she wrote observations about the academic progress and behaviour of each child during her extensive periods of monitoring. Sometimes she did this unobtrusively while at other times – for example, where there was a behavioural transgression – she made eye contact with the child about whom she was writing. The children, she told us, were well aware that they were being continuously monitored and written about. The notes were made on two sheets: 'positive anecdotals' (blue) and 'negative anecdotals' (pink) and along-side each child's name she wrote both comments and codes (for example, 'I' for 'child interrupted teacher or another child' or 'H' for 'child hit a fellow child'). The 'positive anecdotals' were mainly academic:

> If they ask a really intriguing question I write it down. If they're working independently or making new connections in reading, I note that. I also do daily writing and reading anecdotals for every child, to give a running record.

The 'negative anecdotals' mainly focused on behaviour. All such records she then transferred to her computer database and this material provided a very full account of each child's progress to inform her weekly curriculum planning and the meetings with parents four times each school year. In addition, at the end of each week she gave every child his/her 'Friday folder' to take home. This included examples of work and comments ('stories about the kids') based on the positive and negative anecdotals. Parents were encouraged to write their own comments before returning the folder on Monday morning. In contrast to the district sheet, that required teachers to score the pupil's progress ('Has mastered the skill', 'Working on the skill', 'Chooses not to perform the skill or activity', 'Exceptional achievement' and for pupils with special needs 'Modified program') in the teacher's records and reports there were no grades, only 'stories' about the child and examples of his or her work.

The moral judgement exercised by the Michigan form in cases where children were not yet on the starting blocks ('chooses not to perform the skill or activity') contrasted strikingly with the more neutral and matter-of-fact 'not yet acquired' in the French equivalent. But then, children's motivation and behaviour were much more prominent concerns for all the Michigan teachers than they were for those whom we interviewed and observed in southern France (Figure 14.3).

This questionable view of the learning process apart, the Michigan teachers' disdain for their district's record appeared to be justified to the extent that parts of it made very little sense. Teachers were expected to record performance levels against un-specified criteria:

Science	Understands concepts presented
Social studies	Understands concepts presented
Art:	Participates
Music:	Participates
Physical education:	Participates
	Sportsmanship[38]

Perhaps this revealed as much about the school district's curriculum priorities as about its approach to assessment. Art and music, in this corner of the United States at any rate, require no active engagement of either an intellectual or aesthetic kind, only participation. Meanwhile, in the sciences and social sciences it is enough merely to receive and understand whatever unspecified concepts are 'presented'. Thinking and acting scientifically are apparently not on this particular menu.

The Other Three Rs: Routine, Rule and Ritual

The 'three Rs' of routine, rule and ritual are in their way no less important than the three Rs with which all of us – not least those Michigan school administrators – are more familiar. This is more than a stylistic device founded upon alphabetic coincidence, for routine, rule and ritual are distinct concepts, and all three are funda-mental to the culture of the classroom and the work of schools. Teaching is both rule bound and in many of its actions highly routinized; children, too, are expected to internalize and adhere to routines; and as well as the more eye-catching school rituals which are discussed in Chapter 9 – assemblies, teachers' days, the Pledge of Allegiance, and so on – much of classroom life, too, is ritualized.

Routine, rule and ritual have a relationship which is partly hierarchical and partly contingent. A routine is a procedure that through habit and use becomes unvarying. However, 'routine' also shades into the weak sense of 'rule'. In this sense a rule is a routine to which is added an expectation that the unvarying procedure in question is required rather than merely habitual. So in its weak sense a rule is a routine with teeth. In its strong sense a rule is an explicit direction, requirement or regulation which must be obeyed, and whose transgression may well invoke sanctions. 'Ritual' stands slightly apart from the routine–rule continuum when it signifies a prescribed and established ceremony, although here again the word has both a strong and a weak sense. There is the world of difference between the grand ritual events of church, temple, state and indeed school and what people choose to call their 'daily rituals', which may be little more than routines. Yet ritual is also highly dependent upon rules, both to take place successfully and in relation to what is ritualized. So a coronation ritualizes, above all, a set of rules determining the place in a nation of monarch, aristocracy and commoners, the governors and the governed. Finally, ritual can be either pregnant with meaning or utterly meaningless for the people who are involved in it, in which case we complete the journey and find ourselves back in the world of routines. This is the sense in which, in our discussion of learning tasks and activities in the previous chapter, we encountered Edwards' and Mercer's opposition of 'ritual' and 'principled' knowledge.[39]

So routine, rule and ritual are both distinct and intertwined. In classrooms they are the cement which binds together the otherwise anarchic combination of one adult and 15 or 50 children. Educational researchers, by and large, have tended to be more interested in rules than in rituals or routines. One exception is the study by Brown and McIntyre.[40] They worked with experienced secondary teachers to make explicit those aspects of their teaching which had become routinized and therefore taken for granted. Their study allows us to differentiate more sharply two kinds of routines hinted at earlier: the repertoire of ways of acting and managing events on which in their daily encounters with pupils *teachers* draw; and the procedures which *pupils* are expected to follow and internalize in their work and behaviour. Brown and McIntyre dealt with the former.

From their programme of observation and interviews Brown and McIntyre developed a theory of teachers' routines which was more subtle than the rather unfocused notion of 'habitual procedures' allows. Each routine involved teachers in defining a learning or behavioural goal and pursuing it by selecting from their repertoire the action most appropriate to the prevailing classroom conditions (a variant on the 'fitness for purpose' principle). In any one lesson a teacher might face many different combinations of goals, actions and conditions, and the 'speed, fluency and apparent lack of deliberation' with which experienced teachers translated each such encounter into effective action enabled Brown and McIntyre to justify the use of the term 'routine' to describe the process.[41]

Clearly, over many lessons such routines will attend to a large number of issues. However in their work with teachers in England they found the following recurrent foci for teachers' routines:

> A good and easy relationship between the teacher and pupils . . . Pupils to understand what the teacher is asking them to do . . . Pupils who (for whatever reason) are reluctant to work, to be actually working . . . All pupils to be applying themselves well to their work . . . Pupils to be thinking about, and understanding, what they are doing, rather than just doing what they are told.[42]

Routines in this sense, then, are ways that teachers tackle the central challenges of teaching as it happens. Wragg's study dealt with routines in the other sense, those which a teacher expects *pupils* to follow, and which I suggested are on the same continuum as classroom rules. Wragg showed how during the first few encounters between a class of children and a new teacher, typically at the start of a school year, much time is spent in establishing, maintaining and reaffirming the rules and routines until they become, in Edwards' and Westgate's phrase, 'grooved in' and implicit.[43] Wragg identifies nine categories of rules in English primary classrooms, governing movement, talking, on-task behaviour, the presentation of written work, safety, the use of classroom space, the handling of equipment and materials, social behaviour and what counts as appropriate clothing. Under these headings he lists 45 rules which in his early 1990s observational study were laid down by primary teachers at the start of the school year. Of these – significantly in view of this book's insistence on the pedagogical significance of interaction – the largest number relate to talk.[44]

These talk-related rules – 'Put your hands up if you want to ask a question', 'Don't talk when I'm talking to you', 'Be silent during registration', and so on – almost all focus on what discourse analysts call *turns* (which is unusual in the world of jargon in meaning what one would expect it to mean). In a classroom there is only one teacher and a large number of children so it is hardly surprising that the rules of turn-taking are not only prominent but also themselves feature frequently in classroom exchanges – 'How many times do I have to remind you to put your hands up?' 'Let Emma have a turn at answering.' Turn taking remains a prominent preoccupation as children spill out into the playground and enact, contest and bend their own rules for balancing the need for co-operation with the desire to head the pecking order.

Rules become progressively more internalized as the school year proceeds, so that within a few weeks the injunction 'Don't talk when I'm talking to you' either becomes unnecessary or can be signalled by a finger on the lips, by eye-contact or even by the teacher's simply stopping for a couple of seconds to expose the talker to the superior rule-consciousness of the rest of the class. As a variant, to muffle the peremptoriness of such regulation, teachers may use obliquely directed periphrasis. A perennial favourite in English primary classrooms, especially with younger children, is 'Somebody's using a big voice today'. There is no confrontation here, no statement of the rule, and no identification of its transgressor. Curiously, this slightly arch formulation seems to be more effective than the ubiquitous escaping of pedagogical steam – 'Shh . . . shh . . .'. A linguistic anthropologist might be able to make something of the fact that we heard 'Shh' in four of the five countries, and that sound and intent were identical in French, English English, American English and Russian. So there are some universals in teaching, then.

However, there is another set of talk-related rules, and these are rarely made as explicit as those which govern turns. These are the rules that shape what used to be called the 'hidden curriculum' and they stem from, and reinforce, the power-differential which is intrinsic to all teaching. These unwritten rules of classroom discourse are the detailed gloss on the rule of two-thirds which we discussed earlier. Thus (Edwards and Mercer): it is the teacher who asks the questions; it is the teacher who defines the correct answer; and a repeated question signifies a wrong answer.[45] Or (Edwards and Westgate): appropriate participation in classroom talk requires pupils to listen, or appear to listen, at length; to know how to bid for the right to speak; to understand that their contributions will be evaluated, interrupted, terminated or dismissed; to learn that their task in teacher–pupil discourse is to find the 'right' answer ('guess what I'm thinking'); to recognize, in short, that they have *unequal communicative rights.*[46]

While rules in general, as Archer reminds us, 'establish boundaries [of inclusion and exclusion] and boundaries are essential to the continuation of rules',[47] in interaction the social rules are essential to its meaning. Giddens argues that meaning in human interaction depends on Austin's idea of 'mutuality of uptake' together with engagement with its *moral order* of norms, rules, constraints, sanctions, rights and obligations, and with its framework of *power relations* – dominance, subordination, empowerment, personal and collective interests, and so on.[48] Classrooms are thus not unique in the way their interaction is suffused by the agenda of power relations, although they represent a loading of the balance of power that is utterly distinctive.

Penetrating deeper still we come to the rules which govern language itself:

The ingredients of language are words and rules. Words in the sense of memorized links between sound and meaning; rules in the sense of operations that assemble the words into combinations whose meaning can be computed from the meanings of the words and the way they are arranged . . . Much of the richness of language comes from the tension between words and rules.[49]

This is Steven Pinker's summation, and in his study of the psychological and neural origins of regular and irregular forms he acknowledges that the relationship between sounds, words and rules is contested territory. There is more on this later. For now it suffices for us to make the point that in speaking of classroom rules it is simply not good enough to start and stop with those rules which schools make explicit (see Chapter 9) – often writing them down and for good measure communicating them to parents – or even to be content with this canon of formal rules plus the unwritten 'hidden curriculum' rules of unequal communicative rights. Behaviour, classroom interaction, and the linguistic structure of that interaction are all subject to rules with which children in classrooms must come to terms. Further, every school subject has its own rules of engagement: the rules which count one mathematical solution right and another wrong, the rules which judge one piece of scientific or historical evidence valid and another questionable, the rules which elevate one child's painting over another. In the culture of school and classroom, in the hidden curriculum and the formal curriculum, rules are everywhere. Teachers make some explicit. Many more must be detected and unravelled by the children themselves.

If this is so, then it must be apparent that to map out the full array of routines, rules and rituals in any classroom would be a formidable undertaking, and that in a five-country cross-cultural comparison it would verge on the impossible. In the next two chapters we shall probe more deeply the rules of interaction and discourse. Here we try to identify cultural differences within a relatively modest framework.

Most of the rules and routines identified by Wragg (above) were *procedural*. The *Five Cultures* data suggest five categories, of which one is procedural. They are: temporal, procedural, behavioural, interactive, linguistic and curricular.

	Routine	Rule	Ritual
Temporal			
Procedural			
Behavioural			
Interactive			
Linguistic			
Curricular			

Figure 14.5   Mapping classroom routines, rules and rituals

Temporal routines, rules and rituals (RRRs) are manifested in school and class timetables, the structure of the school year, week and day, and the temporal structure of lessons, in as far as any or all of these are regularized and regulated, which they usually are, even in the context of what I earlier termed 'elastic time'. Time, then, is perhaps the pre-eminent regulator of pedagogy. *Procedural* RRRs cover several of the areas identified by Wragg, and deal mainly with how children should conduct themselves in relation to classroom space, equipment and materials and to the tasks and activities set. *Behavioural* RRRs deal with how children should relate to the teacher and each other. *Interactive* RRRs are pre-eminently concerned, as we have noted, with turn taking. *Linguistic* RRRs govern the content of classroom interaction, as opposed to its social dynamics. *Curricular* RRRs set the conceptual boundaries and requirements for the subjects taught and learned.

If one wished to undertake a close study of the routines, rules and rituals in one classroom, or even one lesson, one might map them in terms of a framework such as that contained in Figure 14.5.

I should stress that the *Five Cultures* data allow us to access expected pupil routines much more effectively than teacher routines as defined by Brown and McIntyre. Their study was in the important domain of educational research which engages with teachers' 'craft knowledge', the focus of my own 1986–7 study.[50] Such research is highly intensive and typically requires sustained observation and a progressively focused sequence of interviews, perhaps prompted or illuminated by audio/videotaped lesson extracts. This intensive process serves two purposes: to give the researcher the necessary insight into how the teacher thinks and how professional thought relates to classroom action; and to help the teacher to bring to consciousness, formulate and articulate not just random ideas but the framework of beliefs, theories, dilemmas and decisions of which his or her professional thinking is constituted.[51] Although we did interview teachers after observing their lessons, we did so only once in each case, and covered many issues besides their lesson-related thinking and decision-making. This, combined with the fact that interviewing through an interpreter (as in India and Russia) is decidedly *not* the best way to access the fine grain of another person's thinking, meant that in this project we dealt mainly with required pupil routines.

Comparisons

In Chapter 15 we shall investigate the balance and context of teacher–pupil inter-actions of different kinds – work-related, routine, disciplinary and so on. In the context of our current discussion we might bring forward one or two of the findings. We observed a much higher proportion of *routine* and *disciplinary* interactions in England and Michigan than in any of the other countries (Table 15.5). Thus, the ratio of *task* to *routine* and *disciplinary* interactions at Coulanges (lesson 11.3) was 91:5:0. At Kursk A (lesson 11.7) it was 94:0:6. At Thoreau, however (lesson 11.12), it was 56:20:24; at Ogden (lesson 11.14) 38:46:10 and in the literacy and numeracy hours exemplified in lessons 11.15 and 11.16 the ratios were 75:7:15 and 68:21:11. The contrast between the figures for Kursk and Ogden bear repetition: our analysis of the full transcript for the Kursk A Russian lesson yielded not one routine interac-tion; at Ogden *nearly one half* of the interactions were routine.

To explain differences as marked as these we must consider, as always, the inter-play of culture and organization. The Russian teachers paid unswerving attention to the learning task, to the exclusion of nearly everything else, and their pupils, by and large, complied. Whole class teaching predominated, episodic lesson structures kept pupils on task and reduced the risk of divergence in engagement and outcome. Lessons were highly predictable. Routines were less visible in the Russian classrooms (and indeed in those in France and India) not because there were fewer of them but because they had been much more thoroughly taught and internalized and they therefore, as it were, disappeared from view. A high degree of lesson predictability allowed them to remain relatively invisible.

In most of the English and American classrooms, in contrast, the pupils worked in groups, a pattern of organization which tests teachers' hold on routines much more severely than does whole class direct instruction. Furthermore, there was far less of the predictability that characterized the lessons in Russia and India. Rou-tines, then, were not instilled and embedded in the first few lessons of the first few days of the child's life at school, as they undoubtedly were (and are) in Russia and India, but were subject to constant flux as the child progressed from one teacher to the next and even one lesson to the next. Routines were subject to a continuing process of re-invention. For this organizational reason they were bound to feature much more prominently in the interactions between teachers and their pupils in the English and American contexts.

Returning to the cultural explanation, which of course cannot be detached from matters of organization since classroom organization is in part a working-out of culturally embedded values, we can add a further difference. Routines were a frequent topic of teacher–pupil discourse in the Michigan classrooms because teachers allowed and perhaps encouraged them to be. In an authoritarian teaching culture routines will not be negotiated or contested because teachers will simply not permit this to happen, while in a teaching culture that espouses democratic values routines not only will be negotiated and contested but by definition must be. The combination of complex classroom organization, unpredictable lesson structure and avowedly democratic pedagogy, such as we found in Michigan, is a sure-fire recipe if not for conflict then certainly for the constant testing of regulatory boundaries.

If these explanations are correct, then while one might expect less emphasis on *routines* in contexts where lessons are predictable, structured and teacher dominated, one might also anticipate that in such contexts *rules* and *rituals* will be rather more in evidence, because it is through rules that the boundaries of appropriate action are set and it is through rituals that they are maintained. Let us test this while applying the rest of the framework mapped out in Figure 14.5.

The French lessons were indeed rule bound, but not in the way that our lead into this topic via Michigan might suggest. With the younger classes (for example at Juan-le-grand, lesson 11.1) teachers might need to issue occasional reminders on procedure and behaviour, the areas which were most prominently contested in Michigan – 'You're not sitting properly' . . . 'You shouted out' . . . 'You didn't put your hand up' – but in most French classes neither procedural nor behavioural rules were mentioned. Instead, overt classroom rules concentrated upon the interactive, linguistic and curricular domains of teaching and learning. Thus, the same lesson at Juan-le-Grand was almost entirely preoccupied with the rules of pronunciation and spelling. The Cimiez lesson (11.3) reduced the writing of narrative to the application of a formula. The lesson at St Etienne (11.2) signalled clearly that there were certain quite specific ways to read and interpret texts, before moving on to a classic lesson on conjugation, a central component of French language teaching which has no parallel in English primary schools since the English language has now lost most of its inflexions and verb forms are relatively few. In all the French lessons, whatever the subject, pupils' adherence to the rules of 'correct' spoken and written French was under constant scrutiny. Even the art lessons which we observed were highly formulaic – not quite 'painting by numbers', but almost.

This emphasis was made all the more pointed by the relaxed manner and casual dress of many of the teachers, particularly the men, and by the individualistic and often modish clothing of the children. The message of all this was clear: the procedural and behavioural boundaries are set, understood and not open to question; we don't make a fuss about them unless this is absolutely necessary, and we certainly don't make the mistake of presuming that regulating childrens' and teachers' dress will regulate their conduct or learning; instead we concentrate on what really matters, and the consequent emphasis on the rules governing interaction, language and the disciplines keep procedure and behaviour in line.

The effect of all this was to make the French classrooms far more business-like in their daily dealings than those in the other four countries. Routines were in place, rules concentrated on what was taught and learned, and how, and there was little ritualization.

The Russian classrooms were even more overtly rule bound. Beside every blackboard were the posture diagram and accompanying instructions which can be seen in Plate 8. All lessons began in the same way, with the pupils standing by their desks. If they wished to answer a question (and they vied with each other to do so) they were required not to wave their arms vaguely in the air as in England or Michigan but, starting from a position where their arms were folded, to rotate one arm to the upright position, keeping its elbow firmly cupped in the other hand. If invited to answer a question the pupil would then stand up smartly, step into the gangway, address the teacher and class in ringing tones, and sit down, although only when told to. That of course was the ideal: even in so regimented a setting the rule might be relaxed, and in some lessons teachers themselves deviated from their own regime by encouraging pupils to call out if they wished to generate interest or excitement. However, even this comes nowhere near to deflecting from the purpose-fulness, precision and pace of the teaching.

If procedure, behaviour and interaction in the Russian classrooms were rule bound, language and curriculum were no less so. There was a formulaic thrust to much of the coverage of subject matter, and an even stronger emphasis than in France on 'correct' speaking, reading and writing, and on the rules of spelling, punctuation, syntax and grammar.

However, whereas in the French classrooms there was little evidence of ritual or ritualization, much of what we observed in Russia verged on the ritualistic, especially in respect of procedures such as starting and finishing lessons, arranging desk-tops, answering questions and participating in self-assessment.

The tendency towards ritual was even more marked in the Indian classrooms. Here, routines were again established, implicit and the object of only occasional reminders. As elsewhere these focused mainly on turn-taking. The curriculum, as in France and Russia, was manifestly rule governed, and here too we saw examples of ostensibly free composition that were highly formulaic. However, if teaching was more overtly ritualized in India than in the other four countries, the reasons by now should be clear. Regimentation and ritualization are to some extent the inevitable imperatives of teaching large classes of 50 or 60 children. But, more fundamentally – as we saw in Chapter 4 – two of the main formative traditions in Indian primary teaching, Brahmanical and colonial, also embodied a highly ritualized relationship between teacher and pupil, and indeed between both teacher and pupil and the text (or curriculum). The one shaped the quasi-priestly role and authority of the teacher and the antiphonal character of teaching exchanges. The other reinforced this with the 'rite of rote' of British elementary education. Since both traditions pivoted on particular kinds of teacher–pupil *interaction*, it was not surprising that the inter-active core of the lessons we observed was more highly ritualized than any other aspect. Add to this the daily school assemblies and one realizes why ritual is such an ubiquitous and inescapable feature of mainstream Indian pedagogy, and why so many of the recent experiments and reforms (as reviewed, for example, by John Shotton[52]) have concentrated on transforming the power relationship between teacher and taught which this tradition embodies.

In the English lessons we see the balance of regulatory attention tipping back from interaction and curriculum to procedure and behaviour. Except in denomina-tional schools, the all-important assembly has largely divested itself of serious reli-gious content and has become instead a vehicle for transmitting humanistic values and for reinforcing the idea of the school as a community (see Chapter 9). Consist-ent with this emphasis, school rules dealing with behaviour are explicit, and these frequently invoke communal principles. Classroom rules in the settings we observed sustained this ideal by dwelling less on simple procedural prescription and proscription of the kind seen in Russia and more on moral principle and justification, often underlining the core communal value by making the principle collective. 'In class 6 we do x . . .'. 'In class 6 we don't do y . . .'.

In most of the lessons we observed routines had clearly been established, yet the high proportion of routine interactions indicated the kinds of tensions which I discussed above. Routines were both established and fluid, the relatively complex organization subjected them to fairly constant pressure, and the values which teachers espoused in respect of learner choice, empowerment and autonomy forced them to tread a narrow path between direction and permissiveness. The communal value permeated the discourse however, whatever its actual message. In three sampled sections from lesson 11.13, for example, the teacher initiated what were in effect instructional interactions with 'Let's . . .' or its variant 'Shall we . . . ?' on no fewer than 36 occasions. In Russian, Indian or French classrooms the form, as well as the meaning, would have been that of a command.

This downplaying of rules and accentuating of the ideal of co-operation was for many English teachers eroded by the arrival of the national curriculum in 1988 and still more by the introduction of the Literacy and Numeracy Hours in 1998–9. The National Curriculum imposed on teachers (that, at least, was how they saw it at the time) the rules of subjects, while the Literacy and Numeracy Hours regulated lesson time and teaching method as well. So by 2000 the regulatory context of English primary classrooms embodied at best a slight tension and at worst a downright contradiction, depending on how far individual teachers wished to assert their established professional values in the face of the heavy-handed policing of OFSTED. For OFSTED defined teaching exclusively in terms of strict compliance with rules and was a pretty determined enforcer of those rules.

The tensions in the English situation are therefore somewhat different from those we encountered in Michigan. In England we found teachers responding to the increasing pressure of external regulation either by passing it on to the pupils or by seeking to domesticate or neutralize it in order that the more communal and less overtly directive ethic inherited from the 1960s, the 1970s and early 1980s could also be sustained. Although the Michigan teachers were themselves under pressure from external agencies, especially at the local level (see Chapter 10), this had nothing like the force of England's combination of National Curriculum, national testing, Literacy Hour, Numeracy Hour, OFSTED inspection, naming and shaming, league tables and the frequent assaults on teacher competence by the press, ministers and the chief inspector. The tensions we observed in the regulatory environment of the Michigan classrooms were as likely to be self-induced.

Here the emphasis in classroom rules and routines was at the furthest remove from France and Russia. The emphasis was almost exclusively on procedure and behaviour, including, from the domain of interaction, turn-taking. But by comparison with all the other countries the domains of language and curriculum, although necessarily sustained by routines, were relatively light on rules.

However, what we did notice was a tendency to the ritualization of routines which was more pronounced in some of the Michigan classrooms than anywhere else. So the Emerson language lesson (11.10) was punctuated by a series of 'checks' – 'people check', 'coat check', 'eye check', 'group check' and – mischievously proposed by one of the pupils one cold, wet morning as a parody of these – 'boot check'. The group check was preceded by a three-two-one-zero countdown during which the teacher closed her eyes. When she opened them she expected to see the pupils paying attention (teachers in Russia, India and France would have simply told the children to do so). The ritual striking of the chime bar required all pupils to stop whatever they were doing. At the same time the curriculum routines were procedural rather than epistemological – 'writer's workshop', 'peer conference', 'author's chair'.

At Thoreau (lesson 11.12) the collective ethic penetrated the task- and routine-related interactions to an even greater degree. The normally routine acts of gaining the pupils' attention or of getting them to listen to each other were handled obliquely in order not to sound directive:

T   I have Jane's eyes . . . I don't have Liane's eyes . . . JD's talking. I don't see Group 5 looking at him. I don't see Group 3 looking at him . . . Boy, that Group 5 is doing a lot of talking still . . . I would hate to put Group 5 on my unhappy face list . . .

The same obliqueness conditioned the curricular routines:

T   Where are you gonna begin?
P   Could this be a times problem?
T   I don't know. What do you think?

Clearly, the teacher *did* know. Moreover, the pupil had already hypothesized that solving the mathematical problem in question required multiplication and so did not need to be asked what she thought. Yet the teacher would not commit herself to an explicit judgement in the way a French or Russian teacher would, so in this case 'I don't know' really meant 'No it isn't a times problem', while 'What do you think?' meant 'Try again'. Question was countered by question in a sequence that in theory could have gone on for much longer. On this occasion it did not.

This stance of sometimes extreme equivocation in task-related exchanges and procedural routines leads us to make the probably obvious point that the notion of rules in the context of democratic pedagogy is vastly more problematic than it is in a setting where the authority rests unambiguously with the teacher. For, as Archer proposes, 'rules establish boundaries and boundaries are essential to the continuation of rules'.[53] Here the boundaries were forever shifting, and pupils perceived this and occasionally gave vent to their sense that this was unfair:

T   [*To P1*] Frank, don't holler out. You don't have to do that, you're a good boy.
P2 Why do you keep on calling him a good boy?

I suggested that some of tensions in the routines of Michigan teachers like the one from Thoreau referred to here were self-induced. That they were self-induced rather than externally imposed was demonstrated by the Hawthorne teacher (lesson 11.11), whose classroom regulatory framework was quite unlike that observed in other Michigan classrooms. It lacked the ambiguity and equivocation which we observed elsewhere. Routines were clear and consistent and her six-year-old pupils had internalized them. Rules were never mentioned. Teacher talk was fluent, focused and direct. Yet, lest it be suggested that this was because she was organizationally less adventurous than her fellows, let me add that this was the teacher who used different methods in different lessons, and had the children begin the lessons in question by moving the furniture to match the method. Organizationally, she was the most versatile Michigan teacher that we observed. But she was also very much in charge.

I speculated earlier that lessons which are structured, predictable and subject to a high degree of teacher control focus on *rules*; while those which are more loosely structured and less predictable, and which seek to democratize control, tend to dwell more on *routines*. The speculation would seem to be confirmed. In the first scenario routines rapidly become internalized, and are then sustained by the quotidian round of minor rituals and by the more overtly and frequently reinforced rules of interaction and subject matter. In the second scenario, rules – which require stability to make any kind of sense – are subverted by constant change and may in any case be felt to sit uncomfortably with the ideal of negotiated learning and a reflexive curriculum. Meanwhile, routines, too, are subject to daily challenge, yet in the absence of other regulators must be adhered to at all costs. This time, then, it is the routines that may become ritualized, and in extreme cases this may begin to detract from the very curricular purposes which they are supposed to serve. If I have concentrated more on the second scenario this is because it is rather more problematic than the first. An authoritarian classroom is much more easily managed than a democratic one, unless, that is, teacher and pupils have attained the fine balance of freedom and responsibility which democratic action entails.

15

Interaction, Time and Pace

The Management of Interaction

In 1997 the UK government launched its campaign to raise standards in primary school literacy and numeracy. 'Interactive whole class teaching', which was to play a prominent part in this campaign, was spun to ministers by their advisers, and by ministers to a no doubt grateful nation, as the 'factor x' which would do for primary education in the UK what it had done for education and indeed economic performance in continental Europe and South-east Asia.[1]

Interactive whole class teaching was packaged as a novel strategy, indeed a revolutionary one. In fact research evidence indicated that whole class teaching had been on the increase in English primary schools for several years before New Labour's advisers appropriated it[2] and the power of structured talk in children's learning had been the object of research and development for many years before that.[3] But then, governments sustain their claims to radicalism largely by misrepresenting their predecessors' initiatives. Predecessors' positive achievements, being more problematic, are simply airbrushed from the political record.[4] When educational research had become thoroughly politicized, as in England by the mid 1990s it had,[5] political expediency required that those research findings which were either (in New Labour argot) 'off message', or for that matter on message but off time, be either misrepresented or ignored.

Since interaction of some kind is intrinsic to all teaching, the term 'interactive whole class teaching' is at best tautologous. To assess its usefulness as a tool for reform we need to discover how far the classroom interaction associated with initiatives bearing this particular reformist tag differs from what went before. Thus, for example, one study of the government's Literacy Hour in action concluded that while the quantity of whole class interaction may have increased its character may have changed only marginally, if at all, and closed questions designed to get pupils to recall previously imparted information continued to predominate.[6] We also need to compare the kinds of interaction that have developed in English primary classrooms with those – for example in Russia and France – which reflect a stronger and much more sustained tradition of oral pedagogy.

Yet even when, as in England, the learning tasks which teachers devise require pupils to spend far more of their time engaged in activities such as reading, writing, listening and looking than in talking (Table 13.4), the instructional core of pedagogy remains quintessentially oral. The third question prompted by the proposition with which we started this cross-cultural investigation of the elements of teaching ('teaching . . . is the act of using method x to enable pupils to learn y') was 'By what forms of interaction does the teacher present and sustain the learning tasks and activities?' 'Method', the term more commonly used to encompass the central acts of teaching, is certainly not reducible to interaction alone. Method encompasses the management of time, space and resources. It includes the management, through grouping and differentiation, of the activities of not one pupil but many. It entails socialization into rules, routines and rituals. But all of these too, as well as that instructional core, are to a large extent communicated or framed by interaction.

I have suggested elsewhere and in an earlier chapter that every teaching strategy has three basic dimensions: *organization, discourse* and *values*.[7] 'Organization' is readily understood. 'Discourse' carries both everyday and technical meanings, and is not synonymous with 'interaction', which is an altogether looser notion that includes non-verbal as well as verbal communication.[8] 'Values' suggests part of the domain of meaning but not the whole of it. So with these definitional caveats in mind it might be helpful, in the context of our particular concern at this point with teaching method, to modify the categories to *organization, interaction*, and *meaning*. That allows me to explain a division of attention in these chapters which at first sight may seem inappropriate, indeed illegitimate, but which I think can be defended on methodological as well as practical grounds.

Observational research in the tradition which can be traced back to Ned Flanders in the United States, and indeed earlier, categorizes classroom interaction ('teacher talk', 'student talk', 'questions', 'directions') and in very broad terms defines the meaning of what has been categorized ('accepts', 'praises or encourages' and so on) but does not examine such meanings in detail or treat their ascription to particular utterances as in any way problematic.[9] The systems for coding teacher and pupil talk which were devised by Deanne Boydell and adapted for use in Galton and Simon's ORACLE project and its 1990s sequel, and indeed in the London study of Mortimore and his colleagues, are traceable in their essentials to Flanders, although by the late 1990s such systems were being used in conjunction with qualitative procedures.[10] At some remove from this kind of coding exercise are the contested territories of linguistics and discourse analysis, which move between elucidating language form and structure and eliciting the way meanings are made and conveyed and the manner in which teacher–pupil exchanges are controlled and channelled. To those working in these fields studies in the Flanders tradition are viewed as capable of providing insight into the organization of classroom interaction, but little more.[11]

Yet the organizational context is extremely important, because among the reasons why the discourse of classrooms is so unlike everyday conversation is that it is framed and shaped not only by its pedagogical purposes and the power differential between teacher and taught, but also by the no less pervasive power of the clock and the crowd. Classroom talk is *managed* talk; and to manage classroom talk is to orchestrate events, people and time as well as knowledge, understanding and learning.

Hence the division of attention between this chapter and Chapter 16. We look first at the broad forms, features and logistics of classroom interaction as managed talk, and then introduce the dynamics of time and pace. Then in Chapter 16 we examine in much greater detail the way, within these frameworks, meaning is shaped and conveyed.

The 'rule of two-thirds', the 'rule of three-quarters' and other kinds of asymmetry

Flanders' celebrated 'rule of two-thirds' held it to be a truth universally observable, if not universally acknowledged, that for about two-thirds of the duration of most school lessons somebody is talking; that about two-thirds of this talking is done by the teacher; and that two-thirds of the teacher's talk consists of direct instruction in the form of questions, instructions and exposition.[12]

In similar vein, the first ORACLE study, which involved observing not just whole classes but also individual pupils, found a pervasive 'asymmetry of interaction' which we might now rename the 'rule of three-quarters' and set it alongside Flanders' 'rule of two-thirds'. Three-quarters of teachers' interactions with pupils were with individuals, but for the individual pupil three-quarters of his or her interactions with the teacher were as a member of the class. Although by the mid 1990s, when the ORACLE follow-up was undertaken, English primary teachers were interacting less with individuals and more with whole classes, where each pupil was concerned the rule of three-quarters still applied and '75 per cent of all pupil–teacher exchanges [were still] experienced as a member of a class'.[13]

These forms of pedagogical asymmetry are a direct consequence of the most basic asymmetry of all, the fact that there may be 20, 30 children in a class (or many more than that) but there is only one teacher. 'Learning to live in a classroom', Philip Jackson noted, 'involves learning to live in a crowd'.[14] He might have added that for the teacher it involves not so much managing a crowd – for teaching is not, or ought not to be, merely crowd control – but managing *individuals* in a crowd.

One of the important contributions of the ORACLE study to our understanding of the organizational aspects of classroom interaction, our concern in this section, was the way it related the organizational and interactive components of teaching methods within a typology of teaching 'styles'. Thus, ORACLE postulated 'class enquirers' (teachers who interacted mainly with the class, and used mainly question and answer), 'group instructors' (who dealt mainly with groups and concentrated on supervising pupils' execution of their learning tasks) and 'individual monitors' (who interacted mainly with individuals and spent most of that time checking rather than instructing).[15]

Researchers now prefer to avoid the term 'teaching style' because it implies that it is the overall 'style' – the generalized agglomeration of teaching behaviours and attributes – which produces differential gains in pupil learning, whereas these gains are more likely to stem from particular attributes and strategies which can be generic to several styles.[16] For example, it is now generally accepted that cognitively demanding interaction is a fundamental condition for all successful teaching of young children, however it is organized. Unfortunately, the insistence by OFSTED and the UK government during the late 1990s that whole class teaching was the key to raising standards suggested that in official circles, at least, the teaching style fallacy continued to rule unchallenged. Whole class teaching may yield interaction that positively scintillates with cognitive demand, or it may be mind-numbingly pedestrian.

The other virtue of the ORACLE typology is that it can be adjusted to accommodate different combinations of organization and interaction (class instructors and group enquirers, for example), and indeed the shift from individual to group and whole class interaction in English primary schools which was charted in the 1990s ORACLE follow-up study allowed the original typology to be modified in a way which displayed both the changes and the continuities: 'class enquirer', 'class/group instructor', 'group supervisor' and 'individual monitor'.[17]

Other kinds of asymmetry emerged from my own studies. In Leeds, using systematic observation of teachers and target pupils, we confirmed the ORACLE team's finding about pupils' limited opportunities for interaction with the teacher. The most extreme case was a classroom where

> individual children were involved, on average, in only one work interaction every half hour, and only one interaction of any kind every ten minutes, while the teacher was involved in more then twenty times as many interactions as the pupils, or at least one every half minute.[18]

In both the Leeds study and its predecessor we found that primary teachers themselves were acutely exercised by the dilemma which this finding points up, of how to apportion their interactions among the pupils for whom they were responsible. Typically, they presented their choice as between equal and unequal 'investment' of time and attention, and this remains a central concern in day-to-day classroom management.[19] The dilemma had inescapable implications not just for the quality of classroom interaction but also for what a lesson's learning tasks demanded of the pupils and what its activities demanded of the teacher.

In the Leeds study we classified interactions for the purposes of quantitative analysis and at the same time, mindful of the limitations of this approach, tape-recorded lessons in order to subject the discourse to qualitative scrutiny. The quantitative study revealed the distribution of interactions, over all teachers and lessons, which is shown in Table 15.1.

We then examined the balance of the different kinds of interaction in the ten classrooms. The wide variation between classes was striking. There was variation, first, on a continuum ranging from frequent short interactions to infrequent longer ones; and second, in respect of the proportion of interactions we designated 'work', 'monitoring', 'routine' and 'disciplinary' (Table 15.2).

These figures provoked important questions. It is a reasonable assumption that in teaching we should seek to maximize the number of interactions between ourselves

Table 15.1 Type and frequency of teacher–pupil interaction, based on systematic observation of the lessons of ten English primary teachers over two weeks[20]

	Frequency	%
Work interactions	4,564	37
Monitoring interactions	2,452	20
Routine interactions	3,322	27
Disciplinary interactions	1,260	10
Other interactions	729	6
Total interactions	12,327	100

Table 15.2 Rate of each type of teacher–pupil interaction in ten classes, based on systematic observation of ten English primary teachers over two weeks[21]

Class	Work	Monitoring	Routine	Disciplinary	Other	Total
A	67	56	88	26	8	245
B	44	31	40	19	11	145
C	54	35	131	22	15	257
D	52	26	52	47	14	191
E	68	87	34	4	17	210
F	47	62	55	17	14	195
G	48	15	41	23	4	131
H	59	40	28	19	4	150
I	61	31	45	7	4	148
J	79	43	62	31	13	228
Mean rate	58	43	58	22	10	191

Rate = mean number of interactions per hour

and our pupils which are directly related to the content of the learning tasks we have set, and to minimize those of a routine and disciplinary nature, and for this reason the interaction profile of class E may seem worthier of emulation than that of class D. But the quality of a teacher's work-related interactions is not necessarily defined by their number, and the Leeds evidence suggested that it is equally important for the teacher to ensure that work-related interactions should be as sustained as the task requires. Frequent but brief monitoring of a child's progress with the activities set, especially if the interactions are overwhelmingly routine in their content (class C) may not achieve so much as longer although less frequent interactions. The larger the class, the more the teacher will be forced to compromise between the desire to give each child the attention which the acts of teaching, monitoring and assessment require and the necessity to ensure that interactions are long enough for these purposes to be achieved.

In this form the dilemma is by no means universal. Indeed, it is peculiarly English (and to a degree American too), for it stems from a belief that every child is different and that teaching and learning should therefore be individualized. The belief, which relates to the broader Anglo-American ideology of individualism, was central to the received professional wisdom of English primary education during much of the second half of the twentieth century, and it yielded increasingly complex attempts to deliver on individualization through flexible curricula, multiply targeted learning tasks and complex grouping strategies. By the 1990s the practices and possibly the belief too, were in retreat. Meanwhile, in France, Russia and India – not to mention many other countries – uniform tasks and whole class teaching continued to express the very different view that when we teach children in classes we should concentrate on what they have in common rather than on their differences.

In the CICADA study, which followed the work in Leeds and investigated the impact of the national curriculum on pedagogy, we found that individual interactions were still dominant and that the balance of whole class teaching, group and individual teacher–pupil interactions had not changed significantly during 1986–92. This, however, was in the early days of the national curriculum, when teachers were trying hard to accommodate the new content requirements to existing patterns of pedagogy. By the time the second ORACLE team undertook their classroom observations, in 1996, English primary teachers had begun to capitulate to the demands of an overcrowded curriculum, and perhaps to other pressures too, and the proportional increase in whole class teaching was clearly discernible.[22]

The organization of interaction: international comparisons

The combination of direct observation, field notes and videotape in the *Five Cultures* project allowed us to take our exploration of the organizational aspects of classroom interaction into the international arena. We subjected these data to four kinds of analysis:

(1) *Interaction participants*. The number and proportion of interactions between teacher and class, teacher and groups, teacher and individuals, pupils and class, pupils and pupils, pupils and teacher.
(2) *Utterance length*. Separate calculations for teachers and for pupils.
(3) *Interaction mode*. Teacher–pupil interactions were classified, following the Leeds categories, as 'instructional', 'monitoring', 'routine', 'disciplinary' and 'other'.
(4) *Interaction and lesson stage*. For analytical purposes most of the lessons were treated as single units. That is to say, they yielded figures for each lesson as a whole. However, we have shown in Chapter 13 how important to an understanding of teaching is a recognition of the distinct focus, structure and tempo of the different stages through which lessons pass, and we therefore subjected a sub-sample of the lessons to a stage-by-stage analysis.

An 'interaction' was defined for this essentially computational exercise, as it was in the Leeds and CICADA studies, as an exchange containing either a complete *initiation–response–feedback/follow-up* (IRF) sequence (as defined by Sinclair and Coulthard[23]) or a partial, *initiation-response* (IR) one. The IRF exchange structure is one of the characteristics of classroom talk that differentiates it most sharply from the structure of everyday conversation (where when we answer a question we do not expect the questioner to tell us that our answer is right or wrong). The feedback component is not merely instructional, as we shall see in Chapter 16: it also reflects the power differential between teacher and taught. Teachers ask questions, pupils answer them, and teachers then deliver a judgement on the adequacy of the pupil's response.

One vital difference between the Leeds/CICADA and the *Five Cultures* lesson transcriptions significantly constrains our analysis, and will do so even more when we look at the nexus of interaction and meaning in Chapter 16. In the Leeds and CICADA projects our data were the words as spoken; in the *Five Cultures Project* the data, for three of the countries, were the words as translated.

We cannot overemphasize the hazards of drawing conclusions about interaction from data in which the words analysed, however scrupulously they have been translated, are not the words uttered. However, the present phase of our analysis remains legitimate because it deals with those who participate in interaction (where the words uttered are not the issue), and the focus and mode of interactions (which require only a generalized ascription of meaning, for which translations will serve, rather than an exploration of nuance). Interaction length is both less and more problematic, for while of the four basic analyses it was the only one which used the words as uttered rather than as translated, inferences about the significance of differences in interaction length then become risky because some languages express the same idea with greater brevity than others. Moreover, an informal, conversational style of classroom discourse of the kind used in many of the Michigan and UK lessons tends of its nature to involve longer utterances, and many more pauses and changes of direction, than do the crisp, succinct and highly controlled exchange sequences of classic direct instruction:

T   OK, star or smiley on the top of the paper. Come on kids, hang in, it's a little hard but you can do it. You'll get another chance, OK, so don't go back. Oh good. We're going to back up Jacob for this last page. Page 20. Oh, we haven't done page 23. All right, 23. Rebecca, will you read? I think I'm going to skip some of you boys and girls and just go over so we can get out in time for recess. Rebecca, please read the directions on top of the page. Lamar, please sit down. I'll come to you, I promise.   (Michigan)

T   Correct. Now someone tell me, what is a prefix? Look carefully in your books, find out and tell me. Barantsava, what is a prefix?   (Moscow)

Our response to these constraints is to counsel, and exercise, more than the usual caution in respect of the use and interpretation of the ratings and figures which follow. We present first the overall figures for the lessons from each country. We then take individual lessons to explore how the pattern of interaction changes as a lesson progresses from beginning to end.

Table 15.3 Balance of interactions in primary school lessons in five countries

	(a) Interactions involving both teachers and pupils			(b) Interactions involving pupils only		
	T–C	T–G	T–I	I–C	I–G	I–I
England (a)	2	1	4	1	1	4
England (b)	3	2	3	1	1	4
France	4	1	2	3	1	2
India	5	0	1	5	0	0
Russia	4	0	2	5	0	1
USA	2	1	4	1	1	4

T = teacher; C = class; G = group of pupils; I = individual pupil

For each category, (a) and (b):

5 = most of the interactions observed;

4 = around two-thirds to three-quarters of the interactions observed;

3 = about half of the interactions observed;

2 = around one quarter to one third of the interactions observed;

1 = a small proportion of the interactions observed;

0 = none of the interactions observed

Notes: (i) An interaction is defined here as a complete initiation–response–feedback/follow-up (IRF) or initiation–response (IR) *exchange*.

(ii) In this analysis teacher–class (T–C) interactions include both teachers' interactions with the class as a whole and their interactions with individuals in the context of whole class teaching. By the same token, T–I interactions are those in which teachers dealt with individuals in the context either of monitoring or extended individual attention.

(iii) At any one time I–I interactions may be taking place at the same time as T–G or T–I. Only T–C and I–C interactions preclude others taking place at the same time. For this reason the teacher and pupil counts are dealt with separately.

(iv) England (a) excludes lessons taught in accordance with the UK government's 1998–9 literacy and numeracy strategies. England (b) consists only of lessons taught in accordance with the literacy and numeracy strategies.

Table 15.3 shows the balance of interactions between teachers and whole classes, groups and individuals, and between individual pupils, the class as a whole and – where they are grouped – their groups. Such differences can be represented as numbers (of interactions), percentages, bands or means, but because the precision of numbers in the presentation may imply equal precision in the raw data, they appear as ratings on a scale 0–5.

The figures confirm some of the national differences to which we have already referred. Teachers in the primary schools in England and Michigan interacted substantially with individuals as well as with groups and the class; those in India interacted mainly with the class as a whole; those in Russia also interacted mainly with the class but also to a significant degree with individuals. In France there were slightly more individual interactions and there teachers also dealt occasionally with groups; overall, though, the dominance of teacher–whole-class interactions and the

Table 15.4 Teacher and pupil utterance length in 25 lessons from five countries

| | Utterance length in seconds | | | |
| | Teachers | | Pupils | |
	Range	Mean	Range	Mean
England	1–40	4.6	1–9	2
France	1–55	7	1–12	3
India	1–20	2	1–3	1
Russia	1–30	4	1–40	5
USA	1–90	10	1–15	3

Note: An utterance is defined here as the I, R, or F component of an IRF or IR exchange, that is to say as a discourse *move*.

balance of group and individual interactions corresponds to the findings from the QUEST study.[24] England and Michigan had the highest proportions of interactions with pupil groups, a form of interaction which we did not observe at all in India or Russia (not surprisingly, since in those two countries pupils were seated in rows for all lessons except art). The predominantly whole-class context of interactions in India and Russia is accentuated further by the higher incidence there of pupil interactions with the class. At the other extreme, although grouping was ubiquitous in the observed classes in England and Michigan, teachers still interacted mainly with individuals, and individuals seated in groups tended to interact with other individuals rather than with the group as a collaborative unit. Table 15.3 also shows the increase in whole class teaching and in teachers' working with small groups which occurred with the introduction of the UK government's literacy and numeracy strategies.

Table 15.4 takes as its unit not *exchanges* (IRF or IR) but utterances or *moves* (the separate I, R or F components of an IRF or IR exchange) because we wanted to test our prima facie observation that pupils and teachers talked at greater length in some countries than others. We tried this on just five lessons from each country. The analysis excludes teachers or pupils reading aloud.

The shortest utterances, whether of teachers or pupils, were very short in all countries – 'yes', 'no', a pupil's name, a one-word answer (from a pupil) or the repetition of a pupil's one-word answer (from the teacher). This much is universal, and uncontentious. However, from this point onwards, the warning about comparisons based on translated material must also be remembered. That warning duly noted, we could cautiously observe and tentatively interpret some interesting differences. The Michigan figures for teachers, as noted above, reflect a slower, more conversational and discursive style of teacher talk. Those for the French teachers reflect the relatively high incidence of expository and explanatory teaching.

The differences in the lengths of pupil utterances, most of which were answers to questions or instructions, also merit comment. Short questions and even shorter answers characterized the Indian lesson. With the other countries, the regression effect associated with the calculation of means tends to disguise differences which are in practice quite noticeable and which the figures for pupil utterance range do convey. The most notable of these was the fullness of some of the answers proffered by the Russian pupils:

T   Now these letters, YA and YU, are sometimes called soft consonants, and there is a connection here. What are they connected with? Anyone? Dima? Listen carefully, the rest of you.
P   When we pronounce the letter YA, the sound is soft.
T   Well done so far, you're doing well. Carry on.
P   And when we pronounce the letter A that's called a hard sound because it's not connected to any consonant. The letter YA, when it's pronounced, is similar, but it's joined to a consonant sound and it works in a totally different way. Therefore you can't really put YA together with YU.

(Kursk A, lesson 11.7)

Coming closer now to the meaning of interactions, let us compare the balance of purposes which they served, using the Leeds study's distinction between 'work', 'monitoring', 'routine', 'disciplinary' and 'other' (Table 15.5).

The Russian teachers maintained the most consistent focus on instruction. Among the lessons and teachers observed in the Michigan classrooms there was the widest fluctuation in this regard, with teachers like the one featured in lesson 11.11 (Hawthorne) maintaining an uninterrupted instructional focus while others (for example, lessons 11.10 and 11.12) spent much more time on monitoring, routine

Table 15.5 Balance of teachers' different interaction purposes in primary classrooms in five countries, expressed as proportions of all those interactions observed in each country which involved the teacher

	Instruction	Monitoring	Routine	Disciplinary	Other
England (a)	2	3	1	1	1
England (b)	3	3	1	1	1
France	4	2	1	1	1
India	5	1	1	1	0
Russia	4	2	1	1	0
USA	2–3	3	1–2	1–2	1

5 = most of the interactions observed;
4 = around two-thirds to three-quarters of the interactions observed;
3 = about half of the interactions observed;
2 = around one quarter to one third of the interactions observed;
1 = a small proportion of the interactions observed;
0 = none of the interactions observed

Notes: England (a) excludes lessons taught in accordance with the UK government's 1998–9 literacy and numeracy strategies; England (b) consists only of lessons taught in accordance with the literacy and numeracy strategies.

and disciplinary interactions. The proportion of disciplinary interactions in the French, Indian and Russian classrooms was, with only two exceptions, very small indeed. Those exceptions were a music lesson taught by a pre-service trainee in Russia and an art lesson taught by an experienced teacher in France. The common factor here was the teachers' deviation from the established conventions of whole class teaching, and it provides one clue to the very different balance of interactions that we observed in England and America on the one hand, and France, India and Russia on the other. For in the English classrooms, as in Michigan but unlike those elsewhere, pupils worked as members of groups and they worked on tasks whose constituent activities were heavily biased towards lengthy spells of reading and writing. Such activities make heavy demands on teachers because they make differential demands on pupils, whose responses then become more and more divergent the longer the teacher allows for their completion. As if to reinforce this argument, the lessons in England which followed the prescribed formulae for the UK government's literacy and numeracy hours showed a discernible shift away from monitoring and routine interactions and towards instruction.

Interaction and lesson stage

To tip the balance of analysis back somewhat towards the lesson as a whole, we should note the extent to which the pattern of interaction may change as a lesson progresses from start to finish. In England, where we regularly observed lessons with brief procedural introductions, long unitary central sections, and brief procedural conclusions (see Chapter 11), the changes in interaction were marked. Here is a composite example, based on a pattern frequently observed in the Leeds and CICADA studies but also replicated in the *Five Cultures* data.

> Pupils are seated in three mixed-ability groups, designated 'red', 'blue' and 'green'. During the lesson's introductory stage, interactions are predominantly between the teacher and the class as a whole. They are lengthy, administrative rather than instructional in focus, and, one group at a time, deal with the activity or activities to be undertaken as much as to the substance and purpose of the learning task to which the activities are directed. Pupils then start working in their groups and the lesson's central stage has three sub-phases of interaction. In the first, the teacher moves rapidly from one group to the next, briefly checking to see that pupils understand what they have to do and engaging in interactions with both groups and individuals which are routine in focus and fleeting. Next, the teacher moves round the groups again, this time remaining with each group for longer, often indeed sitting down with them, and she engages in interactions which are more sustained, are mainly with individuals (although they also include occasional shifts to teacher–group and teacher–class interaction to make a wider teaching point or to warn about noise levels) and are more likely to be focused on instruction. This sub-phase is the one with the heaviest concentration of instructional interaction and the most sustained focus on the learning task. Then, and perhaps the most difficult sub-phase for teachers to handle, some pupils finish their activities while others begin to encounter difficulties or to lose concentration. At this point the teacher's systematic group-by-group progress round the class may be interrupted or

even halted by the increasing numbers of pupils who require or demand attention, and interactions become briefer, almost exclusively teacher–individual, and their focus alternates rapidly but unsystematically between instruction, monitoring, routine and – increasingly – discipline. Finally, the teacher ends the lesson either with a sequence of sustained teacher–class and teacher–individual interactions of a recapitulatory kind and with a clear instructional focus ('what have we found out?'), or having run out of time he or she hurriedly tells the pupils to tidy up and has a series of brief, routine or administrative interactions with the class and individuals.

The changes in the character of the interactions during the course of this kind of lesson occur on every dimension that we have discussed in this section: participants (teacher–class, teacher–group, teacher–individual, pupil–class, pupil–pupil, pupil–teacher); utterance length, and interaction focus or purpose (task, routine, disciplinary, administrative, other). In contrast, the pattern of interactions on each dimension is notably more stable in the French lessons and considerably more so in those from Russia and India. Those from Michigan vary from one lesson, and one form of organization, to the next. But the most telling differences emerge when we look at the extent to which teachers managed to secure and maintain a clear concentration in their and the pupils' interactions upon the learning task. The conclusion that there is a connection between the content of interactions and the organizational frame within which they are set is irresistible.

To demonstrate this general point Tables 15.6–15.11 set out the figures for six lessons. Those from England contrast one lesson organized along the lines of the

Table 15.6 The changing pattern of interaction during a lesson – France (Coulanges: lesson 11.3, French)

Lesson stage	1	2	3	4	5	6	7	8	9	Average
Interaction participants										
Teacher %										
T–C	100	88	20		8	88	100			58
T–G										
T–I		12	80	100	92	12				42
Pupils %										
I–C		86	17			86				27
I–G/I			48	55	52					22
I–T	100	14	35	45	48	14	100			51
Teacher–pupil % interaction focus										
Task	100	88	100	100	92	89	66			91
Routine						8	11	17		5
Discipline										
Admin										
Other		12						17		4

Table 15.7 The changing pattern of interaction during a lesson – Russia (Kursk A: lesson 11.7, Russian)

Lesson stage	1	2	3	4	5	6	7	8	9	Average
Interaction participants										
Teacher %										
T–C	100	70	100	29	100					80
T–G										
T–I		30		71						20
Pupils %										
I–C		12		100	7					24
I–G/I										
I–T	100	88	100		93					76
Teacher–pupil % interaction focus										
Task	100	80	94	100	95					94
Routine										
Discipline		20	6		5					6
Admin										
Other										

Table 15.8 The changing pattern of interaction during a lesson – Michigan (Thoreau: lesson 11.12, mathematics)

Lesson stage	1	2	3	4	5	6	7	8	9	Average
Interaction participants										
Teacher %										
T–C	78	6		8	21	43	62			31
T–G			8							1
T–I	22	94	92	92	79	57	38			68
Pupils %										
I–C					90					13
I–G/I	71						57			18
I–T	29	100	100	100	10	100	43			69
Teacher–pupil % interaction focus										
Task	11	75	100	67	75	64				56
Routine	33	19		33	13	7	38			20
Discipline	5	6		12	29	62	24			24
Admin										
Other										

Table 15.9 The changing pattern of interaction during a lesson – England (Ogden: multiple focus lesson: language, maths, art)

Lesson stage	1	2	3	4	5	6	7	8	9	Average
Interaction participants										
Teacher %										
T–C	44							12	14	8
T–C		12	6	54	36	64	7	35		24
T–I	56	88	94	38	64	36	93	53	86	67
Pupils %										
I–C				14						1
I–G/I	80									9
I–T	20	100	100	86	100	100	100	100	100	90
Teacher–pupil % interaction focus										
Task		63	56	38		55	60	65	7	38
Routine	78	37	25	31	91	27	40	29	57	46
Discipline	22		19	23		18		6	7	10
Admin										
Other				18	9				29	6

Table 15.10 The changing pattern of interaction during a lesson – England (Kirkbright: lesson 11.15, Literacy Hour)

Lesson stage	1	2	3	4	5	6	7	8	9	Average
Interaction participants										
Teacher %										
T–C	75	80	25	78						65
T–G										
T–I	25	20	75	22						35
Pupils %										
I–C	25									6
I–G/I										
I–T	75	100	100	100						94
Teacher–pupil % interaction focus										
Task	75	58	88	78						75
Routine		14	12							7
Discipline	25	14		22						15
Admin		14								3
Other										

Table 15.11 The changing pattern of interaction during a lesson – England (St Teresa's: lesson 11.16, Numeracy Hour)

Lesson stage	1	2	3	4	5	6	7	8	9	Average
Interaction participants										
Teacher %										
T–C	100		36							45
T–G										
T–I		100	64							55
Pupils %										
I–C			100							33
I–G/I										
I–T	100	100								67
Teacher–pupil % interaction focus										
Task	58	100	45							68
Routine	42		22							21
Discipline			33							11
Admin										
Other										

one outlined above with two taught in accordance with the 1998–9 literacy and numeracy strategies.

The most obvious explanation for way the Kursk A teacher kept her interactions so firmly on task was that she used the controlling power of whole class direct instruction for most of the lesson. In contrast, the teachers in the Thoreau and Ogden lessons interacted for much of the time with individuals and groups and therefore lost contact with the rest of the class for those periods. The latter teacher, moreover, switched frequently from one interactive mode to another in the manner of the ORACLE 'style changers'.[25] In the Kursk A lesson, as in other lessons we observed in Russia, there was little change in organization and dynamics as the lesson moved from whole class to group mode, and from oral to written work, and back again. However, this is a partial explanation only, for whole class teaching does not rule out interactive variation, and reading and writing tasks feature in whole class lessons too. Sometimes (as in some of the French whole class lessons) the length of time spent reading or writing may be substantial. Indeed, to presume that the high incidence of instructional interactions in the Russian lessons was the result of whole class teaching is to espouse the very teaching style fallacy against which I warned earlier. The form and focus of teacher–pupil interactions are a matter of deliberate professional choice, and are only to a degree dictated by organizational circumstance.

I suggest that there are five reasons why the Russian teachers maintained a consistent instructional focus in their interactions from one lesson stage to the next, and kept routine and disciplinary interactions to a minimum. First, and above all, they were determined, and schooled by training and habit, to do so. Instruction was their task, enabling children to outpace their natural development was their goal. Second, the whole class teaching mode supported this goal, although it certainly did not guarantee it. Third, the teachers adopted the Comenian variant of whole class teaching which breaks lessons down into a developmental sequence of short episodes, several of them to each lesson stage. These allow little time or opportunity for the kinds of pupil responses and behaviours that force teachers to downgrade interactions from instruction to routine or discipline. Fourth, teaching followed a predictable sequence from one lesson to the next, so most of the routines were already known and internalized anyway. Finally, as Elliott, Hufton and Illushin have shown in their comparative studies of Russian, English and American classrooms, pupil motivation was high and pupils understood the importance of effort. By and large, pupils accepted that they were in school to work and did not have to be coaxed into doing so.[26]

This essentially cultural rather than organizational argument makes sense when one notes that the Coulanges lesson was by no means dominated by whole class direct instruction yet maintained a high task focus in its interactions, while the Kirkbright literacy hour, which had more teacher–whole class interactions than Coulanges, was nevertheless interrupted by routine, disciplinary and administrative interactions. Certainly, as both the Leeds and the London studies showed, complex forms of classroom organization militate against maintaining a consistent task focus.[27] Yet the Thoreau lesson, which also failed to achieve a high task focus, was not at all complex organizationally.

So in respect of the maintenance of pupils' task focus, classroom organization is important but it may be transcended by culture. The high incidence of routine and disciplinary interactions in the Thoreau lesson seemed to us to result less from the chosen method of organization – a whole class introduction followed by individual and paired seatwork in a group setting and completed by a whole class plenary during which pairs of pupils came to the board to 'share' their solutions to the mathematical problem which the teacher had given them – than from the teacher's commitment to a 'democratic' mode of pedagogy in which unequivocal command was consciously leavened by suggestion, persuasion and acceptance of pupils' viewpoints (and for which mode of pedagogic discourse the words 'share' and 'sharing' were emblematic):

T   How many are in the circles? How many do you see?
P1   I see three.
P2   I see four.
T   Go count 'em. We'll ask 'em. Wait for them to explain and then they'll tell you. Ssh. Jessica's writing down their solution. Rick's writing down their solution. Trying to think how does their solution match with his. Ssh. Joey's got everybody's solution down.
P3   I'm tired of waiting.
T   I know. Life's tough. It's hard, a lot of work, but it helps you to focus on other people's writing or thinking.

P3   My hand's tired.

T   OK, are you ready to share? [*Whispers to P4*] Did you finish ahead of them? You're doing really well John. I'm so proud of you today. You did a good job today. [*To class*] OK, turn around and see if your classmates are ready. Let them know that you are ready. Ssh. JD's looking at the board. He's starting to talk.

(Michigan, lesson 11.12)

Monitoring: the invisible teaching method

We noted the different proportions of instructional and monitoring interactions in the lessons observed. We can now pull together some of the threads of this brief exploration of the organizational aspects of classroom interaction.

In any lesson, there are three basic ways of organizing pupils for teaching and learning: whole class, group and individual. These alternatives – as the 'simultaneous', 'mutual' and 'individual' method – have been the subject of debate for at least two centuries.[28] There is a contingent connection between these forms of organization and teachers' modes of interaction, although not a necessary one, and it can be represented as in Figure 15.1.

Thus, the main forms of whole class teaching are direct instruction and teacher-led discussion, and these allow teacher–class, teacher–pupil, and pupil–class interactions. Two of the versions of group work identified here reflect the distinction, first noted in the ORACLE research, between pupils working as individuals *within* groups (the group as a 'base') and collaboratively *as* groups (the group as a 'team').[29] However, there is a third form of group work, when the group becomes in effect a mini-class and the teacher sits with them for the purposes of direct instruction or teacher-led discussion. To encompass these three variants, Figure 15.1 distinguishes between group work which is *collective* (teacher led), *collaborative* (pupil led) and

Organizational frame	Interaction mode	Participants
Class	Direct instruction	t–c / t–i / i–c
	Discussion	t–c / t–i / i–c
Group (collective)	Direct instruction	t–g / t–i / i–g
	Discussion	t–g / t–i / i–g
Group (collaborative or 'team')	Discussion	i–i / i–g
Group (individualized or 'base')	Direct instruction	t–i
	Monitoring	t–i
Individual	Direct instruction	t–i
	Monitoring	t–i

Figure 15.1   The relationship between organization and interaction (i)

t = teacher; c = class as a whole; g = group of pupils; i = individual pupil

Note: this framework is extended in Figure 16.2.

individualized. Finally, pupils may work individually within a whole class setting and have one-to-one interactions with the teacher for the purposes of either direct instruction or monitoring.

Now we know a certain amount about the forms of interaction associated with whole-class teaching. From Flanders' enunciation of the two-thirds rule onwards, researchers have devoted considerable attention to teachers' questions, expositions, explanations and instructions.[30] We know much less about interaction between pupils within collaborative groups, and very little about monitoring.

The dearth of material on collaborative group work reflects its rarity as practice, although in England by the late 1990s it was becoming a slightly more familiar feature of classroom life, partly in response to studies like those from Leicester and Exeter universities, and partly from a dawning realization of its considerable potential, when properly organized, simultaneously to advance pupils' cognitive and social learning.[31] Dunne and Bennett, for example, identified and established training protocols for three types of collaborative group work in primary classrooms:

(1)   Group members work on the same task but for different outcomes, sharing ideas while doing so.
(2)   Each group member works on a specific aspect of a single joint task, producing different outcomes which combine somewhat as the pieces in a jigsaw puzzle.
(3)   Group members work together on a single joint task to produce a single joint outcome.[32]

Each of these produces a different form of collaboration, and the discussion imperative varies from weak to strong. When children work individually on the same task such collaboration as takes place is incidental rather than essential. When each child contributes to a joint task the sub-tasks as such may or may not require discussion, but defining them and reconstituting their outcomes almost certainly does. However, when the group has a single task which is expected to produce a single outcome then discussion, and indeed the associated dynamics of negotiation, are inescapable.

In contrast to the emerging literature on classroom discussion, there is little on teachers' monitoring. Yet monitoring is a far more common form of classroom interaction than discussion. Indeed, in some of the lessons we observed in the Leeds study, teachers spent more time engaged in monitoring pupils' progress on their learning tasks than in any other mode of interaction (Table 15.2), and from the *Five Cultures* data we found that monitoring was a particularly prominent mode of interaction not just in the English classrooms but also in those we visited in Michigan (Table 15.5). Actually, all teachers monitor, but only some teachers, and some forms of teaching, tip the balance so far that monitoring outweighs instruction.

If this is so, then we need to know much more about the ways that teachers monitor in order that its dynamics and consequences can be unravelled and so that, if we are in the business of improving teaching, the potential of monitoring may be maximized. At present, it tends to be presumed that monitoring is a relatively homogeneous and low-level activity, which involves keeping an eye on pupils, checking that they are doing what they have been told to do and spotting problems as soon as they begin to develop. The word 'monitoring' is itself more of a hindrance than help, because its connotations of checking, policing and warning suggest activities a long way removed from teaching and learning.

The technology used in the *Five Cultures* project showed us that classroom monitoring is a much more variegated activity than this. The teachers whose lessons we observed and video-recorded wore radio microphones. These allowed us, to an extent which for a normal classroom observer is impossible, to access even the quietest and most intimate of monitoring exchanges between teachers and individual pupils. Indeed it is possible that one reason why monitoring has been ignored by classroom researchers is that until radio microphones became readily available it was difficult to access. (Having said that, I remain convinced that this particular pedagogical practice has been ignored because it has also been viewed as somehow incidental to the instructional process.)

In Chapter 16 some of these monitoring exchanges are examined. Here, based on our organizational analysis of interaction, we can set out a framework that encompasses schematically the wide variation in the use of monitoring which we observed.

Monitoring can be shown to have four dimensions: *purpose, focus, location* and *pattern*. The continuum of monitoring purposes that we observed and recorded ranged from mere supervision (in India) through active instruction, to assessment and (in Michigan) record keeping (several teachers there carried notebooks in which they wrote comments and grades as they moved round the classroom). *Supervisory monitoring* focused mainly on the learning activity and on whether or not pupils were complying with instructions relating to that activity, while *instructional* and *evaluative monitoring* focused on the learning task. Evaluative monitoring sought to establish the extent of pupils' understanding or the adequacy of their performance of the task, while instructional monitoring sought to increase their understanding and improve performance. Supervisory monitoring could be undertaken – and in India and Russia it frequently was – from the front of the room, while other forms of monitoring required the teacher to move from pupil to pupil and interact with them or observe them at close quarters. Finally, monitoring could be random or systematic.

The relationship between the four dimensions (purpose, focus, teacher's location, pattern), and the tendencies in respect of these in the lessons observed in the five countries, are shown in Figure 15.2.

From this it is clear that to treat instruction and monitoring as necessarily rather different forms of interaction is incorrect, and I have to admit that we tended to do this in the Leeds study, defining monitoring as dealing with the progression of the task but not its content. But this was mainly a response to what we observed. In the Leeds classrooms, as in those studied by the ORACLE team, monitoring was overwhelmingly supervisory in nature, and the incidence of instructional monitoring was very low. Thus it was that we came to define monitoring as having, *ipso facto*, little to do with task content.

But the international data, and especially what we observed in some of the French classrooms, showed us that while instruction is not monitoring, monitoring can certainly be instruction. Lesson 11.3, from Coulanges, has a long unitary central

Purpose	Supervision	Instruction	Assessment	Record-keeping
Focus	Activity	Task	Task	Task
Location	Peripatetic or static	Peripatetic	Peripatetic	Peripatetic
Pattern	Random	Random or systematic	Systematic	Systematic

Comparative continua

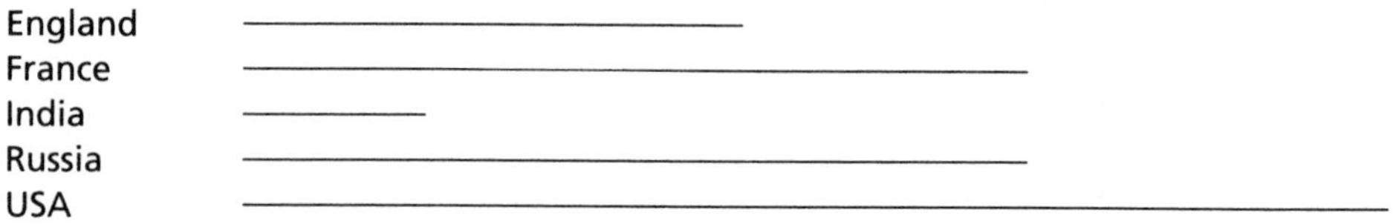

England   ————————————————
France   ——————————————————————
India   ————————
Russia   ——————————————————————
USA   ——————————————————————————

Figure 15.2   Monitoring: an analytical framework based on the *Five Cultures* data

phase. Its structure therefore bears a superficial resemblance to that commonly observed in both England and Michigan. However, what makes the Coulanges lesson markedly different from those which were prominent in the Leeds and CICADA studies is the quality of the teacher's monitoring once the whole class direct instruction phase of the lesson gives way to group-based writing tasks. In Coulanges this monitoring focused exclusively on task content and deployed the question-and-answer technique of direct instruction. It was, in effect, direct instruction at the pupil's desk rather than at the blackboard. Yet it was also different from whole class direct instruction, in that it engaged with the thinking and writing of individual pupils, and did so not before or after they embarked on their tasks but while those tasks were in progress.

All this reinforces my earlier references to the teaching styles fallacy. For the obverse of the assumption that whole class teaching by its nature delivers cognitively challenging interaction is that other teaching methods do not. It is now clear that instructional monitoring may be different from what we usually call direct instruction only by virtue of where it takes place. But it is also clear that because instructional monitoring engages with individual children and intervenes in their thinking processes while tasks are in progress, it has the potential to achieve cognitive outcomes for the individual which generalized whole class direct instruction may achieve less frequently. It is, therefore, a teaching method that has considerable potential to advance pupils' understanding.

However, none of this potential will be unlocked by those teachers whose monitoring is confined to supervision, assessment or record keeping. As I noted earlier in relation to claims made for 'interactive whole class teaching', the form and power of teacher–pupil interactions are a matter of professional choice and competence, and are only to a degree dictated by the pattern of organization.

Time

Is time a problem?

At the height of the 1970s American open education movement (see Chapter 5), Ann and Harold Berlak left the United States to study the English classrooms which had been that movement's inspiration. There, instead of the rural utopia which the open education literature had led them to expect, they found teachers grappling with tensions and dilemmas, and of these the management of time was one of the most fundamental. The Oxfordshire teachers observed by the Berlaks were caught between their desire as progressive educators to cede control of time to their pupils in order to foster autonomy and self-discipline and the fact that time was finite, tasks must be completed and parental and societal expectations of primary schooling must be met.[33]

Two decades later, the teachers interviewed by Brown and McIntyre saw time as 'a condition impinging upon learning', something which constrained and constricted rather than enabled. Mostly there was too little time, occasionally too much, but rarely the right amount.[34] Time, in other words was a problem rather than a blessing. Campbell and his colleagues monitored teachers' use of time after the introduction of the national curriculum in 1988 and found teachers working within tight temporal constraints to deliver what they regarded as a severely overloaded curriculum, yet also losing an appreciable part of each day in 'evaporated' time.[35]

Reviewing some of the UK studies, Bennett found that in English primary classrooms during the 1980s and the early 1990s (when most of the studies were undertaken) time was frequently lost to complex or inefficient teaching strategies which put the teachers under intense pressure while their pupils queued for attention, daydreamed, chattered or gently coasted, ostensibly working but in reality doing so intermittently and with little real engagement in the task set. In Bennett's view, increasing the proportion of time which pupils spend 'on task' would have a dramatic impact on the quality and outcomes of their learning, and by the mid 1990s 'time on task' had become one of the watchwords of school effectiveness.[36]

Yet some years previously Gage in the United States had argued that time on task, or 'time in the form of allocated and engaged learning time', was 'a psychologically empty quantitative concept' because it failed to explicate how time ostensibly spent on task was filled, or in other words to define time qualitatively.[37] In this matter, to compound the problem, even close observation of how children and teachers spend their time may be misleading. John Willcocks, a colleague in the Leeds research, recorded a teacher who judged that a pupil was 'on task' with a dictionary exercise throughout an observed lesson because whenever she looked up the child appeared to be busily turning the pages of the dictionary in search of definitions and spellings. For his part, Willcocks, as observer of that child throughout the lesson in question, suggested that the child was in fact on task for little or none of the time, since he spent the entire lesson slowly, mechanically and dreamily turning the pages of the dictionary, one after the other, from A to somewhere on the way to Z, without attending to what was printed on any of them. And even if the teacher rather than the observer had been right, how would she have known that attention to the task in hand signified cognitive engagement with it?

What this brief circuit shows is not so much the importance of time as pedagogical absolute as its problematic and contested nature as educational concept, in England and the United States at least. The Berlaks understood this to an extent that several later studies did not. Their Oxfordshire teachers were not so much 'wasting' time as trying to find ways to help children turn time from master to servant, for those implacable clanging bells which punctuated the elementary school day during the 1870s continued to resonate in the folk memory of English primary education a century later. Time may well have been spent more profitably – by someone's standards – but what those later researchers pursuing the holy grail of effectiveness failed to grasp was that time is a value in education as well as a measure of it.

On the other hand, it is perhaps only when values of the 1970s Oxfordshire kind matter that time becomes a problem, and one of the intriguing cultural contrasts we have already noted is the way that the Russian teachers tailored their learning tasks and activities to the discipline of the 45-minute lesson apparently without undue effort or pressure, while some of their English and American counterparts had difficulty in accommodating the same or even less within lessons which were twice as long. Were the Russian teachers more efficient in their use of time because they were better organized, or because the Berlak time dilemma had never featured on their agenda and pedagogical time was indisputably teacher-controlled time? Were their pedagogical clocks calibrated so precisely because there was only the one time zone – theirs?

The Berlak thesis sees classroom dilemmas in respect of matters like time as a manifestation of wider societal value-tensions in the context of hegemony and social change. The American open educators portrayed English primary education as cosily consensual, and it was no accident that they sought their idyll in affluent rural Oxfordshire and Leicestershire rather than the decaying and socially riven cities of northern England.[38] In reality, although they were deeply influenced by the arts and crafts nostalgia of gurus like Robin Tanner, even these primary schools were inescapably part of the wider social dialectic.

There are thus two basic ways to account for the prominence of the time dilemma in English and American classrooms, and for its absence in those of Russia. One is in terms of culturally disembedded notions of efficiency, as the ultra-sanitary phrase 'time management' invites. The other understands classroom time as a manifestation of conflicting versions of worthwhile education and conflicting views of what aspects of culture a school should reproduce. The time dilemma signals wider value dissensus; its absence indicates either genuine consensus or the hegemony of a single value system. Primary schooling in post Soviet Russia may have 'de-Sovietized' the prescribed curriculum, but habits of pedagogy are less readily changed. Moreover, as we showed in Chapter 3, it is historically incorrect to view contemporary Russian pedagogy as a purely Soviet product. In fact its origins lie in the much older central European pedagogic tradition which Russia shares with Germany and several other countries, so the habits in question, and the view of the teachers' authority as absolute, are deeply rooted indeed.

Time on task (i)

Yet the alternative 'efficiency' reading cannot be dismissed, for as Bennett's survey showed, 'the relationship between time and learning is strong and consistent'[39] and for this reason time on task – whoever controls it – remains a key indicator of teaching quality. And the figures from English primary classrooms are also remarkably consistent. The 1970s ORACLE study and its 1990s follow-up showed pupils spending between 58 and 61 per cent of classroom time 'actively engaged', 12 per cent 'co-operating on routine' and between 2 and 4.3 per cent waiting for the teacher. In the Leeds study the overall figures were: 59 per cent of lesson time actively engaged, 11 per cent routine, and 8 per cent awaiting attention. The Bristol PACE study figures are similar to these.[40]

Time on task is propelled into the political arena once someone registers that children are not merely not on task for the remaining 20–25 per cent of lesson time, but disengaged and distracted rather than occupied with task-contingent routine activities. It was this revelation which prompted the sensationalist newspaper headlines when the Leeds research was published in 1991, and the immediate rush to lay the blame at the door of Lady Plowden and the progressives:

A GENERATION OF WASTED TIME. The education of millions of primary school children has been blighted in the name of an anarchic ideology, says a new study . . . The 'progressive' theories that have dominated primary school education for the past 25 years have been exposed as a fraud.[41]

There was much more in similar vein from this journalist (John Clare of the *Daily Telegraph*) and others. Time is indeed a value as well as a unit of measure, and Clare's use of 'ideology' is not entirely misplaced. However, beyond the scapegoating ('The Great Betrayal – Do the Plowden Committee accept that they stunted our education?'[42]) there are some important questions about the conditions for learning, and it is certainly the case that if there is a relationship between time and learning, there is also a relationship between time and teaching strategy. The Russian teachers managed time efficiently not just because they were not troubled by the Berlak time-control dilemma, but because they organized their teaching in ways which minimized time spent on contingent routine activities and transitions, and because at any one time the class was engaged in just one activity rather than – as in the typical English primary classroom of the 1960s, the 1970s and the 1980s – in several.

Conscious of some of the limitations of 'time on task', Wragg broadened the domain of teaching–learning time into a bullseye model which had as its outermost ring 'all time' in a week and then progressed inwards to 'time spent in school', 'time assigned to a subject', 'time actually spent on task', 'time spent on a worthwhile task' and 'time spent on task with some degree of success'. Only the inner three rings are within the control of the teacher, and effectiveness in the bullseye time-management model consists in expanding them so that time assigned and time successfully spent on worthwhile tasks come as close to coinciding as possible.[43]

If this seems mechanistic, it does at least attend to Gage's objection that time on task of itself guarantees nothing. Another way to tackle the concept's 'psychological emptiness', which we adopted in the Leeds study, is to identify and plot temporally the pupil activities of which tasks are constituted, for this engages more directly with the learning process and begins to shift attention from *whether* pupils are on task to *how*. For Leeds this yielded the generic activities which we listed and quantified in Table 13.3, and we then extended this line of enquiry into the *Five Cultures* research (Table 13.4). In relation to what we know about the conditions for learning, the Leeds findings were striking:

> Pupils spent a very high proportion of the time working when they were engaged in tasks which involved talking to the class, talking to the teacher, construction, listening or collaboration. Their work levels were lowest in writing, drawing or tasks which involved movement from one part of the room to another, and all three of these activities generated very high levels of routine behaviour . . . In general, the most work and the least distraction occurred in the rarest activities . . . The striking feature of the activities at which children worked for a high proportion of the time was involvement with other people . . . Conversely, all but one of the activities at which children worked for the lowest proportion of the time – writing, movement, drawing and reading – involved no other people . . . This pattern of relationships suggests the possibility that some of the commonest classroom activities may actively discourage pupil engagement because they are more appropriate for individuals in isolation than for a busy classroom setting . . .[44]

So in these classrooms the activities which we know to be particularly potent in generating pupils' cognitive engagement and learning – structured talk and pupil–pupil collaboration – also maintained their attention to task more effectively than reading and writing activities, yet despite that potency they constituted a very small proportion of the school day. These findings prompted us to challenge the conventional assumptions about the distribution of subject time, the widespread British faith in the transforming power of a diet of reading and writing, and the belief that standards in numeracy and literacy will rise simply by giving these subjects an ever larger share of the school day. In any case, as we pointed out from the Leeds findings, 'there is something paradoxical about complaining about the lack of time to deliver the full range of curriculum experiences while simultaneously deploying time-fillers to keep children occupied'.[45]

The Leeds findings illustrate a further – and double – paradox. First, these classrooms, like many in English primary schools during the postwar decades, were social settings dominated by non-social activities (compare the ORACLE finding that children everywhere worked *in* groups but rarely *as* groups[46]). Second, some of the very activities which are most conducive to learning, and which classrooms are particularly well placed to foster, were most conspicuously avoided. Why was this? The answer would seem to have much to do with educational habit – for example, the unthinking ascription of educational value to an unremitting diet of reading and writing – and much also to do with management and control. For these teachers were committed to, or required by their heads, advisers and inspectors to adopt, highly complex teaching strategies and forms of classroom organization which they could control only by giving their pupils tasks which were individual rather than collective, and silent rather than communicative. Moreover, this complexity forced them to spend the bulk of their time on supervisory monitoring of activity rather than on task-focused instructional interaction.

Time, structure and activity

What light do the *Five Cultures* data shed on these matters? In Chapter 8 we noted that at school level (the outer three of the rings in Wragg's bullseye) time was defined and apportioned in ways which would be likely to affect its use in class-rooms and lessons. Time might be *dispersed* to secure frequent alternation between lessons and play, and within lessons between different kinds of activity, or it might be *concentrated* to secure long uninterrupted spells on each such activity in turn. The extremes of this continuum were represented by Russia (dispersed time) and Michigan (concentrated time). However, concentrated time in Michigan and England was also *elastic* time, for the temporal boundaries of lessons were ill defined and indeed flexible, and within lessons time was determined not by allocation in advance but by negotiation. In contrast, in Russian and India time was *rigid* and non-negotiable: the entire school worked to a fixed timetable, and indeed its para-meters might be national rather than local. The introduction of elastic time was what produced the Berlaks' time control dilemma which we referred to earlier, for if the time-frame of a lesson is determined by the state or the school, the room for negotia-tion over the within-lesson distribution of time is strictly limited. Relatedly, while in Russia and India lessons were *short* as well as *regular*, in Michigan, England and, increasingly, France, lessons were, with certain exceptions in each case, inclined to be *irregular* and *long*. Yet temporal regularity and rigidity, we found in Chapter 13, had the effect of making time in some respects less rather than more problematic, for to be predictable is to be secure.

So much for the framing of lessons. Once we started looking at their structure, we were able to contrast the episodic brevity observed in Russia and India with the looser unitary structures of some of the lessons observed in Michigan and England, where everything, from teacher–pupil exchange to teaching episode and whole les-son, was liable to a tendency to expansion.

Some of these differences were straightforwardly attributable to the presence or absence of externally prescribed timetables, but that was clearly only part of the story, for a timetable may specify long as well as short lessons, and I suggested that one key to the startlingly different handling of time was the historical divergence of continental and Anglo-American versions of pedagogic *structure*. This made sense of the contrasting temporalities of Michigan and England on the one hand and Russia on the other, but called for a slightly different explanation for what we found in France in India. The French lessons, we observed, were in transition from regularity and rigidity to irregularity and elasticity, although even in the long lessons professional socialization into the formal structures of *la leçon* kept events on a fairly tight rein. Those in India reflected the formalism not of the Prussian *Gymnasium* but of colonial Britain and its elementary schools – the legacy from which English progressivism fought most fiercely to distance itself.

Then, in chapter 13, our application to the *Five Cultures* data of the Leeds model of generic pupil activities strengthened the sense of divergent models of teaching. The lessons from Russia and France put back into the list those activities which were most conspicuously absent or underused in Leeds: activities which were based on the class rather than the group or the individual, and which centred on talk which was structured and public rather than unstructured and incidental.

Time on task (ii)

Having entered various caveats about time on task while acknowledging its significance if handled sensibly, what did our data reveal? In the Leeds research we had two observers in each lesson, one for the teacher and the other for six target pupils. In the *Five Cultures* classrooms we had just one observer, and the other researcher was fully occupied in recording the lesson with video and camera. The procedure here was to make extensive field notes about the progress of the lesson as a whole, but at the same time to monitor and record the task-related activity of three pupils chosen at random. On the strength of these observations, supplemented by detailed post-lesson analysis of the videotapes, we can make the following observations. We used the same categories of task-related behaviour as in the Leeds study: *working, task-related routine, awaiting attention, distracted,* and *other.*

Pupils were most consistently on task in the Russian classrooms. There, work-rates were high, pupils were rarely distracted, and they spent little time either awaiting the teacher's attention or on task-related routines. Task and activity dominated. The proportion of time on task in the French classrooms was also high, but more time was diverted to routines there than in Russia because the lessons were less predictable and formularistic. Our comparative findings for England and France correspond to those of the QUEST team, although we would estimate the proportion of time spent by French pupils on task higher than the QUEST mean of 68 per cent.[47] Their figures for English pupils of 57 per cent time on task and 24 per cent distracted were very close indeed to the 59 and 21 per cent we found some years earlier in the Leeds study (see above), and indeed to the 1980 and 1999 figures from the original and follow-up ORACLE studies.[48] The consistency of these patterns of task-related behaviour over time and across different research studies reinforces our thesis that the cultural constants and continuities in teaching reach very deep, a fact which should give pause for thought to those close to the UK government who believe that primary teaching can be transformed at a stroke by naming and shaming schools or putting off-the-peg lessons on the DfEE website.

The highest levels of distraction occurred in the Indian and Michigan classrooms, with England following. However, the children were distracted in markedly different ways. While in Michigan we frequently observed the distraction of inattention, casual conversation and misbehaviour, in India we witnessed none of the latter and little of the first two. This, instead, was the distraction of non-comprehension. In the Indian lessons, a significant proportion of pupils was disengaged because they simply did not understand. However, if as a result they were disaffected they did not show it, and the striking cultural difference here was that while some of the Michigan children manifested their distraction noisily or even aggressively, those in the Indian classrooms remained outwardly compliant. When children were off task in a Michigan classroom, the teacher knew immediately, because they made no attempt to disguise the fact. Indeed they drew attention to it.

In India however, most children, including those who were manifestly in difficulties, observed the outward forms of the required collective behaviour, mouthing the words which others chanted, holding their pens or chalks poised above their slates, gazing at the blackboard or the textbook. The classes were large, the rooms were cramped and crowded, the tasks were usually undifferentiated in respect of ability and the teacher monitored mostly from the front. This combination was a recipe for escalating divergence between those who understood and those who did not. One of our interpreters, himself an educational researcher, ran his own discreet checks during the observed lessons and ventured alarmingly high percentages of children who were off task because they did not understand.

In the English classrooms, our figures from the mid 1990s showed some change compared with those of the 1980s in the direction of a slightly higher proportion of time on task. The figures from the lessons that were taught in accordance with the literacy and numeracy strategies showed still greater gains. The gains came with a reduction in the proportion of time spent distracted.

However, what distinguished both the English and Michigan classrooms from those in the other three countries was the much higher proportion of time in both countries which children spent on task-related routine matters and awaiting the teacher's attention. We can explain this in three ways. First, in these classrooms children were invariably seated in groups and it was with groups and individuals that teachers mostly interacted. These teachers did not merely monitor from the front or by patrolling gangways but engaged with groups and individuals, standing over them for lengthy periods and often drawing up an extra chair to sit down with them. For every pupil attended to, therefore, there were others who as a result received no attention that lesson, or perhaps even that day. Second, the combination of organizational complexity (of which grouping is one instance) and variability in the structure and character of lessons meant that much had to be explained afresh and while past routines were not ignored or overturned, they were modified to suit the particular configuration of task, activity and time which the teacher chose for that day and that lesson. Third, the dominant lesson structure in both countries, as we saw in Chapter 13, was one with a long unitary central section. The longer the time allocated to solo reading or writing tasks, the greater the divergence in rates of task completion, so that after a certain point the teacher has to deal with increasing numbers of children who want their work checking. Moreover, if the task is open, it will almost certainly generate queries. Both queries and completed work require the teacher's attention, and there is only one teacher. Finally, and the point at which 'awaiting attention' tips over into 'distracted', the longer the lesson, or the phase of the lesson, the more time there is for attention to wander, for pupils to become bored and restless.

So the relationship between pupils' task-related behaviour and the length and structure of lessons would also seem to be confirmed. But lest this be thought to be another plea for a wholesale shift to fixed-length whole class lessons, let me re-assert two earlier points: first, that we have shown how task-related behaviour is also strongly shaped by culture; second, that there is also a relationship, and possibly a causal one, between pupils' task-related behaviour and the nature of the learning activities through which tasks are undertaken. The Russian lessons were regular in length, by English or American standards they were short, they were predominantly oral, and pupils were taught as a class. Conversely, the lessons in Michigan tended to be long and irregular, pupils worked in pairs and groups, less frequently as a class, and there were prolonged periods of writing and reading. Which of these features contributed most to the very different proportions of pupil time on task? The lessons we observed in France provide a clue. They were often as long as those observed in Michigan or England, pupils were usually seated in groups and spent substantial amounts of time writing and reading. Yet despite these superficial resemblances to lessons observed in England and Michigan, the French pupils were on task for a significantly higher proportion of time.

Part of the explanation must relate to the historical place of elementary education in French culture, to its critical role in positioning children on the competitive, meritocratic ladder, and to the attitudes and indeed anxiety which this legacy is bound to generate. But if we look at the features of the lessons themselves we find that the organizational similarities (which are in any event a recent and partial overlay on what was traditionally a variant on the continental tradition of structured, whole class teaching) may be outweighed by considerable differences in the character of the teacher–pupil interaction, and in this one respect the French lessons are far closer to Russia than either Michigan or England. If in Leeds we found that structured talk kept pupils on task, then there is no reason to suppose that it would not have a similar impact elsewhere.

Pace: another cultural divide

Of all the differences in the way classroom time is handled, pace is the most striking. Some lessons press on relentlessly and even exhilaratingly while others seem to be suspended in time or crawl painfully towards their eventual conclusion.

A fast pace in teaching is not necessarily a virtue. It may prematurely foreclose important lines of enquiry. It may disadvantage those children who need longer to achieve understanding or complete a task, and although it is no longer acceptable to speak of 'slow learners' we know and accept that children learn at different speeds.

Pace is manifested in different aspects of teaching. By comparing the timed sections of the lessons in Chapter 11, it will be found that there are considerable differences in the handling of *preparations*, *introductions*, *transitions* and *conclusions*. In the lessons from France, Russia and India, the typical time taken to settle is one to two minutes, even when this involves pupils coming in at the start of the day. At St Etienne (11.2) the introductory time, which included entering the classroom, locating and arranging books, taking the register and making enquiries about absent pupils was just three minutes. At Ogden (11.14) a similar process took five minutes; at Thoreau (11.12) it took six minutes but at Emerson (11.10) 12 minutes. Yet at Hawthorne – to scotch any suggestion that we are heading for a straightforward East–West demarcation – the teachers and pupils not only prepared for a practical mathematics lesson but also re-arranged the classroom furniture, all within one minute (11.11).

The same differences show in within-lesson transitions. In the Russian lessons the transitions were almost seamless, because they involved no organizational changes and all the materials required for the next phase were already at hand in the form of books on the pupils' desks and prepared sections of blackboard. In England, a transition typically involved a shift from plenary to group or individual mode and this took time. So at St Teresa's (11.16), the numeracy hour was punctuated by a six-minute transition (1102–1108) from whole-class teaching to age-based group work.

Endings may be similarly abbreviated or protracted. The lesson at Kursk A (11.7) is terminated by the bell, and in less than one minute the classroom is empty. At the end of the long French lesson at Coulanges (11.2) the ending also takes under one minute. At Thoreau (11.12) there is a four-minute 'winding down' and at Hamilton (11.13) groups leave the room one at a time, and only when they have shown by their silence and posture that they are ready. This takes six minutes.

It is clear that over the course of a week or year the cumulative effect of these differences will be considerable. We do not have the data to effect a precise calculation, but if we were to extrapolate with due caution from, say the Thoreau lesson (11.12) we would find that over a school year the time taken in preparations, introductions, transitions and conclusions would be the equivalent of a not insignificant number of complete lessons. We would also find that the difference in *teaching time* between, say, a 60-minute lesson conducted on this basis and a 45-minute Russian lesson might be negligible. The Russian lesson might even end up with more teaching time.

This, however, is but one way of looking at pace. If we turn to teaching time itself we find differences no less dramatic, although they are difficult to quantify. The main difference relates to the Berlaks' dilemma 'teacher versus child control (time)' which we discussed earlier. Waiting for pupils to be ready to start a lesson and allowing time for all of them to finish a written assignment at their own rate, even to the extent of this provoking a challenge to the teacher's ability to occupy those who have finished, signal an outlook on the control of time which is markedly different from that adopted by teachers who constantly impose deadlines. The first teacher ascribes to the principle of a degree of child control of time and therefore admits to the time-control dilemma. The second teacher does not. Or so it seems: in practice the operation of a system of apparently firm teacher time control is probably impossible if the deadlines are imposed arbitrarily. Behind the briskness and drive of many of the Russian and French lessons lay – if the system was to work – an understanding of how long, typically, and for the range of abilities contained within a class, a task or activity might take. The negotiations may have been less overt, but subject to the mutual understanding that the teacher was firmly in charge, they were present.

In any event, when tasks are broken down into small subsidiary steps, as in the profiles of 'multiple linked tasks' typically observed in France and Russia (Table 13.1), task completion may entail a single mathematical calculation rather than a page of problems, and it is much easier to keep the class together.

Alongside pace in relation to lesson beginnings, transitions and endings, and pace in relation to task presentation and completion, the matter of pace in *interaction* is the most pervasive and perhaps the most illuminating. In some lessons, including many observed in England and Michigan, the style, and hence the pace, are not unlike those of everyday conversation. Although the teacher's intentions are usually apparent, the interactions have something of the randomness of conversation, too. Their pace is relaxed, and there are the familiar conversational elements of false starts, uncompleted utterances, interruptions and deviations. The configuration of *turns* and *cues* is complex and not always clear. The teacher keeps the interaction on course by negotiation and persuasion, and may do so only with difficulty. In contrast, what we heard in the classrooms of Russia, France and especially India was very different from conversation. This was unambiguously interaction of didactic intent and character. It had a certain urgency, it was highly focused and permitted few if any interruptions or deviations, the teacher controlled turns, and utterances once started were usually completed.

However, although the pace of interaction is one of the features of French or Russian lessons which particularly strikes an English or American observer, to consider the mechanics of interaction without attending to its purpose or meaning is plainly foolish. It is easy to be seduced by the interactive pace of a continental European lesson (and indeed the proponents of 'interactive whole class teaching' may well have succumbed to this surface dazzle), but do such teachers cover their ground any faster than those who adopt the quasi-conversational mode more familiar in English primary classrooms? We need, then, to make a distinction between *interactive* pace (the speed of a sequence of classroom exchanges) and *semantic* or *cognitive* pace (the speed at which ideas are presented and developed, and the demands which this process places upon the child's thought processes). Semantic pace and cognitive pace are the product of several factors: interactive pace, certainly, but also the level of task demand, and characteristics of the interaction other than pace itself – such as the kinds of questions asked and the way responses are received and built upon – which we shall examine in Chapter 16.

We can begin to unpack this complex process, which is clearly vital to the quality of children's learning, by considering three extracts from the lessons summarized in Chapter 11. First, part of the Hindi lesson for 6 year olds at Chanderi (lesson 11.4). The extract comes from the episode beginning at 0957. In these extracts T = teacher, P = pupil, PP = more than one pupil, PPP = all pupils in unison. Square brackets enclosing italicized words or phrases denote explanations, translations or contextual information.

T   Which word begins with an A?
PPP *Anar* [*=pomegranate*].
T   What have we made?

PPP *Anar.*
T   What have we made?
PPP *Anar.*
T   Who likes *anar*? [*Some hands are raised, including Anamika's.*]
     What is her name?
PPP Anamika.
T   What is her name?
PPP Anamika.
T   She is a good [= *acchi*] friend, isn't she?
PPP Yes.
T   *Acchi.*
PPP *Acchi.*
T   What have you learned?
PPP *Aachi.*
T   *Anar.*
PPP *Anar.*
T   *Anamika.*
PPP *Anamika.*
T   What sound can you hear?
PPP The sound 'a'.
etc.

The interactive pace here, and throughout lesson 11.4, is fast. There are no pauses, answers come hard on the heels of questions, and transition time is minimal. Yet in this driving, catechistic style of interaction speed is offset by reiteration, and the outcome of 30 minutes along lines similar to those illustrated is consolidation of pupils' capacity to recognize just three sounds and their associated letters. Cognitive engagement is limited, and the task is essentially a mechanical one.

Lesson 11.7, from Kursk School A is also on letters and sounds, and the children are also in their first year of school. The extract comes from the episode that starts at 0945.

T   [*Writes on the board, changing the existing word* rozy *to* rosy.] What word
     have we created now? Anyone?
P1   *Rosy* [= *dew*].
T   *Rosy*, yes. Now what kind of a word is *rosy*? What does it mean? Nadya?
P2   If you add another letter to it then you get *trosy* [= *ropes*].
T   Yes, you can do that and get *trosy*, but what about *rosy*? What does it
     mean? Tima?
P3   It's the water that appears first thing in the morning and again in the evening.
T   Exactly. The usual word is *rosa* [*singular*] and that produces *rosy* [*plural*],
     and it appears in the morning and the evening. Now, what can we say about
     the sounds 'z' and 's'?
P4   They form a pair because one is voiced and the other is voiceless.

T   Correct. Now we can say that the letter Z designates the sound 'z' and that
      the letter S designates the sound 's'. Is that correct? [*Pupils nod.*] Yes,
      correct. Now [*points to 'soft' symbol on board*] can we say that the letter Z
      designates the soft sound 'z'? Can we? Can someone think of an example?
P5   Zima [= *winter*].
T   Zima. Yes, fine! Another one, please? Masha?
P6   Zayats [= *hare*].
T   Zayats? But surely the sound is hard, not soft? 'z' is a hard sound, remember?
P7   Zerkalo? [= *mirror*]
T   Zerkalo, good. Right, let's go over that again.

Again, interactive pace is fast. This time, however, the teacher packs into a sequence
of similar length to the first not only the identification of sounds and their letters,
but also distinctions between consonants which are hard, soft, voiced and voiceless, the use of softening vowels, and the definition of one of the words which has
been used as an example. She also receives answers from seven different individuals
in succession, on the way handling a small diversion resulting from the ambiguity
in her question 'What kind of a word is *rosy*?' And she leads the pupils steadily
towards the enunciation of the rules governing the impact of one letter on the way
another is sounded depending on their relative positions within a word. There is a
cognitive density to this sequence that makes it totally unlike the one from Chanderi.
In terms of our earlier map of different kinds of learning task (Figure 13.4), the first
sequence is ritualized and mimetic, the second principled and transformative.

The third example is also a language lesson, this time from Emerson (lesson
11.10, from the episode beginning at 1143).

T   OK, Jeremy's ready. My eyes are closed. I'm doing a group check by zero
      [*to gain silence*]. Three, two, one, zero. OK, would Duane start please.
P1   If . . .
T   Just a minute, just a minute, some people aren't ready. Ssh, ssh.
P1   [*Reads*] 'If you could meet anyone in the world it would be the Simpsons'.
P2   Mine's better than that.
T   The Simpsons . . . Did you have a peer conference with anybody?
P1   No.
T   OK, does anybody want to ask Duane a question about his story? [*Several
      pupils raise hands. Teacher points to one.*]
P1   Ooooh!
P2   Why?
P1   What?
P2   Why?
P1   Why what?
P2   Why d'you wanna meet the Simpsons?
P1   Why, do you like them?
P2   No. Why do you wanna meet them?
P1   Because Homer's funny.

T   So you could write, 'Because I think Homer is funny'.
P1   Yeah.
T   Does anyone have another question?
P1   [*To another P*] I thought you had a question.
T   Duane, Duane!
P1   [*Duane points wordlessly to nominated P3.*]
P3   She took my question.
P1   Jim.
P4   Which Simpson, O. J. Simpson, or the Simpsons, the show?
P1   The Simpsons.
P4   Which one?
P1   [*Makes impatient gesture*].
T   Ssh. Jim, he just said he liked Homer Simpson, because he thinks Homer
      Simpson's funny.

The cognitive ground covered in this episode seems at first glance to be minimal.
The 'stories' produced from a lengthy writing session are by any standards cursory
(many others are not much longer than the one-liner offered by Duane). The children put as little real effort into devising their questions about the story written by
this occupant of the 'Author's Chair' as the author has put into writing it, and his
answers are no less casual.

Against that, the teacher would argue, we must set the social ground explored
and, possibly, gained. She has deliberately transferred responsibility to the children
for generating questions and deciding who shall answer them. The rules in this stage
of the lesson are not the rules of orthography, pronunciation and grammar. They
are not – although this is a writing lesson – the rules of writing, except in so far as
the teacher seeks to induct the children into an idealized version of the authorial
process. They are the rules of committee or of the debating chamber, of boardroom,
statehouse and Capitol. One takes the chair and controls proceedings while the
others have the right to put questions and to be heard, subject to their preparedness
to wait their turn. If this particular meeting is a trifle unruly, that is because its members are still procedural novices. This, unlike the Indian example, is not archetypal
recitation teaching, but a serious attempt to shift the interaction into discussion
mode, and the teacher underscores this by introducing some of the roles and rules
by which, in certain formal adult settings, turns are shared and democratized discourse is sustained.

In comparing the pace of these and other lessons, therefore, we should always
be careful to register first the teachers' objectives. The first two lessons are highly
focused in this regard. The third appears to be giving equal weight to two quite
distinct goals, one linguistic-procedural and the other social. Pace appears to be a
casualty of this double agenda, as does the quality of the writing to which the
'Writer's Workshop' was directed, but for this teacher pace is clearly not the
main issue. Yet the Kursk teacher, too, was pursuing several objectives simultaneously, although – critically – hers were conceptually contingent, and untainted by
ambiguity.

The concept of pace in teaching, then, is considerably more complex than it may seem, and we can now distinguish the following aspects:

- *Organizational pace*. The speed at which lesson preparations, introductions, transitions and conclusions are handled.
- *Task pace*. The speed at which learning tasks and their contingent activities are undertaken.
- *Interactive pace*. The pace of teacher–pupil and pupil–pupil exchanges, and contingent factors such as maintaining focus, and the handling of cues and turns.
- *Cognitive* or *semantic pace*. The speed at which conceptual ground is covered in classroom interaction, or the ratio of new material to old and of task demand to task outcome.
- *Learning pace*. How fast pupils actually learn.

The critical issue in a teaching context has to be the relationship of interactive pace to cognition and learning. In the Chanderi extract interactive pace was fast but cognitive pace was slow. In the Kursk lesson both were brisk. In the Emerson lesson, interactive and cognitive pace in respect of both writing and social understanding were compromised because the twin objectives were to some extent in conflict. The Kursk teacher, too, sought to engage children's understanding at different levels, but the lesson was conceptually more tightly composed and orchestrated, and in performance it remained tightly controlled.

These, however, are indeed hints rather than full analyses. Pace is important, but it is one of those elements in teaching which need to be revisited in different contexts. We have come at it here from the standpoints of time, organization and interaction. In Chapter 16 we shall fill out the analysis of the relationships between interactive and cognitive pace, and between time, interaction and pupils' understanding, by examining the control and content of classroom discourse.

Finally, if we seek the cultural roots of some of the differences we have identified in respect of time generally, and pace in particular, we can discern five main traditions at work.

The first is *rote learning*. In this, which remains prevalent in Indian classrooms, time is a precious commodity but its use is severely constrained by the circumstances of large and heterogeneous classes and limited resources. To these constraints teachers respond with heavily reiterative interactions and lesson structures in order to move their 40, 50 or 60 pupils along, more or less, together. Here there is little opportunity for fine judgements about the ratio of practice to incremental tasks, since the spread of prior attainment is so wide. Instead, rote learning is a kind of cognitive blunderbuss which, if fired often enough, eventually has some kind of impact on the learning of most pupils, if not all of them.

Second, we can nominate *democratic pedagogy*, an idea that retains its hold on the thinking of many American and English teachers, although most of the latter have not heard of John Dewey, its progenitor. As we noted in Chapter 3, it also flowered briefly in the Soviet Union during the educational experimentation of the 1920s. It has now reappeared in Russia as an adjunct to the de-Sovietized curriculum, although for reasons we have already discussed at length its impact on the character of teacher–pupil interaction in Russian classrooms could well prove to be limited. Democratic pedagogy rejects the traditional domination–subordination relationship between teacher and taught, makes knowledge reflexive, the child an active agent in his or her learning, and the classroom a workshop or laboratory.[49]

Third, we have *readiness*. This, too, is a key concept in both the American and British progressive movements, and it connotes the Rousseauesque principle that children have their own ways of thinking, seeing and feeling, the Piagetian idea that children go through the same stages of development but at different rates, Froebel's use of organic imagery and the metaphor of growth, and the presumed corollary of all these that children must not be 'pushed' and will learn only when they are 'ready'.

The impact of these ideas on American and English elementary and primary classrooms has been profound, but they have also now been discovered, or rediscovered, in France. A typical English progressive text of the 1970s enjoins us to 'concern ourselves with the individual's sense of time, his rhythms and moods . . . the rhythm of work . . . the ebb and flow between the material and the processes'.[50] This is not too far removed from the thinking which promoted the introduction of cycles in French education. A 1998 Ministry document refers repeatedly to '*les rythmes de vie de l'enfant*', and reminds us that:

> The child of the 21st century is not that of the era of Jules Ferry . . . The new primary school must put in place educational rhythms which are adapted to those of the child.[51]

Fourth, we have the very different principle of *acceleration*. This derives from Vygotsky's famous maxim that 'the only good teaching is that which outpaces development'[52] and is diametrically opposed to the principle of readiness. When we combine this with the arguments of Vygotsky, Luria and their fellows about the critical role of language in learning, the teaching imperative is clear: the momentum of a lesson must be secured and maintained, it must drive forward, and its engine is what we have called interactive and cognitive pace.

Finally, and reaching back to the older tradition of Comenius, there is *conciseness and rapidity*. This, as we also saw in Chapter 12, was one of the central principles of the Comenian method as adumbrated in his *Great Didactic* in 1638, and it found its way to Russia via Bohemia, Germany and Prussia, to be incorporated into the prerevolution pedagogy which remains the bedrock of Russian teaching to this day. There was, then, a prior commitment to economy and pace in teaching, and it fitted as well with the theories of Vygotsky as, in the contrary tradition, Piaget complemented Rousseau.

It is upon time that the principles of acceleration, conciseness and rapidity turn; and it is against the perceived tyranny of time that the principles of growth, readiness and rhythm rebel. The one value-system injects an urgency into the teaching endeavour that the other explicitly rejects, especially when allied to the idea of democratic pedagogy. Time, as I noted earlier, is a value, not merely a unit of measurement. The differences in the handling of time and pace that we discovered when comparing primary teaching across five cultures, are not mere organizational aberrations to be eliminated by the henchmen of school effectiveness. They speak to values in their respective cultures that are deeply ingrained.

Framing these is the value that a culture places on education itself. As Philip Jackson reminds us, to define the time problem in terms of 'time-wasting', and to invoke time-management criteria such as speed, economy and efficiency is to presume that the activities on which time is spent are worth pursuing:

> The problem of eliminating a feeling of wasted time extends beyond keeping students busy and avoiding unnecessary delays. It includes convincing them that the compulsory activities are worthwhile after all and that the things they are busy at are not just 'busy work'. This conviction . . . would probably be more time-saving, in a psychological sense, than would any number of instructional short-cuts.[53]

16

Learning Discourse

Thus far we have compared the interactions of primary teachers and pupils in the five countries by reference mainly to organizational and temporal criteria. The broad pedagogical dimensions of *organizational frame* (whole class, group, individual) and *interaction mode* (direct instruction, discussion, monitoring) allowed us to plot patterns and to classify lessons in relation to their participants and purposes and to the ways their teachers managed time and pace. In this chapter we consider not so much who speaks to whom, when and for how long, but what they actually say. This chapter's polysemic title invites consideration of the character of classroom language, the way that children are taught to use it, the kinds of learning it promotes, and how these three themes relate to those wider, culturally embedded discourses about the nature and purposes of primary schooling which are this book's central concern.

Learning Discourse: the Story So Far

Let us summarize what we have established so far about language in primary classrooms, starting with the seemingly banal observation that it comes in written as well as spoken forms. Since this combination can be observed everywhere, the more important task is to differentiate the forms which classroom talk and writing assume, the balance which is struck between them, and the way they relate to each other. We raised some of these concerns in Chapter 13 when we compared the different classroom *activities* through which children undertake the learning *tasks* that their teachers devise. We registered a clear difference between those classrooms, mainly in England and Michigan, in which there was much informal conversation, a great deal of reading and writing, but relatively little structured talk; and those, especially in Russia, where there was virtually no informal conversation, rather less sustained reading and writing than in England and Michigan, and a predominance of highly structured and indeed tightly controlled talk. The differences represented not so much contrasting methods of teaching as contrasting conceptions of curriculum.

Structured talk, such as we observed in Russia, India and to some extent in France, took place mainly in the context of whole class teaching, and in Chapter 14 we showed how this reflected very different ideas about *differentiation* and *assessment*. Through a predominance of structured whole class interactions, teachers treated their classes as single units and sought to take the learning of all their pupils down the same road at the same time. In contrast, the emphasis on written activities backed by relatively private conversations, such as we observed frequently in Michigan and England and occasionally in France, allowed teachers to differentiate pupils first by ability and task and then by time and attention, so that while teachers in Russia, India and – usually – France sought convergence in pupils' understanding and progress, their counterparts in Michigan and England encouraged divergence. These contrasts are summarized in Table 14.2. Differences in the oral–written emphasis in task and activity then carried through into the forms and foci of pupil *assessment* (Figures 14.1, 14.3 and 14.4). These differences reflected a critical difference in underlying values: on the one hand the importance of the group, on the other individual freedom and self-fulfilment.

Chapter 15 concentrated on the way in which classroom talk is shaped by classroom organization. We plotted the balance of interactions involving different participants, and Table 15.3 summarized the tendencies and differences that this exercise uncovered. Indian and Russian teachers interacted for most of the time with the class as a whole and with individuals only in the context of whole class teaching. French teachers, although they also dealt predominantly with the class as a whole, had more interaction with groups and with individuals in those groups than did their Russian and Indian counterparts, while the Michigan and English teachers had many such interactions. Pupils, for their part, interacted mainly with the teacher and the whole class in Russia, India and France and with the teacher and individual fellow pupils in Michigan and England. The latter interactions were often quite random. We also noted that by 1998 or so the UK government's numeracy and literacy strategies had begun to erode the relative privacy and informality of teacher–pupil interactions which were a significant aspect of the 'progressive' practices which many English primary teachers espoused during the 1960s, the 1970s and the 1980s.

On the whole, teachers everywhere spoke not only much more frequently than their pupils but also for longer at a time (Table 15.4), although the Indian pupils were more monosyllabic in their utterances than those elsewhere. However, because we were dealing here with translated material and the determinants of the length of a classroom utterance are as likely to be linguistic and cultural as pedagogical, any comparisons based on utterance length needed to be treated with caution.

When we started looking at the broad *purposes* of interaction ('instruction,' 'routine', 'monitoring', 'disciplinary') we could be more confident that the trends which were summarized in Table 15.5, and which we plotted in detail for six lessons in Tables 15.6–15.11, actually meant something. The focus upon instruction was more sustained in Russia, India and France than in England and Michigan, where it was more likely to be interrupted by routine or disciplinary interactions. The organizational context of interaction sheds light on these differences (although it does not tell the whole story, as the exceptions demonstrate). Whole class teaching was generally associated with a more sustained instructional focus, while the organizational complexities of group work and differentiated tasks and activities tended to provoke more non-instructional interactions. These increased in proportion to the number of within-lesson organizational transitions.

However, our investigation of the broad purposes of interaction also raised interesting questions about the type of interaction which teachers, inspectors and researchers have loosely termed 'monitoring'. Not only can monitoring consume a great deal of the teacher's time, even in classrooms where the dominant mode of interaction is highly didactic, but its purposes may extend well beyond the mere supervisory 'checking' with which the term is usually associated. In Figure 15.2 we added therefore, on the basis of our international observations, *instructional* and *evaluative* monitoring to monitoring of a mainly *supervisory* kind.

Language also proved a useful test of the routines, rules and rituals by which classroom life is governed, and here again the classrooms of England and Michigan diverged from those of the other three countries. In Russia and India, the conduct of teacher-pupil interactions was regulated and predictable, although in very different ways; in England and Michigan, rather less so. The Russian and French lessons, however, stood out from the others in respect of their teachers' attention to the rules of language itself. Grammar, syntax, spelling, the production and interpretation of text, pronunciation and enunciation all demanded and received constant vigilance in every Russian lesson and a good proportion of those we observed in France. In the sharpest possible contrast – although there were always exceptions – the regulatory culture in the classrooms of England and Michigan focused more insistently than elsewhere on behaviour and organization, and tended to pay considerably less attention to the formal structures of the spoken language through which pupils – and teachers – expressed themselves.

Like interaction, *time* has been one of those aspects of pedagogy which has proved so important and pervasive that it cannot be tidily confined to a single chapter. In Chapter 8 we explored the way in which time shapes the life of the school as a whole. In Chapters 12 and 13 we showed how time and the 'pedagogical clock' ruled lesson structure and form in the five countries to varying degrees and in very different ways. In Chapter 15 we brought the themes of time and interaction together. We first confirmed the power of collaborative and interactive tasks to keep pupils 'on task' in the way we had initially observed in the 1986–91 Leeds study. We then considered the *pace* of teaching, which in England has been brought to the fore by the emphasis in the government's literacy and numeracy strategies on the desirability of 'pacy' interaction. As with other aspects of pedagogy that we have explored in this part of the book, we sought explanations for the culturally specific differences which emerged. We found them in traditions such as rote learning (in India), democratic pedagogy (United States), readiness (England and the United States), acceleration (Russia) and conciseness and rapidity (continental Europe, including Russia and France).

However, we also found that the notion of pace was rather more complex than has been acknowledged by those of its recent advocates who have borrowed from the latter tradition. We argued that it is important to distinguish between *organizational* pace (the speed at which, for example, lesson beginnings, transitions and endings are handled), *interactive* pace (the speed of teacher–pupil and pupil–pupil exchanges) and *semantic* or *cognitive* pace (the speed at which ideas are presented and developed and the demands which they place on the learner's thinking). With this distinction in view we saw how an observer may be deceived into concluding that pace of classroom talk equates with pace of pupil learning. The illusion, or delusion, can cut both ways: the apparently slow pace of those conversational exchanges frequently observed in Michigan and England may achieve cognitively more than they seem to; equally, they may be as undemanding cognitively as they look to be interactively.

That, as they say, all depends; and it depends especially on what actually is *said*, by whom, to whom, and how. That is why our progressive homing-in upon discourse is both inevitable and essential.

It also depends on whether the discourse is sampled in such a way that questions of this kind can be answered. So, for example, to judge a lesson's semantic or cognitive pace we need to study its discourse. That much is self-evident. But we also need to study discourse sequences that are long enough for us to see how teachers and children develop and work on an idea from its launch by the teacher through to what Bruner calls the moment of 'handover'[1] where the idea ceases to be a collection of words to be batted back and forth in question-and-answer exchanges which require only that the child should recall what he or she has been told, and becomes something with which the child can actively engage. Discourse therefore raises theoretical and methodological questions that we need to consider before we investigate this important segment of the *Five Cultures* data.

Language, Learning and Culture

The talk that takes place between teacher and pupil and – less commonly among pupils themselves – is not merely a vehicle for the exchange of information. It is a vital tool of learning. As Jerome Bruner, Margaret Donaldson, Barbara Tizard, Martin Hughes and others have shown in their studies of mother–child dialogue, it is through interaction with others, and especially through speech, that the child constructs and makes sense of its world.[2] Moreover – and here Bruner echoes G. H. Mead as well as Lev Vygotsky:[3]

> That world is a symbolic world in the sense that it consists of conceptually organized, rule-bound belief systems about what exists, how to get to goals, about what is to be valued. There is no way, none, in which a human being could possibly master that world without the aid and assistance of others, for, in fact, *that world is others*. The culture stores an extraordinarily rich file of concepts, techniques and other prosthetic devices . . . The prosthetic devices require for their use certain fundamental skills, notable among them the ability to use the language as an instrument of thought – natural language, and eventually such artificial languages as mathematics . . . and especially written language.[4]

Vygotsky's own thesis, informed as it was by Marx, held that children's development is a complex *dialectical* process involving interaction between the 'natural' and 'social' or cultural-historical lines of development. It is not merely, as English users of Vygotsky's ideas tend to suggest in the context of pre-service teacher training, that interaction is 'helpful' to learning, as if somehow the context beyond those with whom the child interacts is not particularly important. Language is not helpful but essential, for humans live in societies and the goal of human learning is acculturation, and (Vygotsky):

> The very essence of cultural development is in the collision of mature cultural forms of behaviour with the primitive forms that characterize the child's behaviour.[5]

The adult (parent or teacher) enables the child to bridge these two forms, or what Vygotsky elsewhere calls the 'natural' and the 'cultural' lines of development.

This sociocultural view of learning contrasts with the idea of the child as a 'lone scientist'[6] interacting not with people but with objects, which was derived chiefly from Piaget and dominated child development and the training of teachers in both England and the United States for much of the half-century after the Second World War. The attendant concept, as I mentioned at the end of Chapter 15 and elsewhere, was *readiness* rather than the Vygotskian principle of *acceleration*. Vygotsky, while insisting that Piaget had 'revolutionized the study of child language and thought'[7] also firmly rejected the doctrines of both individualism and readiness:

> What the child can do in cooperation today he can do alone tomorrow. Therefore the only good kind of instruction is that which marches ahead of development and leads it . . . For a time, our schools favoured the 'complex' system of instruction, which was believed to be adapted to the child's ways of thinking . . . In offering the child problems he was able to handle without help, this method failed to utilize the zone of proximal development and to lead the child to what he could not yet do. Instruction was oriented to the child's weakness rather than his strength.[8]

Joan Simon, who has translated the work of both Vygotsky and his co-worker Luria, queries the widespread adoption of the 'zone of *proximal* development' (nowadays unthinkingly jargonized as ZPD), preferring 'next' or 'potential' development because it holds more closely to Vygotsky's concern with the child's maturing powers, and indeed to the Russian original, while 'proximal' has a oddly spatial rather than temporal ring.[9] Further, 'potential' enables us to make sense of the Vygotskian idea that the less able child has high potential because he/she has further to travel (see Chapter 14). Whichever version is used – and I prefer 'potential', which Joan Simon says is the translation which Luria sanctioned[10] – the zone underscores the importance of the teacher in the nexus of development, culture, learning and language. Vygotsky defined the zone of potential development as:

> The distance between the actual developmental level as determined by independent problem-solving and the level of potential development as determined through problem-solving under adult guidance or in collaboration with more capable peers.[11]

The task of the adult, then, is – to use Bruner's telling term – to 'scaffold' the child's understanding across the zone through carefully structured learning tasks and especially through language.[12]

To highlight Vygotsky here in a section making a general case for the close study of classroom discourse may seem excessively partisan. I do so for three reasons: first, because Vygotsky, like Jerome Bruner (who has pressed his own distinctive line of enquiry into children's development and learning yet is also clearly influenced by Vygotsky), presents such a clear and convincing case both for the centrality of talk in learning and for a teacher role which is interventive rather than merely facilitative; second, because Vygotsky contrasts with (and complements) Piaget, and between them these two giants of twentieth-century psychology have borne powerfully upon primary education in the particular countries with which in this study we are concerned (although less so in France and India than the others); and third, because in a study of the relationship between schooling and culture, the perspective of Vygotsky is peculiarly apt.

The other parts of my justification for this chapter's emphasis can be expressed much more succinctly. By being the principle tool of acculturation language provides a window on culture and in a comparative study to compare how language is used in the classroom is to achieve some insight into the values and worldview of the wider society. Whether language, by shaping the way we view the world, actually *determines* social structure (as in the Sapir-Whorf hypothesis) or – conversely – is a *product* of social structure, is not my concern here, although it seems implausible to suggest that the development of language and the development of social structure are independent and unconnected. The issue in this study is more straightforward: if we listen to what teachers and children in these five countries say to each other we may understand a little more about what it is to be English, American, Russian, Indian or French. Values will out; identity too, perhaps.

Finally, classroom discourse gives us purchase on the balance and exercise of power and control in teaching and learning, which theme is also central to the present study.

Discourse Structure, Culture and Social Control

The question of how classroom discourse can best be represented, let alone studied, has engendered considerable heat in the academy. This is partly because language is such an absorbing yet complex aspect of human behaviour, and partly because the disciplinary perspectives on language are so many and so diverse. Language engages philosophers, psychologists, physiologists, anthropologists, sociologists and of course semioticians, linguists and applied linguists. A properly conducted debate about classroom language would need to include all of these, as well as teachers and those educational researchers who have an insider's understanding of the dynamics of classroom life.[13]

Here, however, we have to be both selective and brief. The perspectives on which we shall draw are dictated by the questions to which we wish to find answers. They are also steered by the need to give coherence to our developing model of culturally embedded pedagogy. Here are the questions:

- What sorts of discourse are associated with the culturally specific patterns of classroom organization and interaction that we uncovered in Chapters 11–15?
- What kinds of pupil understanding and learning do they appear to promote or encourage?
- What discourse patterns emerge which transcend cultural context and the specific purposes and modes of classroom organization which we exemplify here?

Formal discourse analysis of the kind applied in classrooms by Sinclair and Coulthard offers one basis for a descriptive framework.[14] Their contribution was to create tools for analysis from the familiar proposition that classroom discourse differs from 'normal' conversation in that it is dominated by an exchange structure in which one party consistently both controls and evaluates the exchanges of the other. In this initiation–response–feedback (IRF) structure teachers instruct mainly by asking questions (I) and receiving answers (R) on which they provide feedback or follow-up (F) and which they use as a springboard for further questions. Dillon shows that the context-specificity of IRF does not set teaching as far apart from real life as might be thought, for in most professional encounters where there is a power discrepancy between the parties involved discourse is closed rather than open, although not in the same way as in teaching. He instances and compares the questioning procedures of teaching with psychotherapy, medical consultations, job interviews, criminal interrogation, courtroom examination, journalistic interviewing and survey questioning. Each has its own unique rules of engagement, which are extremely hard for the person at the receiving end to buck.[15]

Sinclair and Coulthard differentiate three key main kinds of classroom discourse: telling or expounding ('informative'), asking questions ('elicitation') and commanding ('directive'). These, following Halliday's earlier scheme, they study in progressively greater detail as they focus in from the levels of 'lesson', 'transaction' and 'exchange' to 'move' and 'act'. The latter two levels or 'ranks' enable an analysis to apply J. L. Austin's celebrated distinction between the *locutionary*, *illocutionary* and *perlocutionary* force of utterances. (An utterance framed in locutionary terms as a question – such as 'Who's making all that noise?' – may have the illocutionary intention of a command and the perlocutionary outcome of producing silence. As speech act it elicits, as move it directs).[16]

In the 1990–2 CICADA project we used a modified version of the Sinclair and Coulthard framework in a computerized study of teacher–pupil discourse in 60 lessons, working at the level of the discourse act. This revealed two sharply differing clusters, one dominated by a combination of directing, commanding and 'formative feedback', the other by explanation and exploratory questioning. The first group of teachers defined a learning task, gave instructions on how it should be undertaken, then monitored and intervened as they saw fit. For want of a better label we termed them 'outside the task'. The second group were firmly 'inside the task' in that rather than stand back and let children follow instructions they conversed constantly with pupils, explaining, questioning, and commenting so that the discourse and the task became inseparable.[17]

This exercise demonstrated the limitations as well as the attractions of the Sinclair and Coulthard approach, for although it usefully glossed the slightly tarnished notion of 'teaching style'[18] it gave us little purchase on the meanings which were being exchanged or the dynamics of the events from which the two teaching clusters were distilled. It stayed on the surface of discourse, patterning structure but little else. Hence the importance of the sociolinguistic perspective, which necessarily attends to both meaning and social context. As Michael Stubbs notes, 'There is no use of language which is not embedded in the culture'[19] and among the defining features of teaching as an activity two are especially important to our understanding of classroom talk. First, the teacher stands between child and culture and mediates that culture to the child. Second, the power differential which is intrinsic to teaching means that once we examine the way exchange structures are chained into sequences, we see the extent to which classroom talk is underpinned by unwritten rules governing who takes a turn and when, what topics may be broached, what count as acceptable and unacceptable pupil utterances, and by what criteria a child is judged to be a competent communicator. Teachers do not just enable – they also define and judge, channel, permit and foreclose.

In the latter context, communicative competence in classrooms may be a long way removed from real life as encapsulated in Grice's conversational maxims of *quantity* (a contribution should be informative), *quality* (it must be well founded and true), *relation* (it must be relevant), and *manner* (it must be clear, orderly and no longer than is necessary).[20] Communicative competence in the very different world of the classroom, suggests Tony Edwards, means following these rules:

- Listen to the teacher, often for long periods at a time.
- When the teacher stops talking, bid properly for the right turn to speak yourself, sometimes when competition for the next turn means balancing the risks of not being noticed against the risks of being ignored as too enthusiastic.
- Answer questions to which the answer will be judged more or less relevant, useful and correct by a teacher who is seeking not to know something but to know if you know something.
- Put up with having anyone's answer treated as evidence of a common understanding or misunderstanding, so that the teacher will often explain something again when you understood it first time, or rush on when you are still struggling with what was said before.
- Look for clues as to what a right answer might be from the way a teacher leads into a question, and evaluates the responses.
- Ask questions about the administration of the lesson but not usually about its content (and certainly never suggest that the teacher may be wrong).
- Accept that what you know already about the topic of the lesson is unlikely to be asked for, or to be accepted as relevant, unless and until it fits into the teacher's frame of reference.[21]

In a cross-cultural study it necessary to note that these rules were based on observation of very specific kinds and contexts of teaching (whole-class direct instruction in English secondary schools). The interaction patterns of primary rather than secondary classrooms, of discussion or monitoring rather than direct instruction, and of classrooms other than in England, may yield different discourse patterns, communicative rules and rights, and versions of communicative competence. And we should not assume that pupils in classrooms in other cultures will necessarily use the same strategies for coping, intervening or evading attention as those characterized above.

Unfortunately, most studies of classroom discourse have tended to confine themselves to just this kind of teaching. They are dominated by what Tharp and Gallimore call the 'recitation script' of a sequence of IRF exchanges in which the teacher asks a question, a pupil answers, the teacher evaluates the response and adds the next question, and in support of which there are both explicit and tacit rules governing bids and turns.[22] Flanders' rule of two-thirds, in other words, with minor variations and endlessly corroborated.

Of course, the dominance of this kind of analysis may genuinely reflect the ubiquity of direct instruction through recitation. Certainly the recitation script is common, and in all probability if any teaching method crosses the boundaries of space, time and culture it is this one (which is why it is such arrant nonsense to claim that international comparisons show whole class teaching correlating with high standards of pupil attainment). Equally, the dominance of discourse studies of recitation may reflect the fact that recitation is the easiest kind of classroom discourse to study.[23] It follows a predictable pattern and – crucial for recording and transcribing – in most cases only one person is talking at any one time. If we wish to record discussion or monitoring or the dialogue of enquiry we cannot simply place an audiocassette recorder on a table and switch it on. We may need several microphones, preferably of the omnidirectional or pressure-zone kind, and – to record monitoring, which is usually peripatetic – the teacher will have to wear a radio microphone. When we come to transcribe what is recorded we need to have ways of representing the way such less formal and tightly controlled modes of discourse are complicated by interruptions, false starts and overlapping turns.

Yet the venture is definitely worth supporting. Dillon's comparison of questioning in two lessons, one recitation and one discussion, shows dramatic differences. In the discussion lesson there was much more pupil talk, more pupils participated, and the unrelenting pace of question and answer in recitation was replaced by a much slower rate of exchange and considerably longer pupil responses. On the other hand, there were far fewer 'higher-cognitive' questions in the discussion lesson. However, Dillon challenges the received wisdom that higher-order questioning of itself produces higher-order thinking, and it is important not to make assumptions about the generic capacity of any mode of interaction to 'scaffold' pupils' understanding or to secure 'handover' in the way discussed above.[24]

One line of enquiry which is particularly pertinent to our own is the one pursued by Edwards and Mercer. It was undertaken mainly in primary schools and it accessed different kinds of discourse, including discussion. Most importantly, it combined linguistic, sociolinguistic and psycholingustic perspectives. Edwards and Mercer examined the relationship between: the *structure* of classroom discourse (the patterns of exchanges, moves and acts in relation to the core classroom discourse functions of *eliciting, directing, informing* and *checking*); its *control* (cues, turns, rules, communicative rights, communicative competence); its *intended meaning* (what propositions and kinds of thinking teachers seek to foster); and – the vital leap at which so many discourse studies balk – the *understanding* which different kinds of discourse actually generate.[25] Moreover, the latter aspects are contained within what one could call a Vygotskian paradigm and the study brings us closer to an understanding of 'scaffolding' and 'handover'.

At the structural level, Edwards and Mercer demonstrate how common in English classrooms are 'cued elicitations' in which 'the teacher asks questions while simultaneously providing heavy clues to the information required'.[26] These contrast with the 'direct elicitations' of classic recitation teaching and tend to be associated with forms of interaction where the teacher prefers 'guided discovery' to telling, or wishes to avoid the appearance of didacticism. We shall have to see whether or not cued elicitations, given their ostensibly progressive credentials, are a peculiarly English formulation. Certainly, in the Leeds discourse study, we found ourselves wondering whether open questions combined with heavy prompts, clues and cues represented a pedagogy which was in reality any more open than exposition or direct elicitation.[27] Alternatively, if the intention behind the cue is to scaffold, we might reasonably suggest that scaffolding implies something more than merely prompting the child to recall a word or phrase which he or she has encountered a few minutes or days earlier. Bruner argues that to scaffold is to 'reduce the degrees of freedom in carrying out some task so that the child can concentrate on the difficult skill she is in the process of acquiring'.[28] By this, clearly, he did not mean the old classroom game of 'guess what the teacher is thinking'.

On the way to providing insights into the relationship between language structure, the classroom context and cognition, Edwards and Mercer usefully classify the elements in different kinds of classroom talk. So, for instance, to elicit knowledge from their pupils, teachers use both *direct elicitations* and *cued elicitations*. And in reponding to what pupils say they use *confirmations, rejections, repetitions, elaborations* and *reformulations*. In contrast, pupil talk in teacher-free discussions can be *disputational, cumulative* or *exploratory*.

While understanding and demonstrating the power of context, the Edwards and Mercer approach falls somewhat short of the kind of understanding to which this book aspires by confining context to the four walls of the classroom. In fact, classroom discourse is embedded in what we might describe as the concentric circles of culture: the micro-culture of the classroom, with its routines, rules and rituals such as we considered in Chapter 14; the culture of the school, as discussed in Chapters 8–10, with its collective values and its unique ways of mediating the values of the community and the requirements of governments and administrative bodies; and the culture of region, state and nation, which are themselves historically embedded, and which bear upon public primary schooling in ways which we considered in Chapters 2–7, not least through the curriculum, both formal and hidden. Microcultures do not exist, cannot exist, in a vacuum: micro presupposes macro.

If we acknowledge this, we immediately make the task of discourse analysis more taxing than if we focus on discourse structure and the mechanics of interaction alone. But then, what exactly *is* being transacted in sequences such as the three at the end of Chapter 15? The technical rules of spelling, pronunciation and writing, or the social rules of communication? What does it signify that in the Russian classrooms, which we visited during two consecutive autumns, the seasonal reality which teachers everywhere mined in their language teaching was a comforting, mythic vision of birch forest, wooden cabin, glowing stove and *babushka*, while in Michigan teachers and pupils turned no less readily to the more disturbing world of television cartoons, murder trials, junk food and baseball games? Both groups of teachers believed in the learning gains to be made when teaching is grounded in real-world situations. But why did the Russian teachers choose to sanitize and romanticize the world outside the school while their Michigan counterparts allowed its most emphemeral and even violent aspects to penetrate the classroom conversation of six year olds? Do we report such differences merely as a very localized matter of pedagogical habit, or can they be taken to say something of real significance about the relationship between culture and classroom discourse?

Few have captured the imperative implied by these questions better than Basil Bernstein. His use of the phrase 'pedagogic discourse' is itself both comprehensive and elusive, for it moves back and forth between classroom and society and between social interaction and social control:

> Education is a relay for power relations external to it . . . The educational system's pedagogic communication is . . . a relay for something other than itself . . . for class relations . . . for gender relations . . . for religious relations . . . for regional relations.[29]

and

> Pedagogic discourse is the rule which embeds a discourse of competence . . . into a discourse of social order in such a way that the latter always dominates the former.[30]

However, although Bernstein is uniquely illuminating on the reproductive function of schooling in terms that are discussed in Chapter 7, his is a theoretical rather than an empirical analysis. He criticizes classroom discourse analysts for being

> less concerned with the question of how the distribution of power and principles of control establish a regulating discourse, but more concerned . . . to articulate the principles of interactional communication and practice within the local context of the classroom.[31]

but in turn his own work requires the evidence of others to substantiate the working-out of the regulatory process at classroom level. It would seem that it is rare to achieve the necessary link between well-articulated social theory and close empirical study of micro-level social transactions. It is certainly difficult.

Text from Talk

The matter of transcription is in its way no less problematic, because the questions it raises are theoretical as well as technical. Do we transcribe words alone, or do we attempt to transcribe also the manner in which they are uttered? And given that every exchange has a history, or as Mercer suggestively has it, is part of a 'long conversation' which spreads back over many lessons, days and weeks,[32] how much of the history and how much of the conversation do we need to include in order to assay a valid interpretation? Stubbs, in his turn, is critical of discourse analysts who work with short extracts, on the grounds that they do not analyse the discourse so much as make claims and then look for discourse examples which will support them.[33]

Here the rock of theory meets the hard places of readability and marketing. I have used the *lesson* as my highest level of detailed pedagogical analysis, and in Chapter 11 I justified this by reference to the everyday intentions of teachers and the experiences of children, to both of which groups the lesson actually has real significance. But in the setting of the 'long conversation' the choice could equally be seen as arbitrary, especially in the primary context where the class-teacher system makes it inevitable that across the boundaries of hours, days, subjects and lessons there will be many continuities and connections. Yet for severely practical purposes our transcribed extracts need to be much shorter even than the lesson. In the *Five Cultures* data the shortest lesson transcript has 14 pages of typescript, while the longest has 57 pages.

Text is emphatically not the same as talk, yet short of supplying a box of videotapes with every copy of this book I have no alternative but to change talk into text in order that I as writer and you as reader can confront it together. Conventions exist for adding to verbal transcription those paralinguistic elements which bring words on the page to life and which are so important in human communication – intonation, emphasis, volume, changes of speed (or, to resume the musical analogy from Chapter 12, timbre, dynamics and tempo), and even kinesic cues such as facial expression and body language. However, to include them all in a transcription may make it unreadable. Yet if words alone are transcribed, Austin's vital distinction between locution, illocution and perlocution will become blurred, and the reader will be forced to 'read into' the text the speaker's intention and the impact of what was said.

Working with both videotape and transcript sensitized us to this problem. The bald text read very differently from the words as we heard and indeed 'saw' them (words cannot be seen, but communication certainly can). The French and Russian teachers, in particular, are more intimidating in unnotated print than on videotape or in real life. Intonation, gesture and facial expression all modified, and as often as not mollified, the force of the language as it was spoken. Stubbs notes the same tendency: 'If interaction is stripped to its logical and semantic content, it may appear much more aggressive than the original'.[34] Yet he too warns against the other extreme, the 'folk phonetics' of extensively notated ethnomethodological transcription, and rejects as entirely misplaced the objective of making a transcript 'look to the eye how it sounds to the ear'.[35]

Then there is the added problem of translation. Some of our tapes were transcribed and translated by professional translators who were used to dealing with legal and commercial documents or to simultaneous translation at conferences. Their house rules forbade semantic ambiguity and frowned on loose grammar and syntax. Once we checked the first batch of these translations against the recordings and the judgements of native speakers of the languages in question we found that many hesitations, false starts, repetitions and uncompleted words or sentences had been removed, and that many utterances which in heard speech hinted at semantic possibilities, but as written text were ungrammatical, had been tidied up. We immediately sent them back to be redone from scratch, with even stricter cross-checks to ensure that those features which make conversation so utterly different from writing were reinstated. However, it is extremely difficult to achieve both 'formal' and 'dynamic' translation, and as Hatim and Mason remind us, there is no such thing as a literal translation because languages do not line up on the basis of word-for-word equivalence.[36] One obvious and irretrievable casualty is the form of address which – as *tu/vous* in French and *ti/vi* in Russian – conveys and reinforces nuances of intimacy, social distance and status in ways which, a few remaining pockets of dialect apart, English cannot. A speaker of English may use intonation and gesture to do what the all-purpose vocative case cannot, but that takes the task well beyond the competence of the translator. There are many other examples.

But the translator of *classroom* discourse faces a more particular challenge. Teachers and pupils do not so much exchange meanings as progressively negotiate and unravel them. Tentativeness, imprecision, solecism and ambiguity are as intrinsic to classroom transactions as are the many variations on the theme of initiation–response–feedback; and classroom meanings are in any case rooted in context and therefore likely to be elliptical. The classroom translator's (and transcriber's) paradox is this: translation has somehow to convey with clarity the sense in which an utterance is opaque; and it must use a vocabulary of explicit meanings to convey the character of discourse in which meaning is often conveyed implicitly.

Our use of translated material rules out close-grained cross-cultural comparison of classroom exchanges at the level of the speech act, other than of a fairly tentative kind, and we simply have to accept that in translation certain meanings will be lost. Subject to this limitation, the presentation and treatment of the extracts which follow is guided by six broad principles.

First, the extracts are of a length which allows them to be be read and understood as coherent acts of *teaching*, not merely as disembedded instances of pedagogical talk of the kind which feature in many studies of classroom discourse. The distinctive features of classroom discourse to which linguists commonly refer – the dominance of the IRF exchange structure and the prevalence of closed or leading questions, for example – begin to make sense only when one sees where a particular exchange or question comes from or leads to. To analyse the structure of such discourse without attending to its meaning is – in this book at least – a pointless exercise. Applying this argument makes the extracts here rather longer than in many other accounts of classroom discourse, although in my view they are no longer than is necessary to avoid doing an injustice to the teachers and teaching in question. The

In margin	
T	Teacher
A, B, C	Pupils, named and identifiable
(P)	Pupil, not identifiable (e.g. off camera)
PP	Several pupils simultaneously
PPP	Whole class simultaneously
(0945)	Time (lessons summarized in Chapter 11 only)
. . .	Omitted section of discourse

In text	
(...)	Indecipherable
/	Pause of less than 2 seconds
//	Pause of more than 2 seconds
bold	Word(s) given particular emphasis
<u>underlining</u>	Overlapping turns/simultaneous utterances
...	Interrupted or unfinished utterance, or explicit cueing for next turn
A, B, Ю, YO	Letter *names* as spoken
'a', 'b', 'yo'	Letter *sounds* as spoken
C-A-T	Spelling, spoken letter by letter
'c'-'a'-'t'	Spelling, spoken sound by sound
[*italics within square brackets*]	Explanation, translation, or contextual information

Figure 16.1   Transcription conventions used in sequences 16.1–16.17

extracts can then be located within their wider settings of lesson, classroom and school by referring to the relevant sections of earlier chapters.

Second, the transcripts are notated in sufficient detail to convey the context, tone and force of the language as spoken, but not so heavily that notation submerges text and disrupts the flow of what it represents. We have also tried to steer a careful course between legitimate interpretation of the actors' moves and the imposition on them of an arbitrary or tendentious authorial voice. This has not been easy. The notation uses conventions for indicating pauses, emphasis, overlapping turns and omissions that are explained in Figure 16.1.

Third, as indicated in Figure 16.1, the exchanges are anonymized by the use of letters of the alphabet. This is a not wholly happy solution to the ethical requirement of confidentiality, for while pseudonyms disguise, letters depersonalize. They also prevent the reader from locating the actors socially: gender is lost, obviously, but so too are ethnicity, region, class and caste. It clearly could be of some significance that in a particular exchange from India an upper caste teacher is talking to a *dalit*; that in Michigan a white female teacher is talking with a black male child; that in France one child comes from Algeria and that in southern Russia another comes from over the border in the Ukraine or Georgia; that in England an indigenous male teacher from a lapsed Protestant background is talking with a second-generation Bangladeshi girl from a devout Muslim family. Conversations are meetings of identities, and when names are removed from transcripts these identities begin to be submerged. A culturally literate English researcher will know which names are appropriate substitutes for, say, Lucinda, Anne, Sharon, Yasmin or Latoya – although even here stereotyping is a danger. However, it is all but impossible to do this in a way which does justice to the social nuances of gender, race, caste, class, geography, time (names come in and out of fashion) and all the other elements of identity – and indeed to social mobility or the intentions of parents who have decided that in naming their child the cultural placing which names suggest will be consciously resisted – and to do it with equal validity for children from southern Russia, northern India, the American Midwest, Provence, and northern England. So we stuck to letters, after all. At least they encourage one to focus on the discourse.

Fourth, the sequences provide a vehicle for a commentary which attempts to bring to bear matters of *structure, control, meaning* and *learning* as we have touched on them above and which relates to the interaction framework which we developed in Chapter 15. The sequences exemplify major organizational variants such as whole class, group and individual interaction, and significant pedagogical functions such as exposition, rote, recitation, discussion and monitoring. They are therefore embedded in two contexts, one situational, the other theoretical.

Fifth, where most discourse analyses make a little text go a long way, here most of the extracts are longer than their accompanying commentaries. Our priority is to enable the different paths to classroom meaning and learning to be picked out. If we were dealing with transactions with which every reader is thoroughly familiar and whose contours and messages could be taken for granted, detailed analysis interspersed with brief illustration would be appropriate. But for most readers of a comparative study such as this a great deal will be unfamiliar and it becomes as important to *show* as to try to explain.

Finally, and not just because they are unusually long, the extracts have a status and force which are independent of the commentaries which follow them. By combining transcription, translation, re-translation and annotation, all of which are double-checked against the videorecording and field notes, a text such as each of those which follow reconstructs, albeit problematically, what actually took place in the classrooms in question. In this sense the transcript text is its own theory and its own analysis. The same might be said for the order in which the sequences have been placed.

India

Sequence 16.1. Ferozabad Primary School, 47 pupils
aged 6, mathematics

T   [*Standing at blackboard, her back to the class, writes a column of numbers: 51, 52, 53, 54, 55, 56. Raises voice.*] Now we shall learn from 50 onwards. What is *this*? 50 and 1 is . . .

PPP   [*They chant their responses, some looking at board, others writing on slates*] 51.

T   50 and 2 is . . .

PPP   52
T   50 and 3 is . . .
PPP   53
T   50 and 4 is . . .
PPP   54
T   50 and 5 is . . .

.

.

.

T   90 and 8 . . .
PPP   98
T   90 and 9 . . .
PPP   99
T   100 and 0 . . .
PPP   100
T   [*Turns to face class*] 100 and 0
PPP   100
T   [*Points to numbers on board*] So this completes the numbers from 51 to 100.
A   (. . .) [*Pupil makes inaudible comment. Teacher smiles and speaks to him quietly*]
T   A, would you get up. [*A leaves his place and comes to the board. Teacher points to number 53*] What is this number?
A   53.
T   [*Raises voice to antiphonal mode again*] What have you **learned**?
PPP   53.
T   What have you **learned**?
PPP   53.
T   What have you **learned**? [*Picks up stick from her desk*]
PPP   53.
T   What have you **learned**?
PPP   53.
T   [*Points stick at A*] Good – sit down . . .
      [*Points stick at B, then to number 57 on board, then back to B*] What is this number?
B   57.
T   [*Raises voice*] What have you **learned**?
PPP   57.
T   What have you **learned**?
PPP   57.
T   What have you **learned**?
PPP   57.

.

.

.

T   [*Points stick at C, who gets up, walks to board and picks up a piece of chalk*] Write 77. [*C pauses to look at numbers written previously by teacher, then writes 77. To class*] What has she **written**?
PPP   77.
T   What has she **written**?
PPP   77.
T   What has she **written**?
PPP   77.
T   What has she **written**?
PPP   77.

This is whole class direct instruction at its most elemental. The dominant IRF classroom exchange structure is here abbreviated to chained sequences of IR only, where the initiation is a closed question requiring recall and the response is a single word. An answer is either correct or incorrect. The core antiphonal structure entails a question delivered with rising tone and volume, its last word drawn out ('What have you **learned**?') and a loudly chanted response, and the exchange has an regular and insistent pulse.

The sequence shows three variants on rote learning. In the first subsequence, pupils count from 51 to 100 without repetition. In the second a succession of individual pupils are called on to recognize numbers that are then confirmed by the rest of the class. In the third subsequence, individuals write numbers on the board, which the class must recognize and then repeat. The teacher's feedback on responses is thus at best tacit, even where individual pupils are concerned. Pupils do not bid for turns but are nominated by the teacher.

Through this procedure how and what do pupils learn? This is a large class and although the task is revision, our observation of the pupils showed that not all of them recognized the numbers or were able to effect the mental calculations required. At the first 'What have you learned?' or 'What has she written?' a fair proportion of the pupils repeated the correct answer. By the third repetition most of the rest had caught on and joined in, but even then some stragglers remained silent or complied strategically by opening and shutting their mouths.

We observed this formula in most of the Indian classrooms, especially those containing younger pupils. Occasionally it lasted for a whole lesson. More commonly rote punctuated other exchange patterns, as below.

Sequence 16.2. Chanderi Primary School, 55 pupils aged 6, Hindi (lesson 11.4, page 284)

(0945)
T   [*Raises her left hand above her head*] One hand up. [*Pupils raise their left hands above their heads*]
T   [*Raises her right hand*] Second hand up. [*Pupils raise their right hands*]
T   Start clapping. [*Pupils clap, their hands still above their heads*]

T	Stop! [*Pupils stop clapping and lower their arms*] How many of you like school?
PPP	[*Raising hands and shouting*] I do!
T	Hands down. [*Pupils lower their hands*] How many of you had a shower before you came here?
PP	[*Some raise hands*] I did!
T	Hands down. [*Hands are lowered*] // What did mummy give you to eat?
PP	Chappati.
T	What else?
PP	Vegetable curry.
T	Did you have some milk?
PP	[*Some raise hands*] Yes!
T	Children, do you eat fruit?
PP	Yes!
T	What kind of fruit do you eat?
PP	[*Calling out, excitedly*] <u>Aam</u> [*mango*]
	<u>Kele</u> [*banana*]
	<u>Sev</u> [*apple*]
	<u>Tadbuch</u> [*melon*]
	<u>Narangi</u> [*orange*]
T	Do you like *aam*?
PP	Yes.
T	[*Looks towards A*] What does A like?
A	*Aam.*
T	You also like *aam*.
PP	Yes I like *aam* too.
T	What does B like?
B	[*Raising her hand*] I like banana.
T	And what does C like?
C	I like *aam*.
T	And D?
D	I like banana.
T	You like bananas better. And E? [*E does not reply. Teacher walks between rows to where she is sitting*] What do you like best? Which fruit do you like? / Don't you like any fruit at all? Don't you even like banana? [*E shakes her head, smiling*]
T	What does F like?
F	[...]
T	[*Walks further down the row and turns to face G*] G?
G	*Aam.*
T	You like *aam*.
T	[*Walking back towards the front of the class*] What does H like?
H	*Aam.*
T	*Aam.* Can anyone draw a picture of *aam*?
I	[*Raises hand and calls out*] I can draw *aam*.

T Right. [*Gestures towards the blackboard*] Come forward and draw an *aam*. [*I goes to the board and starts writing the word 'aam'. Teacher points out she should draw a picture of a mango, which she does. She then puts the chalk on the teacher's desk and returns to her place. The sequence is repeated with other pupils and other fruit*].

.
.
.

T [*Bends down and gestures to B, who stands up. Teacher takes her arm and turns her to face the class*] What is her **name**?
PPP Aarti!
T Is it Aarti?
PPP Yes!
T [*Steers Aarti back to her place. Then inclining her head towards the class and saying the word slowly and with rising inflexion*] **Aam.**
PP Aam.
T [*Spoken Aar-ti*] Aarti.
PP Aar-*ti*.
T What can you hear?
PP Aam, Aarti. [*In strict rhythm: common time, semibreve-crotchet-crotchet, all accented*]
T What can you hear?
PP Aam, Aarti.
T What are the same sounds you can hear in these two words? [*Holds out hands as if to weigh the two words*]
PP [*Calling out*] We can hear 'aa'.
T [*To pupil sitting at front of one row*] What can you hear?
J I can hear 'aa'.
T 'Aa'?
J Yes.
T [*Raises voice*] Which sound can you hear?
PPP I can hear 'aa'.
T Which sound can you hear?
PPP I can hear 'aa'.

.
.
.

T You stay clean don't you?
PPP Yes!
T Do you have a bath everyday?
PPP Yes!
T Is that a good [*acchi*] or a bad habit?
PPP Acchi.
T Aam.
PPP Aam.

T	*Aarti.*
PP	*Aarti.*
T	*Aadat.*
PP	*Aadat.*
T	Which sound can you hear the most in these words?
PP	'<u>Aa</u>'.

[*Other answers, not individually decipherable, but certainly not 'aa'*].

T	Again, what can you hear?
PP	'Aa.'
T	Again, what can you hear?
PPP	'Aa.'
T	And how do we write the sound 'aa'? [*Pupils raise their hands and point, ready to trace the letter. Teacher raises her hand. Together they trace the letter A in the air*].
T	// How do we write 'aa'? [*Teacher and pupils trace the letter again. Teacher then points to a child to come to board and write it*]
T	Does anybody else know? Anamika, will you come and show me? [*Anamika comes to the board and does so*] Well done! Everyone, clap for Anamika. [*Teacher and pupils applaud*]

Here, as throughout sequence 16.1, the exchange structure has two moves – opening and answering – rather than the more usual three. But it is used very differently, and the formal discourse of rote features only at key points where the teacher seeks to drive home the knowledge of specific sounds, letters and words to which the lesson as a whole is directed (at this stage she is concerned with the sound 'aa' and the letter A). Examples appear in the first subsequence, where the teacher has the pupils repeat *aam* and *Aarti* (a child's name), and in the second, by which time *aachi* and *aadat* have been added. Other 'aa' words follow as the lesson develops, and at the end of the extract a second conveniently named child, Anamika, is drawn in to reinforce the point (as is also shown in the extract towards the end of Chapter 15).

Overall, however, the teacher uses questioning as much to engage and maintain the pupils' attention as to instruct them in sounds and letters. The open questions at the start of the lesson prompt a fair proportion of the pupils excitedly to volunteer information about their breakfasts, and the teacher selects from the resulting cornucopia the one fruit (*aam*) which provides the sound on which she intends to work. She maintains engagement by the way she handles turns: she nominates individuals to answer questions, encourages them to bid competitively, and both in this sequence and during the remainder of the lesson brings children to the front to draw or write on the board. This process reaches its climax when, at 10.00, she has three pupils at the blackboard writing letters and asks a fourth to correct their efforts.

Yet this remains a transmission lesson. The mode of instruction is ritualized, the two-move discourse exchange structure precludes feedback on answers and therefore any systematic building upon them. The answers that the teacher seeks, other than during episodes (such as the one at the start of the lesson) where she seeks to gain the pupils' attention and interest, are non-discursive. If, in contrast to what we observed in many lessons in the other four countries, the elicitations are direct rather than cued, this is because the teacher provides the basic cue – that everything which follows is going to involve the sound 'aa' and/or its corresponding letter – early on.

In this and other Indian lessons, the illocutionary force of the first move of an IRF exchange, regardless of its content, was never less than precisely conveyed by its intonation. The pupils know that delivered one way 'What can you hear?' invites the pupils to bid for turns to answer individually; delivered another way it requires a unison response. When the teacher repeats G's 'Aam' she provides confirmatory feedback. When, after an exchange with Aarti she utters the same word the children know that they must chant it back to her. Nothing more is said and no explicit instructions such as 'Now repeat after me, or 'All together now' are necessary. The repertoire is clearly understood; communicative rights and responsibilities are subject to an unvarying formula which obviates the need for those frequent reminders about classroom routines which in Chapter 14 we noted were so prominent in some of the English and American classrooms.

Our third Indian sequence shows a teacher of older children who is breaking out of this pattern. Her science lesson, on substances and their properties, was supported by a limited range of basic practical materials (supplied by her) and the use of such materials was made easier than elsewhere because this classroom, unusually, had desks.

Sequence 16.3. Purana Primary School, 44 pupils aged 9, science (lesson 11.5, page 282)

(0955)

T	[*Walking between rows*] Now I want you to name a few of these substances which cannot be changed, for example, you cannot change their form even when you press on them. Name a few examples of these types of substances. [*Pupils raise hands. Teacher selects A*]
A	[*Stands to speak*] Iron, stone . . .
T	Do these change?
A	No . . .
T	No. What is it that you are sitting on? [*A sits*].
PP	[*Calling out*] Bench.
T	[*Walking towards the back of the room*] Bench. Has the shape of the bench changed as a result of your sitting on it?
PP	No.
T	It has not become any bigger or smaller has it?
PP	No.
T	So what kind of thing is it? // [*Goes to front of room*] <u>Sol</u> . . .
PP	<u>Solid</u>.
T	What kind of thing is it?
PPP	Solid.
T	Yes. Solid. This substance is called a solid. Tell me, what other things are solids? [*A few pupils raise their hands. Teacher nod's in B's direction*]
B	Ice.

T	[*Walks towards back of room. Returns to front*] Yes. [*Emphasizes words with a repeated vertical movement of one hand*] Ice is the solid form of water. Water turns to ice when it is placed in a freezer. It becomes solid like stone. And if we were to warm it up, what would it become? For example, if we warm the ice cube up, what does it become?
PP	Water.
T	[*Walks to rear of room along a different aisle*] Yes, water. Speak up loudly. If we place the ice cube over heat it thaws and become water. And what is the state of water? Is it solid, is it liquid or is it gas?
PP	[*They turn round to look at the teacher, who is standing at the back of the class. Some raise their hands and call out. Two boys stand up in an effort to attract her attention, but in the end join in the collective response*] Liquid.
T	[*Walks to front of room*] Yes, liquid is another form of a substance. There are three types of substance, the first one is . . .
PP	Solid.
T	Yes solid. One minute. [*Goes to board and writes 'What is a substance?'*]. The first question is 'What is known as a substance?' [*Turns to the class*]. So speak up.
PP	Solid, liquid and gas.
T	[*Holds up three fingers*] Solid, liquid and gas are the three main forms that are called substances.
T	[*Writing on the board 'solid, liquid, gas'*] Solid . . .
T/PPP	Liquid, gas.
T	Solid . . .
PPP	Liquid, gas.

.

.

.

(1008)

T	[*Shows the class a teaspoon of sugar*] As I said to you earlier, there are some substances which change their shape in different conditions. If I pour some milk into this glass of water [*pours as she speaks*] what has happened here? It has changed its shape. It has become a full glass, hasn't it?
PP	Yes.
T	Yes, it has become a full glass.
T	[*Places her hand on top of the glass*] And if I put this milk or water into this bowl, then the milk or water would become the shape of the bowl [*points to the bowl*]. And if I mix this sugar into this liquid . . . [*holds up teaspoon of sugar, empties it into the bowl and pours in the water*] C, stir this please [*makes a stirring motion with her finger. C stands, takes the bowl and begins stirring*]
T	Is the sugar dissolving in the bowl?
C	Yes it is.

T	[*To class, raising her voice*] Will the sugar be dissolved into the milk?
PP	Yes it will.
T	So this means that sugar will be dissolved into either milk or water. Right. If we were to . . . This is sand. [*Holds up a piece of paper with a small amount of sand on it*] What is this?
PP	Sand.
T	And sand has a different nature. [*Puts a spoonful of sand into the bowl of sugar dissolved in water, which C is still holding*] Will the sand be dissolved into the liquid or not?
PP	No.
T	Will it dissolve?
PP	No.
T	That's right, and how can I get the sand out of the liquid? Sand does not dissolve but stays at the bottom of the liquid. I can get the sand out by pouring the liquid off, like this and then I am left with the sand at the bottom. What is this? [*Holds up the bowl*]
PP	Sand. [*C sits down*]
T	Yes, sand settles at the bottom of the water. This means that sand is not able to change its form. Sugar changed its form but the sand did not dissolve but stayed . . . [*Pours liquid from the bowl into a glass and walks round the class showing pupils the bowl's remaining contents*]
PP	At the bottom.
T	Yes, this means that sand stayed sand even in water.

In the first episode the familiar catechistic IR pattern is modified when pupils bid for turns to answer, and is then interrupted when, prompted, pupils name the first of the three substances. Each of the subsequent three exchanges has an explicit feedback move, which confirms and repeats correct answers ('Yes, solid' . . . 'Yes, water'), and several elicitations are cued rather than direct. In the second subsequence the teacher uses simple apparatus – water, sugar, sand – to demonstrate the degree to which substances change or resist change in size and/or shape. A pupil dissolves the sugar and fails to dissolve the sand, and through this device and by moving between the rows and nominating individuals the teacher seeks to foster what in her subsequent interview she termed 'activity method'.

> I demonstrate the practical in the class, using simple materials and involving some of the pupils. They then do the same at home and come back next day and tell me about it . . . In our training we were advised not to stand in one place but to be with the children and be totally involved with them. We should teach them in a personal manner, not as though we were giving a political speech.

Yet although in her demonstration lesson this teacher indeed does not harangue or lecture her pupils but seeks to engage their attention and involve some of them in the demonstrations, and although the two-move exchange of the previous sequences is partly replaced by exchanges including feedback on responses, the traditional catechistic discourse retains its hold, just as the English variant did throughout the

Plowdenite ascendancy.[37] Questioning remains largely closed, key words are chanted, and at exactly those points which offer greatest potential for questioning of a more exploratory kind it is replaced by exposition. In these utterances the teacher does not direct the questions to her pupils but answers them herself ('How can I get the sand out of the liquid? I can get the sand out by . . .').

Russia

Sequence 16.4. Kursk School A, 24 pupils aged 6–7, Russian (lesson 11.7, page 284. For analysis of organizational aspects of this lesson's interaction, see Table 15.7, page 403)

(0930)

T   [*Pointing to magnetic letters on blackboard*] Now these letters, YO [Ю] and YA[Я], are sometimes called soft consonants, and there is a connection here. What is the connection? [*A few pupils raise their hands*] Shush. / Please. Anyone? A? [*Gestures towards A, who stands up*] Listen carefully please, the rest of you. [*Raises finger to reinforce this injunction*]

A   When we pronounce the sound '*ya*' . . . /[*the sound is spoken very emphatically*]

T   The sound '*ya*'?

A   . . . the sound the sound is soft.

T   Well done so far, you're doing well. Carry on.

A   // And when we pronounce the sound '*a*' . . .

T   [*Nods encouragingly*] Mmm . . .

A   . . . that's called a hard sound because it's not connected to any consonant. The sound '*ya*', when it's pronounced, is similar, but it's joined up to a consonant sound . . .

T   Right, yes.

A   . . . and it works in a totally different way.

T   Mmm . . .

A   . . . Therefore you can't put A and YO together [*In the Russian, A actually juxtaposes the letter names*].

T   Correct, yes. If you read all four of them . . . I'll put them all together. [*Rearranges the letters* A, Я, O, Ю – A, YA, O *and* YO – *on the board*] It will help us if we put them all together. Now A, which is the better pair? I think they should be arranged in this way [*pointing to letters on board*] because the way they are pronounced is similar. That's my opinion. Now these are the pairs that really work together, I believe. Right, next question. Why are they together? B? [*Gestures to B, who stands up*]

B   Because the pronunciation of '*ya*', the way you pronounce it, is very similar to the pronunciation of the sound, the sound '*a*'.

T   Yes, correct. [*Points to* Я *on board*]

.
.
.

(0941)

T   Let's do some work with words now and everything will become clear. Let's start with one word – *roza* [rose]. No [*raises finger as if to check herself*], *rozy* [roses]. Let's do that one first. One of you out to the board, please. [*Points to C*] C? [*Teacher walks to the back of the room while C goes to board*]

T   *Rozy* [*emphatically rolls the R*] *rrrr-ozy.*

C   *Rozy.*

T   *Rrrr-ozy.*

C. *Rrr.*

T   [*She watches while C writes the phonetic symbol for a consonant –* □ *– then adds a diagonal line from bottom left to top right to indicate that it is hard. The other pupils write it in their exercise books*] What kind of sound is that? Anybody, tell me what kind of sound that is?

C   A consonant.

T   A consonant, good. // [*Briefly monitors a pupil's writing of cyrillic P(R)*] Now, what kind of consonant? Is it a hard sound? Is it voiced? [*Walks back to C at board*]

C   Hard.

T   Hard, yes, and is it voiced or unvoiced? Touch your throat, your throat. [*Puts her hand to her own throat*] Feel your throat with your hand, 'rrrr'. /

C   [*Imitates T, with fingers on her throat to feel her vocal cords vibrating*] 'Rrrr'.

T   What kind of sound is that?

C   Voiced.

T   Voiced, yes, good. [*C places a dot within the left segment of the consonant symbol*] So what do you put into the picture? [*M makes the dot larger*] A little bell, yes. Now let's go a bit further. What is the second sound in the word?

C   [*Puts her hand to her throat*] 'o' – 'o' – 'o'.

T   [*Hurriedly*] Say the word, the **word**. The word.

C   *Ro-o-o-zy.*

T   What is the sound?

C   'o' [*Draws symbol –* O *– for a vowel. Puts hand to her throat*]. 'z'.

T   The word, say the word.

C   *Ro-zzz-y.*

T   *Ro-zy* // Is that a consonant sound? [*Quickly*] Consonant, consonant.

C   Consonant.

T   Consonant, yes. [*C draws the symbol for a second hard consonant*] And it's voiced. [*C adds the 'bell' for voicing*]

T   'z' – that's the third sound of R-O-Z-Y [*P-O-3-ЬI*], so it's a consonant, and a voiced one. And the last sound?

C   *Ro-z-y* [*Stresses last syllable*]

T   Sound?

C   Vowel.

T   Pronounce it.

C   'y'.
T   'y'. Correct, a vowel, good. [*C draws symbol for a second vowel, adds a line to separate the syllables, then places a diacritical mark over the first vowel symbol to signify where the stress falls*]
T   Right. [*To C*] Wait a minute. [*To class*] Now the sounds are as follows. What's the first sound? [*Points to first phonetic symbol on board and holds up her other hand, outstretched*]
PP   'r'.
T   The sound is 'r'. [*Makes a grasping gesture with her outstretched hand*] Yes, and 'r' indicates which letter?
PP   R [*C writes cyrillic letter P under the first of the four phonetic symbols*]
T   And the second sound is?

.
.   [*Teacher, C and the class follow the same procedure with the remaining three letters*]

.
T   Good, well done. Read it please.
C   R-o-z-y [*C adds brackets below each pair of symbols and letters to indicate the two syllables of РОЗЫ*]
T   Good, that is written correctly. Well done C, thank you very much. Sit down please. [*C returns to her seat*]

The organizational mode here is again whole class direct instruction. However, in place of the truncated IR exchanges that predominate in the Indian extracts we now have the classic IRF teaching exchange. Each episode opens with a succinct expository introduction which leads to a rapid series of highly focused questions. The elicitations are mostly direct and where responses are hesitant they are encouraged rather than overtly cued as in the manner noted in the literature on classroom discourse in Britain. This encouragement can be of an effectively supportive kind – 'You're on the right track, keep going' – as in the first subsequence, or may simply involve restating or paraphrasing the question until the pupil works things out for herself, as in 'And the last sound?' 'Ro-z-y.' 'Sound?' 'Vowel.' 'Pronounce it.'

The response pattern alternates between the narrow and the discursive. In the second subsequence the pupil working at the blackboard gives mostly one-word answers. In the first, the length of the responses – in fact it is a single response which is helped on its way by the teacher's encouraging noises and gestures – marks a pattern for which we found no parallels elsewhere, except in France. In Russia, children are expected, and expect, to stand up when questioned and to answer clearly, loudly and, where necessary, at length, using properly constructed sentences and appropriate vocabulary.

It is possible that pupil A was rehearsing a well-established formula, for when we studied the language textbooks used in this and other classes we found that the issue of which letters and sounds go together and which do not featured in reminders at the foot of page after page. On the other hand, pupil C was clearly applying or restructuring prior knowledge in a novel situation, and this is why her responses were shorter and more hesitant, and why in place of the large open question 'What is the connection between YO and YA?' we had a stepwise succession of tightly framed elicitations. However, for both pupils, and in all the Russian language lessons that we observed, learning was framed by rules. Keywords were reiterated, terms were given their formal names – vowels, consonants, soft, hard, voiced, unvoiced – and the combination of rules, categories and symbols provided the framework into which new knowledge was pressed.

This regulatory framing was followed through into the discourse. Pupils were expected not merely to know the rules but also to enact them. Even when the subject matter of a lesson was something other than language itself, there was the same insistence by teachers that pupils should choose their words with precision, combine them with due regard for grammatical convention, and utter them clearly and expressively.

As noted earlier, we could have introduced transcribing conventions such as those which Halliday uses to indicate changes in rhythm, speed, pitch and the many different ways that these combine to give bald words their expressive burden.[38] In the interests of transcript readability, and because intonation patterns are culture-specific and such markings might be misleading if applied in the same way to Russian, French, Hindi and English transcriptions, we chose not to.

However, it is pertinent to note that in the Russian classrooms the style of teacher–pupil discourse in whole class teaching settings was public rather than conversational, and this gave it a somewhat declamatory and even stylized form. In the English and American classrooms, in contrast, not only was much of the discourse relatively private (that is, located in the context of one-to-one monitoring) but the form of individual utterances was closer to everyday conversation. There might be a slight shift in register from the conversational to the formal when the mode of interaction changed from monitoring to whole-class direct instruction, but essentially much of the latter was different from the discourse of monitoring mainly in that it was uttered more loudly. This gave many exchanges an edge of ambivalence – for although 'conversational' they were not really conversation – which we shall look at more closely when we consider the English and American sequences in question.

The pattern of turns in sequences 16.4 and 16.5 provides a further important clue to how learning was conceived and advanced. Direct instruction in an English classroom characteristically entails teachers nominating pupils in turn, or pupils themselves bidding for turns. There is an expectation on both sides that during the course of this kind of teaching a substantial proportion of the class will be called upon. The same expectation guides teachers' sense that when monitoring they must spend time, however brief, with every child, for democratic pedagogy is about having one's share of the teacher's time and attention, however brief or superficial. This was the cultural conditioning which I took to Russia and had to jettison, for during most lessons there we found two quite different patterns of turn taking. One was 'asking round the class', but the other entailed sustained question–answer sequences involving just one pupil, as in both sequence 16.4 and 16.5. As a result, one could come away from some lessons noting that oral participation had been restricted to a relatively small proportion of the class, which in the English context would have been deemed unsatisfactory and indeed unjust, because there 'participation' is not only seen as important but it is also measured orally. Indeed one of the most familiar comments on English primary school reports is 'X seems unwilling to participate', or 'I would like X to participate more in class' – for which verb 'participate' read 'speak'.

To apply this to the Russian lessons would have been to make a decidedly ethnocentric judgement. In Russian classrooms the notion of 'participation' is as likely to mean watching and listening while one of one's peers thinks and reasons aloud at length about a problem which all are tackling as briefly answering one or two questions for oneself. For, as we noted in previous chapters, the school class in Russia has considerable collective resonance and significance and is far more than the sum of its members. The child who comes to the front and works through a problem, aloud and at length, is less an individual being tested and compared with others than their representative. For the moment, that child *is* the class, and all are participating.

This difference has profound consequences for learning. In England and Michigan we see many pupils answering questions but each pupil answers at most one or two questions over the course of a lesson. This yields the interactional asymmetry that the ORACLE team noted and which is discussed in Chapter 15. In Russia we also encountered this pattern of exchange, but alongside it we regularly observed episodes during which the same child answered one question, then another which built on the first, then another and another. In the Anglo-American context each child supplies or is given one small piece of the jigsaw of understanding. In the Russian alternative, a single child provides not just one piece but several, and then goes further and fits all the pieces together. Moreover, if in the English or American classroom the one or two questions are asked and answered in the context of that very private kind of interaction which we call monitoring, the child may be left holding just the one jigsaw piece and nothing else. In Russia, in contrast, the process is invariably a public one, so what pupils do not do themselves they hear and see another doing, in terms and at a conceptual level which they have a good chance of comprehending. If it is indeed the case that one has only understood something if one can explain it to a child, then for one child to explain something to another is double guarantee of understanding.

Let us pursue this idea through our second Russian extract.

Sequence 16.5. Moscow, School B, 28 pupils aged 9–10, mathematics (lesson 11.9, page 286)

(0932)

T   [*To pupil who has just answered a question*] Sit down please. [*To class*] Now what is obtained as a result of working through a process of subtraction? [*Pupils raise their hands high above their heads*] Everybody work on this please. Now all of you lay your arms on the desks, please. [*Some pupils keep their hands up, although in the approved style, cupping one elbow in the other hand*] All of you. Now raise your hands. [*Others raise their hands in the manner required*] That's the way to do it. Right. / Yes, please?

A   [*Stands*] What's obtained is a difference.
T   Yes, so what do we say? From a process of subtraction . . .
A   From a process of subtraction we obtain a difference. ·
T   Good. Sit down please. Now what is meant by 'product'? [*Pupils raise hands
     with undiminished enthusiasm*] From what do we obtain a product? B?
B   [*Stands*] A product is obtained as a result of a process of multiplication.

.

.

.

(0933)

T   [*Holds up card with* 4 × 8 *on it. Pupils raise hands*]. How much? How
     much? [*Nominates C*]
C   [*Stands, hesitates*]
T   [*Urgently*] How much? How much?
D   Thirty-two. [*Other pupils raise discs on sticks, green side facing the teacher,
     to signal that they agree with this answer. The other side is red*]
T   Thirty-two, yes. That's good. Next card please. [*Holds up card bearing* 2 × 9.
     Pupils raise their hands. T nominates E by turning the card towards her]
E   [*Stands*] Eighteen. [*The other pupils wave their green discs*]

.

.

.

(0934)

T   [*Standing at blackboard with a wooden pointer*] Good. // Now what two
     numbers can be added together to make 90?
F   [*Teacher writes F's dictated options on the board, as algorithms*] The number
     90 is obtained by adding together 50 and 40, or by adding together 20 and
     70, or by adding together 10 and 80.
T   [*Pointing to figures on board*] Now what do we get if we divide 96 by 6? /
     What do you think? / [*Points to G*] How much?
G   16.

.

.

.

T   Now, 70 divided by 14 please. Seventy divided by 14, by 14. Quickly please,
     H.
H   We get 5.
T   How can we check that?
H   / We can multiply 14 by 5.
T   That's quite right.

.

.

.

(0948)

T   Now here's another problem. // [*J raises her hand. Teacher reads from the notebook on her desk and writes on the board*] There are 50 chairs distributed between 2 classrooms. // When 10 chairs are removed from one room // the same number of chairs remain in each room. This is the first variant. Now who had a mistake there? [*J promptly lowers her hand. Other pupils raise theirs*] Yes please? [*Points to K*] What do you think? How can we solve this problem? [*J raises her hand again*]

K   [*Stands*] Take 10 away from 50.//

T   Yes, now how do we put together the question? K?

K   How many chairs were left . . .

T   How many chairs were there in both rooms if each room has the same number? How can L work this out? [*Points to L*]

L   [*Stands*] There would be 40 chairs left if . . .

T   No, not 40 in both. We're doing the first variant. Take your time. Think.

L   50 minus 10 equals 40.

T   Yes. And the chairs are distributed equally between the two halls. We've taken the chairs that aren't needed away. So far so good – well done. [*L sits*] Yes please?

K   40 must be divided by 2, which means that you get 20 chairs if there are 40 chairs distributed evenly.

T   But that means that there would be 20 chairs in the first hall as well as in the other. But what about the total left over, not in the first hall? We can't find that out.

K   Well, in that case we have to add 10 to 20, which would mean 30 chairs left over from the first hall. [*Begins to sit, thinking she has finished*]

T   Check that, please.

K   [*Stands again*] You have to add 20 to 30, to get 50.

T   Fifty chairs, yes. [*K sits*]

.
.
.

(0954)

T   Now, who still has, in either the first or the second variant, some mistakes? [*M raises her hand. Other pupils turn to look at her*] If there is anyone, would they like to come out here and get them out right? Come and see me and we'll get them sorted out together, shall we? [*Teacher walks to rear of room and escorts M to the front*] Now, let's have a look at the first variant, with hours and minutes, shall we? [*Pointing to N*]

N   [*Teacher writes the sum on the board as N reads it aloud*] 12 minutes, 23 seconds plus 7 minutes, 52 seconds.

T   Good. [*To M*] Now, would you like to work it out for yourself?

M   [*Nods and picks up chalk. Teacher moves to the side of the room so that the class can see*] 23 plus 52. 2 plus 3 equals 5. [*Writes it*] 5 plus 2 equals 7.

[*Writes it*] That's a total of 75 seconds. [*Adds 'sec'*] Now, 12 plus 7. 2 plus 7 equals 9, and the 1 is brought down by itself. [*Writes '19' as she speaks*] So we have 19 minutes. [*Adds 'min'*] But we can't have 75 seconds.

T   [*Returns to M at the board*] Now we can't have 75 seconds, can we? How many seconds are there in 1 minute?

M   60. We have to take 60 away from 75. 75 take away 60 is 15, so that leaves us 15 seconds [*Adds '15 sec'*] and here we have another minute, so we have to add that on to make 20 minutes [*Adds '20 min'. Teacher nods*] So the answer is: 20 minutes, 15 seconds. [*M places chalk on ledge below board, wipes her hands on a cloth hanging from the ledge, then goes to wash her hands in the basin near the board*]

T   Good. [*Turns to class*] Now who else has a mistake? [*M returns to her seat*]

Here we have patterns of discourse with which English primary teachers, since 1998, have become more familiar, for the brief examples of mental arithmetic (episodes 1–4) bear some resemblance to the version of continental whole class teaching which primary schools were required to use during the first part of the UK government's Numeracy Hour: rapid sequences of direct elicitations which are designed to prompt narrow recall responses. In this kind of discourse many pupils are involved, and feedback confirms rather than elaborates.

Again, however, we encounter the Russian predilection for teaching the class by getting one or two of its members to think aloud and at length. In the fifth sub-sequence K solves the problem of the chairs (with L's help) by being encouraged to break it down into stages according to a predetermined logic: first state the problem clearly; then identify the calculation which is needed; next calculate; finally, reverse the calculation to check that the answer is correct. In place of the phonetic template of sequence 16.4, we have a mathematical problem-solving template. In both cases solutions are reached by the application of previously learned rules.

This time, however, the pupils called upon are not those who might be expected to perform the task with ease but those who have encountered difficulties. As the summary of lesson 11.9 shows, M is one of several whom the teacher brings to the front to work through her problem again. M is reluctant and has to be encouraged, but applies the template successfully. To the principle that pupils can learn by attending to sustained discourse involving just one of their number is added the belief that mistakes are not so much faults to be negatively assessed and privately corrected as an essential aspect of learning. We learn from our own mistakes, the belief goes, and from those of others, and we help each other to correct them. Again and again the strong collective ethic of Russian classroom life asserts itself.

This has implications for how communicative competence is defined. As extrapolated from observation in English classrooms, Edwards' list (page 434) emphasized pupils' strategies for providing the 'right' answer and for avoiding being singled out if they did not know it. English pupils, in this characterization at least, are individuals struggling to survive in a crowd. A context within which mistakes are admissible, as in the Russian classrooms, greatly reduces this element of gamesmanship. Here, communicative competence is defined as answering *well* as much as answering *correctly.* This explains the apparent paradox of why, although the climate of Russian classrooms tends to be viewed by Western observers as authoritarian, even oppressive, Russian pupils are eager to answer questions while in the supposedly more democratic climate of English classrooms they may be reluctant to do so. Equally however, Russian teachers frame their questions in such a way that most pupils are able to address them with some degree of confidence. It is not that the questions are 'easier' in the sense of being cognitively undemanding – comparison with some of the English and Michigan exchanges will show that the level of cognitive demand is often higher in the Russian questions – but that the questions are invariably embedded with some care in prior knowledge.

The pupils in sequence 16.5 were in their third year of primary school. But those in sequence 16.6 were in their first. Clearly, pupils' capacity to handle the rules and rights implicit in this pattern of discourse, which is so unlike the conversation in which they engage outside school, is not instinctive. It is acquired in school and it necessitates training. The next sequence is instructive because, by coming from a kindergarten, it shows both how much is instilled during the first year of compulsory schooling and how much is grounded in a tradition of oral pedagogy which reaches back much earlier to the moment the child enters public education.

Sequence 16.6. Kursk, kindergarten, 12 pupils aged 6, art

T   And the leaves hang on to the branches for a while, and then what happens? / [*Pauses dramatically*] They **fall**. [*Slowly lowers his hands to suggest falling leaves*]

A   Yes, I've seen them.

T   You've seen them, have you?

A   Yes. They fall down ever so slowly [*Waves his hands to and fro*]

T   Yes, they fall ever so, ever so slowly. And on this day Grandma went to the wood. She had to wrap up warm. She put on her shawl [*mimes tying a shawl under his chin*] and covered her body with a thick coat, and picked up her stick [*picks up imaginary walking stick*]. Then she got up and went out. [*In quavering voice*] Oh! She walked along all crooked [*hobbles round the room with stooped back, eyes on the ground*], her back was old and bent, old and bent [*clutching painful hip*] and oh, the stiffness! And she came at last to the wood. She came to the wood and [*looks up*] raised her head, and what do you think she saw? [*Nominates B by bending towards her, still in babushka posture*].

B   [*Rapidly*] The leaves falling, the leaves falling.

T   Yes! But that's not all she saw. / What else did she see?

C   [*Calls out*] The **sky**!

T   [*Stands up straight and sweeps his arm in a celestial arc*] Yes! The sky. And [*bending towards C*] what was the sky like?

D   [*Calls out*] Light blue.

T   Light blue, yes. Now, what we have to do is this. [*Clasps hands, speaks more earnestly*] We have to show this scene, with the leaves falling. [*Mimes falling leaves*] That's what we have to make today. So what do we have to start with? / What do have to do first? Anyone?

E The sky!

T Yes, we start with the sky. Right, let's upen up the paints. Have you all got yellow, red, dark blue and white?

PP Yes.

T Good. Now don't use any others, just keep to the yellow, red, blue and white.

.
.
.

T And now I need a **huge** brush, a really big brush to help me. [*Pupils hold up their paintbrushes*] Oh yes, let me have that for a minute, can you? [*Takes brush offered by A and holds it up*] Now look, this brush is really large, so we'll be able to do everything we need to really quickly using this one, won't we? We can't afford to do it slowly, you know, otherwise we'll never be able to help Grandma, will we? Now look this way, please. The first thing you do is to dip the brush into the water, [*does so*] then get just a very little paint onto the end of the brush. [*Dips brush into paint. To two pupils who are standing up to look*] Sit down please, sit down.

F [*Calls out*] Should we start from the bottom and work up?

T Of course! Now watch the way I do it. First of all, the bottom line. [*Paints a line across a piece of paper fixed to the portable blackboard, then re-charges his brush*] and then some very little blocks, just tiny little ones, like this: one, two, three [*Dabs small blocks of colour above the line and then rinses his brush*] And now what colour paint do we need? Which colour do we need just a little of?

G Dark blue?

T Not dark blue . . . [*Charges his brush*]

G Yellow?

T Yes. Just a little yellow, like this: [*paints four more blocks of colour*] one, two, three, four. And now a few more strokes with the brush, what colour this time? [*Up to the sky now*]

A Dark blue!

T Dark blue, yes.

G Lots and lots of it!

T [*Paints*] One, two, three, four.

H And now we want some white.

T We want some white, yes. And in what direction do we put the white on?

H In little blocks?

T I said in what direction? From the top or from the bottom?

PP <u>From the top.</u>
<u>From the bottom.</u>

T From the bottom, yes. And this is the way I do it, do you see – [*painting as he speaks*] – over everything else that hasn't been painted yet. Here we go!

Here, and here, and all over, and out comes a really beautiful sky. Now. [*Gestures towards the class. Return's A's brush*] You try it please. [*To G*] Hold that brush. Just a little paint to start off with, but you can place the blocks anyhow, it doesn't have to be exactly the same way as I did it.

.
.

.

T   [*Monitoring. Teacher is encouraging C to paint boldly and quickly*] Now [*urgently*] let's get this paint on quick, quick, quick, quick [*each 'quick' prompts a dab of paint*], and put it into little blocks, just like I did, little blocks, **little** blocks [*the child's first blocks are rather large*]. Wonderful! That's just the right amount of paint that you need, just right.

T   [*To F*] Good, mix the yellow up thoroughly with the dark blue, mix them up thoroughly together. [*F finishes mixing and applies paint*] Well done. Bring that blue in there, that's right. Good. [*Points with his brush to the leaves falling from the tree*] Now look at these areas of paint, that isn't the way to do it. // What you need is some more – yes, that's it. [*F has anticipated him and is vigorously painting*] Place it here and here, in little blocks. [*Moves on to D*]

D   Some more yellow in here? I've got a really big brush here, look!

T   Good!

D   And I've got some green here.

T   Yes, that's right. Now [*Points with his brush at the sky in D's painting*] onto this bit. That's the best way to do it. Now this is a bit heavy, look, I'll show you the best way to do it. This blue should come across here, like this, see?

H   [*Painting next to D*] Yellow, yellow, look at this yellow!

This art lesson opened with the teacher telling a story about a *babushka* going into the autumn forest to seek a promised cure for her aches and pains. The sky, grass, autumn trees and falling leaves turning to red, yellow and brown were what these six year olds now had to paint. The lesson sequence ran as follows: story/ exposition; demonstration and instruction; task, monitored by the teacher; plenary discussion at which the children viewed and commented upon each other's paintings. The teacher was a painter who gave his time to this kindergarten unpaid. He was charismatic, avuncular, had a rich bass voice, and his narrative and dramatic flair are evident even in this brief transcript.

These factors might argue for exclusion of this lesson on the grounds of its atypicality. Yet the seeds of mainstream Russian pedagogy are all there. Whole class teaching, with a strong element of direct instruction, predominates, and the self-expression which the teacher seeks to encourage is framed by rules and conventions governing the use of paint and brushes, the number of colours to be used, and precisely how trees, leaves and sky may be depicted. The monitoring, which was unlike the monitoring observed in the Russian language and mathematics lessons but not unlike that we saw in other art lessons, is instructional and evaluative rather than merely supervisory. The IRF exchanges nearly all terminate with a feedback move which confirms ('light blue, yes', 'from the bottom, yes') or rejects but cues ('not dark blue . . .') and in both cases chains to a further elicitation ('yes, but that's not all she saw', 'we want some white, yes. And in what direction do we put the white on?') and in this sense they are characteristic of Russian teaching more generally, even although the exchanges themselves are less formalized.

More than that, where in an English primary classroom the activity of painting is typically characterized by desultory conversation rather than structured interaction,[39] here it is firmly driven by talk. Apart from the story-telling element, which on this occasion effectively blurs the boundaries of art and language teaching, it is the teacher's preparedness to intervene and direct while monitoring which marks the sharpest difference, and behind this difference are contrasting views of young children's artistic development. Here, as in other aspects of Russian pedagogy, the imperative of inducting children into culturally evolved forms and techniques remains important. In English primary schools during the 1960s, the 1970s and the 1980s, children's painting at this age would have been accompanied by as little teacher intervention as possible, for the guiding principles would have been self-expression and respect for the natural line of development. Here, the natural line is being accommodated to the cultural one in a way which seems to confirm my argument in earlier chapters that Vygotskian theory has Russian rather than purely Soviet or Marxist resonance.

When we compare the discourse in this sequence with the previous two sequences, the decisive difference, apart from the obvious domain of content, is in the area of turns and communicative rights. Whereas turns in post-kindergarten Russian schooling, as we observed it, are governed by conventions for pupil bidding and teacher nomination which are both long established and universally applied, here the entire sequence is punctuated by children calling out or volunteering ideas and information *ad libitum*, sometimes in response to questions, sometimes not.

This lesson, then, shows the other side of the coin of oral pedagogy. In all three examples, pupils' capacity to articulate ideas and frame speculations and hypotheses is valued and fostered. Comparing the three shows how teachers both encourage this willing articulation or vocalization and, as the child grows older, progressively shape it to the moulds of epistemic form and communicative convention.

France

Sequence 16.7. St Etienne, 20 pupils aged 9–10, French comprehension (lesson 11.2, page 278)

(0934)

T [*Pupils are working in silence. To A*] Put the number in the margin. //
   [*Teacher cleans blackboard, wipes his hands, then walks around the classroom, monitoring pupils' work. Two pupils in succession go to the basin for a drink of water*]

T   [*To B*] Be careful with your writing. // [*To class*] There are two questions, so
      you need to put . . .
PP   Numbers //
      [*Two more pupils go for a drink of water*]. //
T   [*To class*] Sit up straight, or you'll get round shoulders later. // [*To C*] Head
      up, C.
      [*Teacher stands behind one pupil, watching her writing, then walks on,
      scanning the class. Stands behind another pupil, watching. Moves on. An-
      swers a whispered query from D. Moves on. Stops and points to a pupil's
      text book. Moves on.*
T   [*Quietly*] Head up, E. // [*To F, who approaches him*]. What is it?
F   [*Quietly*] I don't understand . . .
T   Look at the question. 'Where did Tartarin . . .' //
      [*Continues circulating and monitoring. To E, more forcefully this time*]
      Head up, E. Sit up straight.

      .
      .
      .

(0946)
T   [*Stands at front of class, textbook in hand*] Question 4. E.
E   [*Reads*] 'But is it true? Where did Tartarin get the weapons and plants?
      What are his books for?'
T   Can we give a definite answer to this question?
PP   No.
T   No, we can't be sure, we don't know. If it says 'Where did Tartarin get his
      weapons and plants?' How do we know?
PP   We don't know.
T   We don't know. We can only guess. First guess?
PP   [*Raise hands and call out*] He might have bought them.
T   He might have bought them. Second guess?
PP   [*Call out*] He might have been on a journey.
T   He might have really been on a journey, and brought them back with him
      from where they grow. What are the books for then?
G   To know if there are a lots of exotic plants growing there . . . / exotic
      things . . .
T   [*Other pupils begin calling out as G's answer tails off. Some pupils raise
      hands*] Shh. H?
H   To impress his / er, visitors.
T   To impress visitors.
I   To impress people.
T   To impress people. What are the books for if he hasn't been on a journey?/
      If he didn't bring the plants back with him, if he bought them . . .
I   To make people think he goes hunting?
T   Yes, but with regard to the plants and trees?

I   That <u>he</u> . . .

J   [*Calls out*] <u>If he</u> can't travel, the books tell him what it's like.

T   Yes.

H   [*Calls out*] If he bought them, he wouldn't know where he had found them, so he reads about it in books. If he had a visitor who asked him where he bought something, he wouldn't know what to say. If a visitor asked him where he bought, for example [*Glances at her textbook*] the bao . . . bo . . .

T   Baobab.

H   . . . He er, he er bought it in, in Africa. If er, if Tartarin doesn't know the answer and he says he bought it in America, the visitor would know he wasn't a great ***traveller***.

T   ***Yes***. He mustn't make any mistakes in his answers. He mustn't say . . .

PP   Just anything.

T   . . . just anything.

In the first of the three French extracts we find two distinct kinds of interaction, both of which take place in the context of whole class direct instruction. Despite the impression created by the text, the first subsequence lasts considerably longer than the second. This seven-minute episode is conducted largely in silence, as the teacher engages in supervisory monitoring at its most minimal. He moves round the room, looks over the shoulders of seated pupils at their work, scans the class as a whole, and makes occasional comments which are as likely to deal with posture as task. The climate in the classroom during these seven minutes is that of the examination hall, one of total concentration on the task in hand. The silence – there is every reason in the study of discourse, as in music, to comment on silence as well as sound – is palpable. It has a quality more forceful than the mere absence of talk. It carries its own message: silence begets silence.

The second episode is no less archetypal. The pupils are going over the answers they have written to questions about the comprehension passage taken from *Tartarin de Tarascon*. The exchanges are mainly direct elicitations, with the occasional cue (as at the end), and the teacher signals his evaluation of each response mostly by repetition ('No'/'No', 'We don't know'/'We don't know', 'To impress people'/'To impress people' and occasionally by affirmation. Despite this structural formality, the teacher encourages pupils to call out, listens to the range of answers, and selects the one which suits his purpose. We found this practice common in all five countries, even where, as in France, Russia and India, turn taking is on the whole tightly controlled. In these cases the encouragement of calling out appears to be a strategy for securing engagement across the class by inciting competitiveness among pupils in bidding for turns. It also enables teachers to assess how well they are pitching task and content. They use this procedure confident that it will not disintegrate into a shouting match because it marks but a temporary deviation from the more usual procedure of hand-raising and nomination, and the overarching framework of class-room rules and routines is both firmly-established and without ambiguity. Just as in the Indian lessons the children unfailingly know by the teacher's tone of voice which questions they must compete with each other to answer and which require a chanted unison response, so here these French children sense, rather than are told, that in inviting them to guess the teacher is asking them to brainstorm rather than spot the single 'correct' reply.

In this case, what the teacher does with the responses he receives is to use them to build progressively towards the conclusion that the library of Tartarin de Tarascon is a proxy or insurance for the travel to exotic places which he may not really have undertaken. Alongside the substantive theme of the comprehension extract the teacher reinforces the driving idea of his approach to the analysis and comprehension of written text in general: that the text is not so much to be responded to for its literary qualities as interrogated as evidence. The children learn where to draw the line between what the text implies and what it states, what they may read into it and what they can read *in* it. Thus: 'Can we give a definite answer to this question?' 'How do we know?/'We don't know. We can only guess'./First guess . . .'. He then receives the various answers, using repetition to confirm that they are *acceptable* as staging posts to the conclusion rather than necessarily correct in themselves, and reserves the definitive 'Yes' for the two answers which in his view accurately address the question 'What are [Tartarin's] books for?' that he started with ('If he can't travel, the books tell him what it's like' and 'If Tartarin doesn't know the answer . . . the visitor would know he wasn't a great traveller').

There is in this lesson, then a synergy – at any rate a correspondence – between the inherent discipline of the subject (at least as this teacher defines it) and the imposed discipline of the discourse through which the subject is mediated. This was a prominent feature of many of the French lessons which we observed, and no doubt played its part in sustaining *les disciplines* once the pupils moved into secondary education.

However, some teachers sought to accommodate this traditional pedagogic form to the rather different assumptions of recent policy, with their emphasis on individualism and the developmental rhythms of childhood.

Sequence 16.8. Coulanges, 20 pupils aged 6, mathematics

T   [*On the blackboard is the plan of a car park with three bays labelled A, B and C. Teacher stands at board with pupil A who has fixed her worksheet to the board and is explaining her calculation. Addresses pupil B*] Come and show me what you counted. // [*B goes to the board*] How did you count? Listen, children, if I ask people how they did it, it's because all the different ways are interesting. / Most of you are able to find the right answer. I'm not interested in the answer. [*To B, raising her voice*] What are you doing here? Show me how you counted.

.

.

.

T   [*A remains at the board with the teacher. Other pupils are clamouring for attention, shouting out their own explanations. Teacher addresses D, who persistently interrupts, in a fairly severe tone of voice*] We haven't got to 8. Add 8 makes 16 here. If you wait your turn, then we might listen to you.

	[*Turns back to A. Her tone lightens*] Right in Car Park B / there were . . . // [*Draws six small rectangles signifying parked cars, five on one side of bay B, one on the other*].

(P) [*Calls out*] Six // Six.

T [*Pointing to the plan*] In Car Park B there were four spaces, five cars <u>on one side</u> . . .

(P) <u>Six?</u>

T And one on the other. What about Car Park C?

PP (. . .) [*Calling out different versions of the answer simultaneously*]

T [*Takes A's worksheet from the board, bodily turns her round to face the class and puts her arm round her shoulder. Smiles*] Now, let's ask C. [*To A*] Go and sit down. [*To C*] How did you find out how many cars there were in the whole car park? How many were there? [*Goes to look at C's worksheet*] Twenty-six. Right, come and explain how you worked that out. [*Returns to board, C follows*].

T [*To C, but really to the class*] Wait, wait, **wait**. [*To class*] Let her explain. [*T hands C a pointer so that she can reach the plan*]

C (. . .) . . . and ten here [*Very quietly, to teacher rather than class*].

T C said there were ten here [*pointing to bays A and C*] and ten here. That makes 20. That's interesting. Did anyone do it differently? [*Pupils raise hands excitedly. C returns to her desk*]. Right, D.

D [*Goes to board, takes pointer from teacher*]. Yes, I said that 5 add 5 here [*Points to bay A*] made 10, and over here too [*Points to bay C. Teacher begins drawing in ten rectangles/parked cars*] there were 10, and here [*Points to bay B*] there were 6. That makes 26.

T So you added 5 each time. [*Pupils begin calling out again*]. E did it a different way. [*Groans from some pupils, possibly because they wanted to be nominated*] E has been waiting. [*E is on her way to the board*]

E [*At blackboard, pointing to bays A and C*] Here, there are two and two . . .

T [*Raises her hands and frowns*] Can you explain what you mean when you say two and two?

E Two tens.

T Right, **now** I understand. [*E giggles*] You have to explain properly in maths. // If you say there are two tens, that makes 20.

E [*Points to bay B*] And here there are six, that makes 26.

T [*To the several pupils who are clamouring for attention*] We haven't finished. [*Holds up worksheet*]. Here you have . . . [*The head enters the room. She and the teacher speak briefly and quietly. To class again*] On the dotted line, it says write down the sum . . . [*Leans forward, adopts harsher tone of voice*] Madame la Directrice isn't going to do it for you, F, so listen please. [*Tone lightens again*] Write down the sum that helps you to find 26. There are several ways of doing it. Write down the sum, and then we'll discuss it. There are several ways of doing it. Listen / [*Puts finger to lips*] You've already said some, which are right. Now look. [*Draws line on board*] You write down the sum.

G   (. . . ?)
T   Pardon?
G   Do you put the sign?
T   Yes, you do write down the sign. And we know the answer. [*Writes the symbol '=' on the blackboard*]. It's not really the answer we're interested in. We already know the answer. What is the answer?
PP 26.
T   If you have to find the *sum*, what sign will you need?
PP Add.
T   [*Writes the symbol '+' on the blackboard*]. So you will have . . .
G   Two.
T   It depends on how you work it out. Some children will have two signs, some won't. It depends how you do it. Do you understand? We'll talk about it later.

After the lesson, this teacher told us:

My main rule is that the child has a problem to solve and must find an answer. The teacher does not provide everything, but tries to get the most out of the child. So this morning I was not interested in the answer so much as how to find the answer, and there are different ways of doing that . . . There are times when I have to tell them, because they don't know, times when the teacher is the teacher and has to provide information. But there are also occasions when the children tell me, or the starting point is what they say . . . It's a constant give-and-take, I tell them, they tell me.

The concept of the 'problem' in this mathematics lesson is traditional, although it involves cars and car parks rather than maidservants filling baths and workmen digging holes. However, this teacher's message to her pupils, consistent with what she said in interview, was the rather less traditional one that there may be one solution to a mathematical problem but there are several routes to that solution. In the Russian classrooms children came to the board to demonstrate that they knew which specific calculation a given problem called for and that they could effect this calculation. Here, while the lesson was structurally similar – whole class teaching, pupils at the blackboard thinking aloud to their peers – the dynamics were markedly different. The pattern of interaction was less strictly governed, and instead of rehearsing a single correct route to solving the problem of the cars in the car park the children were encouraged to invent their own: 'I'm not interested in the answer'/ '. . . all the different ways are interesting'. / 'There are several ways of doing it'.

The pupils' freedom, however, was in three respects circumscribed. First, like the teacher at St Etienne, the teacher here encouraged her pupils to compete, and to compete vocally, to answer. However, those pupils who exceeded the (unspecified) upper limit of liveliness or persistence were reprimanded in terms that implied that the process, appearances notwithstanding, remained essentially an ordered one: 'If you wait your turn, then we might listen to you.' Spotting the precise dividing line between acceptable and unacceptable behaviour in this regard, given the somewhat paradoxical character of that injunction, may not have been easy. Second, children could speculate about the means to solve the problem but in doing so they had to use the appropriate mathematical vocabulary ('**Now** I understand. You have to explain it properly in maths'). Third, the test of a viable procedure was its capacity to produce the correct solution: 'You've already said some [ways of solving the problem], which are right'. As in all French teaching that we observed, freedom in one area was balanced by constraint in another, and if pupils did not grasp this through the handling of content and turns, teachers did not hesitate to revert to their traditional authoritarian role to remove any ambiguity.

We shall see how in some of the Michigan lessons, in contrast to the situation we found in France, the pedagogical and epistemic boundaries were much harder to discern.

The final French sequence, too, raises questions about the ways teachers balance freedom and constraint in what and how they teach, and how this infuses and problematizes the classroom discourse. In this case the teacher wanted the pupils to write a narrative containing lively dialogue. Their stories were expected to attend to three criteria or disciplines: inventiveness, accuracy in grammar and spelling, and conformity to a specified framework for determining their narrative shape and development.

Sequence 16.9. Coulanges, 26 pupils aged 9–10, French (lesson 11.3, page 279. For analysis of organizational aspects of this lesson's interaction, see Table 15.6, page 402)

(1345)

(1) T   [*Teacher at blackboard, presents a way of charting, for the purposes of structuring narrative prose, the way events unfold. He has drawn a narrative 'line' on the board which starts with 'initial state' and moves through stages of disequilibrium and resolution to a 'final state'*] So there is a disruptive element. [*Writes 'disruptive element' some way along the narrative line on the blackboard*] So, what does that mean? [*Turns to face class*] There is something which causes disruption. What happens? [*Pupils raise hands. Points to C*]

C   There is a change.

T   There is a change. So if, as A said, everything is quiet, what will happen?

PP   (. . .) [*Many competing answers called out simultaneously*]

T   [*Quietly*] Or, there could be a silence. But there is a *change*. [*T writes 'A change' above the narrative line*] A *change*. [*Turns from board to face class*] What will the change cause? [*Pupils call out. Teacher points to D*]

D   Disruption.

T   It will cause disruption. So what happens? [*Gestures towards E*]

E   There's . . .

T   For example, we're having a picnic, as B said. It starts to rain. Then what happens?

PP   (. . .) [*Pupils again call out different answers simultaneously.*

T   [*Teacher picks out the word 'reaction' and gestures towards F who has said it.*] There's a . . . [*Cups his hand to his ear as other pupils continue to call out*]

F   Reaction.

PP   [*Picking up the signal*] Reaction.

T   There's a reaction. What is the reason for the reaction?

(P)   It's caused by a change . . . [*Other pupils call out and drown the rest of the answer*]

T   [*Writing 'reaction' below the narrative line*] A change which produces a . . .

PP   [*Hesitantly*] Reaction.

T & PP   Reaction.

T   And this reaction?

(2) R   Ret . . . [*Begins calling out an answer, but hestitates. Teacher signals to him to continue*] Returns to normal.

T   Is it the reaction which returns to normal?

R   No, the reaction enables us to return to normal, and the final state. [*Teacher writes 'Final state' at the end of the narrative line on the blackboard*]

.
.
.

(1409)

T   [*Monitoring pairs and individuals. Stops at group of four pupils. Checks G's work and asks her to read to the class her narrative so far. He then asks A*] A, read us the beginning of your story.

(3) A   [*Reads aloud to the class*] 'Fear. On 29th January, in an aeroplane, M Jean and M Marc met / in chance. M Jean . . .'

T   Perhaps that should be 'by chance' [*Teacher has corrected the pupil's 'en surprise' to 'par surprise'*]

A   'M Jean said, "Hallo Marc, how are you?" "I'm very busy. I work in accounts" [*Les comptes*] and . . .'

T   *Comptes*. How do you write that?

A   C-O-N-T-E.

T   What do you mean? If you write *conte* it means a fairy tale for children.

A   I mean at a bank.

T   Ah. Then how do you spell it? H?

H   C-O-M-P-T-E-S.

T   Good. What is going to happen next, A?

A   The plane . . . [*Pupil next to A points to his writing. A hasn't anything further to read out*] . . . the plane . . .

T	<u>No</u>, *imagine* <u>the</u> ...
A	[*Fluently again*] <u>The plane</u> takes off, and they fall backwards into their seats, because they are still standing up.
T	Yes?
A	Then they sit down. When the plane gets up into the sky, there will be turbulence. [*Rocks his hand to suggest turbulence*]
T	Yes. Then, what will happen, because of the turbulence? How will they feel?
A	Marc will be afraid ...
T	Yes ...
A	... and other people will try to reassure him ...
T	There!
A	... and many people will be sick.
(4) T	Don't try to put too much into it, but that's good. That is something which might happen. Then everything returns to normal.
A	Then – then the pilot will straighten, er / straighten the plane, and everything will come right again.
T	Good. [*To class*] So you see what it is that I want: a conversation, but with an adventure, too. They are in a ship or an aeroplane or a train. But they go somewhere, the aeroplane takes off, the train starts, the ship sets sail. Right. Come on!
(5) T	[*To group of four pupils*] Whose work haven't I seen yet? [*Leans over I, reading her work*] // There's no dialogue there. Will it come later?
I	[*Looking up as teacher moves on*]. Yes, yes, <u>we</u> ...
T	[*Briskly, over his shoulder*] <u>Fine</u>, fine. [*To J, who is scribe for herself and K*] You should say *rencontré* [*met*].
K	I told <u>her</u> ...
T	[*Over his shoulder, already on his way to the next group*] <u>She doesn't</u> listen, does she? // [*To L*] *J'ai rencontré* [*I met*] ... an old school friend. Where? After you put '*j'ai*' [*I have*], why did you say '*ils*' [*they*]? It should be '*nous*' [*we*]. That's a good idea. Right. In the plane. Come on! Come on! Come on! Hurry up! [*Moves to the next group. To M and N*] So, is the plane taking off? Right. Ah! // [*Reads*] '... are afraid ... take off.' So, what do the passengers do? There's something missing here. The aeroplane won't take off ... So why are they frightened? I'd like you to work together. *Conte* – that means a fairy tale. // [*To O and P*] You would say ... 'How are you, Tom?' Why don't you say, 'Hallo, how are you?' The other man replies, 'Yes, I'm fine.' But you have to ask him a question. *Décollage* [*take-off*] // [*To class*] I think we need some words, er, some expressions, like *comment ça va, comment vas-tu?* // [*Walks to front of class*] Q, how do you write '*Comment ça va?*' – some of your spellings are very inventive? [*Walks towards Q, gestures to him to speak*]
Q	Er, C-O-double M / [*Teacher walks to board*] E-N-T.

T	So. [*Writes* Comment ça va? *on board*] I prefer [*writes as he speaks*] Comment . . .
(P)	. . . vas-tu?
T	Vas-tu. Why is it V-A-S?
PP	[*Calling out*] Because it agrees with *tu*.
T	Because it agrees with *tu*. Now what does an aeroplane do? Does it start [*démarrer – used for road vehicles*] or take off [*décoller*]? What does it do?
(P)	It takes off.
T	[*Writing as he speaks*] Takes off. Two Ls. Look it up in the dictionary, please, A.

.
.
.

(1442)

(6) T	[*To class*] But if you were told that the aeroplane had lost an engine . . . [*Pupils calls out. Teacher nods to A*]
A	You'd be really frightened.
T	That's right, as A says, you would be really frightened. [*Pupils call out. Teacher points to E*]
E	The kerosene . . . the aeroplane would explode . . .
L	Oh, dear!
T	So. If you were told that, you would be uneasy, you'd be afraid.
(P)	[*Calls out*]. I would hide under the seat.
T	[*Other pupils call out. Teacher gestures them to quieten*] Wait. You would listen to the air hostess's instructions. What would she tell you to do? [*Pupils call out very excitedly*]. Now, now, wait, wait, wait. What instructions would she give? B?
A	[*Standing*] You would have to put your table up.
T	So you don't hurt yourself.
B	Take off your shoes. Put your head between your knees.
(P)	Why?
T	You have to take off your shoes? I didn't know that. That's new. / Yes? [*Points to M, who has her hand up*]
(P)	Why?
M	Put your life jacket on.
T	Put your life jacket on. Yes. It depends where you are. If you're over the sea. / Not if you're over the Sahara desert.
(P)	[*Calls out*] Put on a parachute.
T	No, there are no parachutes. Just think about it . . . three hundred passengers. [*To class*] You may have a few more minutes. // Yes? [*Moves to respond to N, who has her hand up*]
N	My mummy gets very scared in aeroplanes, and if they said that / she would faint.

In this extract we find four distinct kinds of discourse. The first episode (1) comes closest to classic recitation. The teacher elicits specific answers to specific questions, often by cueing, and confirms those responses that are correct by repeating them. However, the exchanges chain into a transaction designed not so much to check on existing knowledge as to enable the teacher to validate his framework for imposing pattern upon the apparent randomness of real-life events in order to replay them as narratives having a common form: 'initial state' → 'disruptive element' → 'change' → 'reaction' → 'equilibrium' → 'final state'.

In the second episode, taken from the long central phase of the lesson, the teacher alternates between monitoring pairs and individuals (5) and using pupils' work in progress as a platform for whole class instruction (3). The monitoring is supervisory and evaluative more than it is instructional, for when the teacher wishes to develop a teaching point he stops monitoring and summons the attention of the class as a whole in order that all shall benefit. During this episode, each interaction is relatively brief, although not as brief as the text implies, for each comment is preceded by the teacher's reading and, sometimes, silent correcting or annotating, of what the pupil has written. Finally (6), the teacher leads a class discussion whose purpose is to generate ideas at a juncture in the lesson where his monitoring has persuaded him that pupils are responding to the task less imaginatively than he would like.

The dynamics here are of some importance. The discourse is alert and purposeful. The teacher is constantly on the move and inclusive in both his monitoring of individuals and the way he draws them into whole class interactions. His intentions and expectations are never less than clearly signalled and he consistently demands precision and accuracy. For their part, pupils compete for turns, and indeed in the initial whole-class episode competing is short-circuited as pupils simply call out their ideas and the teacher registers and develops those he deems most appropriate. The interactive pace is fast yet, somehow, unhurried and relaxed, despite the teacher's occasional '*Allez, allez, allez!*' This is partly because the lesson is long, but mainly because, as the overall interaction analysis of this lesson in Table 15.6 shows, routine interactions are kept to a minimum, there are no disciplinary interactions whatever and teacher–pupil talk remains firmly anchored in task content. Most pupils display apparent confidence in handling their side of the discourse, whether volunteering ideas, reading aloud or receiving evaluative feedback. In this lesson, as in all those we observed in France, oral pedagogy is central. However, in this particular case we find a more developed and diverse pattern of oral pedagogy than we encountered in some of the other French lessons. It is unlikely that this has been achieved by the one teacher, confident in the orchestration of classroom interaction although he seems to be. These children are in their fourth year of primary schooling, and by now the rules and routines are well embedded.

Yet there are also clues in the transcript that the teacher in question is consciously testing, and encouraging the pupils themselves to test, the boundaries of these established communicative rules. At (2) a pupil hesitates simply to call out, but the teacher signals to him to do so. At (4), having been invited to speculate about that part of his story which is as yet unwritten, A gets so firmly into his stride that he successfully resists the teacher's attempt to end his turn. He does so having already held the floor for some time. Although the episode which starts with A's being invited to read aloud his story so far represents the seat-based equivalent of thinking aloud at the blackboard such as we observed frequently in both France and Russia, the purpose is exploratory as much as evaluative. The teacher is concerned not just to check and correct, as in the exchange about *conte* and *comptes*, but also to seed new ideas. In this respect the episode can usefully be compared with the one from Kursk in sequence 16.4 where C rehearses the phonetic and literal representation of *rozy*. The exchanges in the Kursk episode are more searching and precise, but also more comprehensively rule-bound.

It is this flexibility in relation to boundaries and conventions which takes the discourse here into domains which the much tighter and more consistent pattern of control in the Russian lessons is unlikely to accommodate. As in Russia the teacher remains firmly in command, yet here he does so in a manner which cedes the capacity and right to initiate turns and ideas to the pupils. This would seem a prerequisite for discussion, and the final episode above moves out of recitation into a mode of discourse which – to use Dillon's typology – may not be dialectical but is certainly moving towards talk of a kind which Mercer calls 'exploratory' rather than merely 'cumulative' or 'disputational'.[40] Nor is it foiled, as Dillon notes that class discussion so often is, by the teacher's interventions.

In our journey through the different patterns of discourse witnessed in primary classrooms in these five countries, we can see how this lesson includes elements which follow the familiar paths of expository and interrogatory teaching but also open up the possibilities of dialogue. Dialogic discourse is a problematic notion in the context of conventional pedagogy, for not only does it sit uneasily with the dynamics of large groups, but it also implies a power relationship between the parties which, if not fully equal, at least has been equalized to the point where there is a shared acceptance of the right of each participant to speak, be heard, and be listened to without the imposition of an overriding view of what counts as a proper or correct contribution. Alongside this necessary change in power relations there is an important element of skill, for handling turns by mutual consent is much more difficult than giving control of them to one person.

It is for these reasons that some argue that class discussion can never be other than recitation in disguise and that the most promising context for the development of the true learning potential of dialogic discourse is the small group discussion in which pupils undertake their tasks with the minimum of intervention from the teacher.

Yet here the teacher manages both to steer and be steered, to maintain control and to cede it. The lesson extract as transcribed, even with the extent of annotation we have here, cannot really convey how this is done. Most of the clues lie beyond this transcript altogether: within the classroom in those aspects of teaching – such as lesson structure, task design, the balance and motivating power of learning activities, the management of time – which we discussed in previous chapters; outside it in the convergence of school, home and societal values relating to primary education, from which a school located, as Coulanges is, in a prosperous and upwardly mobile neighbourhood, is certain to gain special benefit. But other clues come from observation and the videotape. Throughout the lesson, the teacher's tone of voice is relaxed and matter-of-fact. He speaks loudly enough to be heard, but never shouts or declaims. Unlike many teachers we observed in India, Russia, England and Michigan, he does not slip into a 'teacherly' vocabulary and register or deploy those highly localized and semi-secret classroom codes which in the latter two countries are designed to reinforce the micro-community of 'our class'. Unlike the teacher in sequence 16.8, he is even-handed in his dealings with individual children. Wearing slacks and a jaunty red sweater he moves rapidly round the room, engaging with all of them yet providing feedback which is focused and formative rather than – as so often in England – vague and palliative.

For all that, while this teacher and his pupils seem to be discovering a viable middle ground between constraint and freedom in their talk, when it comes to the lesson's written task both prefer to revert to safer and even more authoritarian habits. The teacher contains the children's inventiveness within the bounds of grammatical and orthographic conformity. He gives mixed messages about the narrative line, which remains prominently displayed on both the blackboard and the pupils' worksheets throughout the lesson. He starts by setting it up as a model to be followed. Later (not in this extract) he says, 'You don't have to use the plan I drew out' and 'Now you don't have to follow the plan: it's just there to help you'. But at the very end of the lesson, when talking to the class as a whole about the work they have produced, he reverts:

> T You need more suspense and excitement . . . G and M need to be little bit more original . . . F needs to end her story better . . . You need to correct your work in order to avoid repetition . . . You have all done good work, but not all of you have followed the plan that I gave you.

In the end, whatever kind of talk this teacher is keen to promote, writing is for him a technical matter, and narrative writing follows a path which is as predictable as the chemical reaction which provides its metaphor at the lesson's outset. Yet in the vital matter of the relationship between classroom discourse and pupils' learning I shall want to argue that this lesson is one which brings us very close to the elusive notion of scaffolding.

Perhaps we see here two levels of curriculum in partial conflict: the achievement of understanding and the demonstration of competence. Perhaps, too, the contrast between inventiveness in talk and conformity in writing gives us insight into the finding of a national survey that in their oral language French pupils of the late 1990s expressed themselves more articulately and confidently than those of the mid 1980s while their written self-expression and spelling had deteriorated.[41]

In the next lesson, from England, pupils of the same age as those at Coulanges are also being asked to write. The writing is to be descriptive and impressionistic rather than narrative, but once again the pupils are bound by a formula.

England

Sequence 16.10. Ogden, 31 pupils aged 9–11,
English (lesson 11.14, page 293)

(0946)

(1) T I am really looking for [*writes 'descriptive' on blackboard*] words, right? / I mean in my bedroom I could say, I have a pink carpet. / I could say, I have a pink carpet with tiny flecks of white in it, just to – rather than just pink, y'know, just describing it. Or it is dusky pink with tiny flecks of white. Try and make some description. That will be in your first paragraph. [*Underlines '1st describe' on blackboard*] In your second paragraph / [*writes on blackboard '2nd* →'] which we start a little bit in [*referring to a pupil's answer to an earlier question*] if you like / [*glances at her notes*] I want you to consider // [*writes on blackboard 'How your room is special to you'*] how your / room is / special / to you, / OK? [*Turns to face class*] How it's special to you. Some of you / [*sternly pointing her notes at A*] *A* / some of you might / use it as a place where you go to have a quiet read or where you like to be quiet. Some of you might use it, well **you** tell **me**. / How do you use your bedroom B, or do you simply sleep in it?

(2) B I go upstairs to read most of the time.

T You go upstairs to read. Why do you go upstairs to read?

B Well, it's quieter than going downstairs because my sister's normally practising her clarinet.

T Your sister's practising clarinet. C?

C I read and I listen to music and I do my homework and I sleep and I do everything in there.

T OK. / Er, who do you allow in it? / Or, can, does anybody just walk in at your house?

C Um, I don't let my brother in it very <u>much</u> . . .

T <u>Oh, why not?</u>

C I let my mum in, but only when my room is tidy.

T // Well, a method here isn't there? D?

D I didn't put my hand up.

T No, I know you didn't put your hand up. That's why I'm asking you.

D / Sometimes I go in there to play on my computer and watch telly.

T [*Walks towards D and addresses her*] If you have friends to play. [*To class*] Who has friends to play and they play in the bedroom? [*Most hands are raised*] Why E? Out of your mum's way?

E No.

T OK. Just as a matter of interest, how many of you have a television in your bedroom? [*Most hands are raised*] I find that amazing. Put your hands down. How many of you have a computer in your bedroom? [*Some pupils raise hands*] How many have you a, er, a video in your

bedroom? [*A few pupils raise hands*] I find that even more amazing. /
However / right, OK. /

(3)   [*Walks back to blackboard*] Er, so what I want in your second paragraph
        [*writes 'Personal feelings' on blackboard*] is your own personal feelings.
        Right. [*Underlines what she has written*] Third paragraph. / [*Writes on
        board '3rd other people's views'*] I want to know / [*writing*] what other
        peoples' views are / of your bedroom. [*Faces class*] What your mum might
        think about it, what your dad might think about it, what your friends
        might think about it, how **they** see it.

.
.
.

(0958)

(4) T   [*To F, leaning on his shoulder, checking his work*] Now that **does** want
        an apostrophe. [*Writes one in and continues to read*] / Oh, I like that. /
        That's good. [*Ticks F's work*] OK. [*Moves on to next table. Looks at
        A's work*]. Have you read this A? [*Referring to the worksheet which she
        places in front of him*]

A   Yes.

T   Right. // [*Reading his work*] With a what?

A   Mirror.

T   / And?

A   White plastic on the front.

T   Is that M-I-double R-O-R?

A   Yeah.

T   That's fine. Well done. [*Starts to walk away*]

A   Can I have a, is that a, the first paragraph?

T   [*Stops*] I don't think that's a paragraph A. [*Points towards his work with
        her pen*]

A   Here?

T   Probably. [*Steps towards him for a closer look*] Well I don't really like to
        say in, um, in sort of. / Have you described, have you described the walls?
        Have you described the furniture and the bedcovers . . .

A   . . . I don't wanna, I don't . . .

T   . . . What about the bedcovers? What colour scheme?

A   Yeah. I will but, I don't wanna say the, um, oh . . . / [*Pauses to find the
        word, mimes running his hand across a wall*]

T   What?

A   The wallpaper 'cause it's babyish.

T   // Well / you could, you want, in other words you'd like it changing . . .

A   Mm.

T   . . . to something teenagerish.

A   Mm.

T   Well, / OK, fair enough. [*Moves to another table*]

The prescribed form for the pupils' writing is that of the paragraph. Pupils must construct three of them on the subject of their bedrooms: first, 'Describe', then 'How your room is special to you', and finally 'Other people's views of your room'. The extract illustrates three kinds of discourse. These are whole class exposition (1), whole class questioning (2) reverting to exposition (3), and one-to-one monitoring.

I have chosen this extract not only because it illustrates further the generic tension between constraint and freedom in teaching and therefore compares usefully with the lesson from Coulanges in which children of the same age are also writing to a formula, but also because in this case the tension, being in the realm of meaning and values, shapes the discourse more directly.

In the Coulanges lesson the subject matter was prescribed: the pupils had to construct a story from a picture of two passengers sitting in an aircraft. There were other givens: the passengers were male and wore business suits, while the cabin crew were female. But values, let alone the issue of gender stereotyping, were not the issue there for the task was essentially a technical one. In the Ogden lesson above, however, the subject-matter raises value-questions which cannot be ducked or sidelined, for the teacher has asked the children to write about something which is doubly personal to them: their home, and the particular space within the home which is most distinctively theirs, their bedroom.

This I should stress, is a typically English approach. The teacher has been professionally socialized into the belief that children learn best 'from experience' and that it is therefore in experience that their learning tasks should be grounded. Allied to the belief in individualism this commitment can give to some of those learning tasks which are experientially sited a very personal edge which is missing from comparable tasks set by teachers in France, Russia and India. There, the experiences about which pupils talk and write are more likely to be public and communal (such as what it feels like to be a passenger in an aircraft) than domestic and private. In England (and indeed in Michigan, where teachers advanced similar arguments about the value of a particular version of 'experience') it is common for children to be asked to record, in 'diaries' or 'journals', quite intimate details of their family life, and generations of parents have been routinely embarrassed by what emerges. (We might add that 'My bedroom' would have been an inconceivable topic in the Russian and Indian schools anyway, not just because of its individualistic orientation but also because few of the pupils would have had bedrooms to call their own.)

Having invited these pupils to write three paragraphs on this topic the teacher then has to accommodate to what emerges and the pupils have to accommodate to her reactions. The initial exposition at (1) sets the structural framework for what the pupils are to write before cutting itself short ('Some of you might use it . . . ') and inviting illustrations ('well, *you* tell *me*'). However, the teacher has already signalled her preferred notion of 'bedroom' by invoking pink carpets with white flecks and this comes through ever more strongly as the lesson proceeds. The initial exchanges at (2) are conventional IRF: direct elicitation, focused response and confirmatory feedback ('You go upstairs to read' / 'Your sister's practising clarinet'): conventional because they conform to the preferred vision of childhood bedroom and – by extension – childhood. Thereafter the pattern reflects the children's growing assertion of a less bourgeois vision. Talk of messy bedrooms is first curtailed by the teacher's deviating from her normal procedure for handling turns ('D?' 'I didn't put my hand up.' '. . . That's why I'm asking you'). D's response about her personal computer and television is then reformulated in a manner which effectively dismisses it ('If you have friends to play. Who has friends to play . . . in their bedroom?') – for D has in fact said nothing about having friends to play. However, the true extent of the gulf between the two worlds is revealed when a show of hands shows an extent of material possessions which the teacher seems unable to handle ('I find that amazing . . . I find that even more amazing'). At that point the entire discussion is terminated and the teacher retreats to safer ground ('However / right / OK / So what I want in your second paragraph is . . .').

The monitoring episode (4) is largely supervisory and evaluative in respect of technical aspects of the writing task – punctuation, spellings, what counts as a paragraph – until once again values collide and the IRF structure disintegrates into a series of overlapping turns and silences signalling E's discomfort at being quizzed about his bedcovers and wallpaper. The teacher tries to help by suggesting that he might like a bedroom ambience which is more 'teenagerish', but to this E can manage no more than a guarded response and the teacher moves away with a closing comment ('Well / OK, fair enough') which is more nonplussed than evaluative.

In two of the Michigan extracts later in this chapter we shall find further examples of what happens to teacher–pupil discourse when it attempts to engage pupils' own experiences and concerns for curriculum purposes. We can advance two hypotheses at this stage to explain the tensions and difficulties that fracture the IRF structures which this teacher would no doubt have preferred. First, there is a collision between the teacher's view of childhood and the children's own: in hers nine year olds read improving books, practise their clarinets and politely entertain their friends; in theirs, they watch videos, play computer games and with anticipatory moodiness listen to pop music in untidy bedrooms. (Elsewhere in this lesson the teacher attempts to correct Boyzone to 'Boy's Own', much to the covert contempt of several of the pupils.) Second, there is a tussle for control as the children resist the teacher's attempts to annex and commodify their out-of-school lives as part of an 'experiential' curriculum in which their felt experience is subjected to a process of vetting and adjustment in order to bring it into line with the received view of children and childhood.

Thus we can contemplate here an emerging paradox of pedagogical 'relevance'. Many English teachers would dismiss the subject matter of the Coulanges teacher's writing lesson as arid and, possibly, sexist. Yet it seems more effectively to scaffold the construction of written narrative than the Ogden teacher's choice of 'My bedroom' helps children to construct paragraphs, because its distance from what most matters to the children allows both for greater forensic concentration on the writing process as such and for greater imaginative play.

In the next sequence a teacher at Hamilton uses subject matter which is very remote indeed from the children's experience as a basis for teaching them how to use books to access information. This allows us to reflect on how far the discourse differences between the previous two extracts were related to factors other than the lessons' subject matter.

Sequence 16.11. Hamilton, 31 pupils aged 6–8,
English (study skills) (lesson 11.13, page 291)

(1053)

(1) T   [*Is sitting with the 'castles' group*] F was just saying about jousting. She's just mentioned that word and the second question says, 'What happened in the joust?' So can we find jousting in the index? [*Each pupil begins to turn to the index in his/her book*] <u>And see if it</u> . . .

A   <u>Jousting</u>. How do you spell that?

T   Have a look, look [*Shows him question card*] 'j' – 'ou' – 'st'.

A   There isn't a 'j' in there.

B   Is that joust? Is that joust?

T   [*Pointing to A's book*] Jousting. / No, 'j', 'j'. [*Points to B's book*] No, it's not in that one is it?

(P)   Is that a joust?

T   [*To C*] J, a J / [*drawing letter J in the air*] look. [*Shows C the question card*].

D   I've found one.

T   Found it? Is it the right word? [*Shows D the question card*] What page is it on? What page D? [*D turns to the right page*]

B   There isn't one in this book.

T   Right, see if it's in the other book then.

E   I haven't even got a 'j' in there

T   See if it's in that one. [*Hands her another book*]

C   I don't even have the letter.

T   [*Looking and sounding surprised*] Don't you even have the letter in that one?

E   Jousting, there. [*Shows T the book's index*]

T   Find the right page then. [*F holds her book up for the teacher to see*]

A   [*To himself*] <u>J-O-U</u> . . .

E   . . . <u>22 or 24</u>.

T   <u>Pardon?</u>

E   . . . <u>find which one</u>.

T   Have a look and see. [*To F, who is still holding her book up*] Have a look, er, have you got one, <u>er, F?</u>

(P)   . . . <u>isn't</u> the joust.

T   Have you found <u>the joust?</u>

C   <u>Don't know</u> what's happened to the letter in this either.

T   Right you have a look in mine then. / [*Hands C another book*] Have you got one B?

B   Yeh, I've got two. I've found it.

.

.

.

(1115)

(2) T   [*She has heard F the first time, but has been sidetracked by the more persistent B*] Now what did you say F?

F   Well, I've looked in all the books and I can't . . .

T   You can't find bath. So what do **you** think happened? Do you think they had baths? [*To rest of group*] We've got a problem here. Can we just listen and see if we can solve this problem? F's looked in every single book and she can't find bath.

C   Well maybe they don't have them then.

E   They don't have baths.

T   Do you think maybe they don't have them? [*Looks at F*]

PP   No, no.

D   They don't have baths. There was . . .

C   I knew they don't, they don't have baths.

D   'Cause they don't have water.

A   Yeah, they go in the water in the lake.

C   They just get a bucket of water and tip it over them. [*Teacher, looking in turn at each of the previous speakers, now nods to C*]

D   [*Shakes his head*] No they don't, they go under . . .

A   Yeah they go in this, they go under the water fountain and get washed.

T   Do they?

A   Yes.

D   Yeah, they jump in.

T   How do you know that then?

A   'Cause I've seen it on TV.

T   [*Not looking at him*] Oh.

C   Yeah, 'cause, 'cause I've seen.

D   [*Raising his voice above C's*] I've seen . . .

T   [*Shaking her head, still not looking at A*] Well I, *I* don't know the answer to that question.

A   I do.

T   So you think that's what, you've seen that on the television. [*Nods*]

C   I've seen it before.

T   All right F, does that help then? What do **you** think they did?

F   [*Mimes as she speaks*] I think they got a bucket of water and . . .

T   [*Nods*] A bucket of water and threw it over them.

Here the setting is a group of six children rather than the class as a whole, and the discourse includes teacher-led instruction and discussion, interspersed with periods of unstructured conversation while the pupils work at their assignment cards. As defined in Chapter 15 this is 'collective' rather than 'collaborative' group work: that is, it is largely teacher led, and when the teacher leaves this group to monitor others the pupils work independently, although they converse casually while doing so.

In the first episode the teacher gets the pupils to search the indexes in the reference books which she has placed on their table in order to address the question 'What happened in the joust?' In the second episode F's failure to find 'bath' in any of these books prompts members of the group to volunteer their own ideas on how the inhabitants of medieval castles kept themselves clean. The reduction of the teaching group to just six pupils generates a discourse structure which differs from whole class teaching most obviously in respect of the taking and controlling of turns. The teacher can remove the usual regulatory procedures and allow turn taking to follow a pattern that is closer to that of everyday conversation.

In the first episode we have not so much conversation as a set of overlapping and competing exchanges as each pupil responds to the task of looking up 'joust'. Although the result looks somewhat chaotic, we can register the fact that the range of pupil utterances includes questions as well as statements, and that the latter are mostly in the nature of fragments of commentary on the activity of looking up the word ('There isn't a 'j' in there' / 'I've found one' / 'I don't even have the letter' / 'I've found it') rather than statements about what the word actually means. By and large, pupils do not so much take turns as speak in parallel, and in doing so they put down markers rather than initiate exchanges.

In the second episode the teacher manages the discussion in a different way. The book indexes have failed to turn up the word (*bath*) which will help F to discover the answer to her question about medieval ablutions. This time the teacher encourages the group to treat this as a collective problem and to pool their knowledge and speculation in the absence of the authority of the text. F and the teacher listen as C, E, D and A take over the discussion, and, as so often in conversation, the end of one utterance overlaps with the beginning of another, either because one speaker 'reads' or – correctly or incorrectly – anticipates the meaning of the other's utterance from its first few words, or because the speakers are speaking at or past rather than to each other, or again because they wish to signal their superior knowledge to a third party (the teacher). The teacher intervenes when A shows signs of becoming too dominant, but does so not by ending his turn and nominating another pupil, as in the whole class context she might, but by responding sceptically to his confident assertions and, when this makes little difference, by saying 'Well *I* don't know the answer to that question'.

What is striking about the second episode is that even this evaluation, which in a whole class context would seem quite cutting, does not topple A from his temporary position of the group's authority on the matter of castle baths. The teacher merely turns back to F (whose enquiry started this discussion) and asks her to make up her own mind: 'Does that help then? What do *you* think they did?' For this brief period of time these six to eight year olds have taken collective responsibility for managing their classroom talk and the teacher has subsumed her communicative rights within theirs. Of course, this is not so much a discussion as a series of assertions and counter-assertions, much of it lacking even the tacit sharing of turns which characterizes conversational adjacency pairs. The pattern is no less common among adults than children, and in both cases it reminds us that true discussion is a considerable discipline. The fact remains, however, that the teacher has extended the repertoire of classroom interaction beyond the usual English combination of whole class teaching, individual monitoring, and random pupil–pupil conversation across seating groups, and has begun to shift the latter in the direction of group discussion and collective problem-solving. This being England, however, we know that although the teacher who takes over this class will secure continuity and progression in curriculum content, whether as they progress through the school the pupils' discourse repertoire will be extended in the direction of genuinely dialectical discussion is a matter of chance.

Structurally, conversations are said to consist of *adjacency pairs* – one utterance provoking a response – which chain together on the basis of communicative rules and understandings which are *locally managed*. In the discourse of whole class teaching the IRF exchange predominates and the dynamics of turn taking are managed by the teacher, who also 'owns' the discourse in the sense that he or she determines its topic, decides what direction it may and may not take, and arbitrates on how it shall begin and end.

Although this distinction implies nothing about the vocabulary and syntactical form of the actual language used, we tend to expect conversations, and certainly conversations among children, to be less 'formal' than the stage-managed exchanges of whole class teaching. In Bernstein's terms, everyday conversation is not only managed differently from teacher-controlled talk, but it may also encompass fundamentally different linguistic forms. Together, the mode and control of utterances and exchanges constitute a code: 'A code is a regulative principle, tacitly acquired, which selects and integrates relevant meanings, forms of realizations, and evoking contexts.'[42]

In his early work, Bernstein focused on linguistic form and semantic burden, differentiating first 'public' and 'formal' language and then, as he probed the power relations which provoke these differences and their relationship to social structure, 'restricted' and 'elaborated' codes. The changing terminology reflected an intensifying preoccupation not only with the 'deep structures' of language but also with the relationship between school and society, micro and macro.

Our cross-cultural examination of discourse extracts points to an intriguing problem in respect of the notion of codes. In the Indian and Russian lessons, and to a considerable degree in those from France, the grammatical, syntactical, lexical and semantic 'otherness' of teacher-managed classroom language is very evident. Indeed, the Russian extracts in particular accord closely with Bernstein's original definition of the elaborated code in their attention to grammatical convention and syntactical elaboration, as well as in their overt regulatory character. In contrast, the language of the extract above has the grammatical simplicity and syntactic imprecision of Bernstein's restricted code. It – and this includes the teacher's language as well as the children's – is vernacular rather than scholastic.

The convergence of what one might term playground and classroom codes is as pronounced in the English and American pedagogical data as is their divergence in the same data from India, Russia and France. To some degree, this might be explained as a function of the very different dynamics of whole classes and small groups. However, although code convergence is most obvious in group work, and we observed group work only in France, England and Michigan, in England and

Michigan – especially the latter – it was also common in whole class interaction, although the latter is invariably shaped and managed by the teacher.

At this point we signal the issue. As we move through the remaining extracts we shall explore some of its ramifications, not the least of which is the possibility that conflicting signals in the matter of pedagogical codes connotes disturbance at the deeper level of values.

Sequence 16.12. Kirkbright, 28 pupils aged 6–7, Literacy Hour (lesson 11.15, page 294. For analysis of organizational aspects of this lesson's interaction, see Table 15.10, page 404)

(1343)

(1)   *[Tables 1 and 2 have prominent signs announcing 'We are working with the teacher']*

T   *[To tables 3, 4 and 5]* Right, I'm closing the magic curtain *[Mimes closing a curtain. Some pupils laugh]* / which doesn't work. *[Smiles, puts finger to lips]* Now, if it's a curtain I can still hear you. And I'm working, going to try and work with these two tables and you're trying, / *[frowns at pupil who is talking loudly]* trying to work on your own. *[Goes to table 1]*.

.
.
.

(2)   *[Teacher is walking towards table 4 to help B]*.

C   *[Sitting at table 3, calls out as teacher passes]* Miss, um Miss Newton, can A be in our group?

T   A. / We'll work out where A is sitting. *[To B]* Oh, you've done it! *[Moving to table 5]* Well done! *[Places her hands on D's shoulders]*

D   Miss, can of, off be . . . ?

T   Of, off, it needs 'f' not 'v': of. *[Moves to table 3]*

E   *[Calls out from table 4]* Miss Newton, Miss Newton, *[Teacher stops, looks and smiles in E's direction]* shall I do a short one?

T   *[Nods and moves on to table 1]*

(3) C   Miss, Miss, Miss Newton, Miss Newton . . .

F   *[Table 1, pointing to a word in her word book]* Is it that one?

T   *[Leaning over to look at F's work]* It is, well done! Good girl. 'I want . . .' *[Moves to table 2]*

(4) G   Miss Newton, Miss Newton, can you spell 'what'?

T   *[Leaning towards G with her hands resting on the table]* 'What'? There's a hat in 'what'. *[Picking up G's wordbook, moves round to stand behind him]* Shall we see if it's in here?

G   *[Nods]*

T   *[Notices F is not working, but staring at the teacher's radio microphone]*. Hello F, shall we get on with the third word?

F   [*Pointing to the microphone*] I've seen that on the television, on Count
           Me In.
T   [*Smiling*] It's listening to you, F. [*Continues to scan G's word book. To
           G*] We're looking for 'w'. Help me find 'w'. [*To F*] No you are. 'w', 'w',
           'w', 'w', what! It's the 'w'-'h' page. Sh-sh. [*To F, while walking towards
           her*] Come on now, the best thing you can do would be . . .
H   Mrs Newton, Mrs Newton, [*Reads from his own writing*] 'I will help
           you.'
T   'I will help you.' Very good. [*Moves to table 2, touches I's shoulder. I
           leans back from J*] Let's sit separately. [*Looks over I's shoulder and reads*]
           'Hello, oh no my letter has blown away. Help catch it', 'Shall we help?'
           Right, move you up a little bit J [*Pushes J's worksheet away from I's. J
           moves to the next chair, leaving a space between herself and I*] 'cause
           your stories are very much the same. I stood on your toe, I'm sorry.
           [*Moves to table 1*].
K   Miss, Miss.
T   [*Nods to K as she passes, but has noticed that F is distracted again*] Right,
           F. [*F goes back to work. T sits down next to H*]
H   I've done, 'I will too'.
(5) L   [*Approaches from table 3*] How do you spell 'can't'?
M   Miss Newton, Miss Newton . . .
T   Find the 'c' page in your word book. [*Raises her palm in a calming
           gesture towards M*] Ssh.
N   [*Reads to herself*] 'We are working with the teacher'.
M   Is that how you spell 'shouted'?
T   [*Drawing M's word book towards her*] It's very much like that.
(6) O   [*Queuing behind L*] I need 'that'
T   Bring me your 't' page. [*O goes to fetch her word book. To H, in a
           whisper*] Come on, you're doing ever so well. [*To M, starting to spell
           'shouted' for him*] Sh . . .
N   [*Reads to herself*] 'We are working with the teacher.'

This extract shows a teacher of younger children attempting to accommodate to
the organizational requirements of the UK government's Literacy Hour. The rubric
specifies an hour-long lesson divided into four sections, the first two and last of
which involve whole class instruction while the third entails 'independent reading,
writing or word work, while the teacher works with at least two ability groups each
day on guided text work (reading or writing)'. During this phase those pupils with
whom the teacher is not working should have been trained 'not to interrupt the
teacher and there should be sufficient resources and alternative strategies for them
to fall back on if they get stuck'.[43]

Thus, for all its trumpeted celebration of continentally inspired 'interactive whole
class teaching' the Literacy Hour has as its longest phase a strategy which is English
rather than continental, and indeed has its roots in teachers' attempts during the
post-Plowden period to reconcile the ideal of individualism with the imperatives of

managing a large class. In that context teachers in two of our earlier studies called the strategy one of 'planned unequal investment' and we found it to be fraught with problems in respect not just of management but also of curriculum balance. Thus, the 'independent' tasks being undertaken by pupils who were not in line for the teacher's attention tended to be less challenging and were pursued intermittently and with frequent interruptions and distractions. Observing this we noted then: 'The price that some of these children may pay for demanding little of the teacher may be that they are given work that demands little of them.'[44] Or, as one of the teachers in our 1986 study put it, 'If the work is high demand cognitively for the children, then it's high investment for me as teacher'.[45]

The extract comes from this third stage of the Literacy Hour. The teacher uses a typically oblique formula at (1) for commanding silence (I'm closing the magic curtain') which, as she gracefully notes, 'doesn't work', and then settles down (2) with the groups at Tables 1 and 2 whose status is signalled by the signs 'We are working with the teacher'. Her concentration on these groups is interrupted by a succession of children from the supposedly independent remaining three groups demanding help with spellings (3, 4, 5, 6) and as a result the discourse is highly fragmented. Meanwhile, the loss of continuity and focus allows N, a member of the group at table 1, to pass the time by reading and re-reading the notice 'We are working with the teacher'. At least she is reading.

The result is that the discourse more closely resembles that of supervisory monitoring than instruction, in that it focuses on the mechanics of the learning *activity* rather than the substance of the learning *task* (see Chapter 14). The extract shows clearly the link between discourse form and classroom organization, and the extent to which the management of turns is compromised by events. Had this teacher had the support of a non-teaching assistant (as had the teacher in the previous extract from Hamilton) the discourse would have remained more directly within her control.

Yet although the support of another adult would have made the interaction less subject to interruption and diversion, its content may not have been much different, for this teacher maintained, at every stage of the lesson from which this short extract is taken, a language which veered between the conversational and a form which owed less to the official discourse of the Literacy Hour than to the inherited discourse of English infant education, a sub-phase which, as we found in Chapter 7, has its own genealogy and ideology within the larger domain of British elementary and primary education.

This form is oblique and euphemistic in its handling of matters of control ('Now if it's a curtain I can still hear you'), inclusive (not the oppositional 'I' and 'you' of teacher and pupil, but 'we', as in 'Shall we see what's in here?'), indirect in the management of turns ('Hello F, shall we get on with the third word?') and in tone and mood gentle and approachable. It also eschews the technical vocabulary of the discipline ('take away' and 'times' instead of 'subtract' and 'multiply') and in this context uses an esoteric repertoire of letter sounds instead of letter names ('Curly cuh . . . kicking cuh . . . it's the "w" – "h" page').

This is the classroom manifestation of the wider professional language of child centredness and is as far removed as it is possible to imagine from the discourse in the Kursk extract in sequence 16.4. There we encountered little of the pervasive English early years dissonance between locutionary act and illocutionary force: questions were questions and instructions were instructions. The relationship of teacher and taught was signalled precisely by 'I' and 'you' rather than blurred by 'we', and indeed its status differential was unavoidably underscored by the *ti/vi* usage. Most notably, in the teaching of language the technical vocabulary of vowels, consonants, hard and soft, voiced and unvoiced was introduced from the outset. Children were inducted into this and other subject registers with the minimum of delay.

The Literacy Hour has breached the discourse of infant education, in a conscious emulation of mainstream European practice, by requiring teachers to accelerate the introduction of linguistic terminology (in this lesson, the word 'phoneme' was dutifully used several times but had a somewhat self-conscious ring). Critics have suggested that there is a danger that the knowledge about language argued for in the first version of the National Curriculum will be reduced to the mere 'naming of parts'.[46] This debate apart, the relational colouring of this discourse, as exemplified above, will not be that easily transformed, because it manifests deeply-seated collective professional beliefs about the nature of childhood which go back via the English progressive movement and Piaget to the Froebelian garden and to Rousseau.[47]

If one compares the language of the teacher here with that used in extract 16.11, one finds differences which cannot be put down to the organizational context alone. The pupils are the same age, but only the second teacher deploys with them what I have called the 'inherited discourse of infant education'. The notion of 'psychobiography' reminds us that in classrooms, as in every walk of life, language and the meanings it expresses are embedded in individual experience. To this we must add that teachers have shared as well as unique biographies and that professional socialization into the world of primary teaching may have an impact which is no less readily discernible. Sealey's work, applying Layder's domain theory, shows how psychobiography, social setting and collectivity combine and interweave to create identity and shape transactions.[48] The teacher above was trained in the heyday of Plowden, and her language in this extract and throughout the lessons which we observed was redolent of the developmental, child-centred discourse of that time, as I and others analysed this during the 1970s and the 1980s.[49] In contrast, the teacher whose pupils were working with children on using indexes (16.11) was professionally socialized into a context framed by the National Curriculum and in which the earlier discourse was under attack. Where the earlier discourse was inward looking and strongly protective of its boundaries, the later one had been strongly infiltrated by the world beyond primary teaching. In 1984, I quoted a typical professional text (that garden again):

> Froebel referred to the teacher as a gardener and the children as plants. Many people have broken into this garden . . . parents, administrators, providers of resources and taxpayers.[50]

By 2000, not only would any suggestion that it was the proper job of teachers to exclude parents from their child's education have been treated with derision –

although in the 1980s Kirby was voicing a view to which many primary teachers subscribed – but the new culture of accountability and performance management had radically repositioned the protagonists. In the rhetoric of 2000, parents, tax-payers and OFSTED inspectors were in the garden, protecting children from the mayhem caused by teachers and administrators, and the latter (at LEA level, any-way) were in the process of being banished from it altogether.[51]

This lesson reveals an albeit gentle collision of discourses which manifests a sharper underlying collision of educational values. Our final English extract shows a teacher coming to terms with another plank in New Labour's 'standards' platform, the numeracy hour.

> ### Sequence 16.13. St Teresa's, 29 pupils aged 9–11, Numeracy Hour (lesson 11.16, page 295. For analysis of organizational aspects of this lesson's interaction, see Table 15.11, page 405).

(1059)

T   [*Pupil A has just finished writing his 'make 16' calculation on the black-board. Teacher to class*]. Do you agree with that one? [*Pupils murmur. A returns to his seat*] 100,000 take away 100,000 is going to be nothing. Add 16, and have our 16. Take away 9. / What are we going to get to? Take away 9?

(P) 7.

T   7. Then add 3, A, where are we up to?

A   10.

T   10. Add 4?

A   14.

T   14. Add 2?

(P) 16. [*Pupils raise hands to be chosen to go to the board*]

T   Er, B?

.
.
.

(1102)

T   Right, um, [*walks to side table and picks up worksheets*] Year 5, er, last week we were looking at patterns in number. You're going to be doing a bit more on that today with magic squares. [*Walks to front of class*] So you're working on the sheet, OK? [*Holds up worksheet*] And you're trying to complete the magic squares and these ones there, the examples I've given you, have got a magic number of 15. What do we mean when we say a magic square? [*No response*] Does C know the answer? Come on. I'm sure you'll have come across these before. Magic square, why are they called magic? / Er, D?

D Because all the numbers across and down and diagonally are the same.

T Equal, the same number, very good. So all the numbers [*indicates the dimensions on the worksheet*] across, downwards or diagonally equal the same number. So if I tell you these have got a magic number of 15, what does that mean, E, on these squares? / [*No response*] That if we add the numbers across, they're going to come to what total? / If you add these numbers here, [*points to partly-completed square on worksheet*] if we had the right numbers in, what total would it come to if it's a magic square of 15? / [*No response*] Anyone help her out? F?

F 15.

T It's gonna come to 15. So if we add the top numbers [*points to the numbers*] – that first – the first three numbers across, that's got to come to 15. And then if we add the numbers going down that's got to come to 15 as well. And if we add the diagonal, that's corner to corner, that's got to come to 15 as well. So you've got to fill in the numbers so that they're going to come – add up – total 15. OK? And then, when you've done that, it tells you that you've got a bit more to do further down here. I'll probably come round and help you with that if you get stuck. You've got to see whether you can make up a magic square, add 10 to your numbers and whether that's going to make a difference, whether it's still going to be a magic square, but start with these and then I'll come round to you. So that's Year 5.

.

.

.

(1121)

[*Teacher moves, for the first time this lesson, to one of the Year 5 groups. E and P promptly stop chatting as she approaches*]

T Right. How are we doing on here?

H I did <u>it all</u> . . .

T [*General question, but looking at I, E and G. H stops talking and waits her turn*] <u>Manage</u> to get all the magic squares done? And are they all adding up to / . . .

I Yeah.

T . . . the number 15?

I Yeah.

T And the diagonals as well?

I Yeah. [*E, seated next to I, nods her head in agreement*]

T Excellent, well done. [*Turns to H*]

H [*Showing her worksheet*] I forgot to do the diagonals first and now I've got to start again.

T Oh dear! I did say the diagonals didn't I? [*To I*] Well done, yeah. [*To J*] How're you doing J?

J I'm on my third one.

T   Third one, good, OK. [*Looks again at I's work*]

E   G's writing a different . . . [*G shakes her head*]

T   [*Moving round the table to look at G's work*] Are you all right G? [*G nods.
     Teacher, sympathetically*] She's not, knows how to add these up don't you?
     / Just looking for a pattern aren't we, to make 15. / [*Checks G's work.*]
     Good.
     [*Moves to a Year 6 table*]

.

.

.

(1131)

T   [*Three pupils have their hands raised*] What about you, um, K?

K   We started it.

T   Did you get that far?

K   Yeah.

T   D'you think it would still be a magic square?

K   <u>Yeah.</u>

L   <u>Yes</u>.

T   Why's that?

K   [*Takes a deep breath*] Because, when you times it – the number you've got
     – last number – when you add 10 – from your / magic number square that
     adds up to 15, the number that you add up to 10, such as 9, it – all the sums
     added up to, well 9, then you times all the numbers on the other square by
     3, which the numbers get bigger *again* and the / the magic number which all
     the sums add up to, got bigger as well.

T   [*L, seated next to K, raises his hand*] It got bigger as well, it was still a
     magic square. [*V lowers his hand*]

K   Yeah.

T   'Cause you're doing [*emphasizes with both voice and hands*] the **same thing
     to each** of the numbers aren't you? So it will still stay a magic square and
     you can get a lot bigger – bigger number. Well done. [*Notices that M is
     clattering his ruler*] Right M, could you put your ruler down please. Now
     then Year 6, N, could you tell us what you've been doing this morning?

The first episode is from the tail end of the first of the Numeracy Hour's three
stages. This prescribes 'oral and mental work to rehearse and sharpen skills'[52] and
here one pupil comes to the board to demonstrate his response to the task 'How many
ways can you make 16?' His solution ($100,000 - 100,000 + 16 - 9 + 3 + 4 + 2$)
consists, apart from the initial feint, mainly of counting on, but whereas a Russian
teacher might have challenged him to exploit all four basic number operations, the
teacher here merely confirms each step in the solution by reiteration ('seven'/'seven'),
and the solution as a whole without comment, before passing to the next pupil. This
is the first sign of a tendency in many of the exchanges to focus on the procedural
rather than substantive aspects of the learning task, or – in terms of the distinction

discussed in Chapter 14 – on *activity* rather than on *task* – and it alerts us to the need to probe a central claim in both the literacy and numeracy strategy: that 'interactive whole class teaching' of itself more successfully promotes learning than other strategies. In this case the discourse checks but does not more than marginally engage.

The same can be said for the extracts from the second ('main') and third ('plenary') stages of the lesson. The class, it will be recalled, has two age ranges spread across five seating groups. In the extract's second episode, the teacher sets the task for the Year 5 pupils, which consists of completing numerical 'magic squares' of nine cells in which each horizontal, vertical and diagonal line of cells adds up to 15. They then expand the numbers in the cells first by adding 10 to each and then by multiplying each by 3, and are asked to check whether the squares have retained their mathematical 'magic'. The episode is notable in four respects. First, the teacher does most of the talking. Second, she does so because pupils are reluctant to respond to her non-targeted questions, and because she elicits directly only twice. Thus, a transaction that sets out with heuristic intentions becomes straight exposition. Third, the register is vernacular rather than mathematical. Finally, the most difficult parts of the task – its second and third stages – receive least attention on the basis of her promise to return to help the group when they reach that point.

Studies of classroom discourse tend to presume a high degree of teacher control of turn taking in those exchanges in which the teacher is prominent. In our second English extract (sequence 16.11) the teacher ceded control to the pupils as a matter of deliberate strategy, and indeed ended up saying less. In this extract the pupils take control by remaining silent, and the teacher finds herself saying more. One can too readily assume that the 'rule of two-thirds' (rather more in this episode) is set by the teacher. In fact, if one studies the paralinguistic and organizational context of classroom discourse one finds that pupils may connive at or even actively encourage this dominance by remaining silent or abbreviating their responses.

With 'So that's Year 5' the teacher leaves these two groups to tackle their magic square worksheets. Seventeen minutes later she returns to one of the groups and the ensuing interaction can be classified as monitoring, although it is supervisory rather than instructional, and the promised help with exploring what happens when the numbers in the cells are enlarged is not provided because the teacher needs to move on quickly to each of the other four groups. Here, to begin with, the teacher's non-targeted and semantically open question 'How are we doing on here?' is taken by pupils to invite them to discuss not the substance of the task but whether they have completed it. Anticipating that this is all that is at stake, I confines his responses to a threefold laconic 'Yeah', the first an interruption, the second and third mechanical. This minimal response is strongly confirmed ('Excellent, well done'). H is more forthcoming, but her response to the teacher's silent initiation is merely procedural again. The nearest we get to a substantive exchange occurs when the teacher checks G's work having been alerted by E that the latter is tackling the task differently.

Year 5's final engagement with the teacher is during the plenary session. The pupils are telling her how they have responded to the second and third tasks. K explains why if the number in each of the square's nine cells is increased by the same amount the square's 'magical' property is retained. K understands but, other than fumblingly, cannot explain because he commands neither the register nor the terminology that are necessary for him to do so. In this matter the substitution of 'times' for 'multiply' ('when you times it . . . you times all the numbers') is symptomatic of a prominent characteristic of the English and American classroom discourse which we sampled. This lazy neologism is extrapolated from the recitation of multiplication tables ('two times two is four'). Intriguingly, the politicians who during the late 1990s led the assault on low standards in 'the basics' did so by legitimating this vocabulary. 'We are going to make sure' announced Prime Minister Blair and Education Secretary Blunkett on prime-time radio and television on occasions too frequent to enumerate, 'that before they leave primary school children will be be able to add up, take away and do their times tables.'

So, emulating their country's leaders, K and his teacher stick to the vernacular, and buried somewhere in the interstices of the final exchange above is the mathematical rule which the teacher wishes her pupils to come to know and understand but which they do not have the vocabulary to express. In this lesson, the continental pedigree of the Numeracy Hour is belied by the much greater power of indigenous English pedagogy and discourse. It is true that the lesson has some of the external trappings of the continental form: a high proportion of whole class teaching, much oral work, emphasis on pupils explicating their thinking, for example. However, a typically complex form of classroom organization traps much of the discourse at the level of mere task supervision and prevents its elevation to genuine instruction. The failure to develop an appropriate register and vocabulary for the subject in question means that pupils are ill-equipped to engage in the communal exchanges which are the essence of any teaching which calls itself 'whole class'. Precision with numbers is frustrated by lack of precision with the words that are necessary to handle them.[53] Questions ask but do not enquire or challenge. And pupils are able to manipulate the dynamics to keep matters that way.

In each of the last two examples, the central phase of the lesson is problematic not so much because the government's strategy requires something new of the teachers but because it is content to replicate established practice.

United States

And so to the United States. This first of our Michigan extracts drops us plumb into the problematic domain of personal and social values which loomed large throughout the *Five Cultures* interviews with Michigan teachers, school principals, parents and administrators (Chapters 9 and 10).

Sequence 16.14. Melville, 24 children aged 6–7, personal safety

[*The class is sitting on the carpet at the teacher's feet. She is using a series of photographic enlargements of children and adults to promote discus-*

*sion about 'good and bad touches'. On a previous occasion the pupils
have viewed a videotape which enunciated the rules which they recall at
the end of this extract]*

T   [*Holds up picture showing a girl sitting on the knee of a middle-aged
man*] This is Barbara and she loves her uncle. [*Points to man in the
picture*] This is her uncle. She loves to sit on her uncle's lap and her uncle
tells her lots of stories about what happened to him when he was a little
boy and Barbara just loves to hear those stories. Um, D, what kind of
touch do you think that is for Barbara?

D   Um, I don't know.

T   Do you think that's a good touch or or a bad touch?

D   [*Makes a face*] Mmm.

N   Good touch.

C   What d'you mean?

T   D, N thinks it's a good touch. Would you agree with her?

D   Mmhmm.

T   [*N shakes her head*] And N, why would you guess that's a good touch?

N   I don't know. I think it's a bad touch.

(P)   I think it's a bad touch too.

T   [*Makes a gesture perhaps suggestive of ambivalence*] You're saying good
and bad. Why do you think maybe bad? [*B raises her hand*]

N   Because he looks like he's gonna touch her in a bad way.

T   Be . . . / . . . cause [*B puts her hand down*] Um, he looks like he's **gonna**?
[*N nods*] Can you tell what he didn't do yet, but he's gonna do?

N   <u>Yeah</u>.

(P)   <u>Yes</u> . . .

T   <u>Right, let's, let's look</u> at some of that. <u>N thinks</u> . . .

(P)   <u>'Cause he has</u> a bad face.

T   . . . N thinks maybe she's a – let's talk about that a minute. Look at, look
at Barbara's face. Does she look like she's having that funny feeling and
feeling upset <u>and</u> . . .

C   [*Loudly*] <u>**No**</u>.

T   . . . <u>feeling</u> bad? Or does she look like she's – like she's happy / and, and
<u>she enjoys this?</u>

C   <u>She's having a good time.</u>

PP   Yeah.

T   And look at her uncle. [*Points to the picture*] Does he look <u>like he's</u> . . .

(P)   <u>He's cute.</u>

T   . . . OK and does he, does it look like he's **making** her stay there?

PP   No.

T   Or does it, does it look like if she didn't wanna sit there she could go, / she
could get away? [*No response from pupils, who by now are rather restless*] // Does it look like that? O?

C   No.

O	Um, well yeah, 'cause he knew.
T	// Uhuh. I think he's kinda like just touching her like this, because I think she's smiling and happy. What or – what if this did *not* feel like a good touch to Barbara?
D	Woo!
T	And / <u>um</u> . . .
C	<u>How do</u> you know their names?
T	It tells me, their stories on the back.
D	Oowoo!
T	Um / what, what would Barbara do *if* it was a bad touch for her?
C	<u>Go and call her parents.</u>
P	<u>(. . .)</u>
T	P, what do you think she would do?
P	Um . . .
T	. . . .know what? It doesn't tell the answers. It only tells the questions. You kids / tell the answers.
P	Um, / um, she'll say, um, [*D gets up and walks away*] 'I don't like that touch' in a quiet voice, um / voice <u>and um / and</u> . . .
T	<u>D, D, sit.</u>
P	. . . .and go home and talk / with her mum <u>and dad.</u>
T	<u>OK, OK</u> our rules that we saw on the video were [*D returns to his place and sits down*] – what's the first one? // Say . . . ?
T/PP	. . . *No* . . .
T	Number two?
A	<u>You gotta get away.</u>
M	<u>It's not</u> . . .
T	<u>Leave if</u> you can. // Three?
N	<u>Tell your parents.</u>
C	<u>It's not your fault.</u>
T/PP	It's not your fault.
T	And four?
(P)	Tell your parents.
(P)	<u>Tell a trusted adult.</u>
(P)	<u>And five?</u>
(P)	If it's someone bigger . . . you can still say no.

The teacher is responding to growing public anxiety about children's personal safety not only on the streets but also, as this extract shows, within the extended family. The distinction here between a good and bad 'touch' marks the dividing line between legitimate familial affection or professional contact and potential or actual abuse. This is a tough assignment for teacher and class alike, not least in view of the children's age.

We observed no lesson comparable to this in any other country, although some of the English teachers were beginning to engage with similar issues. On the contrary, the lesson from which this sequence is taken contrasts strikingly with one observed in France (the end of lesson 11.1) where the teacher and children of the same age as these sing – and mime – along to a tape of Henri Dès:

When I was a tiny little baby,
When I did a wee-wee, but didn't do it in the potty,
When I smeared food over the TV,
When I spilled cocoa on the piano,
When I put peas in Daddy's pocket,
When I took off all my clothes in front of strangers,
When I dropped keys down the toilet,
When you used to kiss and cuddle me, in spite of everything,
When I used to snuggle up to you, for fear of the bogey man . . .

. . . and much more besides, all to a compulsively jingly tune. The episode from Juan-le-grand is as jocular and relaxed as the Michigan lesson is serious, and since in the French lesson taboos are nowhere remotely in view the fact that the person who gets six year olds to sing about undressing in front of strangers is male is not an issue either. In England or Michigan it certainly would be, and the defence that the Henri Dès song is about the unconditionality, warmth and security of parent–child relationships would count for less than the apparent condoning of a 'bad touch'.

So, with the very different cultural baggage of Michigan, and having already evaluated the touches involved in undressing for a medical examination by the family doctor, the teacher starts this final stage of her personal safety lesson with the picture of Barbara and her uncle. The open elicitation at the end of her brief exposition ('What kind of a touch do you think that is') yields 'I don't know', although her exposition has cued the pupils into a particular response ('This is Barbara and she loves her uncle'), so the teacher rephrases to shorten the odds. That the pupils have difficulty handling the concept of a good or bad touch, at least on the basis of such pictorial evidence, becomes immediately apparent. N suggests that the touch is good. The teacher asks D if she agrees, and D takes this to mean that N's answer may be wrong – for that is the more usual illocutionary force of this particular feedback move – and contradicts. Since there is no evidence in the picture either way (although Barbara looks happy enough on her uncle's lap) N then has to speculate on what may happen next ('He looks like he's gonna touch her in a bad way').

At this point the teacher tries once more to bring the children back to the evidence of the picture itself ('Look at Barbara's face. Does she look like she's having that funny feeling . . . And look at her uncle. Does he look like he's making her stay there?'). She asks not one question at a time but a rapid sequence thrown together as a single utterance which is cross-cut by fairly random shouted pupil responses ('No' . . . 'She's having a good time' . . . 'Yeah' . . . 'He's cute' . . . 'No'). This line of enquiry being no more productive than those which preceded it, the teacher abandons the task of interpreting the actions and facial expressions in the picture and enters a 'What if . . . ?' scenario with the children. C, encouraged by the discussion mode, asks his own question about the identity of the characters in this and the other picture. P gets closest of all the children to the reasoned response which the teacher seeks ('She'll say "I don't like that touch" in a quiet voice and . . . go home and talk with her mum and dad'). This at least provides the teacher with a cue for recitation. However, she has set the lesson up as a discussion, and so instead of the strict turn-taking which is essential to effective recitation we end with a tumbling series of overlapping turns.

In setting up the discourse in this way the teacher is being consistent with her view that 'it [the picture, and by extension the teacher] only tells the questions. You kids tell the answers'. Elicitations are mostly open. Some respondents are nominated but there is no bidding for turns and pupils mostly speak when the inclination takes them. As a result many turns overlap. The teacher accepts pupils' responses and initiations neutrally, with neither positive nor negative evaluation, and several exchanges have no teacher feedback move at all, which accentuates their conversational dynamic. When the teacher judges that the pupils are heading in the wrong direction she gently tries a different tack. The language is vernacular rather than scholastic, and in this the teacher takes her cue from the pupils rather than vice versa. The teacher tolerates interventions that deviate from the topic. She also tolerates, mostly, deviations such as D's wanderings and owl-like noises (one value of a long extract is that one can track not only the teacher's line of questioning but also the journeys of individual pupils in and out of the recording frame). In all these respects the lesson exemplifies the teacher's commitment to a pedagogy which can be defined as 'democratic' in so far as communicative rights are negotiable, the learner is treated as a more or less equal partner in discussion and neither message is subverted by arbitrary directives or closures.

However, in the matter of pupil learning, we have to ask where this pedagogic encounter leads. By the end of a lesson which contains several episodes of this kind (one for each 'touches' picture discussed) the children recite rules that they have learned some days previously. However, the connection between rules and discussion may well not be what was intended. On the one hand the children have established that in situations of this kind they can deduce little or nothing about human intentions and feelings from outward appearances (which in the context of another kind of lesson, perhaps with older pupils, would have been a valuable outcome). On the other hand, any fear of adults that they have acquired may have been intensified. At the very least, some of these six year olds may have left the classroom believing that henceforth they should suspect the intentions of their uncles and doctors. A long way from Henri Dès indeed.

Sequence 16.15. Emerson, 24 pupils aged 6–7, language arts (lesson 11.10, page 288)

(1114)

(1) T   [*Standing by her desk. Some pupils are also standing; others are sitting*]. We're going to do your journals this morning and [*points towards the blackboard on the other side of the room*] your story-starters are 'If you could meet anyone in the world, who would it be? And why?'

And this can even be somebody that was alive long ago – or it can be someone now. Um, the timer is set, so that we'll do attendance check, closet check [*pupils start moving about*] and people check / um so you can begin.

.
.
.

(1119)
(2) T [*Crouching down next to A, who has told her that he most wants to meet O. J. Simpson*] What would you, what would you wanna talk about with him?
A / Why'd he kill.
T Mm, did, did, did he kill, did he get – we don't know for sure. That's why / that's why he's in court is they're trying to, they're trying to decide.
A Everybody's saying yes *and* no.
T Right, [*nods*] and nobody knows for sure except O. J. O. J. is the only person that knows for certain and he said that he did not.
A That's <u>because</u> . . .
B [*Stands up and points at the teacher*] . . . <u>O. J. and the</u> girl <u>knows.</u>
T [*Ignoring B's intervention, to A*] <u>Maybe</u> . . .
B <u>O. J. is</u> . . .
T [*To A*] . . . <u>or maybe not.</u>
C [*To B*] <u>Yvonne's</u> dead.
B [*To C*] I know but she'd still have known.
T [*To A*] We don't know for sure.

.
.
.

(1120)
(3) T [*Standing up and moving away to talk to D, who is chatting to another pupil. A, B and C continue discussing the O. J. Simpson trial*] D, um [*places her hand on D's shoulder*] do you wanna sit by N [*points*] or by . . . Oh [*to class, hearing her timer ring*] bell ring. // [*Pupils look towards teacher, who makes a face and adopts a conspiratorial, worried voice*]. Closet check – there's a couple of coats – who would like to do closet check for us? D? OK. [*D begins to pick up coats and replace them on pegs. Teacher goes to her desk to check the register*] Closet check now people. / R really is absent, she's run a temperature and S really is absent they run a temperature. [*Raises her little finger*] You did earn your marble for, um, attendance check and people check. / No we did earn one marble this morning. E, you're at your chair, you're working, would you give us our first marble this morning.
D [*Running in from the corridor, shouts*] Boot check yes!

T   Oh, boot check yes? [*Nods*] / All right . . . [*E, in removing the class's marble from the jar sends them all clattering to the floor*] Oops! [*Puts her hand over her mouth and laughs*] E, F will you help him pick those up. OK. Um // [*Teacher makes notes at her desk, while E and F pick up the marbles, helped by the teaching assistant. G approaches her with a finished piece of writing*] OK, you can have a peer conference with a friend or illustrate it or you can have your head down.

(4) C   [*Comes to the desk. G stands and listens. Teacher continues to write as he speaks*] Mrs, Mrs, Mrs Garfield, if um O. J. killed his wife, guess, guess what the police are gonna do to him.

T   [*Stops writing, steps back, and looks at C*] What?

C   They're gonna put him in the gas chamber or the electric chair.

T   Um, he, the, the judge might decide that he would stay in jail for his whole life.

C   Yeah.

T   And, and the police don't do it, the, the courts do it and d'you know who's gonna decide . . .

C   Who? The judge?

T   . . . if they think he really did it or if they think he really didn't?

C   Who?

T   The jury.

G   The judge.

T   The jury those are / those are people that have been picked to listen to both sides. [*C walks away, teacher resumes her paperwork*]

.
.
.

(1130)

(5) T   [*Moving on from a teacher conference with H, sitting next to I*] I, have you done a story today?

H   [*Calling out as she moves away*] Can I write another story?

T   [*Crouches down next to I and looks at his journal*] Um, what are you thinking of for your story today? [*Glances towards the timer*]

I   [*Pointing to his journal*] I already made it.

T   Tell me about it.

I   [*Reads, pointing to each word with his little finger. His other fingers are sticky with Fruit Roll-Up – today's mid-morning snack – which he has not quite finished eating*] 'I am going to Mikey's house'

T   Tell me that again, tell me that again, I . . .

I   [*Teacher slows down his reading by tracing the words with her pen*] 'I – am – going – to Mike- Mike- [*stabs at the page with his little finger*] to Mikey's house – house . . .'.

T   Mmhm . . .

I   '. . . and then we'll get some movies so we can watch . . .'

T	Oh, you're **going** to do this? [*I nods*] Oh, / when are you gonna do this?
I	Um // tomorrow.
T	[*Nods*] Are you?
I	It'll be his birthday party.
T	Oh, do you know what movies you're gonna get? [*I nods*]
T	How old is he gonna be?
I	(. . .) [*Talking about the movies*]
T	Oh, who's gonna pick'em out?
I	Um, me and my brother.
T	Oh, OK and, and it's Mikey's birthday? [*I nods*]
T	How old's Mikey gonna be?
I	I dunno.
T	<u>Oh.</u>
I	<u>Ten,</u> eleven . . .
T	Oh, so he's <u>older than you, huh?</u>
I	<u>Eleven, I think, eleven</u> . . .
T	[*Nods*] Oh, oh, OK. Hey, look what I see you doing. You wrote [*reads, underlines and corrects*] 'I am going to' – I really can read that – 'Mikey's . . .' I can really read that, you're using all the right letters. <u>Good.</u>
J	<u>Hey I,</u> [*stands up and calls to him across the table*] you're really good!
.	
.	
.	

(1150)

[*The class is now divided into two groups for 'author's chair' to hear and discuss what has been written. It is K's turn*]

(6) K	[*Reads from his journal*] 'I am going to Tennessee.'
PP	Oh! Wow!
K	Only for a few days.
T	Did you have a peer conference with anybody?
K	[*Shakes his head*] No.
T	Choose somebody to ask a question about it.
K	Um / [*points*] L.
L	What do you like about it?
K	Well, there's this bridge that's / like forbidden bridge. It goes <u>like this</u> . . . [*moving his hands from side to side*]
M	<u>I want my journal!</u>
T	<u>Ssh</u> [*Stretches her hand towards him in a quietening gesture*]
K	. . . <u>If you swing</u> around it goes . . . [*Several pupils catch their breath as if in alarm*] it rocks like that and then you could fall in the water and you got to be careful lest you die in the water if you don't know how to swim. [*T nominates C by pointing at him with her pen*]
C	K, um / one time I <u>went to</u> . . .

(6) T Oh, I'm gonna, I'm gonna interrupt just a minute 'cause when we
       do . . . when we do peer conferences, talk about somebody's story it's not
       time when we talk about ourselves. It's only when we talk about the
       author's story. OK, do you wanna ask K something about his story?
C   No.
T   OK // [To K] Have you ever been to Tennessee before?
K   No, my mum just told me about it. / And there's . . .
T   So this is your first time?
K   Yeah.
T   [Smiles] Great!
K   Like there's a condo there and we'll spend the night there for seven
       days . . . .
T   Mmm. Great. [Stretches her hand out to take K's journal]
K   . . . and my grandpa can loan us this place, y'know he went there an' he
       said we can take his place . . .
T   Great, oh, that's right . . .
K   [Raising his voice above the teacher's] . . . and there's an indoor pool . . .
J   Where's your . . .
T   . . . at his, uhuh at his, which at, at the condo?
J   I know.
T   Your family's gonna stay at the condo.
J   K! [Urgently, waving his arm in the air. Teacher points at him]
K   [Looking at J] Yeah.
J   Um, does your grandpa own the place?
M   [Thumping the floor and looking at the teacher] I want my journal now!
K   Yeah, he owns it, but it's like . . . // He made, he helped made it when he
       was younger. He helped made it // and he's boss over it.

Where the first Michigan extract deployed a single interaction strategy (teacher-
led class discussion), this one exemplifies, within the one lesson, whole class task
instruction, supervisory, instructional and evaluative monitoring of individuals, and
teacher-steered collaborative group discussion. Apart from when the teacher summons the class's attention, there is a constant buzz of pupil–pupil conversation
which – were one to attempt to transcribe the entire tapestry of discourse in a lesson
such as this – could be captured and represented only with the aid of several microphones, a mixer and a multi-dimensional protocol capable of recording and notating
many simultaneous strands of talk. It would look – the musical analogy again – very
much like an orchestral score. Here we eavesdrop on examples which involve the
teacher only, since she wore the radio-microphone and the overlapping turns which
are shown here are only those within the group with which she, at that moment, is
dealing. The true picture is vastly more complex, and apart from discernible teacher-
led whole class or group episodes such as (1) and (5), the predominant pattern for
this lesson is a network of localized interactions in which topics and turns are,
variously, managed by the teacher, managed locally by pupils, and tossed by the
conflicting currents of the conversational market place.

That the teacher controls only to a degree the lesson's topics as well as its turns accounts for what teachers in Russia, France or India might define as the lesson's many digressions and diversions, but then no teacher whom we observed in those three countries would have presented pupils with a writing task as open as 'If you could meet anyone in the world, who would it be, and why?' and few if any of them would have been happy to countenance classroom talk among six year olds, outside or inside the learning task, about murder, trial and judicial execution. But these are the rules the teacher has defined, and she remains faithful to them.

In fact, the discourse is rule bound to an extent that may need emphasizing. The topic is open, but the pupils are then expected to converse about topic treatment with each other ('peer conference') and/or the teacher ('teacher conference') before assembling to hear from each of their number in turn ('author's chair'). In each case, the explicit message from the teacher is that pupils must take the initiative. 'Author's chair' is bound by an additional and more exacting discipline and the teacher's intervention at (7) confirms the lesson's central purpose, which is not so much to produce a coherent and well-formed piece of writing as to be initiated into a particular version of the writing process, hence 'writer's workshop'. Its particularity resides in its social character. Writers, the teacher proposes, are not study-bound solitaries but social beings who develop and refine their ideas by subjecting them to the judgements of their peers. This is writing for democracy (or is it corporatism?) and chimes with the values of 'joining' and 'sharing' we found the Michigan schools celebrating in their wider institutional missions and rituals. This objective accounts for the difference between the conversationalism of the monitoring episodes and the more formal and pedagogically familiar discourse procedures of the teacher conference at (5) and the author's chair at (6). It also explains what in other countries might be seen as an abdication of the teacher's authority in respect of the quality of what the children write. She accepts, and questions, but her few relatively emphatic judgements are reserved for matters of procedure rather than substance, as when at (7) she interrupts C – to remind him to 'talk about the author's story' rather than himself.

Within this rationale, the direction taken by the discourse makes sense, and the exchanges about O. J. Simpson are in two respects consistent with the teacher's purpose. First, because she does not rule the topic inappropriate; second, because in keeping with the lesson's democratic stance she stresses judicial process and the American legal principle of innocent until proved guilty ('Why he'd kill' / 'Did he kill . . . we don't know for sure . . . O. J. is the only person who knows for certain and he said that he did not'. / 'The police . . . are going to put him in the gas chamber . . .'. / 'The police don't do it, the courts do it, and do you know who's gonna decide? . . . The jury . . . those people who have been picked to listen to both sides'). Admittedly, this strand of argument has to be unpicked from an exchange structure in which turns overlap, speakers interrupt each other and the message may therefore not be transmitted with the force that the teacher would prefer. But the conversational character of these episodes, in respect of both linguistic register and the handling of communicative rights, is again consistent with the rules which she has set.

The long transaction with I is bounded by conventional elicitation / directive and evaluative feedback moves ('Have you done a story today? . . . Tell me about it . . . I can really read that, you're using all the right letters. Good.') In between, the teacher accepts with no more than momentary surprise I's decision to ignore both writing options she has presented to the children at the start of the lesson (a journal entry on something that has happened to them recently, or the speculative 'If you could meet . . .'). She works with what the pupil has written, dodges the glaireous Fruit Roll-Up, and poses a series of questions to which, to underscore I's control, he knows the answer but she does not. The exchange does not, as elsewhere it would, *inform* the writing task which she has set, for I has already completed it and the teacher does not invite him to extend his efforts in the light of what has been seeded by their conversation.

Author's chair is similarly retrospective, confirming again that in this lesson the process of talking about and around the writing matters more than what is written. Like I, K has chosen to write about something that lies ahead. After he has announced his one-liner 'I am going to Tennessee' and the teacher has established that no peer conference was involved, he is given the chair. The other children are interested: Tennessee is exotically distant and the swaying suspension bridge sounds enticingly dangerous. K makes one nomination himself (of L), but the teacher then has to intervene to keep the formula on track. M ('I want my journal . . . I want my journal now!') is quietened; C's attempt to tell his own story is ruled out of order; and J's persistent interruptions are finally channelled into a nominated question ('Does your grandpa own the place?'). By the end of the episode the teacher tries to reintroduce her authority using the locutionary form of enthusiastic feedback ('Great . . . Mmm. Great . . . Great, oh, that's right') not so much to praise as to signal termination, for she has the delicate task of giving every child a turn at controlling the turns of others. This leads to a brief tussle with K, who has author's chair at this moment and wants to hang onto it. He attempts to talk at greater length about his grandfather's condo; the teacher tries to terminate his tenancy of the chair by physically taking his journal from him, albeit gently. K continues talking, and by ignoring one interruption from the teacher and talking over the next he finally wins back control, receiving and answering in full J's question before relinquishing the chair on his own terms.

In the next sequence we shall see further examples of the dilemmas and paradoxes of democratic pedagogy. For the moment there are two final points to make about the complex discourse dynamics which we have discussed here. First, we are now a long way indeed from Tony Edwards' version of classroom communicative competence (itself a sociolinguistic gloss on the Flanders 'rule of two-thirds') as a set of strategies for reading the teacher's mind and avoiding his or her attention. But then, as soon as we reached the sequences in which Russian primary teachers controlled topics and turns if anything even more tightly than their British secondary counterparts, it was clear that Edwards' framework was far from universal, for such control can be exercised in very different ways and with very different consequences for those who are subject to it. However, if Edwards' rules do not travel too well across cultures or even educational phases, his more general argument – that the character and quality of pupil talk are shaped by the way that the teacher manages topics and turns – remains intact.

The other point, of course, concerns language and learning. Once again we apply the test: what kinds of learning does such discourse promote? In her interview this teacher, like others in Michigan, placed affectivity, self-esteem, pupil empowerment, collaboration, sharing and mutual respect at the top of her list of general educational goals, and the idea of 'experiencing what it is like to be a writer' among those goals which were specific to this lesson. To her, it was more important that children should express their ideas than that they should express them in particular ways; more important that they should talk about writing than write. The rules governing the writing process were interpersonal rather than technical, grammatical or semantic, and the act of expression mattered more than its content or quality. Thus a child might append but three words to the formula 'If you could meet anyone in the world . . .', or nominate not a person at all but a television cartoon character, and still be praised as long as he or she had had a peer conference. Even then, the pursuit of process over content could fracture the logic of the peer conference as surely as it had the meaning of 'anyone in the world':

T   Did you have a peer conference?
P   Yes.
T   Who did you have a peer conference with?
P   D.
T   And what did D ask you?
P   Nothing.

Yet it seemed not to matter. In this language arts lesson, then, pupils learn to talk rather than talk to learn. This is not the dismissive comment it may seem, for the conversational fluency and social confidence that this strategy may eventually yield are in themselves important tools for learning. The issue is posed in this quasi-epigrammatic way to register again the question of why classroom talk is so important. If it transmits, what in this case is being transmitted? If it scaffolds, what is being scaffolded? Is it enough that the purpose of talk here seems to be social rather than cognitive?

In our next sequence, with older primary children, we encounter some of these values in a different context. This time, children are learning to be not 'writers' but 'mathematicians'.

Sequence 16.16. Thoreau, 18 pupils aged 9–10, mathematics (lesson 11.12, page 290)

(0934)

(1) T   [*Standing by the blackboard*] Thank you A. / B, [*points to B, then over her shoulder to the board*] Good job, you've had a good morning, working really hard. [*Picks up a piece of chalk and draws a star on board*] Come on C, [*touches C on the shoulder*] turn around, be a good boy, so,

I can, I can put your name on the happy face list, huh? / Ssh. / Boy, that Group 5 is doing a lot of talking still. / [*Group 5 continues to chat*]. Ssh. Oh C, are you ready? No one is going to touch that. [*Points to the computer at which C has been working*] We will save it for you. Don't let that wreck your day. [*Writes on board*] We won't touch it. / Nobody'll touch that computer, we'll save it. / All right. Would you look up here please so you can follow along, it helps you read along as I read it. // It helps you see words and hear words and helps you become a better reader too. / [*Points her thumb over her shoulder at the blackboard*] Look up here. // I've still not – [*shakes her head*] I don't have everybody's eyes up here, so I'm waiting. // [*Group 5 pupils continue to ignore her. A pupil in another group signals to them to stop talking and look at the board*] Seem to be waiting a long time for Group 5 still. There, now I

(2) think I'm ready. [*Points to the words on the blackboard as she reads them*] I wanted to buy 50 math journals / at Office Max – now the math journal or the notebooks, I changed the name here, sorry about that, same thing – the notebooks came / in packages of three, / so when I bought 'em, I bought three in one package. Here's the question. How many **packages** [*puts finger to lips*] do I need to buy . . .

(P) [*Calls out*] Well, 50 makes . . .

T   Ssh – [*puts up hand in a 'stop' gesture*] to make 50? [*To pupil*] Good, good addition. Will the packages come out evenly or will I have note-books left over, or . . . ? [*Shrugs and mimes an unanswered question*] Work by yourself for five minutes [*points to clock, holds up five fingers, then puts finger to lips*], then if you want to talk with someone you may, to explain your solution, you need [*ticks them off on her fingers*] **explanation**, a **solution** and the **problem**. [*Puts finger to lips*] **By yourself** please. K, T. [*Points to board*] Fifty math books / they came in packages of three, [*walks on to next table*] how many packages do I need? [*Underlines '50 math journals' and 'packages of 3'*]. Ssh.

(3) [*Walks towards C, puts hand on his shoulder and turns him to face his table*]. Ssh. So where are you gonna begin? [*Walks on to next table. To A*]. Where are you gonna begin?

A   Could this be a times problem?

T   [*Leans over D's table*] I don't know. What do you think? / [*Stands up and opens her arms wide*] I wanna buy 50 books altogether, OK?

E   Could you give us the answer again?

T   I give, I wanna buy 50 books altogether. They come in packages of three. So what do you think? I wanna buy 50 of them.

E   [*Turning to face the teacher*] I think it's a times problem.

T   Why? How would you do it? [*Points to their math journals*] Can you show me?

E   I could have put 'em in <u>groups of three</u> . . .

T   <u>Do</u> that

E   . . . like we did direct tables.

T   Try it and see. [*Stands up and moves to next table. C has his desk lid up, looking for something. T crouches down and starts to lower the lid*] So what are you gonna do? Where are you gonna to start? [*Raises the lid again*] Got a pencil? Find a pencil. [*C rummages in his desk. Standing up to look inside C's desk*] No pencil?

C   No pencil.

T   [*Goes to her desk to fetch a pencil*] Let's get you a pencil. [*C finds his as soon as she turns her back. Teacher returns with a pencil. C holds up his own*] Good, faster than I am. All right. [*Crouches down facing C*] Now I want to buy 50 notebooks C. / Now I went to the store . . .

C   Why would you wanna do that?

T   [*Looking across the classroom*] Group five / [*puts finger to lips*] ssh. / Because I wanted to have them here so that people could buy them for math notebooks.

C   Oh.

T   All right? They come in packages. They come in three sets.

C   Yeah.

T   Now, how many packages do I have to buy?

C   Four.

T   How do you know that? [*Points to C's math journal*] Show me. [*C makes a move to start writing*] Do you write an explanation? [*Teacher ticks stages off on her fingers. C puts his head down on the desk*] Your thinking, your proof and your problem.

C   [*Shrugs*] I dunno.

T   You're not done 'til you did all that.

.

.

.

(1023)

(4) F   [*F and G are standing at the blackboard. F has written his 'explanation' on the board. G leans against a cupboard while F explains, still facing the board*] First I did five rows of 2s, then I tried five rows of 10s afterwards . . .

T   Turn around, talk to us. [*F turns to face class*] Why did you do five rows of 10?

F   / Because we had 50.

T   OK.

F   [*Half turns back to board and points to his explanation*] And then I put lines through when – for when I made, I made five rows and then I put a line and then I put five rows then a line.

T   You're talking to the board again [*F turns to face the class*] and we can't understand you.

F   I put five threes and then a line. Every time I got five threes I would make
       a line, 'cause those are threes and then I would count how many books I
       had. And *then* when I got to here I put a line right there. There was . . . /

T   [*To class*] He's talking – he's talking different. You need to listen to what
       he's saying.

F   There was a three, and then I put, then there was, um, [*draws one more
       dot*] only two right here and we needed all threes.

T   // How did F think about this problem differently? [*F draws a line under
       his explanation and writes '51'. G smiles and nods to F, fetches a piece of
       chalk and starts to doodle on the blackboard*] H, how did he think about
       it?

H   I, he thought about it differently.

T   Or did he?

H   I think he did . . .

T   Ssh

H   . . . because um he put / five rows / of ten and then, he's cut threes, um,
       five threes in half so that would make it not even.

T   He put five rows of ten and he cut three. / He cut five groups of three in
       half? Is that what you said?

H   He cut, he put a line through the middle and made that so that it's / five
       things on each / on each side of the line.

T   What do you mean by, what does he mean by five things on each side of
       the line? F, would you talk – show us. C, look and see what he means by
       five things on each side of the line. I, look at what he means by five things
       on each side of the line. J.

H   But, the problem's still the same. [*G puts down the chalk, bows and
       performs a brief dance*]

T   But the problem is still the same you said. All right. G would you move to
       the side please. We are having trouble seeing it. [*G moves away*]

F   First I put . . .

T   Ssh.

(P)   We can't see through you. [*F waits*]

T   [*To F*] Go ahead.

F   [*Pointing to first group of three dots*] First there are three, then I count
       one, two, three, four, five. [*Points to the first dot in each group of three*]

T   [*To herself, but audibly, making notes about F's work*] First there are
       three. [*To F*] What do you mean first there are three what? I, would you
       go to your seat please.

(5)   [*F waits*] I'm sorry it's just not working very well there . . .

F   [*Putting finger to his lips*] Ssh.

T   . . . neither one of you are paying attention. / Ssh.

F   All the dots, all the . . . / [*Waits for the teacher's attention*]

T   [*To pupil who is complaining about a faulty pen*] Go throw it away
       maybe. Is it misty? Is there ink?

(P)   No.

T	Oh. / Ssh. [*F is still waiting for the teacher's attention*] OK, sorry F.
F	[*Pointing to board*] All those three dots . . .
T	Ssh!
F	. . . therefore are whole packages
T	/ OK.
F	And see I have got [*counts the threes*] one, two, three, four, five, and there are five packages in that row [*indicates the first column of dots*].
T	Ssh. [*To herself, making notes*] I got it. All right. / [*To F*] And then you did it again? [*F nods*] until you got to what?
F	Seventeen packages.
T	Seventeen packages. [*To class, raising her voice*] All right I want you to write in your journal what was difficult about this / or what did you learn, what d'you learn / [*F picks up his math journal*] / what did you learn about this problem and the different solutions that went up there? [*F returns to his desk. Teacher walks to C's table. To C*] I want you in your shirt now. [*Putting C's arms back into his sleeves*] In your shirt. [*To class*] What was difficult about it or what did you learn?

The extract illustrates four phases from this 66-minute mathematics lesson in which nine- to ten-year-old pupils tackle a problem requiring them to divide 50 by 3. At (1) the teacher waits for the pupils' attention; at (2) she announces the task; having done so, she starts monitoring the progress of individuals (3); and at (4) she initiates a plenary session during which pupils come to the board to share their 'solutions' and 'explanations'. In her interview later that day the teacher identified the lesson's three informing values: learning through sharing; respect for the ideas and opinions of others; and rejection of a priori knowledge legitimated by external authority in favour of a process of personal conjecture tested by observation. Her rationale therefore merges a variant of the 'democratic pedagogy' illustrated in sequence 16.1 with an epistemology that loosely hints at Popper's rejection of inductive logic[54] but in fact is closer to the 1960s idea of 'discovery' learning.

The teacher's initial attempt to secure the pupils' attention is a fragmented monologue. Her utterances have the illocutionary intent of directing the pupils to be silent and pay attention, but they are expressed mainly as statements and questions in the context of a classroom ethic in which pupils may *choose* whether to listen and how to respond and little is mandated. The silences here signal intent no less eloquently than the utterances – the teacher's facial expressions change from confident expectation to studied patience and then to pained resignation (although never to anger) – but with no greater effect than her words. In fact it is in response to pressure from peers rather than the teacher that the recalcitrant Group 5 eventually quietens down. For her part the teacher refuses to shift into authoritarian mode and simply command silence.

Her exposition of the task – working out how many packs of journals or notebooks to buy from Office Max – continues the monologue. There is no engagement through questioning with the mathematical processes involved, for the teacher is not prepared to say or even hint at what those processes might be: that is for the pupils to discover or, if necessary, invent. So the lesson proceeds straight from task-setting to monitoring.

If any part of the teacher-pupil discourse is likely to further the pupils' understanding it is the monitoring, for now the teacher can individualize her interactions in line with her individualistic view of how knowledge is acquired. However, here too she maintains her non-directive stance. D's conjecture 'Could this be a times problem?' is batted straight back to him in an IRF exchange in which question is countered by question. E discerns the technique: to attain a more informative response from the teacher he himself has to inform rather than ask. He tries, but again the feedback is noncommittal: the teacher accepts what he says as *an* answer, but is not prepared to adjudicate on whether it is *the* answer.

Moving to the next table the teacher encounters an extended repertoire of prevaricatory ploys. C is looking in his desk for nothing in particular. The teacher legitimates his search by allowing it to be for a pencil and departs to find one, at which point C produces his own. She acquiesces in this diversion rather than challenges it, and attempts to focus C's attention on the task. He then pre-empts the question which he knows will follow 'Now I went to the store . . .' by interrupting her with his own: 'Why would you wanna do that?' When the direct elicitation 'How many packages do I have to buy?' does come, he tries a random response ('four') which is implausible, although allowable as a conjecture in terms of the teacher's lesson formula. At this point the monitoring could become instructional and engage with the pupil's thinking, but the teacher's request 'Show me' is an invitation to C to get on and write rather than talk to her, and in general this teacher's monitoring nearly always stops short at the point which, in more directive contexts, would be deemed critical to the instructional process, for it would cue a chain of IRF exchanges combining focused questions and responses linked by confirmation, elaboration and follow-up. Here, however, that never happens, and the exchanges follows a consistent pattern throughout this stage of the lesson: focusing elicitation → informative reply → non-evaluative feedback. In terms of the distinction discussed in Chapter 14, the discourse during the monitoring stage focuses on *activity* rather than *task*.

So we come to the plenary, during which, as in several other countries, pupils come to the board to demonstrate their handling of the task they have been given. The comparison with the two other sequences featuring nine year olds explaining their mathematical thinking at the blackboard (16.5 from Russia and 16.13 from England) is instructive. This lesson shares with the one from St Teresa's the problem of register: the children are required to exchange understandings but lack the particular linguistic repertoire which is required if this is to be done in relation to a subject like mathematics. The teacher has presented and reiterated a general working framework – problem, solution and explanation – but her individualized account of children's mathematical learning has made meaningful explanation difficult. In this sense, two components of her professional ideology – individualization and 'sharing' – are in direct conflict. To share we need the language and concepts for sharing, a common discourse and common meanings. Here, children express their ideas with as much clarity as conversational language allows, covering the board with dots and digits but not once assaying an algorithm.

The other striking contrast is in the area of turns. This teacher rarely nominates individual pupils or invites the class to compete for bids, for respecting the ideas and opinions of others implies a communicative order which is mutually regulated, as in conversation, rather than controlled from above as in the classic teaching transaction. Sometimes her aspiration to achieve communicative consensus works, but more often pupils call out and the teacher controls turns not by reverting to the rules of nomination and bidding but by the much more basic device of suppressing unacceptable interventions with a 'Ssh!'.

During the lesson's plenary stage the turn-taking rubric becomes confused and indeed contradictory. At (4) F is given the floor and starts his explanation, although he is hampered, as I have noted, by the mismatch between collective context and individualistic register. The teacher interrupts, twice, to tell him to face the class rather than the board, thus reminding him that she determines the manner in which his turn is exercised, if not its content. He resumes, only to be interrupted again, this time when the teacher reminds other pupils that *their* part in this transaction is to listen. F by now has filled the board with 17 sets of dots grouped in threes – he is counting on, package by package – at the end of which he draws a line and writes '51'. The teacher then invites other pupils to make sense of F's explanation. Prompted by F's graphics and lacking the appropriate mathematical vocabulary H comments in spatial rather than numerical terms ('He put a line through the middle and made it so that it's five things on each side of the line'). The teacher asks F to explain further. He eventually achieves a viable explanation ('All those three dots . . . therefore are whole packages . . . And . . . I have got five packages in that row' / 'Until you got to . . .' / 'Seventeen packages'). However, articulating his explanation becomes increasingly difficult not just in terms of register, but also because the teacher interrupts him no fewer than a further six times. Her purpose in doing so, paradoxically, is to suppress the interruptions of others. At (5) F regains partial control by mimicking the teacher's moves: he adopts an expression of patient resignation; he waits pointedly for her to be silent; he puts his finger to his lips; he says 'Ssh'. Finally, he suspends his explanation in mid-sentence ('All the dots, all the . . .') because the teacher is attending to another child rather than to him. The teacher apologizes, F continues, and eventually he gets to his 17 packages.

In this sequence, and the lesson from which it is taken, paradox rules. Communicative fluency is most conspicuously disrupted by its guardian. The mode of discourse is conversational but the transactions are rarely conversation. The learning ethic is collective but the learning discourse is individualized. Conceptual structure is sought but none is provided.

Yet there is no denying the seriousness of the teacher's intentions. However, the question we have to ask in the context of the relationship between discourse and learning is this: does a commitment to democratized discourse necessarily and inevitably entail the removal of the cognitive structures by which children's thinking is supported and advanced? (For it is clear that the strategy offers nothing whatever to help scaffold pupils' understanding from their various individual ways of conceptualizing the 'real world' problem they have been given to its one authentically mathematical solution). The final extract, also from Michigan, goes some way to answering this. It should also scotch any suggestion that because teaching like that illustrated above can be explained by reference to American values, it is the form of teaching that American values are most likely to produce.

Sequence 16.17. Hawthorne Elementary, 17 pupils aged 6–7, mathematics (lesson 11.11, page 289)

(0951)

(1)   [*Pupils are working in their 'co-operative learning groups', sorting counters by as many attributes as they can identify. Teacher monitors*]

T   [*Leaning forward, with her hands resting on Group 1's table, and looking at the pattern of counters*] What **kind** of pattern did you make? [*A waves her hand and puts it down again*] 'Cause you <u>have the sa</u> . . .

B   <u>It's the same.</u>

T   [*Turning to B*] <u>What?</u>

A   OK . . .

B   It's the same thing,

T   [*To B*] What's the same thing?

B   The yellow and the red.

T   [*Looking at the pattern*] Well, what's the same?

A   [*Pointing to the lines of counters*] Because we got triangle, square and triangle here, [*Teacher leans further forward to hear A's quiet voice against the hum of discussion from the other groups*] and circle and a square right here, and another square right here.

T   OK, that's right. / [*Points at A*] That's one way. There's **another** way that these are the same also. [*C waves her hand*] C?

C   [*Pointing to the counters*] There's these two the same.

T   The same what?

C   Shape.

T   [*Points to the counters*] They're the same shape, but there's something else you've done.

A   [*Waves her hand. Teacher smiles at her*] I know what it is.

T   What is it?

A   It is / [*thinking as she speaks, and smiling*] er / it is . . . / they're um / both alike / and / . . .

T   [*Crouches down so that her eyes and those of the children are level*] What do you . . . Think about your four attributes about the blocks of, I mean the buttons. Think about the four attributes. [*A raises her hand*] You have, what are the four attributes? [*Fingers poised for ticking off the attributes one by one*]

A   They're the same, they're the same shape.

T   They're the sa- well, yeah, they're the same shape! Think about another attribute.

A   [*Smiling*] / Same shape and / different colours.

T   They're different colours, but there's **something** else. There's another at-
     tribute you did [C *raises her hand and waves it, smiling broadly*] that you
     didn't even know you did and that's good / [*stands up*] because I didn't see
     it either. What is it C? [*Points to C*]

C   Size!

.

.

.

(1007)

(2) [*Pupils now embark on the task of finding, by a process of eliminating
     attributes one by one, the missing button of Corduroy the bear*]

T   [*Standing between the tables*] Now, we have to help find Corduroy's button.
     I'm going to give you some clues which will help Corduroy find a button, or
     will help someone find a button for Corduroy. Listen carefully to the clues.
     After I give each clue / talk about what you're going to do [*raises her finger*]
     first, in your group. [A *raises and lowers her hand*] Talk about what you
     will do **first**. Then, after you have agreed, **then** / you may go ahead and do
     what you have agreed to do. Now listen to the clue. Here's clue number
     one. **Corduroy's button / is not yellow.** Talk about what you're going to do.
     // [*Pupils begin discussing in groups*] **Corduroy's button is not yellow.**
     [*Teacher monitors*]

C   [*To her group*] Take off – take the yellows off. [A *and* C *do so,* B *and* D
     watch]
     [*Pupils in Group 2 start raising their hands to show they are ready*].

A   [*To her group*] Corduroy's button / is small, circle, has <u>two holes</u> . . .

T   [*To class*] <u>OK. Oh</u> I like the way this group raised their hands. [*To Group 2
     – the others listen and watch*] OK. E, what did your group decide?

E   We decided to take all the yellow shapes out.

T   Is that – that is what you all decided? That's a group decision?

E   Yeah, <u>we all</u> . . .

T   [*To class*]. <u>OK, the</u> clue was Corduroy's button is not yellow. That group
     decided that you should take all the yellow buttons off. Do we agree?

PP   Yeah!

T   OK. You may take all the yellow buttons off // [*Group 4 does so, 1, 2 and
     3 already have. Teacher looks at her notes*] Clue number two. / Clue number
     two. **Corduroy's button / is not** [*smiles*] / **a triangle.** [*Pupils raise and wave
     their hands*] What should you do? [C *to* A, *both grinning and waving their
     hands*] Talk about what you're going to do. Corduroy's button is **not** a
     triangle. [*Pupils discuss in groups*]

C   [*To* B *and* D] Take off all the triangles!

T   [*To Group 3*] F, what did your group decide?

F   [*Teacher leans towards her to hear what she is saying*] Take all of the
     triangles off.

T   Did every group decide that?

PP   [*Removing their triangles*] Yes!

T   [*Opening her arms wide*] Why are you gonna take all the triangles off? G? /
     [*No reply*] Because? / Why are you gonna take the triangles off? [*Gestures
     to group 2*] H?

H   Because it's not a triangle.

T   Because it's not a triangle! OK. Let's take the triangles. Triangles. [*Pupils
     finish removing triangles*] // Have you all done that? // [*C waves her hand,
     then lowers it*] OK, so it's not yellow . . . //

A   It's not a triangle.

T   It's not yellow and it's not a triangle. / Look at what is left on your mat. /
     Listen to my question. / Look at the, the / buttons left on your mat. What
     can you tell that Corduroy's button **might** be? What can you tell that Cor-
     duroy's button **might** be [*some pupils in Groups 2 and 3 raise their hands*]
     just by looking at the buttons on your mat? [*A in Group 1 raises her hand*]
     What **might** Corduroy's button be? I?

I   A circle.

T   It could be a circle. Anything else? [*A and C wave their hands. Teacher steps
     towards H, ticking off the attributes on her fingers*] H?

H   A square.

T   It might be a square. What else **might** Corduroy's button be? A?

A   A small circle.

T   It might be small. What else, J, might Corduroy's button be?

J   A triangle.

T   Oh, you said it might be a triangle. Your clues were 'It is not yellow. It is
     not a triangle.' Could it be a triangle?

PP   No!

T   But there's one more thing that it might be. We said it might be / a circle,
     [*ticking off the attributes on her fingers*] might be small, [*pupils raise their
     hands excitedly*] might be a square. It might be what? F?

F   A circle.

T   We already said circle. [*Pupils clamour to be chosen*] What's the other one
     – [*steps towards H*] H?

H   Small.

T   Already said small. C?

C   Big.

T   It might be big. Don't you have something on your mat [*steps towards each
     group in turn looking at their mats. Raises a finger for each of the attri-
     butes*] – buttons on your mats that are big . . .

PP   Yeah.

T   . . . buttons on your mats that are small, buttons on your mats that are /
     square . . .

PP   Yeah.

T   . . . buttons on your mats that are circles?

PP   Yeah.

T   [*Holding up four fingers*] What else do we know? What else **might** Corduroy's button be? [*Steps towards group 1, smiles and points at A*]

A   Corduroy's button might have two holes.

T   Corduroy's button might have two holes. What else? [*Points*] K?

K   It might have four holes.

T   It might have four holes. What else? // L? [*A few hands are raised. K waves his hand vigorously*] What else, L? [*Steps towards him*]

L   [*Rocks to and fro as he speaks*] Corduroy's button must be coloured, must have colour on, is going to have colour . . .

T   [*Stepping back*] Is going to have colour. Which colour?

PP Red.

T   Red.

PP Blue.

T   Blue.

PP Green.

T   Green. Do we know what colour it is yet?

PP No.

T   Listen to your next clue. **Corduroy's button has / four holes.** [*C, H and I raise their hands immediately, with great excitement*] What should you do? What's gonna happen first in your groups? [*C, H and I keep their hands up, joined by A. Other pupils look at their buttons*]

.
.

.

T   [*Smiling*] OK. Listen for your next clue. [*A and C start giggling and the teacher laughs with them*] Corduroy / **Corduroy's button** // **is not** / don't take anything off yet [*pupils laugh, teacher smiles*] **Corduroy's button is not small.** // [*Pupils raise their hands immediately. Other pupils start removing the remaining small buttons*] What should you do? [*More hands are raised*] If it's not small? / E?

E   We should, we decided we should, um, take off all the small buttons.

T   Take off all the small buttons. // What should be left on your mat? [*A and C raise their hands*] C?

C   The big buttons.

T   The big buttons. What colour? J?

J   Red and green.

T   What else? Green, red and blue big buttons. Corduroy's button // **Corduroy's button / is not blue.** // [*Pupils remove remaining blue buttons*]

T   **Corduroy's button is not green.**

PP Yeah! [*Pupils remove remaining green buttons*]

T   What is Corduroy's button? [*D raises his hand*]

PP Red!

T   Mmhm. [*C and H wave their hands*] My question to you is, what is Corduroy's button, H? [*Gestures to H*]

H   Corduroy's button is red, square . . . // [*Knock at classroom door. Teaching assistant goes to answer it*] . . . with four holes / two holes // **four** holes.

T   [*Going to H's table*] Where is it? L took the button? OK. Now, tell me – describe Corduroy's button to me. [*L hands back the button*]

H   Corduroy's button is square, four holes, large, // and red.

T   And red, **good**. So / we have found out that Corduroy's button, [*takes the button from table 1 and holds it up*] Corduroy's button has / four things, four / things that we know about. What are those **things** called? It's a big word, those things about Corduroy's button . . .

(P)   Look at the board.

T   I didn't write it on the board // [*Pupils look at board and around classroom for the elusive word*]. What did I – what did we find out about Corduroy's button?

C   Oo! [*She and L raise their hands*]

T   Those four things that H said. He talked about / that it, that it's big, and it's red, and it's square, and it has four holes . . . [*Pupils lower their hands*] What are those four things called? / What are those four things called? / It's a big word. [*I and K raise their hands, other pupils groan with the effort of remembering*] We talked about it yesterday. // I?

I   Atronyms?

T   No / Attri . . . ? [*Hands shoot up, teacher points to M*]

M   Attras-.

T   Attri-

PP   Attri-

T   Attri- **attribute**.

PP   [*Frustrated*] Oh! Attributes!

T   Attributes. / So the four attributes of Corduroy's button are / [*points to the button, raising a finger for each attribute*] the shape is square, the colour is red, the size is large, and the number of holes is four. OK / Good job. / [*Returns Group 1's button*]

A   [*Wagging her finger at the teacher*] You forgot the sides.

T   I **said**. The size is . . .

A   [*Pointing to the button*] Four!

T   Oh, OK [*To class*] A says 'And it has four **sides**.' OK, so we'll throw in that fifth attribute, that's fine. [*Returns the button*] All right, that's – you did – did well. I'm proud of you. Now, we're getting ready to put the attribute blocks away. Put the attributes – stack them up first. [*Pupils start reaching for the blocks*] Listen, listen! // Stack them up first by size / count by twos, make sure you have twelve of each colour, and then you may put them in the box. [*Pupils take about a minute to do so*]

(1025)

This extract illustrates learning discourse within three organizational frames: collaborative group work, whole-class direct instruction, and monitoring. This was the one teacher among all those we observed in the five countries who regularly rearranged the classroom furniture to match the task set and the interaction she intended, and thereby avoided the task/activity conflict we considered in Chapter 14, and the base/team ambiguities which featured so prominently in the Leeds and ORACLE research.[55] In this lesson the children were working in 'co-operative learning groups' but their discussions were regularly and sometimes lengthily punctuated by whole class instructional episodes.

At (1) the teacher is monitoring one group's response to the task 'How can we make these buttons, in some kind of way, look the same?' The monitoring is instructional and evaluative rather than merely supervisory, and the teacher deploys what for her is a recurrent strategy of progressively sharpening the angle of her questioning so as to close off inappropriate responses and nudge the pupils towards the correct answer. So she starts with a broad question, receives a similarly broad response ('What kind of pattern did you make?' / 'It's the same') and keeps pressing the pupils ('It's the same' / 'What?' / 'It's the same thing' / What's the same thing?' / 'The yellow and the red' / 'Well, what's the same?') until they achieve the precision she wants and correctly name the three shapes (triangle, square, circle), the superordinate attribute (shape) and the other attributes (colour and size). She gets there by chaining confirmatory feedback to further elicitation. However, at the point where A shows signs of running up against the limits of conversational language ('it is, they're um, both alike, and . . .') the chain is broken so the teacher has to change tack. She intensifies the questioning paralinguistically as well as lexically, moving from a standing to a crouching position, making eye contact with each of the four children, and reminding them of the word 'attribute'.

At (2) the teacher uses the story of Corduroy the bear (which she has read to the pupils in a previous lesson) as a device for giving meaning to a sorting task which might otherwise seem mechanical. Turning this into a hunt for Corduroy's missing button both motivates the pupils and gives the entire process a tautening logic as each potential attribute – yellow, triangle, two holes, circle, small, blue, green – is progressively eliminated. The hunt is intensified (and the conceptual challenge increased) by the way the teacher's clues switch randomly from colour to shape to size rather than clear one attribute family at a time, and shift similarly between negative attribution ('is not small') and positive ('has four holes'). Midway through this process she gets the children to begin to hypothesize on the basis of the now reduced range of options ('What *might* Corduroy's button be?') and this enables her to address the thinking of those pupils who are not yet working within the discipline she has set ('F?' / 'A circle' / 'We already said circle. H?' / 'Small' / 'Already said small. C?' / 'Big' / 'It might be big'). This is a very different task from the previous teacher's pursuit of mathematical 'conjectures', for here the children's options are restricted and the children are being trained in a replicable procedure for reducing them further still.

The teacher also frequently reiterates the collaborative nature of the task ('Talk about what you will do *first* . . . Then, after you have agreed . . . Talk about what you're going to do . . . What has your group decided? . . . That group decided you should take all the yellow buttons off. Do we agree?') and throughout the lesson she gives clear procedural pointers: 'Listen carefully to the clues . . . Now listen to the

clue . . . Talk about what you're going to do. . . . Look at what is left on your mat . . .
Now listen to my question . . . Listen to your next clue . . . What should you do?'

Turns are closely controlled by an established and carefully enforced combination
of bidding and nomination, and in this and other respects the sequence contrasts
with the other three from Michigan in its reliance on the more traditional classroom formula of chained IRF exchanges, each opened by a directive or elicitation
and closed by unambiguous evaluative feedback, often incorporating repetition
('Because it's not a triangle'/ 'Because it's not a triangle'). The evaluations in turn
lead on to the next directive ('It's not a triangle. Look at what is left on your mat'),
or elicitation ('Corduroy's button might have two holes. What else?').

However, it is no less important here to attend to the motivational impact on these
children of the transaction's paralinguistic and structural aspects. The teacher uses a
great deal of eye contact, smiles and evokes smiles in response, modulates her intonation from soft (commanding attention and concentration) to emphatic. She enunci-
ates her instructions slowly and clearly, pausing before key words and phrases and
although there is fairly liberal use of colloquialisms like 'OK', and although her utterances sometimes include the ellipses, hesitations and false starts of conversation,
especially at the lesson's conceptual transition points, the tenor is not really conversational. The language of this teacher, and hence of her pupils, was in general more
deliberate, precise and economically structured than in any other of the Michigan classrooms we visited, a matter of some significance when one notes the age of her pupils.

Equally, although this teacher in interview endorsed the collective, collaborative
ethic which we commonly encountered in the Michigan lessons, her teaching
entirely lacked the concomitant tensions and ambiguities which were so pronounced
a feature of sequence 16.16 and were hinted at in other lessons in both Michigan and
England. She was in control. If we wish to discover how a teacher could espouse
similar values but achieve different dynamics and outcomes we should examine,
alongside the discourse, the structure and form of her teaching, for in these matters
she is closer, say, to the French teacher in sequence 16.9 than her Michigan peers in
sequences 16.14–16.16. In the physical layout of the classroom, the internal logic of
the lesson, the sequencing of questions, the concentration on one matter at a time,
and in the carefully judged reiterations and adjustments to tempo, this teacher's
lessons displayed that commitment to structure which elsewhere I characterized as
quintessentially central European rather than Anglo-American. Moreover, although
– also like the Coulanges teacher in sequence 16.9 – she had the pupils working for
some of the time in groups, such group work buttressed her prior goal of bringing
the pupils along together as a class, and in interview she was less inclined than
the other three teachers illustrated here to particularize her concerns to individual
children. No less strikingly, and uniquely among the Michigan teachers, there were
very few disciplinary interactions during the three lessons by this teacher which we
observed, routines had been thoroughly internalized, and a clear instructional focus
was sustained throughout.

Turning from how these different dynamics and outcomes were achieved to *why*,
we can suggest two kinds of explanation. The first is experiential. This teacher was
cosmopolitan rather than local. She had taught in North Carolina, Indiana and

downtown Detroit as well as this part of Michigan, and through this experience she had extended her repertoire of contingencies and skills, weighing her values along the way and jettisoning any ideological excess.

The other explanation is cultural, and, since we refer here to one teacher rather than many, it must be more speculative. If we observed none of the loose structuring and conceptual dissonance of Anglo-American pedagogy in this classroom we must register the fact that the teacher, like her students, was African-American. There is evidence to show that black parents and teachers are not particularly comfortable with white middle-class affective rhetoric of the kind that peppered both the interviews and the classroom practice of some of our other Michigan teachers.[56] There was a directness about this teacher's ideas and actions which set her apart from, say, the teachers in extracts 16.14–16.16. Directness was even more strikingly evident in the discourse of her school's principal (see Chapters 10 and 11), which in a white middle-class context might have been viewed as decidedly autocratic.

The teacher did not have it all her own way, however. At the end of the lesson, despite her pointed cueing ('Attri . . . ?' / 'Attras . . .' / 'Attri . . . ?' / 'Attri . . .') the pupils could not recall the vital word 'attribute' from the start of the lesson. On the other hand, the pupil who claimed to have discovered a fifth attribute ('You forgot the sides') understood the concept well enough, as did all the others when, deftly and speedily, they sorted out the counters and packed them away in their boxes. These closing incidents illustrate the difference between transmission, indeed rote, and scaffolded dialogue.

Discussion

These 17 samples of primary classroom talk from our five countries exemplify and illuminate many of the organizational variants of classroom interaction which were set out in Chapter 15, and enable us to expand the taxonomy which appears in its provisional form in Figure 15.1. Thus we have illustrated the kinds of talk which are framed by whole class, collective group, collaborative group and individualized patterns of organization; and within this organizational frame we have encountered as major modes of pedagogical interaction direct instruction, discussion and monitoring.

What kinds of discourse do these forms of pedagogical organization and interaction allow? Broadly, classroom talk can be expository, interrogatory, dialogic or evaluative. That is to say, teachers may transmit information and explain ideas; they may ask different kinds of question; they may nudge the relationship into the less unequal one of fellow discussants; and they may deliver judgements on what has been said and done. Pupils, too, may tell, ask, discuss or evaluate, and they too may do so within the context of the whole class, the group or the one-to-one encounter.

Expressed in terms which are more specific to learning (for much everyday talk outside the classroom also shifts between these forms) classroom discourse serves as a vehicle for rote learning, for recitation, for exposition, for direct and scaffolded instruction, for problem-solving, for enquiry and for discovery.

These different levels or layers of discourse, from broad organizational frame to narrower pedagogical purpose, may tend to form habitual permutations but it is important to understand that few of these are inevitable. Whole class teaching tends to be interrogatory and expository, but it does not need to be. The 'recitation script', which is supposedly an inevitable concomitant of whole class teaching, is readily replaced by the two-move exchange of rote at one extreme or, at the other by discussion whose orchestration is so loose that it borders on conversation and thus also consists of two moves (the adjacency pair) although within a dramatically different dynamic. Children working in groups may discuss, or they may be instructed: usually, but not necessarily, the form of group discourse depends on whether the teacher is present (hence our distinction between 'collective' and 'collaborative' group work). Teachers monitoring individuals may supervise, or check and evaluate, but equally they may instruct and explain.

These possibilities are indicated in Figure 16.2 and the dominant character of each of the 17 extracts can be represented in terms of its dimensions. However, the extracts also demonstrate the considerable range of possibilities which each combination of categories allows, and perhaps the most striking impression created by this material is the discursive variety which lies concealed beneath well-used pedagogical labels such as 'whole class teaching', 'group work', 'direct instruction', 'discussion' and 'monitoring'. Interrogatory whole class direct instruction, which is probably the dominant teaching method internationally, may enable the teacher to recapitulate and supplement knowledge, to scaffold ideas, to generate understanding, or to evaluate pupils' grasp of what has been taught; or indeed it may fail to do any of these things. Group-based discussion may permit pupils, with or without the teacher, to share information and solve problems; or it may allow little more than assertion and counter-assertion as children talk at or past rather than to each other. One-to-one monitoring can be sustained and instructional; or it can be fleeting and only in the most superficial sense supervisory.

All of these possibilities are illustrated in this chapter, and they should serve, if for nothing else, to counter both the claim that certain modes of interaction – interactive whole class teaching and collaborative group work, for example – are *ipso facto* superior in their learning potential to others, and the element of national stereotyping with which these and other ways of categorizing teaching tend to be associated. It is true that Indian and Russian teaching, across all the classes we observed, showed greater consistency than elsewhere, but some of the variety *within* each of these traditions is also evident in just three extracts from each country (16.1–16.3 and 16.4–16.6).

What are the main themes that underlie the similarities and differences in the discourse illustrated here? Most can be left in the extract commentaries as they stand, but seven are generic and so deserve further comment. They are:

(1) structure and form
(2) register and code, conversation and dialogue
(3) directed and democratic discourse
(4) the individual and the group

Organizational frame	Pedagogic mode	Pedagogic function	Main discourse form
Whole class	Direct instruction	Rote learning	Interrogatory
		Instruction	Expository Interrogatory Evaluative
		Scaffolding	Expository Interrogatory Evaluative Dialogic
		Assessment	Interrogatory Evaluative
	Discussion	Information sharing Problem solving Scaffolding	Dialogic
Group (collective)	Direct instruction	Instruction	Expository Interrogatory Evaluative
		Scaffolding	Expository Interrogatory Evaluative Dialogic
	Discussion	Information sharing Problem solving Scaffolding	Dialogic
Group (collaborative)	Discussion	Information sharing Problem solving	Dialogic
Group (individualized)	Monitoring	Supervision Assessment	Evaluative
Individual	Monitoring	Instruction Scaffolding	Expository Interrogatory Evaluative
		Supervision Assessment	Interrogatory Evaluative

Figure 16.2 Classroom discourse: organization, function and form

(5) communicative competence
(6) communicating and knowing
(7) scaffolding and learning.

Structure and form

Our earlier findings on structure and form in teaching (Chapter 12) were mirrored in the talk between teachers and pupils. The Russian and Indian lessons were framed by regular and predictable timetables; lessons followed a pre-ordained sequence; subject boundaries were clearly marked; the parameters of question, response and feedback were explicit and well understood; and subject matter was handled according to a discernible logic. In the English and American lessons none of these tendencies were so pronounced and in many cases the opposite tendencies prevailed: variable lesson length, elastic time, unpredictable lesson structures; unclear or movable subject boundaries; little internal subject logic; ambiguity in discourse between locutionary act and perlocutionary force, especially in relation to questioning. The French lessons (especially the Coulanges French lesson illustrated in extract 16.9) straddled this divide, displaying a fundamental and probably impermeable commitment to epistemic structure alongside greater flexibility in the handling of time and discourse. However the more critical extract here is the mathematics lesson at Hawthorne (extract 16.17), for it went much more strongly against the grain of the other Michigan lessons in the way it displayed a clear regard for form in respect of both subject matter and the handling of discourse. I have suggested that this divergence has ethnic as well as experiential roots.

Thus the relative freedom – or waywardness – of temporal and epistemic form in many of the English and American lessons, which we first identified in our analysis of whole lessons in Chapter 12, is manifested in talk between teachers and pupils. However, if for a moment we recall our discussion there of musical form and the idea of teaching as art, it is also clear that our teachers use form in different ways. For some, form means formula, a set of rules that must be followed to the letter. For others form is the springboard for elaboration and improvisation, and its conventions and boundaries are there to be tested. The most interesting lessons to observe were not those which abandoned form or those which adhered to it slavishly, but those which exploited and experimented with form while respecting it, and which balanced freedom with constraint. This is the sense in which only at the level of discourse can we begin to understand how very different one French or Russian lesson can be from another, despite the structural similarities. Those who observe teaching in countries where lessons follow a predictable structure, sequence and set of routines sometimes presume that the lessons are in all their other essentials pretty well identical and that we can therefore legitimately speak of 'Indian', 'French' or 'Russian' teaching as if they are monolithic. This part of the book has shown that it is what teachers and children *do* with inherited structures which is important, and that the essence of a lesson lies in the detail of its transactions between teacher and taught. Conversely, it is all too easy to read more into the greater structural and organizational diversity of American and English primary teaching than the core teacher–pupil transactions permit.

Register and code, conversation and dialogue

We discerned three main language forms: *subject*, *scholastic* and *vernacular*. Subject registers are shaped by the structures, procedures and terminology of the mature forms of knowledge from which they are derived. Thus it was in respect of the adoption or rejection of a distinctly mathematical register that we found some of the sharpest contrasts between the teaching of mathematics to nine year olds in Russia (extract 16.5), England (16.13) and Michigan (16.16). In each case, children were required to communicate their thinking to others. However, in the latter two cases the absence of a shared mathematical register made such communication difficult, if not impossible, and the learning potential of these collective episodes was greatly reduced.

While subject register facilitates development and continuity from children's understandings to mastery of the subject in its mature form, it is of course modified to meet the circumstances of the learner. So, in extract 16.4, while teacher and pupils structured their exchanges about the Russian language by reference to the linguistic orthodoxies of vowel, consonant, voicing, palatalization and stress, they did so using an invented symbol system. However, unlike the systems invented by pupils in the Michigan mathematics lesson (16.16) this too was a *shared* system, and it was shared not just among all the pupils in that class but also – to ensure continuity and progression – among all classes in the school; and indeed among all adherents to the particular language teaching 'method' to which the school sub-scribed. Properly speaking, therefore, we need to distinguish *subject register* and *subject teaching register*. This distinction corresponds to Shulman's separation of the 'content' and 'pedagogical content' knowledge bases of teaching.[57] It is also significant in a country like Russia where teachers tend to follow or adapt the method of authority x or y rather than devise their own methods and materials.

Subject teaching register is one aspect of the larger scholastic code which children, to a greater or lesser extent, are expected to adopt in school. The scholastic codes in the Indian and Russian classrooms were particularly well defined. In the Indian classrooms talk was shaped by the highly ritualized form of the core IR and IRF exchange; in Russia, the code was characterized chiefly by the way it carried into speech the grammatical and syntactic precision and structure of writing. The English and American classrooms were again very different. Lexically, grammatic-ally and syntactically, the discourse of both teachers and children tended to the vernacular or conversational. Indeed, as I noted in Chapter 13, in interview several Michigan teachers themselves used the word 'conversation' to describe the com-municative ambience of their classrooms and emphasized its democratic as well as demotic overtones. Yet was this really conversation? In respect of lexis and syntax maybe; in respect of communicative rules and rights the position was not so clear. Conversation is by its nature locally managed. Talk that sounds conversational yet is unilaterally managed is perhaps not conversation. The 'conversational' talk of some of the English and Michigan extracts displayed considerable ambiguity and indeed tension in this regard.

This, perhaps, helps us to clarify the somewhat elusive boundary between register and code. While both relate to the forms of language specific to certain social groups and social situations, register emphasizes structural and semantic aspects while code includes in addition the relational elements of position, status and control. The 'conversation' of extracts 16.15 and 16.16 (Michigan) differed from that of 16.11 and 16.13 (England) in respect not so much of its vernacular form as how it was controlled. The locus of control in these Michigan extracts was more overtly contested or ambivalent than in the extracts from England.

The French lessons can be placed in this respect between those of Russia and England. There, the scholastic code combined the registers of written subject and oral dialectic. Argument was as important as content. Although it had vernacular interweavings, this code remained dominant, as did teacher control.

The ambiguities were not confined to Michigan. In interview, several Russian teachers described *their* classroom talk as 'dialogue', and one explicitly distinguished it from conversation:

My main teaching method is dialogue. There are other methods – conversation, for example – but dialogue supports the tasks best and the tasks support the dialogue. I tell them about the problem that lies ahead, they tell me how they are going to look for solutions, and that's how the dialogue goes . . . It's the best way of building relations between us, for it is important that the children feel free to express their opinions.

She did not clarify her distinction between dialogue and conversation, but we can infer that in identifying the mutuality of the relationship between dialogue and task she was attributing to dialogue a degree of structure and deliberation which conversation might not possess. At the same time she sought a dialogic relationship in which pupils recognized her authority but were not inhibited by it.

Given that these teachers will have been aware, if indirectly, of Vygotsky's distinction between 'inner' and 'outer' speech[58], I suspect that what lay behind the Russian view of classroom talk as dialogue was a concern which was psychological rather than – as in the case of the Michigan teachers – social. Certainly the character of the discourse in most of the Russian classrooms would sustain Bakhtin's view that it is the act of *questioning* which differentiates dialogue from conversation. For him, dialogue is 'inquiry and conversation' (that is to say, it combines questioning with the social ease of conversation) and 'if an answer does not give rise to a new question from itself, it falls out of the dialogue.'[59]

In all the lessons we observed, in all five countries, teachers asked questions. However, we can see from the extracts in this chapter how in some lessons questions and responses are chained into meaningful and cognitively demanding sequences which lead somewhere in the way Bakhtin prescribes, while in others such progress is either blocked by the repetitive IR exchanges of rote, or, at the other extreme, questioning is random and responses are immediate and off the cuff rather than considered. Several of the lessons observed in Michigan, and to a degree in England too, were dominated by talk which was casual cognitively no less than socially. This characteristic can be understood by reference to three typical properties of both sets of classrooms: the teachers' preference for the outward forms and relationships of conversation; an organizational pattern of interaction in which teachers speak with many children over the course of a lesson but to few or none of them at length; and an informal ambience – seating groups, free movement, no embargo on talk – which although friendly and non-threatening, may also impede the construction of both speech and thought. Indeed, the very notion of 'constructed' speech or thought may be deemed antithetical to a belief that these things should 'flow'.

Directed and negotiated discourse

The regulatory context of classroom discourse – the combination of register, code and communicative management – is one aspect of the difference between 'democratic' pedagogy and other forms. In the modern English lexicon of authority – rooted as it is in the political histories of Britain and the United States – most of the contrasting epithets to 'democratic' which are available for a context such as the classroom – 'authoritarian', 'autocratic', 'absolute' and so on – are pejorative, for their primary cultural use is negatively to portray opposing political systems. This enables Western commentators to equate Russian pedagogy with Soviet autocracy and ignore the fact that its distinctiveness owes as much to roots that it has in common with the pedagogies of central Europe as to Soviet additions. It is true that in this European tradition the teacher's authority is unquestioned; but it is equally true that this authority can be exercised in different ways.

Apart from the polarities that it invites, 'democratic' carries other kinds of cultural and indeed nationalistic baggage which makes it unsuitable as a descriptive term in the context of pedagogical research. Raymond Williams shows how in modern usage democracy as popular power in the popular interest has diverged from constitutional democracy by election and representation. 'People's democracies' and 'bourgeois democracies' confront each other not as fellow democracies but as opposing ideologies.[60]

Dewey's version of classroom democracy concentrated on the nature of knowledge and the relations between teacher and taught. His democratic pedagogy eschewed the authoritarianism of a teacher instilling information that was open neither to challenge nor exploration, and commended instead a process of running enquiry in which the classroom was a laboratory within which knowledge claims were subjected to scientific and pragmatic tests of truth.[61]

Although the Michigan teachers would have been aware of Dewey and his legacy, to most English teachers he is little more than a name, and for many of them not even that. Some of the Michigan teachers spoke to us of knowledge, enquiry and activity in recognizably Deweyan terms. In England, such notions were more likely to be validated *developmentally*: 'this is the way children grow and develop, and this therefore is how we should teach'. 'Activity and experience', that catchphrase of English progressivism, was imported from Dewey via the 1931 Hadow Report[62] but was used to buttress the report's discussion of child development. Bearing this meaning the phrase entered the professional discourse.

Thus too, in practice: despite similarities between some of the teaching in England and Michigan, only the latter displayed overtly democratic aspirations. In England the teacher was rarely other than unquestionably in charge. In some of the Michigan lessons teachers were venturing along the much more difficult path of devolving real power from themselves to the children. One result, or symptom, was that disciplinary problems were much more evident in the Michigan classrooms. In England, teachers would never hesitate to use the language and mechanisms of authority should the situation warrant them; in Michigan, we found teachers persisting with the language of devolution and shared responsibility well beyond the point at which an English teacher would have seized control.

In light of this I suggest that a more appropriate continuum for our times, and for teaching as we found it, runs from *directed* pedagogy and discourse to *negotiated*. This avoids the problematic overtones of both 'authoritarian' and 'democratic', and enables us to make sense of the fact that teachers could arrive at the same destination from different starting points, democratic and developmental. However, this does not make the *practice* of negotiated pedagogy any more straightforward. Directed pedagogy is steered and controlled by the teacher and authority is for the most part rationally exercised and consistent rather than arbitrary; but negotiated pedagogy is a more difficult ideal to implement, for it, too, is controlled by the teacher and it therefore embraces at best a tension and at worst a contradiction. The teacher's task of steering a course between freedom and constraint is not always easy, and the tension is revealed in some of the discourse extracts above, as is the occasional imposition of arbitrary authority.

If the normal conduct of teaching can be located somewhere between 'directed' and 'negotiated', we must also allow for those situations which exceed the bounds of normality thus defined. Only at this point does it become legitimate to use terms like 'autocratic' and 'anarchic' that have been tainted by their political usage. I use them here advisedly: they represent what happens when direction is taken to excess, or when mutuality or collaboration break down. Figure 16.3 suggests how in relation to this continuum we might compare the full range of lessons observed in each country.

In any event, in the matter of making and keeping classroom talk dialogic, structured and enquiring, rather than loosely conversational, the responsibility is surely

	(Anarchic)	Negotiated	Directed	(Autocratic)
England		– – ————————————		
France		– – ————————————————	– – –
India			————————————	– – –
Russia		– – ————————		
United States	– – ————————————			

Figure 16.3 Pedagogic control in *Five Cultures*

the teacher's. The work of Lindfors, for one, shows how 'self-other balance' in classroom enquiry can be achieved, and how the dilemmas of 'positive and negative politeness' – the way in which the dialogue of enquiry both imposes and compliments – can be addressed.[63] In relation to the Michigan extracts, we might suggest that the Hawthorne extract (16.17) achieves a more viable balance on both of these dimensions than, say, extract 16.16. Having done so, it sets up a dialogue from which children can and must learn rather than a conversation in which they participate only if they so please.

I suggested earlier that we should be prepared to interpret the clear divergence of the Hawthorne extract (16.17) from the other three Michigan examples by reference to American multi-culture as well as the biographies and situations of the teachers concerned. When in the course of preparing this book I showed some of the video extracts to a group of (white) elementary teachers from New Hampshire, they recoiled sharply from what they saw as the Hawthorne teacher's authoritarianism. For their part, a corresponding group of white primary teachers from England found the Hawthorne teacher's style both engaging and effective. In a study of the relationship between culture and pedagogy the Hawthorne case is a salutary reminder that differences within national cultures may be no less illuminating than differences between them.

The individual and the group

Cutting across the distinctions between directed and negotiated pedagogy, and between expository, interrogative and dialogic discourse, is a third. It deals with the relationship of the individual to the group. Here again, the available terms have to be used with some care. Broadfoot and her Bristol colleagues define the difference between English and French education in terms of Tönnies' opposition of Gemeinschaft and Gesellschaft, or 'community' and 'association'.[64] We did the same in our account of primary schools as organizations in Chapter 9 and found that this was not only theoretically apt but also mirrored how heads and teachers themselves spoke of their situation. We were then able to present the schools of the other three countries as variants on this theme. However, the Bristol group take Gemeinschaft/Gesellschaft down to the level of the classroom and pedagogic relations[65] and this, I think, cannot be sustained by the evidence which either we encountered or they provide. In their case, as I noted in Chapter 15, the QUEST project's classroom data are disappointingly thin in respect of both interaction (which they studied, using systematic ORACLE-style procedures) and discourse (on which they comment, but without giving examples).

The reason for the difficulty is this. Whatever can be said about the basis for *professional* relations in an organization such as a school, the defining of relations between teachers and *pupils* is complicated by three factors. First, the gulf in age, status, role and rights between teacher and taught is inherent rather than a matter of choice. Second, the context of such relations is the classroom, where on one side of the relationship there is one adult, and on the other upwards of 20, 30 or 40 children. Third, schooling everywhere is in the business of teaching, assessing and differentiating *individuals*.

The English and American schools made much of the latter, and individualism is supposedly one of the defining values or obsessions of Western society at the start of the twenty-first century. In contrast, although pupils' individual identity was by no means submerged in the French and Russian classrooms, there the superordinate identity of the class powerfully influenced classroom organization, task design, relationships and discourse. In Chapter 15 this difference came through in the pattern and relative frequencies of teacher–class, teacher–individual and pupil–class interactions, and in the balance of whole class teaching and individual monitoring. In this chapter we saw how although children worked at the blackboard in all five countries (although until 1998 this practice was rarely witnessed in English primary schools) the relationship of the one child at the blackboard to the others at their desks was very different.

At classroom level, then, 'community', is insufficient to cover the different bases for solidarity which we observed and heard, while 'association' makes no sense at all in any of our cultural contexts. 'Collectivism' comes closer to the observed reality in both France and Russia, and in both cases has appropriate historical and political resonances. In Russia the school class was a single, coherent unit whose members were expected to pull together and help each other to achieve common goals. In France the ideal was comparable to this, although slightly weaker, since it had also to accommodate, alongside equality and collective endeavour, differentiation through a very visible process of assessment. In Michigan and England, in contrast to both, the school class was a collection of individuals who were encouraged, as far as possible, to co-operate. The 'as far as possible' is the critical proviso, for the balancing of communal and individual interests in a context in which individualism is a paramount value is far from easy. In England, the ubiquitous 'we' was used to encourage collaboration not so much between all members of the class as between individual pupil and teacher. By appealing to community it disguised the force of directives. And it was usually a direct appeal, for co-operation had always to be requested and could never be taken for granted. In England, too, we sensed the unease of some teachers about the managerial consequences of collaboration: 'I don't mind if you co-operate,' announced one teacher 'as long as I can't hear you.' Two of the Michigan extracts (16.15 and 16.16) show the difficulty teachers could have in reconciling the values of individualism and community. The mantra of 'sharing' referred to the bringing together of ideas that had been produced independently and idiosyncratically rather than collaboratively. Having been shared, they still belonged to the individual. This was very different from the Russian ideal of collective learning.

Communicative competence

As anticipated in this chapter's opening paragraphs, the version of communicative competence which Edwards extrapolated from English secondary classrooms[66] did not travel well. In neither Russia nor France did we encounter the assumption that teachers should as far as possible equalize the distribution of their attention among all pupils, a strategy which raised the stakes in the processes of bidding, nominating and turn taking for willing and unwilling pupil alike. The alternative strategy, of having one pupil participate in a conceptually complete cycle of exchanges on behalf of the class, which is illustrated in Russian extracts 16.4 and 16.5 and French extract 16.9, was observed in many other lessons in both of these countries. In contrast, where we observed sustained transactions involving just one pupil in England or Michigan these almost always took place in the more private context of one-to-one or small-group monitoring and discussion (16.11, 16.15). When, rarely, this strategy was tried at whole class level it was likely to be subverted by incompatibilities in register (16.13 and 16.16) or to be fragmented by competing calls on the teacher's attention (16.13, 16.16). The latter could be a problem even when a teacher attempted – as the UK government's Literacy Hour decrees – to secure sustained and developmental transactions by working with just one or two groups (16.12, 16.13).

In a context within which individual pupils are likely to find themselves answering an uninterrupted series of probing questions or explaining to the class as a whole how they have tackled a problem, communicative competence is more exactingly defined than when no pupil is obliged to answer more than once or twice during a given lesson, and then only briefly. The pupils in the Edwards characterization avoid answering questions as far as possible, and answer them willingly only when they believe that they have reduced the risk of unrewarding exposure by anticipating the 'correct' response. But if as a pupil one is to field several questions in a row, the likelihood of answering them all correctly is much reduced. Communicative competence in such a context is defined more by how one performs over the entire transaction than by whether one delivers the single correct answer. Indeed, the English concern with spotting the correct answer became doubly meaningless in a context where pupils were encouraged to talk about their mistakes (16.5). In Russia, the form of a pupil's oral intervention – clearly audible, well articulated, grammatically correct, embedded in the question – was no less important than its substance. In the French classrooms the convention was similar, although less formulaic.

In both Russia and France, then, communicative competence came closer to observing the four maxims that follow from the co-operative principle which Grice identifies as the cornerstone of conversation: quantity, quality, relation and manner[67]. In both countries maintaining this line was made easier by the way teachers' questions were usually well embedded in what had gone before. In this sense, although the classroom context ritualized the processes of bidding, nominating and uttering, the exchanges observed in many of the Russian and French lessons, especially – although not exclusively – where the older pupils were concerned, combined with the 'otherness' of classroom talk the conventions of rational, co-operative behaviour for the real world.

Two further elements reinforced this espousal of communicative rationality (as opposed to what we might call 'communicative gamesmanship'). The first was *continuity*. In several of the extracts from England and Michigan, and many more of the lessons observed but not illustrated, the flow of communication and ideas was constantly subject to interruptions by pupils and indeed the teacher (16.16). The other reinforcing element was *intonation and register*. Many of the English and American teachers reserved a special 'teacherly' voice and register for speaking to their younger pupils (see especially 16.12). In France they rarely did.

Communicating and knowing

All the differences reviewed so far were reinforced by the versions of knowledge on offer. The use of the structures, procedures and terms of established disciplines of knowledge to frame both learning tasks and pupil–teacher discourse about those tasks lent powerful support to collective values in India, Russia and France. Conversely, the strong opposition to the disciplines in the progressive rhetoric of both England and the United States characterizes them as anti-individual ('inconsistent with the child's view of the world, which is not divided into subject compartments . . .'), but fails to acknowledge the vital function performed by the disciplines in providing a language through which children can communicate about what it is to think and act mathematically, scientifically, historically or artistically. Several of the extracts illustrate this major cultural difference, and the problem it can pose. In extracts 16.13 and 16.16, English and American pupils shared their individual solutions to common mathematical problems with rather less success than the Russian pupils in extract 16.5 because they lacked a common language for doing so; and since at no point were the divergent solutions reconciled it was hard to see why they had been shared at all, other than because 'sharing' (like the numeracy hour 'plenary') is credited with some inherent communal value whether or not it yields significant learning outcomes. The discourse form was dialogic, but in the substance of these exchanges there was little dialogue.

The mismatch of discursive form and substance – conversation in lexis and syntax but not in conduct, dialogue in form but not meaning – was a recurrent feature of lessons observed in England and Michigan, although not, I must emphasize, a universal one. Both dissonances greatly hampered the discourse of learning.

Scaffolding and learning

The extracts allow us to set out as a continuum various ways of fostering children's learning through classroom talk. Within the traditional bipolar distinction between 'transmission' and 'discovery' approaches (telling children as opposed to encouraging them to find out for themselves) we find in the extracts examples of the following:

- *Rote (teacher–class)*: the drilling of facts, ideas and routines through constant repetition.
- *Recitation (teacher–class or teacher–group)*: the accumulation of knowledge and understanding through questions designed to stimulate recall of what has been previously learned or to cue the pupil to work out the answer from clues provided in the question.

- *Instruction/exposition (teacher–class, teacher–group or teacher–individual)*: telling the pupil what to do, and/or imparting information, and/or explaining facts or operations.
- *Scaffolded dialogue (teacher–class, teacher–group, teacher–individual or pupil–pupil)*: achieving common understanding through structured and sequenced questioning, and through 'joint activity and shared conceptions',[68] which guide, prompt, reduce choices and expedite 'handover' of concepts and principles.
- *Discussion (pupil–pupil, with or without the teacher)*: talk among members of a group or class intended to enable ideas or information to be shared and problems to be solved.

There is a danger in current educational discourse ('discourse', that is, in the third sense of this chapter's title) that we consign all but the last two of these forms of classroom talk to the despised archive of 'traditional' methods. In fact, exposition and recitation have an important role in teaching, for facts need to be imparted, information needs to be memorized, and explanations need to be provided, and even the deeply unfashionable rote has a place (memorizing tables, rules, spellings and so on). However, the joint solving of problems through discussion and the achievement of common understanding through scaffolded dialogue are undeniably more demanding of teacher skill than imparting information or testing recall through rote or recitation. Moreover, while the reader needs no prompting from me to locate examples of rote, recitation, instruction, explanation or discussion in these extracts, defining which of the talk constitutes scaffolding is more difficult. This is partly because scaffolded dialogue is indeed a sophisticated and therefore relatively less common form of discourse, and partly because it is not so much a discrete category as a characteristic which several kinds of discourse may share. Clearly rote does not scaffold and basic recitation offers few opportunities, but a well-judged explanation or carefully orchestrated discussion may scaffold no less effectively than carefully judged questioning and follow-up.

In these terms, there are examples are scaffolding in all of the extracts except 16.1 (the rote mathematics lesson from Ferozabad) and 16.16 (the math lesson at Thoreau). At Ferozabad, words are repeated but ideas are not exchanged; and at Thoreau the pupils are given a general structure (explanation, solution, problem) but not a mathematical one; moreover, the teacher makes it clear that she seeks not to secure common understanding but to share unique understandings, so the vital ingredient of 'handover' is not so much missing as actively denied. These two lessons are at the opposite extremes of the transmission–discovery continuum.

More common than the total absence of scaffolding, however, is its relative infrequency. The extract from Chanderi (16.2) is mostly recall. The 'My bedroom' lesson at Ogden (16.10) sets up compositional structures but its route to shared understanding is frustrated at other than the technical level of defining a paragraph by the manifest gulf in values between teacher and taught. The Literacy Hour at Kirkbright (16.12) lacks, for organizational reasons, sufficient discursive continuity to allow ideas to be conveyed and developed. The St Teresa's Numeracy Hour (16.13), like the Thoreau math lesson but in less extreme form, has limited realistic basis for communication of the arithmetical concepts in question because the participants are attempting to share meaning by using private languages.

These first six cases, although to varying degrees, sometimes only spasmodically and sometimes more or less continuously, illustrate four kinds of obstacle to that 'mutuality of uptake'[69] which is essential to meaningful communication and hence to scaffolded teaching and the handover of understanding: lack of reciprocity in the communicative act itself (one-way communication); excessive value-dissonance; frequent interruption or dislocation; and incongruent or conflicting registers.

There is a smaller group of lessons where scaffolded understanding is pursued more consistently and of these the Russian lesson from Kursk A (16.4), the mathematics lesson from Moscow B (16.5), the French lesson at Coulanges (16.9) and the mathematics lesson at Hawthorne (16.17) provide good examples. The techniques are not identical. At Kursk A, new understandings are embedded in a secure phonetic, phonemic, morphological and orthographic framework, as are the questions through which understanding is developed; the teacher applies elements of the framework one at a time and in a logical sequence; and the strongly collective orientation of the lesson enables all to benefit from sustained interactive sequences with individual pupils during many of which a complete conceptual cycle is worked through. At Coulanges, the novel structure of the narrative line and the established rules of spelling, grammar, syntax and punctuation frame the pupils' imaginative venture into a scenario from which dialogue can be constructed. This venture is prompted by 'What if?' questions and the sharing of pupils' existing or vicarious experience. The discourse is far less measured than at Kursk but in its way no less effective.

Different again is the exercise in categorizing and sorting at Hawthorne (16.17). The talk, dynamics, social relations and logic of this lesson all exemplify Bruner's maxim that scaffolding involves 'reducing the number of degrees of freedom that the child must manage in the task'.[70] Moreover, the teacher pursues this process of managed elimination of alternatives by combining pupil–pupil problem-solving discussion with a line of questioning which – but for its amiability and the fact, following Bruner again, that it is structured to prevent error rather than induce it[71] – seems more legalistic than pedagogical. And in combining structure, peer collaboration, problem-solving dialogue and reduction in the possibilities of error with the manipulation of materials, this lesson comes closer still to the spirit of Vygotsky's approving quotation from Francis Bacon: '*Nec manus, nisi intellectus, sibi permissus, multum valent; instrumentis et auxilibus res perficitur*'.[72]

Plates

from photographs by Karen Lennox

1. School exterior (Russia), with Lenin.

2. School exterior (India), children on their way to lessons.

3. Playground (England).

4. Playground (India).

5. Playground (France).

6. Internal play area (Russia).

7. Family Center playground (Michigan).

8. Child's view (Russia).

9. Child's view (France).

10. Child's view (India).

11. Child's view
(Michigan).

12. Whole class teaching: music (England).

13. Groups in a whole class setting: art (France).

14. Whole class teaching: mathematics (India).

15. Grouping for mathematics (England): one group works with the teacher, the others work independently with textbooks and apparatus.

16. Teacher's view (Russia): orthodox desk layout, posture, hand-raising (left) and answering (right).

17. Teacher's view (India).

18. Teacher's view
(France).

19. Growing apart? Different tasks, different outcomes (England).

20. Staying together? Same task, different outcomes (India).

21. Listening (Michigan).

22. Working in groups: classroom Reading Center (Michigan).

23. Working as a class: one child reads aloud while the others follow the text (Russia).

24. Working as a class: mental arithmetic with *l'ardoise* (France).

25. Working in pairs: worksheet mathematics with clipboard (England).

26. Sharing ideas: this is the correct way to solve the problem (Russia).

27. Sharing ideas: this is how we thought about the problem (Michigan).

28. Sharing ideas: book reviews (England). Roald Dahl waits his turn.

29. Queueing for marks and *bons points* (France).

30. 'How do you spell . . . ?' (England).

31. Monitoring
(England).

32. Staying alert: mid-lesson exercise with variations (Michigan).

33. Staying alert: mid-lesson exercise without variations (Russia).

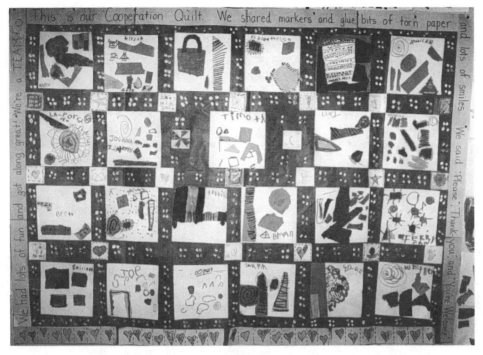

34. Visual values: the Co-operation Quilt (Michigan).

35. Visual values: the skill of painting (Russia).

36. Physical/moral values: courage and co-operation on the climbing wall (France).

37. Physical/moral values: competitive team games – kickball, or baseball with feet (Michigan).

38. Physical/moral values: fitness and posture (Russia).

39. Whole school assembly (England): 'Imagine what it is like to be blind'.

40. Whole school assembly (India): deep breathing.

Part V

Reflections

17

Culture and Pedagogy

Overview

We have taken five countries with contrasting histories and cultures and compared the way they go about the task of educating their young. We have worked down through the levels of system, school and classroom to the transactions of teachers and children as these are expressed in the day-to-day language of teaching and learning. Yet this is not a one-way trip in which one level is presumed to determine the character of the next. Schools and classrooms are microcultures in their own right. They mediate messages and requirements coming from above and add some of their own. And each level is its own kind of window on the larger culture.

Systems, policies and histories

Part II described each of the five systems of primary education in respect of demography, structure, policy and control, before outlining the goals which the system ostensibly pursues and the requirements for curriculum, assessment and inspection which it places upon its schools. We then traced each system back to its roots in order to make sense of some of its defining contemporary characteristics, and sought to identify the forces which had prompted or constrained the system's development and the ideas by which it had been influenced. Finally, we assessed the resulting legacy, adding perspectives from the 'Level 1' interviews from the *Five Cultures* research project which provides the book's empirical core. Inevitably, since one of the book's purposes is to apply the lessons of comparative analysis to the situation and future of primary education in England, the account of the development and condition of primary education in England was the most detailed.

The country chapters in Part II contain condensed and no doubt oversimplified accounts of contemporary educational policies and structures and their historical origins. It is not sensible to try to compress them further simply to suit conventions governing how books should end. Nevertheless it is useful to remind ourselves of some of each system's defining characteristics and values. In France we might emphasize centralization and hierarchy – one nation and one school – and the curricular emphasis on disciplinary understanding, general culture and citizenship. We might also note recent moves towards devolution and the encouragement of a less competitive, more developmental ethos at the primary stage. Although an offspring of revolution, the French system retains features which recall its pre-revolutionary and ecclesiastical origins and the conjunction of institutional secularism and individual liberty is not without its tensions.

In Russia we find another centralized system in the process of ceding power to regional and school levels, and a curriculum which has shed its more obvious Soviet and indoctrinatory trappings and now claims to espouse humanism, pluralism, democracy and individual fulfilment. At the same time, earlier continuities persist, for example in the abiding commitment to *vospitanie*, in the emphasis in schools and classrooms on collective action and responsibility, in accounts of how children develop and learn, and in teaching methods. This is a system, moreover, in which notions of authority, at every level, are deeply ingrained.

The continuities in India reach back even further, and there we found at least four traditions – two indigenous (Brahmanic and post-Independence) and two imposed (colonialist and missionary) combining to influence contemporary practice. Because of the system's size and the country's diversity, as well as for constitutional reasons, much is devolved to the levels of state and district, yet although culturally venerable this country is constitutionally young, so national identity, civic responsibility and patriotism are strongly emphasized and national goals and requirements remain prominent. Policy and intentions, however, are cross cut by the realities of under-resourcing, illiteracy, recruitment, retention and variable teaching quality, and the inequalities of caste, class, wealth, gender and region.

The United States has the most decentralized system of the five studied and the combination of cultural mix, state pride and logistical and policy variation across its 15,000 school districts guarantees considerable diversity at the level of provision and practice. It was for this reason that we concentrated our attention at state level and below, choosing one Midwest state – Michigan – which is no doubt typical and atypical in equal degree. Yet the pull of national identity is strong, and power is now nudging back towards the centre, if not to federal level then certainly from district upwards to state. This may produce a greater consistency but it is unlikely to eradicate the intense value pluralism and volatility that go hand in hand with the American brand of democracy.

England, for long bracketed with the United States as an emblem of decentralization and professional autonomy, became within the space of a decade the most centralized and ruthlessly policed of all our five systems of primary education. At the same time, like the others, it displays powerful historical continuities that counter government claims of 'modernization'. Most prominent are the twin legacies of elementary minimalism and progressive idealism, the one still shaping school structures and curriculum priorities, the other continuing to influence professional consciousness and classroom practice. Yet notwithstanding government control, there is less clarity about the goals of education here than in any other of the five countries and this is reflected in the eclectic mix or morass of values in the government's National Curriculum for the year 2000.

In the final chapter of Part II we compared rather than merely juxtaposed. We explored how official educational goals relate to views of national consciousness and constitutional identity, and showed, after delving beneath their well-documented surface similarities, how the prescribed national curricula for primary schools betray striking differences in values, the more so as one moves into the curriculum domain which deals overtly with the moral and the civic, and into the procedures by which children are assessed and schools are evaluated. National requirements for curriculum, assessment and quality assurance brought us to another of the book's central themes, the balance of control of educational decisions and processes as between governments, regional or local authorities, schools and teachers. To understand the question of control the distinction between centralized and decentralized systems was helpful but, as we were to find later, too stark. Nor does a more exact mapping of the levels at which administrative decisions are taken give us anything like the complete picture. Social control is about much more than this. Here we began to engage with some of our other core themes: cultural transmission and reproduction, hegemony, resistance, identity and of course culture itself.

The international context also highlighted the processes whereby ideas and practice migrate from one culture to another. They may be borrowed, stolen or imperialistically imposed, or they may filter from one collective consciousness to another in more subtle ways.

Schools

Part III took us to the level of the school. A school is a building, a community of people and a community of ideas. We compared the messages conveyed by architecture and the disposition of furniture, equipment and materials. We explored relationships between the way school time is organized and prevailing assumptions about learning and the nature of knowledge; and between pupil grouping and beliefs about the nature of ability and progress.

This brought us to the *idea* of a primary school, as expressed in school documentation and in the interviews with teachers. Here the matter of social relationships and social solidarity was central, and the distinction between Gemeinschaft and Gesellschaft, or 'community' and 'association' (to which we returned in the chapter on classroom discourse) was helpful in identifying the extremes represented by schools in Michigan and France, and in locating those in the other three countries somewhere in between. But many other values and value-differences emerged too: the balance of individual and collective needs and interests; of instrumental and expressive goals; of qualities of mind, body, spirit and the 'whole child'; of the person and the citizen; of education and upbringing.

The last point took us to the relationship between school, home and community. Everywhere we found questions being raised about parental roles and responsibilities *vis-à-vis* those of the school. Teachers and parents in all five countries were worried about the changing and perhaps deteriorating complexion of family life, about the loss of certainty surrounding the family's traditional socializing function and the previously understood division of labour between home and school. Schools' capacity to cope with these changes related in part to the resilience of traditional patterns of upbringing and in part to how, precisely, teachers' roles were defined.

Finally in Part III, at the book's mid-point, we once again took stock of the relationship between school and state, this time from the point of view of school rather than government. In two of the countries – centralized England and the decentralized United States – the balance of control and power generated particularly intense concern at school level, while in France, India and Russia teachers tended, give or take anxieties about resources and curriculum overload, to be more acquiescent. The analysis qualified the account in Chapter 7 in the direction of an even more cautious reading of the conventional antithesis of centralized and decentralized systems. We were particularly exercised by the differential impact of the layers *between* government and school and the power of school and local voices to resist pressures and diktats from above. We noted the strength of Russian local administrations and the closed circuit there of administration, school and professional training, the vulnerability of English LEAs, the seamlessness of the line between school, *académie* and national government in France, the imbalance in power between teachers and local officials in India, and the uneasy and unpredictable counterpoint of teachers, unions, school boards and state in Michigan.

Classrooms

In Part IV we entered the classroom, and from this point onwards the book pursued two tasks in parallel. One was to identify national commonalities and contrasts in respect of the various aspects of teaching and learning that we examined. The other was to construct a framework and vocabulary for studying teaching in general and for documenting and explaining the particular differences which emerge in the practice of primary education both within countries and between them. In pursuit of these goals Part IV ventured a mixture of familiar and somewhat more novel perspectives.

Chapter 11 started with the question of how teaching can be compared across cultures and attempted to come to an accommodation over methodological dilemmas such as statistical and cultural sampling, the balance of researcher and actor perspectives, the contributions of holistic and atomistic analysis, and the familiar question of whether teaching is an art, a craft, a science, or a combination of these. Out of this discussion we constructed a case for taking the whole lesson as our principal and prior unit of analysis and to this end presented timed narrative summaries of 16 lessons from the *Five Cultures* data. These then illustrated Chapter 12's comparison of lesson structure and form and gave us a recurrent point of reference for the remaining chapters in Part IV.

We found important differences in respect of whether lesson timeframes were fixed or open, in the handling and focus of lesson beginnings and endings, and in the unitary or episodic character of what happened in between. The differences which emerged from this analysis were variations on the theme of the significance, regimentation or fluidity of *form*, and in this matter we differentiated distinct central European, Anglo-American and Indian traditions. To account for these we considered the impact of the ideas of of Comenius, Rousseau, Pestalozzi, Herbart and Froebel, and, more recently, Montessori, Dewey, Piaget and Vygotsky. But we also ventured an alternative way of characterizing lesson and structure, using the analogy or metaphor of musical composition and performance.

Chapter 13 sought first to find a model of teaching which would enable us to engage in cross-cultural comparison at a level of analysis smaller than the lesson. We dispensed with school effectiveness and presage–process–product models in favour of one that was more closely grounded in teaching as it happens, working from the proposition that 'teaching, in any school setting, is the act of using method x to enable pupils to learn y'. Our model combined *frame* (space, pupil organization, time, content, routine, rule and ritual) and *act* (task, activity, interaction and judgement) within, again, lesson *form*, and provided our framework for the rest of Part IV.

We started with the organization of space, noting the way that classroom layouts signal distinct views of the relationship between individuals, the group, the class and the teacher, and of the relationship between the learner and what is learned. Beyond superficial resemblances between, say grouping in Michigan, England and France, or whole class layouts in Russia, India and again France, lay profound differences of values in respect of individualism, community, and collectivism to which we found ourselves returning time and time again in subsequent chapters. Teaching materials conveyed similar messages, especially the presence or the absence of standardized texts. But in addition, these also manifested different patterns of educational control, and it was notable that the shifts in the balance of control as between teachers, administrators and policy makers were clearly reflected in changing patterns of textbook use.

Applying the distinction between *task* and *activity* that proved valuable in the Leeds research, we explored how teachers structure pupils' learning. The 'task' dimension of a learning assignment is concerned with cognitive demand, ways of knowing and kinds of learning while 'activity' connotes the way these are packaged for teaching purposes. We found that in the number and structuring of tasks there was a clear relationship with lesson structure as examined earlier: there were unitary and often protracted tasks within the unitary structures of England and Michigan, multiple tasks within the episodic structures of Russia and India, with France exemplifying both. Tasks could be closed or open, and multiple tasks could be developmental (as in Russia and France) or reiterative (as frequently in India). A no less clear difference emerged in respect of task demand: practice and revision tasks predominated, but the Russian and French lessons were most likely to systematically build new knowledge upon old. On the other hand, knowledge was more likely to have a strong propositional emphasis in Russia (as in India and France) than in England and Michigan, where tasks were more likely to be constructed with procedural understanding in view.

These differences, however, were less clear cut than those which emerged from our analysis of learning *activity*. We identified a repertoire of some 23 generic activities through which learning tasks were pursued in the five countries, ranging from listening, talking and looking to reading, writing, drawing and making things; and from solo to group and whole class activities. This analysis confirmed two major dimensions of difference between what we call the Central European and Anglo-American pedagogic traditions. The centre of gravity in the first tradition is the class as a whole; in the second it is the group and the individual. In the first tradition the most prominent activity is structured and public talk; in the second it is seatwork, reading, writing, and relatively unstructured, informal and semi-private conversation.

In Chapter 14, we considered the different kinds of *judgement* to which children in classrooms are subject, making an initial distinction between *differentiation* (identifying differences between children as a basis for deciding where, what and how they should be taught) and *assessment* (judging what and how children have learned). We noted how politically charged these matters can become, not least in England, before examining the criteria by which children in the five countries are (or are not) differentiated within the classroom (age, ability, special need, behaviour, gender, other) and the forms that such differentiation can take (by subject, task, activity, seating or grouping, teacher time and attention, and outcome). Age is a common enough basis for differentiation, but thereafter the countries divide between those that highlight further differences among pupils and those that submerge them. Of all the countries, England seems most prone to within-class differentiation, if not by perceived ability, then by task, teacher time and attention and outcome. To a lesser extent this was true of Michigan, whereas teachers in the other three countries, in a manner which was consistent with their focus on whole class tasks and activities, tended to play down differences and try to keep the class together. The Anglo-American tradition encourages divergence in learning outcomes and levels, the central European tradition fosters convergence.

In the matter of assessment we noted similar variations, and these suggested a cultural difference in the relative emphasis which schools and societies place upon effort as opposed to perceived innate ability in accounting for variation in pupils' progress. Alongside an emphasis on individualism and differentiation in England and Michigan were fatalistic assumptions about ability that tended to downplay the value of effort. Elsewhere, effort was deemed of central importance, and a single standard was set which all should meet or surpass. No less significant were differences in the forms of assessment: mostly written in Michigan, frequently oral in Russia; mostly undertaken by the teacher in India, combining this with self-assessment in France and Russia and peer assessment in Russia and Michigan; strongly affective in Michigan; emphasizing precision, conformity and convergence in Russia, India and France but divergence and creativity in Michigan and to a lesser degree England.

Classroom life is framed by routines, rules and rituals, and these we classified according to whether they were *temporal*, *procedural*, *behavioural*, *interactive*, *linguistic* or *curricular*. A high degree of consistency and predictability in the lessons observed in Russia, France and India was associated with clear and internalized routines which once established were rarely referred to again. The Russian and Indian classrooms, especially the latter, displayed practices which were also highly ritualized. In contrast, matters were much more up for negotiation in the English and Michigan classrooms. However, the differences related not only to the overall balance of rule and negotiation but also to their focus. In Russia and France, administrative and behavioural routines were routinized and the regulatory culture concentrated more on curricular and linguistic control, that is, on the structure of knowledge and communication. These were much more open in the English and Michigan lessons, and in Michigan in particular we encountered a strong belief, allied to the idea of personal and reflexive knowledge, that children should find their own ways of knowing, understanding and communicating rather than have these imposed upon them. At the same time, there was a more overt focus there on the regulation of children's behaviour, but this was greatly complicated by the contrary ethic of collaboration and 'sharing'. All this meant that the regulatory context of the Michigan classrooms, and to lesser degree those in England, displayed far more tension, and many more disciplinary encounters than elsewhere.

The culmination of the account of classroom practice was an organizational, temporal and qualitative analysis of classroom interaction, which was spread over two chapters. Chapter 15 considered interaction participants, utterance length, interaction mode, and the relationship between interaction and lesson stage, referring back to the earlier holistic analysis of lesson structure and form. Teachers in England and Michigan interacted substantially with individuals and groups as well as the class; in India they interacted mainly with the class; in Russia they interacted mainly with the class, but there were more individual interactions in that whole class context, while in France teachers were moving away from predominantly whole class interactions to a greater emphasis on groups and individuals. When we came to the purposes of interaction (*instruction, monitoring, routine, disciplinary*) we found that the Russian teachers maintained the most consistent instructional focus and the Michigan teachers the least, although in Michigan there was also the widest variation across this and several other dimensions of teaching. Relatedly there were hardly any disciplinary interactions in the Russian and Indian lessons, slightly more in the French ones but most in England and Michigan. These differences reflected both organizational and ideological considerations: classrooms which are organizationally complex, which focus on group and individual activity, and which are framed by the values of individualization, collaboration and negotiation, inevitably open themselves up to a greater risk of pupil restlessness and challenge. Democratic pedagogy can carry a high price tag.

Considering how much time teachers spend on monitoring as opposed to direct instruction, this kind of interaction is surprisingly underinvestigated. We attempted to remedy this deficiency by identifying four main purposes which monitoring can serve (*supervision, instruction, assessment* and *record-keeping*) and by plotting the emphasis on each in the five countries. In India, monitoring was strictly supervisory, indeed invigilatory, and this in part reflected the contingency of very large classes. At the other extreme was Michigan, where monitoring not only accounted for a much larger proportion of teacher–pupil interactions but it also encompassed a much wider range of purposes. In England, where teachers also spend a great deal of time monitoring, the focus was more on supervision, with some instruction. Clearly, if monitoring *is* a significant consumer of teacher time, then it is desirable to maximize its potential to contribute to children's learning by making it instructional and task focused rather than supervisory. French teachers were conspicuously more successful in this regard than those in England and Michigan.

Much research attention has been devoted to the variable of 'time on task'. Here, we tried to provide a culturally responsive account of the way time is used rather than a merely arithmetical one. Reminding ourselves of the book's earlier discussions of the handling of time at the levels of the school day and the lesson, we noted that time is a *value* in education, not merely a measure of it, and this illuminated the way time was more likely to be perceived as a problem in England and Michigan than in the other three countries. Time, therefore, relates both to the way lessons are organized and to the beliefs which govern their interactions. The Russian concern with structure, sequence and gradation, and the Indian emphasis on routine and repetition, bore on time-management in ways which were very different to what we found in England and Michigan, where the rule of the clock has been consciously resisted. Yet, when one does look at time on task the differences are clear enough. Pupils were most consistently on task in the Russian lessons and most likely to be distracted in Michigan and India, although for different reasons. In India many pupils were distracted because they did not understand; at the same time they remained outwardly compliant. In Michigan distraction reflected lack of motivation (and lack of pressure) to engage in the task, or was a response to the restlessness of the classroom environment. Those who were distracted tended not to disguise the fact.

In both England and Michigan, especially the latter, we found pupils spending higher proportions of time than in France and Russia on routine matters and awaiting the teacher's attention. These differences could be illuminated by reference to certain characteristics of classroom organization: the focus on groups and individuals; the considerable amount of time given to one-to-one monitoring (which left others expecting, and waiting for, the same degree of attention); variability and unpredictability in lesson routines; and the much greater extent of divergence between one pupil and another which the long, unitary central stages of lessons encourage (but which episodic structures discourage). Yet there were always exceptions, and in this and other matters it was therefore clear that organizational tendencies could be outweighed by cultural considerations and factors such as individual teacher competence. Were this not the case, it would be difficult to explain why some French pupils remained on task in lessons organized in a manner not unlike some encountered in England; or why the collaborative ethic yielded a high task focus in one Michigan classroom and a great deal of distraction in another.

Much has been made recently of apparent differences in the pace of central European and English teaching. On this matter, however, I urged caution, for apart from the obvious differences in the speed at which teachers handle lesson beginnings, endings and transitions (faster in Russia, India and France, slower in the other two countries) it is clear that pace cannot be treated as a property which is seamless or monolithic, any more than tempo in music can be defined solely by reference to metronome markings. In fact, we differentiated five aspects or versions of pace: *organizational, task, interactive, cognitive* or *semantic* and *learning* pace. The brisk teaching of Central Europe and South-east Asia which so impresses English observers must be assessed to establish whether its cognitive pace is as rapid as its organizational and interactive pace suggests, and that requires one to examine the content as well as the mechanics of interaction. On this basis we suggested, for example, that the rapid interactive pace of the Indian lessons was associated with relatively slow cognitive pace, mainly because there was so much repetition. At the other extreme, the slow interactive pace of some of the Michigan lessons might indeed represent a relatively leisurely progress from initiated task to pupil understanding, but it was also clear that in these classrooms at least two layers of meaning were being pursued simultaneously, the academic and the social, whereas in, say, the French and Russian classrooms, the focus was more strictly confined to the inculcation of disciplinary knowledge and understanding. This is not to say that teaching there and in Russia was entirely linear. Thus in Russia we saw teachers orchestrating several conceptual layers simultaneously, for example in their language teaching; crucially, though, each layer formed part of a unified agenda while in Michigan curricular and para-curricular concerns tended to be tangled together and sometimes even in conflict.

We traced many of these temporal differences to culturally specific traditions and/or theories of teaching: in India the practice of rote learning, which merges both indigenous and colonial traditions; democratic pedagogy in the United States and, although more muted, in England; developmental readiness in England and the United States; accelerated development – the exact opposite – in Russia; and conciseness and rapidity in Russia, France and throughout Central Europe. If the last seems an archaic formulation this is hardly surprising, given its Comenian pedigree.

This took us to the final stage of the book's comparative analysis of teaching. Here we used 17 representative extracts of teacher–pupil and pupil–pupil discourse, several of them from the lessons summarized in Chapter 11, as the basis for a detailed investigation of classroom talk. They enabled us to illustrate the different organizational forms of interaction discussed in Chapter 15 – whole class teaching, collective group work, collaborative group work, individual attention, direct instruction, discussion and monitoring. The number, length and diversity of these extracts also allowed us to escape fairly quickly from the commonly held assumption that there are just two types of classroom discourse, recitation and discussion. We found four broad discourse forms – interrogatory, expository, dialogic and evaluative – but many variations upon these. Moreover, by examining the way teachers handled curricular content and participants' communicative rights and responsibilities we gained insights into the relationship between classroom language, pedagogic control and cultural transmission. Above all, the chapter helped us to probe issues in *learning*, and the relative power of different kinds of talk to instruct, to enable children to solve problems and to scaffold their understanding.

The 17 extracts tell their own story, and are each long enough to do so. The story which I chose to read into them highlighted, among other matters, the following: the way the continental concern with structure and form pervades the deeper recesses of classroom talk; the matter of register and code and the relationship between 'disciplinary', 'scholastic' and 'vernacular' forms of classroom language; the distinction between 'conversation' (as espoused especially in Michigan) and the 'dialogue' promoted in France and Russia; the relative emphasis by teachers on the social properties and benefits of classroom talk as opposed to the psychological; the regulatory distinction between, and consequences of, 'directed' and 'negotiated' discourse; the way talk expresses the relationship of the individual to the group and the core values of individualism, community and collectivity; and the cultural specificity of definitions of communicative competence.

Finally, the extracts allowed us to illustrate and evaluate common strategies for fostering children's learning through classroom talk: rote, recitation, instruction/ exposition, scaffolded dialogue. Examples of scaffolding were common, but examples of scaffolding which was sustained or consistent much less so.

What Is Pedagogy?

In Part IV we pursued in parallel the tasks of comparing teaching and defining it. While we are on the subject of definitions it would be as well to clarify the difference between teaching and pedagogy, for despite the fact that the terms are often used interchangeably, there *is* a difference. In brief, it is that teaching is an *act* while pedagogy is both act and *discourse*. Pedagogy encompasses the performance of teaching together with the theories, beliefs, policies and controversies that inform and shape it. So although Part IV was structured in accordance with an ostensibly neutral definition of teaching ('teaching, in any setting, is the act of using method x to enable pupils to learn y') it entered the domain of pedagogy as soon as we started describing, comparing and evaluating the different forms these elements may take and the various ways they may be combined. Every element of teaching which we explored, from task, activity, organization and routine, to judgement, interaction and discourse, raised questions of value, priority and purpose. Pedagogy connects the apparently self-contained act of teaching with culture, structure and mechanisms of social control.

This, I think, is different from a recent exploration of the notion of pedagogy by Watkins and Mortimore. Noting – properly – a tendency for discussion of pedagogy in the UK to dwell on the teacher, they insist that any definition of pedagogy must also take the learner into account and to that end offer as their own corrective 'any conscious activity by one person designed to enhance learning in another'.[1] This, however, is not far removed from my definition of *teaching*, and what it does is to place outside the domain of pedagogy those theories, beliefs, policies and controversies alluded to above and to reflect a characteristically British gulf between theory and practice. In the Watkins and Mortimore account there is 'pedagogy', 'research on pedagogy' and 'practitioners' views of pedagogy' or, if you like, pedagogy as practice and – free-standing, free-wheeling and not necessarily connected with it – pedagogy as theory (for the ideas of researchers and those of teachers are all species of theory).

It was Brian Simon who asked many years ago why there was no pedagogy in England, by which of course he meant not that at that time (the early 1980s) there was no teaching but rather that pedagogic discourse was confused, anecdotal and eclectic rather than coherent, systematic and purposeful.[2] When he revisited his question in the mid 1990s, he held to his original explanation that the problem stemmed mainly from the nineteenth-century public (i.e. private) school view that education should be concerned with 'character' rather than the intellect, a view which also kept the study of education out of Britain's two senior universities until the latter part of the twentieth century.[3] It was for the so-called 'provincial' universities to make the running in the academic study of education. (At the time of going to press, the University of Oxford's very first professor of education is still in post. Other English universities have had chairs in education for over a century). However, elsewhere Simon showed how as the 'foundation' disciplines of educational studies 'became more rigorous and inevitably academic, the historic neglect of pedagogy was accentuated' adding, significantly: 'By pedagogy is meant the *theory and practice* of teaching'.[4]

The divergence of education theory and the practice of teaching is a well documented aspect of the development of teacher training in the UK during the twentieth century. It was exacerbated by the arrival of the BEd degree in 1965, the desire to make teacher training academically respectable and the attendant departmental structures in colleges and departments of education, which generally relegated 'method' to the lowest level of the institutional hierarchy.[5] After a brief period of convergence under the umbrella of 'professional studies' during the 1970s and the 1980s, largely fostered – it must be said – outside the universities in what were then polytechnics, under the auspices of the Council for National Academic Awards, theory in teaching was not so much neglected as officially banished. For during the late 1980s and throughout the 1990s, right-wing luminaries such as O'Hear, Lawlor and Woodhead mounted a strident and successful campaign against the notion that the act of teaching warranted any kind of theoretical underpinning,[6] and their view was supported by the Conservative governments of 1979–97. In 1991 Secretary of State Clarke spoke scathingly of 'barmy theory'.[7] Significantly, in the light of Simon's reference to the ambience of the public schools, Clarke's attack was made at a meeting of the public school Headmaster's Conference. At the Conservative Party Conference the same year, Prime Minister Major damned all those who dared question right-wing orthodoxy as 'progressive' (which by then had been toppled from its 1960s pedestal and become a term of abuse):

> We will take no lectures from those who led the long march of mediocrity through our schools . . . I will fight for my belief. My belief is a return to basics in education. The progressive theorists have had their say and, Mr President, they've had their day.[8]

From 1997, the Conservative Government's Labour successors were more than happy to sanction the continuation of this 'discourse of derision',[9] usually through their chief inspector and a compliant press rather than directly.[10]

For a while, the Council for the Accreditation of Teacher Education (CATE), the government advisory and accrediting body established in 1984, successfully resisted being tainted by this discourse, but in 1994 they were summarily disbanded and their successors, the Teacher Training Agency (TTA), capitulated. The TTA reduced teaching to a set of competencies or 'standards', and teacher training to the task of demonstrating to OFSTED's inspectors that these were complied with. The possibility that teaching was problematic in other than a strictly instrumental sense was not to be entertained. Teachers, by 2000, were expected to confine their questioning to children. Thus, in this all-important arena, British anti-intellectualism demonstrated its longevity.

For good measure TTA then appropriated the word 'pedagogy' itself. In 1999, Anthea Millett, the then head of TTA, urged schools to talk about 'the issues of pedagogy and competence, excellence and failure in teaching methods' adding:

> Pedagogy is a word rarely used in education in England . . . I am always struck by how difficult teachers find it to talk about teaching . . . They prefer to talk about learning. By contrast, they can talk with great clarity about matters such as the curriculum, assessment and testing, classroom organization, examination structures – almost anything except teaching itself . . .[11]

A notion of teaching that excludes curriculum, assessment, classroom organization and *learning*? If she had looked more closely at the European antecedents of the term 'pedagogy' Millett could have avoided this muddle of categories. But then her real message was not about pedagogy at all: it was about performance management and teachers' need to comply with government thinking on just those matters – curriculum, assessment, examinations – that they refused to stop talking about. For whereas in 1991 Education Secretary of State Clarke had said 'Questions about how to teach are not for Government to determine',[12] his successor's controller of teacher training prefaced her comments above by warning that 'pedagogy is not, and should not be at the whim of individual teachers to determine in their classrooms'.[13]

Pedagogy and didactics

The case of pedagogy outside England looks somewhat different. Our Russian fieldwork was negotiated on our behalf by a 'pedagogical university' which, although it trained teachers did so in a way which was far from narrowly instrumental, and in continental Europe generally pedagogy is a prominent and respected intellectual field (especially in Germany). It is also very broad: Watkins and Mortimore cite a Swedish definition of pedagogy as a 'discipline [which] extends to the consideration of health and bodily fitness, social and moral welfare, ethics and aesthetics, as well as the institutional forms that serve to facilitate society's and the individual's pedagogic aims'.[14] At Kursk, the teachers had encountered a similar breadth in their five-year training, ranging from 'general culture' (philosophy, ethics, Russian history, economics, literature, art, anatomy and politics) through psychology, theory of upbringing (i.e. *vospitanie*), child development, pedagogical history, child law, 'defectology', to a wide range of subjects and an equally wide range of 'method' courses in those subjects, and finally options which included religion and folklore. The full list is too long to record here, but this selection serves to make the point: in the continental European tradition pedagogy is both the *act* and the *idea* of teaching, and its knowledge base can be both broad and eclectic.

One important component of this knowledge base is the field known as 'didactics' (*didaktika* in Russia, *la didactique* in France, *die Didaktik* in Germany). While in continental European usage pedagogy is a broad intellectual domain which encompasses the study of education and a variety of forms of human enquiry and endeavour relevant to it, didactics is much more specifically concerned with methods of teaching, and specifically methods of teaching subjects. In Germany, the field subdivides into *allgemeine Didaktik* (general didactics) and *Fachdidaktik* (specialist or subject didactics) and this distinction to a degree holds in Russia. There, however, we found that *metodika* (methods) brought to bear elements of both didactics and wider pedagogical analysis on the question of how this or that particular subject should be taught, for Russian pedagogy traditionally has a strong psychological thrust and developmental and motivational issues are considered no less important for the teaching of, say, mathematics than are epistemic ones.

In France, the importance of didactics was made very evident to us, not just in providing a rationale for classroom decisions, but also because of its critical role in protecting the integrity of *les disciplines*. At the simplest level, we were told, didactics deals with the logical aspects of teaching while pedagogy covers the psychological aspects: on the one hand the disciplines, on the other hand children and learning. This recalls D. W. Hamlyn's discussion of the 'logical' and 'psychological' aspects of teaching in the context of early debates about the nature and purpose of educational studies in Britain.[15]

In France, as some years ago in England and the United States, one has a sense of the logical and the psychological in opposition here, and this problem is partly what Hamlyn tried to address. In English primary education 'subjects' were at one stage anathema to many teachers, and induction into culturally shaped disciplines of enquiry and understanding was held to be fundamentally incompatible with the 'natural' course of children's development. Hence, in the popular slogan of the day (which is still occasionally heard) 'we teach children, not subjects'.[16] An alternative perspective on this dichotomy was revealed to us in France, where some of our Level 1 respondents suggested that universities' initial opposition to the idea of IUFMs – that is to say, to bringing primary teacher training into the university sector – was based partly on the suspicion that the disciplines would be submerged by a tidal wave of 'generalized pedagogy', especially once the 1989 *Loi Jospin* claimed to place the child rather than the subject at the heart of educational policy (two decades after the Plowden report sought to do the same in England).[17]

The French variant on the general/special didactics distinction refines the latter component. The field of didactics, we were told at one IUFM, divides into *didactiques des disciplines* and *transpositions didactiques*. This 'transposition' reflects a separation of *savoir savant* and *savoir enseigné*, or scholarly and taught knowledge, and deals with 'the way in which the subject knowledge to be taught . . . adapts, re-moulds and sometimes disfigures elements borrowed from the broader field of subject knowledge'.[18] This corresponds to the English contrast of 'subject' and 'subject application' and the American 'content' and 'pedagogical content' as propounded by Shulman. Pedagogical content knowledge embodies the aspects of content most germane to its teachability . . . the most useful forms of expression of those ideas, the most powerful analogies, illustrations, examples, explanations and demonstrations – in a word, the ways of representing and formulating the subject that make it comprehensible to others . . .[19]

Thus far, the French, English and American definitions of didactic transposition, subject application and pedagogical content knowledge more or less coincide, and gloss the hopeful maxim, which Jerome Bruner advanced in the early 1960s, that 'any subject can be taught effectively to any child at any stage of development'.[20] But Shulman adds to 'ways of representing and formulating the subject' the important qualification 'including the conceptions that students of different ages and backgrounds bring with them to learning'. Herein lies an important cultural divergence.

For the French academics' objection to IUFMs was precisely targeted at this kind of dilution – as they saw it – of disciplinary purity, while in the United States Shulman for his part was accommodating to a significant tide of academic and professional opinion which argued that children's personal knowledge and unique ways of making sense of the world must be respected. The rationale for this argument, however, varied. To some, especially within the early years movement, children's personal knowledge mattered for its own sake: to respect it was to respect the child, and for some teachers adult ways of knowing counted for little by comparison. The overriding value here was individualism. To others, the case had more to do with finding effective ways to scaffold between Vygotsky's 'natural' and 'cultural' lines of development and move the child via his or her own understandings to those embodied in the mature forms of understanding central to the culture. Bruner's sustained contribution to this complex area of debate over several decades has been his ability to show how not just the logical and psychological, but also the cultural can be reconciled in a viable theory of teaching.

In England, the equivalent figure is Alan Blyth. Blyth approached the question from a social and historical as much as a psychological standpoint and demonstrated the essential mutuality of 'development', 'experience' and 'curriculum'.[21] He defined curriculum as 'planned intervention in the interaction between development and experience' and subsequently applied this principle in an account of the transition from 'subjective' to 'objective' modes of understanding between early childhood and adolescence. However, where Bruner's 'spiral curriculum' kept subjective understanding and discipline-based knowledge in equilibrium from the earliest pedagogical interventions, Blyth's 'dendritic' model began with the unity of experience and consciousness and progressed through subjective knowledge to objective. He suggested that children 'grow into' disciplinary understanding.[22] Blyth's model is more sympathetic to the English developmental tradition in primary education than either Bruner's or Vygotsky's, and indeed he was in part searching for a version of curriculum to which English primary teachers, with their particular inherited professional consciousness, could accommodate.

Such debates seem to have bypassed our French teachers and, to some degree, the teacher trainers. One IUFM director suggested that the researchers at the Institut National de Recherche Pédagogique (INRP) had only lately discovered Piaget and

Bruner and had hardly heard of Vygotsky, but that although it was busy pushing constructivist theories of teaching the INRP in any case had limited influence on practice. The situation was not helped, Beattie suggests, by the fact that until recently French universities showed no interest in education as a discipline and INRP had a monopoly of such educational research as was undertaken.[23] More significantly, while our Russian teachers referred – and deferred – to psychologists, those of their French counterparts who felt the need to legitimate their teaching in this way claimed inspiration from theorists of 'didactic transposition' rather than theorists of learning or human development. So the composition lesson at Coulanges (lesson 11.3, discourse extract 16.9) was based on Larivaille's schematic representation of how events could be transformed into narrative. This was a psychologically uncompromising framework that made no mention of the need to engage with the existing understandings of nine-year-old children. Not for these teachers, as yet anyway, the Anglo-American agonizings of the past four decades about how to bring child and subject into equilibrium. It was not that the French teachers counted the individual of lesser worth: more that cultural and disciplinary induction was unquestionably the most important goal. Brian Simon's question 'Why no pedagogy in England?' might with equal justice have been applied to France; to this the French would almost certainly have retorted, 'Perhaps – but at least we have *la didactique*'.

The only exceptions to this stance that we encountered were two teachers and an IUFM member who referred to the work of Célestin Freinet (1896–1966), the communist and internationalist theorist of education who resisted what he saw as the skewed and unsophisticated educational discourse of France and sought to introduce a pedagogy which was grounded in more than *les disciplines* alone, and above all in a more critical social consciousness. He proposed a balance of collective and individual activity, the one to ensure the child's socialization, the other to respond to his or her specific needs. In the latter case, children would have self-marked files and part of their programme would be individually negotiated. The teachers whom we observed had introduced the latter system and it features in one of the assessment cameos in Chapter 14. Although it is tempting to view Freinet as France's equivalent of the luminaries of the English primary progressive movement of the 1960s, the similarities are balanced or outweighed by contrast. Like them, Freinet challenged the dominance of discipline-based knowledge and urged a pedagogy that respected the individual; unlike them he held to the importance of cultural socialization. Where the English progressives celebrated individualism, Freinet balanced individual and collective needs. He was, after all, not only left wing but also French. Freinet was based near Nice, and locally there was a *mouvement Freinet*, a small Freinet cadre in the IUFM and a few 'Freinet schools'. But in a centralized educational system the chances that someone working at the southern fringes of the country will loosen the grip of so powerful an orthodoxy are slim.[24] Yet it seems probable that the local Freinet influence may be one reason why we observed more group work in Alpes Maritimes and Var than the QUEST team encountered in neighbouring Bouches du Rhône or distant Pas de Calais.[25]

The Indian situation was different again. There the espoused theory of teaching was strongly developmental, and Piaget featured fairly frequently in the teacher interviews. More common, however, were unattributed references, of a generically progressive kind, to 'discovery', 'activity' and 'enquiry' methods. Sometimes these were filled out by reference to one or more of the important learner-centred and community-based initiatives, some of them taking place outside the government system, which are fully reviewed by John Shotton: *Jan Vigyan Manch* in Bihar, *Charvaha Vidalaya* in Bihar, PROPEL in Maharashtra, *Shiksha Karmi* and *Lok Jumbish* in Rajasthan, and the total literacy capaigns in Rajasthan, Kerala, Haryana and Tamil Nadu.[26] These were not, however, methodological reforms so much as more fundamental attacks on the problem of rural illiteracy, low recruitment and poor retention. India has a formidable record of grass roots initiatives in the 'non-formal' sector, and of experimental schools. Some of the ideas thereby generated have been mainstreamed into Government of India initiatives such as the District Primary Education Programme and its successor *Sarva Shiksha Abhiyan* (SSA). 'Pedagogical renewal' is an important component of both.

Three points on the emerging pedagogic discourse of Indian primary education must be made, however. First, it makes much of developmental/progressive imports of the kind noted above. Second, it is not yet clear how far an individualistic, enquiry-based ideology is compatible with either the deeply rooted collective orientation of Indian primary teaching or the unassailable fact of very large classes. Third, our fieldwork was conducted in schools outside the administrative districts in which DPEP has been introduced and is thus more representative of both national resource levels and national practice, at least as these remain until programmes like DPEP and SSA come closer to their objective of universalizing elementary education. The 1999 PROBE report also confirms the typicality of what we saw and heard in our fieldwork classrooms.[27]

Thus in the Indian schools there was no mention of subject transformation or transposition. Rather, subject matter for teaching, like the subjects themselves, was 'given' and the challenge for the teacher in the context of large classes was to devise procedures, and make materials, which would render the concepts more accessible. If we note that teachers in England during the 1970s and the 1980s were advancing a similar rationale to these 1990s Indian teachers, yet that in the one setting children were working on separate tasks in groups while in the other they were working on identical tasks as a class, we have confirmation here, as in the other examples, of another kind of 'transposition', that of pedagogical theory itself. Bruner describes how the ideas advanced in his book *The Process of Education* were turned to very different purposes as they were domesticated to suit the prevailing political and educational ideologies of the various countries into whose languages the book was translated. In Italy the book was used 'for clubbing Marxists and classicists alike'. In the Soviet Union it was used to attack Stalinist education. In Japan it was used to give intellectual legitimacy to technical subjects. In Israel it was seen as a basis for maintaining standards among immigrants. In the United States it was seen to attack rather than sustain a belief in childhood spontaneity.[28] Educational ideas do not just migrate; in speaking to different cultural histories and conditions they also change.

Thus it is that we find the same names crossing national and cultural boundaries to appear in different political guises, for pedagogy, as noted at the start of this section, is discourse, not merely procedure. So, too, in respect of the task of *teaching* 'by method *x* to enable pupils to learn *y*', pedagogy comes into play once we see how in different cultures the various nodal points of this simple formulation – the pupil, the subject matter, the method – take on greater or lesser significance and stand in different relations to each other.

In the Central European tradition, pedagogy is the overarching concept and didactics is that branch of pedagogy which deals with what is to be taught and how. Comenius' *Great Didactic* (perhaps the earliest recognizably modern application of the term) deals with both, setting out a view of humankind, its relation to the divine, to eternity and to nature, the goals of education and the kinds of institutions – common 'mother schools', 'vernacular schools' and gymnasia – in which formal education should be pursued, together with principles of instruction. In respect of the latter, Comenius makes a clear distinction between what later became 'general' and 'special' or subject didactics, differentiating 'the universal requirements of teaching and learning' before expounding on key principles such as 'facility', 'thoroughness' and 'conciseness and rapidity' and setting out 'the methods of the sciences', 'the methods of languages' and other subjects.[29] Comenius justifies his central place in European pedagogy not just in respect of the continuing resonance of some of his institutions and instructional principles (for example pages 310, 425) but also to the extent that he mapped out the territory of pedagogy in ways many continue to find persuasive.

I have referred frequently to this 'Central European' pedagogic tradition. It is rooted in the humanism of Erasmus, the empiricism of Bacon and the Protestantism of Luther. The line crystallizes with Comenius and passes by way of Pestalozzi, Herbart, Froebel and Montessori into modern educational thought. In placing French education close to this line it is important to stress that French education accommodated the didactic element much more readily than the pedagogic one. In this, religion is probably the important variable. Comenius was a member of one of the earliest Protestant churches, Unitas Fratrem or the Moravian Brethren. His concern with education was about much more than 'method' alone. His relatively democratic view of schooling, who should have access to it and how it should be organized, not to mention his resistance to the tyranny of Latin and his advocacy of the vernacular, were all at variance with pre-revolution education in Catholic France. Even now, Sharpe suggests, French education may be secular but it still has the structure and stamp, even the catechistic pedagogy, of ecclesiastical hierarchy, absolutism and social control.[30]

Pedagogy and curriculum

In English and American pedagogical discourse curriculum issues are of central importance, although the Anglo-American concept of curriculum connotes a field which is rather different from 'didactics'. During the postwar period curriculum studies expanded rapidly in American universities, spawning societies, journals, books and – especially after the 1957 Sputnik panic – federal grants.[31] The national spur was curriculum development and renewal, and academics grabbed the opportunities afforded by this bonanza with both hands. The scope of the term 'curriculum' widened in proportion to the growth in activity (for few wished to be left out and careers were there for the making) and by the 1960s 'instruction' and much else besides were gathered under the one umbrella term 'curriculum'. Indeed, few aspects of the educational enterprise were able to escape its clutches, for curriculum was defined as most of what went on in schools. Thus a typical (and impressive) representative text of the early 1960s, Taba's *Curriculum Development: theory and practice*, is positively Germanic in its scope and aspirations. Its theoretical stance, however, is unambiguously American, especially in relation to social reconstruction and the nature of knowledge, and in common with other texts of the period it has a strong emphasis upon 'process'.[32]

Bruner's interventions in this debate were important. His idea of a 'spiral curriculum' which enabled a child to revisit the conceptual and structural foundations of a discipline at different levels as he/she progressed from 'enactive' to 'iconic' and 'symbolic' stages of development and representation seemed to resolve the logic/psychologic tension I referred to earlier, for

> a curriculum reflects not only the nature of knowledge itself but also the nature of the knower and of the knowledge-getting process . . . We teach a subject not to produce little living libraries . . . but rather to get a student to think mathematically . . . to consider matters as an historian does, to take part in the process of knowledge-getting. Knowing is a process, not a product.[33]

This Deweyan last assertion became the epistemic credo for a generation of teachers, teacher trainers and administrators on both sides of the Atlantic. For many, it still is, and the one dichotomy was happily absorbed into others. For example, prominently displayed on the classroom wall of one of our Michigan schools we found this notice:

> *Important issues to me –*
> Process orientation vs product orientation
> Teaching students vs teaching programs
> Teacher as facilitator vs teacher as manager
> Developing a set of strategies vs mastering a set of skills
> Celebrating approximation vs celebrating perfection
> Respecting individual growth vs fostering competition
> Capitalizing on student's strengths vs emphasizing student's weaknesses
> Promoting independence in learning vs dependence on the teacher.

Similar lists could be found in British texts and courses for primary teachers during the 1970s and the 1980s (the second item in the manifesto above is recognizably the Michigan version of 'we teach children, not subjects'), and the habit of setting up complex areas of educational debate in such adversarial terms remains the stock-in-trade of popular speakers at primary teachers' conferences.

Try replacing the 'versus' in the list above by 'and' and you create a refreshingly new and inclusive pedagogy. That is all it takes, but for many teachers and education ideologues such inclusivity is inconceivable; for what is education without its barricades? This adversarialism lies behind some of the problems in American and English pedagogy to which we have already alluded.

In Britain, too, curriculum development and curriculum studies expanded, the one during the 1960s and the 1970s under the auspices of the Schools Council and the other in universities and colleges. In effect, then, the Anglo-American academic–professional nexus inflated 'curriculum' far beyond its original meaning. However, in the process, the new curriculum discourse became normative as well as to a degree scholarly; and the terms 'pedagogy' and 'didactic' acquired undeniably adverse overtones, suggesting nothing so strongly as the chalk-and-talk, fact-transmitting Gradgrinds of progressive folklore. In this context, although they may not have intended this, it strikes me as symptomatic of the English view of curriculum that in the Watkins and Mortimore definition of pedagogy ('any conscious activity by one person designed to enhance learning in another') *what* is to be learned is not a variable.

There is, however, another reason for the prominence of curriculum themes in England and the United States. If we draw back from the all-inclusive definition to one which deals with *what* is to be taught and how (the field covered in central Europe by didactics) we find that one of the clearest differences within the *Five Cultures* data is the degree to which teachers in each country see curriculum in this sense as problematic. Broadly, in Russia, France and India, teachers took the prescribed curriculum as given and talked about how to implement it; those in Michigan and England were much more inclined to contest it. In Russia, the very notion of curriculum – conceptually, I think, rather than linguistically – provoked difficulties in some of the teacher interviews.

The reasons for this difference seem clear. Until 1988 England did not have a national curriculum, so instead of being pre-empted by national government curriculum questions were open for debate. 'Minister', remarked 1940s education minister George Tomlinson, 'knows nowt about curriculum' (non-English readers will have to unpick the dialect which is essential to this well-worn and possibly apocryphal quotation). Although in 1960 another minister, David Eccles, mused darkly about entering the 'secret garden of curriculum', his successors showed little inclination to do so until the late 1970s. Even in 1986, just two years before it arrived, ministers insisted that the idea of a national curriculum was unthinkable. So teachers were not only able to debate such matters for themselves; they were actively encouraged by government to do so. In the primary sector, the abolition of secondary school selection in effect made the curriculum open territory (at secondary level there was less debate about the scope and balance of the curriculum as a whole, because this was to a greater degree shaped by the external pressures of public examinations and the requirements of university entrance and employment).

Therefore, when the National Curriculum was summarily imposed by the Thatcher government in 1987–8 in the teeth of professional opposition, not only was it widely condemned as an affront to professional autonomy and local democracy, but the government's behaviour also guaranteed that education professionals would continue to resist long after the proposals became law, especially as the government's railroading tactics set the style for their subsequent handling of national curriculum matters.

Although the United States has not experienced this kind of curriculum takeover (nor, without a change in the American Constitution, is it likely to) we were made aware in Michigan of a growing pressure washing down through the system, from federal to state and from state to district, to secure greater curriculum uniformity in the interests of 'standards' and international competitiveness ('By the year 2000, United States students will be first in the world in mathematics and science achievement'[34]) following the publication of *A Nation at Risk* in 1983.[35] However, although by the year 2000 more and more state education departments had produced curriculum statements, these were far less prescriptive than the English national curriculum, and many states were content to promulgate 'frameworks' or 'guides' and leave the detail to be worked out by teachers. The professional subject associations frequently did that job.

All this, of course, relates to a narrower definition of 'curriculum' – curriculum as content, subject matter or outcomes – than the imperialist 'curriculum as everything the school does in pursuit of its goals' which emerged from American and English universities during the 1960s and the 1970s. But this only sharpens the difference between these two countries and the other three. In the central European tradition, the debate concerns not curriculum but didactics, the transposition of knowledge rather than its initial specification. In Russia, questioning either version has only recently become possible; and in India an underpowered and dispersed teaching force is not in a strong position to do more than voice concern about the 'burden' of curriculum on pupils, by which it is as likely to mean the weight of books in the child's satchel as conceptual overload. But we have also to consider the strong possibility that what we have in post-Soviet Russia, France and India is a classic illustration of the Gramscian hegemonic process as discussed in Chapter 7: domination with consent, at least where the curriculum is concerned. In the United States, as has become clear at so many levels of our data, educational values are everywhere contested as a matter of habit and cultural circumstance as well as by constitutional right. In England, the memories of decentralization die slowly, and power-coercive policies are strongly resisted (for the time being, anyway: conceivably something approaching the French curriculum settlement may begin to prevail, if only as those in field discover that the battle is lost).

Let us reconsider our map of pedagogy in the light of this. In the Anglo-American tradition, pedagogy – in so far as the word is used in professional contexts – is subsidiary to curriculum. Curriculum has both a broad sense (approaching the continental usage of 'pedagogy') and a narrow one (what must be taught) which is closer to continental 'didactics'; and pedagogy is defined no less narrowly as teaching method. In the Central European tradition it is the other way round. Pedagogy frames everything else, including curriculum (in so far as *that* word is used) and didactics. So in professional discourse pedagogy and curriculum are differentiated. As we look at our five countries we see sharp variations in the counterpoint of pedagogy, curriculum and didactics which intimate how the cultures perceive the central pedagogical relationship between learner, the process of learning, and what is learned.

The case of academic discourse is different. Although, as I have noted, 'curriculum' has become a considerable edifice in England and the United States, there is a growing parallel literature on pedagogy more broadly defined, in which cultural critique is dominant and which tends to focus on pedagogy and pedagogic discourse as mechanisms of social control and cultural reproduction. Thus, as we saw in Chapter 7, 'poisonous pedagogy' enslaves, 'critical pedagogy' liberates.[36]

Is the question of definition of genuine importance, or are we just playing with words? I believe that these differences are indeed significant. First, the emphases within a culture's educational discourse say a great deal about what matters most and least to those engaged in that discourse: the whole curriculum and the whole child; efficient induction into an accepted version of culture, citizenship and knowledge; moral, personal and civic upbringing; cultural reproduction; cultural transformation; and so on. Second, one of the definitions actually works better. The inherent ambiguities of meaning surrounding 'curriculum' – is it everything the school does or merely what is prescribed to be taught, the formal curriculum or the not-so-hidden 'hidden' curriculum'? – cause communication on such matters to be more difficult than it deserves. And for teachers and administrators in countries with national curricula, which in this book means all of them except the United States, there is no longer any ambiguity about the term, for curriculum is what is prescribed. Further, once content is detached in this way it encourages the narrow treatment of matters of teaching strategy and style to which I referred in a previous chapter.

My own preference, therefore, is to eschew the ambiguities of 'curriculum' and the resulting tendency to downgrade pedagogy, and use the latter term to encompass the entire field. The model of the narrower idea of 'teaching' remains as I advanced it at the beginning of Chapter 13. 'Pedagogy' contains both teaching as defined there and its contingent discourses about the character of culture, the purposes of education, the nature of childhood and learning and the structure of knowledge. These discourses bear on, and are manifested in the various aspects of teaching which I identified: space, pupil organization, time, routine, rule, ritual, task, activity, interaction, judgement – and, of course curriculum. This is close to Bernstein's judgement that 'pedagogic discourse . . . selectively relocates, refocuses, and relates other discourses to constitute its own order and orderings'.[37] Defining pedagogy rather than curriculum as the overarching term allows us to understand how it is not just curriculum, which, in Lawton's words, is a 'selection from culture',[38] but every other aspect of what goes on in schools and classrooms as well. Moreover, because 'pedagogy' in both its broad and narrow senses retains an inescapable whiff of the classroom, we are constantly reminded that the real power of pedagogy resides in what happens between teachers and pupils and can avoid qualificatory distinctions like 'curriculum as prescribed'/'curriculum as transacted'.

I hope that this usage also makes the book's treatment of curriculum more comprehensible. In Chapters 2–7, curriculum was identified as a free-standing theme because at that level we were discussing policy rather than practice. At that level curriculum was a written specification, a 'paper curriculum' with a life of its own. When we entered the classroom, however, we noted that curriculum requirements merged with curriculum transactions, and we found ourselves teasing out generic properties of pedagogy which impacted not just on the treatment of curriculum content, but also on the use of space, the handling of time, the grouping of pupils, the formulation of tasks, the balance of activities, the focus and criteria of judgements and, above all, the structure, content and control of pupil–teacher talk. These generic properties were what most fundamentally differentiated the teaching that we observed in the five countries, for they were our links to the defining characteristics of the culture.

In fact, the curriculum is probably best viewed as a series of *translations*, *transpositions* and *transformations* from its initial status as published statutory requirements or non-statutory guidance. At the beginning of this process of metamorphosis is the national or state curriculum. At its end is the array of understandings in respect of each specified curriculum goal and domain that the pupil acquires as a result of his or her classroom activities and encounters. In between is a succession of shifts, sometimes bold, sometimes slight, as curriculum moves from specification to transaction and as teachers and pupils interpret, modify and add to the meanings that it embodies. Sometimes the change may be slight, as a school takes a required syllabus or programme of study and maps it onto the timetable. This we might call a *translation*. Then a school or teacher may adjust the nomenclature and move parts of one curriculum domain into another to effect a *transposition*, which then leads to a sequence of lesson plans. But the real change, the *transformation*, comes when the curriculum passes from document into action and is broken down into learning tasks and activities and expressed and negotiated as discourse. Figure 17.1 schematizes this process, and ties it into the families of 'frame', 'form' and 'act' from the model of teaching in Figure 13.1.

In this sense, therefore, curriculum is a 'framing' component of the act of teaching, as suggested by Figure 13.1, only before it is transformed into task, activity, interaction, discourse and outcome. From that point on it becomes inseparable from each of these. In the classroom, curriculum *is* task, activity, interaction and discourse, and they are curriculum.

However faithful to government, state or school requirements a teacher remains, teaching is always an act of curriculum transformation. On the other hand, the

1	*Specification*	National or state curriculum	
2	*Translation*	School curriculum	*Frame*
3	*Translation and/or transposition*	Class curriculum and timetable	
4		Lesson plan	
5	*Transformation*	Lesson	*Form*
6		Task	
7		Activity	*Act*
8		Interaction	
9		Task product	*Outcome*
10		Learning outcome	

Figure 17.1   Curriculum metamorphosis

degree of transformation varies, sometimes a great deal. Teachers in Russia, India and France generally worked within the labels and syllabuses laid down for them, often using centrally produced textbooks. There, the journey from specification to the first stage of transformation was short and direct. In Michigan it could be longer and more complex, as teachers took curriculum guides (which in any case did not have the force of law), extracted those components which they and their schools deemed important, moved them around, relabelled the resulting combinations, and set about teaching them. Some stuck closely to the official terminology; others introduced stipulative variants. Most were influenced by personal and local belief systems that made the transformation more radical than mere terminological adjustment. The degree to which teachers can interpose their own 'critical pedagogies' between the child and the transmission pedagogy of the state may be, I suggest, seriously underestimated by macro-level pedagogical theorists. It would be hard to find much common ground between the pedagogy of sequences 16.14, 16.15 and 16.16 and the 'standards' rhetoric emanating from further up the system.

In England, teachers worked within a national framework that combined the obligatory with the optional:

> For each subject and for each key stage, programmes of study set out what pupils should be taught, and attainment targets set out the expected standards of pupils' performance. It is for schools to choose how they organize their school curriculum to include the programmes of study . . . The programmes of study [defined in the Education Act of 1996 as the 'matters, skills and processes' that should be taught] set out what pupils should be taught in each key stage, and provide the basis for planning schemes of work . . . The national frameworks for teaching literacy and mathematics published by DfEE, and the exemplar schemes of work published jointly by the DfEE and QCA, show how the programmes of study can be translated into practical, manageable teaching plans.[39]

In practice, the direct and indirect pressures of assessment, inspection and target-setting might seem to lead the teaching of literacy and numeracy towards translation rather than transformation, while the other subjects, especially history and geography (the core of traditional 'topic work') remained free to emerge in the classrooms in somewhat different guises. Certainly, the UK government understood the power of external assessment and inspection to minimize transformation in those subjects in which it had the greatest political investment. But the pedagogical intensity of the final act of transformation is such that control can never be absolute: in sequences 16.12 and 16.13 the literacy and numeracy hours have been domesticated to – or compromised by – mainstream 1980s pedagogy.

Pedagogy and culture: teaching

Prema Clarke of Bangalore and Harvard has set out a number of 'cultural models of teacher thinking and teaching'. Working from the research literature she conflates studies from Europe, North America and Australia into 'Western European models' and those from eastern and southern Asia, Africa and South America into 'non-Western models'. She uses six 'pedagogical categories' ('teacher presentation', 'instructional goals', 'attitudes towards the curriculum', 'communication of knowledge', 'teacher–student verbal interaction' and 'discipline'). This framework allows her to locate research studies which between them point to several of the differences which have been explored in this book: curriculum as given, teacher as authority, the importance of the group (non-Western); curriculum as negotiable, teacher as carer, the importance of the individual (North America); curriculum as given but methods as negotiable, teacher as controller, group/individual ambivalence (Europe).[40] However, the limitations of the research surveyed ensure that these perspectives remain mainly in the domain of teachers' espoused values rather than observed practice, and we know how far apart values and practice may be. The adoption of a single 'non-Western model' is surely unacceptable (Clarke's includes material from three continents under that heading) especially as within her 'Western' category she is prepared to differentiate Europe and North America.

Reynolds and Farrell do a similar job with Europe (drawing on material from Germany, Holland, Switzerland and Hungary) and the Pacific Rim, both of which they contrast with England.[41] In this, again, they itemize culturally specific tendencies: homogeneous teaching groups, textbooks, whole class teaching, high expectations (Europe); emphasis on effort rather than ability, high parental aspirations, high pupil motivation, sharp task focus, whole class interactive instruction, textbooks, predictable school day, the class as a single unit (Pacific Rim).

Then there are the many comparative studies that treat cultures separately rather than grouping them within categories such as 'Pacific Rim', 'European', 'Western-European' or 'non-Western'. Many of these are referred to in this book, and some attempt to construct coherent 'cultural models' out of their comparisons. Thus the Tobin study of pre-schooling in Japan, China and the United States identifies the powerful strand of individualism which runs through American culture, language and education, but also draws attention to its downside and a growing anxiety among Americans that 'in our celebration of individualism the threads that bind people to one another have been stretched too thin and . . . the fabric of American society, already frayed at the edges, has begun to unravel'.[42] Bronfenbrenner had already made a similar point in 1970, on the basis of comparisons with the Soviet Union, adding that the American tendency to age-segregation separates children from adult models and further erodes social cohesiveness.[43] Using data from the same three countries, Stevenson and Stigler work at the recurrent divide between individualism/innate ability (United States) and collectivism/effort (eastern Asia), noting that the latter orientation is much more appropriate to the context of a crowded classroom. They also – and are rare in this regard for doing so – examine classroom discourse and note differences such as the way Chinese and Japanese teachers use and build on pupils' answers while American teachers merely – if that is the right word – praise them.[44] Broadfoot and her colleagues make much of the Gemeinschaft/Gesellschaft distinction in comparing primary education in England and France and link this with 'national orientations' such as charisma, achieved roles, particularism, individualism, diffuse interaction, affectivity and personalized discourse (England); and bureaucracy, role ascription, universalism, collectivism, focused interaction, affective neutrality and objectified discourse (France).[45]

In this study I have dealt with five separate countries and have taken pains to identify not just national differences but also within-country differences, and one of the values of using lesson transcript extracts in combination with narrative lesson summaries, as in Chapters 11 and 16, is that these within-country differences readily show themselves. I have also ventured a broader classification, however, of 'Anglo-American' and 'Central European' pedagogy which I believe is justified by history as well as the patterns revealed by the *Five Cultures* data. This is at variance with both of Clarke's groupings. Her 'Western European' category rightly picks up transatlantic divergence, but fails to identify divergence within Europe. Her 'non-Western' category, as I have said, needs refinement. Crucially, as far as India (which is included in the latter category) is concerned, the grouping disregards the colonial legacy, and the way that as a result Indian pedagogy is both European and Asian.

In loosely pairing English pedagogy with that of the United States rather than continental Europe, I have tried not to imply that the classrooms of the two countries represent a single pattern of teaching or a single cultural orientation. After a century of what some see as unremitting American cultural imperialism and a half-century of British prostration to American foreign policy interests, England and the United States remain resolutely different, educationally no less than culturally. Values are expressed in the classrooms of Michigan, and events take place there, which would never be expressed or take place in England, and vice versa. The UK government's adoption of Americanisms like 'zero tolerance' and 'intervention in inverse proportion to success', which suggest convergence, should be seen as the opportunistic slogans that they are.

In particular, I argued that the negotiated pedagogy that seems to unite some of the classrooms of England and Michigan reflects values which are in fact both distinctive and divergent. In Michigan we observed the uneasy working out of the tensions of individualism and democracy within the context of compulsory school-ing. In England, there was no obvious democratic commitment within the class-rooms, but rather a strong allegiance to a developmental view of the individual within a framework of unambiguous teacher authority. The challenges for this version of negotiated pedagogy were organizational rather than ideological.

Yet for all that, the balance of pedagogical commonalities and differences as between England, Michigan, France and Russia suggests that the Dover Strait is a more fundamental cultural barrier than the Atlantic and that when it comes to some of the defining practices and values of primary education, France appears to look east and England appears to look west.

However, even if we can sort out the family resemblances and locate them cultur-ally and historically, how far does this allow us to define them as supranational cultural *models* of pedagogy? The claim seems to present three main problems.

First, commentators such as those cited are surely right to seek out the ideas which underpin the practice, and in doing so may well find themselves straying into social and political theory. This is not a problem; on the contrary, it reinforces the 'situatedness' of what goes on in schools and classrooms, and is in accordance with the broad definition of pedagogy and pedagogic discourse adopted here. However, most such accounts are stronger on the ideas than the practice, for as I noted in the book's early pages, comparative educationists have until recently had disappointingly little truck with close and sustained observation of teaching and learning as they happen. Pedagogic practice may well be theory-soaked but pedagogic theory without practice is meaningless. Without observational research it is impossible to test whether or to what degree a cited idea or value which may have considerable cultural currency really does impact on children and the learning in schools. And without the voices of participants it will be hard, if not impossible, to separate from the tangle of ideas those which engage with practice and those that merely surround it, or to tease out craft knowledge from researcher interpretation and official propaganda. Thus, do French teachers *themselves* set out to be 'affectively neutral' or is that just how they appear to an observer used to the English rhetoric of 'caring' and child centredness, and to English teachers' generous use of terms of endearment? And who says that the curriculum in American schools is negotiable and that the teacher is a carer? Teachers? Children? Researchers? And which, if any, is right?

Second, this latter barrage of questions indicates that we probably need to take greater care to differentiate the prescriptive from the descriptive here, and the quasi-objective from the subjective and intersubjective. Otherwise we end up with something about whose purpose or claim to truth one can never be sure. Does a 'cultural model of pedagogy' say 'Pedagogy is . . .' or 'Pedagogy ideally should be . . .' or again, 'No, I work there and I'm telling you that pedagogy *really* is . . .'?

Third, a random collection of values or beliefs, even when practices are thrown in, does not make a model. Something more coherent is implied. I do not want to replay the discussion at the beginning of Chapter 13 that led to my model of *teaching*, except to repeat Leach's warning that descriptive models are best kept simple while prescriptive models are likely to be complex. But if the act of teaching is the *sine qua non* of pedagogy, then a reasonably coherent account of teaching must be at the heart of any pedagogic model.

Pedagogy and culture: learning

Another way to approach the question of cultural models of pedagogy is to start with the process of learning rather than the act of instruction. Jerome Bruner, by his own account, has moved from a 'solo, intrapsychic' view of knowing and learning to one which engages with the relationship between learning and culture:

> Culturalism's task is a double one. On the 'macro' side, it looks at the culture as a system of values, rights, exchanges, obligations, opportunities, power. On the 'micro' side, it examines how the demands of a cultural system affect those who must operate within it . . . it is much concerned with intersubjectivity – how humans come to know 'each other's minds'.[46]

This sounds familiar – it is the same task as G. H. Mead set himself[47] and during the 1970s it entered educational research in the UK via symbolic interactionism

– except that Bruner advances upon culture by way of the individual psyche and continues to give to individual cognition much closer attention than do, by and large, sociologists and anthropologists. He has also been closely involved with the thinking and development of young children and therefore has always had a great deal to say to those involved in early years and primary education. Bruner identifies four 'dominant models of learners' minds that have held sway in our times' as the basis for his quest to reposition educational psychology more firmly in the cultural domain:

(1) seeing children as imitative learners
(2) seeing children as learning from didactic exposure
(3) seeing children as thinkers
(4) seeing children as knowledgeable.[48]

The prefix 'seeing' is important: Bruner is characterizing the way in which, in educational contexts, children and their capacities have been defined by teachers, whatever those capacities really are. Age is an objective fact but childhood is a construct. The first model – seeing children as imitative learners – is the basis of apprenticeship, a system for 'leading the novice into the skilled ways of the expert'. Expertise requires practice, and implies not just propositional or procedural knowledge but also talents, skills and abilities. The second – seeing children as learning from didactic exposure – informs the classic transmission model of teaching; it is heavily geared to the acquisition of facts, principles and rules, and presumes that children are not knowledgeable until they have demonstrated that they can recall and repeat the facts, principles and rules in question. The third – seeing children as thinkers – presupposes that children can and do think for themselves, that it is the task of the teacher to uncover and understand that thinking and through discussion and a 'pedagogy of mutuality' to help the child move from a private to a shared frame of reference. The main pedagogical tool is dialogic discourse. Finally, seeing children as knowledgeable starts with the premise that in any culture there is a 'given' of knowledge, that knowledge is not exclusively personal or intersubjective or relative, and that it is the teacher's task to 'help children grasp the distinction between personal knowledge . . . and "what is taken to be known" by the culture'.[49]

Bruner adds that what distinguishes the 'given' cultural knowledge in the fourth model from the 'received' knowledge in the second is that children learn why such knowledge stands up to scrutiny. They engage with its history. This, then, is Karl Popper's 'World Three' – 'the world of the logical contents of books, libraries, computer memories and suchlike'[50] and it is not dead information but ideas which live because children are encouraged to pursue how they impact upon Popper's 'World Two' of subjective knowledge, 'the world of our conscious experiences'.[51]

We can now bring together our culturally located versions of primary teaching and Bruner's four models or views of learning and the learner. The first point to make is that there is no necessary connection between any of the latter and the patterns of interaction and discourse summarized in Figure 16.2. It is a fairly standard fallacy to presume that whole class direct instruction equates with transmission or that collective discussion respects children's capacities as thinkers. As I tried to show by interrogating extended examples of classroom discourse in Chapter 16, it is the character of the talk *as talk*, rather than its organizational framing, which determines the kind of learning to which it leads.

Let us consider each country in turn. In France, much of the teaching we observed appeared to be premised on the importance of children's encountering and engaging with the culture's stock of World 3 objective knowledge, but was in fact steered by the more limited objective of didactic exposure. As Bruner points out, there are good reasons why, for some kinds of knowledge, simple transmission is appropriate and necessary (we made a similar point earlier about rote and recitation teaching). However, we also observed lessons, for example in comprehension, where teachers would take a cultural artefact such as a section of literary text and get children to work with it in a way that encouraged them to see it as meaningful in terms of their personal understandings. The other deviation from didactic exposure was in the direction of Bruner's dialogic or dialectical third model, when teachers sought to promote scaffolded understanding, although it is a matter of debate whether sequence 16.9, which I suggested was a good example of such teaching in the French context, goes as far as Bruner urges and finds 'in the intuitions of the child the roots of systematic knowledge'.[52] Indeed, Bruner's 'model 3' comes closest to scaffolding as he defines it elsewhere but seems to give the natural line of development (as opposed to the cultural) rather greater weight than in his earlier writing.

Russia presents a somewhat similar case, initially at any rate. Teaching there had a strong emphasis upon the acquisition of facts, principles and rules, and some of this was narrowly and very instrumentally directed at memorization and recall. However, we saw how teachers' collective pedagogical theorizing emphasized the scaffolding function of interrogatory classroom discourse, and how, in practice, teachers implemented this by working publicly on the understandings of individual children until the scaffolding process was complete. Further, like France, Russia values rather than ossifies its World 3 cultural stock. However, the dividing line between a 'pedagogy of mutuality' and 'didactic exposure' was not the culture so much as, quite simply, the difference between good and run-of-the-mill teaching. The Russian model at best generates far more cognitive dynamism than some Western observers are prepared to admit. At worst, as with whole class direct instruction in France, India or anywhere else, it very easily regresses to rote and ritualized rather than principled knowledge.[53]

India, in its pedagogy as in so many other respects, is a culture of extremes. The teaching which we observed, which was within the mainstream of government primary education rather than innovations such as the District Primary Education Programme or *Lok Jumbish*, was dominated by fact transmission, propositional knowledge and ritualized understanding. The reiterative discourse exemplified in sequences 16.1 and 16.2 restricts children's responses to one or two words, provides limited feedback, and offers few opportunities for ideas to be developed, let alone turned around and examined from other angles. Yet we did observe teachers who, within the considerable constraints of small and overcrowded classrooms, were able to secure dialogue and scaffolded understanding, and sequence 16.3 illustrates the aspiration. However, the true alternative to rote in the Indian context was not this version of teaching but apprenticeship (Bruner's first model), as we witnessed it in a few music and dance lessons and in experimental settings like Bal Bhawan. Now this form of pedagogy, and its assumptions about the learner and the learner–teacher relationship, have a central place in Indian culture and the quality and longevity of Indian artistic life testifies to its effectiveness. Although it is predicated on teacher authority, it is not the same as the Brahmanic ashram education that Kumar claims has degenerated into modern-day rote learning,[54] for its form of initiation develops skills which can allow the novice eventually to disengage from, and perhaps surpass – rather than merely copy – the expert. We might note that a similar pedagogy may be witnessed in instrumental master classes in some Western conservatoires. The question we have to ask, then, is why Indian primary education generally makes so little use of the culture's other indigenous pedagogic tradition. In this matter it is important to differentiate the 'simple theory of imitative learning', which Bruner insists does not suit an advanced society, from its more sophisticated counterpart, which – as we observed in India, and as one may observe it in music conservatoires – combines imitation with dialogue and knowledge transformation.

In Michigan we saw no examples of apprenticeship, some of straightforward didacticism, and many which aspired to Bruner's third model. Some reflected it, and I believe that sequence 16.17 is a good example of teaching which is intersubjective, respects children's understandings, and through group collaboration and the careful narrowing of options seeks to take all the class towards a shared and systematic way of knowing mathematically. However, the more common condition was one which never quite managed to square the circle of learning. The professional discourse of some of the teachers made much of respecting the child's ways of making sense of the world, but having encouraged them to make that sense, they too often left it at that. So we observed teachers, who out of respect for the child's autonomy and understanding, simply accepted from nine year olds brief fragments of writing on topics which required discussion but did not receive it and at a level which showed little advance on what had been done one year previously. The classroom poster referred to earlier in this chapter reveals the extent of the problem, for by setting up pedagogical values as mutually exclusive you end up with a view of teaching which is in danger of going nowhere: 'process orientation . . . teacher as facilitator . . . developing strategies . . . celebrating approximation'. Yes, but what next? The other side of the coin, that which moves processes and approximations towards shared understanding, has been ruled out of court.

In England, again, we saw no examples of initiation into expertise as defined in Bruner's first model, except at the lowest level of imitation without engagement, skill or independent judgement such as can be all too often observed in ill-taught music or art lessons (in which depressing practice England was certainly not alone). Propositional knowledge predominated, although because teaching leaned away from collective dialogue and towards reading, writing and semi-private conversational talk, knowledge was there to be 'looked up' rather than 'listened to'.[55] This can be a characteristically English sleight of hand, for at first sight the group ambience, buzz of conversation and movement to and from the class library suggests nothing more strongly than pedagogy of both enquiry and mutuality. But again we have to ask what children *do* with what they look up and find out. If they simply write it down without examining either its substance or status then this is mere canonical knowledge. Worse, because it lacks the cognitive challenge that goes with the discourse of well-conducted direct instruction it may yield facts but not principles and rules. If we put this tendency with three others that teachers themselves may not espouse but to which they are vulnerable because they are prominent in English society and government, we have a serious problem. The tendencies are institutionalized anti-intellectualism, the reduction of history and culture to prepackaged 'heritage', and an overweening admiration for electronic information. In this scenario, classroom discourse may lack the structure, continuity and precision needed for real dialogue and handover, while World 3 knowledge remains inert.

The UK government's literacy and numeracy strategies may offer an alternative. Consciously emulating continental European practice, they seek to stiffen and collectivize classroom talk and – in the numeracy strategy at least – to encourage children to make public their private understandings in order that they can move towards a shared frame of reference. The *Five Cultures* data contain too few examples to allow a judgement on whether or not the strategies are proving successful in these respects, although at the time of writing the evidence from research and inspection is in conflict and inspectors are more optimistic than researchers.[56] This is perhaps because inspectors are concentrating on the numeracy and literacy targets which the government set itself for the year 2002, rather than on the strategies' broader pedagogic claims. However, extracts 16.12 and 16.13 expose some of the difficulties of accommodating the strategies to existing pedagogic thinking and practice. In 16.12 (the Literacy Hour), a traditional pattern of organization and monitoring disrupts what is intended to be sustained interaction with a few children; while in 16.13 (the Numeracy Hour), we find a less extreme version of the Michigan condition of children being encouraged to articulate their thinking but lacking a shared vocabulary for doing so. A 'pedagogy of mutuality' requires a shared language.

Bruner's four models of learners' minds, derived from the 'vernacular' or 'folk' pedagogy,[57] therefore take us further along the road towards a coherent set of cultural models of pedagogy. But they also remind us how, when one confronts adult assumptions about how children think and learn, the range of possibilities is not so very great and some models have near-universal currency. Which is why, as a footnote to this section, it is interesting and symptomatic to find a recent English book on pedagogy using the Bruner account so selectively. Watkins and Mortimore refer only to Bruner's third and fourth versions (seeing children as thinkers, and seeing children as knowledgeable).[58] They do this for a good reason – to encourage teachers to abandon mere didacticism – but in doing so overstate, I think, the hierarchy implied by Bruner, seeing apprenticeship as 'primitive', transmission as 'traditional', and only the third and fourth models as appropriate to Western schooling in the twenty-first century. For their part, Gipps and MacGilchrist, writing about 'primary school learners', use the first three but not the fourth.[59] In justification, they cite Bruner's conclusion that 'achieving skill and accumulating knowledge are not enough' (his first and second model), and so presumably set up the third as the appropriate 'modern' pedagogy for primary schools. But again, have they overstated the objections to skill apprenticeship and the acquisition of propositional knowledge? And why leave out the fourth model (through which pupils engage with Popper's 'World 3' of 'what is taken to be known by the culture') unless they are saying that for primary children this realm of knowledge is of no account?

If that is what they propose, then it confirms my earlier concern (and Eric Hobsbawm's, which we encountered in Chapter 7) about the loss of historical consciousness and the restricted treatment of culture in English primary education.[60] Equally serious, to focus the entire pedagogical enterprise upon Bruner's third model is to confine children to a limbo of intersubjectivity in precisely the way we encountered in some of the discourse extracts from England and Michigan in Chapter 16, where children and teachers talk but do not communicate. This, in other words, is the Michigan poster problem of process without product, and approximation without perfection.

The virtue of Bruner's framework, I take it, is that it allows us to test the place in a modern pedagogy of four contrasting stances on learning and knowledge and to allow for the possibility that all may have some part to play. Its limitation, certainly in the use made of it by Gipps and MacGilchrist, is that it takes little account of *curriculum*, and the fact that different ways of knowing and understanding demand different ways of learning and teaching. Mathematical, linguistic, literary, historical, scientific, artistic, technological, economic, religious and civic understanding are not at all the same. Some demand much more than others by way of a grounding in skill and propositional knowledge, and all advance the faster on the basis of engagement with existing knowledge, understanding and insight. That, I know, is an unfashionable standpoint.

This, perhaps, replays or rather transposes an old, old theme in English and American educational thinking: the status of received and reflexive knowledge, and the contrast between reproductive and empowering views of education. In English and American progressivism, World 3 knowledge is dismissed as *ipso facto* 'inert', or at best as 'information' to be treated as authoritative and never challenged. In postmodernist critique World 3 knowledge, as embodied in the 'technology and culture of the book', is so much 'high learning' which regulates, sorts and controls.[61] Both characterizations of knowledge do a disservice to children as well as to their culture; they also reflect an abiding failure to distinguish between the character of the knowledge in question and how it is, or might be, taught. If it is inert, that is because teachers make it so. Whether school knowledge imprisons or liberates depends in part on its cultural currency, but in part too on how it is taught and what the learner does with it.

Pedagogy and culture: control

The control of education and the controlling power of education have been prominent themes throughout this book. It makes no sense to advance a cultural model of learning or teaching, or a theory of pedagogy, which ignores the place of public education in societies where power, wealth and influence are unequally shared. The controlling function, as we have seen, is exercised at different levels. At national level (or state level in the United States) governments devise policies and structures, allocate budgets, determine goals, define curricula and institute mechanisms for assessing and policing what goes on at the system's lower levels. At regional and local levels such systems may be replicated or, depending on the balance of control, they may simply be implemented. At school level, heads exercise varying degrees of influence or direct control over what goes on in classrooms; and at the end of the line, in classrooms, children are every day subjected to the pedagogic controls of teaching and curriculum. These controls extend into the furthest recesses of task, activity and interaction, and are mediated through routine, rule and ritual.

Comparative macro–micro analysis illuminates the way these stack up and cumulatively impact upon the child. If we confine ourselves to the level of the national or state system the variable of centralization–decentralization seems persuasive. Certainly it provides a way of differentiating systems such as the five which have featured here. But if we study a system at meso and micro levels as well as macro we soon perceive the limitations of this mode of analysis, and, by extension, of simple reproductive models of public education. The intermediate levels may transmit; alternatively they may mediate, selectively gate keep, reshape or replace what comes from above, even when governments introduce procedures to prevent or discourage them from doing so. Conversely, in a decentralized system the power available at local level is open to challenge both from other local quarters and above.

Meanwhile, in the classroom, as was discovered several decades ago, 'open' or 'child-centred' pedagogy may no more free the child from external controls than does traditional didactic pedagogy.[62] Pedagogy is by its nature a shaping process, and freedom, say, in choice of task may be offset by control through differentiation and assessment. Above all, we have seen the power of talk to define not just communicative competence, rights and responsibilities, but what it is to know, to understand, to learn and to be a child.

If pedagogy is, in Bernstein's words, a 'cultural relay' governed by the rules of hierarchy, sequence, pacing, appropriateness and acceptability – the 'regulative' rules of structure and hierarchy and the 'discursive' rules of instruction – the workings of that relay are nevertheless complex and variable.[63] The mechanisms are universal: structure, curriculum, assessment, inspection, qualifications, school organization and teaching. At the top of the system is the regulatory power of government and ministry; at the bottom is the regulatory power of classroom discourse. At one end is a view of the social worth of a group: qualified or unqualified, rich or poor, male or female, white or black, employed or unemployed, brahman or dalit, young or old, urban or rural, metropolitan or provincial; at the other end is a view of the communicative competence of the individual. Bernstein's studies since the 1950s have emphasized the overriding force of social class, as is inevitable in an English context.[64] To these, now, in an era more sensitive to the cultural politics of difference, we add gender, age, income, religion and ethnicity, and in India caste. Yet our detailed encounters with Bernstein's 'discursive' level in Chapters 15 and 16 show clearly that even when these many and profound structural divisions and inequalities are factored in we must avoid an overdetermined view of what education does to people.

Schools and classrooms are places where meanings are, depending on the mode of pedagogy adopted, transmitted, negotiated and/or created. The formal curriculum sets out the meanings which a government, administration or school expects teachers to transmit; and this version of curriculum presumes that the primary function of teaching is transmission, for no government is in the business of prescribing subversive curricula or critical pedagogy. These meanings are variously reinforced, confused or subverted as the curriculum goes through its various phases of translation, transposition and transformation on its way to its final transformation by the child (Figure 17.1). The greater the degree of external control, the shorter the line and the closer the congruence between curriculum as prescribed, curriculum as transacted and curriculum as experienced.

As far as the prescribed curriculum is concerned, we have learned to look well beyond the surface international similarities that are revealed by OECD data or the Benavot study.[65] It *does* matter whether children encounter information technology, the arts, science or citizenship alongside the universal 'basics' of literacy and numeracy, for these can enable them to gain access to and participate in different cultural domains. Equally, a badly skewed curriculum will deny access to, and ultimately belittle and weaken, the aspects of the culture which are underrepresented. In England, at the time of writing, the critical question in this regard is whether the government's electoral pledge of raising standards in basic literacy and numeracy has been at the expense of the arts and humanities, and of the kinds of understanding and skill which these domains are uniquely able to foster. Needless to say, when they observe the impact of this policy on the curriculum as transacted, few are reassured by the official rhetoric of 'breadth and balance'.

Empowering through Comparing:
Many Possibilities, One Example

Although I have identified many of this study's implications as we have gone along, I would wish to insist that this task is as much for others as myself. I can make a reasonable stab of answering the question 'What can English primary education, and English pedagogy, learn from the pedagogy of France, India, Russia and the United States?'. I have said much on this already and add a further and final note below. But I would be much less prepared to suggest what, say, Russia can learn from France, or India from the United States, or any of these from England. In this matter the book's ideas, histories, evidence and interpretations must speak for themselves, and those in the countries in question are best placed to decide what, if anything, the book can offer them.

It also depends on what they are looking for. The book has engaged with primary education at the levels of system, school and classroom, so it may also speak to the condition of those who work at these levels: policy-makers and administrators, school heads, principals and directors, parents, teachers. However, the levels are not discrete – pedagogy manifests the values and demands of nation, community and school as well as classroom – and no level in this model can be understood fully without reference to the others, so to extract this or that policy or practice without regard to how it fits into the total picture would be ill advised.

The other variable is motive. We compare across cultures in order to illuminate and understand (the Sadler credo), to confirm our existing practices or to change them. We change in order to entrench, reform, or transform (and sometimes use one of these words when we really mean another). Thus the idea of studying other systems of education in order to find teaching strategies which will deliver those raised standards which are deemed necessary to strengthen a country's position in the global market place is worlds apart from

> Critical pedagogy [which] calls for the construction of a praxis where peripheralized peoples . . . are no longer induced to fear and obey the white Gaze of Power, where bonds of sentiment and obligation can be formed among diverse groups of oppressed peoples, where resistance can enable schools to become more than instruments of monitorization and social replication, where contrasting cultural styles and cultural capital among diverse groups cease to be tokens of estrangement . . .[66]

Again, this is a matter of choice, although I suspect that however hard a book like this tries to de-centre from its author's biography and nationality, and however strenuously it points to the damage done by the extreme forms of political centralization, domination and control to which recent English experience testifies (for that *is* one of the book's messages, and I surely don't need to labour it), and however many questions it raises about the disempowering tendencies of mainstream English pedagogy (for that is another) it will be deemed insufficiently radical. Unlike Edward Said, who writes as a self-avowed 'exile', I write about education as a citizen of a country whose imperialist past cannot but have shaped its – and my – educational present.[67] When I commend the clarity, structure, logic and communicative power of central European pedagogy at its best, although I show how alien this pedagogy is to that of my own country, and how in the wrong hands it can degenerate into something mechanical and repressive, my advocacy may read to a citizen of India or the United States as just another example of that European cultural imperialism to which the education systems of both countries have for far too long been subject.

And yet, my overriding concern with how through primary education children can be empowered (for this is the book's most fundamental message of all) surely offers a chance to reconcile some of the competing positions, since most will claim that empowerment is what they, too, are interested in.

However, for those who would like me to nominate my own empowering example among the many which are possible, let us consider one which dominated these final chapters: the pedagogy of spoken language.

In England the debates about grammar, standard English and received pronunciation continue to rage, but the UK government's literacy strategy confines knowledge about language to the relatively mechanical 'naming of parts'. As we have seen, young children in both France and Russia do not merely name parts but begin from a fairly early age to explore linguistic structure and through a disciplined approach to spoken language become aware of its possibilities for empowerment as well as for communication and self-expression. In contrast, the National Curriculum for 2000 gives language a more restricted purpose and pupils a more passive and conformist role:

> Pupils should be taught . . . to express themselves correctly and appropriately and to read accurately and with understanding . . . Pupils should be taught to recognize and use standard English.[68]

Further, the prescribed English language curriculum for the primary stage – and indeed the secondary as well – makes far less of the development of *spoken* language than do the equivalent statements in France and Russia. France's *Bâtir l'école du XXI siècle* emphasizes reading and writing but gives speaking curricular pride of place.[69] In Russia, reading, writing and talk as systematically taught aspects of the language curriculum are held in something approaching balance, and this is followed through into both formal and informal assessment (the Russian prepared oral examination has no English equivalent). This difference in emphasis is really quite striking, and it manifests itself in the characteristically episodic lesson structures with their relatively fast interactive and cognitive pace that I described earlier. The quality and power of children's spoken language gain immeasurably from this approach, as one would expect. Further, there is no evidence that the development of children's reading and writing are in any way disadvantaged as a result. On the contrary, the relationship and function of each seem to be better understood.

The status of the spoken word in English education has been a recurrent cause for concern since the 1975 Bullock Report argued the need for a policy of 'language across the curriculum' and for children to develop different registers and forms of spoken and written language to meet varying cognitive and social purposes.[70] From the late 1970s onwards, linguistic, psycholinguistic and sociolinguistic research added greatly to our understanding of how through language children learn, how the language environment of the classroom may help or hinder such learning, and what in fact children learn about the micropolitics of communication over and above what educators claim. We reviewed some of this material in Chapter 16 and during 1987–91 much of it was brought together by the National Oracy Project. This attempted to raise the profile of spoken language in schools and developed strategies to enable oral and communication skills to be taught systematically.[71]

Yet by 2000, 'language across the curriculum' had been reduced to a sparse 22 lines in the 150-page National Curriculum handbook for primary teachers, the National Oracy Project was fast becoming a mere memory of high ideals, and despite the new National Curriculum's coherent and well-founded programmes of study in 'speaking and listening' the overriding governmental emphasis on the literacy and numeracy targets effectively relegated these to quasi-optional status. Meanwhile, during 1989–91 another project – Language In the National Curriculum (LINC) – set out to provide materials to compensate for the fact that most teachers had undertaken no formal language study as part of their training. In 1991, possibly as a result of right-wing unease over the questions that it raised about 'standard' or 'correct' English, the government banned its publication.[72]

Then, as we saw in Chapters 15 and 16, pedagogic interaction and discourse in English classrooms, across all subjects, has a very different dynamic from that which we observed in France and Russia. It is relatively informal, conversational, unstructured and above all private. There is little attention to precision and appositeness in the forms of oral expression which children learn to use, and although much is made of sharing (even more in Michigan, where there is a similar problem), the implications of this collective commitment have not been followed through into a strategy for developing genuinely collective forms of talk. Close analysis of all the videotapes and transcripts from the *Five Cultures* project – which of course far exceed the few examples contained in Chapter 16 – force me unambiguously to the conclusion that in English primary classrooms, although much may be made of the importance of talk in learning, and a great deal of talking goes on, its function is seen as primarily social rather than cognitive, and as 'helpful' to learning rather than as fundamental to it.

Behind this difference – and it really is a yawning gulf between the English and central European pedagogies rather than a modest difference in emphasis – are, I think, four problems.

First, there is the hegemony of the English language itself. It is now the main international language. In 2000 there is not yet mandatory second language teaching in English primary schools – compare the situation across the rest of Europe – and outside certain concentrated urban areas where families from minority ethnic groups have settled, the vast majority of English children hear no language other than English. Even when they travel overseas on holiday, as many now do, they get by without speaking more than a few words, if that, of the language of the country they visit. This situation is not conducive to the development of children's ability to look at language objectively. In contrast, it seems likely that the reason why we found Indian primary children to be so articulate is that the linguistic limitations and restrictions within their classrooms were abundantly compensated for by the linguistic vitality outside it – a large number of languages in use, within a small area, at any one time, and a strongly oral culture.

Second, we need to remind ourselves of the legacies of nineteenth-century elementary education, one of which was the received view, up to 2000 and no doubt beyond, of what is 'basic' to the primary curriculum. The 3Rs were directed not at the social and cultural plurality that is typical of today's primary schools, but at the working classes alone; and they were devised not to liberate those working classes, but to contain them. The great fear expressed by opponents of universal public education was that it would give the masses ideas above their 'station' and empower them to question and challenge what they were expected simply to accept. Control was more effectively exercised by commanding the silent completion of mechanical reading and writing tasks than by uncorking the volatile possibilities of talk.

This imbalance was challenged as part of the 1960s progressive backlash against the elementary legacy, but the watchword then was 'informality'. Structure of any kind, including in the newly liberated oral culture of classrooms, was anathema. Informality extended from curriculum (themes and topics rather than subjects) and organization (collaborative groups rather than regimented classes), to time (variable lesson length, fluid task and lesson boundaries), personal style, and – mediating all of these – talk.[73] English primary pedagogy failed to work out a structured middle ground between silence, rote and chanting on the one hand, and easy-going chatter on the other. It was a missed opportunity of the utmost gravity.

Third, many of the English (and American) lessons shared a tendency to complexity and ambiguity in pedagogical structure and message which contrasted with the clarity and unity of organization, purpose and discourse which we frequently observed in Russia and France. This militated against considered dialogue and discussion. Thus the organizational ambience was collaborative but tasks were more usually individual. Grouping encouraged talk, but tasks were pursued through mainly written activities. Even when discussion took place it was individualistic (pupil–teacher rather than pupil–group or class) rather than collective. Pupil–teacher discourse was conversational in structure, syntax and lexis, but was managed as recitation and thus was not really conversation at all. But it was not dialogue either. And so on. Where talk in these settings was concerned, the messages of pedagogic frame, form and act spelled ambivalence or even conflict between the various elements of our model of teaching in Chapter 13.

Finally, and allied to the contradictions of conversational recitation and individualized discussion, research on the different functions of *written* and *spoken* language has not found its way into mainstream professional debate. Children spend a great deal of time writing not because they are thereby expected to acquire the distinct cognitive and linguistic capacities which writing is best suited to develop, but because there is an atavistic belief that written work is the only 'real' work.

Lexically and syntactically, written and spoken registers can take very different forms and operate in different time frames. Written English uses longer words, greater lexical variety, is more Latinate, has more nouns, passive verbs and subordinate clauses, and is more explicit and less embedded in context than talk.[74] We speak about 180 words a minute but write between 20 and 40 – typing and keying are faster. In writing our thoughts get ahead of our expression of them; in speech it is the other way round and we 'lose the thread'.[75] Oral communication relies on shared knowledge and meanings; written communication can make no such assumptions.[76]

The work of Shirley Brice Heath, and especially her study of literacy in use in one American community (Trackton), challenges the belief that writing is a prerequisite for rationality.[77] Graff provocatively itemizes this and other elements in what he calls the 'literacy myth'. Thus, literate persons are said to be empathetic, innovative, achievement-oriented, cosmopolitan, politically aware, urban and technically adaptable; and literacy is said to correlate with economic growth, productivity, political stability, participatory democracy, urbanization, consumption and contraception.

Graff cites a wide array of (mostly American) literature to show how some of these assumptions can be sustained as correlations. The relationship between increased literacy, lowered fertility and female emancipation is of clear and critical importance in India and many other countries, developed as well as developing, and it bears directly on the global imperatives which I discussed in Chapter 1. However, some of the claims in Graff's list are much less convincingly demonstrated, and a glance back at the history of the twentieth century will show that others are entirely fallacious.[78] Behind them, of course, is what Goody calls the 'grand dichotomy' (to be literate is to be civilized, to be illiterate is to be primitive). Brice Heath, too, challenges the assumption that speech is somehow a less developed or sophisticated form of language than writing:

> Instead, it seems more appropriate to think in terms of two continua, the oral and the written. Their points, and extent of overlap, and similarities in structure and function, follow one pattern for Trackton, but follow others for communities with different cultural features. And it is perhaps disquieting to think that many of these cultural features seem totally unrelated to features usually thought to help account for the relative degree of literacy in any social group.[79]

Nevertheless, there is a widely held view that the extremes of the two forms are suited to the promotion and expression of very different kinds of thinking, and what is beyond dispute is that literacy is a passport to jobs and social advancement, and that a vast array of information, and a massive amount of cultural capital of different kinds, is stored in written form. The ability to read, and to read fluently, discriminatingly and in different genres, is a truly vital skill. Of that there can be no question. In societies where literacy has acquired this kind of currency public education has no alternative but to give it the highest priority, however debatable the arguments may be about the precise relationship between literacy and cognition, and especially about the claim that literacy promotes 'higher forms' of thought.

None of this, however, justifies the downgrading of oracy for, manifestly, most human beings do more talking than writing. The 'passport' argument, when one contemplates the very different contexts and oral registers that we all encounter in a mobile and changing society, applies no less to speech than to writing. But the most immediate case for upgrading oracy in primary schools concerns the international evidence about what talking contributes to learning and understanding. The consequences of a failure to give proper attention to the management of talk in primary classrooms are evident in some of the English and American sequences in Chapter 16.

Much writing on this issue deals mainly with the *structure* of classroom talk. Because our analysis is embedded in a comprehensive account of the different elements of teaching, which in turn are related to the overall form and context of lessons, we can see that improving and exploiting classroom talk is about much more than discourse structures alone. To upgrade oracy requires changes at every level of the teaching model as I have presented it, from frame and form to act. We might, for instance, rethink curriculum specifications and rationales; change classroom organization and layout to meet the requirements of different forms of discourse, especially dialogue and discussion; rethink and adjust the balance of writing and talk in the language curriculum; redress the balance of written and oral tasks and activities across the curriculum as a whole; differentiate scholastic and conversational registers, and teach pupils to operate within different registers and codes, and to switch from one to another, as appropriate; balance collective, collaborative and individual discourse; shift from random, brief interactions to sustained and longer ones; and manage talk, and especially turn taking, in a way which enables pupils to develop ideas, raise questions and solve problems.

Coda

I have given much attention to the spoken word in this book, so let us close with some writing. Here are five short pieces, one from each of the five countries. Each was written by a nine-year-old child in a primary classroom that we visited. The pieces are presented here to discourage rather than sanction claims about comparative 'standards', which on the basis of this evidence alone would have no validity, and to allow a more suggestive, culturally engaged act of comparing. Together with the data analysis, the lesson summaries, the discourse extracts and the photographs, these brief samples offer their own intimations of how culture and pedagogy relate. It is proper that children should have the last word on this matter; but whose words are they really?

My room

My room is very important because of the privacy. It has a very happy and relaxed atmosphere, because I have a good time there with my friends and alone. I don't allow my brother in there without my permission because it's my place, not anyone else's. I let my parents in if it's tidy, but I can't really stop them. Mum comes in the most. I spend a lot of time there listening to music, drawing, writing, reading, doing homework and sleeping.

Most people think of it as a mess, but when it's tidy they really like it. My brother says my room is a mess and it's weird. Mum and Dad say it would be nice if it wasn't messy. My sister says it's like a student's room. John likes it all, except for my desk. I think he's jealous. I like my room the way it is, messy, because I feel too cramped and organized when it's tidy.

(England)

The delay

One day two childhood friends met in an aeroplane. One asked the other, 'How are you? How's business?' The other said, 'I'm fine, and so is my business. What about you?' 'I'm fine. I'm a teacher now'. The two started to recall their childhood memories. Suddenly, the air hostess said, 'The pilot cannot get the aircraft to take off. If the problem cannot be sorted out it will mean at least an hour's delay'. The men were worried because it was two o'clock in the afternoon and they were travelling from Paris to Marseilles for a meeting at 4.15. One of them fastened his safety belt, and so did the other. Monsieur Robert, the teacher, said 'As it is going to take at least an hour, we might as well unfasten our safety belts'. The air hostess served refreshments to calm down the passengers. A quarter of an hour later, sweat was pouring down their faces. At last the hostess announced, 'The plane has been repaired. We are about to take off. Please fasten your safety belts'.

(France)

Friendship

The name of my friend is Sangita.
She is studying in the same class as me.
She is the monitor.
Her mother and father are doctors.
She has three sisters.
She never comes to school in dirty clothes.
She always accompanies me to school and in the playground.
She is my neighbour.
She always does her household duties.
She has a kind nature.
She helps me with my school work.
She prays to God for a long life.

(India)

The punk

The four girls were at school. They were best friends and their names were Rachel, Sherry, Christie and Amanda. When they went outside for recess a punk named Richard and almost everybody was there, but the four girls, they weren't scared of him at all. As Richard walked over to the girls they were talking about Christmas, how Santa was real. Richard said, 'You girls are stupid believing in Santa'. 'No we're not. If you say that one more time Santa won't bring you any presents this year' said the girls. 'So. I don't get any presents any year, and I don't care' yelled Richard in a mad way. After recess Mrs Hanrahan told the class that she would be going to South Sandwich Island so there will be a substitute teacher called Miss Smith. At first the kids thought she was going to be mean. Well, when Mrs Hanrahan left Miss Smith said 'Let's party!' When she said that the class was stunned. Then the assistant principal walked in, then said, 'Miss Smith, my office, now'.

(United States)

Autumn

Autumn is the most beautiful season of the year. It is shot through with colours: red, orange, brown, green and gold. The wind tears the leaves from the trees and whirls them in the air, and at some moments it seems as if a golden bird is flying above your head. We walk between the trees and the leaves flutter down to our feet. At sunset they lie as a multicoloured carpet. Now the trees have fewer leaves. The sun emerges from time to time but it gives less and less warmth. The birds sing rarely, and the cranes have departed for warmer countries. The forest stands despondent, but fairy-beautiful. Soon the leaves will be covered with snow and we shall be left only with memories of autumn.

(Russia)

Notes

Introduction

1. DES, 1986, 1990, 1991; DfE, 1992; OFSTED, 1994.
2. Arnold, 1861, p. 109.
3. Ibid., pp. 158–9.
4. Much of the material is pulled together in the series *Education at a Glance*, most recently revised in 1998 (OECD, 1998).
5. Psacharopoulos and Woodhall, 1985; World Bank, 1990; Lockheed and Verspoor, 1991; World Bank, 2000.
6. United Nations, 1999, pp. 176–9.
7. The sequence of achievement studies conducted by the IEA and IAEP from 1960 onwards, the first, second and third international mathematics and science studies (for the third and most recent see Keys, Harris and Fernandes, 1996; Harris, Keys and Fernandes, 1997). The implications of these studies for England up to 1991 were reviewed in Alexander, Rose and Woodhead, 1992, paras 24–50; a later and more detailed analysis was undertaken by Reynolds and Farrell (1996).
8. For a critique of this line of analysis, see Alexander, 1996; Winter, 1998; Morris, 1998; Galton, 1998; Robinson, 1999.
9. The main staging posts were Alexander 1984, 1988, 1989, 1992, 1995 and 1997.
10. King, 1979.
11. Archer, 1979.
12. Green, 1990.
13. Tobin, Wu and Davidson, 1989.
14. Broadfoot and Osborn, 1993; Planel, Osborn, Broadfoot and Ward, 1998; Osborn and Planel, 1999; Broadfoot *et al.*, 2000.
15. Muckle, 1988, 1990.
16. Richards, 1990, p. 81.
17. During 1997–9 some Russian teachers were not paid their salaries for 18 months. Even a three-day strike in January 1999 failed to resolve the problem. Other public workers, and soldiers, were paid in kind (pickled vegetables, for instance). See Holdsworth, 1998, 1999; TES 1998; Pirani 1999; Womack, 1998; Lloyd, 1998.
18. Much of the classroom material from the three projects is brought together in Alexander, 1995, chs 2–6.

19. Edwards and Mercer, 1987, p. 101.
20. I have criticized the International School Effectiveness Research Project (ISERP) of David Reynolds and his colleagues (Reynolds *et al.*, 1994, 1996; Reynolds, 1999) on these grounds: Alexander 1996, 1999a.

Chapter 1. The Comparative Context

1.   Blair, 1998; Giddens, 1998.
2.   Department of Trade and Industry, 1998, p. 6.
3.   Department for Education and Employment, 1998c.
4.   Department for Education and Employment, 1988d, p. 5.
5.   Qualifications and Curriculum Authority, 1998a.
6.   Confederation of British Industry, 1998.
7.   Hobsbawm, 1987, p. 149.
8.   Colley, 1994.
9.   Hobsbawm, 1995, p. 12.
10. Cuttingly quoted and savaged by Matthew Arnold in 'The Twice-Revised Code' (Arnold, 1862).
11. Board of Education, 1931; CACE, 1967.
12. CACE, 1967, ch. 15.
13. Alexander, 1984, p. 32.
14. White, 1982, p. 203.
15. Taylor, 1969, p. 12.
16. I develop the argument about the different and sometimes competing traditions and ideologies that coexist in modern primary education, which make the hybrid metaphor particularly apposite, in Alexander, 1988, 1995.
17. It is as well to remind our selves of the depths of the ecological and political pessimism during this period, as witnessed by the phenomenal growth of the Campaign for Nuclear Disarmament (CND) and the Green movement. See, e.g., Ehrlich and Ehrlich, 1970; Ward and Dubos, 1972; Meadows *et al.*, 1972.
18. Hobsbawm, 1995, pp. 6–12.
19. See Brown, Halsey *et al.*, 1998, and Simon's detailed discussion of the five 'Black Papers' produced by an alliance of Conservatives and academics during 1969–77 (Simon, 1991, especially pp. 396–403). Some of the academics recanted when they saw how the Black Paper agenda of the 1970s translated into the Conservative education policy of the 1980s and the 1990s.
20. Giddens, 1998, pp. 28–33.
21. Bayliss, 1998, pp. 7–8, 11, 51–2.
22. United Nations, 1999, p. 63.
23. Kennedy, 1996.
24. Kennedy, 1996.
25. Landes, 1998, pp. 515, 522.
26. Giddens, 1998, pp. 54–64.
27. Landes, 1978, p. 515.
28. Landes, 1978, p. 517.
29. Hutton, 1998, p. 28.
30. Castells, 1996, 1997, 1998.
31. Summarized from Castells, 1996, pp. 1–4.

32. Notably the 1992–7 Major government's Superhighways Initiative launched throughout the UK in 1995, and the Blair government's National Grid for Learning (DfEE, 1997a, 1998e).
33. Landes, 1998; Hobsbawm, 1995.
34. Kumar, 1997.
35. Giddens, 1998, pp. 27–68.
36. Phillips, 1996.
37. In the introduction to *Literature and Dogma* (Arnold, 1873). The argument is also central to his *Culture and Anarchy* (Arnold, 1869).
38. These are summarized and discussed in Simon, 1991, pp. 396–401.
39. United Nations, 1999, pp. 134–7.
40. UNICEF, 1998.
41. IIEP, 1995.
42. UNESCO, 1999; Oxfam, 1999.
43. Oxfam, 1999.
44. Lockheed and Verspoor, 1991.
45. Sen, 1999, quoting Mahbub ul Haq, the originator of the UN's Human Development Report.
46. United Nations, 1999, pp. 134–7.
47. National Education Goals Panel 1991. Some of these goals, it has to be said, are wholly unrealistic, and both Bush's and Clinton's advisers surely knew that.
48. UNICEF, 1998, p. 34.
49. At the OECD conference *Shaping the 21st Century*.
50. Brown, 1998.
51. The most striking example of this global educational convergence is the primary curriculum, whose range and balance of subjects shows remarkable similarities across most countries for which information is available (Benavot and Kamens, 1989; Benavot *et al.*, 1991). However, as later chapters will show, such comparability at the level of curriculum labels conceals a fair degree of divergence in how each subject is perceived and enacted.
52. Raivola, 1986; Good, 1960.
53. Sadler, 1900, 1902.
54. King, 1979, pp. 31–2.
55. Phillips, 1999, p. 16.
56. Schweisfurth, 1999.
57. Crossley, 1999, p. 255.
58. Reynolds and Farrell, 1996, p. 53.
59. Holmes, 1981; Noah, 1986.
60. Reynolds and Teddlie, 1996, p. 28.
61. Ernest Boyer, reporting to the Carnegie Foundation for the Advancement of Teaching. Quoted in Noah, 1986, p. 156.
62. Precisely how each of these bears on the teacher's planning and action is examined in Alexander, 1984, pp. 114–33. The argument is taken further in a more recent publication, where I try to unpack the much used and abused term 'good' (or 'best' or 'effective') practice as it applies to teaching (Alexander, 1997, pp. 267–87). Defining good classroom practice is not merely a technical matter: it requires the reconciliation of empirical, pragmatic, political, conceptual and ethical imperatives, and in any given context this resolution may not be straightforward.

63. Broadfoot, 1999, p. 24.
64. For example, Broadfoot and Osborn, 1993; Broadfoot, 1996; Broadfoot *et al.*, 2000.
65. Watson, 1999.
66. Crossley, 1999, 2000.
67. Eurydice, 1994.
68. QCA, 1998b; UNICEF, 1998.
69. Eurydice, 1994, p. 77.
70. OECD, 1994, 1995a, 1995b.
71. OECD, 1998a, 1998b.
72. OECD, 1994, 1995a, 1995b.
73. OECD, 1995a, p. 27.
74. Reynolds and Farrell, 1996.
75. Keys, 1996a.
76. Brown, 1998. See also Keys 1996b; Tabberer and Le Métais, 1996.
77. Reynolds *et al.*, 1994.
78. Creemers, 1994a, pp. 10–11.
79. Sammons, Hillman and Mortimore, 1995.
80. Hamilton, 1996.
81. Reynolds and Teddlie, 1995; Reynolds *et al.*, 1996; Reynolds, 1999.
82. Fuller and Clarke, 1996.
83. Creemers, 1994b, 1997.
84. For a more detailed critique of this aspect, see Alexander, 1997b.
85. Watson, 1993.
86. Lockheed and Verspoor, 1991, p. 87.
87. Dearing, 1993.
88. Psacharopoulos and Woodhall, 1985; Government of India Ministry of Human Resource Development, 1993.
89. Luxton and Last, 1997; Prais, 1997; Luxton, 2000.
90. Brown, Halsey *et al.*, p. 9.
91. Levin and Kelly, p. 240.
92. Robinson, 1999.
93. Galton, 1998; Reynolds and Farrell, 1996; Keys, 1996a.
94. Alexander, 1996, 1999a.
95. In the United States, e.g., even more than the UK. The postwar panic about comparative standards started with the Sputnik episode of 1957 (Ravitch, 1983). Latterly, Americans have been no less seduced than the British by the promise of East Asian teaching methods (see, e.g., Stevenson and Stigler, 1992).
96. Tobin, 1999, p. 129.
97. Castells, 1998, pp. 161–2.

Chapter 2. Primary Education in France

1. UNICEF, 1999.
2. The statistics in the Ministry's regular publication *Géographie de l'Ecole* are presented with exemplary clarity. The question about *diversité, disparité ou inégalité*, and the reminder of the responsibility of the state in France's centralized system, come at the beginning of a 1994 issue of this publication (Ministère de l'Education Nationale, 1994).
3. *Loi d'orientation*, 1989; *Circulaire*, 15 Feb. 1990; Centre National de Documention Pédagogique, 1992.

4. Ministère de l'Education Nationale, decree 90–788, 6 Sept. 1990. See Ministère de l'Education Nationale, 1993.
5. OECD, 1998a
6. Centre National de Documention Pédagogique, 1991.
7. UNICEF, 1998b.
8. UNICEF, 1998b; Ministère de l'Education Nationale, 1993.
9. Ministère de l'Education Nationale, 1995a.
10. Ministère de l'Education Nationale, 1995a.
11. Centre National de Documention Pédagogique, 1991, pp. 29–37; Ministère de l'Education Nationale, 1995a.
12. Centre National de Documention Pédagogique, 1991, 1992b; Ministère de l'Education Nationale, 1995b.
13. For a detailed comparative study of the processes and consequences of formal assessment in France and England, see Broadfoot, 1996. The OECD review of education policy in France deems *redoublement* one of the features of the French education system that aggravates social exclusion (OECD, 1996b, pp. 173–7).
14. OECD, 1996b, pp. 43, 48.
15. Ministère de l'Education Nationale, 1998. At the time of going to press, Minister Allègre has been succeeded by former Minister of Culture Jack Lang.
16. Reboul-Scherrer, 1989, pp. 29–31.
17. Pollard, 1956; Bowen, 1981.
18. Green, 1990, p. 157.
19. Good, 1960, p. 299.
20. Reboul-Scherrer, 1989, pp. 31–2.
21. Arnold, 1861, pp. 100, 155.
22. Pollard, 1956, pp. 100–10.
23. Archer, 1979, p. 307.
24. Good, p. 301.
25. Green, 1990.
26. Jules Ferry's address of 1876, quoted by Good, 1960, p. 304.
27. Corbett, 1996; Price, 1994.
28. Prost, 1996, pp. 355–6.
29. Moon, 1996.
30. Ardagh, 1995, p. 458.
31. Centre National de Documentation Pédagogique, 1992a.
32. Centre National de Documentation Pédagogique, 1991.
33. Broadfoot *et al.*, 1993; Planel *et al.*, 1998; Osborn and Planel, 1999.
34. OECD, 1998a, pp. 292–304.
35. Castells, 1997, p. 51.
36. Ministère de l'Education Nationale, 1998. See the last part of Ch. 17.
37. Arnold, 1861, p. 152.
38. Ardagh, 1995, p. 453.
39. Arnold, 1861, p. 153.
40. Bourdieu, 1973, p. 80.
41. Beriss, 1996; Lemosse 1997.
42. Lichfield, 1999; Marshall, 1999.
43. See Harry Judge's account of the relationship between the universities and the teaching profession in France (where such relationships are usefully compared with England and the United States) in Judge, Lemosse, Paine and Sedlak, 1994, pp. 37–94. Lemosse's

account, in the same book, of his experience as a working-class French boy who – in his own words – 'crossed the enemy lines and betrayed my side' by passing a succession of stiff competitive examinations to teach at a *lycée* rather than the primary school for which he was intended, confirms the significance of status to an understanding of the workings of the French educational system.

44. Bourdieu, 1973; Bourdieu and Passeron, 1990; Finkielkraut, 1996.
45. Corbett, 1996, p. 17.
46. Meirieu, 1996.
47. Corbett and Moon, 1996, p. 47.

Chapter 3. Primary Education in Russia

1. The UN projection is from 147.7 million in 1997 to 142.9 million by 2015 (United Nations, 1999, p. 198).
2. World Bank, 2000.
3. Ibid.
4. UNICEF, 1998c.
5. World Bank, 1996.
6. World Bank, 2000.
7. Sutherland, p. 185.
8. OECD, 1998b, pp. 27–54.
9. Pirani, 1999.
10. Kerr, 1994.
11. Modified from OECD, 1998a, and UNICEF, 1998a.
12. OECD, 1998b, pp. 17–20.
13. Ministry of Education of the Russian Federation, 1993.
14. Ibid.
15. Ibid.
16. Ibid.
17. Ibid., UNICEF, 1998b.
18. Leonid Illushin, in personal correspondence.
19. UNICEF, 1998c, p. ix.
20. World Bank, 1996; OECD, 1998a.
21. Ben Eklof, at a seminar of the Study Group on Education in Russia, the Independent States and Eastern Europe, 11 Nov. 1999.
22. Lloyd, 1998, p. 442.
23. Ibid., p. xxi.
24. Ibid., p. 158.
25. Figes, 1996, p. 62.
26. Hobsbawm, 1995, p. 390.
27. Thubron, 1985, p. 37.
28. Archer, 1979, p. 284.
29. Thompson, 1994, p. 125.
30. Muckle (1988) notes that the first *gimnaziya* (based on the German *Gymnasium*) was founded in 1726.
31. 'What a miracle', says a character in *The Squire's Daughter* of his daughter's apparently rapid mastery of reading and writing, 'This is going faster than it could under the Lancasterian system'. Pushkin [1830] (1999), p. 138.
32. Johnson, 1969; Bowen, 1981.

33. Johnson, 1969, p. 34.
34. Sutherland, 1999, gives the lowest figure, which Soviet statistics revised upwards to 28 per cent. The figure of 40 per cent is from Service, 1998.
35. Education Interchange Council, 1956.
36. Figes, 1996, p. 39.
37. Medynskii, quoted in Johnson, 1969.
38. Quoted from Ignatiev, Odinetz and Novgorotsev (1929) *Russian Schools and Universities in the World War*, by Bowen, pp. 492–3.
39. Archer, 1979, pp. 300–1.
40. Sidney and Beatrice Webb visited Russian schools during this period and described them in terms – 'luxuriant experiment' . . . 'joyous bedlam' . . . neglect of discipline and 'formal lessons' – which anticipated later reactions against both American and English progressivism (Webb, 1936, p. 897).
41. Sutherland, 1999, pp. 9–10.
42. Sutherland, p. 10.
43. Vygotsky, 1962. For a comprehensive set of papers on different aspects of Vygotsky's work, see Wertsch, 1995 and Sylvia Scribner's account of the sociohistorical and Marxian dimensions of Vygotsky's psychological theory. It should be noted, however, that there are those who believe that the cultural dimension of Soviet psychology may have been overplayed, especially in the United States, to the detriment of the important experimental work of both Vygotsky and A. R. Luria. Joan Simon (1987) notes that Wertsch even seems unprepared to count Vygotsky as a psychologist. See also Bruner, 1990.
44. One of my interviewees in the *Five Cultures* project was Leontiev's son, Professor Alexei Alexeivitch Leontiev of the Russian Academy of Education.
45. Education Interchange Council, 1956.
46. Muckle, 1988, pp. 171–4, and in personal correspondence.
47. Muckle, 1988. His remains one of the fullest and most perceptive available analyses of late Soviet curriculum and pedagogy.
48. Jeanne Sutherland (1999) provides a detailed and often first-hand account of the changes from the 1980s onwards.
49. OECD, 1998b.
50. World Bank, 1996.
51. Ibid., and OECD, 1998b.
52. OECD, 1998b, p. 100.
53. As the Third International Mathematics and Science Study demonstrated (Keys, Harris and Fernandes, 1996; Harris, Keys and Fernandes, 1997).
54. UNICEF, 1998c.
55. Jones, 1994; Sutherland, 1999, pp. 131–45.
56. Jones, 1994, pp. 13–14.
57. Bronfenbrenner, 1974, p. 7.
58. James Muckle, in personal correspondence.
59. Bronfenbrenner, 1974, pp. 26–37. Bronfenbrenner's source was N. I. Boldyrev (ed.) (1960) *School Vospitanie Programme*, Moscow: Academy of Pedagogical Sciences.
60. Ministry of Education of the Russian Federation, 1993.
61. Nikandrov, 1995, and in interview.
62. Ibid., p. 51. The 'pedagogy of co-operation' was a catch-all for the experimental ideas of the 1970s and 1980s in which V. F. Shatalov, Nikandrov's fellow vice-president V. V. Davydov and others had been prominent and which led to a series of meetings

and declarations during the late 1980s. Both the Ministry and the Academy of Pedagogical Sciences resisted these.

63. Khrushchev was at that time a full member of the Politburo and of the Praesidium of
the Supreme Soviet. Mikoyan had supported Stalin against Trotsky and was one of his
chief henchmen.

64. Simon, 1981b; Alexander, 1984, pp. 9–82; Alexander, 1995, pp. 8–44, 277–88; Alexander, Rose and Woodhead, 1992, pp. 9–10. On espoused theory and theory in use, see
Argyris and Schön, 1974.

65. Sutherland, 1999.

66. Ministry of General and Professional Education, 2000.

Chapter 4. Primary Education in India

1. The figure of one billion, a threefold increase since India gained independence in 1947,
was reached in 1999.

2. UNICEF, 1999.

3. World Bank, 2000.

4. World Bank, 2000.

5. By 2000, software companies such as Wipro, Styam, Infosys and Tata Consultancy
Services were spearheading the Indian IT revolution and Wipro's chief executive, Azim
Premji, was the richest person in India and reputedly the third richest in the world.
Yet affluent Bangalore and Hyderabad, the IT centres, 'sit amid vast poverty-stricken
hinterlands, where millions of people have barely enough to eat' (Popham, 2000).

6. Paz, 1995, p. 67.

7. Government of India, 1993a, p. 12.

8. From 1981 India census data: quoted by Stern, 1993.

9. Delige, 1999.

10. The figures in these paragraphs are culled from various sources, principally: Government of India 1993a, 1998; PROBE 1999; Lockheed and Verspoor, 1991. It is a fact
of statistical life in this country of 1 billion people that different sources give different
figures, and the disparities can be considerable. For our purposes what matters is that
the scale of the basic education problem is indisputable; that it affects some groups –
rural families, girls, the urban poor, scheduled castes and scheduled tribes – much more
than others; that there are considerable geographical disparities between the extremes
of, say, high-achieving Kerala and low-achieving Rajasthan; and that the improvements
since independence are as substantial as the current figures remain dramatic.

11. Bennett, 1993, pp. 44–5. For a detailed analysis of the demography of gender and basic
education in India, allied to passionate advocacy of strategies for universalizing the
education of rural girls, see the many publications by Usha Nayar and her colleagues in
the Department of Women's Studies at the National Council of Educational Research
and Training in Delhi (e.g. Nayar, 1993).

12. PROBE, 1999, p. 39.

13. Government of India, 1993a, p. 116.

14. Little, 1995.

15. PROBE, 1999, p. 44.

16. OECD, 1998a, p. 145.

17. Government of India, 1992, paras 2.1–2.4.

18. Ibid., paras 4.1–4.14.

19. Ibid., para. 5.5.

20. Ibid., para. 5.6.
21. NCERT, 1991, p. 1.
22. NCERT, 1991, pp. 19–182.
23. 'MLLs: Meaningless Levels of Learning', in PROBE, 1999, pp. 79–80.
24. Said, 1978.
25. Landes, 1998, p. 163.
26. Ibid., p. 164.
27. Goody, 1993, p. 113.
28. Kumar, 1991, pp. 71–3.
29. Ibid.; Clarke and Fuller, 1997, p. 243.
30. Paz, 1997, p. 139.
31. I am grateful to Tony Davison (formerly of the British Council in Delhi) for first alerting me to the parallels between Vedic texts and official documents and procedures in India.
32. Neil Mercer cites another study, an unpublished Open University doctoral thesis by G. D. Jayalakshmi (in Mercer, 1995, p. 23) which traces the continuing influence of the traditional *Gurukala and Harikatha* styles of instruction and storytelling in Indian secondary classrooms. The tradition again depends on the combination of charismatic teacher authority and passive pupils. However, I should point out that some – e.g. Jean Drèze of the University of Delhi (oral communication) – caution against making too much of the argument that Brahmanic pedagogy persists in modern classroom practice, and indeed against an over-romanticized view of indigenous Indian education generally. It is true that rote learning of the kind we saw in Indian classrooms can also be seen in many other countries where very large classes make it almost inevitable. This would suggest that the impetus is as much economic as cultural. Yet for all that, the qualities of antiphony and endless chanted repetition in some of the Indian classrooms were very distinctive.
33. Nayar, 1993, pp. 13–14.
34. Stein, 1998, pp. 57–8.
35. Nayar, 1993, pp. 13–14.
36. Kumar, 1991, pp. 53–5.
37. Macaulay's 1835 Minute on Education, quoted in Paz, 1997, pp. 104–5, and in Stein, 1998, p. 266.
38. Kumar (1993, p. 73) cites Chaturvedi's *History of Rural Education in the United Province of Agra and Oudh (1840–1928)*.
39. See, e.g., King, 1979, p. 433.
40. Quoted in Paz, 1997, p. 104.
41. Quoted in Stein, 1998, pp. 265–6.
42. Scrase, 1993.
43. Stern, 1993, pp. 1–11.
44. Shotton, 1996, ch. 1.
45. Kumar, 1991.
46. Nayar, 1993, p. 15.
47. Ibid., pp. 14–16.
48. Pollard, 1956.
49. Shotton, 1996, ch. 1.
50. Government of India, 1993a, p. 9.
51. In this and the following paragraphs, I am indebted to the account of the development of Indian public education by Krishna Kumar (1991). It chimes with mainstream

accounts of colonial and postcolonial Indian history, such as that of Burton Stein (1998) but in respect of the particular matter of education he lays greater stress than many on the intertwining not just of colonial and postcolonial, but of these together with pre-colonial forms of education and the disparate strands in the Independence movement. The result is an illuminating parallel to the essentially conflictual model of the development of English primary education that I ventured in Alexander, 1984, 1989.

52. Government of India, 1993a, pp. 9–10; Government of India, 1992, p. 9.
53. Government of India, 1993a, p. 13.
54. Government of India, 1993a; NCERT, 1986.
55. OECD, 1998a, pp. 292–304.
56. Morris, 1977.
57. NCERT, 1991.
58. PROBE, 1999, p. 138.
59. Kumar, 1991, pp. 71–93.
60. PROBE, 1999, pp. 83–94.
61. Government of India, 1998a, 1998b.
62. See, e.g., Government of India, 1998c, 1998d, 1998e.
63. PROBE, 1999, p. 12.
64. Professor Ambasht of NCERT offered me two indicative statistics: in 1994, 1 per cent of wage earners in India were aged 5–9 years; 8 per cent were aged 10–14. The scale of the problem is also documented in Castells, 1998, pp. 143–65.
65. PROBE, 1999.
66. Nayar, 1989, 1993.
67. Nautiyal, 1993. He reports, *inter alia*, that in 1985–6 one half of the population of Delhi lived in extreme poverty, and that in 1991, 90 per cent of Delhi illiterates were slum dwellers. He also replicates, in the urban context, the PROBE claim that lack of parental interest is a myth: his own research showed that many parents of urban slum children wanted their children to be educated but this was frustrated by a combination of poor facilities, negative teacher attitudes and a culturally alienating curriculum.
68. From M. C. Chagla's autobiography *Roses in December*. For this quotation I am grateful to Dr K. Gopalan, formerly director of NCERT and Vice-Chancellor of Cochin University of Science and Technology.

Chapter 5. Primary Education in the United States of America

1. O'Donnell *et al.*, 1998; Crystal, 1990. The O'Donnell publication is a CD produced for the UK Qualifications and Curriculum Authority by the National Foundation for Educational Research: one of the new wave of international education databases.
2. World Bank, 2000.
3. OECD, 1998b.
4. *Education Week*, 2000.
5. US Bureau of the Census figures, quoted by McKay, 1994, UNICEF, 1999, and O'Donnell *et al.*, 1998. Here, as elsewhere in my search for reliable statistics on each of the five countries, I have encountered considerable differences between supposedly authoritative sources. It baffles me somewhat that in a country as thoroughly documented as the United States it is possible to find one authority claiming that there are 15,000 school districts while another, at the same point in time, claims 16,000. Similarly, the number of public elementary schools in the United States is apparently somewhere

between 60,000 and 80,000. Maybe it is possible in a decentralized system simply to mislay 20,000 schools.

6. Joseph Zimmerman, quoted by McKay, 1994, pp. 61–2.
7. Cohen and Spillane, 1993.
8. Lansing School District, 1994a, 1994b; Holt School District, 1994; Flint School District, 1994.
9. National Commission on Excellence in Education, 1983.
10. This is the final version, as signed into law on 31 March 1994, of Section 102 of the *Goals 2000: Educate America Act*.
11. Michigan State Board of Education, 1994.
12. State of Michigan, 1996. As this material is also available on the Michigan State Department of Education website, I rechecked for an update just before going to press. Curiously, the most recent report on the state's progress towards the National Education Goals was still that dated 1996.
13. See examples from Kentucky, Maryland, Massachusetts and Wisconsin in O'Donnell *et al.*, 1998.
14. Michigan State Board of Education, 1994.
15. UNICEF, 1998b.
16. Michigan State, 1995.
17. O'Donnell *et al.*, 1998.
18. O'Donnell *et al.*, 1998. They state that elementary school lessons last for 45 minutes. I witnessed no such standardization, and few lessons of that length. See chs 9, 12.
19. Lansing School District, 1994a, 1994b; Flint School District, 1994; Holt School District, 1994.
20. OECD, 1998a.
21. Archer, 1979, p. 248.
22. Freedland, 1998.
23. Young, 1932, pp. 89–95.
24. Bowen, 1981, pp. 270–1.
25. Ibid., p. 268. The relationship between literacy and Protestantism is historically extremely important, though in some countries (Germany and Sweden, for example) more than in others (Graff 1991).
26. Good, 1960, p. 393.
27. Thomas Jefferson, writing from Paris in 1785 (quoted by Bowen, 1981, p. 277).
28. Green, 1990, pp. 171–207.
29. Graff, 1991, pp. 251–2.
30. Green, 1990, pp. 171–207.
31. See McCrum, Cran and MacNeil, 1992. Webster's efforts to have every syllable fully articulated influenced published readers and primers for generations. The hugely successful McGuffey series, for example, contains long lists of exercises for children to work at daily: 'ev-*er*-y', 'be-lief', 'trav-*e*-ler', 'his-*to*-ry', 'rhet-o-ric', 'si-lent', for example, rather than 'ev'ry', 'b'lief', 'trav'ler', 'hist'ry', 'rhet-*er*-ic', 'si-l*u*nt'. These examples are from the 1897 edition of *McGuffey's Fourth Eclectic Reader*, now available in facsimile.
32. Green, 1990, pp. 187–8.
33. de Beauvoir, 1954, pp. 273, 302.
34. Dewey, 1900, p. 173.
35. Quoted in Ravitch, 1983, p. 59.
36. In a letter to Edmund King: King, 1979, p. 343.

37. Ibid., pp. 43–4, 79.
38. Ibid., pp. 89–110.
39. The literature is extensive, and had its counterpart during the 1960s and the 1970s in the UK. Key texts were Ralph Tyler's *Basic Principles of Curriculum and Instruction*, and the mighty Bloom taxonomies of educational objectives, which started confidently in the 'cognitive domain', looked less assured in the 'affective' and terminally ill-conceived in the 'psycho-motor'. See, e.g., Tyler, 1950; Bloom, 1956.
40. Ravitch, 1983, p. 78.
41. Chafe, 1995, p. 175.
42. Indeed, even during the post-Thatcher 1990s I still occasionally received requests from US teachers' colleges for advice about which Oxfordshire schools they should visit to see British open education in action. They received my accounts of the National Curriculum, national tests, national testing, naming and shaming, league tables and so on with stunned disbelief.
43. Alexander, 1984, p. 9.
44. See, e.g., Silberman, 1973.
45. National Commission on Excellence in Education, 1983.
46. For example, Stevenson and Stigler, 1992.
47. McKay, 1993.
48. Kirst, 1995, p. 31. The argument about WASP hegemony in the United States is taken further by Green, 1990, pp. 171–207, and can be compared with the Bowles and Gintis (1976) thesis – referred to earlier in this chapter – about the congruence of schooling and capitalism.
49. Ibid., p. 25.
50. Ibid., pp. 50–2.
51. Goertz *et al.*, 1995; Floden, 1997.
52. State of Michigan, 1993, Section 1279c.
53. Ibid., Section 5(5).
54. I suppose I should follow Webster and Americanize this spelling, especially as an American is talking. My prerogative: I like to be reminded of All Hallows Even.
55. Freedland, 1998.
56. As summarized in Archer, 1979, p. 616.
57. United Nations, 1999, p. 149.
58. Figures from US official statistics quoted by McKay, 1993, pp. 17–27.
59. Michigan State Department of Education, 2000 (website last updated 1996).
60. United States Department of Education, 2000a.
61. United States Department of Education, 2000b (last updated 1995).

Chapter 6. Primary Education in England

1. World Bank, 2000.
2. In 1997–9, the UK government legislated for devolution of a limited range of powers to Scotland and Wales, and with the cessation of hostilities in Northern Ireland the Assembly at Stormont (suspended in 1973 at the height of the troubles) was reopened. At the time of going to press it has been suspended again.
3. OECD, 1996, p. 331.
4. O'Donnell *et al.*, 1998.
5. Ibid. The same claim is made in UNCEF, 1988, and Eurydice, 1994, using statements provided by the UK government.

6. In 1997 England had 6,585 voluntary (religious) primary schools: 4,615 Church of England, 1,854 Roman Catholic, 30 Methodist, 18 Jewish and 68 of other religions, including Islam (O'Donnell *et al.*, 1998).
7. School Standards and Framework Act 1998.
8. Figures from OFSTED, 1999c.
9. DES, 1978a.
10. A 1999 OFSTED survey raised concerns about the adequacy of provision for children from Bangladeshi, Pakistani and Caribbean backgrounds (OFSTED, 1999a).
11. O'Donnell *et al.*, 1998.
12. The push to secure specialist subject co-ordination alongside generalist primary teaching was initiated by the national inspectorate in DES, 1978b. Despite the progressive institutionalization of the role, it was still, in 1998, highly problematic in terms of expertise, time and resources (Alexander, 1998).
13. OECD, 1998a, gives the following national percentages of women primary teachers: England 90, Denmark 62, Canada 67, France 77, United States 86. The proportion of male teachers is significantly higher in many poorer countries – only 30 per cent of primary teachers in India, for example, are female. However, the OECD figure of 90 per cent for England is so markedly different from the 84 per cent given by UK government sources for UK consumption that one wonders how much credence can be attached to any of these statistics.
14. Blyth, 1965a, p. 152.
15. Figures from DES, 1982 and OFSTED, 1999c.
16. DfEE, 1997c.
17. Education Act 1996, Section 351.
18. DfEE/QCA, 1999, pp. 12–13.
19. DfEE/QCA, 1999, pp. 11–12.
20. DfEE, 1997c.
21. DfEE 1998a, 1998b.
22. DfEE/QCA, 1999, pp. 16–19.
23. DfEE/QCA, 1999, pp. 136–41.
24. Dearing, 1993.
25. O'Donnell *et al.*, 1999.
26. See, e.g., OFSTED, 1999b.
27. Two characteristic comments on late Victorian complacency in the face of Germany's economic power have come my way. One is Brian Simon's account of his German grandfather Henry (Heinrich) Simon's celebrated 'practical man' speech in Manchester in 1898, when he berated British industrialists for presuming that they could maintain British market supremacy by their wits and experience alone, and without investing heavily in science and technology (Simon 1997). The other is an example of just this attitude in one of Henry Simon's contemporaries. Birmingham industrialist John Shakespeare Manton records visiting German factories in 1876 'to find out whether the superiority of German machines and German mechanics were fact or fable' but announces 'I had seen many things of great interest, but I did not see the superiority of the German over the British mechanic, for it does not exist . . . The Germans took advantage of our Free Trade and built a wall of protection around themselves, but they could not beat us . . .' (and more in this vein) (Manton, 1912).
28. Graff, 1987, pp. 50–2.
29. Ibid., pp. 66–73.
30. Lawson and Silver, 1973, pp. 44–5.

31. Graff, 1987, p. 105.
32. Ibid., pp. 99–106.
33. Ibid., pp. 108–72.
34. Simon, 1966.
35. Lawson and Silver, 1973, pp. 101–2.
36. Quoted in Cressy, 1980, p. 20.
37. Blyth, 1965b, pp. 20–35.
38. For a detailed accounts of Comenius's visit to England and assessment of his influence on events leading up to the establishment of the Royal Society, see Young, 1932 and Sadler, 1966.
39. Green, 1990, p. 239.
40. Graff, 1987, pp. 230–48. Graff notes that evidence on literacy levels became more reliable after the 1754 Marriage Act, which required brides and bridegrooms to sign marriage registers. Study of these registers by Schofield and others has yielded what look like very precise figures broken down by locality and occupation. It seems reasonable to ask, however, what level of literacy is indicated by the ability to sign one's name. On the pros and cons of this measure, see also Cressy, 1980, ch. 3.
41. Butler, 1984.
42. Paine, 1792, pp. 297–8.
43. Mary Wollstonecraft, in *A Vindication of the Rights of Women* (Butler, 1984, pp. 76–7).
44. See the second volume of Richard Holmes' magnificent biography of Coleridge (Holmes, 1998, pp. 130–2, 441).
45. Simon, 1974, especially pp. 17–71.
46. In Butler, 1984, pp. 179–84.
47. 'James Bonwick – an octogenarian's reminiscences', in Burnett, 1982, pp. 171–6.
48. Holmes, 1998, pp. 130–2.
49. Blyth, 1965b, p. 36.
50. Thompson, 1991, pp. 857–87.
51. Ibid., pp. 806–7.
52. Ibid., pp. 783, 806–50.
53. Simon, 1974, pp. 223–70.
54. Ibid., pp. 151–2.
55. In 1999 the spectre of 'payment by results' was frequently evoked by the teaching unions to signal their unease with the government's proposals to link teachers' pay to appraisal of their performance, to reward 'superteachers' and to institute a School Performance Award Scheme (DfEE, 1999a).
56. Arnold, 1862, p. 220.
57. Ibid., pp. 223–4.
58. Ibid., p. 231.
59. Alexander, 1999b, p. 154.
60. Quoted in Selleck, 1972, p. 53. In Alexander, 1984, pp. 1–20, I cite other examples of what became the received view of board schools among primary educationists during the mid twentieth century.
61. Burnett, 1982, pp. 157–70.
62. The passage of the 1902 Act, and the controversies surrounding it, are described in Simon, 1965.
63. *Secondary Education for All*, quoted in Simon, 1974, p. 27.
64. Board of Education, 1927.
65. Simon, 1974, pp. 139–41.

66. Board of Education, 1931.
67. Simon, 1992, citing the Chief Inspector of Schools of the day, Miss A. L. Murton.
68. I examine critically the false dichotomies of progressivism in Alexander 1984, and the characteristics and functions of what I call 'primaryspeak', with its heavy use of slogans and shibboleths, in Alexander, 1995, pp. 8–44.
69. Simon, 1974, pp. 240–50. Simon has consistently provided the most detailed critiques of the models of human intelligence, and the regimes of intelligence testing, which dominated the schooling of older primary children until the late 1960s.
70. Sharp and Green, 1975; King, 1978; Alexander, 1984, pp. 21–47; Alexander, 1997, pp. 11–26.
71. For a study of the postwar progressive network see Cunningham, 1988.
72. CACE, 1967.
73. Notably from Brian Jackson and Brian Simon: see Jackson's classic and influential 1964 study, and Simon, 1991, pp. 342–69, for an account of the campaign which persuaded the Plowden Committee to rule against streaming at the primary stage. Simon's autobiography (Simon 1998) takes the story further, and provides first-hand accounts of life for teachers and pupils in streamed inner-city primary schools in the 1940s and the 1950s and of his debate with Plowden Committee member and distinguished analytical philosopher A. J. Ayer.
74. CACE, 1967.
75. I have examined these strands in some detail in Alexander, 1995, pp. 277–88. See also Selleck, 1972; Cunningham, 1988.
76. The key documents here are the 'Black Papers' published during the late 1960s and the early 1970s (Cox and Dyson, 1971, 1975). For a detailed account of the growing polarization of educational debate, and the part in this played by the Black Paper authors, see Simon, 1991, pp. 405–71.
77. In 1975, the extreme form of progressivism in London's William Tyndale school prompted parental protest, press 'outrage' and a judicial enquiry: see White, 1977.
78. The *Daily Telegraph*, 19 Sept. 1991. The media's handling of the Leeds report and of the subsequent 'three wise men' government initiative are discussed in Alexander, 1997, pp. 183–266; Wallace, 1993; Woods and Wenham, 1995.
79. Alexander, Rose and Woodhead, 1992, p. 9. This, the so-called 'three wise men report', drew on research and inspection evidence. The first full conceptual critique of Plowden was provided by R. S. Peters and his colleagues at the London Institute of Education (Peters, 1968). The main empirical studies of primary teaching and learning during this period were: Bennett, 1976; Galton and Simon, 1980a, 1980b; Bennett *et al.*, 1984; Mortimore *et al.*, 1988; Tizard *et al.*, 1988; Alexander 1992. The question of whether there really was an English primary progressive 'revolution' is examined in Simon, 1980, 1991; also in Alexander, 1984.
80. The final report on the Leeds research is in Alexander, 1992 (revised edn 1997). The project's contributory studies appear in Alexander, Willcocks and Kinder, 1989; Alexander, 1995, chs 3, 4.
81. House of Commons, 1999a, pp. 67–76.
82. The 'three wise men' of Alexander, Rose and Woodhead, 1992, were the author, the Chief Inspector for Primary Education (Jim Rose), and the Chief Executive of the National Curriculum Council (Chris Woodhead). Woodhead went on to become Chief Inspector and head of OFSTED, with Rose as his deputy. The full text of the Leeds report which prompted this initiative, together with an account of its impact and the 'three wise men' sequel, appear in Alexander, 1997.

83. DfEE, 1998a, 1998b.
84. Haviland, 1988.
85. Simon, 1991, pp. 538–49.
86. Archer, 1979. See discussion of her thesis in Ch. 7.
87. The relationship between education, government and the press during 1975–2000 is a story requiring its own separate book. Two cases are provided in Alexander, 1997, and independent commentary on the same episodes is provided by Wallace, 1993, and by Woods and Wenham, 1995.
88. The entire seven-element schema was first set out and applied in a chapter I contributed to Blyth, 1988. The piece is reprinted in revised form in Alexander, 1995, pp. 8–44.
89. Board of Education, 1931, pp. 13–14; CACE, 1967, para. 1170; House of Commons, 1986, paras 9.30, 9.32; Alexander, Rose and Woodhead, 1992, paras 4, 149; House of Commons, 1994a, 1994b.
90. Alexander, Rose and Woodhead, 1992, paras 139–50; Alexander, 1998b, pp. 6–13, 79–86; see also 'specialists in a generalist culture', in Alexander, 1984, pp. 186–93.
91. The Curriculum I/II idea is argued fully in Alexander, 1984, pp. 48–82.
92. Alexander, 1998b, p. 85.
93. Phillips, 1996, p. 219.
94. Castells, 1997.
95. Colley, 1996.
96. Stein Ringen, quoted in Cannadine, 1998, p. ix.
97. Smelser, 1991.
98. Ibid., p. 362.
99. Ibid., p. 368.
100. For example: Douglas 1964; Halsey, Floud and Anderson, 1961; Halsey and Ridge, 1980; Halsey, 1995.
101. Cannadine, 1998, p. 164.
102. Ibid., p. 89.
103. Sharp and Green, 1975.
104. King, 1978.
105. Alexander, Willcocks and Kinder, 1989, pp. 25–86.
106. Woodhead, 1996.
107. In 1986 the Commons Select Committee calculated that England's 20,000 primary schools needed some 15,000 additional teachers to manage the curriculum more effect- ively by using co-ordinators – that is, one extra teacher for all but the smallest schools. This was before the introduction of the national curriculum and was hardly a radical proposal, since it merely glossed a procedure that had been recommended by HMI in 1978. Secretary of State Keith Joseph accepted the calculation, but was removed from his post before he had time to implement it (House of Commons, 1986; DES, 1978b).
108. The 1992 'three wise men' report commended schools to consider a wider range of teaching roles than class teacher and curriculum co-ordinator, to the extent of exploring the possibility of introducing some specialist and semi-specialist teaching. Many teachers objected to extending the teaching vocabulary in this way on the grounds that it struck at very the heart of primary education. It is easy to forget that the original rationale for the class teacher system was financial, not educational.

Chapter 7. Primary Education and the State

1. With the passage of time it is perhaps necessary to note that this was Margaret Thatcher talking (or hectoring) (Young, 1989, p. 490).

2. I have questioned the continuing hegemony of the Victorian concept of 'basics' in England, and for my pains have incurred the ridicule of the chief inspector of schools and the tabloid press. See Alexander, 1998a; Woodhead, 1998; Halpin, 1998.

3. Hobsbawm, 1995, p. 522.

4. England's nine and thirteen year olds performed well in comparison with other countries in the Third International Mathematics and Science Study: at age nine the mean scores for English pupils were significantly lower than only three of the other 25 countries; at age thirteen England came fourth out of the 14 Western European TIMSS countries and first out of the six English-speaking countries (Harris, Keys and Fernandes, 1997; Keys, Harris and Fernandes, 1996).

5. Benavot et al., 1989, 1991.

6. Education Act 1996; Centre National de Documention Pédagogique, 1991.

7. QCA, 1998b. Bernard Crick chaired the government's advisory group on citizenship that produced this report.

8. DfEE/QCA, 1999.

9. Eurydice, 1994; O'Donnell et al., 1998.

10. The House of Commons Education Sub-Committee set up an enquiry on the work of OFSTED in 1998 (House of Commons, 1999).

11. Michael Eraut and his colleagues made this important distinction in the 1970s (East Sussex, 1979). Their model is applied in the context of primary education in Alexander, 1984, pp. 170–2.

12. World Bank, 2000, p. 124.

13. Dale, 1997.

14. World Bank, 2000, pp. 216–7.

15. OECD, 1998b, pp. 292–304.

16. Archer, 1979.

17. Ibid., p. 217.

18. Ibid., p. 278.

19. Ibid., p. 616.

20. Ibid., p. 784.

21. For example, King, 1979b; Anderson, 1986.

22. Green, 1990, pp. 26–75.

23. Ibid., p. 77.

24. Ibid., p. 81.

25. Ibid., pp. 111–70.

26. Ibid., pp. 171–207.

27. Ibid., pp. 208–307.

28. Williams, 1976, p. 76.

29. Althusser, 1972.

30. Bowles and Gintis, 1976.

31. Bourdieu and Passeron, 1977.

32. Ibid., pp. 71–139.

33. Bernstein, 1971, 1975, 1990.

34. Giroux, 1999, p. 100.

35. Macedo, 1999.

36. Giroux, 1983, p. 84.

37. Apple, 1995, pp. xi, 35.

38. Giroux, 1997, p. 128. See also Giroux, 1999.

39. Archer, 1989, p. 178.

40. In 1998–9 there was a surge of publications on the theme of British – and especially English – identity. Compare, e.g., Paxman, 1998; Heffer, 1999; Kidd, 1999; Collini, 1999; Hall and Du Gay, 1996. One common theme is the strength and vitality of those cultures – Scottish, Irish, Welsh – which have been historically subjugated and exploited by England, in comparison with England itself.
41. Hobsbawm, 1995, p. 3.
42. Castells, 1996, p. 3.
43. Ibid., p. 4.
44. Castells, 1997; West, 1997; Hall and Du Gay, 1996.
45. PROBE, 1999.
46. I referred in Ch. 1 to Patricia Broadfoot's hierarchical classification of comparative studies, from (1) single site descriptions through (2) contextualized case studies, (3) more systematic empirical studies, and (4) theoretically-informed studies to studies which are more about theory-generation than comparison (Broadfoot, 1999, pp. 22–7).

Chapter 8. Buildings and People

1. The School Inspections Act 1996 states that 'Special measures are required to be taken in relation to a school if the school is failing or likely to fail to give its pupils an acceptable standard of education' (OFSTED, 1999d, p. 166).
2. CACE, 1967.
3. Sammons, Hillman and Mortimore, 1995; Creemers, 1997.
4. DfEE, 1997c, p. 12.
5. In the Leeds Report of 1991: Alexander, 1991, paras 8.32–8.42; Alexander, 1997, pp. 159–63.
6. Government of India, 1993, p. 116. The 1986 figures were 13.54 per cent without buildings, 13.92 per cent with *kachha* (makeshift) buildings and 72.54 per cent with *pucca* (permanent) or partly *pucca* buildings. The District Primary Education Programme (DPEP) has had an appreciable impact on school buildings, in respect of quality as well as number. By 1998, 4,500 new schools and 5,000 additional classrooms had been built in the seven DPEP states (Government of India, 1998d).
7. The important distinction between seating groups and working groups was first noted in the ORACLE project in the mid 1970s (Galton and Simon, 1980a). Subsequent studies replicated the ORACLE finding that children in English primary schools tend to sit *in* groups but work relatively rarely *as* groups (Mortimore *et al.*, 1988; Alexander, 1995, 1997; Galton *et al.*, 1999).
8. Galton *et al.*, 1999, pp. 85–7.
9. For example, Schweisfurth, 1999b; Muckle, 1988; Education Interchange Council, 1956. Brian Simon noted that our Russian classroom photographs taken in the mid 1990s could without the slightest adjustment have been exchanged for those he and Joan Simon took in the mid 1950s. This observation is important because it confirms not only the historical continuity in Russian pedagogy but also its geographical consistency.
10. DfEE, 1998b; Luxton and Last, 1997; Prais, 1997; Luxton, 2000.
11. McNamara and Waugh, 1993; McNamara, 1994.
12. Alexander, 1995, pp. 53–61; Galton *et al.*, 1999, pp. 39–55.
13. Jackson, 1968, p. 5.
14. Ibid., pp. 10, 33–4.
15. Taylor *et al.*, 1974.
16. Alexander *et al.*, 1989, pp. 161–90; Alexander, 1997, pp. 113–19.

17. Campbell, 1985.
18. Alexander, 1998b.
19. Holmes Group, 1986, 1990, 1995.
20. OFSTED, 1999c, p. 18.
21. Flint Community Schools, 1994a
22. Flint Community Schools, 1994b.
23. Centre Nationale de Documentation Pédagogique, 1991.
24. DfEE, 1997c, p. 7.
25. Ibid., p. 39.
26. Alexander, 1994, pp. 156–60.
27. DES, 1978b.
28. This management typology is set out in detail in Alexander, 1997, pp. 119–20.

Chapter 9. The Idea of a School

1. Argyris and Schön, 1974.
2. Alexander, 1988.
3. Especially in Alexander, 1984, chs 1–3. 'Primaryspeak' is coined as a label and discussed as to its functions, in Alexander, 1995, ch. 1, and Alexander, 1988.
4. Alexander, 1995, pp. 8–44. This study was originally reported in Blyth, 1988, pp. 148–88. My co-researcher on this project was Kay Kinder.
5. Alexander, 1995, pp. 261–4, contrasts the dominant dilemmas of primary teachers in 1986, 1988 and 1992 – i.e. before and after the introduction of the national curriculum.
6. Tönnies, 1887.
7. Broadfoot *et al.*, 1993, 2000.
8. In Judge, Lemosse, Paine and Sedlak, 1994, pp. 47–54.
9. Ardagh, 1995, p. 488.
10. Montaigne: Essais, Book 1, ch. 25: 'Je voudrais aussi qu'on fût soigneux de lui choisir un conducteur qui eût plutôt la tête bien faite que bien pleine et qu'on y requît tous les deux mais plus les moeurs et l'entendement que la science'. In the typically embroidered Florio translation of 1603 Montaigne desires parents to be 'very circumspect and careful in chusing' their son's tutor, 'whom I would rather commend for having a well composed and temperate braine, than a full stuft head, yet both will doe well. And I would rather prefer wisdome, judgement, civill customes, and modest behaviour, than bare and meere literall learning' (Florio, [1603], pp. 154–5).
11. Holmes Group, 1990.
12. Here I have supplemented the *Five Cultures* data with material on primary school subject co-ordinators from one of my concurrent projects (Alexander, 1998b).
13. Williams, 1976, p. 75–6.
14. Muckle, 1988, p. 176.
15. These correspondences are close but certainly not exact. I would certainly not wish to imply that *culture* in the English sense is synonymous with *culture générale*, still less with *kultura*.
16. The contrasting levels of concern with violence in the Russian and American schools in the 1990s can usefully be compared with the differences in the behaviour of Russian and American children which Urie Bronfenbrenner noted in the 1960s (Bronfenbrenner, 1974). The seventh of *Goals 2000* reflects this concern.
17. See p. 71, and Johnson, 1969, pp. 237–47.
18. See p. 70.

Chapter 10. Beyond the Gates

1. Alexander, 1997, pp. 99–107.
2. Saldanha, 1993, 1995.
3. Bronfenbrenner, 1974.
4. Department of Education and Science, 1991b.
5. The head is referring to the UK government's 1997 literacy and numeracy targets, which aimed to take 80 per cent of 11 year olds to Level 4 (the mid-point on the scale for 5–16 year olds) in mathematics, and 75 per cent to Level 4 in reading, by 2002. Her argument is that Level 4 had become an obsession, and nobody was interested in the strides schools in less advantaged areas had made in bringing children up to test levels below Level 4. The 'value added' reference is to the plea schools and academics made after test results were first published for parallel information to be made available about the starting point from which schools had moved and the amount of 'value' which they had added, on the assumption that achieving the government's Level 4 targets would be considerably easier for teachers at, say, Hamilton, than at St Teresa's or Cheetham.
6. Alexander, 1997, p. 61.
7. Department for Education and Empoyment, 1999b.
8. Hartley-Brewer, 1999.
9. CACE, 1967.
10. For an account of the *cycles* see pp. 53–4 and Centre Nationale de Documentation Pédagogique, 1991.
11. Sharpe, 1997, later incorporated in Broadfoot *et al.*, 2000.
12. For discussion of the Minimum Levels of Learning see p. 96 and NCERT, 1991.
13. Government of India, 1993b.
14. Michigan State Department of Education, 1994; Lansing School District, 1994a; Michigan State Department of Education, 1996.
15. Kirst, 1995.
16. Reese, 1995.
17. McKay, 1994.
18. Dearing, 1993.
19. The Audit Commission (1989) managed to predict an optimistic future for LEAs in the era of budgetary delegation to schools and government control of curriculum and assessment.
20. As noted by the House of Commons Select Committee Enquiry set up in 1988 to investigate OFSTED: House of Commons, 1999a, paras 214–27.
21. Ibid., pp. 67–76.
22. House of Commons, 1999b. The tone of the government's response, and of OFSTED's (which appears in the same volume) is arrogantly dismissive. The committee's more serious and closely argued reservations, grounded in a large body of evidence drawn from different professional and political constituencies, are either airily waved away or ignored. Although New Labour would not care to admit it, their handling of this matter is almost identical to the way their Conservative predecessors dealt with the massive chorus of concern about the national curriculum in 1987–8. By the end of the twentieth century the symptoms of government abuse of its powers within a newly centralized education system were very evident.
23. See the discussion on pp. 163–6 of Gramsci on hegemony; Bowles, Gintis, Bourdieu, Passeron and Bernstein on cultural reproduction; Apple and Giroux on resistance.

24. Doyle and Ponder, 1977; Campbell and Neill, 1994; Pollard and Broadfoot, 1997; Galton and Fogelman, 1998.
25. For example, Ardagh, 1995, pp. 452–93.
26. New criteria for accrediting four-year and one-year teacher training courses, each set superseding the previous one, were promulgated by the UK government in 1984, 1989, 1992, 1993, 1996 and 1998 (DES, 1984, 1989; DFE, 1992b, 1993; DfEE, 1996; TTA, 1998). On each occasion government justified the changes on the grounds that courses were not good enough. In fact the timescale made a proper judgement on this matter impossible, especially for four-year courses. In any case, by the 1990s the government's consistently negative claims about the state of teacher training had to be a comment on their own criteria and procedures as much as the courses themselves, for by then all the courses were run in accordance with government requirements and all had been inspected and accredited by government agencies. Naturally, this did not stop them from blaming the teacher training providers for most that was wrong with schools.

Chapter 11. Comparing Teaching

1. These figures are intended to make a point about the scale of the country's teaching operations. The exact figures are difficult and perhaps impossible to ascertain, since although the school year is fixed at 190 days and the government recommends minimum weekly lesson times (21 hours for five to seven year olds and 23.5 hours for seven to eleven year olds) many schools exceed these minima (OECD, 1998, pp. 281–4; O'Donnell *et al.*, 1998). Moreover, I have perhaps arbitrarily treated a lesson as a one-hour session. But though difficult to pin down, the figures here are unlikely to be seriously inaccurate.
2. Geertz, 1973. Joseph Tobin, whose own three-culture study of pre-school education is a worthy example to emulate, argues that ethnography merits the name only if it satisfies two conditions: first it should entail the researcher's studying in depth, *in situ*, and ideally over a sustained period of time, a culture other than his or her own; second, it must generate an encounter between the understandings of the insider and the out-sider (i.e. the researcher). Tobin *et al.*, 1989; Tobin, 1999, pp. 122–5.
3. Reynolds and Farrell, 1996, pp. 52–9.
4. Stevenson and Stigler, 1992; HMI, 1992; Thomas and Postlethwaite, 1983; Smithers and Robinson, 1991; Prais and Wagner, 1965; Bierhoff, 1996; Bierhoff and Prais, 1996; Burghes, 1995.
5. The concept of 'best' (or 'good') practice is discussed in detail in Alexander, 1997, pp. 267–87. The term is never other than saturated with all kinds of values, so when governments, government agencies or local education authorities prescribe the versions of teaching which schools should adopt they run the risk of reducing the complexities of pedagogy to the mere exercise of power politics.
6. Tobin *et al.*, 1989. For the authors' discussion of typicality and an account of audience reactions to their single-school case material, see pp. 7–8 (general), 82–3, 109–22 (China), 44–57 (Japan) and 168–78 (United States).
7. Woods and Jeffrey, 1996, p. 5 (in the context of their case, following Elliot Eisner, that teaching is an art).
8. Gage, 1978, p. 34.
9. Pollard, 1985; Pollard *et al.*, 1994; Pollard and Filer, 1999; Doddington, Flutter and Ruddock, 1999.
10. See, e.g., Dunkin and Biddle's influential study (Dunkin and Biddle, 1974).
11. Gage, 1978.

12. As in the 1995 OFSTED review of school effectiveness research (Sammons, Hillman and Mortimore, 1995), or the various edited collections from the International School Effectiveness Research Project (e.g. Reynolds *et al.*, 1994, 1996).

13. As used in the Barking and Dagenham primary mathematics programme or the UK government's literacy and numeracy strategy (Luxton and Last, 1997; Luxton, 2000; DfEE, 1998a, 1998b).

14. See Chs 5 and 6, pp. 111–14, 137–41.

15. In Alexander, 1984, pp. 13–20, I noted some typical 1970s sentiments on this score. In one, primary teaching was characterized in terms of 'the rhythm of work . . . an ebb and flow between the material and the processes of sketching, observing, looking for references . . . This gives a sensual base to the educational process, where concentration on increasing awareness and sensitivity is a priority . . . No need for the externally-imposed authority of the teacher' (Marsh, 1973, p. 14).

16. Reynolds, 1999b.

17. After the 1997 general election Reynolds became the UK government's chief academic adviser on pedagogical matters. Government publications on the teaching of literacy and numeracy in primary schools then gave attention to school effectiveness research out of proportion to either its scale or significance (e.g. DfEE, 1997b). Elsewhere Reynolds claimed that only American research on teaching has anything to offer to British teachers (Reynolds, 1999b; Reynolds and Lawlor, 1999).

18. Eisner, 1969, 1979, 1985.

19. Eisner, 1979, pp. 153–5.

20. Ibid., p. 155.

21. Gage, 1978. See also Simon 1985, p. 99; Galton *et al.*, 1999, pp. 183–5.

22. Alexander, Rose and Woodhead, 1992, para. 101.

23. Woods, 1996; Woods and Jeffrey, 1996.

24. Alexander, 1995, pp. 8–102.

Chapter 12. Lesson Structure and Form

1. This tendency was first monitored systematically in the UK by Galton, Simon and their ORACLE colleagues (Galton and Simon, 1980; Galton, Simon and Croll, 1980). In the subsequent Leeds study we found a direct relationship between pupils' levels of distraction and the character of the work they were undertaking. Working solo (e.g., on reading or writing tasks) they were much more likely to be distracted than when they were working collaboratively (Alexander, 1995, pp. 134–58). The teacher contributes to this problem if he or she has complex patterns of classroom organization, such as obtain in many British and American primary and elementary schools (see also Bennett, 1992, 1995).

2. This practice was common in English primary classrooms during the last three decades of the twentieth century (although less so during the 1990s). The practice, and its consequences for both pupils and teachers, is analysed in the studies of Galton, Simon, Bennett, Mortimore and Alexander (Galton and Simon, 1980; Galton, Simon and Croll, 1980; Galton *et al.*, 1999; Bennett *et al.*, 1984; Mortimore *et al.*, 1988; Alexander, 1995, 1997).

3. For example, Kumar, 1991.

4. Clarke and Fuller, 1997.

5. Denzil Saldanha, of the Tata Institute of Social Sciences in Mumbai, in conversation.

6. Broadfoot, 1995.

7. Sharpe, 1996.

8. Bourdoncle, 1996.
9. Sharpe, 1995; Broadfoot *et al.*, 2000, pp. 95–6.
10. Vygotsky, 1979, p. 89.
11. Sadler, 1966, p. 34.
12. Comenius [1657], in the 1896 translation of the Latin version which was completed in 1638 and published in Amsterdam in 1657, pp. 316, 276. The extracts are taken from the chapter on 'The principles of conciseness and rapidity in teaching'.
13. Pestalozzi [1802].
14. See Bowen, 1981, pp. 358–74, for a clear account of the development of instructional theory in the United States during the late nineteenth century.
15. Mayo, 1832.
16. Bowen, 1981, p. 335.
17. Alexander, 1995, pp. 25–30.
18. Alexander, 1996, pp. 21–7.
19. For a critique of the theoretical basis of the UK Government's 1998 literacy strategy, see Sealey, 1999.
20. Blyth, 1965b, p. 38; Blyth, 1988, pp. 9–12.
21. Montessori, 1912.
22. See Ch. 6, pp. 139–41; Alexander, 1984, 1995, ch. 6; Cunningham, 1988.
23. The Leeds research investigated and evaluated the practice of curriculum-specific bays (Alexander, 1995, ch. 2; Alexander, 1997, ch. 4). The problems of multiple-focus teaching had been raised earlier in the London study of Mortimore *et al.*, 1988.
24. Pollard *et al.*, 1994, pp. 118–20.
25. Cf. Raymond Williams, 1976, pp. 137–40.
26. David Hargreaves of the University of Surrey at Roehampton is currently researching improvizational thinking in teaching, drawing on parallel work by Baker-Sennett and Matusov (1997) which uses the analogy of jazz musicians.
27. This is a large topic in its own right. Elsewhere (Alexander, 1988) I examine Froebelian metaphors such as growth, unfolding, budding, the garden and the gardener, and relate their impact upon progressive thinking in English primary education to the contrasting re-orderings of nature represented by, say, the geometrical landscaping of André Le Nôtre in France and the pastoral informality of Lancelot 'Capability' Brown in England. (Compare the gardens at Versailles and Stowe, and see also Jenkins' early (1975) exploration of 'classical' and 'romantic' in the curriculum). Though I have applied to lesson structure the language of music, I fully understand that one can also understand it by reference to accounts of the natural world. I think that this strengthens rather than weakens my central argument that we need to place pedagogy within a much larger framework of ideas than educationists normally attempt.
28. As footnote to this tentative line of enquiry, I would draw attention to Jamie James' intriguing account of the relationship between music, mathematics and science, a relationship which until the emergence of modern science was about symbiosis rather than mere analogy (James, 1995).

Chapter 13. Organization, Task and Activity

1. Gage suggests that scientific (in effect quantitative) analysis of teaching can handle convincingly the relationship of no more than four variables.
2. See the review by Wragg, 1984a, pp. 8–10. As an indicator of the longevity and scope of this tradition, see Biddle and Ellena, 1964, or Dunkin and Biddle, 1974. The latter

contains exhaustive lists of correlations (several hundred in all) demonstrated in American classroom research up to that time (e.g. 'higher pupil achievement is associated with greater amounts of pupil initiation', 'amount of pupil talk is unrelated to pupil achievement').

3. The studies of Bennett, 1976; Galton and Simon, 1980; Galton, Simon and Croll, 1980; Bennett *et al.*, 1984; Mortimore *et al.*, 1988; Tizard *et al.*, 1988; and Galton *et al.*, 1999 are the most notable UK examples. To these should be added systematic process studies such as those of Wragg, 1993. From the secondary sector the main instance in a much smaller field remains Rutter *et al.*, 1979.

4. Sammons, Hillman and Mortimore, 1995.

5. Creemers, 1994, 1997; Creemers *et al.*, 1997.

6. Wragg, 1984a, p. 9.

7. OECD, 1995b, p. 49.

8. Creemers, 1997.

9. Creemers writes that in broad terms his model is based on Carroll's 1963 model of school learning, but this seems to apply mainly to his use of levels. This seems to support my view that the Creemers model is not so much a model of teaching (or learning) as a list of some of the factors that may affect its conduct.

10. Dunkin and Biddle, 1974, p. 38.

11. Johnson and Brooks, 1979, cited in Wragg, 1984, p. 22, and 1993, p. 20.

12. Leach, 1964.

13. I can trace this usage back to education Secretary of State and ardent monetarist Keith Joseph, in the early 1980s.

14. See Giddens, 1993, chs 2, 3.

15. Alexander, 1995, pp. 52–8.

16. Galton *et al.*, 1999, pp. 41–2. The quotation is from Galton and Simon, 1980, and refers to what the Leicester team found in 1976.

17. Government of India, 1993b.

18. In 1998 the UK government distributed to each primary school a videotape *Learning from the Best: raising standards through sharing good practice* (DfEE, 1998f), and began to make available a much larger range of lessons and lesson plans on its website, which was linked with the National Grid for Learning (DfEE, 1998e). The videotape propagandized government policies rather than described them. It was mischievously oppositional in its treatment of alternative teaching methods (its voice-over commentary gave teachers the choice between the approved strategy of 'interactive whole class teaching' and 'running around the class looking after individuals', and told teachers to 'teach children to read rather than listen to them read'). It was patronizing to parents on the matter of homework. And the supposedly model lessons were far from exemplary, by any standard.

19. Norman, 1978; Bennett *et al.*, 1984, pp. 22–3. I am much indebted here to the Exeter team's clear presentation of both Norman's theory and their own adaptation and application of it.

20. Bennett *et al.*, 1984, pp. 24–6.

21. Ibid., p. 29.

22. Kerry, 1984, p. 164.

23. Kerry, 1984, pp. 177–8.

24. Wragg, 1993; Wragg and Brown, 1993; Brown and Wragg, 1993; Galton and Simon, 1980; Galton, Simon and Croll, 1980.

25. Bloom, 1956.

26. NCERT, 1991.

27. This resistance is exemplified and discussed in Alexander, 1984, chs 3, 5. For a thoroughly argued presentation of the 'reflexive' or anti-subject view of curriculum knowledge at the primary stage, see Blenkin and Kelly, 1981 (and its several subsequent editions) and Kelly, 1990.

28. Eggleston, 1977, discussed in Alexander, 1984, ch. 3. The received/reflexive distinction is shorthand for ideas in the sociology of knowledge which became prominent in the early 1970s for which the key text was Young, 1971 and in respect of which the leading figure was Basil Bernstein (e.g. 1971).

29. Eisner, 1967, 1969, 1979, 1985.

30. Galton *et al.*, 1999, pp. 185–9; P. Alexander *et al.*, 1991.

31. Bruner and Haste, in Bruner and Haste, 1987, p. 24; Bruner, 1990.

32. Edwards and Mercer, 1987, pp. 92–127.

33. Ibid., p. 97.

34. Jackson, 1968.

35. Alexander, 1995, p. 154.

36. Based on Alexander, 1995, p. 155.

37. Jackson, 1968, pp. 19–28.

Chapter 14. Judgement, Routine, Rule and Ritual

1. As I write, the parents of schoolchildren in Ripon, North Yorkshire, are voting on whether to make the city's grammar school, one of a handful which survived the drive for comprehensive schooling in the 1960s and the 1970s, non-selective. In contrast, selection for grammar schools by the '11-plus' examination was retained for most of Northern Ireland long after it was phased out by most English LEAs, and there it was complicated by the social divide of religion. In 1998 the UK government commissioned a report on the future of the 11-plus in Northern Ireland from a team headed by Tony Gallagher and Alan Smith. At the time of writing, with the Stormont Assembly suspended because of the continuing impasse over the decommissioning of IRA weapons, the fate of this important document remains uncertain. (The outcome of the Ripon vote was a resounding 'No': parents decided to retain selective secondary education.)

2. DfEE, 1999c, p. 4.

3. In a public lecture at the London School of Economics in 1998, HMCI Woodhead claimed that the tests were unreliable and were being administered 'creatively' (Cassidy, 1998).

4. DfEE, 1999c, p. 5.

5. Prime Minister Blair, at a conference for new head teachers on 21 Oct. 1999. This was hardly an encouraging induction into their new roles.

6. DfEE, 2000.

7. DES, 1978b, 1982b.

8. Sharp and Green, 1975; King, 1978.

9. Alexander, 1997, p. 23.

10. There is a vast literature on this issue. The famous 'Pygmalion' experiment of Rosenthal and Jacobson (1968) in the United States alerted people to the close connection between how the teacher views a pupil and how that pupil performs. The build-up of the UK evidence in the context of the English debate about streaming is reviewed in Simon, 1991.

11. Alexander, 1997, p. 26. In this I was reapplying in the Leeds context an argument which I had developed at length in Alexander, 1984, pp. 20–47. Teachers define children's potential and performance on the basis of what they (teachers) know

as well as what pupils do, and what pupils do is in any case strongly influenced, for better or worse, by what teachers know.

12. Stevenson and Stigler, 1992; Reynolds and Farrell, 1996.
13. DES, 1978b. Illuminating the problem of 'match' was one of the most important contributions of the 1978 HMI primary survey. With hindsight, however, we might also suggest that it served to reinforce still further the unattainable Plowdenite ideal of fully individualized teaching.
14. See, for example, the primary science materials of Harlen *et al.*, 1977.
15. Bennett *et al.*, 1984.
16. Galton and Simon, 1980; Galton, Simon and Croll, 1980; Alexander, 1997.
17. Alexander, Rose and Woodhead, 1992, para. 31.
18. Broadfoot, 1996, p. 76.
19. This is a common finding in UK classroom research, including the Leeds study (Alexander, 1997, pp. 71, 76).
20. Weston, Taylor, Lewis and MacDonald, 1998.
21. Alexander, 1995, p. 87.
22. Alexander, 1995, p. 87.
23. Bennett *et al.*, 1984, pp. 217–19.
24. Alexander, 1995, pp. 242–7.
25. Stevenson and Stigler, p. 94.
26. McKay, 1993, pp. 31–4.
27. Elliott *et al.*, 1999; Hufton and Elliott, 1999.
28. Bempechat and Drago-Severson, 1999.
29. Muckle, 1998, pp. 15–16.
30. Broadfoot, 1999b.
31. Reynolds and Farrell, 1996.
32. Osborn and Planel, 1999.
33. Sharpe, 1997.
34. PROBE, 1999, pp. 80–82.
35. Alexander, 1995, pp. 261–3.
36. Alexander, 1997, pp. 87–8.
37. Ministère de l'Éducation Nationale, 1995b.
38. Lansing School District, 1994c.
39. Edwards and Mercer, 1987.
40. Brown and McIntyre, 1993.
41. Ibid., pp. 91–106.
42. Ibid., pp. 102–3.
43. Wragg, 1993, pp. 48–52, 83; Edwards and Westgate, 1994, p. 119.
44. Wragg, 1993, pp. 49–50.
45. Edwards and Mercer, 1987, p. 45.
46. Edwards and Westgate, p. 40.
47. Archer, 1989, p. 180.
48. Giddens, 1993, p. 110.
49. Pinker, 1999, p. 269.
50. Alexander, 1988, and 1995, ch. 1.
51. There is now a substantial body of research on teachers' thinking and craft knowledge, and one journal in particular, *Teaching and Teacher Education*, featured many articles on this theme during the 1990s. Most of this material has come from the United States where in 2000 it remains a fertile field. In the UK, apart from Brown and McIntyre,

much of the running has been made by James Calderhead (1984, 1987), though among the first to open up teacher craft knowledge as a field of empirical enquiry in the UK were David McNamara and Charles Desforges (1978). They later sought to apply their perspectives to courses of pre-service teacher training (McNamara and Desforges, 1979).

52. Shotton, 1998, pp. 64–159.
53. Archer, 1989, p. 180.

Chapter 15. Interaction, Time and Pace

1. Actually, the promotion of interactive whole class teaching started under the Conservative government of 1993–7, with the important and courageous Barking and Dagenham mathematics experiment (Luxton and Last, 1997; Prais, 1997, Luxton, 2000) and OFSTED's report on England's place in the international standards league table (Reynolds and Farrell, 1996). For a contemporary commentary on this episode, see Alexander, 1996. For a critique of the cause–effect assumptions which informed both the OFSTED report and subsequent government policy, see Robinson, 1999. Note that Roger Luxton, Chief Inspector for Barking and Dagenham LEA, presents a more carefully qualified view of the necessary attributes of this mode of teaching than that presented by DfEE (Luxton, 2000).

2. Pollard et al., 1994; Galton et al., 1999. The increase in whole class teaching from the early 1990s onwards can probably be attributed to two circumstances in particular: the need to cover the heavy content demands of the 1989 version of the National Curriculum as speedily and economically as possible; and sustained pressure on teachers to change the balance of whole class, group and individual work, following the 1992 'three wise men' paper (Alexander, Rose and Woodhead, 1992) and subsequent HMI and OFSTED reports (e.g. OFSTED, 1993, 1994b, 1995).

3. 'Higher order cognitive interaction' featured prominently as a key factor in successful teaching in the ORACLE study, and in subsequent classroom studies by Mortimore and Alexander (Galton and Simon, 1980; Mortimore et al., 1988; Alexander, 1992). During the 1970s the Schools Council funded an influential curriculum development project on primary classroom communication skills based on the work of, and directed by, Joan Tough (Tough, 1976, 1979), and the scope of this development activity was greatly widened by the 1987–93 National Oracy project (Norman, 1992), which in turn drew on the seminal 1960s and the 1970s studies of Douglas Barnes, James Britton, Gordon Wells and many others (Barnes, Britton and Rosen, 1969; Britton, 1970; Wells, 1987), and indeed on the strong boost to 'language across the curriculum' given by the Bullock Report (DES, 1976). Much of this excellent work was sidelined or buried by the national curriculum and New Labour's 'Year Zero' rewriting of educational history. See also the last part of Ch. 17.

4. Alexander, 1998c, p. 37.

5. During 1998, two reports, one commissioned by OFSTED, the other by DfEE, raised serious questions about the quality, relevance and bias of much educational research (Tooley and Darby, 1998; Hillage et al., 1998). Notwithstanding questions about the quality and bias of these documents, they gave DfEE and TTA the leverage they needed to extend their control of the focus, funding and reporting of educational research.

6. Mroz, Smith and Hardman, 1999.

7. Alexander, 1996, pp. 21–4.

8. In 1972, David Hargreaves produced an excellent book on the social psychology of teaching (Interpersonal Relations and Education) which demonstrated the almost endless

analytical possibilities of 'interaction'. For a more specialized treatment of one particular kind of classroom interaction, the non-verbal, see Neill, 1991.

9. See Amidon and Flanders, 1967, for the ancestor of most modern schedules for systematic analysis of classroom interaction, the Flanders Interaction Analysis Categories System (FIAC) which first appeared in 1963. However, the Amidon and Flanders collection also includes category systems going back to the 1930s, for example that devised by H. H. Anderson in 1939.

10. Galton and Simon, 1980; Galton *et al.*, 1999; Mortimore *et al.*, 1988.

11. For a comprehensive review of different approaches, see Edwards and Westgate, 1994. For contrasting sociolinguistic and structural perspectives see Stubbs, 1983, 1987, and Coulthard, 1992.

12. Flanders, 1970.

13. Galton *et al.*, 1999, pp. 83–4.

14. Jackson, 1968, p. 10.

15. Galton and Simon, 1980, pp. 36–9.

16. Bennett, 1988.

17. Galton *et al.*, 1999, pp. 117–21.

18. Alexander, 1995, p. 139.

19. Alexander, 1988, pp. 179–81; Alexander, 1995, pp. 68–87.

20. Alexander, 1995, p. 136.

21. Alexander, 1995, p. 137.

22. Galton *et al.*, 1999, pp. 82–5.

23. Sinclair and Coulthard, 1975. A revised version appears in Sinclair and Coulthard, 1992.

24. Broadfoot *et al.*, 2000, pp. 91–4.

25. Galton and Simon, 1980, pp. 37–9.

26. Elliott, Hufton, Hildreth and Illushin, 1999; Hufton and Elliott, 1999.

27. Mortimore *et al.*, 1988; Alexander, 1991.

28. In early nineteenth-century France, for instance. See Ch. 2, and Reboul-Scherrer, 1989.

29. Galton and Simon, 1980, p. 31. The base/team distinction is used in the follow-up study (Galton *et al.*, 1999).

30. The field is summarized in Wragg, 1993, 1994, in Wragg and Brown, 1993, and Brown and Wragg, 1993. For a more detailed study of questioning in a variety of contexts, not just classrooms, see Dillon, 1990.

31. Dunne and Bennett, 1990; Galton and Williamson, 1992.

32. Adapted from Dunne and Bennett, 1990, pp. 13–15.

33. Berlak and Berlak, 1981, especially ch. 7.

34. Brown and McIntyre, 1993, pp. 73–6.

35. Campbell and Neill, 1994; Evans, Packwood, Neill and Campbell, 1994.

36. Bennett, 1995.

37. Gage, 1978, p. 75.

38. In Alexander, 1995, pp. 277–88, I develop the argument about the relationship between the values of postwar primary progressivism and its concentration in rural areas.

39. Bennett, 1995, p. 279.

40. Galton *et al.*, 1999, p. 90; Alexander, 1995, p. 110; Pollard *et al.*, 1994, pp. 182–4.

41. *Daily Telegraph*, 19 Sept. 1991. There were many more headlines and stories in similar vein. An account of the media handling of the Leeds report is contained in Alexander 1997.

42. Davison *et al.*, 1992 (article in the *Sunday Times*).

43. Wragg, 1993, p. 25; Wragg, 1984, p. 27.

44. Alexander, 1995, p. 158; Alexander 1997, p. 78.
45. Alexander, 1995, pp. 210–14.
46. Galton and Simon, 1980, p. 29.
47. Broadfoot *et al.*, 2000, p. 90.
48. Broadfoot *et al.*, 2000, p. 91; Alexander, 1997, p. 75; Galton and Simon, 1980, p. 26; Galton *et al.*, 1999, p. 90.
49. Dewey, 1916.
50. Marsh, 1973, p. 132.
51. Ministère de l'Education Nationale, 1998, p. 2.
52. Vygotsky, 1979, p. 89.
53. Jackson, 1968, p. 169.

Chapter 16. Learning Discourse

1. Bruner, 1983; Bruner and Haste, 1987.
2. Bruner, 1983; Donaldson, 1978, 1992; Tizard and Hughes, 1984.
3. Mead, 1934, Vygotsky, 1962, 1978.
4. Bruner, 1995, p. 32 (my italics).
5. Vygotsky, 1981, p. 151.
6. It was Jerome Bruner who pointed up this fundamental difference in the pedagogies based on Piagetian and Vygotskian perspectives. See, e.g., Bruner 1987, 1995.
7. Vygotsky, 1962, p. 9.
8. Vygotsky, 1962, p. 104.
9. The case for and against 'proximal', 'potential' and 'next' development, and the origins of each, are discussed in Simon, 1987, pp. 611–12. See also Simon and Simon, 1963, pp. 21–34.
10. Simon, 1987, p. 612.
11. Vygotsky, 1978, p. 86.
12. For an early presentation of the now much-used idea of 'scaffolding', see Bruner, 1976.
13. Two of the most useful British texts – useful because they are grounded in both the particularities of classroom talk and the wider disciplinary debates – are Edwards and Westgate (1994) and Stubbs (1984). Edwards and Westgate review the field as a whole, while Stubbs takes a decidedly sociolinguistic stance.
14. Sinclair and Coulthard, 1975; Coulthard, 1987, 1992.
15. Dillon, 1990.
16. Austin, 1962. See also Sealey, 1999b, for a study of the interplay of requests and directives in adult–child talk.
17. Alexander, Willcocks and Nelson, 1996.
18. See p. 393.
19. Stubbs, 1984, p. 8.
20. Grice, 1975, p. 45.
21. Edwards, 1992, pp. 235–6.
22. Tharp and Gallimore, 1988.
23. Examples of recent work which has moved away from the preoccupation with recitation to study collaborative classroom discourse include: Galton and Williamson, 1992; Barnes and Todd, 1995; Wells *et al.* in Sharan, 1990.
24. Dillon, 1990, p. 11.
25. Edwards and Mercer, 1987; Edwards and Potter, 1992; Mercer, 1995.
26. Edwards and Mercer, 1987, pp. 142–6.

27. Alexander, 1995, pp. 158–96.
28. Bruner, 1978, p. 19.
29. Bernstein, 1990, p. 168.
30. Bernstein, 1990, p. 183.
31. Bernstein, 1990, p. 167.
32. Mercer, 1995, p. 68.
33. Stubbs, 1983.
34. Stubbs, 1983, p. 180.
35. Stubbs, 1983, p. 229.
36. Hatim and Mason, 1990, pp. 5–7.
37. DES, 1978; Galton and Simon, 1980; Alexander, Willcocks and Nelson, 1996.
38. Halliday, 1989.
39. This characteristic was first noted by the national inspectorate in the early 1980s (DES, 1982b) and was confirmed in the Leeds study (Alexander, 1997, pp. 54; Alexander, 1995, pp. 156–7).
40. Mercer, 1995, p. 93; Dillon, 1990, p. 208.
41. Court, 1999. This was a report in *Le Figaro* of a survey conducted by the Syndicat National des Instituteurs.
42. Bernstein, 1990, p. 101.
43. DfEE, 1998a, pp. 9–12.
44. Alexander, 1995, p. 87.
45. Alexander, 1985, p. 37.
46. Sealey, 1999a, 2000a.
47. See Ch. 7; Alexander, 1984, chs 1–3; Alexander, 1995, ch. 6.
48. Layder, 1997; Sealey, 2000b, pp. 104–26.
49. Alexander, 1984, chs 1–3; King, 1978; Sharp and Green, 1975.
50. Kirby, 1981, quoted and discussed in Alexander, 1984, pp. 18–19.
51. Elsewhere I have looked at the conflict of educational language and values which the terminology of the National Curriculum began to expose from 1987 onwards (Alexander, 1989).
52. DfEE, 1998b, p. 18.
53. A year after we observed this teacher, DfEE itself became aware of this problem and published a 'Mathematical Vocabulary' for primary teachers (DfEE, 1999d).
54. Popper, 1963, ch. 1.
55. Galton and Simon, 1980; Galton *et al.*, 1999; Alexander, 1997. See Ch. 14.
56. I am grateful to Joseph Tobin (Universities of Hawaii and Chicago) and members of his anthropology and education network for insights on this matter. Key writers cited by this group include Michele Foster, Lisa Delpit, Gloria Ladson-Billings, Jackie Jordan Irvine, and Ray Rist.
57. Shulman, 1987.
58. Vygotsky, 1962, ch. 7.
59. Bakhtin, 1981, and 1986, pp. 114, 168.
60. Williams, 1976, pp. 93–8.
61. Dewey, 1916. See Ch. 5.
62. 'The curriculum is to be thought of in terms of activity and experience rather than knowledge to be acquired and facts to be stored' (Board of Education, 1931, para. 75). See Ch. 6.
63. Lindfors, 1999, especially pp. 191–209.
64. Broadfoot *et al.*, 2000.

65. Broadfoot *et al.*, 2000, pp. 105–12.

66. Edwards, 1992, pp. 235–6.

67. Grice, 1975, p. 45.

68. Edwards and Mercer, 1987, p. 86.

69. Austin, 1962.

70. Bruner, 1995, p. 29. A slightly different formulation to the one from Bruner, 1978, p. 19 quoted earlier (see note 28).

71. Bruner, 1995, p. 27. With respect to the power of questioning to induce or prevent error, note Dillon's point (Dillon, 1990, p. 23) that courtroom cross-examination is premised on the assumption that testimony is fallible.

72. 'Neither the hand, nor the mind, left to themselves, are worth much; the job is done with tools and aids.' Vygotsky quoted the Bacon epigraph in his *Studies in the History of Behaviour*.

Chapter 17. Culture and Pedagogy

1. Watkins and Mortimore, 1999, p. 3.

2. Simon, 1981a.

3. Simon, 1994.

4. Simon, 1983, p. 10 (my italics).

5. The considerable literature on this matter is reviewed by various contributors to the symposium edited by Alexander, Craft and Lynch in 1984. For a history of teacher training in England from the 1944 Education Act to the arrival of national accreditation in 1984, see the chapter by Alexander (pp. 103–60) in the same publication.

6. See, e.g., Lawlor 1990, the many articles by Anthony O'Hear in the *Daily Telegraph* and the accusations of HMCI Woodhead in his annual RCA lectures (e.g. Woodhead, 1998) and elsewhere.

7. In his circular to primary schools announcing the launch of the 'three wise men' enquiry (DES, 1991c).

8. Prime Minister John Major at the Conservative Party Conference, Oct. 1991.

9. Ball, 1990.

10. For example, Woodhead, 1998, and linked articles in the tabloid press which actually targeted supposed members of the progressive conspiracy under headlines such as 'The men failing our children, by school chief', 'Trio at heart of darkness' (I was one of those so named) and 'Luddites at the school gates' (Halpin, 1998; *Mail on Sunday*, 1999).

11. Millett, 1999.

12. DES, 1991c.

13. Ibid.

14. Marton and Booth, quoted in Watkins and Mortimore, 1999, p. 2.

15. Hamlyn, 1970 ('The logical and psychological aspects of learning').

16. In Alexander, 1984, I provide a detailed critique of this line of argument, which at that time – before the arrival of the national curriculum – was accepted unconditionally by many English primary teachers, and indeed was actively fostered in their teacher training courses.

17. See Judge's account of this episode in Judge, Lemosse, Paine and Sedlak, 1994, pp. 87–93.

18. The gloss is from Chévellard, 1991, cited by Moon, 1998.

19. Shulman, 1987.

20. Bruner, 1963, p. 33.

21. Blyth, 1984.
22. Blyth, 1990, especially pp. 11–16.
23. Beattie, 1998.
24. Ibid.
25. Broadfoot *et al.*, 2000.
26. Shotton, 1998, pp. 64–159.
27. PROBE, 1999, especially pp. 68–82.
28. Bruner, 1972, pp. 100–1.
29. The references here are to the fine 1896 Keatinge translation of *Didactica Magna*.
30. Sharpe, 1997; Broadfoot *et al.*, 2000.
31. See Ravitch, 1983, ch. 7, and in this book p. 112.
32. Taba, 1962.
33. Bruner, 1968, p. 72.
34. From the 1994 Educate America Act (see Ch. 6).
35. National Commission on Exellence in Education, 1983 (see Ch. 5).
36. Macedo, 1999; Mclaren, 1997.
37. Bernstein, 1990, p. 184.
38. Lawton, 1983.
39. DfEE/QCA, 1999, p. 17.
40. Clarke, 1997.
41. Reynolds and Farrell, 1996, pp. 52–9.
42. Tobin, Wu and Davidson, 1989, ch. 5.
43. Bronfenbrenner, 1974.
44. Stevenson and Stigler, 1992.
45. Broadfoot *et al.*, 2000, chs 3, 6.
46. Bruner, 1996, pp. 11–12.
47. In *Mind, Self and Society* (Mead, 1934).
48. Bruner, 1996, pp. 53–63.
49. Ibid. I have reduced a complex argument to its essentials without, I trust, doing it harm.
50. Popper, 1972, p. 74.
51. Popper, 1972, p. 73.
52. Bruner, 1996, p. 57.
53. See Edwards and Mercer, 1987, and our application of the ritual/principled distnction in Ch. 14.
54. Kumar, 1991. See Ch. 5.
55. Bruner, 1996, p. 55.
56. Compare Galton *et al.*, 1999, and Mroz, Smith and Hardman 1999, with OFSTED, 1998a, 1998b.
57. 'Folk pedagogy' is Bruner's usage. It is similar to David McNamara's idea of 'vernacular pedagogy' (McNamara, 1994) or Brown and McIntyre's 1993 account of 'craft knowledge'.
58. Watkins and Mortimore, 1999, p. 7.
59. Gipps and MacGilchrist, pp. 50–52.
60. Hobsbawm, 1995, p. 3.
61. Giroux, 1999, p. 100.
62. Sharp and Green, 1975.
63. Bernstein, 1990, pp. 63–93.
64. I suggested in Ch. 6 that this remains a powerful determinant of education and pedagogy, and of children's educational prospects.

65. OECD, 1998a; Benavot *et al.*, 1991.
66. McLaren 1997, pp. 537–8.
67. One of the central themes of Said, 1994.
68. DfEE/QCA, 1999, p. 38.
69. Ministère de l'Education Nationale, 1998.
70. DES, 1975.
71. Norman, 1992.
72. Carter, 1997, pp. 36–54.
73. Cf. Blyth, 1988b.
74. Goody, 1993, p. 263.
75. Chafe, 1982, pp. 36–7.
76. Tannen, 1982, p. 2.
77. Heath, 1983.
78. Graff, 1987, p. 83.
79. Heath, 1982, p. 111.

Bibliography

Adonis, A. and Pollard, S. (1997) *The Myth of Britain's Classless Society*. London: Penguin Books.

Alexander, P., Schallert, D. and Hare, V. (1991) 'Coming to terms: how researchers in learning and literacy talk about knowledge', *Review of Educational Research* 61:3, 315–43.

Alexander, R. J. (1984) *Primary Teaching*. London: Cassell.

Alexander, R. J. (1988) 'Garden or Jungle? Teacher development and informal primary education', in W. A. L. Blyth (ed.) *Informal Primary Education Today: Essays and Studies*, pp. 148–88. London: Falmer Press.

Alexander, R. J. (1989) 'Core subjects and autumn leaves: the national curriculum and the languages of primary education', *Education 3 to 13*, 17:1.

Alexander, R. J. (1991) *Primary Education in Leeds*. Leeds: University of Leeds.

Alexander, R. J. (1992) *Policy and Practice in Primary Education*. London: Routledge.

Alexander, R. J. (1995) *Versions of Primary Education*. London: Routledge.

Alexander, R. J. (1996) *Other Primary Schools and Ours: hazards of international comparison*, Warwick: Centre for Research in Elementary and Primary Education.

Alexander, R. J. (1997a) *Policy and Practice in Primary Education: local initiative, national agenda*. London: Routledge.

Alexander, R. J. (1997b) 'Unfinished journey: pedagogy and discourse in school effectiveness research', in NCERT (ed.) *Studies in Classroom Processes and School Effectiveness at Primay Stage*, pp. 3–26. Delhi: NCERT.

Alexander, R. J. (1998a) 'Basics, cores and choices: towards a new national curriculum.' *Education 3 to 13*, 26:2, 60–69.

Alexander, R. J. (ed.) (1998b) *Time for Change? Curriculum managers at work*. Warwick: Centre for Research in Elementary and Primary Education in conjunction with the National Primary Centre.

Alexander, R. J. (1998c) 'Reinventing pedagogy, rewriting history', *Parliamentary Brief* 5:7, 37–8.

Alexander, R. J. (1999a) 'Culture in pedagogy, pedagogy across cultures', in R. J. Alexander, P. Broadfoot and D. Phillips (eds) *Learning from Comparing: new directions in comparative educational research. Volume I: Contexts, Classrooms and Outcomes*, pp. 149–80. Oxford: Symposium Books.

Alexander, R. J. (1999b) Memorandum to the Inquiry of the Commons Education and Employment Committee into the Work of OFSTED, in House of Commons *Report of the Inquiry into the Work of OFSTED, Volume 2*, pp. 144–54. London: The Stationery Office.

Alexander, R. J., Craft, M. and Lynch, J. (eds) (1984) *Change in Teacher Education: context and provision since Robbins*. London: Holt, Rinehart and Winston (published by Praeger in New York as *Change in Teacher Education: context and provision in Great Britain*).

Alexander, R. J., Rose, A. J. and Woodhead, C. (1992) *Curriculum Organisation and Classroom Practice in Primary Schools: a discussion paper*. London: DES.

Alexander, R. J., Willcocks, J. and Kinder, K. M. (1989) *Changing Primary Practice*. London: Falmer Press.

Alexander, R. J., Willcocks, J. and Nelson, N. (1996) 'Discourse, pedagogy and the National Curriculum: change and continuity in primary schools', *Research Papers in Education* 11:1, 81–120.

Althusser, L. (1972) 'Ideology and ideological state apparatuses', in B. R. Cosin (ed.) *Education: Structure and Society*, pp. 242–80. London: Penguin Books.

Amidon, E. J. and Hough, J. B. (eds) (1967) *Interaction Analysis: theory, research and application*. Reading, MA: Addison-Wesley.

Anderson, R. D. (1986) 'Sociology and history: M. S. Archer's Social Origins of Educational Systems', *European Journal of Sociology* 27:1, 149–60.

Apple, M. W. (1995) *Education and Power*, 2nd edn. London: Routledge.

Archer, M. S. (1979) *Social Origins of Educational Systems*. London: Sage.

Archer, M. S. (1989) *Culture and Agency: the place of culture in social theory*. Cambridge: Cambridge University Press.

Ardagh, J. (1995) *France Today*. London: Penguin Books.

Argyris, C. and Schön, D. (1974) *Theory in Practice: increasing professional effectiveness*. San Francisco: Jossey-Bass.

Arnold, M. [1861] (ed. R. H. Super 1962) *The Popular Education of France,* in M. Arnold, *Democratic Education*. Ann Arbor, MI: University of Michigan Press.

Arnold, M. [1862] (ed. R. H. Super 1962) *The Twice-Revised Code,* in M. Arnold, *Democratic Education*. Ann Arbor, MI: University of Michigan Press.

Arnold, M. [1869] (ed. S. Lipman 1994) *Culture and Anarchy*. New Haven, CT: Yale University Press.

Audit Commission (1989) *Losing an Empire, Finding a Role: the LEA of the future*. (Audit Commission Occasional Paper 10). London: HMSO.

Austin, J. L. (1962) *How To Do Things With Words*. Oxford: Oxford University Press.

Baker-Sennett, J. and Matusov, E. (1997) 'School "performance": improvisational processes in development and education', in K. Sawyer (ed.) *Creativity in Performance*. Greenwich, CT: Ablex.

Bakhtin, M. M. (1981) *The Dialogic Imagination*. Austin, TX: University of Texas.

Bakhtin, M. M. (1986) *Speech Genres and Other Late Essays*. Austin, TX: University of Texas.

Ball, S. J. (1990) *Politics and Policy-making in Education*. London: Routledge.

Ball, S. J. (1994) *Educational Reform: a critical and post-structural approach*. Buckingham: Open University Press.

Barnes, D., Britton, J. and Rosen, H. (1969) *Language, the Learner and the School*. Harmondsworth: Penguin Books.

Barnes, D. and Todd, F. (1995) *Communication and Learning Revisited: making meaning through talk*. London: Heinemann.

Bayliss, V. (1998) *Redefining Work: an RSA initiative*. London: RSA.

Beattie, N. (1998) 'Freinet and the Anglo-Saxons', *Compare* 28:1, 33–47.

de Beauvoir, S. [1954] (tr. C. Cosman 1998) *America Day by Day*. London: Gollancz.

Bempechat, J., Drago-Severson, E. (1999) 'Cross-cultural differences in academic achievement: beyond etic conceptions of children's understandings', *Review of Educational Research*, 69 (3) pp. 287–314.

Benavot, A., Cha, Y-K., Kamens, D., Meyer, J. W. and Wong, S-Y. (1991) 'Knowledge for the masses: world models and national curricula, 1920–1986', *American Sociological Review 56*.

Benavot, A. and Kamens, D. (1989) *The Curriculum Content of Primary Education in Developing Countries*. Washington, DC: World Bank.

Bennett, L. (1992) *Women, Poverty and Productivity in India*. Washington, DC: World Bank.

Bennett, S. N. (1976) *Teaching Styles and Pupil Progress*. London: Open Books.

Bennett, S. N. (1988) 'The effective primary school teacher: the search for a theory of pedagogy', *Teaching and Teacher Education* 4:1, 19–30.

Bennett, S. N. (1992) *Managing Learning in the Primary School*. Stoke on Trent: ASPE/ Trentham Books.

Bennett, S. N. (1995) 'Managing time', in C. Desforges (ed.) *An Introduction to Teaching*, pp. 275–87. Oxford: Blackwell.

Bennett, S. N., Desforges, C., Cockburn, A. and Wilkinson, B. (1984) *The Quality of Pupil Learning Experiences*. Hove: Lawrence Erlbaum.

Beriss, D. (1996) 'Scarves, schools and segregation', in A. Corbett and B. Moon (eds) *Education in France: continuity and change in the Mitterand years, 1981–1995*, pp. 377–87. London: Routledge.

Berlak, A. and Berlak, H. (1981) *Dilemmas of Schooling: teaching and social change*. London: Methuen.

Bernstein, B. (1971) 'On the classification and framing of educational knowledge', in M. F. D. Young (ed.) *Knowledge and Control*, pp. 47–69. London: Collier Macmillan.

Bernstein, B. (1990) *The Structuring of Pedagogic Discourse* (Class, Codes and Control, Volume 4). London: Routledge.

Biddle, B. J. and Ellena, W. J. (eds) (1964) *Contemporary Research on Teacher Effectiveness*. New York: Holt, Rinehart and Winston.

Bierhoff, H. (1996) *Laying the Foundation of Numeracy: a comparison of primary school textbooks in Britain, Germany and Switzerland*. London: National Institute for Economic and Social Research.

Bierhoff, H. and Prais, S. J. (1995) *Schooling as Preparation for Life and Work in Switzerland*. London: National Institute for Economic and Social Research.

Blair, A. (1998) *The Third Way: new politics for the new century*. London: Fabian Society.

Blenkin, G. M. and Kelly, A. V. (1981) *The Primary Curriculum*. London: Harper & Row.

Bloom, B. S. (1956) *Taxonomy of Educational Objectives: the classification of educational goals. Handbook 1: cognitive domain*. New York: Longmans, Green.

Blyth, W. A. L. (1965a) *English Primary Education: a sociological description. Volume I: Schools*. London: Routledge and Kegan Paul.

Blyth, W. A. L. (1965b) *English Primary Education: a sociological description. Volume II: Background*. London: Routledge and Kegan Paul.

Blyth, W. A. L. (1984) *Development, Experience and the Curriculum in Primary Education*. London: Croom Helm.

Blyth, W. A. L. (ed.) (1988a) *Informal Primary Education Today: essays and studies*. Lewes: Falmer Press.

Blyth, W. A. L. (1998b) 'Five aspects of informality in primary education', in W. A. L. Blyth (ed.) *Informal Primary Education Today: essays and studies*, pp. 7–24. Lewes: Falmer Press.

Blyth, W. A. L. (1990) *Making the Grade for Primary Humanities*. Buckingham: Open University Press.

Board of Education (1927) *Report of the Consultative Committee on the Education of the Adolescent*. (1927 Hadow Report) London: HMSO.

Board of Education (1931) *Report of the Consultative Committee on the Primary School* (1931 Hadow Report). London: HMSO.

Bourdieu, P. (1973) 'Cultural reproduction and social reproduction', in R. Brown (ed.) *Knowledge, Education and Cultural Change: Papers in the Sociology of Education*. London: Tavistock Publications.

Bourdieu, P. and Passeron, J.-C. (1990) *Reproduction in Education, Society and Culture*, 2nd edn. London: Sage.

Bourdoncle, R. (1996) 'From the schoolteacher to the expert: the IUFM and the evolution of training institutions', in A. Corbett and B. Moon (eds) *Education in France: continuity and change in the Mitterand years, 1981–1995*, pp. 309–20. London: Routledge.

Bowen, J. (1981) *A History of Western Education. Volume Three: The Modern West, Europe and the New World*. London: Methuen.

Bowles, S. and Gintis, H. (1976) *Schooling in Capitalist America: educational reform and the contradictions of economic life*. London: Routledge and Kegan Paul.

Britton, J. (1970) *Language and Learning*. London: Allen Lane.

Broadfoot, P. (1995) 'Primary schooling and policy change'. Paper presented at a conference on French primary education at the School Curriculum and Assessment Authority, 6 November. London: SCAA.

Broadfoot, P. (1996) *Education, Assessment and Society*. Buckingham: Open University Press.

Broadfoot, P. (1999a) 'Not so much a context, more a way of life? Comparative education in the 1990s', in R. J. Alexander, P. Broadfoot and D. Phillips (eds) *Learning from Comparing: new directions in comparative educational research. Volume I: Contexts, Classrooms and Outcomes*, pp. 21–32. Oxford: Symposium Books.

Broadfoot, P. (1999b) 'Comparative research on pupil achievement: in search of validity, reliability and utility', in R. J. Alexander, P. Broadfoot and D. Phillips (eds) *Learning from Comparing: new directions in comparative educational research*, pp. 237–60. Oxford: Symposium Books.

Broadfoot, P., Osborn, M., Gilly, M. and Bûcher, A. (1993) *Perceptions of Teaching: primary school teachers in England and France*. London: Cassell.

Broadfoot, P., Osborn, M., Planel, C. and Sharpe, K. (2000) *Promoting Quality in Learning: does England have the answer?* London: Cassell.

Bronfenbrenner, U. (1974) *Two Worlds of Childhood: US and USSR*. London: Penguin Books.

Brown, G. and Wragg, E. C. (1993) *Questioning*. London: Routledge.

Brown, M. (1998) 'The tyranny of the international horse race'. London: Kings College.

Brown, P., Halsey, A. H., Lauder, H. and Wells, A. S. (1998) 'The transformation of education and society', in A. H. Halsey, H. Lauder, P. Brown and A. S. Wells (eds) *Education: Culture, Economy, Society*. Oxford: Oxford University Press.

Brown, S. and McIntyre, D. (1993) *Making Sense of Teaching*. Buckingham: Open University Press.

Bruner, J. S. (1963) *The Process of Education*. New York: Random House.

Bruner, J. S. (1968) *Toward a Theory of Instruction*. New York: W. W. Norton.

Bruner, J. S. (1972) *The Relevance of Education*. London: George Allen and Unwin.

Bruner, J. S. (1976) 'Early social interaction and language acquisition', in H. R. Schaffer (ed.) *Studies in Mother-Infant Interaction*. London: Academic Press.

Bruner, J. S. (1978) 'The role of dialogue in language acquisition', in A. Sinclair, R. Jarvella and W. Levelt (eds) *The Child's Conception of Language*. New York: Springer-Verlag.

Bruner, J. S. (1983) *Child's Talk*. Oxford: Oxford University Press.

Bruner, J. S. (1990) *Acts of Meaning*. Cambridge, MA: Harvard University Press.

Bruner, J. S. (1995) 'Vygotsky: a historical and conceptual perspective', in J. V. Wertsch (ed.) *Culture, Communication and Cognition: Vygotskian Perspectives*. Cambridge: Cambridge University Press.

Bruner, J. S. (1996) *The Culture of Education*. Cambridge, MA: Harvard University Press.

Bruner, J. S. and Haste, H. (eds) (1987) *Making Sense: the child's construction of the world*. London: Routledge.

Burghes, D. (1995) 'Britain gets a minus in maths', *Sunday Times*, 14 May.

Burnett, J. (1982) *Destiny Obscure: autobiographies of childhood, education and family from the 1820s to the 1920s*. London: Allen Lane.

Butler, M. (ed.) (1984) *Burke, Paine, Godwin and the Revolution Controversy*. Cambridge: Cambridge University Press.

Calderhead, J. (1984) *Teachers' Classroom Decision-making*. London: Holt Rinehart and Winston.

Calderhead, J. (ed.) (1987) *Exploring Teachers' Thinking*. London: Cassell.

Campbell, R. J. (1985) *Developing the Primary School Curriculum*. London: Cassell.

Campbell, R. J. and Neill, S. R. St J. (1994) *Primary Teachers at Work*. London: Routledge.

Cannadine, D. (1998) *Class in Britain*. New Haven, CT: Yale University Press.

Carroll, J. B. (1963) 'A model of school learning', *Teachers College Record* 64, 723–33.

Carter, R. (1997) *Investigating English Discourse: language, literacy and literature*. London: Routledge.

Cassidy, S. (1999) 'Tests are unreliable, says chief inspector', *Times Educational Supplement*, 18 December.

Castells, M. (1996) *The Rise of the Network Society* (*The Information Age: Economy, Society and Culture*, Vol. 1). Oxford: Blackwell.

Castells, M. (1997) *The Power of Identity* (*The Information Age: Economy, Society and Culture*, Vol. 2). Oxford: Blackwell.

Castells, M. (1998) *End of Millennium* (*The Information Age: Economy, Society and Culture*, Vol. 3). Oxford: Blackwell.

Central Advisory Council for Education (England) (CACE) (1967) *Children and Their Primary Schools* (Plowden Report). London: HMSO.

Centre National de Documention Pédagogique (1991) *Les Cycles à l'Ecole Primaire*. Paris: Hachette.

Centre National de Documention Pédagogique (1992a) *Le Project d'Ecole*. Paris: Hachette.

Centre National de Documention Pédagogique (1992b) *La Maîtrise de la Langue à l'Ecole*. Paris: Hachette.

Chafe, W. H. (1995) *Unfinished Journey: America since World War II*. Oxford: Oxford University Press.

Chafe, W. L. (1993) 'Integration and involvement in speaking, writing and oral literature', in D. Tannen (ed.) *Spoken and Written Language: exploring orality and literacy*. Norwood, NJ: Ablex.

Chévellard, Y. (1991) 'La transposition didactique: du savoir savant au savoir enseigné'. Paris: la Pensée Sauvage.

Clarke, P. (1996) 'Cultural models of teacher thinking and teaching'. Unpublished paper. Cambridge, MA: University of Harvard.

Clarke, P. and Fuller, B. (1997) 'Life in Indian classrooms: the influence of culture and caste', in K. Kumar (ed.) *Studies on Classroom Processes and School Effectiveness at Primary Stage,* pp. 239–57. New Delhi: NCERT.

Cohen, D. K. and Spillane, J. P. (1993) 'Policy and practice: the relationship between governance and instruction', in S. H. Fuhrman (ed.) *Designing Coherent Education Policy: improving the system,* pp. 35–95. San Francisco: Jossey-Bass.

Colley, L. (1996) *Britons: forging the nation 1707–1837.* London: Vintage Books.

Collini, S. (1999) *English Pasts.* Oxford: Oxford University Press.

Comenius, J. A. [1657] tr. M. W. Keatinge (1896), *The Great Didactic.* London: A. & C. Black.

Confederation of British Industry (1998) *Greater Expectations: priorities for the future curriculum.* London: CBI.

Corbett, A. (1996) 'Secular, free and compulsory: republican values in French education', in A. Corbett and B. Moon (eds) *Education in France: continuity and change in the Mitterand years, 1981–1995,* pp. 5–21. London: Routledge.

Coulthard, M. (1987) *An Introduction to Discourse Analysis.* London: Longman.

Coulthard, M. (1992) *Advances in Spoken Discourse Analysis.* London: Routledge.

Court, M. (1999) 'Les écoliers ont la parole facile', *Le Figaro,* 12 Novembre.

Cox, B. and Dyson, A. E. (1971) *The Black Papers on Education.* London: Davis-Poynter.

Cox, B. and Dyson, A. E. (1975) *The Fight for Education: Black Paper 1975.* London: J. M. Dent.

Creemers, B. P. M. (1994a) 'The history, value and purpose of school effectiveness studies', in D. Reynolds, B. P. M. Creemers, P. S. Nesselrodt, E. C. Schaffer, S. Stringfield and C. Teddlie (eds) (1994) *Advances in School Effectiveness Research and Practice,* pp. 9–24. Oxford: Pergamon.

Creemers, B. P. M. (1994b) 'Effective instruction: an empirical basis for a theory of educational effectiveness', in D. Reynolds, B. P. M. Creemers, P. S. Nesselrodt, E. C. Schaffer, S. Stringfield and C. Teddlie (eds) (1994) *Advances in School Effectiveness Research and Practice,* pp. 189–206. Oxford: Pergamon.

Creemers, B. P. M. (1997) *Effective Schools and Effective Teachers: an international perspective.* Warwick: University of Warwick Centre for Research in Elementary and Primary Education.

Creemers, B. P. M., Reezigt, G. J., Van der Werf, G. P. C. and Hoeben, W. T. J. G. (1997) 'Developments in educational effectiveness theory and research in the Netherlands', in K. Kumar (ed.) *Studies in Classroom Processes and School Effectiveness at Primay Stage,* pp. 197–235. Delhi: NCERT.

Cressy, D. (1980) *Literacy and the Social Order: reading and writing in Tudor and Stuart England.* Cambridge: Cambridge University Press.

Crossley, M. (1999) 'Reconceptualising comparative and international education', *Compare* 29:3, 248–67.

Crystal, D. (ed.) (1990) *The Cambridge Encyclopaedia.* Cambridge: Cambridge University Press.

Cunningham, P. (1988) *Curriculum Change in the Primary School Since 1945: dissemination of the progressive ideal.* London: Falmer Press.

Dale, R. (1977) 'The state and the governance of education', in A. H. Halsey, H. Lauder, P. Brown and A. S. Wells (eds) *Education: Culture, Economy, Society,* pp. 273–82. Oxford: Oxford University Press.

Davison, J., Driscoll, M. and Hymas, C. (1992) 'The Great Betrayal', *Sunday Times*, 26 January.

Dearing, R. (1993) *The National Curriculum and its Assessment: final report*. London: School Curriculum and Assessment Authority.

Delige, R. (1999) *The Untouchables of India*. London: Berg.

Department for Education (1992a) *Teaching and Learning in Japanese Elementary Schools*. London: HMSO.

Department for Education (1992b) *Initial Teacher Training (Secondary Phase) (Circular 9/92)*. London: DFE.

Department for Education (1993) *The Initial Training of Primary School Teachers: criteria for courses (Circular 14/93)*. London: DFE.

Department for Education and Employment (1996) *Teacher Training Circular Letter 1/96*. London: DfEE.

Department for Education and Employment (1997a) *Preparing for the Information Age: synoptic report of the Education Departments' Superhighways Initiative*. London: DfEE.

Department for Education and Employment (1997b) *The Implementation of the National Literacy Strategy*. London: DfEE.

Department for Education and Employment (1997c) *Excellence in Schools*. London: The Stationery Office.

Department for Education and Employment (1998a) *The National Literacy Strategy: framework for teaching*. London: DfEE.

Department for Education and Employment (1998b) *The Implementation of the National Numeracy Strategy: the final report of the Numeracy Task Force*. London: DfEE.

Department for Education and Employment (1998c) *The Learning Age: a renaissance for a new Britain*. London: HMSO.

Department for Education and Employment (1998d) *Towards a National Skills Agenda*. London: DfEE.

Department for Education and Employment (1998e) *National Grid for Learning*. London: DfEE.

Department for Education and Employment (1998f) *Learning From the Best: raising standards through sharing good practice* (videotape). London: DfEE.

Department for Education and Employment (1999a) *Teachers: meeting the challenge of change* (Government Green Paper). London: The Stationery Office.

Department for Education and Employment (1999b) *Meeting the Challenge: Education Action Zones*. London: DfEE.

Department for Education and Employment (1999c) *Weighing the Baby: the report of an independent scrutiny panel on the 1999 Key Stage 2 National Curriculum tests in English and mathematics*. London: DfEE.

Department for Education and Employment (2000) *Pay and Conditions for Teachers in England and Wales, 2000–1*. London: DfEE.

Department for Education and Employment and Qualifications and Curriculum Authority (1999) *The National Curriculum: handbook for primary teachers*. London: DfEE and QCA.

Department of Education and Science (1975) *A Language for Life* (Bullock Report). London: HMSO.

Department of Education and Science (1978a) *Special Educational Needs: Report of the Committee of Enquiry into the Education of Handicapped Children* (Warnock Report). London: HMSO.

Department of Education and Science (1978b) *Primary Education in England: a survey by HM Inspectors of Schools*. London: HMSO.

Department of Education and Science (1982a) *Statistics of Education 1981*. London: HMSO.

Department of Education and Science (1982b) *Education 5–9: an illustrative survey of 80 first schools in England*. London: HMSO.

Department of Education and Science (1984) *Initial Teacher Training: approval of courses (Circular 3/84)*. London: DES.

Department of Education and Science (1986) *Education in the Federal Republic of Germany: aspects of curriculum and assessment*. London: HMSO.

Department of Education and Science (1989) *Initial Teacher training: approval of courses (Circular 24/89)*. London: DES.

Department of Education and Science (1990) *Aspects of Education in the USA: teaching and learning in New York city schools*. London: HMSO.

Department of Education and Science (1991a) *Aspects of Primary Education in France*. London: DES.

Department of Education and Science (1991b) *The Parent's Charter: you and your child's education*. London: DES.

Department of Education and Science (1991c) *Primary Education: statement by the Secretary of State for Education and Science*. London: DES.

Department of Trade and Industry (1998) *Our Competitive Future: building the knowledge-driven economy*. London: HMSO.

Dewey, J. (1900) *The School and Society*. Chicago: Chicago University Press.

Dewey, J. (1916) *Democracy and Education*. New York: Macmillan.

Dillon, J. T. (1990) *The Practice of Questioning*. London: Routledge.

Doddington, C., Flutter, J. and Ruddock, J. (1999) *Improving learning: the pupils' agenda*. Cambridge: Homerton College.

Donaldson, M. (1978) *Children's Minds*. London: Fontana.

Donaldson, M. (1992) *Human Minds: an exploration*. London: Allen Lane.

Douglas, J. W. B. (1964) *The Home and the School*. London: Macgibbon and Kee.

Doyle, W. and Ponder, G. (1977) 'The practicality ethic and teacher decision-making', *Interchange* 8, 1–12.

Drummond, M. J. (1999) *Comparisons in Early Years Education: history, fact and fiction* (CREPE Occasional Paper 10). Warwick: University of Warwick Centre for Research in Elementary and Primary Education.

Dunkin, M. J. and Biddle, B. J. (1974) *The Study of Teaching*. New York: Holt Rinehart and Winston.

Dunne, E. and Bennett, S. N. (1990) *Talking and Leraning in Groups*. London: Macmillan.

Dunstan, J. (1994) 'Clever children and curriculum reform: the progress of differentiation in Soviet and Russian state schooling', in A. Jones (ed.) *Education and Society in the New Russia*. London: M. E. Sharpe.

East Sussex Accountability Project (1979) *Accountability in the Middle Years of Schooling: an analysis of policy options*. Brighton: University of Sussex.

Education Interchange Council (1956) *Education in the Soviet Union: report of a study tour, 1956*. London: EIC.

Education Week (2000) 'Quality counts 2000', *Education Week* 19:18.

Edwards, A. D. (1992) 'Teacher talk and pupil competence', in K. Norman (ed.) *Thinking Voices: the work of the National Oracy Project*. London: Hodder & Stoughton.

Edwards, A. D. and Westgate, D. P. G. (1994) *Investigating Classroom Talk*, 2nd edn. London: Falmer Press.

Edwards, D. and Mercer, N. (1987) *Common Knowledge: the development of understanding in the classroom*. London: Routledge.

Eggleston, S. J. (1977) *The Sociology of the School Curriculum*. London: Routledge and Kegan Paul.

Ehrlich, P. R. and Ehrlich, A. H. (1970) *Population, Resources, Environment: issues in human ecology*. San Francisco: W. H. Freeman.

Eisner, E. W. (1967) 'Educational objectives: help or hindrance?', *School Review* 75, 250–56.

Eisner, E. W. (1969) 'Instructional and expressive objectives', in E. W. Popham, E. W. Eisner, H. J. Sullivan, L. L. Tyler, *Instructional and Expressive Objectives*. Chicago: Rand McNally.

Eisner, E. W. (1979) *The Educational Imagination*. London: Macmillan.

Eisner, E. W. (1985) *The Art of Educational Evaluation*. Lewes: Falmer Press.

Elliott, J., Hufton, N., Hildreth, A. and Illushin, L. (1999) 'Factors influencing educational motivation: a study of attitudes, expectations and behaviour of children in Sunderland, Kentucky and St Petersburg', *British Educational Research Journal* 25:1, 75–97.

EURYDICE (1994) *Pre-School and Primary Education in the European Union*. Brussels: EURYDICE.

Evans, L., Packwood, A., Neill, S. R. St J. and Campbell, R. J. (1994) *The Meaning of infant teachers' work*. London: Routledge.

Figes, O. (1996) *A People's Tragedy: the Russian Revolution 1891–1924*. London: Jonathan Cape.

Finkielkraut, A. (1996) 'A pair of boots is as good as Shakespeare', in A. Corbett and B. Moon (eds) *Education in France: continuity and change in the Mitterand years, 1981–1995*, pp. 335–48. London: Routledge.

Flanders, N. (1970) *Analysing Teacher Behavior*. Reading, MA: Addison-Wesley.

Flint Board of Education (1989) *Strategic Plan 1989–1994*. Flint, MI: Flint Board of Education.

Flint Board of Education (1994a) *Multiage Primaries: how they help our children succeed*. Flint, MI: Flint Board of Education.

Flint Board of Education (1994b) *What is Multiage and Why is it Beneficial for My Children?* Flint, MI: Flint Board of Education.

Floden, R. E. (1997) *Changing School Mathematics: systemic reform and teacher decisions*. Warwick: Centre for Research in Elementary and Primary Education.

Florio, J. [1603] (1910) *The Essays of Michael, Lord of Montaigne, Translated by John Florio*, Vol. I. London: J. M. Dent.

Freedland, J. (1998) *Bring Home the Revolution: how Britain can live the American dream*. London: Fourth Estate.

Fuller, B. and Clarke, P. (1996) 'Raising school effects while ignoring culture? local conditions and the influence of classroom tools, rules and pedagogy', *Review of Educational Research* 94:1, 119–57.

Gage, N. (1978) *The Scientific Basis of the Art of Teaching*. New York: Teachers College Press.

Galton, M. (1998) 'What do the tests measure?', *Education 3 to 13*, 26:2, 50–59.

Galton, M. and Fogelman, K. (1998) 'The use of discretionary time in the primary school', *Research Papers in Education*.

Galton, M., Hargreaves, L., Comber, C., Wall, D. and Pell, A. (1999) *Inside the Primary Classroom: 20 Years On*. London: Routledge.

Galton, M. and Simon, B. (eds) (1980) *Progress and Performance in the Primary Classroom*. London: Routledge.

Galton, M., Simon, B. and Croll, P. (1980) *Inside the Primary Classroom*. London: Routledge.

Galton, M. and Williamson, J. (1992) *Group Work in the Primary Classroom*. London: Routledge.

Giddens, A. (1993) *New Rules of Sociological Method*. Cambridge: Polity Press.

Giddens, A. (1998) *The Third Way: the renewal of social democracy*. Cambridge: Polity Press.

Gipps, C. and MacGilchrist, B. (2000) 'Primary school learners', in P. Mortimore (ed.) *Pedagogy and its Impact on Learning*, pp. 45–67. London: Paul Chapman.

Giroux, H. A. (1983) *Theory and Resistance in Education*. London: Heinemann.

Giroux, H. A. (1997) 'Crossing the boundaries of educational discourse: modernisim, postmodernism and feminism', in A. H. Halsey, H. Lauder, P. Brown and A. S. Wells (eds) *Education: Culture, Economy, Society*, pp. 113–30. Oxford: Oxford University Press.

Giroux, H. A. (1999) 'Border youth, difference and postmodern education', in M. Castells, R. Flecha, P. Freire, H. A. Giroux, D. Macedo and P. Willis, *Critical Education in the New Education Age*, pp. 93–116. Lanham: Rowman & Littlefield.

Goertz, M. E., Floden, R. E. and O'Day, J. (1995) *Studies of Education Reform: systemic reform*. New Brunswick: Consortium for Policy Research in Education.

Good, H. G. (1960) *A History of Western Education*. New York: Macmillan.

Goody, J. (1993) *The Interface Between the Written and the Oral*. Cambridge: Cambridge University Press.

Graff, H. (1991) *The Legacies of Literacy: continuities and contradictions in western culture and society*. Bloomington, IN: Indiana University Press.

Green, A. (1990) *Education and State Formation: the rise of education systems in England, France and the USA*. London: Macmillan.

Grice, H. P. (1975) 'Logic and conversation', in P. Cole and J. Morgan (eds) *Syntax and Semantics*, Volume 3, *Speech Acts*. New York: Academic Press.

Hall, S. and du Gay, P. (eds) (1996) *Questions of Cultural Identity*. London: Sage.

Halliday, M. (1989) *Spoken and Written Language*. Oxford: Oxford University Press.

Halpin, T. (1998) 'The men failing our children, by schools chief', *Daily Mail*, 25 February.

Halsey, A. H. (1995) *Change in British Society*. Oxford: Oxford University Press.

Halsey, A. H., Floud, J. and Anderson, C. A. (eds) (1961) *Education, Economy and Society*. New York: Free Press.

Halsey, A. H. and Ridge, J. (1980) *Origins and Destinations: family, class and education in modern Britain*. Oxford: Oxford University Press.

Hamilton, D. (1995) 'Peddling feel-good fictions: reflections on "Key characteristics of effective schools"'. Liverpool: University of Liverpool School of Education.

Hamlyn, D. W. (1970) 'The logical and psychological aspects of learning', in R. S. Peters (ed.) *The Concept of Education*, pp. 24–43. London: Routledge and Kegan Paul.

Hargreaves, D. H. (1972) *Interpersonal Relations and Education*. London: Routledge and Kegan Paul.

Harlen, W., Darwin, A. and Murphy, M. (1977) *Match and Mismatch: raising questions*. Edinburgh: Oliver and Boyd.

Harris, S., Keys, W. and Fernandes, C. (1997) *Third International Mathematics and Science Study, Second National Report, Part 1*. Slough: NFER.

Hartley-Brewer, E. (1999) 'Are home-school deals just pie in the sky?', *The Independent*, 29 July.

Hatim, B. and Mason, I. (1990) *Discourse and the Translator*. London: Longman.

Haviland, J. (1988) *Take Care, Mr Baker*. London: Fourth Estate.

Heath, S. B. (1982) 'Protean strategies in literacy events: ever-shifting oral and literate traditions', in D. Tannen (ed.) *Spoken and Written Language: exploring orality and literacy*, pp. 91–113. Norwood, NJ: Ablex.

Heath, S. B. (1983) *Ways with Words*. Cambridge: Cambridge University Press.

Heffer, S. (1999) *Nor Shall My Sword: the reinvention of England*. London: Weidenfeld & Nicolson.

Hillage, J., Pearson, A., Anderson, A. and Tamkin, P. (1998) *Excellence in Research on Schools*. London: DfEE.

Hobsbawm, E. J. (1987) *The Age of Empire 1875–1914*. London: Abacus.

Hobsbawm, E. J. (1995) *Age of Extremes: the short twentieth century 1914–1991*. London: Abacus.

Holdsworth, N. (1998) 'Stoical staff survive by growing vegetables', *Times Educational Supplement*, 27 November.

Holdsworth, N. (1999) 'Starving teachers demand wages', *Times Educational Supplement*, 29 January.

Holmes, B. (1981) *Comparative Education: some considerations of method*. London: Allen & Unwin.

Holmes, R. (1998) *Coleridge: darker reflections*. London: Harper Collins.

Holmes Group (1986) *Tomorrow's Teachers*. East Lansing, MI: The Holmes Group.

Holmes Group (1990) *Tomorrow's Schools: principles for the design of professional development schools*. East Lansing, MI: The Holmes Group.

Holmes Group (1995) *Tomorrow's Schools of Education*. East Lansing, MI: The Holmes Group.

Holt School District (1994) *Holt Public Schools*. Holt, MI: Holt Board of Education.

House of Commons (1986) *Achievement in Primary Schools: Third Report from the Education, Science and Arts Committee*. London: HMSO.

House of Commons (1994a) *The Disparity in Funding Between Primary and Secondary Schools: Education Committee Second Report*. London: HMSO.

House of Commons (1994b) *Education Committee Third Special Report: Government Response to the Second Report from the Committee, Session 1993-4 (The Disparity in Funding Between Primary and Secondary Schools)*. London: HMSO.

House of Commons (1999a) *The Work of Ofsted: fourth report of the Education and Employment Committee* (3 volumes). London: The Stationery Office.

House of Commons (1999b) *Government's and Ofsted's Reponse to the Fourth Report from the Committee, Session 1998–99: the work of OFSTED*. London: the Stationery Office.

Hufton, N. and Elliott, J. (1999) 'Motivation to learn: the pedagogical nexus in the Russian school – some implications for transnational research and policy borrowing', *Educational Studies*.

Hutton, W. (1998) 'Big Boom Bang', *Marxism Today*, Nov.–Dec., 28.

India, Government of, Ministry of Human Resource Development (1992) *National Policy on Education, 1986 (with modifications undertaken in 1992)*. Delhi: MHRD.

India, Government of, Ministry of Human Resource Development (1993a) *Education for All: the Indian Scene*. Delhi: MHRD.

India, Government of, Ministry of Human Resource Development (1993b) *Learning Without Burden: report of the National Advisory Committee*. Delhi: MHRD.

India, Government of, Ministry of Human Resource Development (1998a) *Three Years of DPEP: assessment and challenges*. Delhi: MHRD.

India, Government of, Ministry of Human Resource Development (1998b) *DPEP Moves On . . . Towards Universalising Basic Education*. Delhi: MHRD.

India, Government of, Ministry of Human Resource Development (1998c) *Aide Memoire: District Primary Education Programme, Seventh Joint Supervision Mission*. Delhi: MHRD.

India, Government of, Ministry of Human Resource Development (1998d) *Access and Retention: the impact of DPEP*. Delhi: MHRD.

India, Government of, Ministry of Human Resource Development (1998e) *Three Years of DPEP and Learners' Achievement*. Delhi: MHRD.

International Institute for Educational Planning (IIEP) (1995) *Education Aid Policies and Priorities*. Paris: IIEP.

Jackson, B. (1964) *Streaming: an education system in miniature*. London: Routledge and Kegan Paul.

Jackson, P. W. (1968) *Life in Classrooms*. New York: Holt, Rinehart and Winston.

James, J. (1995) *The Music of the Spheres: music, science and the natural order of the universe*. London: Abacus.

Jenkins, D. (1975) 'Classical and romantic in the curriculum landscape', in M. Golby, J. Greenwald and R. West (eds) *Curriculum Design*. London: Croom Helm.

Johnson, M. and Brooks, H. (1979) 'Conceptualising classroom management', in D. L. Duke (eds) *Classroom Management*. Chicago: University of Chicago Press.

Johnson, W. H. E. (1969) *Russia's Educational Heritage*. New York: Octagon Books.

Jones, A. (ed.) (1994) *Education and Society in the New Russia*. Armonk, NY: M. E. Sharpe.

Judge, H., Lemosse, M., Paine, L. and Sedlak, M. (1994) *The University and the Teachers: France, the United States, England*. Oxford: Triangle Books.

Kellmer-Pringle, M. (1980) *The Needs of Children*. London: Hutchinson.

Kelly, A. V. (1990) *The National Curriculum: a critical review*. London: Paul Chapman.

Kennedy, P. (1996) 'Globalisation and its discontents', *BBC 1996 Analysis Lecture*. London: British Broadcasting Corporation.

Kerr, S. T. (1994) 'Diversification in Russian Education', in A. Jones (ed.) *Education and Society in the New Russia*, pp. 47–74. Armonk, NY: M. E. Sharpe.

Kerry, T. (1984) 'Analysing the cognitive demand made by classroom tasks in mixed-ability classes', in E. C. Wragg (ed.) *Classroom Teaching Skills*, pp. 163–79. London: Routledge.

Keys, W. (1996a) 'Take care when you compare', *Times Educational Supplement*, 14 June.

Keys, W. (1996b) 'What do international comparisons of educational achievement really tell us?' Slough: National Foundation for Educational Research.

Keys, W., Harris, S. and Fernandes, C. (1996) *Third International Mathematics and Science Study: First National Report, Part 1*. Slough: NFER.

Kidd, C. (1999) *British Identities Before Nationalism*. Cambridge: Cambridge University Press.

King, E. J. (1979a) *Other Schools and Ours: comparative studies for today*. London: Holt Rinehart and Winston.

King, E. J. 'Social origins of education systems: a review'. *Comparative Education* 15:3, 350–52.

King, R. (1978) *All Things Bright and Beautiful? A sociological study of infants' classrooms*. Chichester: Wiley.

Kirby, N. (1981) *Personal Values and Education*. London: Harper & Row.

Kirst, M. W. (1995) 'Who's in charge? Federal, state and local control', in D. Ravitch and M. A. Vinovskis (eds) *Learning from the past: what history teaches us about school reform*. Baltimore: Johns Hopkins University Press.

Kumar, Krishan (1997) 'The post-modern condition', in A. H. Halsey, H. Lauder, P. Brown and A. S. Wells (eds) *Education: Culture, Economy, Society*. Oxford: Oxford University Press.

Kumar, Krishna (1991) *Political Agenda of Education: a study of colonialist and nationalist ideas*. New Delhi: Sage.

Landes, D. S. (1998) *The Wealth and Poverty of Nations: why some are so rich and some so poor*. London: Little, Brown.

Lansing School District (1994a) *Great Expectations: Lansing School District Annual Report*. Lansing, MI: Lansing Board of Education.

Lansing School District (1994b) *Schools of Choice Plan*. Lansing, MI: Lansing Board of Education.

Lansing School District (1994c) *Student Progress Report, Grade 1*. Lansing, MI: Lansing Board of Education.

Lawlor, S. (1990) *Teachers Mistaught*. London: Centre for Policy Studies.

Lawson, J. and Silver, H. (1973) *A Social History of Education in England*. London: Methuen.

Lawton, D. (1983) *Curriculum Studies and Educational Planning*. London: Hodder & Stoughton.

Lawton, D. (1989) *Education, Culture and the National Curriculum*. London: Hodder & Stoughton.

Layder, D. (1997) *Modern Social Theory: key debates and new directions*. London: UCL Press.

Leach, E. (1964) 'Models', *New Society*, 14 June.

Lemosse, M. (1997) *Education, Race and Religion in France and Great Britain*. Warwick: Centre for Research in Elementary and Primary Education.

Levin, H. M. and Kelly, C. (1997) 'Can education do it alone?', in A. H. Halsey, H. Lauder, P. Brown and A. S. Wells (eds) *Education: Culture, Economy, Society*, pp. 240–52. Oxford: Oxford University Press.

Lichfield, J. (1999) 'Mother tongue divides France', *Independent*, 28 June.

Lindfors, J. W. (1999) *Children's Inquiry: using language to make sense of the world*. New York: Teacher's College, Columbia University.

Little, A. (1995) *Multi-Grade Teaching: evidence from practice and research*. London: Overseas Development Administration.

Lloyd, J. (1998) *Rebirth of a Nation: an anatomy of Russia*. London: Michael Joseph.

Lockheed, M. and Verspoor, A. M. (1991) *Improving Primary Education in Developing Countries*. Washington, DC: World Bank in conjunction with Oxford University Press.

Luxton, R. G. (2000) *Interactive Whole Class Teaching: a briefing note*. London: London Borough of Barking and Dagenham Department of Education.

Luxton, R. and Last, G. (1997) *Underachievement and Pedagogy*. London: National Institute for Social and Economic Research.

Macedo, D. (1999) 'Our common culture: a poisonous pedagogy', in M. Castells, R. Flecha, P. Freire, H. A. Giroux and P. Willis (eds) *Critical Education in the New Information Age*, pp. 117–38. Lanham: Rowman & Littlefield.

Mail on Sunday (1999) 'Luddites at the school gates'. London: *Mail on Sunday*, 14 March.

Manton, F. (1912) *Life of John Shakespeare Manton*. Birmingham: Frank Manton.

Marsh, L. G. (1973) *Being a Teacher*. London: A. & C. Black.

Marshall, J. (1999) 'Chirac's "non" to local dialects', *Times Educational Supplement*, 9 July, 24.

Mayo, E. (1832) *Lessons on Objects*. London: Seeley & Burnside.

McCrum, R., Cran, W. and MacNeil, R. (1992) *The Story of English*. London: Faber & Faber.

McKay, D. (1994) *American Politics and Society*. Oxford: Blackwell.

McLaren, P. (1997) 'Multiculturalism and the postmodern critique: toward a pedagogy of resistance and transformation', in A. H. Halsey, H. Lauder, P. Brown and A. S. Wells (eds) *Education: culture, economy and society*, pp. 520–40. Oxford: Oxford University Press.

McNamara, D. R. and Desforges, C. (1978) 'The social sciences, teacher education, and the objectification of craft knowledge', *British Journal of Teacher Education* 4:1, 17–36.

McNamara, D. R. (1979) 'Professional studies as a source of theory', in R. J. Alexander and E. Wormald (eds) *Professional Studies for Teaching*, pp. 46–60. Guildford: Society for Research into Higher Education.

McNamara, D. R. (1994) *Classroom Pedagogy and Primary Practice*. London: Routledge.

McNamara, D. R. and Waugh, D. (1993) 'Classroom organisation: a discussion of grouping strategies in the light of the "Three Wise Men's Report"', *School Organisation* 13:1, 41–50.

Mead, G. H. (1934) *Mind, Self and Society*. Chicago: University of Chicago Press.

Meadows, D. H., Meadows, D. L., Randers, J. and Behrenes, W. W. (1972) *The Limits to Growth*. London: Earth Island.

Meirieu, P. (1996) 'Is differentiated teaching out of date?', in A. Corbett and B. Moon (eds) *Education in France: continuity and change in the Mitterand years, 1981–1995*, pp. 359–68. London: Routledge.

Michigan, State of (1993) *Enrolled House Bill No. 5121*. Lansing, MI: State of Michigan Government.

Michigan State Department of Education (1995) *Content Standards and Draft Benchmarks*. Lansing, MI: Michigan State Board of Education.

Michigan State Department of Education (2000) *A Report to the Citizens: Michigan's progress toward the National Educational Goals*. Lansing, MI: Michigan State Board of Education.

Millett, A. (1999) 'Why we need to raise our game', *The Independent*, 11 Feb.

Ministère de l'Education Nationale (1993) *Primary Education in France*. Paris: Ministère de l'Education Nationale.

Ministère de l'Education Nationale (1994) *Géographie de l'Ecole*. Paris: Ministère de l'Education Nationale.

Ministère de l'Education Nationale (1995a) *Projet: programmes de l'école primaire*. Paris: Ministère de l'Education Nationale.

Ministère de l'Education Nationale (1995b) *Aide à l'Evaluation des Elèves*. Paris: Ministère de l'Education Nationale (six volumes, two for each cycle).

Ministère de l'Education Nationale (1998) *Bâtir L'Ecole du XXI Siècle*. Paris: Ministère de l'Education Nationale.

Ministry of Education, Russian Federation (1993) *State Educational Standard, General Secondary Education: Basic Curriculum for Secondary General Education*. Moscow: Ministry of Education of the Russian Federation.

Ministry of General and Professional Education, Russian Federation (2000) *National Doctrine of Education in the Russian Federation* (draft, Feb. 2000). Reprinted in *Education in Russia, the Independent States and Eastern Europe* 18:1, 36–41.

Montessori, M. (1912, tr. A. E. George) *The Montessori Method: scientific pedagogy as applied to child education in the 'Children's Houses'*. New York: F. A. Stokes.

Moon, B. (1996) 'Challenging the idea of centralised control: the reform of the French curriculum in a European context', in A. Corbett and B. Moon (eds) *Education in France: continuity and change in the Mitterand years, 1981–1995*, pp. 142–63. London: Routledge.

Moon, B. (1998) *The English Exception: international perspectives on the initial education and training of teachers*. London: Universities Council for the Education of Teachers.

Morris, B. (1977) *Some Aspects of the Professional Freedom of Teachers*. Paris: UNESCO.

Morris, P. (1998) 'Comparative education and educational reform: beware of prophets returning from the Far East', *Education 3 to 1*, 26:2, 3–8.

Mortimore, P., Sammons, P., Stoll, L., Lewis, D. and Ecob, R. (1988) *School Matters: the Junior Years*. London: Open Books.

Mroz, M., Smith, F. and Hardman, F. (1999) 'The discourse of the literacy hour', *Cambridge Journal of Education* 30:3.

Muckle, J. (1988) *A Guide to the Soviet Curriculum: what the Russian child is taught in school*. London: Croom Helm.

Muckle, J. (1990) *Portrait of a Soviet School under Glasnost*. London: Macmillan.

National Commission on Excellence in Education (1983) *A Nation at Risk: the imperative for educational reform*. Washington, DC: US Government Printing Office.

National Council of Educational Research and Training (1986) *Fifth All-India Survey: a concise report*. Delhi: NCERT.

National Council of Educational Research and Training (1991) *Minimum Levels of Learning at Primary Stage*. Delhi: NCERT.

National Education Goals Panel (1991) *The National Education Goals Report: building a nation of learners*. Washington, DC: US Government Printing Office.

Nautiyal, K. C. (1993) *Basic Education in Slums of Delhi: growing menace*. Delhi: NCERT.

Nayar, U. (1989) 'Universalisation of elementary education for girls in India: some basic issues.' Conference paper. Delhi: NCERT.

Nayar, U. (1993) *Universal Primary Education of Girls in Rural India*. Delhi: NCERT.

Neill, S. R. St J. (1991) *Classroom Non-Verbal Communication*. London: Routledge.

Nikandrov, N. D. (1995) 'Russian education after Perestroika: the search for new values', *International Review of Education* 41:1–2, 47–57.

Noah, H. J. (1986) 'The use and abuse of comparative education', in P. G. Altbach and G. P. Kelly (eds) *New Approaches to Comparative Education*, pp. 153–66. Chicago: University of Chicago Press.

Norman, K. (ed.) (1992) *Thinking Voices: the work of the National Oracy Project*. London: Hodder & Stoughton.

O'Donnell, S., Le Métais, J., Boyd, S. and Tabberer, R. (1998) *INCA: the International Review of Curriculum and Assessment Frameworks Archive* (CD-ROM). London: Qualifications and Curriculum Authority.

Office for Standards in Education (1993) *Curriculum Organisation and Classroom practice in Primary Schools: a follow-up report*. London: OFSTED.

Office for Standards in Education (1994a) *Aspects of Primary Education in Italy*. London: HMSO.

Office for Standards in Education (1994b) *Primary Matters: a discussion on teaching and learning in primary schools*. London: OFSTED.

Office for Standards in Education (1995) *Teaching Quality: the primary debate*. London: OFSTED.

Office for Standards in Education (1997) *National Curriculum Assessment: results and the wider curriculum at Key Stage 2*. London: OFSTED.

Office for Standards in Education (1998a) *The National Literacy Project: an HMI evaluation*. London: OFSTED.

Office for Standards in Education (1998b) *The National Numeracy Project: an HMI evaluation*. London: OFSTED.

Office for Standards in Education (1998c) Letter from HMCI to the Secretary of State for Education and Employment, 5 January. London: OFSTED.

Office for Standards in Education (1999a) *Raising the Attainment of Minority Ethnic Pupils*. London: OFSTED.

Office for Standards in Education (1999b) *Standards and Quality in Education: the Annual Report of Her Majesty's Chief Inspector of Schools*. London: The Stationery Office.

Office for Standards in Education (1999c) *Primary Education 1994–8: a review of primary schools in England*. London: The Stationery Office.

Office for Standards in Education (1999d) *Handbook for Inspecting Primary and nursery Schools*. London: the Stationery Office.

Office for Standards in Education with the Department for Education and Employment (1997) *National Curriculum Assessment Results and the Wider Curriculum at Key Stage 2: some evidence from the OFSTED database*. London: OFSTED and DfEE.

Organization for Economic Co-operation and Development (1994) *Quality in Teaching*. Paris: OECD.

Organization for Economic Co-operation and Development (1995a) *Measuring the Quality of Schools*. Paris: OECD.

Organization for Economic Co-operation and Development (1995b) *Measuring What Students Learn*. Paris: OECD.

Organization for Economic Co-operation and Development (1996a) *Education at a Glance: OECD indicators 1996*. Paris: OECD.

Organization for Economic Co-operation and Development (1996b) *Reviews of National Policies for Education: France*. Paris: OECD.

Organization for Economic Co-operation and Development (1998a) *Education at a Glance: OECD indicators 1998*. Paris: OECD.

Organization for Economic Co-operation and Development (1998b) *Reviews of National Policies for Education: Russian Federation*. Paris: OECD.

Osborn, M. and Planel, C. (1999) 'Comparing children's learning, attitude and performance in French and English primary schools', in R. J. Alexander, P. Broadfoot and D. Phillips (eds) *Learning from Comparing: new directions in comparative educational research. Volume I: Contexts, Classrooms and Outcomes*, pp. 259–81. Oxford: Symposium Books.

Oxfam (1999) *Education Now*. Oxford: Oxfam.

Paine, T. [1792] 'The Rights of Man: part the second combining principle and practice', in M. Philp (ed.) (1995) *Thomas Paine, Rights of Man, Common Sense and Other Political Writings*. Oxford: Oxford University Press.

Paxman, J. (1998) *The English*. London: Penguin Books.

Paz, O. (1997, tr. by E.Weinberger) *In Light of India*. London: Harvill Press.

Pestalozzi, J. H. [1802] (1907, tr. by L. E. Holland and F. C. Turner, ed. E. Cooke) *How Gertrude Teaches Her Children*. London: Swan Sonnenschein.

Peters, R. S. (ed.) (1968) *Perspectives on Plowden*. London: Routledge and Kegan Paul.

Phillips, D. (1999) 'On comparing', in R. J. Alexander, P. Broadfoot, D. Phillips (eds) (1999) *Learning from Comparing: new directions in comparative educational research. Volume I: Contexts, Classrooms and Outcomes*, pp. 15–20. Oxford: Symposium Books.

Phillips, M. (1996) *All Must Have Prizes*. London: Little, Brown.

Pinker, S. (1999) *Words and Rules: the ingredients of language*. London: Weidenfeld & Nicolson.

Pirani, S. (1999) 'War over wages reaches impasse', *Times Educational Supplement*, 19 March.

Planel, C., Osborn, M., Broadfoot, P. and Ward, B. (1998) *A Comparative Analysis of English and French Pupils' Attitudes and Performance in Mathematics and Language*. Bristol: University of Bristol School of Education.

Pollard, A. (1985) *The Social World of the Primary School*. London: Cassell.

Pollard, A. and Broadfoot, P. (1997) 'PACE: Primary Assessment, Curriculum and Experience'. Bristol: CLIO.

Pollard, A., Broadfoot, P., Croll, P., Osborn, M. and Abbott, D. (1994) *Changing English Primary Schools: the impact of the Education Reform Act at Key Stage One*. London: Cassell.

Pollard, A. and Filer, A. (1999) *The Social World of Pupil Careers: strategic biographies through primary school*. London: Cassell.

Pollard, H. M. (1956) *Pioneers of Popular Education, 1760–1850*. London: John Murray.

Popham, P. (2000) 'Software from city of rickshaws breathes down Microsoft's neck', *The Independent*, 22 Feb.

Popper, K. (1963) *Conjectures and Refutations: the growth of scientific knowledge*. London: Routledge and Kegan Paul.

Popper, K. (1972) *Objective Knowledge: an evolutionary approach*. Oxford: Oxford University Press.

Prais, S. J. (1997) *School Readiness, Whole Class Teaching, and Pupils' Mathematical Achievement*. London: National Institute for Economic and Social research.

Prais, S. J. (1998) 'Raising schooling attainments by grouping pupils within each class', *National Institute Economic Review* 165, 83–8.

Prais, S. J. and Wagner, K. (1965) 'Schooling standards in England and Germany: some summary comparisons based on economic performance', *Compare* 16, 5–36.

Price, R. (1993) *A Concise History of France*. Cambridge: Cambridge University Press.

PROBE (1999) *Public Report on Basic Education in India*. Delhi: Oxford University Press.

Prost, A. (1996) 'The educational maelstrom', in A. Corbett and B. Moon (eds) *Education in France: continuity and change in the Mitterand years, 1981–1995*, pp. 349–58. London: Routledge.

Psacharopoulos, G. and Woodhall, M. (1985) *Education for Development: an analysis of investment choices*. Washington, DC: World Bank in conjunction with Oxford University Press.

Pushkin, A. S. [1830] (1999) 'The Squire's Daughter', in Alexander Pushkin (tr. Paul Debreczeny) *The Collected Stories*. London: Everyman.

Qualifications and Curriculum Authority (1998a) 'Skills for adult and working life' (working paper). London: QCA.

Qualifications and Curriculum Authority (1998b) *Education for Citizenship and the Teaching of Democracy in Schools*. London: QCA.

Qualifications and Curriculum Authority (1998c) *The Review of the National Curriculum in England: consultation materials*. London: QCA.

Qualifications and Curriculum Authority (1999a) *Developing the School Curriculum*. London: QCA.

Qualifications and Curriculum Authority (1999b) *The Review of the National Curriculum in England: the consultation materials*. London: Qualifications and Curriculum Authority.

Raivola R. (1986) 'What is comparison? Methodological and philosophical considerations', in P. G. Altbach and G. P. Kelly (eds) *New Approaches to Comparative Education*, pp. 261–73. Chicago: University of Chicago Press.

Ravitch, D. (1983) *The Troubled Crusade: American education 1945–80*. New York: Basic Books.

Reboul-Scherrer, F. (1989) *Les Premiers Instituteurs, 1833–1882*. Paris: Hachette.

Reese, W. J. (1995) ' "Reefer Madness" and "A Clockwork Orange" ', in D. Ravitch and M. A. Vinovskis, *Learning About the Past: what history teaches us about school reform*, pp. 355–81. Baltimore: Johns Hopkins University Press.

Reynolds, D. (1999a) 'Creating a new methodology for comparative educational research: the contribution of the International School Effectiveness Research Project', in R. J. Alexander, P. Broadfoot and D. Phillips (eds) *Learning from Comparing: new directions in comparative educational research. Volume I: Contexts, Classrooms and Outcomes*, pp. 135–48. Oxford: Symposium Books.

Reynolds, D. (1999b) 'Woodhead has failed to grasp that teaching is a complex applied science, not a craft', *Observer*, 25 April.

Reynolds, D., Bollen, R., Creemers, B., Hopkins, D., Stoll, L. and Lagerweij, N. (1996) *Making Good Schools: linking school effectiveness and school improvement*. London: Routledge.

Reynolds, D., Creemers, B. P. M., Nesselrodt, P. S., Schaffer, E. C., Stringfield, S. and Teddlie, C. (1994) *Advances in School Effectiveness Research and Practice*. Oxford; Pergamon.

Reynolds, D. and Farrell, S. (1996) *Worlds Apart? A review of international surveys of educational achievement involving England*. London: HMSO.

Reynolds, D., and Lawlor, S. (1999) 'Can good teaching be measured?', *Times Educational Supplement*, 13 Aug.

Reynolds, D. and Teddlie, C. (1995) *World Class Schools: a preliminary report from the international School Effectiveness Research Project*. Newcastle upon Tyne: University of Newcastle upon Tyne School of Education.

Richards, S. (1990) *Epics of Everyday Life: encounters in a changing Russia*. London: Penguin.

Robinson, P. (1999) 'The tyranny of league tables: international comparisons of educational attainment and economic performance', in R. J. Alexander, P. Broadfoot and D. Phillips (eds) (1999) *Learning from Comparing: new directions in comparative educational research. Volume I: Contexts, Classrooms and Outcomes*, pp. 217–35. Oxford: Symposium Books.

Rosenthal, R. and Jacobson, L. (1968) *Pygmalion in the Classroom: teacher expectations and pupils' intellectual development*. New York: Holt.

Rutter, M., Maughan, B., Mortimore, P. and Ouston, J. (1979) *Fifteen Thousand Hours: Secondary schools and their effects on children*. London: Open Books.

Sadler, J. E. (1966) *J. A. Comenius and the Concept of Universal Education*. London: George Allen & Unwin.

Sadler, M. [1900] 'How can we learn anything of practical value from the study of foreign systems of education?', in J. H. Higginson (ed.) *Selections from Michael Sadler: studies in world citizenship*. Liverpool: Dejall & Meyorre.

Sadler, M. (1902) 'The unrest in secondary education in Germany and elsewhere', in Board of Education, *Education in Germany: Special Reports on Education Subjects, Volume 9*. London: HMSO.

Said, E. (1979) *Orientalism*. London: Vintage.

Said, E. (1994) *Culture and Imperialism*. London: Vintage.

Saldanha, D. (1993) 'Cultural communication in literacy campaigns: social relational contexts, processes and hegemonic organisation', *Economic and Political Weekly* (India), 28:2, 981–90.

Saldanha, D. (1995) 'Literacy campaigns in Maharashtra and Goa: issues, trends and direction', *Economic and Political Weekly* (India), 20:20, 1172–96.

Sammons, P., Hillman, J. and Mortimore, P. (1995) *Key Characteristics of Effective Schools: a review of school effectiveness research*. London: OFSTED.

Schaffer, E. C., Nesselrodt, P. S. and Stringfield, S. (1994) 'The contributions of classroom observation to school effectiveness research', in D. Reynolds, B. P. M. Creemers, P. S. Nesselrodt, E. C. Schaffer, S. Stringfield and C. Teddlie (eds) *Advances in School Effectiveness Research and Practice*, pp. 133–52. Oxford: Pergamon.

Schweisfurth, M. (1999a) 'Resilience, resistance and responsiveness: comparative and international education in United Kingdom universities', in R. J. Alexander, P. Broadfoot, D. Phillips (eds) *Learning from Comparing: new directions in comparative educational research. Volume I: Contexts, Classrooms and Outcomes*, pp. 89–102. Oxford: Symposium Books.

Schweisfurth, M. (1999b) *A Comparative Study of Teachers and Social Change in Russia and South Africa*. (PhD thesis). Warwick: University of Warwick.

Scrase, T. J. (1993) *Image, Ideology and Inequality: cultural domination, hegemony and schooling in India*. New Delhi: Sage.

Sealey, A. (1999a) *Theories About Language in the National Literacy Strategy*. Warwick: University of Warwick Centre for Research in Elementary and Primary Education.

Sealey, A. (1999b) '"Don't be cheeky": requests, directives and being a child', *Journal of Sociolinguistics* 3:1, 24–40.

Sealey, A. (2000a) 'Grammar in the schools: notes from the British front', *Syntax in the Schools*, 16:3, 1–5.

Sealey, A. (2000b) *Childly Language: children, language and the social world*. London: Longman.

Selleck, R. J. W. (1972) *English Primary Education and the Progressives, 1914–39*. London: Routledge and Kegan Paul.

Sen, A. (1999) 'Assessing human development' in United Nations Development Programme, *Human Development Report 1999*. New York: Oxford University Press.

Service, R. (1998) *A History of Twentieth Century Russia*. London: Penguin Books.

Sharan, S. (1990) (ed.) *Cooperative Learning: theory and research*. New York: Praeger.

Sharp, R. and Green, A. (1975) *Education and Social Control: a study in progressive primary education*. London: Routledge and Kegan Paul.

Sharpe, K. (1995) 'Children's experience of primary schooling in England and France'. Paper presented at a conference on French primary education at the School Curriculum and Assessment Authority, 6 Nov. London: SCAA.

Sharpe, K. (1996) 'Educational homogeneity in French primary education', in A. Corbett and B. Moon (eds) *Education in France: continuity and change in the Mitterand years, 1981–1995*, pp. 216–37. London: Routledge.

Sharpe, K. (1997) 'The Protestant ethic and the spirit of Catholicism: ideological and instructional constraints on system change in English and French primary schooling', *Comparative Education* 33:3, 329–48.

Shotton, J. (1996) *Education, Empire and Resistance in India, 1854–1937*. PhD thesis, University of London.

Shotton, J. (1998) *Learning and Freedom: policy, pedagogy and paradigms in Indian education and schooling*. New Delhi: Sage.

Shulman, L. (1987) 'Knowledge and teaching: foundations of the new reform', *Harvard Educational Review* 57:1, 1–22.

Silberman, C. (ed.) *The Open Classroom Reader*. New York: Random House.

Simon, B. (1965) *Education and the Labour Movement, 1870–1920*. London: Lawrence & Wishart.

Simon, B. (1974) *The Two Nations and the Educational Structure, 1780–1870*. London: Lawrence & Wishart.

Simon, B. (1981a) 'Why no pedagogy in England?', in B. Simon and W. Taylor (eds) *Education in the Eighties: the central issues*, pp. 124–45. London: Batsford.

Simon, B. (1981b) 'The primary school revolution: myth or reality?', in B. Simon and J. Willcocks (eds) *Research and Practice in the Primary Classroom*, pp. 7–25. London: Routledge.

Simon, B. (1983) 'The study of education as a university subject', *Studies in Higher Education* 8:1, 1–13.

Simon, B. (1985) *Does Education Matter?* London: Lawrence & Wishart.

Simon, B. (1991) *Education and the Social Order, 1940–1990*. London: Lawrence & Wishart.

Simon, B. (1992) 'Curriculum Organisation and Classroom Practice: a discussion paper' (review article), *Curriculum Journal* 3:1.

Simon, B. (1994) *The State and Educational Change: essays in the history of education and pedagogy*. London: Lawrence & Wishart.

Simon, B. (1997) *Henry Simon of Manchester*. Leicester: Pendene Press.

Simon, B. (1998) *A Life in Education*. London: Lawrence & Wishart.

Simon, B. and Simon, J. (1963) *Educational Psychology in the U.S.S.R.* London: Stanford University Press.

Simon, J. (1966) *Education and Society in Tudor England*. Cambridge: Cambridge University Press.

Simon, J. (1987) 'Vygotsky and the Vygotskians', *American Journal of Education*, Aug.

Sinclair, J. McH. and Coulthard, R. M. (1975) *Towards an Analysis of Discourse*. Oxford: Oxford University Press.

Sinclair, J. McH. and Coulthard, R. M. (1992) 'Towards an Analysis of Discourse', in M.Coulthard (ed.) *Advances in Spoken Discourse Analysis*, pp. 1–34. London: Routledge.

Smelser, N. J. (1991) *Social Paralysis and Social Change: British working-class education in the nineteenth century*. Berkeley, CA: University of California Press.

Smithers, A. and Robinson, P. (1981) *Beyond Compulsory Schooling: a numerical picture*. London: Council for Industry and Higher Education.

Stein, B. (1998) *A History of India*. Oxford: Blackwell.

Stern, R. W. (1993) *Changing India: bourgeois revolution on the subcontinent*. Cambridge: Cambridge University Press.

Stevenson, H. W. and Stigler, J. W. (1992) *The Learning Gap: why our schools are failing and what we can learn from Japanese and Chinese Education*. New York: Simon & Schuster.

Stubbs, M. (1983) *Discourse Analysis: the sociolinguistics of natural language*. Oxford: Blackwell.

Stubbs, M. (1986) *Educational Linguistics*. Oxford: Blackwell.

Sutherland, J. (1999) *Schooling in the New Russia: innovation and change 1984–95*. Basingstoke: Macmillan, in association with the School of Slavonic and East European Studies, University of London.

Taba, H. (1962) *Curriculum Development: theory and practice*. New York: Harcourt, Brace and World.

Tabberer, R. and Le Métais, J. (1996) 'Why different countries do better: evidence from examining curriculum and assessment frameworks'. Slough: National Foundation for Educational Research.

Tannen, D. (ed.) (1982) *Spoken and Written Language: exploring orality and literacy*. Norwood, NJ: Ablex.

Taylor, P. H., Reid, W. A., Holley, B. J. and Exon, G. (1974) *Purpose, Power and Constraint in the Primary School Curriculum*. London: Macmillan.

Taylor, W. (1969) *Society and the Education of Teachers*. London: Faber.

Teacher Training Agency (1998) *National Standards for Qualified Teacher Status*. London: TTA.

Tharp, R. G. and Gallimore, R. (1988) *Rousing Young Minds to Life: teaching, learning and schooling in social context*. Cambridge: Cambridge University Press.

Thomas, R. and Postlethwaite, N. (1983) *Schooling in East Asia: forms of change*. Oxford: Pergamon Press.

Thompson, E. P. (1991) *The Making of the English Working Class*, revd edn. London: Penguin.

Thompson, J. M. (1994) *Russia and the Soviet Union*. Boulder, CO: Westview Books.

Thubron, C. (1985) *Among the Russians*. London: Penguin Books.

Times Educational Supplement (1997) 'Advisers clash on primary timetable', *Times Educational Supplement*, 16 Feb.

Times Educational Supplement (1998) 'Teacher dies in pay protest', *Times Educational Supplement*, 4 Dec.

Tizard, B., Blatchford, P., Burke, J., Farquhar, C. and Plewis, I. (1988) *Young Children at School in the Inner City*. London: Lawrence Erlbaum.

Tizard, B. and Hughes, M. (1984) *Young Children Learning: talking and thinking at home and at school*. London: Fontana.

Tobin, J. J. (1999) 'Method and Meaning in Comparative Classroom Ethnography', in R. J. Alexander, P. Broadfoot, D. Phillips (eds) *Learning from Comparing: new directions in comparative educational research. Volume I: Contexts, Classrooms and Outcomes*, pp. 113–34. Oxford: Symposium Books.

Tobin, J. J., Wu, D. Y. and Davidson, D. H. (1989) *Preschool in Three Cultures: Japan, China and the United States*. New Haven, CT: Yale University Press.

Tönnies, F. [1887] (1955) trans. C. P. Loomis, *Community and Association*. London: Routledge and Kegan Paul.

Tooley, J. and Darby, D. (1998) *Educational Research: a critique*. London: OFSTED.

Tough, J. (1976) *Listening to Children Talking*. London: Ward Lock Educational.

Tough, J. (1979) *Talk for Teaching and Learning*. London: Ward Lock Educational.

Tyler, R. W. (1971) *Basic Principles of Curriculum and Instruction*. Chicago: University of Chicago Press.

United Nations (1999) *Human Development Report 1999*. New York: Oxford University Press.

United Nations Educational, Scientific and Cultural Organisation (UNESCO) (1999) *State of the World's Children*. Geneva: UNESCO.

United Nations Children's Fund (UNICEF) (1998a) *The Progress of Nations*. New York: UNICEF.

United Nations Children's Fund (UNICEF) (1998b) *World Data on Education*, 2nd edn. Geneva: UNICEF International Bureau of Education (compact disk).

United Nations Children's Fund (UNICEF) (1998c) *Education for all? Regional Monitoring Report 5, CEE/CIS/Baltics*. Florence: UNICEF.

United Nations Children's Fund (UNICEF) (1999) *Statistics*. New York: UNICEF website.

United States Department of Education (1983) *A Nation at Risk*. Washington, DC: US Government Printing Office.

United States Department of Education (2000a) *National Goals Panel Report (1998)*. Washington, DC: Department of Education Website.

United States Department of Education (2000b) *Misconceptions about the Goals 2000 Educate America Act*. Washington, DC: Department of Education Website.

Vygotsky, L. S. (1962) *Thought and Language*. Cambridge, MA: M.I.T. Press.

Vygotsky, L. S. (1978) *Mind in Society*. Cambridge, MA: Harvard University Press.

Vygotsky, L. S. (1981) 'The genesis of higher mental functions', in J. V. Wertsch (ed.) *The Concept of Activity in Soviet Psychology*. London: M. E. Sharpe.

Wallace, M. (1993) 'Discourse of derision: the role of the mass media within the educational policy process', *Journal of Educational Policy* 8:4.

Ward, B. and Dubos, R. (1972) *Only One Earth: the care and maintenance of a small planet*. London: Pelican.

Watkins, C., Mortimore, P. (1999) 'Pedagogy: what do we know?', in P. Mortimore (ed.) *Pedagogy and its Impact on Learning*, pp. 1–19. London: Paul Chapman.

Watson, G. and Seiler, R. M. (eds) (1992) *Text in Context: contributions to ethnomethodology*. London: Sage.

Watson, K. (1993) 'Changing emphases in educational aid', in T. Allsop and C. Brock (eds) *Key Issues in Educational Development*. Wallingford: Triangle Books.

Watson, K. (1999) 'Comparative educational research: the need for reconceptualisation and fresh insights', *Compare* 29:3, 233–48.

Webb, S. and Webb, B. (1936) *Soviet Communism – a New Civilization?* New York: Scribner.

Wells, G. (1986) *The Meaning Makers: children learning language and using language to learn*. London: Hodder & Stoughton.

Wertsch, J. V. (1995) *Culture, Communication and Cognition*. Cambridge: Cambridge University Press.

West, C. (1977) 'The new cultural politics of difference', in A. H. Halsey, H. Lauder, P. Brown and A. S. Wells (eds) *Education: Culture, Economy, Society*, pp. 509–19. Oxford: Oxford University Press.

Weston, P., Taylor, M., Lewis, G. and MacDonald, A. (1998) *Learning from Differentiation: a review of practice in primary and secondary schools*. Slough: NFER.

White, J. P. (1977) 'Tyndale and the Left', *Forum* 19:2.

White, J. P. (1982) 'The primary teacher as servant of the state', in C. M. Richards (ed.) *New Directions in Primary Education*. Brighton: Falmer Press.

Williams, R. (1976) *Keywords: a vocabulary of culture and society*. London: Fontana.

Winter, S. (1998) 'International comparisons of student achievement: can they tell us which nations perform best and which nations are most successful?', *Education 3 to 13*, 26:2, 26–32.

Womack, H. (1998) 'A rotten, decaying nation', *The Independent*, 17 Aug.

Woodhead, C. (1996) 'Boys who learn to be losers', *The Times*, 6 Feb.

Woodhead, C. (1998) 'Blood on the tracks: lessons from the history of education reform' (RSA HMCI Annual Lecture, 1998). London: OFSTED.

Woods, P. (1996) *Researching the Art of Teaching: ethnography for educational use*. London: Routledge.

Woods, P. and Jeffrey, B. (1996) *Teachable Moments: the art of teaching in primary schools*. Buckingham: Open University Press.

Woods, P. and Wenham, P. (1995) 'Politics and pedagogy: a case study in appropriation', *Journal of Educational Policy* 10:2.

World Bank (1990) *Primary Education: a World Bank Policy Paper*. Washington, DC: World Bank.

World Bank (1996) *Russia: Education in the Transition*. Washington, DC: World Bank.

World Bank (2000) *Entering the 21st Century: World Development Report 1999–2000*. New York: Oxford University Press.

Wragg, E. C. (1984a) 'Teaching skills', in E. C. Wragg (ed.) *Classroom Teaching Skills*, pp. 1–20. London: Routledge.

Wragg, E. C. (ed.) (1984b) *Classroom Teaching Skills*. London: Routledge.

Wragg, E. C. (1993) *Primary Teaching Skills*. London: Routledge.

Wragg, E. C. (1997) *The Cubic Curriculum*. London: Routledge.

Wragg, E. C. and Brown, G. (1993) *Explaining*. London: Routledge.

Young, H. (1989) *One of Us: a biography of Margaret Thatcher*. London: Macmillan.

Young, M. F. D. (ed.) (1971) *Knowledge and Control*. London: Collier-Macmillan.

Young, R. F. (1932) *Comenius in England: the visit of Jan Amos Komensky the Czech philosopher and educationist to London in 1641–42; its bearing on the origins of the Royal Society, on the development of the encyclopaedia, and on plans for the higher education of the Indians of New England and Virginia*. Oxford: Oxford University Press.

Index

Note: entries for the book's most pervasive terms and names – *children, culture, curriculum, learning, pedagogy, primary education, teaching, England, France, India, Russia, United States* – list only those pages where these are treated in detail or at length.

Abbott, D., 619
ability and effort, 369–71
académie, 52, 242, 258, 308
acceleration (Vygotsky), 425–6
activities in teaching, 350–5
Adonis, A., 151, 604
African-American values, 515, 523, 600n
Agrégation, 63
Alexander II of Russia, 71–2
Alexander, P., 344–5, 604
Alexander, R. J., 571–4n, 578n, 582–6n, 588–90n, 592–3n, 595–601n, 604–5
    see also CICADA project, Leeds project, 'three wise men' report
Allègre, C., 55, 60, 575n
Althusser, L., 164, 587n, 605
Ambasht, N. K., 99, 580n
Amidon, E. J., 598n, 605
Anderson, A., 613
Anderson, C. A., 586n, 613
Anderson, H. H., 598n
Anderson, R. D., 587n, 605
Anglesey, 139
Apple, M., 165, 587n, 590n, 605
Archer, M. S., 3, 70, 78, 107, 144, 160–2, 166, 168, 262, 383, 389, 571n, 575n, 576n, 581n, 582n, 586n, 587n, 596n, 597n, 605
Ardagh, J., 60, 199, 589n, 591n, 605
Argyris, C., 578n, 589n

Arnold, Matthew, 1, 23, 26, 28, 57, 60–1, 89, 135–6, 146, 163, 201, 571, 572–3n, 575n, 605
Arnold, Thomas, 89–90
Arnold, William, 89–90
art teaching, 458–61
Ashram, 94
assembly, school, 158–9, 181, 209–10, 213–15
assessment
    classroom, 368–80
    criteria, 375–8
    national, 34–5, 69, 88, 106–7, 127, 356–8, 371–3
    oral/written, 373–4
    peer/self/teacher, 374–5
Audit Commission, 590n, 605
Austin, J. L., 383, 433, 438, 599n, 601n, 605
Australia, 171, 272
Austria, 101
Ayer, A. J., 585n

Bacon, Francis, 26, 130, 201, 319, 528, 547, 601n
Baker-Sennett, J., 593n, 605
Bakhtin, M. M., 520, 600n, 605
Bal Bhawan, 308, 559
Balfour, Lord, 137
Ball, S. J., 605

Barking and Dagenham LEA, 41, 183
Barnes, D. R., 597n, 599n, 605
basics in primary education, 147–8
Battersea Training College, 93
Bayliss, V., 572n, 606
Beattie, N., 602n, 606
Behrenes, W. W., 617
Bell, Andrew, 91, 132, 311 *see also*
    monitorial system
Bempechat, J., 370, 596n, 606
Benavot, A., 156, 563, 573n, 587n, 603n,
    606
Bengal, 92
Bennett, L., 578n, 606
Bennett, S. N., 342, 343, 346, 359, 367,
    408, 411, 585n, 592n, 594n, 596n,
    598n, 606, 611
Beriss, D., 575n, 606
Berlak, A. and H., 411–13, 415, 419, 598n,
    606
Bernstein, B., 165, 437, 481–92, 551, 562,
    587n, 596, 600n, 602n, 606
bhadralok, 92
Biddle, B. J., 322, 591n, 593n, 594n, 606,
    611
Bierhoff, H., 591n, 606
Birmingham (Alabama), 113
Birmingham (England), 113, 132, 237
Black Papers on Education, 23, 572n, 585n
Blackie, John, 139
Blair, Tony, 18, 21, 149–50, 169, 235,
    274, 490, 572n, 595n, 606
Blake, William, 140
Blatchford, P., 623
Blenkin, G. M., 595n, 606
Bloom, B. S., 112, 343–5, 582n, 594n, 606
Blunkett, David, 40, 157, 210, 254, 484
Blyth, W. A. L., 134, 146, 313, 544, 583n,
    584n, 586n, 589n, 593n, 602n, 603n,
    606, 607
Board of Education, 607
Bobbitt, F., 112
Boldyrev, N. I., 577n
Bollen, R., 620
Bombay/Mumbai, 82, 92
Bonwick, J., 132, 584n
Borough Road, School, Southwark, 56, 91,
    132
Bourdieu, P., 60, 164, 260, 575n, 576n,
    587n, 590n, 607
Bourdoncle, R., 593n, 607

Bowen, J., 576n, 581n, 593n, 607
Bowles, S., 164–5, 582n, 587n, 590n, 606
Boyd, S., 618
Boydell, D., 392
Boyer, E., 30, 573n
Boyle, Robert, 130
Brahmanic legacy in Indian education,
    88–9, 168, 307, 532, 559, 579n
Brearley, Mollie, 139
Brezhnev, L., 78, 246
British and Foreign Schools Society, 132,
    134
British Council, 28
Britton, J., 597n, 605, 607
Broadfoot, P., 3, 30–3, 43, 58, 197, 308,
    359–62, 370, 523, 554, 571n, 574n,
    575n, 587n, 588n, 589n, 591n, 592n,
    593n, 596n, 598n, 599n, 600n, 602n,
    604, 607, 619
Bronfenbrenner, U., 76–7, 231, 554, 577n,
    589n, 590n, 602n, 607
Brooks, H., 322–3, 594n, 615
Brougham, Lord, 134
Brown, G., 598n, 607, 625
Brown, Lancelot 'Capability', 593n
Brown, M., 35, 573n, 607
Brown, P., 41, 572n, 607
Brown, S., 381, 384, 411, 596n, 598n,
    602n, 608
Bruner, J. S., 345, 430, 432, 528, 544–5,
    546, 548, 556–61, 577n, 595n, 599n,
    601n, 602n, 607, 608
Bryanston School, 138
Bûcher, A., 607
Buell Elementary School, 252
Bullock Report, 565, 597n, 610
Burghes, D., 591n, 608
Burke, Edmund, 132
Burke, J., 623
Burnett, J., 136, 584n, 608
Burt, Cyril, 138
Bush, George, 114
Butler, M., 608

Calcutta, 82, 92
Calderhead, J., 597n, 608
Cambridge, 129, 151–2
Campaign for Nuclear Disarmament, 572n
Campbell, R. J., 411, 589n, 591n, 598n,
    608, 612
Canada, 24, 101, 123, 171, 583n

Cannadine, D., 151, 586n, 608
Carroll, J. B., 594n, 608
Carter, R., 603n, 608
Cassidy, S., 595n, 608
Caste in India, 83, 90, 99–100
Castells, M., 21–2, 45, 149, 167, 572n,
    574n, 575n, 580n, 586n, 588n, 608
Catherine II (the Great) of Russia, 70
Caxton, William, 129
Central Advisory Council for Education
    (CACE), 588n, 590n, 608
centralization/decentralization in education,
    60–1, 95–7, 107, 114–15, 142–5,
    159–63, 240–61
Centre Nationale de Documentation
    Pédagogique, 574n, 575n, 587n, 589n,
    590n, 608
Cha, Y-K., 606
Chafe, W. H., 582n, 608
Chagla, M. C., 100, 580n
Charity Commissioners, 134
Chechnya, 76
Chévellard, Y., 601n, 608
Chevènement, J-P., 58
children
    ability and effort, 360, 362, 369–71
    ages and grades, 191–3
    behaviour, 360, 362
    classroom discourse, 441–515
    condition of in different countries, 23–5,
        44
    development, 370–1, 424–5
    differentiation in classrooms, 360–8
    grouping in classrooms, 334–7
    interaction with teachers and peers,
        391–410
    models of learning, 556–61
    personal safety, 490–4
    special needs, 123, 360, 362
China, 82, 98, 267, 369, 554
Chirac, Jacques, 62
Church of England, 108, 132, 134, 149–50,
    161
church schools, 220–3
CICADA project, 4, 368, 372, 396–7, 401,
    433
citizenship, 61, 87, 106, 126, 157, 162,
    168
civil rights, 113
Clare, John, 413
Clarke, Kenneth, 143, 541–2

Clarke, P., 38, 307, 554–7, 574n, 592n,
    602n, 608, 612
class teacher system, 113–14, 147, 191
class, social, 151–3, 164–5
classrooms
    descriptions, 9–14, 181–6, 325–38
    layout, 333–7
    organization, 181–6, 325–38
    plans, 326–9
    resources, 337–8
    teaching and learning, 265–528
Clegg, Alec, 139
Clinton, Bill, 104
Cobbett, William, 134
Cockburn, A., 342, 607
code, 481–2, 519–21
Cohen, D. K., 581n, 609
Coleridge, Samuel Taylor, 132, 133, 319,
    595n
collective values, 73, 454, 523–4, 539–40
Colley, L., 16, 149, 572n, 586n, 609
Collini, S., 588n, 609
Columbine High School, 252
Comber, C., 613
Comenius, J. A. (Jan Amos Komensky), 26,
    75, 108, 310, 319, 406, 425, 535, 547,
    584n, 593n, 609
Committee on Un-American Activities, 112
communes (France), 52
communicative competence/rights, 380,
    434–5, 457–8, 461, 572, 499, 507,
    524–7
communism, 70–4, 77–9, 319 see Russia
community, 169, 197, 201–3, 205, 206–7,
    209–10, 213, 221, 224–5, 523–4,
    539–40
comparative education, 26–45
    history, 25–7
    critiques, methods, 30–42
    'old' and 'new', 27–9
compétences transversales, 54, 126
comprehensive schools, 139, 151
Condorcet, Marquis de, 55
Confederation of British Industry (CBI), 15,
    572n, 609
Congress Party, 92
Conservative Party, 14, 36, 143, 153, 372,
    541
conversation and dialogue, 312–13, 453,
    481, 519–21
Corbett, A., 63, 575n, 576n, 609

Coulthard, M., 397, 433, 598n, 599n, 609, 623
Council for the Accreditation of Teacher Education (CATE), 142, 541
Council for National Academic Awards, 541
Council of Europe, 62
Court, M., 600n, 609
Cox, B., 585n, 609
Craft, M., 601n, 605
craft knowledge, 384
Cran, W., 581n, 617
Creemers, B. P. M., 38, 321, 588n, 594n, 609, 620
Cressy, D., 584n, 609
Crick, Bernard, 157, 587n
critical pedagogy, 165–6, 564
Croll, P., 592n, 594n, 596n, 612, 619
Cromwell, Oliver, 130
Crossley, M., 29, 31, 573n, 574n, 609
Crystal, D., 580n, 609
culture
  definitions, 163–4
  education and, 5, 20, 29, 163–72, 265–70, 384, 531–4, 561–3
  England, 120, 148–54
  France, 61–3
  general, 61, 542
  India, 82–3, 87, 89, 100
  language, 430–8, 440–1
  learning, 556–61
  reproduction/transmission, 163–6
  Russia, 75–6, 84
  teaching, 306–14, 369–71, 424–6, 553–6
  United States, 101, 115–17
Cunningham, P., 585n, 593n, 609
curriculum areas/bays/centres, 183–4, 333
Curriculum I/II, 147
curriculum
  control, 141–2
  didactics, 542–7
  England, 126–7, 141–2
  France, 53–4
  global convergence, 156, 563
  hidden, 383, 551
  India, 87–8
  national, 155–8
  pedagogy and, 547–53
  Russia, 68–9
  spiral, 548
  subjects, 542–7
  transformation, 552
  United States, 105–6

Daily Telegraph, 413, 598n
Dale, R., 159, 587n, 609
dalits ('Untouchables'), 83
Dalton Plan, 73
Darby, D., 597n, 624
Darlington, T., 27
Dartington School, 94, 138, 171
Darwin, A., 613
Davidson, D. H., 267, 571n, 602n, 623
Davison, J., 598n, 610
Davison, Tony, 579n
Davydov, V. V., 218, 248, 308, 577n
de Beauvoir, S., 111, 606
Dearing R./Dearing Report on the National Curriculum, 39, 126, 255–6, 574n, 581n, 590n, 604, 610
Declaration of Independence (USA), 109
defectology, 74
Defferre, Gaston, 58
Delhi, 82, 189, 211, 213, 229
Delige, R., 578n, 604, 610
Delpit, Lisa, 600n
Democratic Party, 249
democratic pedagogy, 111–12, 424–5, 500–12
Denmark, 101, 123, 160, 171, 583n
Department for Education (DFE), 591n, 610
Department for Education and Employment (DfEE), 15, 37, 43, 122, 254, 553, 572n, 583n, 588n, 589n, 590n, 591n, 592n, 594n, 595n, 600n, 602n, 603n, 610
Department for International Development (DfID), 28, 83
Department of Education and Science (DES), 589n, 590n, 591n, 596n, 600n, 601n, 603n, 610, 611
Department of Trade and Industry (DTI), 15, 572n, 611
Dès, Henri, 493–4
Descartes, René, 26, 55, 60, 227, 319
Desforges, C., 342, 597n, 606, 616
Detroit, 252
development, concepts of, 370–1, 424–5
Dewey, John, 26, 73, 94, 111–13, 138, 140, 146, 311, 319, 424, 521–2, 535, 548, 581n, 599n, 600n, 611

dialogue and dialogic discourse, 312–13,
    515–16
didactics, 542–7
Diderot, Denis, 71
differentiation in teaching, 360–8
Dillon, J. T., 435, 472, 598, 599n, 600n,
    601n, 611
direct instruction, 407, 428, 515–18
directed and negotiated discourse, 521–3
director of school, see head teacher
discourse in teaching and learning, 427–528
    adjacency pairs, 481
    analysing, 432–41
    communicative competence and rights,
        434–5, 458, 461, 472, 499, 507,
        524–7
    conversational, 453, 481
    culture and, 430–2
    dialogic, 515–18, 519–21
    directed and negotiated, 521–3
    discussion, 436, 480–1, 492–4, 500–1
    elicitations, 436, 457
    evaluative, 515–16, 517
    examples, 441–515
    expository, 515–16
    individual and collective, 523–4
    interrogatory, 515–16
    IRF structure, 396, 433–4
    learning, 430–2
    pedagogic, 437–8
    questions and questioning, 434–5, 443,
        446, 449, 452–4, 463–4, 515–17
    recitation, 449, 471–2, 516
    register and code, 519–21
    rote, 441–3, 517
    scaffolding, 526–8
    structure and form, 518–19
    transcribing/translating, 438–41, 453
    vernacular, 490
discussion in teaching, 436, 480–1, 492–4,
    500–1
display in English classrooms, 184–5
District Institutes of Education and
    Training (DIETs), 96, 307
District of Columbia, 111
District Primary Education Programme
    (DPEP), 83, 88, 98, 100, 168, 177,
    245–6, 546, 558, 588n
Doddington, C., 591n, 611
Donaldson, M., 430, 599n, 611
Douglas, J. W. B., 611

Doyle, W., 261, 591n, 611
Drago-Severson, E., 370, 596n, 606
Drèze, J., 579n
Driscoll, J., 610
dropout from school, 24–86
Drummond, M. J., 611
Dubos, R., 572n, 624
Dunblane, 179
Dunkin, M. J., 322, 591n, 593n, 594n, 611
Dunne, E., 408, 598n, 611
Dunstan, J., 611
Dyson, A. E., 585n, 609

East Sussex, 611
Ecob, R., 617
Eccles, David, 549
école maternelle, 51, 53, 99
ecology, 20
economy and education, 15–20, 23–5,
    34–5, 39–40, 40–3, 51, 64, 82, 101,
    120
Educate America Act 1994, 25, 104, 602n
Education Act 1870, 136
Education Act 1902, 137
Education Act 1944, 72, 122, 139, 151,
    356
Education Act 1980, 234
Education Act 1996, 124
Education Action Zone, 237
Education Interchange Council, 577n,
    588n, 611
Education Reform Act 1988, 4, 122, 124,
    126, 141, 144, 193
Education Reform Bill 1997, 144
Education Week, 611
Educational Testing Service (ETS), 114
Edwards, A. D., 381–2, 433, 457, 500,
    524–5, 598n, 599n, 601n, 602n, 611
Edwards, D., 345, 381–2, 435–6, 571n,
    595n, 596n, 599n, 601n, 611
effort and ability, 369–71
Eggleston, S. J., 344, 595n, 612
Ehrlich, A. H. and P. R., 20, 572n, 611
Eisner, E. W., 273–4, 344, 591n, 592n,
    595n, 612
Eklof, B., 596n
elementary tradition in English primary
    education, 145–9
Elkonin, D. B., 218, 248, 308
Ellena, W. J., 593n, 606
Elliott, J., 369, 406, 596n, 598n, 612, 614

Elmhirst, Dorothy and Leonard, 94, 171
England
  assessment, 127
  church schools, 220–3
  classroom plans, 326–9
  context of education, 120
  control of education, 253–9
  curriculum, 126–7
  demography and statistics, 120–3
  goals of education, 124–6
  history of primary education, 128–43
  inspection of schools, 127
  lesson examples, 291–6
  parents and teachers, 234–9
  primary education, 120–53
  teaching extracts, 474–90
  teachers, 188–90, 252–7
  school and state, 252–7
  schools, 13–14, 190, 206–10, 225
  structure of education system, and policy, 120–4
  values and identity, 149–53
Enlightenment, 55, 60, 71, 132–3, 319
episodic lesson structure, 300–4
Erasmus, Desiderius, 547
Eraut, M. R., 587n
espoused theory, 195, 578n
Eton College, 129
European/central European pedagogy, 272, 319
European Union, 32, 157
Eurydice, 33, 582n, 587n, 612
Evans, L., 598n, 612
Exon, G., 623
expectations of children, 358–9
expository teaching, 515–16

Falklands War, 249
Farquhar, C., 623
Farrell, S., 35, 42, 359, 554, 573n, 574n, 591n, 596n, 602n, 621
Featherstone, J., 113
Fernandes, C., 571n, 577n, 587n, 613, 615
Ferry, Jules, and *loi Ferry*, 57, 59, 60, 198, 425, 575n
Figes, O., 71, 576n, 577n, 612
Filer, A., 591n, 619
Finkielkraut, A., 576n, 612
Five Cultures project, aims, methods and data, 3–6, 43–5, 177, 265–78, 396, 589n

Flanders, N., 392, 408, 435, 500, 597n, 598n, 612
Flint Board of Education, 612
Flint School District, 192, 612
Floden, R. E., 582n, 612, 613
Florio, J., 590n, 612
Floud, J., 586n, 613
Flutter, J., 591n, 611
Fogelman, K., 612
form in teaching, 297–319
Forster, W. E., 136
Foster, Michele, 600n
France
  assessment, 54–5, 378–9
  classrooms, 183–4, 186, 325–58
  control of education, 242–3
  context, 51
  curriculum, 53–4
  demography and statistics, 51–2
  goals of education, 53
  history of primary education, 55–63
  home and school, 227–9
  inspection of schools, 52
  lesson examples, 278–81
  primary education, 49–63
  school and state, 242–3
  schools, 9–10, 189, 197–201, 223
  structure of education, 51–2
  teachers, 188–90, 242–4
  teaching extracts, 461–73
  values and identity, 58–63
Francke, A. H., 108, 310
Franklin, Benjamin, 109
Freedland, J., 108, 581n, 582n, 612
Freinet, Célestin, 378, 545
Frensham Heights School, 138
Froebel, Friedrich, 26, 94, 140, 313, 319, 425, 485, 535, 547
Froebel Society, 138
Fuller, B., 38, 307, 574n, 592n, 608, 612

Gage, N., 268, 270, 274, 411, 414, 591n, 592n, 593n, 598n, 612
Gallimore, R., 435, 599n, 623
Galton, M. J., 42, 182–3, 274, 336, 343–4, 346, 392, 571n, 574n, 585n, 588n, 592n, 594n, 595n, 596n, 597n, 598n, 599n, 600n, 602n, 612
Gandhi, Mohandas K., 94, 180–1, 213
Gardner, Dorothy, 140
Geertz, C., 591n

Gemeinschaft/Gesellschaft, 197–8, 523–4, 533, 534

gender and education, 24–5, 82–3, 85, 93, 96, 98, 99–100, 110, 125, 129, 132, 360–1, 367, 493, 578n

Germany, 1–2, 16, 42–3, 70–1, 128, 166, 171, 183, 246, 272, 311, 425, 584n

Giddens, A., 18, 20, 23, 382, 572n, 573n, 594n, 596n, 612

Gilly, M., 607

Gintis, H., 164–5, 582n, 587n, 590n, 607

Gipps, C., 560–1, 602n, 613

Giroux, H. A., 165–6, 167, 587n, 590n, 602n, 613

Glasnost, 77

globalization, 18–25

Goals 2000, 25, 104–5, 114, 117–18, 249

Godunov, Boris, 71

Godwin, William, 132

Goertz, M. E., 582n, 613

Goethe, J. W. von, 319

Good, H. G., 573n, 575n, 581n, 613

good/best practice, 573n

Goody, J., 89, 568, 579n, 603n, 613

Gopalan, K., 580n

Gorbachev, M. S., 71, 222

Government of India, 83, 245, 338, 579n, 580n, 588n, 590n, 594n, 614

Graff, H., 129, 567–8, 581n, 583n, 584n, 603n, 613

grammar schools, 595n

grammar teaching, 383, 386, 473, 564–5

Gramsci, A., 162, 166, 550, 590n

green movement, 572n

Green Revolution, 20

Green, A., 152, 357, 571n, 585n, 622

Green, Andy, 3, 109, 162–3, 575n, 581n, 582n, 584n, 586n, 587n, 595n, 599n, 600n, 602n, 613

Grice, H. P., 434, 525, 613

grouping and group work, 334–7, 398, 402–6, 407–8

Guinea, 24

Guizot, F., 56

Gutenberg, Johannes, 129

gymnasium, 71, 171, 415

Haby, René, 58

Hadow Reports, 17, 137–8, 139, 147, 171, 521

Hall, S., 588n, 613

Halle, 310

Halliday, M., 433, 453, 600n, 613

Halpin, T., 587n, 613

Halsey, A. H., 41, 572n, 586n, 607, 613

Hamilton, D., 38, 574n, 613

Hamlyn, D. W., 543, 601n, 613

Hardman, F., 597n, 602n

Hare, V., 604

Hargreaves, D. H., 597n, 613

Hargreaves, D. J., 593n

Hargreaves, L., 613

Harlen, W., 596n, 613

Harris, S., 571n, 577n, 587n, 613, 615

Hartley-Brewer, E., 590n, 613

Harvard, 108

Haryana, 11, 211

Haste, H. E., 595n, 599n, 608

Hatim, B., 439, 600n, 613

Haviland, J., 585n, 613

Hazlitt, William, 134

Headmasters' Conference, 541

head teachers/principals/directors of schools, 188–90, 194, 198–9, 203–5, 206, 208–9, 211–12, 218–19, 221, 223–5

Heath, S. B., 567–8, 603n, 613

Heffer, S., 588n, 613

hegemony, 162–4

Her/His Majesty's Inspectorate (HMI), 1, 74, 127, 134, 141–2, 193, 359

Herbart, J. F., 26, 94, 111, 138, 310–11, 319, 535, 547

Herbartianism, 311, 313

Hildreth, A., 598n, 612

Hillage, J., 597n, 613

Hillman, J., 574n, 588n, 592n, 594n, 621

Hinduism, 83, 88–90, 319

Hirsch, E. D., 165

Hobsbawm, E. J., 16–17, 23, 70, 167, 561, 572n, 576n, 587n, 588n, 602n, 614

Hoeben, W. T. J. G., 610

Holdsworth, N., 571n, 614

holistic analysis of teaching, 271–2

Holley, B. J., 623

Holmes Group, 190, 206, 589n, 614

Holmes, B., 573n, 614

Holmes, R., 584n, 614

Holt School District, 614

home and school, 226–40

Hopkins, D., 620

Hough, J. B., 605

House of Commons, 136, 142, 147, 257, 586n, 587n, 590n, 614
Hufton, N., 406, 596n, 598n, 612, 614
Hughes, M., 430, 599n, 623, 624
Human Development Index (HDI), 224, 574n
Hume, David, 319
Hungary, 1–2, 272
Hunter Commission, 93
Hutton, W., 21, 572n, 614
Hyderabad, 82
Hymas, C., 610

ideological state apparatus (ISA), 164, 166
Illushin, L., 577n, 598n, 612
India
  assessment, 88
  classrooms, 325–38
  constitution, 83, 94–5
  control of education, 82–6, 99–100, 243–6
  curriculum, 87–8
  goals of education, 86–7
  history of primary education, 88–95
  independence, 82, 94–5
  inspection of schools, 244–5
  languages, 82–3
  lesson examples, 281–4
  parents and teachers, 227–9
  primary education, 82–100
  reforms, 95–100
  school and state, 243–6
  schools, 11–12, 189–90, 211–15, 224
  structure of education system, and policy, 82–8
  teachers, 188–90, 243–6
  teaching extracts, 420–1, 441–50
  values, 211–15
India, Government of, Ministry of Human Resource Development (MHRD), 95, 588n, 614
Indian Civil Service, 92
individualization in teaching, 359–60
individualism, 73, 75, 111, 169, 202–3, 213, 219, 221, 224–5, 523–4, 539–40
industrialization, 127–8, 162–3
Infant School Society, 134
information technology/information and communications technology (IT/ICT), 15, 21–2, 167

initiation-response-feedback/follow-up (IRF) exchange structure, 396, 399, 433, 435, 447, 449, 452, 477, 481, 506, 519
Inner London Education Authority (ILEA), 258
inspection of schools, 52, 59–60, 142, 244–5, 246, 256–7, 260–1 see also HMI, OFSTED
Institut National de Recherche Pédagogique (INRP), 544–5
Instituts Universitaires de Formation des Maîtres (IUFM), 63, 199, 303, 543–5
interaction in classrooms
  analysing, 391–3
  length, 399–400
  lesson stage, 401
  monitoring, 407–10
  organization of, 391–410
  participants, 398–9
  types, 394–5, 400–1
  see also discourse
interactive whole class teaching, 321, 483, 597n
International Assessment of Educational Progress (IAEP), 35, 114
International Association for the Evaluation of Educational Achievement (IEA), 35, 39, 41, 114
international comparisons in education, 30–43 see also comparative education
International Institute for Educational Planning, 616
Iowa Test of Basic Skills, 107
Irvine, Jackie Jordan, 600n
Isaacs, Susan, 140
Islam, 62
Israel, 546
Italy, 162, 546

Jackson, B., 585n, 615
Jackson, P. W., 186–7, 321, 346, 393, 426, 588n, 595n, 598n, 599n, 615
Jacobson, L., 595n, 621
James, J., 593n, 615
James, William, 111
Japan, 1–2, 267, 369, 546, 555
Jayalakshmi, G. D., 579n
Jefferson, Thomas, 109, 581n
Jeffrey, B., 591n, 592n, 625
Jenkins, D., 593n, 615

Johnson, Lyndon B., 113
Johnson, M., 322–3, 594n, 615
Johnson, W. H. E., 576–7n, 589n, 615
Jomtien, 25
Jones, A., 76, 77, 577n, 615
Joseph, Keith, 586n, 594n
Jospin, Lionel and Loi Jospin 1989, 52–3,
    58–9, 62, 199, 243, 543
Judge, H., 199, 575n, 589n, 601n, 615
judgement in teaching, 356–80
Jullien, Marc-Antoine, 27

Kamens, D., 573n, 606
Kant, Immanuel, 319
Kay-Shuttleworth, J., 93, 135, 151, 171
Keatinge, M. W., 602n
Kellmer-Pringle, M., 615
Kelly, A. V., 595n, 606, 615, 616
Kelly, C., 42, 574n
Kempe, William, 130
Kennedy, John F., 113
Kennedy, P., 20–1, 572n, 615
Kennedy, Robert, 113
Kerr, S. T., 576n, 615
Kerry, T., 594n, 615
Keys, W., 36, 571n, 574n, 577n, 587n,
    613, 615
Khrushchev, N., 73, 74, 78, 579n
Kidd, C., 588n, 615
Kilpatrick, W. H., 112
Kinder, K. M., 585n, 586n, 589n, 605
Kindergarten, 66, 458–61
King, E. J., 3, 27, 573n, 579n, 581n, 587n,
    615
King, Martin Luther, 113
King, R., 152, 357, 571n, 585n, 586n,
    595n, 600n, 615
Kirby, N., 486, 600n, 615
Kirst, M. W., 114, 582n, 590n, 615
knowledge
    curriculum, 547–53
    conceptual, declarative, metacognitive, 345
    didactics, 542–7
    disciplines, 61–3, 202, 526, 548–50
    mimetic and transformative, 346
    personal, 346, 505
    propositional and procedural, 343–4
    ritual and principled, 345–7
    school subjects, 53–4, 61–3, 68–9, 67–8,
        105–6, 126–7, 202, 340–1, 548–50
    teachers', 542–7

Komensky, J. A., see Comenius
Komsomol, 74, 76, 231
Krupskaya, N., 73
Kumar, Krishan, 23, 572n, 615
Kumar, Krishna, 89–90, 91, 92, 97, 559,
    579–80n, 592n, 602n, 615
Kursk, 3, 189, 246–7, 277

Labour/New Labour, 14, 21, 23, 29, 36,
    117–18, 124, 137, 142, 146, 153, 176,
    235, 257, 339, 372, 391
Ladson-Billings, Gloria, 600n
Lagerweij, N., 620
Lancaster, Joseph and Lancasterian method,
    56, 91, 110, 132 see also monitorial
    system
Landes, D. S., 20–1, 23, 88, 572n, 573n,
    579n, 615
Lang, Jack, 60, 575n
Language In the National Curriculum
    (LINC), 565
language teaching, 61–2, 278–82, 283–6,
    288–9, 291–5, 443–7, 450–4, 462–4,
    467–75, 476–86, 494–8, 564–9
Lansing, Michigan, 190, 615
Last, G., 574n, 588n, 592n, 597n, 616
Lauder, H., 607
Lawlor, S., 541, 592n, 601n, 616, 621
Lawson, J., 616
Lawton, D., 551, 602n, 616
Layder, D., 485, 600n, 616
Le Nôtre, André, 594
Leach, E., 323, 556, 594n, 616
learning
    activities, 350–5
    assessment, 368–80
    culture and, 424–6, 556–61
    differentiation, 360–8
    discourse, 428–528
    models, 557–62
    pace, 418–26
    readiness, 425
    rote, 441–3
    routines, rules and rituals, 380–90
    scaffolding, 526–8, 557–61
    tasks, 339–40
Leeds Project/Report, 4, 141, 142–4, 152,
    183, 189, 191, 193, 210, 226–7, 237,
    256, 336, 351–2, 358, 362, 363, 369,
    394–5, 397, 401, 409, 413–14, 436,
    585n, 600n

Leibniz, G. W., 130
Leicestershire, 139, 412
Le Métais, J., 574n, 618, 623
Le Monde, 63
Lemosse, M., 575n, 589n, 601n, 615, 616
Lenin, V. I., 73, 215
Leontiev, A. A., 577n
Leontiev, A. N., 73
lesson form and structure
  cultural and historical determinants,
    306–14
  national differences, 209–301
lessons
  analysed and compared, 276–7
  England, 291–6, 474–90
  examples, 278–96
  extracts, 441–512
  France, 278–81, 461–73
  India, 281–4 , 420–1, 441–50
  length, 297–8, 305–6
  Russia, 284–8, 421–2, 450–61
  teachers' planning, 306–14
  United States, 288–91, 422–3, 490–515
Levin, H. M., 42, 574n, 616
Lewis, D., 617
Lewis, G., 595n, 625
Lichfield, J., 575n, 616
Lindfors, J. W., 600n, 616
literacy, 15, 24–5, 44, 71, 85, 88, 129,
  143, 229–30, 564–70
literacy/language teaching, examples,
  192–3, 278–82, 283–6, 288–9, 291–5,
  402–4, 443–7, 450–4, 461–3, 466–73,
  473–85
Literacy Hour, see National Literacy
  Strategy
Little Rock, 113
Little, A., 578n, 616
livret scolaire, 54, 371, 378
Lloyd, J., 70, 571n, 576n, 616
local education authorities (LEAs), 122–3,
  139, 144–5, 253, 258–61
Locke, John, 26, 131, 319
Lockheed, M., 39, 571n, 573n, 574n,
  578n, 616
Lok Jumbish, 558
London University, 37
Lowe, Robert, 135
Lunar Society, 132
Luria, A. R., 73, 425, 432, 577n
Luther, Martin, 547

Luxton, R. G., 574n, 588n, 594n, 597n,
  616
Lynch, J., 601n, 605

Macaulay, Thomas B., 88–9, 90–2, 93
MacDonald, A., 595n, 625
Macedo, D., 165, 587n, 602n, 616
MacGilchrist, B., 560–1, 602n, 613
MacNeil, R., 581n, 616
Madras, 91–2, 132
magnet schools, 249
Mail on Sunday, 601n, 616
Major, John, 150, 169, 237, 253, 541, 601n
Makarenko, A., 73–4
Mandela, Nelson, 19
Manton, F., 616
Manton, J. S., 583n
Marsh, L. G., 592n, 599n, 616
Marshall, J., 575n, 616
Marx, Karl, 20, 162, 431
Mason, I., 439, 600n, 613
Mason, Stewart, 139
Massachusetts, 108, 110
'match', 359
mathematical achievement, 35–6, 40–2, 69,
  104–5, 106–7, 127
mathematics teaching, examples, 286–8,
  289–92, 295–6, 403–5, 441–3, 454–8,
  464–7, 486–90, 501–15
Matusov, E., 593n, 605
Maughan, B., 621
Mayo, Elizabeth, 311, 616
McCarthy, Joseph, 112, 145
McCrum, R., 581n, 616
McGuffey Readers, 581n
McKay, D., 580n, 582n, 590n, 596n, 616
McIntyre, D., 381, 384, 411, 596n, 598n,
  602n, 607
McLaren, P., 602n, 603n, 616
McNamara, D., 183, 588n, 597n, 602n,
  616
Mead, G. H., 599n, 602n, 615
Meadows, D. H. and D. L., 572n, 617
Meirieu, P., 575n, 576n, 617
Mercer, N., 345–6, 381–2, 435–6, 438,
  472, 579n, 595n, 596n, 599n, 600n,
  601n, 602n, 611
Meyer, J. W., 606
Michigan
  assessment, 106–7, 379–80
  classrooms, 181–6, 326–9

control of education, 248–52
curriculum, 105–6, 114–17
Goals 2000, 118
lesson examples, 288–91, 403
outcomes-based education, 115–16, 118
parents and teachers, 231–4
schools, 12-13, 179–80, 190, 201–6, 224–5
statistics, 103
teacher-pupil discourse, 490–515
teachers, 188–90, 248–52
testing, 106–7, 115–16, 354, 372
values, 115–16
Michigan Educational Assessment Program (MEAP), 106–7, 115–16, 357, 372
Michigan State Board of Education, 108
Michigan State Department of Education, 581n, 582n, 590n, 617
Mikoyan, A. I., 578n
Mill, James, 89
Mill, John Stuart, 89
Millett, A., 542, 601n, 617
Millfield School, 138
Milosovic, S., 167
Milton, John, 130–1, 319
Minimum Levels of Learning (MLLs), 87, 96, 244, 344, 579n, 590n
Ministère de l'Education Nationale, 59–60, 192, 197, 199, 243, 378, 425, 576n, 596n, 599n, 603n, 617
Ministry of Education/Ministry for General and Professional Education (Russia), 66, 68, 77, 81, 260, 310, 576n, 578n, 617
Mitterand, François, 59, 220
models of teaching, 320–5, 553–6
monitorial system, 56, 110, 132, 171
monitoring, 407–11, 460, 463, 477, 484, 513
Montaigne, Michel de, 201, 589n
Montessori, Maria, 26, 94, 138, 140, 313, 319, 518, 535, 547, 593n, 617
Moon, B., 63, 575n, 576n, 601n, 617
Moorhouse, Edith, 139
Moravia, 310
Moravian church/Unitas Fratrem, 108, 547
More, Hannah, 132
Morozov, Pavel (Pavlik), 77
Morris, B., 617
Morris, Estelle, 254
Morris, P., 571n, 617

Morris, William, 274
Mortimore, P., 283, 392, 540, 542, 549, 561n, 574n, 585n, 588n, 592n, 593n, 597n, 598n, 601n, 602n, 617, 621, 624
Moscow, 66, 77, 215, 246–7, 277
Mroz, M., 597n, 602n, 617
Muckle, J., 3, 74, 215, 370, 571n, 576n, 577n, 588n, 589n, 596n, 617
Mulcaster, Richard, 130
Murphy, M., 613
Murton, A. L., 585n
music teaching, 308
music and the analysis of lesson structure and form, 315–18
Muslim children in schools, 62, 168, 180, 236
mutual teaching method, 56, 91
see monitorial system

names, cultural significance, 440–1
Napoleonic Code, 55, 60, 62, 198
National Assessment of Educational Progress (NAEP), 106
National Association of Headteachers (NAHT), 124, 254
National Commission on Excellence in Education, 581n, 582n, 602n, 617
National Council of Educational Research and Training (NCERT), 87–8, 96, 99, 100, 579n, 590n, 594n, 617, 618
National Curriculum Council (NCC), 141
National Curriculum, 33, 39, 46, 565, 600n
National Doctrine on Education 2000, 81
National Education Goals, 104
National Education Association (NEA), 250, 252
National Educational Goals Panel, 573n, 618
National Foundation for Educational Research (NFER), 361–2
National Grid for Learning, 573n, 594n
National Institute of Educational Planning and Administration (NIEPA), 88
National Literacy Strategy and Literacy Hour, 118–19, 122, 143, 147, 254, 256, 271, 294–5, 303–4, 482–6, 525, 527
National Numeracy Strategy, 35–6, 41, 118–19, 122, 143, 147, 183, 254, 256, 271, 295–6, 303–4, 457, 486–90, 528

National Oracy Project, 565, 597n
National Rifle Association (NRA), 252
National Society for Promoting the
    Education of the Poor, 132
National Skills Task Force, 15
National Union of Teachers (NUT), 254
Nautiyal, K. C., 580n, 618
Nayar, U., 90, 93, 99, 578n, 580n, 618
Nehru, Jawaharlal, 94
Neill, S. R. St J., 591n, 598n, 609, 612, 618
Nelson, N., 599n, 600n, 605
Nesselrodt, P. S., 620, 621
Netherlands, 83
New Education Fellowship, 138
New England, 109, 130
New Hampshire, 523
New Jersey, 101
New Lanark, 133–4, 138
New Zealand, 272
Newcastle Commission and Report, 16,
    134, 156
Nice, 189, 227, 308, 545
Nicholas II of Russia, 72
Niger, 24
Nikandrov, N. D., 77–8, 577n, 618
Nixon, Richard, M., 113
Noah, H. J., 30–2, 43, 573n, 618
normal school/école normale/Normalschule,
    93–4, 111, 171
Norman, K., 594n, 603n, 618
Northern Ireland, 169, 583n
numeracy, see mathematics

O'Day, J., 613
O'Donnell, S., 580n, 581n, 582n, 583n,
    587n, 591n, 618
O'Hear, Anthony, 541, 601n
Octobrists, 73–4, 76, 231
Office for Standards in Education
    (OFSTED), 13, 35, 37, 40, 43, 58,
    107, 122, 127, 134, 142, 158, 191,
    209, 237, 256–7, 259, 266–7, 320,
    357, 388, 542, 571n, 583n, 587n,
    588n, 589n, 590n, 591n, 597n, 602,
    618
'open education', 113–14
Operation Blackboard, 97, 177
ORACLE and ORACLE follow-up projects,
    183, 336, 343–4, 392–5, 397, 405,
    407, 409, 413–14, 416, 420, 588n,
    591n, 592n, 597n

oracy, 228, 563–9
Organization for Economic Co-operation
    and Development (OECD), 1, 34–5,
    40, 69, 75, 80, 96, 107, 159–60, 321,
    563, 571n, 575n, 576n, 577n, 591n,
    603n, 618, 619
Osborn, M., 371, 571n, 574n, 575n, 596n,
    607, 619
Ouston, J., 621
outcomes-based education, 115–16, 118
Owen, Robert, 133–4, 140, 311
Oxfam, 573n, 619
Oxford, 129, 151–2, 541
Oxfordshire, 139, 140, 411, 412, 583n

pace in teaching, 418–26, 471–3
Pacific Rim, 19–20, 41, 42, 554
Packwood, A., 598n, 613
Paine, L., 575n, 589n, 601n, 615, 619
Paine, T., 132
Panchayati Raj, 83, 87, 96, 246
parents and teachers, 226–40
Parents' Charter, 235
Parkhurst, Helen and Dalton Plan, 73
Passeron, J.-C., 164, 260, 576n, 587n,
    590n, 607
Paxman, J., 588n, 619
payment by results, 135–6
Paz, O., 82, 89, 578n, 579n, 619
Pearson, A., 613
pedagogical content knowledge, 519,
    543–4
pedagogy
    conceptualizing and researching, 269–76,
        320–5, 540–63
    critical, 165–6, 564
    cultural models, 306–14, 318–19,
        553–61
    curriculum, 547–52
    definitions, 540–2
    didactics, 542–7
    directed/negotiated, 521–3
    folk/vernacular, 560
    lesson extracts, 441–515
    organization, interaction and discourse,
        517
    teaching examples, 441–515
    see also activity, assessment, curriculum,
        differentiation, discourse, interaction,
        learning, pace, routine, rule and ritual,
        schools, task, teachers, teaching, time

Pell, A., 613
Pennsylvania, 108
petty schools, 130
People's Commissariat of Enlightenment (Narkompros), 72, 73
perestroika, 71, 74
personal safety of children, 492–4
Pestalozzi, J. H., 26, 72, 75, 94, 138, 139, 171, 310–11, 313, 319, 535, 547, 593n, 619
Peter I (the Great) of Russia, 70–1
Peters, R. S., 585n, 620
Phillips, D., 28, 573n, 605
Phillips, M., 23, 149, 573n, 586n, 619
Piaget, J., 140, 146, 319, 431–2, 485, 535, 544–5
Pierce, C. S., 111
Pinker, S., 383, 596n, 619
Pioneers, 73–4, 76, 231
Pirani, S., 571n, 576n, 619
Planel, C., 371, 571n, 575n, 596n, 618, 620, 621
Plewis, I., 623
Plowden, Lady B., 413
Plowden Report, 17, 113, 139–41, 147, 171, 175–6, 195, 239, 413, 450, 483, 543
policy borrowing, 27, 40–3
Pollard, A., 269, 591n, 593n, 619
Pollard, H. M., 575n, 579n, 619
Pollard, S., 151, 591n, 597n, 598n, 604
Ponder, G., 260, 591n, 612
Popham, P., 619
Popper, Karl, 505, 557, 560–1, 600n, 602n, 603n, 619, 620
Postlethwaite, N., 591n, 623
Prais, S. J., 574n, 588n, 591n, 597n, 606, 620
Price, R., 575n, 620
Priestley, Joseph, 132
'primaryspeak', 195–6, 589n
principal of school, see head teacher
printing, 129–30
Professional Development School, 190, 196
Progressive Education Association (PEA), 112
Progressive education movements, 73, 114, 139–41, 171, 545
Projet d'école, 52, 199–200
Prost, A., 575n, 620

Protestantism, 16, 149–50, 163, 319, 547, 581n
Prussia, 16, 111, 163, 415, 425
Psacharopoulos, G., 571n, 574n, 620
psychobiography, 485
public (i.e. private) schools in UK, 541
Public Report on Basic Education (PROBE), 97–8, 99, 168, 371, 546, 578n, 579n, 588n, 596n, 602n, 620
Puritans, 108, 131
Pushkin, A. S., 71, 576n, 620
Putin, Vladimir, 65

Qualifications and Curriculum Authority (QCA), 15, 32–3, 122, 124, 142, 254–5, 572n, 583n, 620
Queen's scholarships, 134
QUEST project, 370, 398, 416, 523, 545

Raivola, R., 573n, 620
Randers, J., 617
Rathbone, J., 113
Ravitch, D., 112, 113, 574n, 581n, 582n, 602n, 620
readiness, 425
Reboul-Scherrer, F., 575n, 598n, 620
redoublement, 56, 192, 243, 575n
Reese, W. J., 590n, 620
Reezigt, G. J., 610
Reformation, 129, 130
register, 481–2, 519–21
Reid, W. A., 623
Rein, W., 311
religion and education, 51, 57, 70, 75, 86, 89, 90, 108, 116, 126, 131, 133–4, 136, 150, 157, 210, 220–2
Renaissance, 319
Republican Party, 249
Restoration period, 131
Revised Code, 135–7, 156, 192
Reynolds, D., 29–31, 35, 38, 42, 273, 359, 370, 554, 572n, 573n, 574n, 591n, 592n, 595n, 596n, 602n, 620, 621
Richards, S., 3, 571n, 621
Richardson, Marion, 139
Ridge, J., 586n, 613
Ringen, S., 149, 586n
Ripon, North Yorkshire, 595n
Rist, Ray, 600n
Robinson, Pamela, 624

Robinson, Peter, 42, 574n, 621
Rochefoucauld, Duc de la, 56
Roman Catholic Church/Catholicism, 13, 150, 220–3, 243, 256, 319, 547
Rose, A. J., 274, 571n, 578n, 585n, 586n, 592n, 596n, 605
Rosen, H., 597n, 605
Rosenthal, R., 595n, 621
rote learning, 424, 443
Rousseau, J.-J., 26, 94, 132, 138, 139, 171, 313, 319, 425, 485, 535
routines, rules and rituals in the classroom, 380–90, 536–7
Royal Society, 130
Royal Society of Arts, 18
Ruddock, J., 269, 611
Rugg, H., 112
rules, school and classroom, 381–4, 386–90, 521–3, 524–7, 536–7
Rush, Benjamin, 109, 110
Ruskin, John, 94
Russia/Russian Federation/Soviet Union
    assessment, 69
    context, 64
    control of education, 64–70, 78–80, 246–8
    curriculum, 68–9
    demography and statistics, 64–6
    goals of education, 67–8
    history of primary education, 70–4
    lesson examples, 284–8, 403
    lesson structure and form, 298–314
    parents and teachers, 230–1
    post-Soviet period, 74–6
    primary education, 64–81
    schools, 10–11, 189, 215–23
    Soviet period, 72–4
    structure of education system, policies and laws, 64–7, 81
    teachers, 188–90, 246–8
    teaching extracts, 422–3, 490–515
    Tsarist period, 70–2
    values and identity, 74–81
Russian Academy of Education/Soviet Academy of Pedagogical Sciences, 66, 77, 79–80, 310, 338, 578n
Russian Orthodox Church, 70–1, 75, 220, 221–3, 319
Russian Revolution, 72
Rutskoi, A., 246
Rutter, M., 591n, 594n, 621

Sadler, J. E., 584n, 593n, 621
Sadler, M., 27–8, 172, 564, 573n, 621
Said, E., 88, 564, 579n, 603n, 621
Saldanha, D., 229, 307, 590n, 592n, 621
Sammons, P., 574n, 588n, 592n, 594n, 617, 621
Sapir-Whorf theory, 432
Sarva Shiksa Abhiyan (SSA), 100, 546
Savary, Alain, 58, 220
scaffolding and learning, 431–2, 516–18, 526–8, 557–61
Schaffer, E. C., 620, 622
Schallert, D., 604
scheduled castes/tribes, 245
Schiller, Christian, 139
Scholastic Aptitude Test (SAT), 107
Schön, D., 578n, 589n, 605
School Curriculum and Assessment Authority (SCAA), 141
school districts (USA), 248–52
school effectiveness research, 36–9
School Examinations and Assessment Council (SEAC), 141
Schools Council, 549
schools, 175–262
    association/community, 197–8
    buildings, 177–86
    church, 220–3
    classrooms, 181–6, 325
    management, 193–4
    organization, 188–94
    resources, 337–9
    staffing, 188–91
    student grouping, 191–3
    use of time, 186–7
    values, 195–6
'Schools of choice', 235
Schweisfurth, M. A., 573n, 588n, 621
Scotland, 120, 166, 169, 582n
Scrase, T. J., 92, 621
Sealey, A. J., 485, 593n, 599n, 600n, 621, 622
secularism in education, 58, 161, 170, 220
    see also religion and education
Sedlak, M., 575n, 589n, 601n, 615
Seiler, R. M., 624
Selleck, R. J. W., 584n, 585n, 622
Sen, A., 573n, 622
Serbia, 167
Service, R., 577n, 622
Shakespeare, William, 201

Sharan, S., 622
Sharp, R., 152, 357, 585n, 586n, 595n, 600n, 602n, 622
Sharpe, K., 243, 371, 547, 590n, 592n, 593n, 596n, 602n, 607, 622
Shastri, Lal Bahadur, 181
Shatalov, V. F., 577n
Shepherd, Gillian, 41
Shotton, J., 546, 579n, 597n, 602n, 622
Shulman, L., 519, 543–4, 600n, 601n, 622
Sierra Leone, 23–4
Silberman, C., 582n, 622
Silver, H., 616
Simon, B., 132, 134, 274, 343, 392, 540–1, 545, 572n, 573n, 583–6n, 588–90n, 592–6n, 598–601n, 612, 622
Simon, H., 583n
Simon, J., 129, 431, 577n, 599n, 623
Simpson, O. J., 415–16, 499
Sinclair, J. McH., 396, 433, 598n, 599n, 623
Smelser, N. J., 150, 586n, 623
Smith, F., 597n, 602n, 617
Smithers, A., 591n, 623
Société pour l'Instruction Elémentaire, 56
Society for Promoting Christian Knowledge (SCPK), 131
Solomon's House, 130
Soros, George, 21
Soviet psychology, 528
Soviet Union *see* Russia
Spain, 171
special educational needs, 123, 360, 372
Spillane, J. P., 581n, 609
spiral curriculum, 548
Sputnik, 112, 146, 547, 574n
St Petersburg/Leningrad, 66, 76, 77, 247, 369
Stalin, J., 73, 76, 78, 578n
Standards and Effectiveness Unit, 37, 122, 344
Standards Task Force, 37
state and school, 154–72, 240–61
State Councils of Educational Research and Training (SCERT), 96
Stein, B., 579n, 623
Stern, R. W., 579n, 623
Stevenson, H. W., 359, 369–70, 554, 574n, 582n, 591n, 596n, 602n, 623
Stigler, J. W., 359, 369–70, 554, 574n, 582n, 591n, 596n, 602n, 623

Stoll, L., 620
Stone, Arthur, 139
Straw, Jack, 144
Stringfield, C., 620, 621
structure and form in teaching, 297–319
Stubbs, M., 434, 438, 598n, 599n, 600n, 623
Summerhill School, 138
Sutherland, J., 576n, 577n, 623
Sweden, 171, 542
Switzerland, 2, 42–3, 101, 171, 183, 272, 310
Syndicat National des Instituteurs, 600n

Taba, H., 548, 603n, 623
Tabberer, R., 574n, 618, 623
Tagore, Rabindranath, 94, 171, 180, 319
Taiwan, 1–2, 42
talking and learning
  classroom interaction, 391–410
  oracy in the curriculum, 563–9
  teacher-student discourse, 427–528
Tamkin, P., 613
Tannen, D., 603n, 623
Tanner, Robin, 139, 140, 412
tasks in teaching, 339–50
Tawney, R. H., 137–8
Taylor, M., 596n, 625
Taylor, P. H., 188, 588n, 623
Taylor, W., 17, 572n, 623
Teacher Training Agency (TTA), 40, 43, 122, 142, 341, 541–2, 591n, 623
Teachers' College, Columbia, 112
teachers, 188–91, 240–61, 540–53
  England, 206–10, 225, 252–7
  France, 197–201, 223, 242–3, 244
  India, 211–15, 224, 243–6
  Russia, 215–20, 223, 246–8
  United States, 201–6, 224–5, 248–52
teaching style, 393
teaching
  activities, 350–5, 535–6
  analysing and comparing, 265–76, 320–5
  as art/craft/science, 272–6
  assessment, 368–80, 536
  atomism/holism, 271–2
  classroom discourse, 427–528
  conceptualizing, 272–6, 320–5, 534–5
  culture and, 553–6
  differentiation, 360–8, 536
  learning and, 534–40, 556–61

interaction, 391–410, 537–8
judgement, 356–9
models, 320–5
pace, 418–26
pupil organization, 334–7
resources, 334–9
routines, rules and rituals, 380–90,
    536–7
space, 325–34
tasks, 339–50
textbooks, 79–80, 247–8, 338–9
time, 411–26, 538–9
see also learning, pedagogy, teachers
Teddlie, C., 573n, 574n, 620, 621
Tharp, R. G., 435, 599n, 623
Thatcher, Margaret, 18, 60, 76, 143–4,
    150, 156, 169, 239, 258, 549
Third International Mathematics and
    Science Study (TIMSS), 35–6, 42, 69,
    156, 577n
Thomas, R., 591n, 623
Thompson, E. P., 134, 623
Thompson, J. M., 576n, 623
'three wise men' report, 113, 147, 274–5,
    585n, 586n
Thubron, C., 70, 576n, 620
time in teaching
    classroom and school time, 186–8
    conceptualizing and measuring, 411–15
    dilemmas, 412
    lesson time, 278–96, 297–8, 305–6,
        415–16
    on task, 413–15, 416–18
    pace, 418–26
    pulse and tempo, 316
Times Educational Supplement, 571n,
    623
Tizard, B., 430, 585n, 594n, 599n, 623,
    624
Tobin, J. J., 3, 44, 267, 554, 571n, 574n,
    591n, 600n, 602n, 624
Todd, F., 599n, 605
Tolstoy, Leo, 72, 94, 319
Tomlinson, George, 549
Tönnies, F., 197, 523, 589n, 624
Tooley, J., 597n, 624
Tough, J., 597n, 624
Trackton, 567
transcription and translation in comparative
    research, 438–41, 453
Trevelyan, C. E., 89

Trotsky, Leon, 73, 578n
Tudor education, 129–30
Tyler, R. W., 112, 582n, 624

Unified Workers' School, 72
unitary lesson structure, 300–4
Unitas Fratrem, 547
United Kingdom, 40–1, 120–1
United Nations Children's Fund (UNICEF),
    23–4, 33–4, 83, 573n, 576n, 579n,
    580n, 582n, 624
United Nations Educational, Scientific and
    Cultural Organization (UNESCO), 96,
    624
United Nations, 2, 19, 69, 571n, 572n,
    573n, 577n, 624
United States Department of Education,
    582n, 624
United States of America
    assessment, 106–7, 379–80
    classrooms, 12–13, 181, 183–4, 185–6,
        325–38
    colonial period, 108–9
    Constitution, 110
    context, 101, 103
    control of education, 101–4, 248–52
    curriculum, 105–6
    demography and statistics, 101, 103,
        117
    elementary education, 101–19
    goals of education, 104–5
    history of primary education, 107–14
    independence, 109–10
    lesson examples, 288–91, 403
    lesson structure and form, 298–319
    parents and teachers, 231–4
    primary education, 101–19
    school and state, 101–4, 114–19,
        248–52
    schools, 12–13, 178–80, 190, 201–6,
        225
    structure of education system, and
        federal policy, 101–19
    teachers, 188–90, 248–52
    teaching extracts, 422–3, 490–515
    values and identity, 114–19, 201–6
    see also Michigan
University of France, 198
Ushinsky, K. D., 71–2, 73–5, 221
Utah, 101
Uttar Pradesh, 11, 211

'value-added', 237
value-for-money research, 39–40
Van der Werf, G. P. C., 610
Vermont, 111
Verspoor, A. M., 39, 571n, 573n, 574n,
    578n, 616
videorecording in classroom research,
    276–7
Vietnam, 17, 113, 165
village education committees (VEC), 83, 96
Voltaire, 71
Vospitanie, 66, 76–7, 81, 193, 216–17,
    240, 532
Vygotsky, L. S., 73, 309, 319, 345, 370,
    425–6, 430–2, 436, 461, 520, 535,
    577n, 593n, 599n, 601n, 624

Wagner, K., 591n, 620
Wales, 129, 166, 169, 582n
Wall, D., 613
Wallace, M., 585n, 586n, 624
Ward, B., 571n, 619, 624
Watkins, C., 540, 542, 549, 601–2n, 624
Watson, G., 624
Watson, K., 31, 39, 574n, 624
Waugh, D., 588n, 616
Webb, Beatrice and Sydney, 73, 577n, 624
Webster, Noah, 109, 110
Wells, A. S., 607
Wells, G., 597n, 599n, 625
Wertsch, J. V., 577n, 625
West Riding of Yorkshire, 139
West, C., 588n, 625
Westgate, D. P. G., 381–2, 590n, 598n,
    599n, 611
Weston, P., 361, 596n, 625
Whitbread, Samuel, 134
White, J. P., 572n, 585n, 625
Wilkinson, B., 342, 607
Willcocks, J., 411, 585n, 586n, 599n,
    600n, 605

William Tyndale school, 141
Williams, Raymond, 163, 209, 521, 585n,
    587n, 589n, 593n, 600n, 625
Williamson, J., 598n, 599n, 600n, 613
Winchester College, 129
Winter, S., 571n, 625
Wollstonecraft, Mary, 132, 584n
Womack, H., 571n, 625
Wong, S.-Y., 606
Woodhall, M., 571n, 621
Woodhead, C., 23, 41, 235, 541, 571n,
    574n, 578n, 585n, 586n, 587n, 592n,
    595n, 596n, 601n, 605n, 625
Woods, P., 268, 275, 585n, 591n, 592n,
    625
Wordsworth, William, 132
World Bank, 1, 39, 69, 75, 83, 159, 571n,
    576n, 577n, 578n, 587n, 625
World Education Forum, 25
Wragg, E. C., 321, 322, 342–3, 381–4,
    413, 415, 593n, 594n, 596n, 598n,
    607, 625
writing
    examples, 569–70
    literacy and oracy, 564–9
Wu, D. Y., 267, 571n, 602n, 623

Yeltsin, Boris, 78, 222, 246
Young, H., 625
Young, M. F. D., 595n, 625
Young, R. F., 108, 581n, 584n, 625
Yugoslavia, 60

Zankov, L. V., 218, 248, 308
zemstvo, 71
Zhirinovsky, V., 76, 222
Ziller, T., 311
Zimmerman, J., 581n
zone of next/potential/proximal
    development, 431–2
Zyuganov, G., 76